THE APPALACHIAN MOUNTAIN CLUB'S

White Mountain Guide

28th Edition

Hiking Trails in the
White Mountain National Forest

Compiled and Edited by
Gene Daniell and Steven D. Smith

Appalachian Mountain Club Books
Boston, Massachusetts

P9-DBY-687

THE STAFF OF AMC BOOKS

Vanessa Torrado, Senior Editor   Bryan Davidson, Production Manager

Eric Hague, Editorial and Production Assistant

The AMC is a non-profit organization and sales of AMC books fund our mission of protecting the Northeast outdoors. If you appreciate our efforts and would like make a donation to the AMC, contact us at Appalachian Mountain Club, 5 Joy Street, Boston, MA 02108.

http://www.outdoors.org/publications/books/

Cartography by Larry Garland
Book Design by Jennie Sparrow
White Mountain Guide Centennial Logo by Eric Hague
Front-Cover Photograph by Robert Kozlow
Back-Cover Photographs by Robert Kozlow

Library of Congress Cataloging-in-Publication Data

The Appalachian Mountain Club's White Mountain guide : hiking trails in the White Mountain National Forest / compiled and edited by Gene Daniell and Steven D. Smith. -- 28th ed.
    p. cm.
Includes index.
ISBN-13: 978-1-929173-34-1 (pbk. : alk. paper)
ISBN-10: 1-929173-34-2 (pbk. : alk. paper)
1. Hiking--White Mountains (N.H. and Me.)--Guidebooks. 2. Trails--White Mountains (N.H. and Me.)--Guidebooks. 3. White Mountains (N.H. and Me.)--Guidebooks. I. Daniell, Gene. II. Smith, Steven D., 1953- III. Appalachian Mountain Club. IV. Title: White Mountain guide.

GV199.42.W47A67 2007
796.5109742'2--dc22   2006103179

The paper used in this publication meets the minimum requirements of the American National Standard for Information Sciences—Permanence of Paper for Printed Library Materials, ANSI Z39.48-1984.∞

Due to changes in conditions, use of the information in this book is at the sole risk of the user.

Printed in the United States of America.

Printed on recycled paper.

07   10 9 8 7 6 5 4 3 2

A

CLASS A. XXc. No. 181761.

Library of Congress, to wit:

Be it remembered,

That on the *thirteenth* day of *July*, 1907,
Appalachian Mountain Club, of
Boston, Mass., hath deposited in this Office the title of a
BOOK, the title of which is in the following words, to wit:

Guide to the Paths and Camps in the
White Mountains. Part I.
        The Department of Improvements
                of the
        Appalachian Mountain Club
                Boston, Mass.
                    1907

the right whereof *it* claims as author—and proprietor in conformity
with the laws of the United States respecting Copyrights.

Office of the Register of Copyrights,
Washington, D. C.

Herbert Putnam
Librarian of Congress.

By *Thorvald Solberg,*
Register of Copyrights.

Written
Revised
Entered
Mailed

(10, vi, 1907—5,000.)

Editions of the White Mountain Guide

First Edition	1907	Fifteenth Edition	1955
Second Edition	1916	Sixteenth Edition	1960
Third Edition	1917	Seventeenth Edition	1963
Fourth Edition	1920	Eighteenth Edition	1966
Fifth Edition	1922	Nineteenth Edition	1969
Sixth Edition	1925	Twentieth Edition	1972
Seventh Edition	1928	Twenty-First Edition	1976
Eighth Edition	1931	Twenty-Second Edition	1979
Ninth Edition	1934	Twenty-Third Edition	1983
Tenth Edition	1936	Twenty-Fourth Edition	1987
Eleventh Edition	1940	Twenty-Fifth Edition	1992
Twelfth Edition	1946	Twenty-Sixth Edition	1998
Thirteenth Edition	1948	Twenty-Seventh Edition	2003
Fourteenth Edition	1952	Twenty-Eighth Edition	2007

FOREWORD

With this, its 28th edition, the *White Mountain Guide* celebrates one century of providing trail information to White Mountain hikers, giving those of us who are involved in producing it a chance to reflect on those who have made it into a strong and durable White Mountain tradition.

The AMC *Guide to the Paths and Camps in the White Mountains* (as the *White Mountain Guide* was originally titled) first appeared in 1907, published by the AMC's Department of Improvements, of which Harland A. Perkins was chairman. The second and third editions were edited by William W. Bryant under Perkins's chairmanship. Thereafter the editor was officially designated as chairman of the White Mountain Guidebook Committee; these editors were Ralph C. Larrabee (editions 4–9), Charles W. Morse (10), Howard M. Goff (11–21), Richard M. Dudley (22), and Vera V. Smith and Eugene S. Daniell III (23). Subsequent editors (having formally reassumed that title) were Daniell (24), Daniell and Jonathan Burroughs (25–26), and Daniell and Steven D. Smith (27–28). Of the multitude of hikers who served on the Guidebook Committee over the years, many were also prominent in building and maintaining the trails that we enjoy today: Warren W. Hart (who supervised the building of the Great Gulf trail system), Nathaniel L. Goodrich, Charles W. Blood, Paul R. Jenks, Karl P. Harrington, and Arthur C. Comey are particularly notable names in White Mountain trail history. Louis Cutter, whose maps graced the book for many decades, deserves special mention, as well as Larry Garland, who has ushered the AMC's mapmaking into a new era.

We salute those who have created and maintained this book, which has guided hikers through our beloved mountains for the last 100 years.

—Gene Daniell

ACKNOWLEDGMENTS

A book like the *White Mountain Guide* is the product of the efforts of many people. Properly recognizing everyone, past and present, who contributed to this book would require a small book of its own, but the editors would like to recognize a few people whose contributions were especially indispensable.

First, we would like to thank our families, and particularly our wives, Carol Smith and Debi Clark. We dedicate our part of the life of this venerable book to them, with love and gratitude. Among the others who made unusually important contributions to this book, we wish to recognize the following:

We want to thank the staff of AMC Books, including Vanessa Torrado, Bryan Davidson, and Eric Hague. We also want to thank the AMC's staff cartographer Larry Garland. We thank those who made other contributions to this book, including those individuals from the trail-maintaining organizations and other individuals who provided information, suggestions, corrections, and advice: Rebecca Oreskes, Don Muise, Dave Govatski, Dave Neeley, Roger Collins, Jenny Preiss, and Brian Johnston of the White Mountain National Forest; Andrew Norkin of AMC Trails; Doug Mayer and Jack Stewart of the Randolph Mountain Club; Al Cressy of the Chatham Trails Association; Peter Smart of the Wonalancet Outdoor Club; Mike Micucci; Dave Salisbury; David Hooke; Mohamed Ellozy; Richard Curry; Carl Schildkraut; Roy Schweiker; Rioioli Schweiker; Dave and Marita Wright; Ken and Ann Stampfer; Keith D'Alessandro; Ben English; Bob Fuller; Ruth Jamke; Kevin and Joanne Jones; Dave Raymond; Steve Snyder; Rich Strazdas; John Compton; Richard Ashley; Cath Goodwin; Jane Gibbons; Roger Doucette; Tom Ryan; Ed Robertson; and J.R. Stockwell.

CONTENTS

TO THE READER OF THIS BOOK

This book aims to provide complete coverage of hiking trails located in the White Mountain National Forest (WMNF) in New Hampshire and Maine. Several trails outside the boundary of the forest deemed important by the editors—most of which are in northern New Hampshire and adjacent parts of Maine—have also been included in this work. For other regions in Maine, consult the AMC's *Maine Mountain Guide, 9th Edition.* The *White Mountain Guide* also covers the Appalachian Trail (AT) and its side trails from the New Hampshire–Vermont boundary at the Connecticut River to Grafton Notch in Maine, just east of the Maine–New Hampshire boundary. New Hampshire's Route 25 (NH 25)—the highway that runs west to east across the state of New Hampshire and separates the White Mountain Region from the Lakes Region and the Dartmouth-Sunapee Region—has been chosen as the southern boundary of the areas covered in the *White Mountain Guide;* however, the Middle Connecticut River region, which the AT crosses between Hanover and Glencliff, is included for this book to provide complete coverage of the section of the AT that runs through New Hampshire. Several cross-country (ski-touring) trails are mentioned in this book because they happen to intersect hiking trails.

It cannot be emphasized too strongly that trails can be rerouted or abandoned or closed by landowners, and almost any trail might be closed unexpectedly or suddenly become obscure or hazardous under certain conditions. Momentary inattention to trail markers, particularly arrows at sharp turns or signs at junctions, or misinterpretation of signs or guidebook descriptions, can cause hikers to become separated from all but the most heavily traveled paths—or at least lead them into what may be a much longer or more difficult route. All the trail-maintaining organizations, including the AMC, reserve the right to discontinue any trail without notice and expressly disclaim any legal responsibility for the condition of any trail.

SUGGESTED HIKES

At the end of each section of this guide is a list of suggested hikes designed to supply readers with a number of options for easy, moderate, and strenuous hikes within a region. A short (easy) hike can be completed in about 2 hr. or less by an average hiker, a moderate hike in 3 to 4 hr., and a longer (strenuous) hike in 7 or 8 hr. The numbers in brackets indicate distance, elevation gain, and time calculated by the formula of 30 minutes for each mile of distance or 1,000 ft. of elevation gain. The time allowances are merely a rough estimate—many parties will require more time, and many will require less—and they do not include time for extensive stops for scenery appreciation or rest.

When choosing a hike, readers should consider distance, elevation gain, time required, and special factors such as brook crossings and rough footing. A 6-mi. hike on easy terrain will require considerably less effort, though perhaps more time, than a 3-mi. hike over rocky trails with 1,500 ft. of elevation gain. A hike should be tailored to the amount of time (and daylight) available, and to the experience, fitness, and ambition of the group. Larger groups will generally move at a slower pace.

DISTANCES, TIMES, AND ELEVATION GAINS

The distances, times, and elevation gains that appear in the tables at the end of trail descriptions are cumulative from the starting point at the head of each table. Elevation gains are given for the reverse direction only when they are significant, and are not cumulative—they apply only to the interval between the current entry and the next one (which will be the entry before the current one in the list). Reverse elevation gains are not given for trails that have summaries in both directions. The following example shows users how to read the tables that are at the end of trail descriptions.

Boott Spur Link (map 1:F9)

Distance from Tuckerman Ravine Trail (3,875 ft. **[elevation]**) to
- Boott Spur Trail (4,650 ft. **[elevation]**): 0.6 mi. **[distance]**, 850 ft. **[elevation gain]** (rev. 50 ft.**[reverse elevation gain]**), 45 min **[time]**.

Elevation gains are estimated and rounded to the nearest 50 ft.; some elevation gains can be determined almost to the foot, but others (such as where several minor ups and downs are traversed) are only roughly accurate. Elevations are estimated as closely as possible when not given precisely by our source maps. The USGS maps are used as the basis for all such information except for the area covered by Bradford Washburn's map of the Presidential Range, where that map supersedes the USGS maps.

There is no reliable method for predicting how much time a particular hiker or group of hikers will actually take to complete a particular hike on a particular day. However, to give inexperienced hikers a rough basis for planning, estimated times have been calculated for this book by allowing 30 minutes for each mile of distance or 1,000 ft. of climbing. No attempt has been made to adjust these times for the difficulties of specific trails. During winter, with heavy packs or in deep snow, hikes may take two or three times the summer estimate.

MAPS

The six maps featured in the guidebook provide complete coverage of the WMNF. These maps (except map 1, Presidential Range) are designed at the same size and scale, allowing the user to easily read from one map to the next. Universal Transverse Mercator (UTM) grid coordinates are included on the map sheets to facilitate the use of global positioning system (GPS) receivers in the field. Waterproof Tyvek® versions of the maps that accompany the *White Mountain Guide* can be purchased through the AMC's Web site, bookstores, many outdoor equipment stores, as well as the AMC information centers in Boston, Pinkham Notch, and Crawford Notch.

Detailed maps are available from the U.S. Geological Survey for most of the United States, including all of New Hampshire and Maine. They are published in rectangles of several standard sizes called quadrangles ("quads"). All areas in the regions covered in this guide are now covered by detailed 7.5-minute quads, some of which are in metric format. Although topography on the newer maps is excellent, some of these recent maps unfortunately are very inaccurate in showing the location of some trails. These maps can be obtained at a number of local outlets and from the USGS (800-USA-

MAPS, www.usgs.gov). Index maps showing the available USGS quads in any state and an informative pamphlet titled *Topographic Maps* are available free on request from the USGS. Maps by the USGS are now also available on compact disc from a number of sources, including Maptech and National Geographic/TOPO! It is possible to purchase map sets covering all of New Hampshire or New England.

The WMNF (though not all of the North Country) is covered by two *National Geographic Trails Illustrated Maps: Franconia Notch/Lincoln* (#740) and *Presidential Range/Gorham* (#741), which were produced in partnership with the AMC.

PARKING FEES AND THE HIKER SHUTTLE

Hikers need to display an annual parking pass sticker on their windshield or should be prepared to pay for a parking pass when parking at established trailhead parking sites that have a posted fee sign. Almost all the proceeds from these passes are used for improvements in the WMNF. Parking passes are available at WMNF ranger offices, information centers, outdoor retail stores, as well as at the AMC's information centers in Boston, Pinkham Notch, and Crawford Notch. See the WMNF Web site for details.

To reduce the difficulty of finding a parking spot at trailheads, during summer and fall, the AMC offers a hiker shuttle service between Pinkham Notch Visitor Center, the Highland Center at Crawford Notch, and several major trailheads, including those serving popular routes to the AMC huts. For trips beginning and ending at different trailheads, many hikers leave their cars at their final trailhead and take the shuttle to their starting trailhead. Reservations are recommended, and a fee is charged. For information, contact the AMC's Reservations Office (603-466-2727) or visit the AMC's Web site (www.outdoors.org).

LEAVE NO TRACE

The AMC is also a national educational partner of Leave No Trace, a nonprofit organization dedicated to promoting and inspiring responsible outdoor recreation through education, research, and partnerships. The Leave No Trace Program seeks to develop wildland ethics—ways in which people think and act in the outdoors to minimize the impact they have on the areas they visit and to protect our natural resources for future enjoyment.

The Leave No Trace ethic is guided by these seven principles:

- Plan ahead and prepare
- Travel and camp on durable surfaces
- Dispose of waste properly
- Leave what you find
- Minimize campfire impacts
- Respect wildlife
- Be considerate of other visitors

hikeSafe HIKER RESPONSIBILITY CODE

You are responsible for yourself, so be prepared:

1. With knowledge and gear. Become self reliant by learning about the terrain, conditions, local weather and your equipment before you start.

2. To leave your plans. Tell someone where you are going, the trails you are hiking, when you will return and your emergency plans.

3. To stay together. When you start as a group, hike as a group, end as a group. Pace your hike to the slowest person.

4. To turn back. Weather changes quickly in the mountains. Fatigue and unexpected conditions can also affect your hike. Know your limitations and when to postpone your hike. The mountains will be there another day.

5. For emergencies. Even if you are headed out for just one hour, an injury, severe weather or a wrong turn could become life threatening. Don't assume you will be rescued; know how to rescue yourself.

6. To share the hiker code with others.

HikeSafe: It's Your Responsibility. The Hiker Responsibility Code was developed and is endorsed by the WMNF and New Hampshire Fish and Game. www.hikesafe.com.

INTRODUCTION

WHITE MOUNTAIN NATIONAL FOREST

Most of the higher peaks of the White Mountains are within the WMNF, which was established under the Weeks Act and now comprises about 794,000 acres, of which about 47,000 acres are in Maine and the rest in New Hampshire. This is not a national park but, rather, a national forest; parks are established primarily for preservation and recreation, whereas national forests are managed for multiple use. In the administration of national forests, the following objectives are considered: recreation management, timber production, watershed protection, and wildlife habitat management. It is the policy of the United States Forest Service (USFS) to manage logging operations so that trails, streams, camping places, and other spots of public interest are protected. Mountain recreation has been identified as the most important resource in the WMNF. The boundaries of the WMNF are usually marked wherever they cross roads or trails, usually by red-painted corner posts and blazes. Hunting and fishing are permitted in the WMNF under the state laws; state licenses are required. Organized groups, including those sponsored by nonprofit organizations, must apply for an outfitter-guide permit if they conduct trips on WMNF land for which they charge any kind of fee; contact any WMNF office for details. Much information has been published by the WMNF and is available free of charge at the forest supervisor's office in Laconia, the ranger district offices, and other information centers.

The national Wilderness Preservation System, which included the Great Gulf Wilderness, was established in 1964 with passage of the Wilderness Act. Since then, in the WMNF the Presidential Range–Dry River Wilderness, Pemigewasset Wilderness, Sandwich Range Wilderness, and Caribou–Speckled Mountain Wilderness areas have been added to the system. In 2006, Congress passed legislation adding 10,800 acres to the Sandwich Range Wilderness, which created the new 23,700-acre Wild River Wilderness. This addition brought the WMNF's total wilderness area to

150,000 acres, which is almost 19 percent of its area. Regulations for these areas prohibit logging and road building, as well as any use of mechanized equipment or vehicles, including bicycles. Wilderness areas are established by an act of Congress, though the recommendations of the USFS are a critical part of the process of selecting areas for congressional designation. Management of these areas in accordance with guidelines contained in the Wilderness Act is entrusted to the USFS. Most important is the protection of the natural environment, and among other qualities that the USFS is charged with preserving is the opportunity for visitors to enjoy solitude and challenge within this natural environment. As a consequence, for example, "structures for user convenience" such as shelters are not permitted in wilderness. In general, visitors to wilderness areas should look forward to a rougher, wilder, more primitive experience than in other parts of the WMNF, and should expect USFS regulations to emphasize the preservation of wilderness qualities even when substantial inconvenience to hikers results. As a consequence, there are no mileages on signs and few if any blazes, and "easy-over, easy-under" blowdowns may be intentionally left in place to add to the wild character. Group size is limited to 10, and camping and fire regulations vary by wilderness. The USFS has also established nine scenic areas in the WMNF to preserve lands of outstanding or unique natural beauty: Gibbs Brook, Greeley Ponds, Pinkham Notch, Lafayette Brook, Rocky Gorge, Lincoln Woods, Sawyer Pond, Mt. Chocorua, and Snyder Brook.

Additionally, three natural research areas—the Alpine Garden, The Bowl, and Nancy Brook—have been established as areas where "natural processes will be predominate" and recreation use will be incidental.

Camping is restricted in many areas under the Forest Protection Area (FPA) program to protect vulnerable areas from damage. To preserve the rare alpine plants of the Mt. Washington Range and other significant and uncommon ecosystems within the entire WMNF, rules prohibit removal of any tree, shrub, or plant without written permission. Federal law also protects cultural sites and artifacts on public lands. If you discover such remains, please leave them undisturbed.

The AMC earnestly requests that those who use the trails, shelters, and campsites heed the rules (especially those having to do with camping) of the WMNF and the New Hampshire Department of Resources and Economic Development Division of Parks and Recreation (NHDP). The same consideration should be shown to private landowners because trails can be closed forever if a landowner finds the way the public treats them objectionable. Trails must not be cut in the WMNF without the approval of the forest supervisor, or elsewhere without consent of the owners and definite formal provision for maintenance.

APPALACHIAN TRAIL

With the passage of the National Trails System Act by Congress on October 2, 1968, the Appalacian Trail (AT) became the first federally protected footpath in this country and was officially designated the Appalachian National Scenic Trail. Under this act, the AT is administered primarily as a footpath by the secretary of the interior in consultation with the secretary of agriculture and representatives of the several states through which it passes. The footpath runs more than 2,000 mi. from Springer Mountain in Georgia to Katahdin in Maine, and traverses the White Mountains for about 170 mi. in a southwest to northeast direction, from the New Hampshire–Vermont boundary in the Connecticut River Valley at Hanover to Grafton Notch, a short distance past the Maine–New Hampshire boundary. Its route traverses many of the major peaks and ranges of the White Mountains. Except for a few short segments between Hanover and Glencliff, the trails that make up the AT in the White Mountains are all described in this book. In each section of this guide through which the AT passes, its route through the section is described in a separate paragraph near the beginning of the passage.

CLIMATE AND VEGETATION

The climate gets much cooler, windier, and wetter at higher elevations. The summit of Mt. Washington is under cloud cover about 55 percent of the time. On an average summer afternoon, the high temperature on the summit is only about 52 degrees Fahrenheit; in winter, about 15 degrees Fahrenheit. The record low temperature is −46 degrees Fahrenheit. Average winds throughout the day and night are 26 MPH in summer and 44 MPH in winter. Winds have gusted more than 100 MPH in every month of the year, and set the world record of 231 MPH on April 12, 1934. During the storm of February 24–26, 1969, the observatory recorded a snowfall of

97.8 in. Within a 24-hr. period during that storm, a total of 49.3 in. was recorded, at that time a record for the mountain and for all weather observation stations in the United States. Other mountains also experience severe conditions in proportion to their height and exposure.

The forest on the White Mountains is of two major types: the northern hardwood forest (birch, beech, and maple), found at elevations of less than about 3,000 ft., and the boreal forest (spruce, fir, and birch), found from about 3,000 ft. to the timberline. At low elevations, oaks and white pines may be seen, and hemlocks are found in some deep valleys; red pines may grow up to elevations of about 2,000 ft. in ledgy areas. Above the timberline is the "krummholz," the gnarled and stunted trees that manage to survive wherever there is a bit of shelter from the violent winds, and the tiny wildflowers, some of which are extremely rare. Hikers are encouraged to be particularly careful in their activities above treeline because the plants that grow there already have to cope with the severity of the environment.

TRIP PLANNING

The normal hiking season runs approximately from Memorial Day to Columbus Day. In some years ice or snowdrifts may remain at higher elevations until the early part of June and possibly much later than that in some of the major ravines, on north-facing slopes, and in other sheltered places such as Mahoosuc Notch. Such conditions vary greatly from year to year and place to place. When snow or ice are present, trails are often far more difficult to follow, and usually far more dangerous to hike on.

Winterlike conditions can occur above treeline in any month of the year. Even on sunny days in midsummer, hikers above treeline should always be prepared for cold weather with at least a minimum of a wool or synthetic fleece sweater, hat, mittens, and a wind parka, which will give comfort on sunny but cool days and protection against sudden storms. Spring and fall are particularly difficult seasons in the mountains because the weather may be pleasant in the valleys but brutal on the summits and ridges. A great number of the serious incidents in the mountains occur in spring and fall, when hikers deceived by mild conditions at home or even at trailheads may find themselves facing unanticipated severe, perhaps life-threatening, hazards.

Plan your trip schedule with safety in mind. Consider the strength of your party and the general strenuousness of the trip: the overall distance, the amount of climbing, and the roughness of the terrain. Get a weather report, but be aware that most forecasts are not intended to apply to the mountain region; a day that is sunny and pleasant in the lowlands may well be inclement in the mountains. The National Weather Service in Gray, Maine, issues a recreational forecast for the White Mountain Region's valleys and higher summits and broadcasts it on its radio station each morning approximately from 5 A.M. to 10 A.M.; the forecast from the Mt. Washington Observatory is posted at Pinkham Notch Visitor Center at about 8 A.M. and is also available on the Web sites for both the observatory and the AMC. Plan to finish your hike with daylight to spare (remember that days grow shorter rapidly in late summer and fall). Hiking after dark, even with flashlights (which frequently fail), makes finding trails more difficult and crossing streams hazardous. Let someone else know where you will be hiking, and avoid letting people get separated from the group, especially inexperienced ones. Many unpaved roads are not passable until about Memorial Day, and from November to May the WMNF closes with locked gates many of its roads that are normally open during the summer season (see http://www.fs.fed.us/r9/forests/white_mountain/recreation/roads_status.php); many trips are much longer when the roads are not open.

FOLLOWING TRAILS

Hikers should always carry a map and compass and carefully keep track of their approximate location on the map. The maps included with this guide are topographic maps (maps with the shape of the terrain represented by contour lines). They are designed as an aid to planning trips and following well-established trails, and for determining a reasonable course of action in an emergency. They therefore cover fairly large areas, which necessarily limits the amount of detail that can be shown on them. Maps with more detail (which cover much smaller areas) are published by the U.S. Geological Survey.

The editors consider the protractor compass (a circular, liquid-filled compass that turns on a rectangular base made of clear plastic, also known as a baseplate or orienteering compass) the best for hiking. Such a compass is easily set to the bearing you want to follow, and then it is a simple matter of keeping the compass needle aligned to north and following the arrow on the base. Directions for the compass given in the text are based on true north instead of magnetic north, unless otherwise specified. There is a deviation (usually called *declination*) of 16 degrees to 17 degrees between true north and magnetic north in the White Mountains. This means true north will be about 17 degrees to the right of (clockwise from) the compass's north needle. If you take a bearing from a map, you should add 17 degrees to the bearing when you set your compass. On the maps included with this guide, the black lines that run from bottom to top are aligned with true north and south.

Global Positioning System (GPS) units are becoming increasingly popular, but to use them effectively, hikers have to understand exactly what they will and will not do. Hikers are advised to remember GPS reception can be poor, particularly in deep valleys and under heavy foliage. Furthermore, all electronic devices are subject to damage, battery failure, and other problems that can render them totally useless. A GPS unit should not be relied on to orient anyone traveling through wilderness, nor should it be considered a satisfactory substitute for a compass. Without a good map and a regular compass, the usefulness of a GPS unit is very limited. In the field, it is difficult to obtain precise coordinates from a map, and it is equally difficult to determine a location on a map from the coordinates provided by a GPS unit. More sophisticated and pricey models allow a user to purchase and download maps to the device, but the usefulness of this feature is limited because of the small display area. If GPS units will be used, we recommend preparing a list of coordinates for a number of useful landmarks before leaving for the field; this can be done easily by using one of the many versions of the USGS maps available on CD-ROM, or by using Maptech's free services online (www.maptech.com/mapserver). Finally, learn how to use the device effectively before setting off on any trip. Experiment with a GPS unit in a place with which you are familiar and where it would be difficult to get lost so that you are accustomed to using it.

In general, trails are maintained to provide a clear pathway while protecting the environment by minimizing erosion and other damage. Some may offer rough and difficult passage. Trails in officially designated wilderness areas, by policy, are managed to provide a more primitive experience. As a result, they are maintained to a lesser degree, are sparsely marked, and have few signs. Hikers entering wilderness must be prepared to make a greater effort to follow their chosen route. Most hiking trails are marked with paint on trees or rocks, though a few still only have ax blazes cut into trees. The trails that compose the AT through the White Mountains are marked with vertical rectangular white paint blazes throughout. Side trails off the AT are usually marked with blue paint. Other trails are marked in other colors, the most popular being yellow. Except for the AT and its side trails, and trails maintained by clubs such as the Chocorua Mountain Club (CMC) and the Wonalancet Out Door Club (WODC), the color of blazing has no significance and may change without notice; therefore blazing color is not a reliable means of distinguishing particular trails from intersecting ones. Above timberline, cairns (piles of rocks) mark the trails. Below treeline, the treadway is usually visible except when it is covered by snow or fallen leaves. In winter, signs at trailheads and intersections and blazes also are often covered by snow. Trails following or crossing logging roads require special care at intersections to distinguish the trail from diverging roads, particularly because blazing is usually very sparse while the trail follows the road. Around shelters or campsites, beaten paths may lead in all directions, so look for signs and paint blazes.

If you lose a trail and it is not visible to either side, it is usually best to backtrack right away to the last mark seen and look again from there; this will be much easier if you carefully note each trail marking and keep track of where and how long ago you saw the most recent one. Even when the trail cannot be immediately found, it is a serious but not desperate situation. If you have carefully kept track of your location on the map, it will usually be possible to find a nearby stream, trail, or road to which a compass course may be followed. Most distances are short enough (except in the North Country, north of New Hampshire's Route 110) that it is possible, in the absence of alternatives, to reach a highway in half a day, or at most in a whole day, simply by going downhill, carefully avoiding any dangerous cliffs (which will normally be found in areas where the map's contour lines are unusually close together), until you come upon a river or brook. The stream should then be followed downward.

WHAT TO CARRY AND WEAR

Adequate equipment for a hike in the White Mountains varies greatly according to the length of the trip and the difficulty of getting to the nearest trailhead if trouble arises. If you plan to take a stroll in good weather that will amount to less than a mile of territory away from a main road, then perhaps a light jacket, a candy bar, and a bottle of water will suffice. If, however, you are going above, you will need a good pack filled with plenty of warm clothing, food for emergency use, and other equipment. No determination of what one needs to take along can be made without considering the length of a trip and the hazards of the terrain it will cross.

Good things to have in your pack for an ordinary summer day hike in the White Mountains include a guidebook; maps; at least 2 quarts of water per person; a compass, a knife (good-quality stainless steel); rain gear; a windbreaker; a wool or synthetic sweater(s); a hat; mittens; waterproof matches; enough food per person, plus extra high-energy foods for an emergency reserve (such as dried fruit or candy); first-aid supplies (adhesive bandages, gauze, surgical gloves, nonprescription painkiller [such as aspirin, acetaminophen, or ibuprofen], and antiseptic); an emergency supply of any personal medicines; needle and thread; safety pins; nylon cord; a trash bag; toilet paper; and a headlamp or small flashlight, with extra batteries and a spare bulb.

Wear comfortable hiking boots. Lightweight boots, which are sturdier than sneakers, are popular these days and they provide ankle support. Jeans, sweatshirts, and other cotton clothes are popular but, once wet, dry very slowly and may be uncomfortable; in adverse weather conditions, they seriously drain a cold and tired hiker's heat reserves. Those planning to travel to remote places or above treeline should seriously consider wearing (or at least carrying) wool or synthetics, which keep much of their insulation value even when wet.

CAMPING

Those who camp overnight in the backcountry tend to have more of an impact on the land than day-hikers. Backpacking hikers should take great care to minimize their effect on the mountains by practicing low-impact camping and making conscious efforts to preserve the natural forest. If available on your chosen trip route, the best alternative is to use formally designated campsites to concentrate impact and minimize damage to vegetation. Many popular campsites and shelters have caretakers. In other areas, choose previously established campsites to minimize the impact caused by the creation and proliferation of new campsites. When selecting an established campsite, choose the ones that are farther away from surface water to protect the water quality for future and downstream users. Several Web sites (including www.lnt.org) are now devoted to encouraging Leave No Trace principles.

There are more than 50 backcountry shelters and tentsites in the White Mountain area, open on a first-come, first-served basis. Some sites have summer caretakers who provide trail and shelter maintenance, educate hikers on low-impact camping methods, and oversee the environmentally sound disposal of human waste. An overnight fee is charged at these sites to help defray expenses. Most sites have shelters, a few have only tent platforms, and some have both. Shelters are intended as overnight accommodations for persons carrying their own bedding and cooking supplies. The more popular shelters are often full, so be prepared to camp at a legal site off-trail with tents or tarps. Make yourself aware of regulations and restrictions before your trip.

Each year, the 14 AMC-managed backcountry sites host an average of 20,000 overnight visitors. Nine of the most popular sites host an average of 11,000 visitors. More than one-third of those visitors—35 percent—are part of an organized group. The heavy use of these popular sites leads to the deposit of human waste, erosion of heavily used trails, and trampling of vegetation—all of which have an impact on the forest. The AMC requests pre-notification from large groups concerning the sites they plan to use. If you are planning a group trip with six or more people during the peak summer or fall season, see the following Web page for notification forms and updates on availability to groups: http://www.outdoors.org/lodging/campsites/campsites-notification.cfm

If you camp away from established sites, look for a spot more than 200 ft. from the trail and from any surface water, and observe Forest Service camping regulations for the area. Bring all needed shelter, including whatever poles, stakes, ground insulation, and cord are required. Do not cut boughs or branches for bedding or firewood, or young trees for poles. Avoid clearing vegetation, and never make a ditch around the tent. Wash your dishes and yourself well away from streams, ponds, and springs. Heed the rules of neatness, sanitation, and fire prevention, and carry out everything—food, paper, glass, cans—that you carry in. Food should not be kept in your tent; hang it from a tree—well down from a high, sturdy branch and well away from the tree trunk—to protect it from raccoons and bears.

In some popular camping areas, a "human browse line" where people have gathered firewood over the years is quite evident: limbs are gone from trees, the ground is devoid of dead wood, and vegetation has been trampled. The use of portable stoves is often mandatory in popular areas, and is encouraged everywhere by all groups concerned with environmental protection to prevent damage to vegetation. Wood campfires should not be made unless there is ample dead and down wood available near your site and it is legal in your particular camping area. Before you build a fire, clear a space at least 5 ft. in radius of all flammable material down to the mineral soil. Under no circumstances should a fire be left unattended. All fires must be completely extinguished with earth or water before you leave a campsite, even temporarily. Campers should restore the campfire site to as natural an appearance as possible (unless using a preexisting fire ring) before leaving the campsite.

Camping Regulations

Trailside camping is practical only within the WMNF, with a few limited exceptions, such as the established campsites on the AT. The laws of the states of Maine and New Hampshire require that permission be obtained from the owner to camp on private land and that permits be obtained to build campfires anywhere outside the WMNF, except at officially designated campsites. Camping and campfires are not permitted in New Hampshire state parks except in campgrounds.

Overnight camping is permitted in almost all of the WMNF. To limit or prevent some of the adverse impacts of concentrated, uncontrolled camping, the USFS has adopted regulations for a number of areas in the WMNF that are threatened by overuse and misuse. The objective of the Forest Protection Area (FPA) program (formerly called the Restricted Use Area program) is to disperse their use of the land so that people can enjoy themselves in a clean and attractive environment without causing deterioration of natural resources. Because hikers and backpackers have cooperated with FPA rules, many areas once designated as FPAs have recovered and are no longer under formal restrictions. However, common sense and self-imposed restrictions are still necessary to prevent damage.

Stated briefly, the 2006 FPA rules prohibit camping and wood or charcoal fires above timberline (where trees are less than 8 ft. in height), or within a specified distance of certain roads, trails, streams, and other locations, except at designated sites. Some of these restrictions are in force throughout the year and others only from May 1 to November 1. This guide provides information on FPAs as of 2002 in each relevant section. Because the list of restricted areas changes from year to year, however, hikers should get current information from the USFS in Laconia, New Hampshire, the AMC at Pinkham Notch Visitor Center, or any ranger district office for up-to-date information. A brochure outlining the current backcountry camping rules is available at WMNF ranger stations and information centers.

Roadside Campgrounds

The WMNF operates a number of roadside campgrounds with limited facilities; fees are charged, and most of these campgrounds are now managed by private concessionaires. Consult the WMNF offices for details or call the campground hotline. Many of these campgrounds are full on summer weekends. Reservations for sites at some WMNF campgrounds can be made through the National Recreation Reservation Service. Several New Hampshire state parks also have campgrounds located conveniently for hikers in the White Mountains and other parts of the state. Reservations can now be made at all state campgrounds. Brochures on state parks and state and private campgrounds are usually available at New Hampshire highway rest areas throughout the normal camping season.

FIRE REGULATIONS

Campfire permits are no longer required in the WMNF, but hikers who build fires are still legally responsible for any damage they may cause. Fires are forbidden in FPAs, above treeline (where trees are less than 8 ft. tall), and in the Great Gulf Wilderness. Fires are not permitted on state lands except at explicitly designated sites, and on private land the owner's permission is required. During periods when there is a high risk of forest fires, the forest supervisor may temporarily close the entire WMNF against public entry. Such closures are given wide publicity so that local residents and visitors alike may realize the danger of fires in the woods.

WINTER ACTIVITIES

Snowshoeing and cross-country skiing on White Mountain trails and peaks have steadily become more popular in the last decade. Much more experience is required to foresee and avoid dangerous situations in winter than in summer. Winter on the lower trails in the White Mountains often requires only snowshoes or skis and some warm clothing. Summer hiking boots are usually inadequate, flashlight batteries fail quickly (a headlamp with battery pack works better), and water in canteens freezes unless carried in an insulated container or wrapped in a sock or sweater. The winter hiker needs good physical conditioning from regular exercise and must dress carefully to avoid overheating and excessive perspiration, which soaks clothing and soon leads to chilling. Cotton clothes are useless in the winter because they cannot be kept perfectly dry (thus the winter climbers' maxim "cotton kills"); only some synthetic fabrics and wool retain their insulating values when wet. Fluid intake must increase, as dehydration can be a serious problem in the dry winter air.

It is important to note that some trails go through areas that may pose a severe avalanche hazard. Gulfs, ravines, and open slopes are especially prone to avalanches, though they can also occur below treeline. Avalanche danger for Tuckerman Ravine is posted daily at the Pinkham Notch Visitor Center. These areas should be regarded as technical terrain and strictly avoided unless group leaders have been trained in avalanche safety; avalanches have become a major cause of death and serious injury in the White Mountains in recent years, largely because of inexperienced, untrained hikers wandering into dangerous terrain.

Above timberline, conditions often require specialized equipment and skills and experience of a different magnitude. The conditions on the Presidential Range in winter are as severe as any in North America south of the great mountains of Alaska and the Yukon Territory. On the summit of Mt. Washington in winter, winds average 44 MPH, and daily high temperatures average 15 degrees Fahrenheit. There are few calm days, and even on an average day conditions will probably be too severe for any but the most experienced and well-equipped climbers. The Mt. Washington Observatory routinely records wind velocities in excess of 100 MPH, and temperatures are often far below zero. The combination of high wind and low temperature has such a cooling effect that the worst conditions on Mt. Washington are approximately equal to the worst reported from Antarctica, despite the much greater cold in the latter region. Extremely severe storms can develop suddenly and unexpectedly. But the most dangerous aspect of winter in the White Mountains is the extreme variability of the weather: it is not unusual for a cold, penetrating, wind-driven rain to be followed within a few hours by a cold front that brings below-zero temperatures and high winds.

No book can begin to impart all the knowledge necessary to cope safely with the potential for such brutal conditions, but helpful information can be found in *Winterwise: A Backpacker's Guide by John M. Dunn* (published by the Adirondack Mountain Club). Hikers who are interested in extending their activities into the winter season are strongly advised to seek out organized parties with leaders who have extensive winter experience. The AMC and several of its chapters also sponsor numerous evening and weekend workshops, in addition to introductory winter hikes and regular winter schedules through which participants can gain experience

BACKCOUNTRY HAZARDS

If you find yourself in an emergency situation, please refer to the Helpful Information and Contacts section in this book. Hikers should be aware that cell phone coverage in the White Mountains can be very unreliable, and there is absolutely no assurance that a cell phone call will get through to authorities during an emergency.

Courses that teach the principles of backcountry safety and incident management are offered by the AMC and many other outdoor organizations. Dozens of books are available on such subjects. On backcountry travel, the classic book is *Mountaineering: The Freedom of the Hills* (7th ed., 2003), published by Mountaineers. For first aid techniques while in the mountains, useful books are *Medicine for Mountaineering & Other Wilderness Activities* (5th ed., 2001), also by Mountaineers, and *NOLS Wilderness First Aid*, by Tod Schimelpfenig and Linda Lindsey, from Stackpole Books.

Hypothermia

Hypothermia, the most serious danger to hikers in the White Mountains, is the loss of ability to preserve body heat and may be caused by injury, exhaustion, lack of sufficient food, and inadequate or wet clothing. Moderate and advanced hypothermia—the form usually encountered in hiking situations—develops over the course of several hours because a person loses body heat faster than it can be generated and can occur during any season and in any condition.

In the earliest stages, often referred to as mild to moderate hypothermia, the symptoms include uncontrollable shivering, impaired speech and movement, lowered body temperature, and drowsiness. Be on the look out for what current hypothermia education programs refer to as the *umbles*—stumbles, mumbles, and bumbles—which amount to a loss of agility, an inability to speak clearly, difficulty with knots and zippers, and similar issues that indicate loss of control over normal muscular and mental functions. As the situation becomes more serious, the body begins to shiver violently, which produces a substantial amount of heat but consumes the body's last remaining energy reserves very rapidly. Uncontrollable shivering should be regarded as a sure sign of mild to moderate hypothermia and indicates the person's body temperature has dropped significantly but is still more than 90 degrees Fahrenheit; this shivering will eventually cease on its own even if the state of hypothermia is still present. A victim should be given dry clothing and placed in a sleeping bag, then given quick-energy food to eat and something warm (not hot) to drink.

In cases of severe hypothermia, which occurs when a body's temperature has reached a point below 90 degrees Fahrenheit, shivering ceases, but a victim becomes afflicted by an obvious lack of coordination to the point that walking becomes impossible. Sure indicators are slurred speech, mental confusion, irrational behavior, disorientation, and unconsciousness. Only prompt evacuation to a hospital offers reasonable hope for recovery. Severe hypothermia cannot be treated in the field because it requires advanced techniques such as circulating warm water through the abdominal cavity to rewarm a victim's body from its core outward. Any attempt to rewarm such a person in the field will cause cold blood from the extremities to return to the heart, almost certainly causing death from heart failure. Extreme care must also be used in attempting to transport such a person to a trailhead because even a slight jar can bring on heart failure. The victim should be protected from further heat loss as much as possible and handled with extreme gentleness, and trained rescue personnel should be called for assistance.

Heat Exhaustion

Excessive heat can also be a serious problem in the mountains, particularly during mid-summer. Heat exhaustion, usually in a mild form, is quite common. A hiker suffering from heat stroke will feel tired, perhaps lightheaded or nauseous, and may have cramps in large muscles. The principal cause of the condition is dehydration and loss of electrolytes (mostly salt) through perspiration, often combined with overexertion.

Treatment for heat exhaustion includes the immediate intake of water and possibly salt (salt without adequate water will make the situation worse). Help the victim cool down and minimize further exertion. Drinking untreated water must often be considered despite the risk, as the consequences of heat injury can be much more dangerous than the pathogens normally found in water in the White Mountain area.

Dehydration contributes to cardiac problems by placing great strain on the heart. The volume of blood is reduced and becomes thicker, so the heart works much harder to supply nutrients and oxygen to both the muscles and the brain and, at the same time, carry excess heat to the skin to disperse it. If ignored, heat exhaustion can also lead to heat stroke, a medical emergency in which the body's temperature rises above the level that allows the body's control mechanisms to operate; irreversible damage to the brain and other vital organs can occur if body temperature rises above 107 degrees Fahrenheit for even a few minutes. This condition requires immediate cooling of the victim.

Lightning

When thunderstorms are likely, avoid bare ridges or summits. Look for shelter in thick woods as quickly as possible if an unexpected "thumper" is detected. Most thunderstorms occur when a cold front passes, or on very warm days; those produced by cold fronts are typically more sudden and violent. Weather forecasts that mention cold fronts or predict temperatures much above 80 degrees Fahrenheit in the lowlands and valleys should arouse concern.

Wildlife

The most risky part of hiking in the White Mountains, in the opinion of many people, has always been the drive to the trailhead. During the first nine months of one recent year, for example, collisions between moose and automobiles caused the deaths of four people and more than 160 moose. Most of such collisions occur from early May to the middle of July, when moose leave the woods to avoid the black flies and seek out the road salt that has accumulated in ditches near highways. Motorists need to be aware of the seriousness of the problem, particularly at night when these huge, dark-colored animals are both active and very difficult to see. Instinct often causes them to face an auto rather than run from it, and they are also apt to cross the road unpredictably as a car approaches.

Bears are common but tend to keep well out of sight. The bear is a large and unpredictable animal that must be treated with respect. Several recent serious incidents have been unnecessarily provoked by deliberate feeding of bears, or by harassment by a dog leading to an attack on people nearby. Bears live mostly on nuts, berries, and other plants, and dead animals, and rarely kill anything larger than a mouse. Since the closing of many of the town dumps in the

White Mountain Region, where some bears routinely foraged for food, bears have become a nuisance and even a hazard at some popular campsites; any bear that has lost its natural fear of humans and gotten used to living off us is extremely dangerous. Hikers confronted by a bear should attempt to appear neither threatened nor frightened, and should back off slowly—never run—but not abandon food unless the bear appears irresistibly aggressive. A loud noise, such as one made by a whistle or by banging metal pots, is often useful. Careful protection of food at campsites is mandatory; it must never be kept overnight in a tent, but should be hung between trees well off the ground—at least 10 ft. high and 4 ft. away from the tree trunk.

Moose-hunting season is in mid to late October; deer-hunting season (with rifles) is in November, at which time you'll probably see many more hunters than deer. Seasons involving muzzle-loader and bow-and-arrow hunters extend from mid-October through mid-December. Most hunters usually stay fairly close to roads, and, in general, the harder it would be to haul a deer out of a given area, the lower the probability that a hiker will encounter hunters there. In any case, avoid wearing brown or anything that might give a hunter the impression of the white flash of a white-tailed deer running away. Wearing bright-orange clothing, as is often done by hunters, is strongly recommended.

There are no poisonous snakes in the White Mountains. Mosquitoes and black flies are the woodland residents most frequently encountered by hikers. Mosquitoes are worst throughout the summer in low, wet areas, and black flies are most bloodthirsty in June and early July. Fishermen's head nets can be useful. The most effective repellents are based on the active ingredient diethyl-meta-toluamide, generally known as DEET, but there are growing doubts about its safety. Ticks have been an increasing problem in recent years, becoming common in woods and grassy or brushy areas at lower elevations, especially in oak forests. At present the most feared tick (the tiny, easily overlooked deer tick, which can transmit Lyme disease, is not yet common in the White Mountains, though its range seems to be steadily increasing. The common tick in the White Mountains is the larger wood tick (also known as the dog tick), which can also carry serious diseases such as Rocky Mountain spotted fever. Countermeasures include using insect repellent, wearing light-colored long pants tucked into your socks, and frequent visual checks of clothing and skin.

Brook Crossings

Use caution crossing rivers and brooks without bridges. Note that many crossings that may only be a nuisance in summer may be a serious obstacle in cold weather when one's feet and boots must be kept dry. Another kind of hazard can occur in late fall, when cold nights may cause exposed rocks to be coated with a treacherous thin layer of ice. Higher waters, which can turn innocuous brooks into virtually uncrossable torrents, come in spring as snow melts, or after heavy rainstorms, particularly in fall when trees drop their leaves and take up less water. Avoid trails with potentially dangerous stream crossings during these high-water periods. If you are cut off from roads by swollen streams, it is better to make a long detour, even if you need to wait and spend a night in the woods. Rushing current can make wading extremely hazardous, and several deaths have resulted. Floodwaters may subside within a few hours, especially in small brooks. It is particularly important not to camp on the far side of a brook from your exit point if the crossing is difficult and heavy rain is predicted.

Drinking Water

The presence of cysts of the intestinal parasite *Giardia lamblia* in water sources in the White Mountains is thought to be common, though difficult to prove. The safest course is for day-hikers to carry their own water, and for those who use sources in the woods to treat the water before drinking it. There are also various kinds of filters available, which are constantly becoming less bulky and expensive and more effective; they also remove impurities from water, often making it look and taste better, so that sources that are unappealing in the untreated state can be made to produce drinkable water. Water should be brought to a rolling boil or disinfected with an iodine-based disinfectant. Chlorine-based products, such as Halazone, are ineffective in water that contains organic impurities, and all water-purification chemicals tend to deteriorate quickly. Remember to allow extra contact time (and use twice as many tablets) if the water is very cold. Be sure to keep human waste at least 200 ft. away from water sources. If there are no toilets nearby, dig a hole 6 to 8 in. deep (but not below the organic layer of the soil) for a latrine and cover it completely after use.

KEY TO LOCATOR MAPS

The numbers within the boxes on the locator map presented at the beginning of each section indicate which maps show trails discussed in that section.

The page numbers listed at the beginning of each section indicate the start of trail descriptions covering a given area; the trail description text does not necessarily make note of the transition to different areas.

Map 1: Presidential Range

Map 2: Franconia–Pemigewasset

Map 3: Crawford Notch–Sandwich Range

Map 4: Moosilauke–Kinsman

Map 5: Carter Range–Evans Notch

Map 6: North Country–Mahoosuc Range

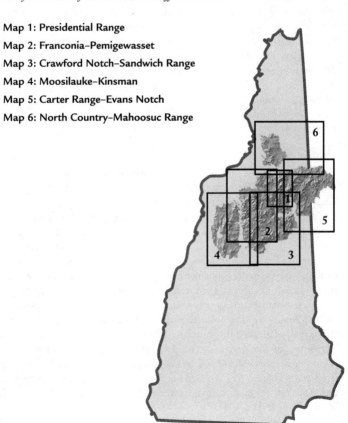

KEY TO ABBREVIATIONS AND ACRONYMS

The following abbreviations are used in this book.

AMC	Appalachian Mountain Club	**mts.**	mountains
ASNH	Audubon Society of New Hampshire	**Mt.**	Mount
		NC	Nature Conservancy
AT	Appalachian Trail	**NHDP**	New Hampshire Department of Resources and Economic Development Division of Parks and Recreation
ATC	Appalachia Trail Conservancy		
ATVs	all-terrain vehicles		
CMC	Chocorua Mountain Club		
CTA	Chatham Trails Association	**ow**	one way
CU	Camp Union	**PEAOC**	Phillips Exeter Academy Outing Club
DOC	Dartmouth Outing Club		
est.	estimated	**rd.**	road
FPA	Forest Protection Area	**rev.**	reverse elevation
FR	Forest Road (WMNF)	**RMC**	Randolph Mountain Club
ft.	foot, feet	**rt**	round trip
GPS	Global Positioning System	**RTC**	Rivendell Trail Council
HA	Hutmen's Association	**SLA**	Squam Lakes Association
hr.	hour(s)	**SPNHF**	Society for the Protection of New Hampshire Forests
in.	inch(es)		
JCC	Jackson Conservation Commission	**SSOC**	Sub Sig Outing Club
		st.	street
km.	kilometer(s)	**TCTA**	The Cohos Trail Association
LCC	Littleton Conservation Commission	**USFS**	United States Forest Service
		USGS	United States Geological Survey
lp	loop	**UTM**	Universal Transverse Mercator
LRCT	Lakes Region Conservation Trust	**WMNF**	White Mountain National Forest
MBPL	Maine Bureau of Parks and Lands	**WODC**	Wonalancet Out Door Club
mi.	mile(s)	**WVAIA**	Waterville Valley Athletic and Improvement Association
min.	minutes(s)		
MPH	miles per hour	**yd.**	yard(s)

HELPFUL INFORMATION AND CONTACTS

Organization	Office Locations	Phone Number
Appalachian Mountain Club (AMC)	Main Office	617-523-0636 (membership, headquarters), 603-466-2727 (reservations)
	Pinkham Notch Visitor Center	603-466-2725
AMC Four Thousand Footer Club		
Appalachian Trail Conservancy (ATC)	Main Office	304-535-6331
	ATC New England Regional Office	603-795-4935
Chocorua Mountain Club (CMC)		
Cohos Trail Association (TCTA)		
Dartmouth Outdoor Programs Office		603-646-2428
Dartmouth Outing Club (DOC), Director of Trails and Shelters		(603) 646-2429
Green Hills Preserve		603-356-8833
Leave No Trace	Main Office	800-332-4100
Mount Washington Observatory	Mount Washington	603-356-2137
National Recreation Reservation Service		877-444-6777
National Weather Office		207-688-3216 (office) 603-225-5191(forecast)
The Nature Conservancy, Green Hills Preserve		603-356-8833
New Hampshire Camping Information		603-726-7737 (in state) 888-CAMPSNH (888-226-7764) (out of state)

Address or Location	Web Site
5 Joy St., Boston, MA 02108	www.outdoors.org
Route 16, Box 298, Gorham, NH 03581-0298	
P.O. Box 444, Exeter, NH 03833	http://www.amc4000footer.org/
P.O. Box 236, Harpers Ferry, WV 25425	www.appalachiantrail.org
18 On the Common, Unit 7 P.O. Box 312, Lyme, NH 03768	
Chocorua Mountain Club, Chocorua, NH 03817	
252 Westmoreland Rd., Spofford, NH 03462	http://www.cohostrail.org/
Dartmouth College, P.O. Box 9, Hanover, NH 03755	
113 Robinson Hall, Dartmouth College, Hanover, NH 03755	http://www.dartmouth.edu/~doc/
P.O. Box 310, North Conway, NH 03860	
P.O. Box 997, Boulder, CO 80306	www.lnt.org
P. O. Box 2310, North Conway, NH 03860	www.mountwashington.org
	www.reserveusa.com
P.O. Box 1208, 1 Weather Lane, Route 231, Gray, ME 04039	http://www.erh.noaa.gov/er/gyx/
P.O. Box 310, North Conway, NH 03860	http://www.nature.org/
Box 1354, Campton, NH 03223	www.campsnh.com

Organization	Office Locations	Phone Number
New Hampshire Department of Resources and Economic Development, Division of Parks and Recreation (NHDP)		603-271-3556
New Hampshire State Park Campground Reservations		603-271-3628
New Hampshire State Police		800-525-5555 (emergency)
Pinkham Notch Visitor Center		603-466-2727
Randolph Mountain Club		
Society for the Preservation of New Hampshire Forests (SPNHF)		603-224-9945
The Squam Lakes Association (SLA)		603-968-7336
United States Forest Service (USFS) in Laconia, NH		603-524-6450
WMNF Offices and Ranger Districts (RDs)	Androscoggin Ranger District	603-466-2713; TTY 603-466-2856
	Campton Visitor Center	603-726-3804
	Evans Notch Visitor Center	207-824-2134; TTY 207-824-3312
	Forest Supervisor	603-528-8721; TTY 603-528-8722
	Gateway Visitor Center	603-745-3816
	Lincoln Woods Visitor Center	603-630-5190
	Pemigewasset Ranger District, Bethlehem Office (former Ammonoosuc Ranger District)	603-869-2626; TTY 603-869-3104
	Pemigewasset Ranger District, Plymouth Office	603-536-1315; TTY 603-536-3281
	Saco Ranger District	603-447-5448; TTY 603-447-3121
Wonalancet Outdoor Club (WODC)		

Address or Location	Web Site
172 Pembroke Road, P.O. Box 1856, Concord, NH 03302-1856	www.nhstateparks.org
Camping Reservations, Division of Parks and Recreation, P.O. Box 1856, Concord, NH 03302-1856	http://nhparks.state.nh.us/
	http://www.nh.gov/nhsp/
Route 16, Box 298, Gorham, NH 03581-0298	
P.O. Box 279, Gorham, NH 03581	www.randolphmountainclub.org
54 Portsmouth St., Concord, NH 03301	www.spnhf.com
P.O. Box 204, Holderness, NH 03245	http://www.squamlakes.org/
719 Main Street; Box 638, Laconia, NH 03247	
300 Glen Rd., Gorham, NH 03581 (at south end of town along NH 16)	
Exit 28 of I-93	
RFD 2, Box 2270, Bethel, ME 04217	
P.O. Box 638, Laconia, NH 03247 (at 719 North Main St., across railroad tracks from downtown section)	www.fs.fed.us/r9/white
Exit 32 of I-93	
Lincoln Woods Trail trailhead on the Kancamagus Highway	
660 Trudeau Rd., Bethlehem, NH 03574 (just north of US 3 opposite Gale River Rd.)	
RFD 3, Box 15, Rte. 175, Plymouth, NH 03264 (from I-93 Exit 25, turn left uphill, bear left at fork at top of hill onto NH 175 north; the office is on the left in 1 mi. at 1171 NH 175)	
RFD 1, Box 94, Conway, NH 03818 (at 33 Kancamagus Highway, just west of NH 16)	
HCR 64, P.O. Box 248, Wonalancet, NH 03897	http://www.wodc.org/

SECTION ONE
MOUNT WASHINGTON AND THE SOUTHERN RIDGES

This section includes the summit of Mt. Washington and the major ridges that run south from it, which constitute the southern portion of the Presidential Range. The region is bounded on the north approximately by the line formed by the Mt. Washington Cog Railway and the Mt. Washington Auto Rd., on the east by NH 16, on the south by US 302, and on the west by US 302 and the Base Rd. The northern portion of the Presidential Range, including Mts. Clay, Jefferson, Adams, and Madison, and the Great Gulf, is covered in Section Two of this book. Many of the trails described in Section Two also provide routes to Mt. Washington. The AMC's *Presidential Range Map* (map 1) covers this entire section except for the Iron Mountain Trail and several trails in the southern Montalban region in the south part of the section. All these trails (and much of the rest of this section as well) are covered by the AMC's *Crawford Notch–Sandwich Range Map* (map 3). The Davis Path is the only trail not completely covered by one map or the other; however, all but the southern end is on map 1 and all but the northern end on map 3.

Note: No hotel or overnight lodging for the public is available on the summit of Mt. Washington. No camping is permitted above treeline in summer. In winter, above-treeline camping is permitted in places where there is at least 2 ft. of snow cover on the ground, but not on frozen bodies of water nor on the east face of Mt. Washington's summit cone (the area above Tuckerman and Huntington Ravines and the Alpine Garden, running up to the summit).

In this section, the Appalachian Trail (AT) follows the entire Webster Cliff Trail from Crawford Notch to its intersection with the Crawford Path near the summit of Mt. Pierce, then follows the Crawford Path to the summit of Mt. Washington. On the way, it also crosses the summits of Mts. Webster, Jackson, and Pierce, and passes near Mts. Eisenhower, Franklin, and Monroe. From Mt. Washington, it descends to the Gulfside Trail (see Section Two) via the Trinity Heights Connector. Then, after passing over the ridge of the Northern Peaks (although missing most of the summits) and through the Great Gulf—areas also covered in Section Two—the AT returns to Section One at the Mt. Washington Auto Rd. and follows the Old Jackson Rd. to Pinkham Notch Visitor Center and NH 16.

MOUNTAIN SAFETY

Caution: Mt. Washington has a well-earned reputation as the most dangerous small mountain in the world. Storms increase in violence with great rapidity toward the summit. The greatest wind velocity ever recorded at any surface weather station was attained on Mt. Washington (231 MPH on April 12, 1934). Based on windchill temperatures, the worst conditions on Mt. Washington are approximately equal to the worst reported in Antarctica, although actual temperatures on Mt. Washington are not as low. If you begin to experience difficulty from weather conditions, remember that the worst is yet to come, and turn back, without shame, before it is too late.

Good weather conditions during winter hiking can be deceptive and give hikers a sense of confidence that can turn out to be dangerous. Terrible weather conditions can materialize with little warning and prove to be inconceivably brutal, so the best practice is to be prepared for the worst at all times. Safe ascents of Mt. Washington and all mountains during winter require much warm clothing, experienced leadership, and some special equipment such as crampons and an ice ax. From Columbus Day to Memorial Day, no building is open to provide shelter or refuge to hikers.

Inexperienced hikers sometimes misjudge the difficulty of climbing Mt. Washington by placing too much emphasis on the relatively short distance from the trailheads to the summit. To a person used to walking around their neighborhood, the trail distance of 4 mi. or so sounds rather tame. But the most important factor in the difficulty of the trip is the altitude gain of around 4,000 ft. from base to summit, give or take a few hundred feet depending on the route chosen. To a person unused to mountain trails or in less than excellent physical condition, this unrelenting uphill grind can be grueling and intensely discouraging. If you are not an experienced hiker or a trained athlete, you will almost certainly enjoy the ascent of Mt. Washington a great deal more if you build up to it with easier climbs in areas with less exposure to potentially severe weather.

Visitors ascending the mountain on foot should carry a compass and should take care to stay on the trails. If you are forced to travel in conditions of reduced visibility, favor the main trails with their large yellow-topped cairns over the lesser-used connecting trails that are often far less clearly marked. It is a grave predicament when a hiker above treeline accidentally abandons a trail in dense fog or a whiteout, particularly if the weather is rapidly deteriorating. There is no completely satisfactory course of action in this situation because the objective is to get below treeline as quickly as possible—with or without a trail—but the weather exposure is generally worse to the west while cliffs are more prevalent in the ravines to the east. If you know where the nearest major trail should be, then it is probably best to try to find it. If you have adequate clothing, it may be best to find a scrub patch and shelter yourself in it. In the absence of alternatives, take note that the Cog Railway on the western slope and the Mt. Washington Auto Rd. on the eastern slope make a line, although a rather crooked one, from west to east. These landmarks are difficult to miss in even the darkest night or the thickest fog, except in winter conditions when snowdrifts may conceal them. Remember which side of the mountain you are on, and travel clockwise or counterclockwise, skirting the tops of the ravines; sooner or later you will reach either the Cog Railway or Mt. Washington Auto Rd. Given a choice, aim for the Auto Rd., as the railroad is on the side of the mountain that faces the prevailing winds.

Winterlike storms of incredible violence occur frequently, even during the summer months. Winds of hurricane force exhaust even the strongest hiker, and cold rain driven horizontally by the wind penetrates clothing and drains heat from the body. When a person's body temperature falls, brain function quickly deteriorates; this is one of the first, and most insidious, effects of excessive heat loss (hypothermia). For more information on this lethal condition, read the passage on hypothermia in the Backcountry Hazards section of this book's Introduction.

All water sources in this heavily used area should be suspected of being unfit to drink; the safest course is to avoid drinking from trailside sources (for more information about drinking water and safety see p. xxix). Water is available at the Sherman Adams summit building during the months in which it is open, roughly from Memorial Day to Columbus Day.

SUMMIT BUILDINGS

No hotel or overnight lodging for the public is available on the summit of Mt. Washington. From Columbus Day to Memorial Day no buildings are open to hikers for shelter or refuge. The principal summit building serving tourists and hikers was named to honor Sherman Adams, a former New Hampshire governor and special assistant to President Eisenhower who was also a legendary White Mountain woodsman and, in his youth, trailmaster of the AMC's Trail Crew. Operated by the New Hampshire Division of Parks and Recreation during the summer season (mid-May to mid-October), it has food service, a pack room, a souvenir shop, public restrooms, telephones, and a post office. It houses the Mt. Washington Observatory, the Mt. Washington Museum, and facilities for park personnel.

The first Summit House on Mt. Washington was built in 1852. The oldest building still standing on the summit is the Tip Top House, a hotel first built in 1853 and rebuilt after it suffered a fire in 1915. This stone building, now owned by the state of New Hampshire and part of Mt. Washington State Park, has been restored and is open to the public as a historical site when the public summit facilities are in operation, but is not available for lodging or emergency shelter. The second Summit House, 1873–1908, was destroyed by fire.

There are several other buildings on the summit of Mt. Washington, none of them open to the general public. The Yankee Building, built in 1941 to house transmitter facilities for the first FM radio station in northern New England, houses two-way radio equipment for various organizations. The Mt. Washington Auto Road Company owns the Stage Office, built in 1975 to replace a similar building constructed in 1908. Two other summit buildings—the Yankee Powerhouse and the former WMTW-TV building—were destroyed by fire in February 2003.

MOUNT WASHINGTON OBSERVATORY

There has been a year-round weather observatory on Mt. Washington from 1870 to 1886, and from 1932 onward. The observatory maintains museum exhibits in the Sherman Adams summit building on Mt. Washington and in a new location on NH 16 just south of North Conway village. The Mt. Washington Observatory is operated by a nonprofit corporation, and individuals from the general public are invited to become members and contribute to the support of its important work. For details, contact the Mt. Washington Observatory.

MOUNT WASHINGTON AUTO ROAD

This road from the Glen House site on NH 16 to the summit, often called the Carriage Rd., was constructed from 1855 through 1861. Vehicles are charged a toll at the foot of the mountain. With long zigzags and an easy grade, the road climbs the prominent northeast ridge named for Benjamin Chandler, who died on the upper part from the effects of hypothermia in 1856. Hiking on the road is not forbidden, but despite easier grades and smoother footing than hiking trails, the distance is long and the competition with automobile traffic is annoying and potentially dangerous. After dark, however, its advantages increase markedly while its disadvantages decrease greatly, so this road may well be the best escape route for hikers faced with the likelihood of becoming benighted on the trails of Mt. Washington. In winter, severe icing and drifting, along with ruts from official snow-vehicle traffic, make the section above treeline a less pleasant and more difficult route than might be anticipated, particularly for skiers. The emergency shelters that were formerly located along the upper part of the road have been removed. The first 4 mi. of the road (below treeline), although still used by snow vehicles, are now officially maintained as a part of the Great Glen cross-country ski trail network and receive considerable use by skiers.

Because of the continual theft and destruction of trail signs, they are often placed on the trails at some distance from the Auto Rd. The names of some trails are painted on rocks at the point where they leave the road.

The Auto Rd. leaves NH 16 opposite the Glen House site (elevation about 1,600 ft.), crosses the Peabody River, and starts the long climb. Just above the 2-mi. mark, after sharp curves right and then left, the AT crosses. To the south, the AT follows the Old Jackson Rd. (now a foot trail) past junctions with the Nelson Crag Trail and the Raymond Path to Pinkham Notch Visitor Center. To the north the AT follows the Madison Gulf Trail toward the Great Gulf and the Northern Peaks. Low's Bald Spot, a fine viewpoint, can be reached by an easy walk of about 0.3 mi. from the road via the Madison Gulf Trail and a short side path.

The Auto Rd. continues to treeline, passing to the left of the site of the Halfway House (3,840 ft.), and soon swings around the Horn, skirting a prominent shoulder known as the Ledge, where there is a fine view to the north. A short distance above the Ledge, the Chandler Brook Trail descends into the Great Gulf on the right, and soon the route used by snow vehicles in winter diverges right.

Just above the 5-mi. mark, on the right exactly at the sharp turn, there are some remarkable folded strata in the rocks beside the road. Here, near Cragway Spring, the Nelson Crag Trail comes close to the left side of the road. At about 5.5 mi., the road passes through the patch of high scrub in which Dr. B. L. Ball survived two nights in a winter storm in October 1855. (Dr. Ball's account of his ordeal, *Three Days on the White Mountains: The Perilous Adventure of Dr. B. L. Ball on Mt. Washington,* published in 1856, is now available in a reprint edition from Bondcliff Books.) A short distance above the 6-mi. mark, where the winter route rejoins, the Wamsutta Trail descends on the right to the Great Gulf, and the Alpine Garden Trail diverges left. The trenchlike structures near the road are the remains of the old Glen House Bridle Path, built in 1853. The road soon makes a hairpin turn and circles the left edge of a lawn sometimes called the Cow Pasture, where the Huntington Ravine Trail enters on the left and the remains of an old corral are visible on the right a little farther along. Beyond the 7-mi. post, the Cog Railway approaches and runs above the road on the right; near the tracks, just below the summit, the Bourne monument stands at the spot where Lizzie Bourne perished in September 1855 at the age of 23, the second recorded death on the mountain. Soon the road crosses the Nelson Crag Trail, which enters on the left and climbs to the summit from the right side. The Tuckerman Ravine Trail enters on the left just below the parking-lot complex at about 8 mi., from which the summit buildings are reached by a wooden stairway.

MOUNT WASHINGTON COG RAILWAY

The Mt. Washington Cog Railway, an unusual artifact of 19th-century engineering with a fascinating history, was completed in 1869. It roughly follows the route of Ethan Allen Crawford's second trail up the mountain, which he cut to provide a shorter and more direct route to Mt. Washington than the Crawford Path over the Southern Peaks. Its maximum grade, 13.5 in. to the yd., is equaled by only one other railroad in the world (excluding funicular roads), the railroad on Mt. Pilatus in the Alps. The location of the Base Station is called Marshfield, in honor of Sylvester Marsh, an inventor of meatpacking machinery who was the chief promoter and builder of the railway, and Darby Field, leader of the first recorded ascent of Mt. Washington.

When the Cog Railway is in operation, walking on the track is not permitted; at other times, it is a poor pedestrian route at best. A WMNF public parking area is located on the Base Rd. about 0.5 mi. west of Marshfield. Hikers who wish to visit or park at the Base Station itself should expect to pay a fee. In recent years, the Cog Railway has operated in winter, taking skiers partway up for a 1-mi. downhill run beside the tracks. It is currently planned to operate trains part way up the mountain for passengers during weekends in the winter; the service for skiers that has been offered in the recent past has been discontinued.

The Cog Railway ascends a minor westerly ridge in a nearly straight line to the treeline, which is reached near the trestle called Jacob's Ladder (4,800 ft.). This trestle, standing as much as 30 ft. above the mountainside, is the steepest part of the railroad. After crossing the shoulder that extends toward Mt. Clay, the line curves to the right and runs close to the edge of the Great Gulf; there is a fine view across the gulf toward the Northern Peaks from the vicinity of the Gulf Tank (5,600 ft.). It is 3 mi. from Marshfield to the summit, and trains ascend in about 1 hr. 10 min.

SKIING IN THE MOUNT WASHINGTON AREA

A number of cross-country ski trails have been constructed in the vicinity of Pinkham Notch Visitor Center, making it a fine destination for those who wish to enjoy this sport. In addition, several of the hiking trails in the area are also suitable for ski touring. Information on these trails can be obtained at the center's Trading Post and on the AMC's *Winter Trails Map*.

The slopes of Tuckerman Ravine and the snowfields on and near the summit cone are justly famous for the opportunities they offer for alpine skiing. The skiing season on the Tuckerman headwall starts about the middle of March and may last into June in some years. The ravine area and the John Sherburne Ski Trail (see later) are patrolled by Forest Service rangers and the Mt. Washington Volunteer Ski Patrol. Warning notices about sections that are unsafe because of ice or possible avalanche danger are posted at Pinkham Notch Visitor Center and in the Tuckerman shelter area.

The Tuckerman Ravine Trail affords an easy ascent route on foot because it is normally well packed, but skiing downhill on it is prohibited because people walking on the trail would be put in jeopardy. Skiers should descend from Tuckerman Ravine on the John Sherburne Ski Trail (WMNF). This trail—named for John H. Sherburne Jr., whose efforts contributed greatly to its establishment—leaves the south end of the parking lot at Pinkham Notch Visitor Center at the same point as the Gulf of Slides Ski Trail. It ascends by a zigzag course, always to the left (south) of the Tuckerman Ravine Trail and the Cutler River, to the foot of the Little Headwall of the ravine, above the shelter area, where it ends. It is 10 to 50 ft. wide, and although the slope is suitable for expert and intermediate skiers at some points, many less expert skiers can also negotiate this trail because of its width. It is not open to hiking in any season.

The Gulf of Slides, which is situated somewhat similarly to Tuckerman Ravine, receives a large volume of snow that remains in the ravine, so open-slope skiing is possible well into spring (April and May). Its slopes, though less severe than those in Tuckerman Ravine, are more uniform and avalanche frequently. The Gulf of Slides Ski Trail leaves the south end of the parking lot at Pinkham Notch Visitor Center at the same point as the John Sherburne Ski Trail, and ascends west about 2,200 ft. in 2.5 mi. to the bowl of the Gulf of Slides. It is wet in places with a footway that is frequently overgrown, and is not maintained or recommended for summer hiking.

The Old Jackson Rd. is a good run for intermediate skiers. It drops 650 ft. and can be run in 30 min. The ascent takes 1 hr. Skiers should use the old trail route instead of the relocation; enter the old route below the 2-mi. mark, about 0.2 mi. below where the relocated section and the Madison Gulf Trail meet at the Auto Rd.

The upper half of the Mt. Washington Auto Rd. is not usually suitable for skiing because of windblown bare and icy spots and ruts from snow-vehicle traffic. The snowfields between the top of the Tuckerman headwall and the summit cone, and also those on Chandler Ridge near the 6-mi. mark on the Auto Rd., afford good spring skiing at all levels of skill, but are far more exposed to bad weather and require much more effort to reach because of their elevation. The lower half of the Auto Rd. is maintained as a cross-country ski trail by Great Glen Trails. In particular, it affords a link between the Old Jackson Rd. at the 2-mi. mark and Connie's Way, a ski trail that runs from Pinkham Notch Visitor Center to the 1-mi. mark on the road.

GEOGRAPHY

The tallest peak east of the Mississippi River and north of the Carolinas, Mt. Washington (6,288 ft.), is a broad, massive mountain. Mt. Washington has great ravines cut deeply into its steep sides, leaving buttress ridges that reach up through the timberline and support the great upper plateau. The timberline occurs at an elevation of 4,500 to 5,000 ft., depending on the degree of exposure to the mountain's fierce weather. The upper plateau, varying in elevation from 5,000 to 5,500 ft., bears comparatively gentle slopes interspersed with wide grassy areas strewn with rocks, which are called lawns. The summit cone, covered with fragments of rock and almost devoid of vegetation, rises steeply above this plateau. The upper part of the mountain has a climate similar to that of northern Labrador, and its areas of alpine tundra support a fascinating variety of plant and animal life adapted to the extreme conditions of the alpine environment. Many of these species are found only on other high mountaintops or in the tundra many hundreds of miles farther north, and a few plants are found only or primarily on the Presidential Range. The alpine plants in particular have attracted many professional and amateur scientists (including, among the well-known amateurs, Henry David Thoreau), and many of the features of the mountain are named for early botanists such as Manasseh Cutler, Jacob Bigelow, Francis Boott, William Oakes, and Edward Tuckerman. Great care should be exercised not to damage the plant life in these areas, as their struggle for survival is already sufficiently severe. Hikers should avoid unnecessary excursions away from the trails, and should step on rocks rather than vegetation wherever possible. The AMC publishes the *AMC Field Guide to the New England Alpine Summits,* a handbook covering the ecological relations of the plants and animals found above treeline. The New Hampshire Department of Resources and Economic Development publishes booklets on geology intended for the general public. The Presidential Range area is covered by *The Geology of the Mt. Washington Quadrangle* (currently out of print) and *The Geology of the Crawford Notch Quadrangle.*

The slopes of Mt. Washington are drained by tributaries of three major rivers: the Androscoggin, the Connecticut, and the Saco. The tall, massive Northern Presidentials or Northern Peaks (see Section Two) continue the rocky alpine terrain of Mt. Washington to the north and northeast in an arc that encloses the Great Gulf, the largest glacial cirque in the White Mountains. (A glacial cirque is a landform that results when an alpine glacier [a small local glacier in a mountain valley] excavates a typical V-shaped brook valley with a narrow floor and fairly uniform slopes, turning it into the classic U-shaped cirque with a broad, fairly flat floor and almost vertical walls.)

Moving clockwise from the Great Gulf around the east side of the mountain, Chandler Ridge (by which the Mt. Washington Auto Rd. ascends the upper part of the mountain) passes over the small peak of Nelson Crag before merging into the summit cone; this ridge divides the Great Gulf from the great ravines of the east face: Huntington Ravine, the Ravine of Raymond Cataract, Tuckerman Ravine (which is one of the finest examples of the glacial cirque), and the Gulf of Slides. Chandler Ridge also forms the north boundary of the lawn that is called the Alpine Garden for its colorful displays of alpine flowers in late June, which lies at the foot of the summit cone just above the three eastern ravines. Lion Head, a pinnacled buttress named for its appearance when seen from points on NH 16 just north of Pinkham Notch Visitor Center, caps the north wall of Tuckerman Ravine.

The steep eastern slopes of the mountain bear several notable waterfalls. Raymond Cataract falls through a series of wild and beautiful cascades in the Ravine of Raymond Cataract, but brush has covered a former footway, so this series of falls can be reached only by those intrepid explorers who are highly skilled in off-trail travel. Crystal Cascade is easily reached from Pinkham Notch Visitor Center by a walk of about 0.4 mi. on the Tuckerman Ravine Trail. Glen Ellis Falls, located deep in the Ellis River valley, can be easily reached from the parking area located on NH 16, 0.8 mi. south of Pinkham Notch Visitor Center, by a gravel path 0.3 mi. long, with rock steps and handrails, that passes under the highway through a tunnel. The main fall is 70 ft. high, and below it are several pools and smaller falls.

Boott Spur (5,500 ft.), the great southeast shoulder of Mt. Washington, forms the south wall of Tuckerman Ravine and the north wall of the Gulf of Slides. The flat ridge connecting Boott Spur with the cone of Mt. Washington bears Bigelow Lawn, the largest of the Presidential Range lawns. Both the Montalban Ridge and the Rocky Branch Ridge descend from Boott Spur and quickly drop below treeline, continuing south in thick woods with occasional open summits. Oakes Gulf, at the headwaters of the Dry River, lies west of Boott Spur and east of Mt. Monroe. The Southern Presidentials or Southern Peaks, running southwest from Mt. Washington, form the second most prominent ridge in the range (after the Northern Peaks), dropping to the treeline slowly and rising above it again several times before the final descent into the woods below Mt. Pierce. The Mt. Washington Cog Railway ascends the minor unnamed ridge that separates the much less spectacular (but still quite impressive) principal ravines of Mt. Washington's western face, Ammonoosuc Ravine and Burt Ravine, which lie between the Southern Peaks and the Northern Peaks.

Three major ridges run southwest or south from Mt. Washington, separated by deep river valleys from each other and from the ranges to the west and east. The most impressive of these ridges, formed by the Southern Peaks, runs southwest from Mt. Washington and ends abruptly at the cliffs of Mt. Webster, which make up the most impressive section of the eastern wall of Crawford Notch. The peaks that rise along this ridge are (from northeast to southwest) Mts. Monroe, Franklin, Eisenhower (formerly called Pleasant), Pierce (also commonly known as Clinton), Jackson, and Webster. To the northwest, the headwaters of the Ammonoosuc River (a Connecticut River tributary) flow across the Fabyan Plain—a broad, relatively flat expanse that separates the Southern Peaks from the much lower Cherry-Dartmouth Range; on the other side of the Southern Peaks ridge, the Dry River begins high on Mt. Washington in Oakes Gulf and runs to the Saco River below Crawford Notch through a deep, steep-sided valley between the Southern Peaks and the Montalban Ridge. Beyond the Dry River valley rises the Montalban Ridge, the longest of all Mt. Washington's subsidiary ridges, extending about 20 mi. from the summit. This ridge first runs generally south over Boott Spur, Mt. Isolation, Mt. Davis, Stairs Mountain, Mt. Resolution, and Mt. Parker, then swings east to Mts. Langdon, Pickering, and Stanton, the low peaks above the intervales of Bartlett and Glen near the confluence of the Rocky Branch and Saco River. The Bemis Ridge is a significant spur running from Mt. Resolution southwest over Mt. Crawford, then south to Hart Ledge, which overlooks the great bend in the Saco. East of the Montalbans lies the Rocky Branch of the Saco River, and to the east of that stream rises the Rocky Branch Ridge, a long, wide-spreading assortment of humps and flat ridges running south from Boott Spur via Slide Peak, with no noteworthy summit except Iron Mountain at the far south end. Still farther east, the Ellis River flows down from Pinkham Notch, with NH 16 running through the valley and the ridges of Wildcat Mountain rising on the opposite side.

The Southern Presidentials or Southern Peaks—the names are used interchangeably—form a great ridge that extends about 8 mi. southwest from the summit of Mt. Washington to the Webster Cliffs above Crawford Notch. The Ammonoosuc River lies to the northwest and the Dry River to the southeast. The summits on this ridge decrease steadily in elevation from northeast to southwest.

The tallest of the Southern Peaks, Mt. Monroe (5,372 ft.), is a sharply pointed pyramid that rises abruptly from the flat area around the Lakes of the Clouds, with a secondary summit, a small crag sometimes called Little Monroe (5,225 ft.), on its west ridge. The summit, crossed by the Mt. Monroe Loop, is completely above treeline and affords fine views of the deep chasm of Oakes Gulf on the east, the Lakes of the Clouds, and the nearby summit of Mt. Washington. The Lakes of the Clouds are two small alpine tarns that lie in a small bowl on the northwest side of the ridge near the low point between Mt. Washington and Mt. Monroe. The larger lake, often called the Lower Lake, is at an elevation of 5,025 ft., while the much smaller Upper Lake lies to the north of the Lower Lake at an elevation of 5,050 ft. The flat region between Mt. Monroe and the Lakes of the Clouds supports a bountiful number of alpine plants, including the extremely rare Robbins' cinquefoil *(Potentilla robbinsiana),* making it the most significant and thus the most vulnerable habitat in the White Mountains. Part of this area is closed to all public entry because of damage caused in the past by hikers coming to admire these plants, which can withstand the full violence of above-treeline weather but not the tread of hikers' boots. Sadly, we can now pay homage to some of these rare survivors only from a distance.

Mt. Franklin (5,001 ft.) is a flat shoulder of Monroe that appears impressive only when seen from below, in the Eisenhower-Franklin col. The summit's exact location (and even existence) among a group of low, rolling ridges is not entirely obvious; it lies a short distance to the east of the Crawford Path and commands an excellent view straight down into Oakes Gulf.

Previously called Mt. Pleasant, Mt. Eisenhower (4,760 ft.) was renamed after the former president's death. While there is a good deal of scrub on the lower slopes of this dome-shaped mountain, the top is completely bald. Its summit is crossed by the Mt. Eisenhower Loop.

The New Hampshire legislature named Mt. Pierce (4,312 ft.) for Franklin Pierce, the only U.S. president born in New Hampshire, in 1913. Although this name is officially recognized by the Board of Geographic Names and appears on all USGS maps, it was not universally accepted, and the mountain's former name, Mt. Clinton, persists in the Mt. Clinton Rd. and the Mt. Clinton Trail, which ascends the southeast slope of the mountain. Mt. Pierce is wooded almost to the top of its flat summit on the west, but a broad open area on the east side affords fine views. Its summit lies on the Webster Cliff Trail just above its junction with the Crawford Path.

Named for Charles Jackson, a 19th-century New Hampshire state geologist, and not (as many would suppose) for President Andrew Jackson, Mt. Jackson (4,052 ft.) has a square, ledgy summit with steep sides and a flat top, affording possibly the finest views overall among the Southern Peaks. Its summit is crossed by the Webster Cliff Trail and is also reached by the Jackson branch of the Webster-Jackson Trail.

Once called Notch Mountain, Mt. Webster (3,910 ft.) was renamed for Daniel Webster, the great 19th-century orator, U.S. senator, secretary of state, and unsuccessful aspirant to the presidency. The summit of Mt. Webster is crossed by the Webster Cliff Trail, which is intersected by the Webster branch of the Webster-Jackson Trail not far from the top.

To the southeast of the Southern Peaks lies the Dry River, running down the central valley of the Presidential–Dry River Wilderness. This river has also been called the Mt. Washington River, but Dry River has won the battle, possibly because of the ironic quality of the name. The Dry River runs from Oakes Gulf to the Saco through a deep, narrow, steep-walled ravine. Though in a dry season the flow is a bit meager, with lots of rocks lying uncovered in the streambed, its watershed has extremely rapid runoff and its sudden floods are legendary—it has drowned unwary hikers. No other logging railroad ever constructed in the White Mountains had as many river crossings in so short a distance as the railroad that was built up this valley, and no other logging railroad ever had all its trestles swept away by floods so quickly after ceasing operations.

Access to the Dry River area has always been somewhat difficult, and ascents of the Southern Peaks from this side have always been relatively arduous. But since the Presidential Range–Dry River Wilderness was established and the number of wilderness-seeking visitors increased sharply, the WMNF has made access somewhat easier by eliminating many river crossings through trail relocations and the construction of a major suspension bridge at the first (and usually most difficult) remaining crossing. However, it is still an area where visitors need to keep a careful watch on the weather and take account of any substantial rainfall in the previous few days. In accordance with USFS Wilderness policy, the trails in the Dry River area are in general maintained to a lower standard than trails outside Wilderness.

The Montalban Ridge extends southward from Boott Spur, forming the longest subsidiary ridge in the Presidential Range, running for about 20 mi. between the Rocky Branch on the east and the Dry River and Saco River on the west. At Mt. Resolution the main ridge curves to the east along the Saco valley, while the short Bemis Ridge carries the line of the upper ridge south to the great bend in the Saco. The peaks of the Montalban Ridge, in order from the north, include Mt. Isolation (4,003 ft.), Mt. Davis (3,819 ft.), Stairs Mountain (3,463 ft.), Mt. Resolution (3,415 ft.), Mt. Parker (3,004 ft.), Mt. Langdon (2,390 ft.), Mt. Pickering (1,930 ft.), and Mt. Stanton (1,716 ft.). The peaks of the Bemis Ridge include Mt. Crawford (3,119 ft.), Mt. Hope (2,505 ft.), and Hart Ledge (2,020 ft.). Cave Mountain (1,439 ft.), a low spur of the range near Bartlett village, is much better known for the cave on its south face than for its summit.

The views from the summits of Mts. Isolation, Davis, and Crawford are among the finest in the White Mountains, and Mts. Resolution and Parker also offer excellent outlooks. The Giant Stairs are a wild and picturesque feature of the region, offering a spectacular view from the top of the cliff that forms the upper stair. These two great steplike ledges at the south end of the ridge of Stairs Mountain are quite regular in form, and are visible from many points. A third and somewhat similar cliff, sometimes called the Back Stair, lies east of the main summit but has no trail. Mt. Stanton and Mt. Pickering are wooded, but several open ledges near their summits afford interesting views in various directions.

All of the peaks named above are reached by well-maintained trails, except Mt. Hope and Hart Ledge. Mt. Hope is heavily wooded and very seldom climbed. The fine cliff of Hart Ledge rises more than 1,000 ft. above the meadows at the great bend in the Saco River just above Bartlett and affords commanding views to the east, west, and south. There is no regular trail, but intrepid bushwhackers may follow the roads that run west along the north side of the river, passing under the cliffs, then climb up the slope well to the west of the cliffs.

East of the Montalban Ridge, beyond the Rocky Branch but west of the Ellis River valley, lies the Rocky Branch Ridge. This heavily wooded ridge runs south from Slide Peak, and is sharply defined for only about 3 mi., then spreads out and flattens. It has no important peaks. Iron Mountain (2,726 ft.), a small mountain near Jackson with a fine north outlook and a magnificent bare ledge at the top of its south cliff, is the most significant summit on this long stretch of uplands between the Rocky Branch and the Ellis River—though the Rocky Branch Ridge ceases to be an outstanding ridge long before it reaches Iron Mountain. Green Hill (2,181 ft.) is a shoulder of Iron Mountain with an interesting view but no official path.

HUTS AND LODGES

For current information on the AMC's huts, Pinkham Notch Visitor Center, Joe Dodge Lodge, or the Highland Center at Crawford Notch, contact the AMC's Reservation Office (603-466-2727) or visit www.outdoors.org/lodging.

Pinkham Notch Visitor Center (AMC)

Pinkham Notch Visitor Center is a unique mountain sports facility in the heart of the WMNF. This facility, originally built in 1920 and greatly enlarged since then, is located on NH 16 practically at the height-of-land in

Pinkham Notch, about 20 mi. north of Conway and 11 mi. south of Gorham. It is also 0.8 mi. north of Glen Ellis Falls and 0.5 mi. south of the base of the Wildcat Mountain Ski Area. Pinkham Notch Visitor Center offers food and lodging to the public throughout the year. Pets are not allowed inside any building of the visitor center. Concord Trailways offers daily bus service to and from Logan Airport and South Station in Boston, and the AMC operates a hiker shuttle bus from the visitor center to most of the principal trailheads in the White Mountains during the summer.

The Joe Dodge Lodge accommodates more than 100 guests in a variety of bunk and family rooms. It also offers overnight guests a library that commands a spectacular view of the nearby Wildcat Ridge, and a living room where accounts of the day's activities can be shared around an open fireplace. The center features a 65-seat conference room equipped with audiovisual facilities.

The Trading Post, a popular meeting place for hikers, has been a center of the AMC's educational and recreational activities since 1920. Weekend workshops, seminars, and lectures are conducted throughout the year. The building houses a dining room, and an information desk where basic equipment, guidebooks, maps, and other of the AMC's publications are available. The pack room downstairs is open 24 hours a day for hikers to stop in, relax, use the coin-operated showers, and repack their gear.

Pinkham Notch Visitor Center is the most important trailhead on the east side of Mt. Washington. Free public parking is available, although sleeping in cars is not permitted. Additional parking is available in designated areas along NH 16 in both directions, but a USFS recreational permit is required. Though the permit is not legally required for parking at Pinkham Notch Visitor Center, the AMC requests that hikers purchase one to support the USFS recreation program. The Tuckerman Ravine Trail, the Lost Pond Trail, and the Old Jackson Rd. all start at the center, giving access to many more trails, and a number of walking trails have been constructed for shorter, easier trips in the Pinkham vicinity. Among these are the Crew-Cut Trail, George's Gorge Trail, Liebeskind's Loop, and the Square Ledge Trail. There are also several ski-touring trails; for information, consult personnel at the Trading Post main desk.

The Highland Center at Crawford Notch (AMC)

Located on 26-acres of privately owned land at the head of Crawford Notch, the Highland Center, opened in 2003, is a lodging and education center open to the public year-round. It is located at the site of the former Crawford House grand hotel on US 302, about 20 mi. west of North Conway and 8.5 mi. east of the traffic lights in Twin Mountain village. The Highland Center is a stop on the AMC's Hiker Shuttle routes during summer and fall.

The Highland Lodge contains 34 lodging rooms accommodating a total of 122 beds, including shared rooms with shared baths and private rooms with private baths. The adjacent Shapleigh Bunk House includes 16 beds in two bunkrooms, as well as a common room and pantry with refrigerator and microwave. Reservations are encouraged. The center's construction utilizes energy-efficient materials and is designed to complement the landscape while paying tribute to the intriguing human history in Crawford Notch. Meals consisting of hearty mountain fare are served in a family-style setting.

A wide variety of educational programs and skills training for children, teens, and adults are offered at the Highland Center, aiming to help participants increase their understanding of the natural environment and gain proficiency in outdoor skills such as map and compass use or wilderness first aid. Day-hikers, backpackers, and other visitors can access trail and weather information at the center.

The Macomber Family Information Center, open during summer and fall, is located in the historic Crawford Depot, a former train station renovated by the AMC, and houses interpretive displays, an information desk, and a small store that stocks last-minute hiker supplies, guidebooks, the AMC's publications, and souvenir items. It is also a major stop and transfer point for the AMC's Hiker Shuttle, which operates during the summer and early fall, and serves as a depot for the excursion trains that run on the Crawford Notch line during the tourist season.

From the AMC's Crawford Notch property, many trails can be accessed, including the Mt. Willard Trail and the Avalon Trail. Parking next to the Macomber Family Information Center is limited to 30 minutes. Parking for overnight guests is located on the Highland Center property near the main building. Parking for the Crawford Path is available in the

USFS lot (recreational permit required) located just off Mt. Clinton Rd. near its junction with US 302. Other trails easily accessed from the Highland Center include the Around-the-Lake Trail, Red Bench Trail, Saco Lake Trail, and Webster-Jackson Trail.

Lakes of the Clouds Hut (AMC)

The original stone hut was built in 1915 and has been greatly enlarged since then. It is located on a shelf near the foot of Mt. Monroe about 50 yd. west of the larger lake at an elevation of 5,012 ft. It is reached by the Crawford Path or the Ammonoosuc Ravine Trail, and has accommodations for 90 guests. Pets are not permitted in the hut. The hut is open to the public from June to mid-September, and closed at all other times. Space for backpackers is available at a lesser cost. A refuge room in the cellar is left open in the winter for emergency use only.

Mizpah Spring Hut (AMC)

The newest of the AMC huts was completed in 1965 and is located at about 3,800 ft. elevation on the site formerly occupied by the Mizpah Spring Shelter, at the junction of the Webster Cliff Trail and the Mt. Clinton Trail, near the Mizpah Cutoff. The hut accommodates 60 guests, with sleeping quarters in 8 rooms containing from 4 to 10 bunks. This hut is open to the public from mid-May to mid-October (caretaker basis in May). Pets are not permitted in the hut. There are tentsites nearby (caretaker, fee charged).

CAMPING

Presidential Range–Dry River Wilderness

Wilderness regulations, intended to protect Wilderness resources and promote opportunities for challenge and solitude, prohibit use of motorized equipment or mechanical means of transportation of any sort. In accordance with USFS Wilderness policy, the trails in the Dry River area are in general maintained to a lower standard than trails outside Wilderness. They may be rough, overgrown, or essentially unmarked with minimal signage, and considerable care may be required to follow them. Camping and wood or charcoal fires are not allowed within 200 ft. of any trail except at designated campsites. Hiking and camping group size must be no larger than 10 people. Camping and fires are also prohibited above the treeline (where trees are less than 8 ft. tall) except in winter, when camping is permitted above the treeline in places where snow cover is at least 2 ft. deep, but not on any frozen body of water. Many shelters have been removed, and the remaining ones will be dismantled when major maintenance is required; one should not count on using any of these shelters.

Forest Protection Areas

The WMNF has established a number of Forest Protection Areas (FPAs)—formerly known as Restricted Use Areas—where camping and wood or charcoal fires are prohibited throughout the year. The specific areas are under continual review, and areas are added to or subtracted from the list in order to provide the greatest amount of protection to areas subject to damage by excessive camping, while imposing the lowest level of restrictions possible. A general list of FPAs in this section follows, but because there are often major changes from year to year, one should obtain current information on FPAs from the WMNF.

(1) No camping is permitted above treeline (where trees are less than 8 ft. tall), except in winter, and then only in places where there is at least 2 ft. of snow cover on the ground—but not on any frozen body of water, and not on the east face of Mt. Washington's summit cone from Boott Spur to Nelson Crag (the area above Tuckerman and Huntington Ravines, including the Alpine Garden area). The point where the above-treeline restricted area begins is marked on most trails with small signs, but the absence of such signs should not be construed as proof of the legality of a site.

(2) No camping is permitted within 0.25 mi. of any trailhead, picnic area, or any facility for overnight accommodation such as a hut, cabin, shelter, tentsite, or campground, except as designated at the facility itself. In the area covered by Section One, camping is also forbidden within 0.25 mi. of Glen Ellis Falls.

(3) No camping is permitted within 200 ft. of certain trails. In 2006, designated trails included the Ammonoosuc Ravine Trail.

(4) No camping is permitted on WMNF land within 0.25 mi. of certain roads (camping on private roadside land is illegal except by permission of

the landowner). In 2006, these roads included US 302 west of Bartlett, New Hampshire, NH 16 north of Dana Place Inn, the Base Rd. (FR 173), the Jefferson Notch Rd. from the Base Rd. to the Caps Ridge Trail trailhead, and the Rocky Branch Rd. (FR 27, a.k.a. Jericho Rd.).

(5) In Tuckerman and Huntington Ravines (Cutler River drainage, including the Alpine Garden and the east face of the Mt. Washington summit cone), camping is prohibited throughout the year; the only year-round exception is the Hermit Lake Shelters and adjoining tent platforms (management policies described later under campsites). Visitors in the ravine areas may not kindle charcoal or wood fires; people intending to cook must bring their own small stoves. Day visitors and shelter users alike are required to carry out all their own trash and garbage—no receptacles are provided. This operating policy is under continual review, so it can change from time to time; current information is available at Pinkham Notch Visitor Center or the Tuckerman Ravine caretaker's residence, or from WMNF offices. There is no warming room open to the public, and refreshments are not available.

Crawford Notch State Park

No camping is permitted in Crawford Notch State Park, except at the public Dry River Campground (fee charged).

Established Trailside Campsites

During peak summer and fall periods, groups of six or more planning to use AMC-managed backcountry campsites are asked to use the AMC's group notification system. For more information visit http://www.outdoors.org/lodging/campsites/campsites-notification.cfm.

Hermit Lake Campsite (AMC/WMNF), located in Tuckerman Ravine, consists of eight open-front shelters with a capacity of 86 and three tent platforms open to the public. Tickets for shelter and tentsite space (nontransferable and nonrefundable) must be purchased for a fee at Pinkham Notch Visitor Center in person (first come, first served). Campers are limited to a maximum of seven consecutive nights, and pets are not allowed to stay overnight.

Nauman Tentsite (AMC) consists of seven tent platforms near Mizpah Spring Hut. In summer, there is a caretaker and a fee is charged.

Lakes of the Clouds Hut (AMC) has limited space available for back-packers at a substantially lower cost than the normal hut services.

Rocky Branch Shelter #1 and Tentsite (WMNF) is located near the junction of the Rocky Branch and Stairs Col Trails, just outside the Presidential Range–Dry River Wilderness.

Rocky Branch Shelter #2 (WMNF) is located at the junction of the Rocky Branch Trail and Isolation Trail, within the Presidential Range–Dry River Wilderness. Following the established policy for management of Wilderness, this shelter will be removed when major maintenance is required.

Dry River Shelter #3 (WMNF) is located on the Dry River Trail, 6.3 mi. from US 302, within the Presidential Range–Dry River Wilderness. This shelter will be removed when major maintenance is required.

Resolution Shelter (AMC) is located on a spur path that leaves the Davis Path at its junction with the Mt. Parker Trail, within the Presidential Range–Dry River Wilderness. The water source is scanty in dry seasons. This shelter will be removed when major maintenance is required.

Mt. Langdon Shelter (WMNF) is located at the junction of the Mt. Langdon and Mt. Stanton Trails, at the edge of the Presidential Range–Dry River Wilderness.

TRAIL DESCRIPTIONS

Tuckerman Ravine Trail (WMNF)

This trail to the summit of Mt. Washington from NH 16 at Pinkham Notch Visitor Center is probably the most popular route of ascent on the mountain. From Pinkham Notch Visitor Center, it uses a rocky tractor road to the floor of Tuckerman Ravine. From there to the top of the head-wall, it is a well-graded path, steady but not excessively steep. Its final section ascends the cone of Mt. Washington steeply over fragments of rock. In spring and early summer, the WMNF often closes the section of trail on the ravine headwall because of snow and ice hazards including dangerous crevasses, and notice is posted at Pinkham Notch Visitor Center. In these circumstances, the Lion Head Trail is usually the most convenient alternative route. In winter conditions, the headwall is often impassable except by experienced and well-equipped technical snow and ice climbers, and it is frequently closed by the WMNF even to such climbers because of avalanche and icefall hazards. The winter route of the Lion Head Trail, which begins on the Huntington Ravine Fire Rd. 0.1 mi. from the Tuckerman Ravine Trail, bypasses the headwall and usually provides the easiest and safest route for ascending Mt. Washington from the east in winter.

The Tuckerman Ravine Trail starts behind the Trading Post at Pinkham Notch Visitor Center; the Old Jackson Rd. diverges right 50 yd. from here. Be careful to avoid numerous side paths, including the Blanchard Ski Trail, in this area. In 0.3 mi., it crosses a bridge to the south bank of the Cutler River, begins its moderate but relentless climb, and soon passes a side path leading 20 yd. right to the best viewpoint for Crystal Cascade. The Boott Spur Trail diverges on the left at a sharp curve to the right, 0.4 mi. from Pinkham Notch Visitor Center, and at 1.3 mi., the Huntington Ravine Trail diverges on the right. At 1.5 mi., the Tuckerman Ravine Trail crosses a tributary, then at 1.6 mi., the main branch of the Cutler River. At 1.7 mi., the Huntington Ravine Fire Rd., which is the easiest route to Huntington Ravine in winter but offers very rough footing on some parts in summer, leaves on the right. The Lion Head winter route now begins about 0.1 mi. up this road. At 2.1 mi., the Raymond Path enters on the right at a point where the Tuckerman trail turns sharp left, and at 2.3 mi., the Lion Head Trail leaves on the right. In another 0.1 mi., the Boott Spur Link leaves on the left, opposite the buildings located at the floor of Tuckerman Ravine near Hermit Lake. Views from the floor of the ravine are impressive: the cliff on the right is Lion Head, while the more distant crags on the left are the Hanging Cliffs of Boott Spur.

The main trail keeps to the right (north) of the main stream and ascends a well-constructed footway into the upper floor of the ravine. At the foot of the headwall, it bears right and ascends a steep slope, where the Snow Arch can be seen on the left in spring and early summer of most years. In the early part of the hiking season, the snowfield above the Snow Arch usually extends across the trail, and the trail is often closed to hiking until this potentially hazardous snow slope has melted away. Some snow may persist in the ravine until late summer. The arch (which does not always form) is carved by a stream of snowmelt water that flows under the snowfield. *Caution:* Do not approach or get too close to the arch, and under no circumstances cross over it or venture beneath it because sections weighing many tons may break off at any moment. One death and several narrow escapes have occurred. When ascending the headwall, be careful not to dislodge rocks and start them rolling—this may put hikers below you in serious danger. There have been several serious accidents in recent years involving hikers who slipped off the side of the trail on the upper part of the headwall, often in adverse weather conditions, especially when the trail was slippery. Though the trail itself is relatively easy and quite safe, it passes within a very short distance of some extremely dangerous terrain, so a minor misstep off the side of the trail can have grave consequences.

Turning sharp left at the top of the debris slope and traversing under a cliff, the trail emerges from the ravine and climbs almost straight west up a grassy, ledgy slope. At 3.4 mi., a short distance above the top of the headwall, the Alpine Garden Trail diverges right. At Tuckerman Junction, located on the lower edge of Bigelow Lawn at 3.6 mi., the Tuckerman Crossover leads almost straight ahead (southwest) to the Crawford Path near the Lakes of the Clouds Hut; the Southside Trail diverges from the Tuckerman Cross-over in 30 yd. and leads west, skirting the cone to the Davis Path; and the Lawn Cutoff leads left (south) toward Boott Spur. The Tuckerman Ravine Trail turns sharp right at this junction and ascends the steep rocks, marked by cairns and paint on ledges. At 3.8 mi., at Cloudwater Spring about a third of the way up the cone, the Lion Head Trail reenters on the right. The Tuckerman trail continues to ascend to the Auto Rd. a few yards below the lower parking area, from which wooden stairways lead to the summit area.

Tuckerman Ravine Trail (map 1:F9)

Distances from Pinkham Notch Visitor Center (2,032 ft.) to
- Boott Spur Trail (2,275 ft.): 0.4 mi., 250 ft., 20 min.
- Huntington Ravine Trail (3,031 ft.): 1.3 mi., 1,000 ft., 1 hr. 10 min.
- Huntington Ravine Fire Rd. (3,425 ft.): 1.7 mi., 1,400 ft., 1 hr. 35 min.
- Raymond Path (3,675 ft.): 2.1 mi., 1,650 ft., 1 hr. 55 min.
- Lion Head Trail (3,825 ft.): 2.3 mi., 1,800 ft., 2 hr. 5 min.
- Boott Spur Link and Hermit Lake shelters (3,875 ft.): 2.4 mi., 1,850 ft., 2 hr. 10 min.
- Snow Arch (4,525 ft.): 3.1 mi., 2,500 ft., 2 hr. 50 min.
- Alpine Garden Trail (5,125 ft.): 3.4 mi., 3,100 ft., 3 hr. 15 min.
- Tuckerman Junction (5,383 ft.): 3.6 mi., 3,350 ft., 3 hr. 30 min.
- Lion Head Trail, upper junction (5,675 ft.): 3.8 mi., 3,650 ft., 3 hr. 45 min.
- Mt. Washington summit (6,288 ft.): 4.2 mi., 4,250 ft., 4 hr. 15 min.

Lion Head Trail (AMC)

The Lion Head Trail follows the steep-ended ridge—aptly named for the appearance of its upper portion when viewed from points on NH 16 north of Pinkham Notch Visitor Center—that forms the north wall of Tuckerman Ravine. The trail begins and ends on the Tuckerman Ravine Trail and thus provides an alternative route to that heavily used trail, although it is much steeper in parts. It is especially important as an alternative when the Tuckerman Ravine Trail over the headwall is closed during the spring or whenever snow and ice create hazardous conditions. The winter route of the Lion Head Trail is considered the least dangerous route for ascending Mt. Washington in winter conditions, and is the most frequently used winter ascent route. An avalanche late in 1995 destroyed the former winter route, and a new winter route was constructed; this route leaves the Huntington Ravine Fire Rd. just past the crossing of the Raymond Path, about 0.1 mi. from the Tuckerman Ravine Trail, and rejoins the summer Lion Head Trail at treeline. The signs and markings are changed by the USFS according to prevailing conditions at the beginning and end of the winter season (which on Mt. Washington extends from late fall through much of the spring in most years) to ensure that climbers take the proper route. The winter route is not open at times when it is not signed and marked as the currently open route.

The Lion Head Trail diverges right from the Tuckerman Ravine Trail 2.3 mi. from Pinkham Notch Visitor Center and 0.1 mi. below Hermit Lake. Running north, it passes a side path on the left to one of the Hermit Lake shelters and crosses the outlet of Hermit Lake. It soon begins to climb the steep slope by switchbacks, scrambling up several small ledges with very rough footing. It reaches treeline at 0.4 mi., where the winter route enters on the right as the main trail bears left. (Descending, the summer trail turns right and the winter route descends almost straight ahead.) The trail then ascends an open slope to the lower Lion Head and continues to the upper Lion Head at 0.9 mi., where it runs mostly level, with impressive views from the open spur, until it crosses the Alpine Garden Trail at 1.1 mi. After passing through a belt of scrub, it ascends to the Tuckerman Ravine Trail, which it enters at Cloudwater Spring about a third of the way up the cone of Mt. Washington, about 0.4 mi. and 600 ft. below the summit.

Lion Head Trail (map 1:F9)

Distances from lower junction with Tuckerman Ravine Trail (3,825 ft.) to
- Alpine Garden Trail (5,175 ft.): 1.1 mi., 1,350 ft., 1 hr. 15 min.
- upper junction with Tuckerman Ravine Trail (5,675 ft.): 1.6 mi., 1,850 ft., 1 hr. 45 min.

Distance from Pinkham Notch Visitor Center (2,032 ft.) to
- Mt. Washington summit (6,288 ft.) via Lion Head Trail and Tuckerman Ravine Trail: 4.4 mi., 4,250 ft., 4 hr. 20 min.

Huntington Ravine Trail (AMC)

Caution: This is the most difficult regular hiking trail in the White Mountains. Many of the ledges demand proper use of handholds for safe passage, and extreme caution must be exercised at all times. Although experienced hikers who are reasonably comfortable on steep rock will probably encounter little difficulty when conditions are good, the exposure on several of the steepest ledges is likely to prove extremely unnerving to novices and to those who are uncomfortable in steep places. Do not attempt this trail if you tend to feel queasy or have difficulty on ledges on ordinary trails. Hikers encumbered with large or heavy packs may experience great difficulty in some places. This trail is very dangerous when wet or icy, and its use for descent at any time is strongly discouraged. Retreat under unfavorable conditions can be extremely difficult and hazardous, so one should never venture beyond the Fan in deteriorating conditions or when weather on the Alpine Garden is likely to be severe. During late fall, winter, and early spring, this trail (and any part of the ravine headwall) should be attempted only by those with full technical ice-climbing training and equipment. In particular, the ravine must not be regarded as a feasible escape route from the Alpine Garden in severe winter conditions.

This trail diverges right from the Tuckerman Ravine Trail 1.3 mi. from Pinkham Notch Visitor Center. In 0.2 mi., it crosses the Cutler River and, at 0.3 mi., the brook that drains Huntington Ravine. At 0.5 mi., it goes straight across the Raymond Path. It crosses the Huntington Ravine Fire Rd. and then climbs to meet it again, turning left on the road; at this junction a fine view of the ravine can be obtained by following the road to a small rise about 100 yd. in the opposite direction. Above this point the trail and road separate, rejoin, or cross several times; the junctions are not always well marked, but both routes lead to the same objective, and the major advantage of the trail is somewhat better footing. At 1.2 mi., the recently relocated first-aid cache in the floor of the ravine is reached. Just beyond here there are some interesting boulders near the path whose tops afford good views of the ravine. Beyond the scrubby trees is a steep slope covered with broken rock, known as the Fan, whose tip lies at the foot of the deepest gully. To the left of this gully are precipices; the lower one is called the Pinnacle.

After passing through the boulders, the path ascends to the left side of the Fan and, marked by yellow blazes on the rocks, crosses the talus diagonally. It then turns left and ascends in scrub along the north (right) side of the Fan to its tip at 1.8 mi., crossing a small brook about two-thirds of the way up. The trail then recrosses the brooklet and immediately attacks the rocks to the right of the main gully, climbing about 650 ft. in 0.3 mi. The marked route up the headwall follows the line of least difficulty and should be followed carefully over the ledges, which are dangerous, especially when wet. The first pitch above the Fan—a large, fairly smooth, steeply sloping ledge—is probably the most difficult scramble on the trail. Above the first ledges, the trail climbs steeply through scrub and over short sections of rock, including some fairly difficult scrambles. About two-thirds of the way up, it turns sharp left at a promontory with a good view, then continues to the top of the headwall, where it crosses the Alpine Garden Trail at 2.1 mi. From this point, it ascends moderately, and at 2.3 mi., it crosses the Nelson Crag Trail, by which the summit can be reached in 0.8 mi. by turning left at this junction. Soon the Huntington Ravine Trail reaches the Mt. Washington Auto Rd. just below the 7-mi. mark, 1.1 mi. below the summit.

Huntington Ravine Trail (map 1:F9)

Distances from Tuckerman Ravine Trail (3,031 ft.) to
- Raymond Path (3,425 ft.): 0.5 mi., 400 ft., 25 min.
- first-aid cache in ravine floor (4,075 ft.): 1.3 mi., 1,050 ft., 1 hr. 10 min.
- Alpine Garden Trail crossing (5,475 ft.): 2.1 mi., 2,450 ft., 2 hr. 15 min.
- Auto Rd. (5,725 ft.): 2.4 mi., 2,700 ft., 2 hr. 35 min.

Distance from Pinkham Notch Visitor Center (2,032 ft.) to
- Mt. Washington summit (6,288 ft.) via Tuckerman Ravine, Huntington Ravine, and Nelson Crag Trails: 4.4 mi., 4,250 ft., 4 hr. 20 min.

Nelson Crag Trail (AMC)

This trail, which now runs to the summit of Mt. Washington, begins on the Old Jackson Rd. at a point 1.7 mi. from Pinkham Notch Visitor Center and 0.2 mi. from the Auto Rd. It is an attractive trail, relatively lightly used, fairly steep, and rough in the lower part and greatly exposed to weather in the upper part.

Leaving the Old Jackson Rd., this trail follows and soon crosses a small brook, then climbs steadily, soon becoming quite steep. At about 1.1 mi., it rises out of the scrub, emerging on the crest of Chandler Ridge, from which there is an unusual view of Pinkham Notch in both directions. From this point, the trail is above treeline and very exposed to the northwest winds. It then bears northwest, climbs moderately over open ledges, and passes close by the Auto Rd. near Cragway Spring (unreliable), at the sharp turn about 0.3 mi. above the 5-mi. mark. The trail then climbs steeply to the crest of the ridge. It passes over Nelson Crag and crosses the Alpine Garden Trail, swings left and crosses the Huntington Ravine Trail at 2.8 mi. It climbs up the rocks to Ball Crag (6,112 ft.), then finally runs across the Auto Rd. and the Cog Railway to the summit. To descend on this trail, follow the walkway down along the lower side of the Sherman Adams summit building.

Nelson Crag Trail (map 1:F9)

Distances from Old Jackson Rd. (2,625 ft.) to
- closest approach to the Auto Rd. near Cragway Spring (4,825 ft.): 1.7 mi., 2,200 ft., 1 hr. 55 min.
- Huntington Ravine Trail (5,725 ft.): 2.8 mi., 3,100 ft., 2 hr. 55 min.
- Mt. Washington summit (6,288 ft.): 3.6 mi., 3,700 ft. (rev. 50 ft.), 3 hr. 30 min.

Boott Spur Trail (AMC)

This trail runs from the Tuckerman Ravine Trail near Pinkham Notch Visitor Center to the Davis Path near the summit of Boott Spur. It follows the long ridge that forms the south wall of Tuckerman Ravine and affords fine views. Grades are mostly moderate, but it has some rough footing. This trail is above treeline and thus greatly exposed to any bad weather for a considerable distance.

This trail diverges left from the Tuckerman Ravine Trail at a sharp right turn 0.4 mi. from Pinkham Notch Visitor Center, about 150 yd.

above the side path to Crystal Cascade. It immediately crosses the John Sherburne Ski Trail, then climbs through a ledgy area, crosses a tiny brook, and climbs steeply up a ladder to the ridge crest. At 0.5 mi., the trail climbs over a ledge with a view of Huntington Ravine, then turns sharp right where a side trail (left) leads in 50 yd. to a very limited view east. The trail next crosses a level, muddy area and then ascends northwest up a steeper, rougher slope toward a craggy shoulder. Halfway up this section, an obscure side trail leads left 100 yd. to a small brook (last water). At the ridge crest, 1.0 mi. from the Tuckerman Ravine Trail, the main trail turns left and a side trail leads right (east) 25 yd. to an interesting though restricted outlook to Huntington Ravine. The main trail continues upward at moderate grades with several short scrambles, reaching a ledgy ridge crest that affords some views, and at 1.7 mi., a side trail on the right leads in 30 yd. to Harvard Rock, which provides an excellent view of Tuckerman Ravine and of Lion Head directly in front of the summit of Mt. Washington.

The trail emerges from the scrub at 1.9 mi., then soon bears left and angles up the slope to Split Rock, which one can pass through or go around, at 2.0 mi. The trail then turns right, passes through a final patch of fairly high scrub, and rises steeply over two minor humps to a broad, flat ridge, where, at 2.2 mi., the Boott Spur Link descends on the right to the Tuckerman Ravine Trail near Hermit Lake. Above this point, the trail follows the ridge, which consists of a series of alternating steplike levels and steep slopes. The views of the ravine are excellent, particularly where the path skirts around the potentially dangerous Hanging Cliff, 1,500 ft. above Hermit Lake. After passing just to the right (north) of the summit of Boott Spur, the trail ends at the Davis Path.

Boott Spur Trail (map 1:F9)

Distances from Tuckerman Ravine Trail (2,275 ft.) to

- Harvard Rock (4,046 ft.): 1.7 mi., 1,750 ft., 1 hr. 45 min.
- Split Rock (4,337 ft.): 2.0 mi., 2,050 ft., 2 hr.
- Boott Spur Link (4,650 ft.): 2.2 mi., 2,400 ft., 2 hr. 20 min.
- Davis Path junction (5,450 ft.): 2.9 mi., 3,200 ft., 3 hr. 5 min.

Distances from Pinkham Notch Visitor Center (2,032 ft.) to

- Davis Path junction (5,450 ft.): 3.4 mi., 3,400 ft., 3 hr. 25 min.
- Mt. Washington summit (6,288 ft.) via Davis and Crawford Paths: 5.4 mi., 4,300 ft., 4 hr. 50 min.

Boott Spur Link (AMC)

This steep but interesting trail climbs the south wall of Tuckerman Ravine, connecting the main floor of the ravine with the upper part of Boott Spur. It now leaves the south side of the Tuckerman Ravine Trail at the southeast corner of the clearing opposite the buildings at Hermit Lake, 2.4 mi. from Pinkham Notch Visitor Center. From this clearing, it descends south-southeast and soon crosses the Cutler River on a bridge, then crosses the John Sherburne Ski Trail and swings to the left, reaching a junction with a former route of the trail at 0.2 mi. Here it turns right and climbs straight up the slope very steeply through woods and scrub, with rapidly improving views back into the ravine. It then continues to climb steeply over open rocks to the crest of Boott Spur, where it meets the Boott Spur Trail.

Boott Spur Link (map 1:F9)

Distance from Tuckerman Ravine Trail (3,875 ft.) to
* Boott Spur Trail (4,650 ft.): 0.6 mi., 850 ft. (rev. 50 ft.), 45 min.

Glen Boulder Trail (AMC)

This trail ascends past the famous Glen Boulder to the Davis Path 0.5 mi. below Boott Spur. It begins on the west side of NH 16 at the Glen Ellis Falls parking area 0.8 mi. south of Pinkham Notch Visitor Center. Parts of it are rather rough, but it reaches the treeline and views relatively quickly.

The trail leaves the parking area and ascends gradually for about 0.4 mi. to the base of a small cliff, then climbs around to the right of the cliff and meets the Direttissima, which enters from the right (north) coming from Pinkham Notch Visitor Center. At this junction the trail turns sharp left (south) and soon passes a short branch trail that leads left to an outlook on the brink of a cliff, which commands a fine view of Wildcat Mountain and Pinkham Notch. The main trail turns west, rises gradually, then gradually becomes steep. At 0.8 mi., it crosses the Avalanche Brook Ski Trail, which is marked with blue plastic markers (but not maintained for hiking). The Glen Boulder Trail soon reaches the north bank of a brook draining the minor ravine south of the Gulf of Slides. After following the brook, which soon divides, the trail then turns southwest and crosses both branches. It is level for 200 yd., then rapidly climbs the northeast side of the spur through conifers, giving views of the minor ravine and spur south of the Gulf of Slides. Leaving the trees, it climbs over open rocks with one fairly difficult scramble and, at 1.6 mi., reaches the Glen Boulder, an immense rock perched on the end of the spur that is a familiar landmark for travelers through Pinkham Notch. The view is wide, from Chocorua around to Mt. Washington, and is particularly fine of Wildcat Mountain.

From the boulder, the trail climbs steeply up the open ridge crest to its top at 2.0 mi., then reenters high scrub and ascends moderately. At 2.3 mi., a side trail descends right about 60 yd. to a fine spring. The main trail continues to Slide Peak (also called Gulf Peak) at 2.6 mi.; this rather insignificant peak at the head of the Gulf of Slides offers fine views. It then turns north and descends slightly, leaving the scrub, and runs entirely above treeline—greatly exposed to the weather—to the Davis Path just below a minor crag.

Glen Boulder Trail (map 1:G9)

Distances from Glen Ellis Falls parking area on NH 16 (1,975 ft.) to
- the Direttissima (2,300 ft.): 0.4 mi., 350 ft., 25 min.
- Avalanche Brook Ski Trail (2,600 ft.): 0.8 mi., 650 ft., 45 min.
- Glen Boulder (3,729 ft.): 1.6 mi., 1,750 ft., 1 hr. 40 min.
- Slide Peak (4,806 ft.): 2.6 mi., 2,850 ft., 2 hr. 45 min.
- Davis Path junction (5,175 ft.): 3.2 mi., 3,200 ft., 3 hr. 10 min.
- Boott Spur Trail (5,450 ft.) via Davis Path: 3.7 mi., 3,500 ft., 3 hr. 35 min.
- Mt. Washington summit (6,288 ft.) via Davis and Crawford Paths: 5.7 mi., 4,400 ft. (rev. 100 ft.), 5 hr. 5 min.

The Direttissima (AMC)

For hikers desiring access to the Glen Boulder Trail from Pinkham Notch Visitor Center, this trail eliminates a road walk on NH 16. Although in general it is almost level, there are several significant ups and downs. The trail begins about 0.2 mi. south of Pinkham Notch Visitor Center, just south of the highway bridge over the Cutler River, indicated by a sign at the edge of the woods. Marked by paint blazes, the trail turns sharp left about 30 yd. into the woods and follows a cleared area south. It turns slightly west at the end of this clearing and winds generally south, crossing a small brook. It skirts through the upper (west) end of a gorge and then crosses the gorge on a bridge at 0.5 mi. The trail continues past an excellent viewpoint looking down Pinkham Notch, passes along the top of a cliff and then the bottom of another cliff, and ends at the Glen Boulder Trail.

The Direttissima (map 1:F9–G9)

Distance from NH 16 near Cutler River bridge (2,025 ft.) to
  • Glen Boulder Trail (2,300 ft.): 1.0 mi., 400 ft. (rev. 100 ft.), 40 min.

Alpine Garden Trail (AMC)

This trail leads from the Tuckerman Ravine Trail to the Mt. Washington Auto Rd. through the grassy lawn called the Alpine Garden. Although its chief value is the beauty of the flowers (in season) and the views, it is also a convenient connecting link between the trails on the east side of the mountain, making up a part of various routes for those who do not wish to visit the summit. It is completely above treeline and exposed to bad weather, although it is on the mountain's east side, which usually bears somewhat less of the brunt of the mountain's worst weather.

The tiny alpine flowers that grow here are best seen in the middle to late part of June. Especially prominent in this area are the five-petaled white diapensia, the bell-shaped pink-magenta Lapland rosebay, and the very small pink flowers of the alpine azalea. (See the AMC's *Field Guide to the New England Alpine Summits* and *Wildflowers of the White Mountains,* published by Huntington Graphics.) No plants should ever be picked or otherwise damaged. Hikers are urged to stay on trails or walk very carefully on rocks so as not to kill the fragile alpine vegetation.

The trail diverges right from the Tuckerman Ravine Trail a short distance above the ravine headwall, about 0.2 mi. below Tuckerman Junction. It leads northeast, bearing toward Lion Head, and crosses the Lion Head Trail at 0.3 mi. Beyond this junction, the trail ascends gradually northward, its general direction from here to the Auto Rd. It traverses the Alpine Garden and crosses a tiny stream that is the headwater of Raymond Cataract. (This water may be contaminated by drainage from the summit buildings.) The trail soon approaches the top of Huntington Ravine and crosses the Huntington Ravine Trail at 1.2 mi. Here, a little off the trail, there is a fine view down into this impressive ravine. In winter and spring, take care not to approach too close to the icy gullies that drop precipitously from the edge of the Alpine Garden. Rising to the top of the ridge leading from Nelson Crag, the trail crosses the Nelson Crag Trail at 1.4 mi., then descends and soon enters the old Glen House Bridle Path, constructed in 1853, whose course is still plain although it was abandoned more than a century ago. In a short distance the Alpine Garden Trail turns left and in a few yards enters the Auto Rd. a short distance above the 6-mi. mark, opposite the upper terminus of the Wamsutta Trail.

Alpine Garden Trail (map 1:F9)

Distances from Tuckerman Ravine Trail (5,125 ft.) to
- Lion Head Trail (5,175 ft.): 0.3 mi., 50 ft., 10 min.
- Huntington Ravine Trail (5,475 ft.): 1.2 mi., 350 ft., 45 min.
- Nelson Crag Trail (5,575 ft.): 1.4 mi., 450 ft., 55 min.
- Auto Rd. junction (5,305 ft.): 1.8 mi., 450 ft. (rev. 250 ft.), 1 hr. 10 min.

Southside Trail (AMC)

This trail, which is completely above treeline, forms a direct link between Tuckerman Ravine and the Crawford Path and Westside Trail. It diverges right (west) from the Tuckerman Crossover about 30 yd. southwest of the Tuckerman Ravine Trail at Tuckerman Junction and, skirting the southwest side of Mt. Washington's summit cone, enters the Davis Path near its junction with the Crawford Path.

Southside Trail (map 1:F9)

Distance from Tuckerman Junction (5,383 ft.) to
- Davis Path (5,575 ft.): 0.3 mi., 200 ft., 15 min.

Tuckerman Crossover (AMC)

This trail connects Tuckerman Ravine with Lakes of the Clouds Hut. It is totally above treeline and crosses a high ridge where there is much exposure to westerly winds. It leaves the Tuckerman Ravine Trail left (southwest) at Tuckerman Junction, where the latter trail turns sharp right to ascend the cone. In 30 yd., the Southside Trail diverges to the right. The Tuckerman Crossover then rises gradually across Bigelow Lawn, crosses the Davis Path, and descends moderately to the Crawford Path, which it meets along with the Camel Trail a short distance above the upper Lake of the Clouds. After a left turn on the Crawford Path, the Lakes of the Clouds Hut is reached in 0.2 mi.

Tuckerman Crossover (map 1:F9)

Distances from Tuckerman Junction (5,383 ft.) to
- Davis Path (5,475 ft.): 0.3 mi., 100 ft., 10 min.
- Crawford Path (5,125 ft.): 0.8 mi., 100 ft. (rev. 350 ft.), 25 min.
- Lakes of the Clouds Hut (5,012 ft.) via Crawford Path: 1.0 mi., 100 ft. (rev. 100 ft.), 35 min.

Lawn Cutoff (AMC)

This trail provides a direct route between Tuckerman Junction and Boott Spur, entirely above treeline. It leaves the Tuckerman Ravine Trail at Tuckerman Junction and ascends gradually southward across Bigelow Lawn to the Davis Path about 0.6 mi. north of Boott Spur.

Lawn Cutoff (map 1:F9)

Distance from Tuckerman Junction (5,383 ft.) to
- Davis Path (5,475 ft.): 0.4 mi., 100 ft., 15 min.

Camel Trail (AMC)

This trail, connecting Boott Spur with the Lakes of the Clouds Hut, is named for ledges on Boott Spur that resemble a kneeling camel when seen against the skyline.

This is the right-hand trail of the two that diverge right (east) from the Crawford Path 0.2 mi. northeast of Lakes of the Clouds Hut (the Tuckerman Crossover, the other trail that also diverges here, is the left-hand trail of the two). The Camel Trail ascends easy grassy slopes, crosses the old location of the Crawford Path, and continues in a practically straight line across the level stretch of Bigelow Lawn. It aims directly toward the ledges that form the camel, passes under the camel's nose, and joins the Davis Path about 200 yd. northwest of the Lawn Cutoff.

Camel Trail (map 1:F9)

Distance from Crawford Path (5,125 ft.) to
- Davis Path (5,475 ft.): 0.7 mi., 350 ft., 30 min.

Westside Trail (WMNF)

This trail was partly constructed by pioneer trail maker J. Rayner Edmands; as was Edmands's practice, many segments are paved with carefully placed stones. It is wholly above timberline, very much exposed to the prevailing west and northwest winds. However, as a shortcut between the Gulfside Trail and Crawford Path that avoids the summit of Mt. Washington, it saves about 0.7 mi. in distance and 600 ft. in elevation between objectives in the Northern Peaks and Southern Peaks regions.

The trail diverges left from the Crawford Path at the point where the latter path begins to climb the steep part of the cone of Mt. Washington. It skirts the cone, climbing for 0.6 mi. at an easy grade, then descends moderately, passes under the tracks of the Mt. Washington Cog Railway, and soon ends at the Gulfside Trail.

Westside Trail (map 1:F9)
Distance from Crawford Path (5,625 ft.) to
- Gulfside Trail (5,500 ft.): 0.9 mi., 50 ft. (rev. 150 ft.), 30 min.

Trinity Heights Connector (NHDP)

This trail was created to allow the AT to make a loop over the summit of Mt. Washington; formerly the true summit was a side trip, albeit a very short one, from the AT, so technically the AT did not pass over it. Trinity Heights is a name formerly used for the summit region of Mt. Washington. From the true summit (marked by a large sign), the path runs approximately northwest over the rocks to the Gulfside Trail less than 0.1 mi. to the north of its junction with the Crawford Path.

Trinity Heights Connector (map 1:F9)
Distance from true summit of Mt. Washington (6,288 ft.) to
- Gulfside Trail (6,100 ft.): 0.2 mi., 0 ft. (rev. 200 ft.), 5 min.

Raymond Path (AMC)

This trail, one of the older paths in the region, begins on the Old Jackson Rd. 1.7 mi. from Pinkham Notch Visitor Center and 0.2 mi. from the Auto Rd., at a point about 100 yd. south of the beginning of the Nelson Crag Trail. Raymond Path ends at the Tuckerman Ravine Trail about 0.3 mi. below Hermit Lake. Its grades are mostly easy to moderate.

After diverging from the Old Jackson Rd., the trail crosses several small branches of the Peabody River, climbing moderately to the crest of a small ridge at 0.8 mi. where there is a restricted view to Lion Head and Boott Spur. It then descends moderately for a short distance to a small mossy brook, then begins to ascend easily, crossing Nelson Brook at 1.2 mi. and the Huntington Ravine Trail at 1.8 mi. From here, the trail drops down a steep bank to cross the brook that drains Huntington Ravine on a ledge at the brink of Vesper Falls—one should use great care here in high water or icy conditions, and perhaps consider a detour upstream. (This crossing can be avoided entirely by following the Huntington Ravine Trail north 0.1 mi. to the Huntington Ravine Fire Rd., then following the Fire Rd. south until it crosses the Raymond Path.) Soon the path crosses the brook coming from the Ravine of Raymond Cataract (sign) and then the Huntington Ravine Fire Rd., then climbs 0.3 mi. at a moderate grade to the Tuckerman Ravine Trail.

Raymond Path (map 1:F9)

Distances from Old Jackson Rd. (2,625 ft.) to
- Huntington Ravine Trail (3,425 ft.): 1.8 mi., 800 ft., 1 hr. 20 min.
- Tuckerman Ravine Trail (3,675 ft.): 2.4 mi., 1,050 ft., 1 hr. 45 min.
- Hermit Lake (3,850 ft.) via Tuckerman Ravine Trail: 2.7 mi., 1,250 ft., 2 hr.

Old Jackson Road (AMC)

This trail runs north from Pinkham Notch Visitor Center to the Mt. Washington Auto Rd., providing access to a number of other trails along with the most direct route from the visitor center to the Great Gulf. It is part of the AT and is blazed in white. Because it is used as a cross-country ski trail in winter, it is usually also marked with blue diamonds year-round.

Old Jackson Rd. diverges right from the Tuckerman Ravine Trail about 50 yd. from the trailhead at the rear of the Trading Post. After about 0.3 mi., the Blanchard and Connie's Way Ski Trails cross, and at 0.4 mi., the Link Ski Trail enters right just before a bridge and the Crew-Cut Trail leaves right (east) just after the bridge. Soon the Old Jackson Rd. begins to ascend moderately—more steeply in fact than one would expect of an old road—and crosses a small brook that runs in an interesting gorge with a small waterfall just above the trail. At 0.9 mi., George's Gorge Trail enters on the right (east), and the Old Jackson Rd. rises easily across the flat divide between the Saco and Androscoggin drainages and then descends slightly, crossing several small brooks. Just before reaching a larger brook, it makes a sharp left turn uphill, then after a short, steep climb, it turns right and runs nearly level. At 1.7 mi., the Raymond Path leaves on the left, and in another 100 yd., just after a small brook is crossed, the Nelson Crag Trail leaves on the left. Continuing north, the trail climbs slightly up an interesting little rocky hogback, passes through an old gravel pit, and meets the Auto Rd. just above the 2-mi. mark, at a small parking area opposite the Madison Gulf Trail trailhead.

Old Jackson Road (map 1:F9)

Distance from Pinkham Notch Visitor Center (2,032 ft.) to
- Mt. Washington Auto Rd. (2,675 ft.): 1.9 mi., 700 ft. (rev. 50 ft.), 1 hr. 20 min.

Crew-Cut Trail (AMC)

The Crew-Cut Trail, George's Gorge Trail, and Liebeskind's Loop, a small network of paths in the region north of Pinkham Notch Visitor Center, were originally located and cut by Bradford Swan. These trails provide pleasant walking at a modest expenditure of effort, passing through fine woods with small ravines and ledges.

The Crew-Cut Trail leaves the Old Jackson Rd. on the right about 0.4 mi. from the visitor center, just after a stream crossing and just before the point where the Old Jackson Rd. starts to climb more steeply. After crossing a stony, dry brook bed it runs generally east-northeast, crossing two small brooks. On the east bank of the second brook, at 0.2 mi., the George's Gorge Trail leaves left. The Crew-Cut Trail continues generally northeast, rising moderately up the slope through open woods and crossing several gullies. It skirts southeast of the steeper rocky outcroppings until, at 0.5 mi. from the Old Jackson Rd., Liebeskind's Loop enters left, coming down from George's Gorge Trail. The spur path to Lila's Ledge, which affords fine views, leaves Liebeskind's Loop less than 0.1 mi. from this junction. The Crew-Cut Trail passes under the base of a cliff and turns right, then descends steeply over a few small ledges and through open woods until it passes east of a small high-level bog formed by an old beaver dam. Shortly thereafter, it crosses a small stream and the Connie's Way Ski Trail, and goes through open woods again, emerging at the top of the grassy embankment on NH 16 0.1 mi. south of the entrance to Wildcat Ski Area.

Crew-Cut Trail (map 1:F9–F10)

Distances from Old Jackson Rd. (2,075 ft.) to
- Liebeskind's Loop (2,350 ft.): 0.5 mi., 300 ft., 25 min.
- NH 16 (1,950 ft.): 1.0 mi., 300 ft. (rev. 400 ft.), 35 min.

George's Gorge Trail (AMC)

This trail leaves the Crew-Cut Trail on the left 0.2 mi. from the Old Jackson Rd., on the east bank of a small brook (the infant Peabody River). It leads up the brook, steeply in places, passing Chudacoff Falls (often dry) and crossing the brook twice, then swings rather sharply away from the brook. Liebeskind's Loop leaves on the right at 0.5 mi., and George's Gorge Trail then climbs nearly to the top of a knob and descends west to the Old Jackson Rd. in the flat section near its halfway point, 0.9 mi. from Pinkham Notch Visitor Center.

George's Gorge Trail (map 1:F9)

Distance from Crew-Cut Trail (2,100 ft.) to
- Old Jackson Rd. (2,525 ft.): 0.8 mi., 600 ft. (rev. 150 ft.), 40 min.

Liebeskind's Loop (AMC)

Liebeskind's Loop makes possible a loop hike starting on the Old Jackson Rd. 0.4 mi. from the Pinkham Notch Visitor Center (using the Crew-Cut, George's Gorge, Loop, and Crew-Cut Trails) without resorting to returning either by NH 16 or by the section of the Old Jackson Rd. that is markedly steeper than the rest of the trail. This loop hike is best made in the sequence referred to earlier because George's Gorge is more interesting on the ascent and Liebeskind's Loop is more interesting on the descent.

Liebeskind's Loop leaves right (east) near the high point of the George's Gorge Trail, 0.3 mi. from Old Jackson Rd., and descends to a swampy flat, then rises through a spruce thicket to the top of a cliff, where there is a fine lookout called Brad's Bluff with a good view to the south down Pinkham Notch. Here the trail turns left and runs along the edge of the cliff, finally descending by an easy zigzag in a gully to a beautiful open grove of birches. The trail continues east, descending through a small gorge and skirting the east end of several small swells until it finally descends to a small notch in the ridge crest. Here a spur trail leads left 0.1 mi. to Lila's Ledge (named by Brad Swan in memory of his wife), which affords excellent views of Pinkham Notch and the eastern slope of Mt. Washington; the lower ledge is accessed by a short, steep descent that may be dangerous in wet or icy conditions. Liebeskind's Loop then descends on the other side of the ridge to join the Crew-Cut Trail, which can then be followed back to the starting point by turning right (west-southwest).

Liebeskind's Loop (map 1:F9–F10)

Distances from George's Gorge Trail (2,575 ft.)

- to Crew-Cut Trail (2,350 ft.): 0.6 mi., 0 ft. (rev. 250 ft.), 20 min.
- for complete loop from Pinkham Notch Visitor Center (2,032 ft.) via Old Jackson Rd., Crew-Cut Trail, George's Gorge Trail, Liebeskind's Loop, Crew-Cut Trail, and Old Jackson Rd.: 2.8 mi., 650 ft., 1 hr. 45 min.

Crawford Path (WMNF)

This trail is considered the oldest continuously maintained footpath in the United States. The first section, leading up Mt. Pierce (Mt. Clinton), was cut in 1819 by Abel Crawford and his son Ethan Allen Crawford. In 1840, Thomas J. Crawford, a younger son of Abel, converted the footpath into a bridle path, but more than a century has passed since it was used regularly for ascents on horseback. The trail still follows the original path, except for the section between Mt. Monroe and the Westside Trail, which was relocated to take it off the windswept ridge and down past the shelter at Lakes of the Clouds. From the junction just north of Mt. Pierce to the summit of Mt. Washington, the Crawford Path is part of the AT and is blazed in white.

Caution: Parts of this trail are dangerous in bad weather. Several lives have been lost on the Crawford Path because of failure to observe proper precautions. Below Mt. Eisenhower, a number of ledges are exposed to the weather, but they are scattered, and shelter is usually available in nearby scrub. From the Eisenhower-Franklin col, the trail runs completely above treeline, exposed to the full force of all storms. The most dangerous part of the path is the section on the cone of Mt. Washington, beyond Lakes of the Clouds Hut. Always carry a compass and study the map before starting. If trouble arises on or above Mt. Monroe, take refuge at Lakes of the Clouds Hut or go down the Ammonoosuc Ravine Trail. The Crawford Path is well marked above treeline with large cairns; in poor visibility, great care should be exercised to stay on it because many of the other paths in the vicinity are much less clearly marked. If the path is lost in bad weather and cannot be found again after diligent effort, one should travel west, descending into the woods and following streams downhill to the roads. On the southeast, toward the Dry River valley, nearly all the slopes are more precipitous, the river crossings are potentially dangerous, and the distance to a highway is much greater.

The main parking area at the south end of this trail is now located on the west side of Mt. Clinton Rd. a short distance north of its junction with US 302. The former parking lot on US 302 has been closed, and Crawford Path hikers are requested to use the Mt. Clinton Rd. lot because the parking spaces at other lots in the area are needed for the trails that originate from them. For historical reasons, the name Crawford Path continues to be attached to the old route of the trail that leads directly from US 302, and the short path that connects the Crawford Path to the Mt. Clinton Rd. parking lot is called the Crawford Connector. However, in the descriptions that follow, the main route will be described and distances given starting from Mt. Clinton Rd. via the Crawford Connector, which will now be the usual route for most hikers using this trail.

The following description of the path is in the northbound direction (toward Mt. Washington). See later for a description of the path in the reverse direction.

Leaving the parking lot and soon crossing Mt. Clinton Rd., the Crawford Connector climbs gradually for 0.4 mi. until it reaches the bridge over Gibbs Brook. Here the Crawford Cliff Spur diverges left.

Crawford Cliff Spur. This short side path leaves the Crawford Connector at the west end of the bridge over Gibbs Brook and follows the brook to a small flume and pool. It then climbs steeply above the brook, turns left at an old illegible sign, becomes very rough, and reaches a ledge with an outlook over Crawford Notch and the Willey Range, 0.4 mi. (20 min.) from the Crawford Path.

The Crawford Connector continues across the bridge and ends at the Crawford Path 0.2 mi. from its trailhead on US 302 opposite the AMC's Highland Center at Crawford Notch. To continue ascending on the Crawford Path, turn left here. The Crawford Path follows the south bank of Gibbs Brook, and at 0.6 mi., a side path leads 40 yd. left to Gibbs Falls. Soon the trail passes an information sign for the Gibbs Brook Scenic Area, then climbs moderately but steadily. At about 1.2 mi., from Mt. Clinton Rd. the trail begins to climb away from the brook, angling up the side of the valley. At 1.9 mi., the Mizpah Cutoff diverges east for Mizpah Spring Hut. The Crawford Path continues to ascend at easy to moderate grades, crossing several small brooks, then reaches its high point on the shoulder of Mt. Pierce and runs almost level, breaking into the open with fine views. At 3.1 mi., it reaches the junction with the Webster Cliff Trail, which leads right (south) to the summit of Mt. Pierce in about 0.1 mi.

From Mt. Pierce to Mt. Eisenhower, the path runs through patches of scrub and woods with many open ledges that give magnificent views in all directions. Cairns and the marks left by many feet on the rocks indicate the way. The path winds about heading generally in a northeasterly direction, staying fairly near the poorly defined crest of the broad ridge, which is composed of several rounded humps. At 3.8 mi., the trail crosses a small stream in the col, then ascends mostly on ledges to the junction with the Mt. Eisenhower Loop, which diverges left at 4.3 mi. The trip over this summit adds only 0.2 mi. and 300 ft. of climbing and provides excellent views in good weather. The Crawford Path bears somewhat to the right at this junction and runs nearly level—though with somewhat rough footing—through scrub on the southeast side of the mountain; this is the better route in bad weather. The Mt. Eisenhower Loop rejoins the Crawford Path on the left at 4.8 mi., just above the sag between Mt. Eisenhower and Mt. Franklin, on a ledge that overlooks Red Pond, a small alpine tarn of stagnant water. The Edmands Path can be reached from this junction by following the Mt. Eisenhower Loop for a short distance.

At 5.0 mi., the Mt. Eisenhower Trail from the Dry River valley enters right. The Crawford Path then begins the ascent of the shoulder called

Mt. Franklin, first moderately, then steeply for a short distance near the top. At 5.5 mi., the trail reaches the relatively level shoulder and continues past an unmarked path on the right at 6.0 mi. that leads in 130 yd. to the barely noticeable summit of Mt. Franklin, from which there are excellent views, particularly into Oakes Gulf. At 6.2 mi., the Mt. Monroe Loop diverges left to cross both summits of Monroe, affording excellent views. It is about the same length as the parallel section of the Crawford Path but requires about 350 ft. more climbing. The Crawford Path is safer in inclement conditions because it is much less exposed to the weather. The Crawford Path continues along the edge of the precipice that forms the northwest wall of Oakes Gulf, then follows a relocated section, passing an area that has been closed to public entry to preserve the habitat of the dwarf cinquefoil, an endangered species of plant. The area between the two ends of the Mt. Monroe Loop is one of great fragility and botanical importance. To protect this area—probably the most significant tract of rare vegetation in the entire White Mountain region—the most scrupulous care is required on the part of visitors. At 6.9 mi., the Mt. Monroe Loop rejoins on the left, and the Crawford Path descends easily to Lakes of the Clouds Hut at 7.0 mi.

The Ammonoosuc Ravine Trail enters on the left at the corner of the hut, and in another 30 yd., the Dry River Trail enters on the right. The Crawford Path crosses the outlet of the larger lake and passes between it and the second lake, and in a short distance the Camel Trail to Boott Spur and the Tuckerman Crossover to Tuckerman Ravine diverge right at the same point. The Crawford Path then ascends moderately on the northwest side of the ridge, always some distance below the crest. The Davis Path, which has been following the original, less sheltered location of the Crawford Path, enters on the right at 7.9 mi., at the foot of the cone of Mt. Washington. In another 50 yd., the Westside Trail, a shortcut to the Northern Peaks, diverges left. The Crawford Path runs generally north, switching back and forth as it climbs the steep cone through a trench in the rocks. At the plateau west of the summit, it meets the Gulfside Trail at 8.3 mi., then turns right, passes through the old corral in which saddle horses from the Glen House used to be kept, and from there ascends past buildings to the summit.

Crawford Path (map 1:G8–F9)

Distances from Mt. Clinton Rd. parking area (1,920 ft.) via Crawford Connector to

- Mizpah Cutoff (3,480 ft.): 1.9 mi., 1,550 ft., 1 hr. 45 min.
- Webster Cliff Trail (4,250 ft.): 3.1 mi., 2,350 ft., 2 hr. 45 min.
- south end of Mt. Eisenhower Loop (4,425 ft.): 4.3 mi., 2,650 ft., 3 hr. 30 min.
- Mt. Eisenhower Trail (4,475 ft.): 5.0 mi., 2,750 ft., 3 hr. 55 min.
- Lakes of the Clouds Hut (5,012 ft.): 7.0 mi., 3,450 ft., 5 hr. 15 min.
- Westside Trail (5,625 ft.): 7.9 mi., 4,050 ft., 6 hr.
- Gulfside Trail (6,150 ft.): 8.3 mi., 4,600 ft., 6 hr. 25 min.
- Mt. Washington summit (6,288 ft.): 8.5 mi., 4,750 ft., 6 hr. 40 min.

Crawford Path (WMNF) [In Reverse]

Descending from the summit of Mt. Washington, the path is on the right (west) side of the railroad track. After passing between the buildings, it leads generally south, then west. After passing the old corral, the path reaches a junction where the Gulfside Trail turns sharp right. Here the Crawford Path turns sharp left and zigzags downward through a trench in the rocks. At 0.6 mi., the Westside Trail enters on the right, and in another 50 yd., the Davis Path diverges left, following the original, less sheltered route of the Crawford Path. The Crawford Path now descends moderately on the northwest side of the ridge well below the crest, and the Tuckerman Crossover and the Camel Trail enter on the left at the same point just before the trail reaches the Lakes of the Clouds. It then passes between the lakes and reaches Lakes of the Clouds Hut at 1.5 mi., where the Dry River Trail enters on the left and the Ammonoosuc Ravine Trail enters on the right.

The Crawford Path now climbs up to the base of Mt. Monroe, where the north end of the Mt. Monroe Loop diverges right to cross both summits of Monroe, affording excellent views. The loop over the summits is about the same length as the parallel section of the Crawford Path but requires about 350 ft. more climbing. The Crawford Path is safer in inclement conditions, because it is much less exposed to the weather. It circles around the foot of this sharp peak, following a relocated section past an area that has been closed to public entry to preserve the habitat of the dwarf cinquefoil, an endangered species of plant. The area between the two ends of the Mt. Monroe Loop is one of great fragility and botanical importance. To protect this area—probably the most significant tract of rare vegetation in the entire White Mountain region—the most scrupulous care is required on the part of visitors. The Crawford Path continues along the edge of the precipice that forms the northwest wall of Oakes Gulf, the Mt. Monroe Loop rejoins on the right, and the main path continues along the flat ridge, passing an unmarked path on the left at 2.6 mi. that leads in 130 yd. to the barely noticeable summit of Mt. Franklin, from which there are excellent views, particularly into Oakes Gulf. At 3.0 mi., the trail drops rather steeply off the end of the shoulder, then descends moderately to the sag, passing the Mt. Eisenhower Trail on the left at 3.5 mi. The Mt. Eisenhower Loop leaves on the right at 3.7 mi. on a small ledge overlooking Red Pond, a small alpine tarn of stagnant water. The Edmands Path can be reached from this junction by following the Mt. Eisenhower Loop for a short distance. The trip over Mt. Eisenhower adds only 0.2 mi. and 300 ft. of climbing and provides excellent views in good weather. The Crawford Path bears left and runs nearly level—though with somewhat rough footing—through scrub on the southeast side of the mountain; this is the better route in bad weather.

The Mt. Eisenhower Loop rejoins on the right at 4.2 mi., and the Crawford Path descends on ledges to cross a small stream in the col, then climbs moderately to the junction with the Webster Cliff Trail at 5.4 mi., on an open ledge just below the summit of Mt. Pierce. From here, the trail soon enters the scrub and then full woods, descends moderately past the Mizpah Cutoff at 6.6 mi., and continues through the Gibbs Brook Scenic Area. At 8.1 mi., where the Crawford Path continues straight another 0.2 mi. to US 302 opposite the AMC's Highland Center at Crawford Notch, the main route turns right on the Crawford Connector, immediately crosses a bridge over Gibbs Brook and passes the side path on the right to Crawford Cliff (see earlier), and continues 0.4 mi. to the Mt. Clinton Rd. parking area.

Crawford Path [In Reverse] (map 1:G8–F9)

Distances from the summit of Mt. Washington (6,288 ft.) to

- Gulfside Trail (6,150 ft.): 0.2 mi., 0 ft., 5 min.
- Westside Trail (5,625 ft.): 0.6 mi., 0 ft., 20 min.
- Lakes of the Clouds Hut (5,012 ft.): 1.5 mi., 0 ft., 45 min.
- Mt. Eisenhower Trail (4,475 ft.): 3.5 mi., 150 ft., 1 hr. 50 min.
- south end of Mt. Eisenhower Loop (4,425 ft.): 4.2 mi., 200 ft., 2 hr. 10 min.
- Webster Cliff Trail (4,250 ft.): 5.4 mi., 350 ft., 2 hr. 55 min.

- Mizpah Cutoff (3,480 ft.): 6.6 mi., 350 ft., 3 hr. 30 min.
- Mt. Clinton Rd. parking area (1,920 ft.) via Crawford Connector: 8.5 mi., 350 ft., 4 hr. 25 min.

Mount Eisenhower Loop (AMC)

This short trail parallels the Crawford Path, climbing over the bare, flat summit of Mt. Eisenhower, which provides magnificent views. It diverges from the Crawford Path 4.3 mi. from Mt. Clinton Rd. at the south edge of the summit dome, climbs easily for 0.1 mi., then turns sharp left in a flat area and ascends steadily to the summit at 0.4 mi. From there, it descends moderately to a ledge overlooking Red Pond, then drops steeply over ledges, passes through a grassy sag just to the left of Red Pond, and finally climbs briefly past a junction on the left with the Edmands Path to rejoin the Crawford Path on a small, rocky knob.

Mount Eisenhower Loop (map 1:G8)

Distances from south junction with Crawford Path (4,425 ft.) to
- Mt. Eisenhower summit (4,760 ft.): 0.4 mi., 350 ft., 25 min.
- north junction with Crawford Path (4,475 ft.): 0.8 mi., 350 ft. (rev. 300 ft.), 35 min.

Mount Monroe Loop (AMC)

This short trail runs parallel to the Crawford Path and passes over the summits of Mt. Monroe and Little Monroe. The views are fine, but the summits are very exposed to the weather. The trail diverges from the Crawford Path 6.2 mi. from Mt. Clinton Rd. and quickly ascends the minor crag called Little Monroe, then descends into the shallow, grassy sag beyond. It then climbs steeply to the summit of Mt. Monroe at 0.4 mi., follows the northeast ridge to the end of the shoulder, and drops sharply to the Crawford Path 0.1 mi. south of Lakes of the Clouds Hut.

Mount Monroe Loop (map 1:F9)

Distances from south junction with Crawford Path (5,075 ft.) to
- summit of Mt. Monroe (5,372 ft.): 0.4 mi., 350 ft. (rev. 50 ft.), 20 min.
- north junction with Crawford Path (5,075 ft.): 0.7 mi., 350 ft. (rev. 300 ft.), 30 min.

Ammonoosuc Ravine Trail (WMNF)

The Ammonoosuc Ravine Trail ascends to Lakes of the Clouds Hut from a parking lot on the Base Rd., 1.1 mi. east of its junction with the Mt. Clinton Rd. and the Jefferson Notch Rd. The parking area is a stop for the AMC's Hiker Shuttle. The trail can also be reached on foot from the Jefferson Notch Rd. via the Boundary Line Trail (see Section Two). Together with the upper section of the Crawford Path, this trail provides the shortest route to Mt. Washington from the west. The trail follows the headwaters of the Ammonoosuc River with many fine falls, cascades, and pools, and affords excellent views from its upper section. It is the most direct route to Lakes of the Clouds Hut, and the best route to or from the hut in bad weather, because it lies in woods or scrub except for the last 200 yd. to the hut. The section above Gem Pool is extremely steep and rough, and is likely to prove quite arduous to many hikers, particularly those with limited trail-walking experience. Many hikers also find it somewhat unpleasant to descend this section because of the steep, often slippery rocks and ledges.

Leaving the parking lot, this trail follows a path through the woods, crossing Franklin Brook at 0.3 mi. then passing over a double pipeline as it skirts the Base Station area. It joins the old route of the trail at the edge of the Ammonoosuc River at 1.0 mi., after a slight descent. (The lower section of the old route, marked by a sign, leads left from here 0.3 mi. to the Base Station.) The main trail bears right along the river, following the old route for the rest of the way. It ascends mostly by easy grades, though with some rough footing, crossing Monroe Brook at 1.7 mi. At 2.1 mi., it crosses the outlet of Gem Pool, a beautiful emerald pool at the foot of a cascade.

Now the very steep, rough ascent begins. At 2.3 mi., a side path (sign) leads right about 80 yd. to a spectacular viewpoint at the foot of the gorge. Above this point, the main brook falls about 600 ft. down a steep trough in the mountainside at an average angle of 45 degrees, while another brook a short distance to the north does the same, and these two spectacular water slides meet in a pool at the foot of the gorge. The main trail continues its steep ascent, passes an outlook over the cascades to the right of the trail and at 2.5 mi. crosses the main brook on flat ledges at the head of the highest fall, a striking viewpoint. The grade now begins to ease, and the trail crosses several more brooks. Ledges become more frequent and the scrub becomes smaller and more sparse. At 3.0 mi., the trail emerges from the scrub and follows a line of cairns directly up some rock slabs (which are slippery when wet), passes through one last patch of scrub, and reaches the Crawford Path at the south side of Lakes of the Clouds Hut.

Ammonoosuc Ravine Trail (map 1:F8–F9)

Distances from the Base Rd. parking lot (2,500 ft.) to
- Gem Pool (3,450 ft.): 2.1 mi., 950 ft., 1 hr. 30 min.
- brook crossing on flat ledges (4,175 ft.): 2.5 mi., 1,700 ft., 2 hr. 5 min.
- Lakes of the Clouds Hut (5,012 ft.): 3.1 mi., 2,500 ft., 2 hr. 50 min.
- Mt. Washington summit (6,288 ft.) via Crawford Path: 4.5 mi., 3,800 ft., 4 hr. 10 min.

Edmands Path (WMNF)

The Edmands Path climbs to the Mt. Eisenhower Loop near its junction with the Crawford Path in the Eisenhower-Franklin col, starting from a parking lot on the east side of the Mt. Clinton Rd. 2.3 mi. north of its junction with US 302 and 1.3 mi. south of its junction with Base Rd. and Jefferson Notch Rd. This trail provides the shortest route to the summit of Mt. Eisenhower, and a relatively easy access to the middle portion of the Crawford Path and the Southern Presidentials. The last 0.2-mi. segment before it joins the Mt. Eisenhower Loop and Crawford Path is very exposed to northwest winds and, although short, can create a serious problem in bad weather. The ledgy brook crossings in the upper part of the trail can be treacherous in icy conditions.

J. Rayner Edmands, the pioneer trail maker, relocated and reconstructed this trail in 1909. The rock cribbing and paving in the middle and upper sections of the trail testify to the diligent labor that Edmands devoted to constructing a trail with constant comfortable grades in rather difficult terrain. Most of his work has survived the weather and foot traffic of many decades well, and though erosion has made the footing noticeably rougher in recent years, the trail retains what is probably the easiest grade and footing of any comparable trail in the White Mountains. It is nearly always comfortable, and almost never challenging.

From its trailhead, the path runs nearly level across two small brooks, then at 0.4 mi., it crosses Abenaki Brook and turns sharp right onto an old logging road on the far bank. At 0.7 mi., the trail diverges left off the old road and crosses a wet area. Soon it begins to climb steadily, undulating up the west ridge of Mt. Eisenhower, carefully searching out the most comfortable grades. At 2.2 mi., the trail swings left and angles up the mountainside on a footway supported by extensive rock cribbing, then passes through a tiny stone gateway. At 2.5 mi., it crosses a small brook running over a ledge, and soon the grade becomes almost level as the trail contours around the north slope of Mt. Eisenhower, affording excellent views out through a fringe of trees. At 2.8 mi., it breaks into the open, crosses the nose of a ridge on a footway paved with carefully placed stones, and reaches the Mt. Eisenhower Loop a few yards from the Crawford Path.

Edmands Path (map 1:G8)

Distances from Mt. Clinton Rd. (2,000 ft.) to
- stone gateway (4,000 ft.): 2.2 mi., 2,000 ft., 2 hr. 5 min.
- Mt. Eisenhower Loop junction (4,450 ft.): 2.9 mi., 2,450 ft., 2 hr. 40 min.
- Mt. Eisenhower summit (4,760 ft.) via Mt. Eisenhower Loop: 3.3 mi., 2,750 ft., 3 hr.

Webster-Jackson Trail (AMC)

This trail connects US 302 at a small parking area just south of the Macomber Family Information Center (Crawford Depot) with the summits of both Mt. Webster and Mt. Jackson, and provides the opportunity for an interesting loop trip, because the two summits are linked by the Webster Cliff Trail.

The trail, blazed in blue, leaves the east side of US 302 0.1 mi. south of the Crawford Depot and 0.1 mi. north of the Gate of the Notch. It runs through a clearing, enters the woods, and at 0.1 mi. from US 302 passes the side path leading right to Elephant Head.

Elephant Head Spur. Elephant Head is an interesting ledge that forms the east side of the Gate of the Notch, a mass of gray rock striped with veins of white quartz providing a remarkable likeness to an elephant's head and trunk. The path runs through the woods parallel to the highway at an easy grade, then ascends across the summit of the knob and descends 40 yd. to the top of the ledge, which overlooks Crawford Notch and affords fine views; it is 0.2 mi. (10 min.) from the Webster-Jackson Trail.

The main trail climbs along the south bank of Elephant Head Brook, well above the stream, then turns right, away from the brook, at 0.2 mi. Angling up the mountainside roughly parallel to the highway, nearly level stretches alternating with sharp uphill pitches, it crosses Little Mossy Brook at 0.3 mi., and at 0.6 mi. from US 302, a side path leads right 60 yd. to Bugle Cliff. This is a massive ledge overlooking Crawford Notch, where the view is well worth the slight extra effort required; if ice is present, exercise extreme caution. The main trail rises fairly steeply and crosses Flume Cascade Brook at 0.9 mi. At 1.4 mi., within sound of Silver Cascade Brook, the trail divides, the left branch for Mt. Jackson and the right for Mt. Webster.

Mount Webster Branch

The Webster (right) branch immediately descends steeply to Silver Cascade Brook, crosses it just below a beautiful cascade and pool, then bears left and climbs steeply up the bank. The trail then climbs steadily south 1.0 mi., often with wet, rough footing, meeting the Webster Cliff Trail on the high plateau northwest of the summit of Mt. Webster, 2.4 mi. from US 302. The ledgy summit of Mt. Webster, with an excellent view of Crawford Notch and the mountains to the west and south, is 0.1 mi. right (south) via the Webster Cliff Trail. For Mt. Jackson and Mizpah Spring Hut, turn left.

Mount Jackson Branch

The Jackson (left) branch ascends gradually until it comes within sight of Silver Cascade Brook, then begins to climb moderately. About 0.5 mi. above the junction, it crosses three branches of the brook in quick succession. At 1.0 mi. from the junction, a short distance below the base of the rocky summit cone, it passes Tisdale Spring (unreliable, often scanty and muddy). The trail soon swings right and ascends steep ledges to the open summit, 2.6 mi. from US 302.

Webster-Jackson Trail (map 1:G8)

Distances from US 302 (1,900 ft.)

- to Bugle Cliff (2,450 ft.): 0.6 mi., 550 ft., 35 min.
- to Flume Cascade Brook (2,500 ft.): 0.9 mi., 600 ft., 45 min.
- to Mt. Webster–Mt. Jackson fork (2,800 ft.): 1.4 mi., 900 ft., 1 hr. 10 min. ▶

- to Webster Cliff Trail (3,840 ft.) via Webster branch: 2.4 mi., 2,050 ft. (rev. 100 ft.), 2 hr. 15 min.
- to summit of Mt. Webster (3,910 ft.) via Webster Cliff Trail: 2.5 mi., 2,100 ft., 2 hr. 20 min.
- to summit of Mt. Jackson (4,052 ft.) via Jackson branch: 2.6 mi., 2,150 ft., 2 hr. 25 min.
- for loop trip over summits of Webster and Jackson (via Webster Cliff Trail): 6.5 mi., 2,450 ft., 4 hr. 30 min.

Webster Cliff Trail (AMC)

This trail, a part of the AT, leaves the east side of US 302 opposite the road to Willey House Station, about 1 mi. south of the Willey House Recreation Area at the Willey House site. The parking area is a stop for the AMC's Hiker Shuttle. The trail ascends along the edge of the spectacular cliffs that form the east wall of Crawford Notch, then leads over Mts. Webster, Jackson, and Pierce to the Crawford Path 0.1 mi. north of Mt. Pierce.

From US 302, it runs nearly east 0.1 mi. to a bridge on which it crosses the Saco River. The Saco River Trail joins from the left at 0.2 mi. and departs on the right at 0.3 mi. Then the Webster Cliff Trail climbs steadily up the south end of the ridge, winding up the steep slope, swinging more to the north and growing steeper as it approaches the cliffs, with one tricky scramble across the top of a small slide. At 1.8 mi. from US 302, it reaches the first open ledge, and from here on, as the trail ascends the ridge with easier grades, there are frequent outlook ledges giving ever-changing perspectives of the notch and the mountains to the south and west. At 2.4 mi., a ledge affords a view straight down to the state park buildings, and a short distance farther there is a ledge with an outlook to Mt. Washington and another with a view east to the Montalban Ridge. After climbing steadily and scrambling up a few fairly steep pitches with more good outlooks, the trail reaches the jumbled, ledgy summit at 3.3 mi.

The trail then descends north, and in 0.1 mi., the Webster branch of the Webster-Jackson Trail from US 302 near the Macomber Family Information Center (Crawford Depot) enters left. The Webster Cliff Trail swings east and crosses numerous wet gullies, finally ascending the steep, ledgy cone of Mt. Jackson to reach the summit at 4.7 mi., where the Jackson branch of the Webster-Jackson Trail enters left.

The trail leaves the summit of Mt. Jackson toward Mt. Pierce, following a line of cairns running north, and descends the ledges at the north end of the cone quite rapidly into the scrub, then enters and winds through open alpine meadows. At 5.2 mi., where an overgrown side path leads right 40 yd. to an outlook, the trail turns sharp left and drops into the woods. It continues up and down along the ridge toward Mt. Pierce, then descends gradually to the junction at 6.3 mi. with the Mizpah Cutoff, which leads left (west) to the Crawford Path. At 6.4 mi., Mizpah Spring Hut (where there are also tentsites for backpackers) is reached, and the Mt. Clinton Trail to the Dry River valley diverges right (southeast), heading diagonally down the hut clearing. Continuing past the hut, the trail soon ascends a steep, rough section with two ladders, and reaches an open ledge with good views south and west at 6.6 mi. The grade lessens, and after a sharp right turn in a ledgy area the trail reaches the summit of the southwest knob of Mt. Pierce, which affords a view of the summit of Mt. Washington rising over Mt. Pierce. The trail descends into a sag and ascends easily through scrub to the summit of Mt. Pierce at 7.2 mi., where it comes into the open. It then descends moderately in the open in the same direction (northeast) about 150 yd. to its junction with the Crawford Path.

Webster Cliff Trail (map 1:G8)

Distances from US 302 (1,275 ft.) to
- first open ledge (3,025 ft.): 1.8 mi., 1,750 ft., 1 hr. 45 min.
- summit of Mt. Webster (3,910 ft.): 3.3 mi., 2,700 ft. (rev. 50 ft.), 3 hr.
- summit of Mt. Jackson (4,052 ft.): 4.7 mi., 3,050 ft. (rev. 200 ft.), 3 hr. 50 min.
- Mizpah Spring Hut (3,800 ft.): 6.4 mi., 3,250 ft. (rev. 450 ft.), 4 hr. 50 min.
- Crawford Path (4,250 ft.): 7.3 mi., 38,00 ft. (rev. 100 ft.), 5 hr. 35 min.

Mizpah Cutoff (AMC)

This short trail provides a direct route from the Macomber Family Information Center (Crawford Depot) area to Mizpah Spring Hut. It diverges right (east) from the Crawford Path 1.9 mi. from the Mt. Clinton Rd. parking area, climbs the ridge at a moderate grade, passes through a fairly level area, and descends slightly to join the Webster Cliff Trail 0.1 mi. south of Mizpah Spring Hut.

Mizpah Cutoff (map 1:G8)

Distance from Crawford Path (3,480 ft.) to
- Mizpah Spring Hut (3,800 ft.): 0.7 mi., 300 ft., 30 min.

Distance from Mt. Clinton Rd. parking area (1,920 ft.) to
- Mizpah Spring Hut (3,800 ft.) via Crawford Connector, Crawford Path, Mizpah Cutoff, and Webster Cliff Trail: 2.6 mi., 1,900 ft., 2 hr. 15 min.

Sam Willey Trail (NHDP)

This trail provides a short, easy walk at the base of the Webster Cliffs from the Willey House site on US 302, starting from the parking area on the east side of the road.

Leaving the road, the trail crosses the wooden dam over the Saco River. Beyond a sign, the Sam Willey Trail bears right, and the Pond Loop Trail (providing a 0.2-mi. loop walk beside Willey Pond, with views up to the surrounding mountains, returning to a point near the dam) bears left. The Sam Willey Trail follows a graded path south and comes to its loop junction at 0.4 mi. Going left (clockwise), the loop reaches the junction at 0.5 mi. where the Saco River Trail continues ahead (south). The Sam Willey Trail swings around back to the north, passes a scenic spot by the Saco River and a view up to the Webster Cliffs, and returns to the loop junction in another 0.1 mi. To return to the Willey House site, turn left.

Sam Willey Trail (map 1:G8)

Distance from Willey House site (1,300 ft.)
- to Saco River Trail (1,300 ft.): 0.5 mi. (0.8 km), 0 ft., 15 min.
- for complete loop: 1.0 mi., 0 ft., 30 min.

Saco River Trail (NHDP)

This trail, blazed in blue, provides easy walking through attractive forests along the floor of Crawford Notch, linking the Willey House site (via the Sam Willey Trail) with the Webster Cliff Trail and Dry River Trail.

Leaving the most southerly point of the southern loop section of the Sam Willey Trail, 0.5 mi. from the Willey House site, the trail runs briefly alongside the Saco River, then bears left away from the river and traverses several minor ups and downs. At 0.5 mi., it dips to the edge of an open swamp, where there is a view of Mt. Willey. At 0.7 mi., the Saco River Trail meets the Webster Cliff Trail (0.2 mi. from its trailhead on US 302) and turns left on it. The two trails coincide, climbing steadily eastward. At 0.8 mi., the Saco River Trail turns right off the Webster Cliff Trail and descends easily, working down to the floor of the valley. At 1.2 mi., it crosses several channels of Webster Brook and continues south through open hardwoods; in places, the footway must be followed with care. At 1.6 mi., the trail passes a rustic bench and skirts a beaver swamp, crossing a small brook. After traversing a rocky section it ends at the Dry River Trail, 0.5 mi. from that trail's trailhead on US 302 and directly across from the junction with the Dry River Connection 0.4 mi. from Dry River Campground.

Saco River Trail (map 1:G8–H8)

Distances from Sam Willey Trail (1,300 ft.) to
- lower (west) junction with Webster Cliff Trail (1,350 ft.): 0.7 mi., 50 ft., 25 min.
- Dry River Trail (1,300 ft.): 2.4 mi., 150 ft. (rev. 150 ft.), 1 hr. 15 min.

Saco Lake Trail (AMC)

This very short trail makes a loop around the east shore of Saco Lake, beginning and ending on US 302. About halfway along the shore a short side path on the left climbs steeply to a ledgy area called Idlewild, where there is a view of the lake and the Willey Range (use care if wet). The path starts opposite the AMC's Highland Center at Crawford Notch and ends after crossing the dam at the south end of Saco Lake. In addition to being an attractive short walk, it provides an alternative to part of the road walk between the beginning points of the Crawford Path and Webster-Jackson Trail.

Saco Lake Trail (map 1:G8)

Distance from north junction with US 302 (1,890 ft.) to
- south junction with US 302 (1,890 ft.): 0.3 mi., 0 ft., 10 min.

Dry River Trail (WMNF)

The Dry River Trail is the main trail from US 302 up the valley of the Dry River and through Oakes Gulf to Lakes of the Clouds Hut, giving access to Mt. Washington, the Southern Peaks, and the upper portion of the Montalban Ridge. It leaves the east side of US 302, 0.3 mi. north of the entrance to Dry River Campground and 2.6 mi. south of the Willey House site. This trail in general is somewhat rougher than most similar valley trails elsewhere in the White Mountains. The first 5 mi. follows fairly close to the route of an old logging railroad, although the river and its tributaries have eradicated much of the old roadbed, and the relocations cut to eliminate the numerous potentially hazardous river crossings have bypassed much of the remaining grade. When water levels are high, the few Dry River crossings that remain on this trail—and on the trails that diverge from it—are at best difficult and can be very dangerous. At such times, it is prudent not to descend into this valley if major stream crossings lie between you and your destination. This trail is almost entirely within the Presidential Range–Dry River Wilderness. Dry River Shelters #1 and #2 have been removed; Dry River Shelter #3 will be removed whenever major maintenance is required (contact Saco Ranger District office for information).

From the highway the trail follows a wide woods road generally northeast for 0.5 mi. to its junction with the bed of the old logging railroad (signed as the Dry River Connection), which reaches this point from Dry River Campground in 0.4 mi. At this junction, the Saco River Trail, connecting to the Webster Cliff Trail and (via the Sam Willey Trail) the Willey House site, enters on the left. From here the Dry River Trail follows the railroad bed, enters the Presidential Range–Dry River Wilderness at 0.7 mi., and leaves the railroad grade sharp left at 0.9 mi., staying on the west side of the river where the railroad formerly crossed it. Just downstream from this point there is a pleasant pool. The trail climbs over a low bluff, rejoins the roadbed, then leaves it again and climbs over a higher bluff, where there is a restricted but beautiful outlook up the Dry River to Mt. Washington, Mt. Monroe, and the headwall of Oakes Gulf. At 1.7 mi., after a short, fairly steep descent, the trail crosses the Dry River on a suspension bridge and continues up the east bank with minor ups and downs, occasionally using portions of the old railroad grade. (*Note:* The suspension bridge was damaged in the spring of 2005 and is closed until repairs are made; the resulting unbridged crossing is difficult at ordinary water levels and extremely dangerous at high water.) At 2.9 mi., it turns sharp right off the railroad grade where the Mt. Clinton Trail diverges left to cross the river and ascend to Mizpah Spring Hut. At 4.2 mi., the Dry

River Trail makes a sharp turn away from the river, then turns left and continues along the bank at a higher level. At 4.9 mi., it crosses Isolation Brook, turns right along the brook bank, and in 60 yd., the Isolation Trail diverges right, heading up along the brook.

The Dry River Trail continues straight along the high east bank of the Dry River and passes a cleared outlook over the river and up to Mt. Pierce; at 5.2 mi., the Mt. Eisenhower Trail diverges sharp left and descends the steep bank to cross the river and climb to the Crawford Path. The Dry River Trail continues along the east bank, passing at 5.4 mi. an unsigned obscure side path on the left that leads down 40 yd. to the pool at the foot of Dry River Falls, a very attractive spot. The top of the falls, with an interesting pothole, can also be reached from here. At 5.6 mi., the trail crosses the river to the west side; the crossing is normally fairly easy but could be a serious problem at high water. At 6.3 mi., Dry River Shelter #3 is passed; it will be removed when major maintenance is required. In another 60 yd., the trail crosses a major tributary of the Dry River at the confluence and continues along the bank of the main stream, gradually rising higher above the river.

At 7.4 mi., the trail begins to swing away from the river, which has been at least audible to this point, and gradually climbs into Oakes Gulf. After it crosses a small ridge and descends sharply on the other side, views begin to appear, although the trail remains well sheltered in the scrub. At 8.7 mi., there is a good outlook perch just to the right of the trail. The trail soon climbs out of the scrub, turns left, and crosses a small brook at a right angle. At 9.1 mi., the trail turns sharp right from the gully it once ascended, where signs forbid public entry into the area formerly crossed by the trail. (The closed area is the habitat of the dwarf cinquefoil, an endangered plant species.) The trail continues to climb, passing the Presidential Range–Dry River Wilderness boundary sign in a patch of scrub, and reaches the height-of-land on the southwest ridge of Mt. Washington at 9.4 mi. It then descends to the larger of the two Lakes of the Clouds, follows its south edge, and ends at Lakes of the Clouds Hut.

Dry River Trail (map 1:H8–F9)

Distances from US 302 (1,205 ft.) to
- Dry River Connection and Saco River Trail (1,300 ft.): 0.5 mi., 100 ft., 20 min.
- suspension bridge (1,600 ft.): 1.7 mi., 500 ft. (rev. 100 ft.), 1 hr. 5 min. ▶

- Mt. Clinton Trail (1,900 ft.): 2.9 mi., 800 ft., 1 hr. 50 min.
- Isolation Trail (2,600 ft.): 4.9 mi., 1,500 ft., 3 hr. 10 min.
- Mt. Eisenhower Trail (2,650 ft.): 5.2 mi., 1,550 ft., 3 hr. 25 min.
- Dry River Shelter #3 (3,125 ft.): 6.3 mi., 2,000 ft., 4 hr. 10 min.
- Lakes of the Clouds Hut (5,012 ft.): 9.6 mi., 4,100 ft. (rev. 200 ft.), 6 hr. 50 min.

Mount Clinton Trail (WMNF)

This trail connects the lower part of the Dry River to Mizpah Spring Hut and the southern part of the Southern Peaks, and lies almost entirely within the Presidential Range–Dry River Wilderness. This trail is lightly used and much of it, especially below the Dry River Cutoff, is rough, wet and in places overgrown. It may require considerable care to follow, especially at stream crossings. *Caution:* The crossing of the Dry River on this trail near its junction with the Dry River Trail can vary from an easy skip over the stones to a waist-high ford in a torrent, and there may be no safe way across. In high-water conditions, it would be prudent not to descend from Mizpah Spring Hut by this trail because the only safe course on reaching the Dry River (other than returning to the hut) might be a rough bushwhack south along the riverbank for about 1.2 mi.

The trail diverges left from the Dry River Trail 2.9 mi. from US 302, and immediately makes the potentially hazardous crossing of the Dry River. On the west side of the river it follows a short stretch of old railroad grade upstream, then swings left up the bank of a major tributary, following an old logging road at a moderate grade much of the way. At 0.5 mi., the trail crosses this brook for the first of seven times, then scrambles up a washed-out area on the other bank. At 1.2 mi., the trail turns sharp left off the road and descends to the brook, crosses at a ledgy spot, and soon regains the road on the other side. It follows close to the brook, crossing several tributaries as well as the main brook, to the seventh crossing of the main brook at 1.8 mi. Above an eroded section where a small brook has taken over the road, the walking on the old road becomes more pleasant, and the Dry River Cutoff enters on the right at 2.5 mi. From here, the trail crosses two small streams and ascends past a large boulder to the Presidential Range–Dry River Wilderness boundary at 2.9 mi., and soon enters the clearing of Mizpah Spring Hut, where it joins the Webster Cliff Trail.

Mount Clinton Trail (map 1:G8)

Distances from Dry River Trail (1,900 ft.) to
- Dry River Cutoff (3,425 ft.): 2.5 mi., 1,550 ft., 2 hr.
- Mizpah Spring Hut (3,800 ft.): 3.0 mi., 1,900 ft., 2 hr. 25 min.

Mount Eisenhower Trail (WMNF)

This lightly used trail connects the middle part of the Dry River valley to the Crawford Path at the Eisenhower-Franklin col and lies almost entirely within the Presidential Range–Dry River Wilderness. Its grades are mostly easy to moderate and it runs above the treeline for only a short distance at the ridge crest.

The trail diverges left from the Dry River Trail about 5.2 mi. from US 302, and descends rather steeply on a former route of the Dry River Trail through an area with many side paths; care must be taken to stay on the proper trail. The trail crosses the Dry River (may be difficult or impassable at high water) and follows the bank downstream. At 0.2 mi., it joins its former route and bears right up a rather steep logging road, and the Dry River Cutoff diverges left at 0.3 mi. Soon the grade on the Mt. Eisenhower Trail eases as it leads generally north, keeping a bit to the west of the crest of the long ridge that runs south from a point midway between Mts. Franklin and Eisenhower. At 1.3 mi., it passes through a blowdown patch with views of Mt. Pierce, and from here on there are occasional views to the west from the edge of the ravine. At 1.8 mi., it turns sharp right, then left, and soon ascends more steeply for a while. At 2.4 mi., the trail finally gains the crest of the ridge and winds among rocks and scrub, passing the Presidential Range–Dry River Wilderness boundary 50 yd. before reaching the Crawford Path in the Eisenhower-Franklin col, at a point 0.2 mi. north of the Crawford Path's northern junction with the Mt. Eisenhower Loop.

Mount Eisenhower Trail (map 1:G8)

Distances from Dry River Trail (2,650 ft.) to
- Dry River Cutoff (2,650 ft.): 0.3 mi., 100 ft. (rev. 100 ft.), 10 min.
- Crawford Path (4,475 ft.): 2.7 mi., 1,950 ft., 2 hr. 20 min.

Dry River Cutoff (AMC)

This trail connects the middle part of the Dry River valley to Mizpah Spring Hut and the southern section of the Southern Peaks. Grades are mostly easy with some moderate sections. This trail is entirely within the Presidential Range–Dry River Wilderness.

The trail diverges left from the Mt. Eisenhower Trail 0.3 mi. from the latter trail's junction with the Dry River Trail. In 0.1 mi., it crosses a substantial brook after a slight descent, turns sharp left and climbs the bank, crosses a tributary, then swings back and climbs above the bank of the tributary. It crosses several branches of the tributary and gains the height-of-land on the southeast ridge of Mt. Pierce at 1.3 mi., then runs almost on the level with wet footing in places to its junction with the Mt. Clinton Trail at 1.7 mi. Mizpah Spring Hut is 0.5 mi. to the right from this junction via the Mt. Clinton Trail.

Dry River Cutoff (map 1:G8)

Distance from Mt. Eisenhower Trail (2,650 ft.) to
- Mt. Clinton Trail (3,425 ft.): 1.7 mi., 800 ft., 1 hr. 15 min.

Davis Path (AMC)

The Davis Path, completed by Nathaniel T. P. Davis in 1845, was the third (and longest) bridle path constructed to the summit of Mt. Washington. It was in use until 1853 or 1854 but became impassable soon afterward; eventually, it went out of existence entirely until it was reopened as a foot trail by the AMC in 1910. At that time, it was so overgrown that some sections could be located only by one of the original laborers, then a very old man, who relied on his memory of where the path had been built. The sections leading up the dauntingly steep southern slopes of Mt. Crawford and Stairs Mountain give some idea of the magnitude of the task Davis performed in building a trail passable to horses along this ridge. The resolution that enabled Davis to push forward with this apparently hopeless task was the inspiration for the naming of Mt. Resolution. This trail is almost entirely within the Presidential Range–Dry River Wilderness.

The path leaves US 302 on the west side of the Saco River at a paved parking lot near the Notchland Inn, 5.6 mi. south of the Willey House site in Crawford Notch State Park.

It follows the bank of the river about 200 yd. upstream to the new suspension footbridge (Bemis Bridge). Beyond the east end of the bridge, the trail passes through private land, continuing straight east across an overgrown field near a camp, then turns left into a path along a power line and crosses a small brook. It then swings right and enters the woods and the WMNF, and soon joins and follows a logging road along the bed of a small brook (normally dry in summer). It crosses the brook bed at a point where there may be running water upstream, soon crosses a tributary, and begins to climb away from the main brook, shortly passing into the Presidential Range–Dry River Wilderness. At 0.9 mi., it turns sharp right and soon enters the old, carefully graded bridle path and begins to ascend the steep ridge between Mt. Crawford and Mt. Hope by zigzags. Attaining the crest at 1.9 mi., the Davis Path follows this ridge north, rising over bare ledges with good outlooks, particularly to Mt. Carrigain and the Tripyramids. At 2.2 mi. from US 302, at the foot of a large, sloping ledge, a side trail diverges left and climbs 0.3 mi. and 200 ft. (15 min.) to the bare, peaked summit of Mt. Crawford, from which there is a magnificent view of Crawford Notch, the Dry River valley, and the surrounding ridges and peaks.

From this junction the Davis Path turns northeast, descends slightly to the col between the peak of Mt. Crawford and its ledgy, domelike east knob (sometimes called Crawford Dome), and resumes the ascent. It soon passes over a ledgy shoulder of Crawford Dome, with good views back to the impressively precipitous face of the small peak of Mt. Crawford, and dips to the Crawford-Resolution col. Leaving this col, the path runs north, rises slightly, and keeps close to the same level along the steep west side of Mt. Resolution.

At 3.7 mi., the Mt. Parker Trail diverges right (east) and leads in about 0.5 mi. to open ledges near the summit of Mt. Resolution, then continues to the Mt. Langdon Trail and Bartlett village. Fine views can be obtained from open ledges by ascending this trail for only a little more than 0.1 mi. from the Davis Path junction.

At this junction also, a spur trail leaves opposite the Mt. Parker Trail and descends steeply for about 120 yd. to the AMC's Resolution Shelter, an open camp with room for eight, situated on a small branch of Sleeper Brook. (WMNF Wilderness policies call for removal of this shelter when major maintenance is required.) Ordinarily there is water just behind the shelter, but in dry seasons, it may be necessary to go down the brook a short distance. In most seasons, this is the first water after the brook at the base of the climb up from the Saco valley; in dry seasons, it may be the last water available on the entire remainder of the trail unless one descends well down one of the branches of the Isolation Trail because all of the water sources near this ridge-crest trail are unreliable.

At 4.0 mi., the path passes just west of Stairs Col, the small, wild pass between Mt. Resolution and Stairs Mountain. Here the Stairs Col Trail to the Rocky Branch diverges right. The Davis Path now veers northwest, passing west of the precipitous Giant Stairs, ascending gradually along a steep mountainside, then zigzagging boldly northeast—with occasional steep scrambles on ledges—toward the flat top of Stairs Mountain. As the path turns sharp left shortly before reaching the top of the slope, a branch trail leads right a few steps to the Down-look, a good viewpoint at the brink of a cliff. (On the descent, where the main trail turns sharp right, take care not to follow this side path inadvertently because it ends at the drop-off very abruptly.) At the top of the climb, 4.4 mi. from US 302, a branch trail leads right at easy grades (southeast) 0.2 mi., passing just south of the summit of Stairs Mountain, to the top of the Giant Stairs, where there is an inspiring view to the east and south.

The Davis Path descends moderately along the north ridge of Stairs Mountain for 1.0 mi., then runs east in a sag for about 0.1 mi. Turning north again and crossing a small brook (watch for this turn), it passes over a small rise and descends into another sag. The path next begins to ascend the long north and south ridge of Mt. Davis, keeping mostly to the west slopes. Grades are mostly easy along this wild, little-used section, but the footing is rough in places and blowdown and overgrown sections may be encountered.

At 6.1 mi., there is a small spring on the right, and at 6.5 mi., a small brook is crossed. At 8.5 mi., a side path diverges right (east) and climbs steeply 0.2 mi. to the summit of Mt. Davis, which commands perhaps the finest view on the Montalban Ridge and one of the best in the mountains. The main path now descends to the col between Mt. Davis and Mt. Isolation, where it crosses a small brook and then ascends Mt. Isolation. At

9.7 mi., a spur path (which is signed, but easily missed) diverges left at a ledgy spot, leading steeply in 125 yd. to the open summit of Mt. Isolation, which provides magnificent views in all directions.

The path descends moderately for 0.2 mi. and then runs north along the ridge at easy grades. At 10.5 mi., the path leads past the site of the former Isolation Shelter, and at 10.6 mi., the east branch of the Isolation Trail enters on the right from the Rocky Branch valley. Water can be obtained by going down the Isolation Trail to the right (east); decent-appearing water (which is nevertheless unsafe to drink without treatment) may be a considerable distance down. The Davis Path now climbs steadily, and at 10.9 mi., as it reaches the top of the ridge and the grade decreases, the west branch of the Isolation Trail diverges and descends to the left into the Dry River valley. The Davis Path passes over a hump and runs through a sag at 11.5 mi., then ascends steadily to the treeline at 12.1 mi. From here, the trail is above the treeline and completely exposed to the weather. At 12.5 mi., the Glen Boulder Trail joins on the right just below a small crag; at 13.0 mi. the path passes just west of the summit of Boott Spur, and the Boott Spur Trail from the AMC's Pinkham Notch Visitor Center enters on the right (east).

Turning northwest, the path leads along the almost level ridges of Boott Spur and crosses Bigelow Lawn. At 13.6 mi., the Lawn Cutoff diverges right to Tuckerman Junction, and, 200 yd. farther on, the Camel Trail diverges left (west) to the Lakes of the Clouds Hut. At 14.0 mi., the Davis Path begins to follow the original location of the Crawford Path and crosses the Tuckerman Crossover, and in another 0.3 mi., the Davis Path is joined on the right by the Southside Trail. At 14.4 mi., the Davis Path ends at the present Crawford Path, which climbs to the summit of Mt. Washington in another 0.6 mi.

Davis Path (maps 1/3:H8–F9)

Distances from parking area near US 302 (1,000 ft.) to

- Mt. Crawford spur path (2,900 ft.): 2.2 mi., 1,900 ft., 2 hr. 5 min.
- Mt. Parker Trail (3,040 ft.): 3.7 mi., 2,200 ft. (rev. 150 ft.), 2 hr. 55 min.
- Stairs Col Trail (3,020 ft.): 4.0 mi., 2,250 ft. (rev. 50 ft.), 3 hr. 10 min.
- Giant Stairs spur path (3,450 ft.): 4.4 mi., 2,650 ft., 3 hr. 30 min.
- Mt. Davis spur path (3,600 ft.): 8.5 mi., 3,550 ft. (rev. 750 ft.), 6 hr.
- Mt. Isolation spur path (3,950 ft.): 9.7 mi., 4,000 ft. (rev. 100 ft.), 6 hr. 50 min.

▶

- Isolation Trail, east branch (3,850 ft.): 10.6 mi., 4,150 ft. (rev. 250 ft.), 7 hr. 25 min.
- Isolation Trail, west branch (4,150 ft.): 10.9 mi., 4,450 ft., 7 hr. 40 min.
- Glen Boulder Trail (5,175 ft.): 12.5 mi., 5,550 ft. (rev. 100 ft.), 9 hr.
- Boott Spur Trail (5,450 ft.): 13.0 mi., 5,850 ft., 9 hr. 25 min.
- Lawn Cutoff (5,475 ft.): 13.6 mi., 5,950 ft. (rev. 100 ft.), 9 hr. 45 min.
- Crawford Path (5,625 ft.): 14.4 mi., 6,150 ft. (rev. 50 ft.), 10 hr. 15 min.
- Lakes of the Clouds Hut (5,012 ft.) via Camel Trail: 14.4 mi., 5,950 ft. (rev. 450 ft.), 10 hr. 10 min.
- Mt. Washington summit (6,288 ft.) via Crawford Path: 15.0 mi., 6,800 ft., 10 hr. 55 min.

Stairs Col Trail (AMC)

This trail connects the Rocky Branch valley with Stairs Col on the Davis Path, providing, in particular, the easiest route to the Giant Stairs. Note that there is usually water in small streams in the upper part of this trail, but very little on the Davis Path. This trail is almost entirely within the Presidential Range–Dry River Wilderness.

It leaves the Rocky Branch Trail opposite the side path to the Rocky Branch Shelter #1 area and follows an old railroad siding for 50 yd. It then turns sharp left, crosses a swampy area, and climbs briefly to a logging road, where it enters the Presidential Range–Dry River Wilderness. From here nearly to Stairs Col, the trail follows old logging roads along the ravine of Lower Stairs Brook, becoming quite steep at 1.3 mi. and crossing the headwaters of the brook at about 1.5 mi., where it enters a birch glade. The trail becomes gradual as it approaches Stairs Col, with an impressive view up to the cliffs of Stairs Mountain, then it crosses this small, ferny pass and continues down the west slope a short distance to meet the Davis Path. For the Giant Stairs, turn right.

Stairs Col Trail (map 1:H9)

Distance from Rocky Branch Trail (1,420 ft.) to
- Davis Path junction (3,020 ft.): 1.8 mi., 1,650 ft., 1 hr. 45 min.

Rocky Branch Trail (WMNF)

This trail provides access to the valley of the Rocky Branch of the Saco River, which lies between the two longest subsidiary ridges of Mt. Washington: the Montalban Ridge to the west and the Rocky Branch Ridge to the east. In the upper part of the valley, the forest is still recovering from fires that swept the slopes in 1912 to 1914. The lack of mature trees, particularly conifers, is evident in many areas. *Caution:* There are four river crossings between the junctions with the Stairs Col Trail and the Isolation Trail, and one just beyond the Isolation Trail junction; these crossings are wide, difficult, and possibly dangerous at high water. The northeast terminus of this trail is located at a paved parking lot on NH 16 about 5.5 mi. north of Jackson, just north of the highway bridge over the Ellis River. The Jericho (south) trailhead is reached by following Jericho Rd.—called Rocky Branch Rd. (FR 27) by the USFS—which leaves US 302 just east of the bridge over the Rocky Branch, 1 mi. west of the junction of US 302 and NH 16 in Glen; it is paved for about 1 mi., then a good gravel road up to the beginning of the trail about 4.4 mi. from US 302.

At the northeast terminus, on NH 16 below Pinkham Notch, the trail leaves the north end of the parking lot (avoid a gravel road that branches left just below the parking lot) and climbs moderately by switchbacks on an old logging road. At about 0.5 mi., the Avalanche Brook Ski Trail enters from the left and leaves on the right at 0.7 mi. At 1.3 mi., the trail swings left, away from the bank of a small brook, and continues to ascend, then turns sharp left at 1.8 mi. and follows an old, very straight road on a slight downhill grade. After about 0.5 mi. on this road, it swings gradually right and climbs moderately, following a brook part of the way, and reaches the Presidential Range–Dry River Wilderness boundary just east of the ridge top. Passing the almost imperceptible height-of-land at 2.8 mi., the trail follows a short bypass to the left of a very wet area and runs almost level, then descends easily, with small brooks running in and out of the trail.

At 3.5 mi., the trail begins to swing left, descends gradually to the Rocky Branch and follows it downstream for a short distance, then crosses it at 3.7 mi. This crossing may be very difficult, and the trail can be difficult to follow from this crossing for travelers going toward NH 16 because it is poorly marked and there are well-beaten side paths to campsites—heading for NH 16, the main trail first parallels the river going upstream and then swings gradually away from the river on a well-defined old road. (*Note:* If you are climbing to Mt. Isolation from NH 16, and the river is high, you can avoid two possibly difficult crossings by bushwhacking upstream along the east side of the river for 0.4 mi. because the Isolation Trail, which begins on the opposite bank, soon crosses back to the east bank. Please avoid areas along the river that are signed as vegetation rehabilitation areas.)

On the west bank of the river at this crossing is the junction with the Isolation Trail, which turns right (north), following the riverbank upstream on the old railroad grade. The Rocky Branch Trail turns left downstream, also following the old railroad grade from this junction, and passes Rocky Branch Shelter #2 in 60 yd. (USFS Wilderness policies call for removal of this shelter when major maintenance is required.) The trail then runs generally south along the west bank for about 2.4 mi., at times on the old railroad grade, then follows the grade more closely, crossing the river four times. These crossings are difficult at high water; it may be practical to avoid some or all—particularly the upstream pair, which are a bit more than 0.1 mi. apart, while the downstream pair are 0.4 mi. apart—by bushwhacking along the west bank. After the fourth crossing at 6.8 mi., the trail leaves the Presidential Range–Dry River Wilderness, crosses Upper Stairs Brook, and begins a bypass on the uphill side of the old railroad grade that is almost 0.5 mi. long. Returning to the grade, the trail reaches a junction at 7.8 mi. with the Stairs Col Trail on the right, and, 20 yd. farther along the trail, a spur path on the left leads 60 yd. to WMNF Rocky Branch Shelter #1 and tentsite. Continuing south along the river on the railroad grade, the trail crosses Lower Stairs Brook, makes a shorter bypass on the uphill side of a boggy section of the grade, crossing another brook, and at 9.4 mi., enters a new gravel logging road and follows it for another 0.4 mi. to Jericho Rd., crossing the river and Otis Brook on logging-road bridges just before reaching its south terminus.

In the reverse direction, where the new road swings to the left about 0.4 mi. from the Jericho Rd. (south) terminus, the trail continues straight ahead into the woods at a kiosk on the old railroad grade, which looks like an old grassy road.

Rocky Branch Trail (map 3:G10–H9)

Distances from parking lot off NH 16 (1,200 ft.) to
- height-of-land (3,100 ft.): 2.8 mi., 1,950 ft. (rev. 50 ft.), 2 hr. 20 min.
- Isolation Trail (2,800 ft.): 3.7 mi., 1,950 ft. (rev. 300 ft.), 2 hr. 50 min.
- Stairs Col Trail (1,420 ft.): 7.8 mi., 1,950 ft. (rev. 1,400 ft.), 4 hr. 50 min.
- Jericho Rd. (1,100 ft.): 9.8 mi., 1,950 ft. (rev. 300 ft.), 5 hr. 50 min.

Isolation Trail (WMNF)

This trail links the Dry River valley (Dry River Trail), the Montalban Ridge (Davis Path), and the Rocky Branch valley (Rocky Branch Trail), crossing the ridge crest north of Mt. Isolation. It is entirely within the Presidential Range–Dry River Wilderness. The section west of the Davis Path is lightly used, rough, wet, and often overgrown, and may require considerable care to follow. East of the Davis Path, the trail receives much more use but is still wet and rough in places and not well-marked. This trail diverges from the Rocky Branch Trail just north of Rocky Branch Shelter #2 (which will be removed when major maintenance is required), on the west bank of the river at the point where the Rocky Branch Trail crosses it. The Isolation Trail follows the river north along the west bank on what is left of the old railroad grade, crossing the river at 0.4 mi. At 0.7 mi., the trail turns sharp right off the railroad grade, climbs briefly, then follows a logging road that at first runs high above the river. The trail crosses the river three more times; the next two crossings are only 70 yd. apart and so can be fairly easily avoided by a short bushwhack along the riverbank. The last crossing comes at 1.7 mi., after which the trail swings away from the main stream and climbs easily along a tributary with wet and rocky footing, reaching the Davis Path at 2.6 mi. after passing through an area of confusing side paths among bootleg campsites where the main trail must be followed with care.

Now turning right, coinciding with the Davis Path, the Isolation Trail climbs steadily north for about 0.3 mi. until it approaches the ridge crest and the grade decreases, where it turns left off the Davis Path. It runs level for 0.2 mi., then descends moderately southwest into the Dry River valley. At 4.3 mi., the trail reaches Isolation Brook, a branch of the Dry River, and follows its northwest bank on an old logging road disrupted by numerous small slides until it ends at the Dry River Trail, 4.9 mi. from US 302.

Isolation Trail (map 1:G9–G8)

Distances from Rocky Branch Trail (2,800 ft.) to
- fourth crossing of the Rocky Branch (3,423 ft.): 1.7 mi., 600 ft., 1 hr. 10 min.
- Davis Path, south junction (3,850 ft.): 2.6 mi., 1,050 ft., 1 hr. 50 min.
- Davis Path, north junction (4,150 ft.): 2.9 mi., 1,350 ft., 2 hr. 10 min.
- Isolation Brook (3,300 ft.): 4.3 mi., 1,400 ft. (rev. 900 ft.), 2 hr. 50 min.
- Dry River Trail (2,600 ft.): 5.3 mi., 1,400 ft. (rev. 700 ft.), 3 hr. 20 min.

Distances from Rocky Branch Trail at parking area on NH 16 (1,200 ft.) to
- Isolation Trail (2,800 ft.) via Rocky Branch Trail: 3.8 mi., 1,950 ft. (rev. 350 ft.), 2 hr. 50 min.
- Davis Path, south junction (3,850 ft.): 6.4 mi., 3,000 ft., 4 hr. 40 min.
- Mt. Isolation summit (4,003 ft.) via Davis Path: 7.3 mi., 3,300 ft. (rev. 150 ft.), 5 hr. 20 min.

Mount Langdon Trail (WMNF)

This trail runs to the Mt. Langdon Shelter from the road on the north side of the Saco near Bartlett village, meeting both the Mt. Parker Trail and the Mt. Stanton Trail, and thus gives access to both the higher and lower sections of the Montalban Ridge. It should be noted that despite its name this trail does not get particularly close to the summit of Mt. Langdon, which is crossed by the Mt. Stanton Trail. Most of this trail is either within or close to the boundary of the Presidential Range–Dry River Wilderness; Mt. Langdon Shelter is just outside the Wilderness.

From the four corners at the junction of US 302 and the Bear Notch Rd. in Bartlett village, follow River St. (the road that leads north) across a bridge over the Saco to a T-intersection at 0.4 mi. and bear left a short distance to the trailhead parking area (sign) on the right. The trail follows a logging road, bearing left at a fork at 75 yd., and at 0.3 mi., the path to Cave Mountain (unsigned and easily missed) diverges left. The road gradually becomes older and less evident. The trail enters the Presidential Range–Dry River Wilderness just before it crosses a brook at 1.0 mi. After recrossing the brook, it climbs more steadily with gravelly footing, bearing sharp right twice as the road fades away.

The Mt. Langdon Trail crosses Oak Ridge at 2.2 mi. after passing through an unusual stand of red oak, and descends, sharply at times, to the Oak Ridge–Mt. Parker col, where it bears right at 2.5 mi. at the junction with the Mt. Parker Trail. The Mt. Langdon Trail then descends gradually to the WMNF Mt. Langdon Shelter, capacity eight, where this trail and the Mt. Stanton Trail both end. Some care is required to follow the trail near the shelter. Water may be found in a brook 60 yd. from the shelter on the Mt. Stanton Trail, although in dry weather the brook bed may have to be followed downhill for a distance.

Mount Langdon Trail (map 3:I9–H9)

Distances from the road on the north bank of the Saco River (700 ft.) to
- Mt. Parker Trail (1,894 ft.): 2.5 mi., 1,450 ft. (rev. 250 ft.), 2 hr.
- Mt. Langdon Shelter (1,760 ft.): 2.9 mi., 1,450 ft. (rev. 150 ft.), 2 hr. 10 min.
- high point on Mt. Langdon (2,380 ft.) via Mt. Stanton Trail: 3.7 mi., 2,050 ft., 2 hr. 55 min.

Mount Parker Trail (SSOC)

This pleasant, rugged, lightly used trail passes several excellent viewpoints and provides access from Bartlett to Mt. Parker, Mt. Resolution, the Stairs Col area, and the upper Montalban Ridge. It runs almost entirely within or close to the boundary of the Presidential Range–Dry River Wilderness. Parts of the trail may require care to follow because of blowdown and encroaching brush, although experienced hikers should have little problem. There is no reliable water on this trail.

This trail begins in the Oak Ridge–Mt. Parker col 2.5 mi. from Bartlett, continuing straight ahead to the north where the Mt. Langdon Trail turns right (east). It climbs moderately with many switchbacks through brushy beech and oak woods severely damaged by the January 1998 ice storm, descends briefly to the right, and then swings left and continues its winding ascent to the open summit of Mt. Parker at 1.4 mi., where there are excellent views, especially north up the Rocky Branch valley to Mt. Washington.

The trail now descends and then continues north following the long ridge between Mt. Parker and Mt. Resolution and passing over three bumps, in spruce woods nearly all the way. Some blowdown may be encountered in this area. It then runs along the west and south slopes of the remainder of the ridge (swinging inside the Presidential Range–Dry River Wilderness for the rest of its length) until it reaches the southeast corner of Mt. Resolution. Here it turns sharp right and zigzags up to the col between the main summit ridge and a southerly knob at 3.2 mi., where an unmarked, badly overgrown branch trail leads left 0.1 mi. to the top of this knob, which is a large flat open ledge with excellent views; the beginning of the side path is next to a sawed-off stub along a flat section of the trail. Beyond this junction, the trail climbs moderately, then winds along the flat top of Mt. Resolution until it reaches a large cairn on an open ledge with excellent views at 3.8 mi. The true summit is probably just above this cairn; there is another knob of almost equal elevation about 0.1 mi. east-northeast that affords excellent views north, but there is no path to it through the dense scrub. From the cairn the trail descends into a gully where it crosses a small, sluggish brook (unreliable water), then heads down northwest over fine open ledges and finally drops steeply to the Davis Path, opposite the branch trail to Resolution Shelter.

Mount Parker Trail (map 3:H9)

Distances from Mt. Langdon Trail (1,894 ft.) to

- summit of Mt. Parker (3,004 ft.): 1.4 mi., 1,100 ft., 1 hr. 15 min.
- branch trail to open southerly knob (3,200 ft.): 3.2 mi., 1,600 ft. (rev. 300 ft.), 2 hr. 25 min.
- high point on Mt. Resolution (3,400 ft.): 3.8 mi., 1,800 ft., 2 hr. 45 min.
- Davis Path junction (3,040 ft.): 4.3 mi., 1,800 ft. (rev. 350 ft.), 3 hr. 5 min.

Mount Stanton Trail (SSOC)

This trail passes over the low eastern summits of the Montalban Ridge and affords many views from scattered ledges. To reach the relocated east trailhead (the west trailhead is at Mt. Langdon Shelter), leave the north side of US 302 1.8 mi. west of its junction with NH 16 in Glen and a short distance east of the bridge over the Saco River. Follow a paved road (Covered Bridge Ln.) west, bearing left at 0.2 mi. The road swings right (north), and at 0.9 mi., the trailhead (sign) is on the left where the road swings right again to head east as Hemlock Drive. Park on the roadside, taking care not to block any driveways. (The new trailhead is 0.1 mi. west of the old trailhead, which was on Hemlock Drive.)

The yellow-blazed trail follows the left edge of a driveway for 80 yd. and enters the woods. It swings right, passing around the house and climbs, turning left onto the older route of the trail at 0.3 mi. At 0.4 mi., it turns sharp left where the red-blazed WMNF boundary continues straight ahead. It climbs moderately, levels briefly, then ascends a steep gravelly section with poor footing. At the top of this pitch it turns left and ascends at an easier grade, and the first of several outlooks from White's Ledge is passed at 0.9 mi. The trail climbs steeply again, with gravelly, slippery footing, after passing a large boulder on the right of the trail, and at 1.3 mi., it turns sharp right on a ledge, where there is a good viewpoint just to the left of the trail and climbing becomes easier. At 1.4 mi., it passes about 15 yd. to the right of the true summit of Mt. Stanton. The summit area is covered with a fine stand of red (Norway) pines, and there are good views from nearby scattered ledges.

The trail descends past a north outlook to the Stanton-Pickering col, then ascends steadily, crosses a ledgy ridge and descends slightly, then climbs steeply and passes 30 yd. to the right of the true summit of Mt. Pickering at 2.2 mi. It then leads to ledges on a slightly lower knob, where there are excellent views. The trail descends to a minor col, then crosses over several interesting small humps sometimes called the Crippies (the origin of this peculiar name is one of the mysteries of White Mountains nomenclature). These humps have scattered outlook ledges, and the best view is from the fourth and last Crippie, which is crossed at 3.4 mi.

After the last Crippie, the trail may be less well cleared and harder to follow. It descends somewhat along the north side of the ridge toward Mt. Langdon, then climbs north moderately with a few steep pitches, passing a restricted outlook to Carter Dome, Carter Notch, and Wildcat Mountain. At 4.6 mi., the trail passes about 35 yd. to the right of the summit of Mt. Langdon, which is wooded and viewless, then descends easily to a gravel slope, turns right, and continues downward to a brook that is crossed 60 yd. east of Mt. Langdon Shelter, where the Mount Stanton Trail ends.

Mount Stanton Trail (map 3:H10–H9)

Distances from the trailhead off Covered Bridge Lane (700 ft.) to

- high point on Mt. Stanton (1,710 ft.): 1.5 mi., 1,000 ft., 1 hr. 15 min.
- high point on Mt. Pickering (1,920 ft.): 2.2 mi., 1,450 ft. (rev. 250 ft.), 1 hr. 50 min.
- Fourth Crippie (1,888 ft.): 3.4 mi., 1,800 ft. (rev. 400 ft.), 2 hr. 35 min.
- high point on Mt. Langdon (2,380 ft.): 4.6 mi., 2,500 ft. (rev. 200 ft.), 3 hr. 35 min.
- Mt. Langdon Trail at Mt. Langdon Shelter (1,760 ft.): 5.4 mi., 2,500 ft. (rev. 600 ft.), 3 hr. 55 min.

Cave Mountain Path

Cave Mountain (located on private property) is remarkable for the shallow cave near its wooded summit. It is reached from Bartlett by following the Mt. Langdon Trail for 0.3 mi. to an unsigned but well-worn branch path that forks left (watch for it carefully) and skirts the east side of Cave Mountain. After 0.3 mi., this path swings right and leads up a steep gravel slope to the cave. A rough, poorly marked trail to the right of the cave leads, after a short scramble, to the top of the cliff in which the cave is located, where there is a good view of Bartlett and the Saco River.

Cave Mountain Path (map 3:H9)

Distances from Mt. Langdon Trail (800 ft.) to
- cave (1,200 ft.): 0.3 mi., 400 ft., 20 min.
- outlook (1,350 ft.): 0.4 mi., 550 ft., 30 min.

Winniweta Falls Trail (WMNF)

This trail provides easy access to a waterfall. Its trailhead (limited parking) is located on the west side of NH 16, 3 mi. north of the bridge over the Ellis River in Jackson. Hikers using this trail must ford the wide bed of the Ellis River, which is often a rather shallow stream, but the crossing can require wading in even moderate flow and may be dangerous or impassable at high water. During the winter months, the crossing is even more treacherous, because there is often considerable running water under a seemingly stable snowpack and ice pack. This trail makes use of several cross-country ski trails maintained by the Jackson Ski Touring Foundation. During the winter months, hikers should avoid walking on ski tracks and should yield to skiers, who have the right of way.

After reaching the far bank of the Ellis River, this trail bears right and skirts the north side of an open field, crossing the Ellis River Ski Trail at 0.2 mi. It then follows the Winniweta Falls Ski Trail upstream along the north bank of Miles Brook on an old logging road. At an arrow, the path turns left from the road and soon reaches the falls. The ski trail continues uphill along the logging road for over a mile and ends at the Hall Ski Trail, which connects Dana Place with Green Hill Rd.

Winniweta Falls Trail (map 1:G10)

Distance from NH 16 (950 ft.) to
• Winniweta Falls (1,350 ft.): 0.9 mi., 400 ft., 40 min.

Iron Mountain Trail (JCC)

The summit of this mountain is wooded with restricted views, but an outlook on the north side and the fine south cliffs provide very attractive views for relatively little effort. Somewhat down the slope to the east of the cliffs are abandoned iron mines. A prominent easterly ridge, on which there was once a trail, descends over the open summit of Green Hill to the cliff called Duck's Head, named for its shape when seen from a point on NH 16 just north of the Jackson covered bridge. The trail is reached by leaving NH 16 in Jackson, next to the golf course and 0.3 mi. north of the red covered bridge that leads to Jackson village, and following a road prominently signed Green Hill Rd. to the west. At 1.2 mi., the pavement ends (from here the road is called Iron Mountain Rd.), and at 1.4 mi., the road (FR 119) bears left at a fork where FR 325 bears right. The road now becomes fairly steep, a bit rough, and very narrow (be prepared to back up if required for other cars to pass); above the fork, the road is not passable in mud season and winter. At 2.6 mi. from NH 16, where the road ahead soon becomes very poor, park in a designated area generously provided by the landowner on either side of the road just before reaching the house of the former Hayes Farm (now a summer residence).

The trail starts at a sign on the left 10 yd. up the road. It crosses a field, where there are fine views, traverses a smaller field, then passes through a band of trees and emerges at the base of a clear-cut slope. Marked with wooden stakes and small cairns, it ascends the open slope, swinging left, then right, and enters the woods at the top edge at 0.2 mi. The path climbs up a badly eroded footway, steeply at times, entering the WMNF at 0.3 mi. At 0.6 mi., there is a side path right 20 yd. to a fine outlook up the Rocky Branch valley to Mt. Washington, with the Southern Presidentials visible over the Montalban Ridge, and at 0.7 mi., a ledge on the left affords a view to the east. The main trail continues to the summit at 0.9 mi., where there are remains of the former fire tower. The trail descends steadily along a rocky ridge, dropping about 300 ft., then crosses several small humps in thick woods; follow cairns and blazes carefully. At 1.5 mi., a faintly marked side path descends left 0.2 mi. and 250 ft. to the old mines (tailings, water-filled shaft, tunnel), while the main trail ascends in a short distance to ledges and the edge of the cliffs, where wide views to the south and west can be enjoyed; swing right to reach the best viewpoint. On the return, the trail leaves the northeast corner of the ledge area behind the cliffs and soon makes a right turn.

Iron Mountain Trail (map 3:H10)

Distances from Hayes Farm (1,920 ft.) to
- summit of Iron Mountain (2,726 ft.): 0.9 mi., 800 ft., 50 min.
- south cliffs (2,430 ft.): 1.6 mi., 850 ft. (rev. 350 ft.), 1 hr. 15 min.

SUGGESTED HIKES

For more information on suggested hikes, see p. ix.

Easy Hikes

Crystal Cascade [rt: 0.6 mi., 200 ft., 0:25]. A short jaunt up the Tuckerman Ravine Trail to a fine waterfall.

Elephant Head [rt: 0.6 mi., 150 ft., 0:25]. An easy climb up the Webster-Jackson Trail and a spur trail to a ledge with a view of Crawford Notch.

Liebeskind's Loop [lp: 2.8 mi., 650 ft., 1:45]. An interesting loop—including the short side trip to Lila's Ledge—with views of Pinkham Notch and Mt. Washington, using the Old Jackson Rd., Crew-Cut Trail, George's Gorge Trail, and Liebeskind's Loop.

Iron Mountain [rt: 3.2 mi., 1,200 ft., 2:10]. This small mountain, reached by the Iron Mountain Trail, has a fine north outlook and a broad ledge with an excellent view on its south end.

Moderate Hikes

Glen Boulder [rt: 3.2 mi., 1,750 ft., 2:30]. A fairly steep and rough but short route to the treeline via the Glen Boulder Trail, with good views and a huge boulder perched on the mountainside.

Low's Bald Spot [rt: 4.4 mi., 950 ft., 2:40]. An attractive walk from Pinkham Notch Camp via the Old Jackson Rd., Madison Gulf Trail, and a side path, with an outlook providing interesting views of the Presidentials.

Hermit Lake [rt: 4.8 mi., 1,850 ft., 3:20]. A moderate climb up the Tuckerman Ravine Trail to views into the famed glacial cirque.

Harvard Rock [rt: 4.2 mi., 2,000 ft., 3:05]. This outlook on the Boott Spur Trail offers a magnificent view into Tuckerman Ravine.

Mt. Crawford [rt: 5.0 mi., 2,100 ft., 3:35]. This beautiful rock peak, reached by the Davis Path, offers extensive views. It is also part of an excellent longer trip that includes Stairs Mountain [rt: 9.8 mi., 3,050 ft., 6:25], Mt. Resolution [rt: 9.0 mi., 2,900 ft., 6:00], or both of these excellent viewpoints [rt: 10.8 mi., 3,400 ft., 7:05].

Mts. Jackson and Webster. The open summit of Mt. Jackson is reached by the Jackson branch of the Webster-Jackson Trail [rt: 5.2 mi., 2,150 ft., 3:40]. Mt. Webster, another fine viewpoint, is reached by the Webster branch of the Webster-Jackson Trail [rt: 5.0 mi., 2,200 ft., 3:35]. A loop can be made over both summits via the Webster Cliff Trail [lp: 6.5 mi., 2,450 ft., 4:30]. If a car spot is available, one can ascend Mt. Webster by the Webster-Jackson Trail and then make a leisurely descent of the magnificent Webster Cliff Trail down to the notch [lp: 5.8 mi., 2,150 ft., 4:00]. The Webster Cliff Trail can also be enjoyed as an out-and-back route to Mt. Webster [rt: 6.6 mi., 2,750 ft., 4:40].

Mt. Pierce and Mizpah Spring Hut [lp: 6.6 mi., 2,450 ft., 4:30]. This interesting loop provides good views and a sampling of the alpine zone on Mt. Pierce, with additional views and a visit to a high country hut on the return trip. Use the Crawford Connector, Crawford Path, Webster Cliff Trail, and Mizpah Cutoff.

Mt. Eisenhower [rt: 6.6 mi., 2,750 ft., 4:40]. The Edmands Path and Mt. Eisenhower Loop provide a moderate, graded route to this bald summit.

Strenuous Hikes

Mt. Monroe [rt: 7.0 mi., 2,900 ft., 5:00]. This craggy peak is an excellent alternative to its more notorious neighbor, Mt. Washington, offering superb views. Ascend via the Ammonoosuc Ravine Trail, Crawford Path, and Mt. Monroe Loop. With a car spot, a magnificent open ridge walk can be enjoyed along the Crawford Path, with descent via the Edmands Path [lp: 8.2 mi., 2,950 ft., 5:35].

Mt. Washington. Few hikers will be able to resist the urge to climb the highest mountain in the Northeast, despite the crowds on the popular trails and the hordes of tourists on the summit. The easiest way to climb it is probably the Jewell Trail–Gulfside Trail combination on the west side [rt: 10.2 mi., 4,000 ft., 7:05], which begins at a parking lot on the road to the Cog Railway. Most hikers climbing from this side will be tempted to turn the hike into a loop by combining the Jewell and Gulfside Trails with the Ammonoosuc Ravine Trail, which begins at the same parking lot [lp: 9.7 mi., 3,900 ft., 6:50]. The Ammonoosuc Ravine Trail [rt: 9.2 mi., 3,800 ft., 6:30] is a much more interesting and beautiful route to Mt. Washington than the Jewell Trail, but the section between Gem Pool and Lakes of the Clouds Hut can be extremely discouraging to a person in poor physical condition. On the descent, this section passes mostly over ledges and rocks, some of which are wet and slippery, and it can be quite tedious and tiring for a person whose agility is limited. On the whole, it is probably better to ascend the Ammonoosuc Ravine Trail and descend the Jewell Trail, but if afternoon thunderstorms are threatening, the descent by the Jewell Trail is probably more hazardous, as it is far less sheltered; on the other hand, in rain without lightning the steep wet rocks on the Ammonoosuc Ravine Trail may be more of a problem, but if it is both cold and rainy the exposure on the Jewell Trail may be more hazardous.

From the east side, the Tuckerman Ravine Trail is the easiest and most popular route to the summit [ow: 4.2 mi., 4,250 ft., 4:15; rt: 8.4 mi.,

4,250 ft., 6:20]. There are many other routes available, but though all of them are substantially less crowded they are also either longer or more strenuous. In good weather, the Boott Spur Trail offers better views, and though it is longer, it is not substantially more difficult; one can ascend by this trail and then descend through Tuckerman Ravine with the crowds, or make the easier, faster ascent through Tuckerman Ravine and then make a leisurely descent via Boott Spur [lp: 9.5 mi., 4,300 ft., 6:55]. The Lion Head Trail is about the same length as the Tuckerman Ravine Trail and offers better views, but it has steeper sections and is generally rougher; for most people, it is probably a better route for the ascent than for descent [ow: 4.4 mi., 4,250 ft., 4:15].

SECTION TWO
THE NORTHERN PEAKS AND THE GREAT GULF

This section covers the high peaks of Mt. Washington's massive northern ridge, which curves north and then northeast as a great arm embracing the magnificent glacial cirque called the Great Gulf. This ridge runs for 5 mi. with only slight dips below the 5,000-ft. level, and each of the three main peaks rises at least 500 ft. above the cols. The AMC's *Presidential Range Map* (map 1) covers the entire area except for the Pine Mountain Trail, which is covered by the AMC's *Carter Range–Evans Notch Map* (map 5). The Randolph Mountain Club (RMC) publishes a map of the Randolph Valley and Northern Peaks, printed on plastic-coated paper, and a guidebook, *Randolph*. The map covers the dense trail network on the northern slope of this region, and it is useful for people who want to explore some of the attractive, less crowded paths in this section. The RMC maintains a considerable number of paths on the Northern Peaks; many of these paths are very lightly used and are wilder and rougher than most trails in the White Mountain National Forest (WMNF). Traditionally, they have been less plainly marked, cleared, and trampled out than the heavily used primary trails, but in recent years they have been thoroughly cleared and marked so they are now suitable for almost any hiker. Adventurous hikers will find them a delightful alternative to the heavily used principal throughways on the range. This network of paths also provides opportunities for less strenuous, varied walks to the many waterfalls and other interesting places on the lower slopes of the range. Additional information can be obtained from the RMC.

Caution: The peaks and higher ridges of this range are nearly as exposed to the elements as Mt. Washington, and should be treated with the same degree of respect and caution. Severe winterlike storms can occur at any time of the year, and many lives have been lost in this area from failure to observe the basic principles of safety. In addition, all of the major peaks are strenuous climbs by even the easiest routes. The distances quoted may not seem long to a novice, but there is only one route to a major peak, the Caps Ridge Trail to Mt. Jefferson, that involves less than 3,000 ft. of climbing, and that trail is not an easy one. Although the Caps Ridge Trail is relatively short, it is also quite steep with numerous scrambles on ledges that a person unfamiliar with mountain trails might find daunting. Most other routes to the summits involve 4,000 to 4,500 ft. of climbing, because of the lower elevations of the major trailheads, thus making these ascents roughly equivalent in strenuousness to the ascent of Mt. Washington. Another consideration is the very rough, rocky footing on the upper slopes, which can slow travel times considerably. The substantial amount of effort required to climb these peaks, together with the threat of sudden and violent storms, should make the need to avoid overextending oneself quite apparent.

The highest points from which to climb the Northern Peaks, not including the summit of Mt. Washington, are Jefferson Notch Rd. at the Caps Ridge Trail (3,008 ft.); the parking lot on the Cog Railway Base Rd., 1.1 mi. east of the Jefferson Notch Rd., for the Jewell Trail (2,500 ft.); Pinkham Notch Visitor Center (2,030 ft.); and the Pinkham B Rd. (Dolly Copp Rd.) at the Pine Link (1,650 ft.). Other important parking areas are at the Great Gulf trailhead located 1.5 mi. south of Dolly Copp Campground on NH 16; at Randolph East, on Pinkham B (Dolly Copp) Rd. near its junction with US 2; at Appalachia, on US 2 about 1 mi. west of Pinkham B Rd. (a stop for the AMC's Hiker Shuttle); at Lowe's Store on US 2 (nominal fee charged by owner); and at Bowman, on US 2 about 1 mi. west of Lowe's Store. Several of the trailheads in the region, such as Randolph East, Appalachia, and Bowman, owe their names and locations to their former status as stations on the railroad line, whose tracks were removed in the summer of 1997; the railroad grade is now the Presidential Range Rail Trail and available for hiking. The USFS requires a parking permit (fee) for areas located on WMNF land.

The Northern Peaks were observed by Thomas Gorges and Richard Vines from the summit of Mt. Washington in 1642, but the men evidently considered these peaks to be merely a part of Mt. Washington, for on their return the explorers wrote, with considerable geographic confusion, "The mountain runs E. and W. 30 mi., but the peak is above all the rest." In the early summer of 1820, a party consisting of Adino N. Brackett, John W. Weeks, Gen. John Wilson, Charles J. Stuart, Noyes S. Dennison, Samuel A. Pearson, Philip Carrigain, and Ethan Allen Crawford visited Mt. Washington, and from that summit named Mts. Jefferson, Adams, and Madison, but did not explore them. On August 31, 1820, Brackett, Weeks, and Stuart made a second visit to the summit of Mt. Washington in company with Richard Eastman, Amos Legro, Joseph W. Brackett, and Edward B. Moore. Two members of this party spent a part of the day on the Northern Peaks and were probably the first persons of European extraction to visit these summits. Dr. J. W. Robbins, who spent considerable time there collecting botanical and other specimens, made a more thorough exploration in 1829.

The first trail on the Northern Peaks was probably the Stillings Path, which was cut about 1852 primarily for transporting building materials from Randolph to the summit of Mt. Washington and did not cross any of the summits. In 1860 or 1861, a partial trail was made over the peaks to Mt. Washington, of which some sections still exist as parts of current trails. Lowe's Path was cut between 1875 and 1876, the branch path through King Ravine was made in 1876, and the Osgood Path was opened in 1878. Many trails were constructed between 1878 and the beginning of lumbering in about 1902, but this network was greatly damaged by the timber cutting, and many trails were obliterated, at least temporarily. The more important ones were restored after the most intensive period of lumbering ceased.

In the Randolph Valley, where the Link crosses Cold Brook just below scenic Cold Brook Fall, Memorial Bridge stands as a memorial to J. Rayner Edmands, Eugene B. Cook, and other pioneer path makers who helped construct the superb trail network in the Presidential Range, including Thomas Starr King, James Gordon, Charles E. Lowe, Laban M. Watson, William H. Peek, Hubbard Hunt, William G. Nowell, and William Sargent.

In this section, the Appalachian Trail (AT) follows the Gulfside Trail from its junction with the Trinity Heights Connector near the summit of Mt. Washington to Madison Spring Hut. It then follows the Osgood Trail over Mt. Madison and down into the Great Gulf, proceeding to the Auto Rd. via the Osgood Cutoff, Great Gulf Trail (for a very short distance), and Madison Gulf Trail.

GEOGRAPHY

The upper part of the mass of the Northern Peaks is covered with rock fragments; above 5,000 ft., there are no trees and little scrub. The southeast side of the range is dominated by the Great Gulf and the two smaller cirques that branch off from it, Jefferson Ravine and Madison Gulf. The two Jefferson "knees," fairly prominent buttresses truncated by the Great Gulf, are the only significant ridges on this side of the range that survived the massive excavations by the glaciers that hollowed out the gulf. Many ridges and valleys radiate from this range on the north and west sides, the most important being, from north to south: on Mt. Madison, the Osgood Ridge, Howker Ridge, Bumpus Basin, Gordon Ridge, and the ravine of Snyder Brook, which is shared with Mt. Adams; on Mt. Adams, Durand Ridge, King Ravine, Nowell Ridge, Cascade Ravine, the Israel Ridge, and Castle Ravine, which is shared with Mt. Jefferson; on Mt. Jefferson, the Castellated Ridge and the Ridge of the Caps; and on Mt. Clay, an unnamed but conspicuous ridge extending westerly. The Great Gulf, Bumpus Basin, King Ravine, and Castle Ravine are glacial cirques, a landform that results when an alpine glacier (a small local glacier in a mountain valley) excavates a typical V-shaped brook valley with a narrow floor and fairly uniform slopes, turning it into the classic U-shaped cirque with a broad, fairly flat floor and almost vertical walls.

The Great Gulf is the largest cirque in the White Mountains, lying between Mt. Washington and the Northern Peaks and drained by the West Branch of the Peabody River. The headwall, bounded on the south by the slopes of Mt. Washington and on the west by the summit ridge of Mt. Clay, rises about 1,100 to 1,600 ft. above a bowl-shaped valley enclosed by steep walls that extend east for about 3.5 mi. The gulf then continues as a more open valley about 1.5 mi. farther east. The glacial action that formed the Great Gulf and its tributary gulfs is believed to have occurred mainly before the most recent ice age. The views from its walls and from points on its floor are among the best in New England, and steep slopes and abundant water result in a great number of cascades. The first recorded observation of the Great Gulf was by Darby Field in 1642, and the name probably had its origin in 1823 from a casual statement made by Ethan Allen Crawford, who, having lost his way in cloudy weather, came to "the edge of a great gulf." For a time it was sometimes called the "Gulf of Mexico," but this name is no longer used. J. W. Robbins, a botanist, visited the region in 1829, but even then little was known about the area until Benjamin F. Osgood blazed the first trail, from the Osgood Trail to the headwall, in 1881.

The first peak on the ridge north of Mt. Washington is Mt. Clay (5,533 ft.). Strictly speaking, it is only a shoulder, comparable to Boot Spur on the southeast ridge of its great neighbor, because it rises barely 150 ft. above the connecting ridge. But it offers superb views from the cliffs that drop away practically at the summit to form the west side of the Great Gulf headwall.

The remarkable features of Mt. Jefferson (5,716 ft.) are its three summits, which are a short distance apart, in line northwest and southeast, with the tallest in the middle. Perhaps the most striking view is down the Great Gulf with the Carter Range beyond (better views of the gulf itself are obtained from points on the Gulfside Trail to the north of the summit). There are other fine views from the peak, most notably those to Mt. Washington and the other Northern Peaks, to the Fabyan Plain on the southwest, and down the broad valley of the Israel River on the northwest. The Castellated Ridge, sharpest and most salient of the White Mountain ridges, extends northwest, forming the southwest wall of Castle Ravine; the view of the Castles from US 2 near the hamlet of Bowman is unforgettable. The Ridge of the Caps, similar in formation but less striking, extends to the west from the base of the summit cone. Jefferson's Knees, the two eastern ridges that are cut off abruptly by the Great Gulf, have precipitous wooded slopes and gently sloping tops. South of the peak of Mt. Jefferson is a smooth, grassy plateau called Monticello Lawn (about 5,400 ft.). In addition to its share of the Great Gulf proper, Jefferson's slopes are cut by two other prominent glacial cirques: Jefferson Ravine, a branch of the Great Gulf northeast of the mountain, and Castle Ravine, drained by a branch of the Israel River, on the north. The boundary between these two cirques is the narrow section of the main Northern Presidential ridge that runs from Mt. Jefferson through Edmands Col to Mt. Adams.

The second highest of the New England summits, Mt. Adams (5,799 ft.) has a greater variety of interesting features than any other New England mountain except Katahdin: its sharp, clean-cut profile; its large area above the treeline; its inspiring views, the finest being across the Great Gulf to Mts. Washington, Jefferson, and Clay; its great northern ridges, sharp, narrow Durand Ridge and massive, broad-spreading Nowell Ridge; and its five glacial cirques, King Ravine and the four that it shares with its neighbors, which are the Great Gulf, Jefferson Ravine, Madison Gulf, and Castle Ravine. The two most prominent of the several lesser summits and crags of Mt. Adams are Mt. Sam Adams (5,585 ft.), a rather flat mass to the west, and Mt. Quincy Adams or J. Q. Adams (5,410 ft.), a sharp, narrow shark-fin ridge to the north.

The farthest northeast of the high peaks of the Presidential Range, Mt. Madison (5,366 ft.) is remarkable for the great drop of more than 4,000 ft. to the river valleys east and northeast from its summit. The drop to the Androscoggin River at Gorham (4,580 ft. in about 6.5 mi.) is probably the closest approach in New England, except at Katahdin, of a major river to a tall mountain. The views south and southwest to the neighboring Presidential peaks and into the Great Gulf are very fine; the distant view is excellent in all other directions, and it includes Chocorua, which is visible just to the left of Mt. Washington.

Edmands Col (4,938 ft.), named for pioneer trail maker J. Rayner Edmands, lies between Mt. Adams and Mt. Jefferson, and Sphinx Col (4,959 ft.) lies between Mt. Jefferson and Mt. Clay. The col between Mt. Adams and Mt. Madison has an elevation of about 4,890 ft., so there is a range of only about 70 ft. between the lowest and highest of the three major cols on this ridge. In the unnamed Adams-Madison col lies Star Lake, a small, shallow body of water among jagged rocks, with impressive views, particularly up to Mt. Madison and Mt. Quincy Adams. Nearby is the Parapet, a small crag that offers magnificent views into the Great Gulf.

Pine Mountain (2,405 ft.) is a small peak lying to the northeast, between Mt. Madison and the great bend of the Androscoggin River at Gorham. Though low compared to its lofty neighbors, it is a rugged mountain with a fine cliff on the southeast side, and it offers magnificent, easily attained views of its Northern Presidential neighbors and of the mountains and river valleys to the north and east.

HUTS

Madison Spring Hut (AMC)

In 1888 at Madison Spring (4,800 ft.), a little north of the Adams-Madison col, the AMC built a stone hut that was later demolished. The present hut, rebuilt and improved after a fire in 1940, accommodates 50 guests in two bunkrooms operated on a coed basis. It is open to the public from early June to mid-September and is closed at all other times. Pets are not permitted in the hut. It is located 6.0 mi. from the summit of Mt. Washington via the Gulfside Trail, and 6.8 mi. from Lakes of the Clouds Hut via the Gulfside Trail, Westside Trail, and Crawford Path. In bad weather, the best approach (or exit) is via the Valley Way, which is sheltered to within a short distance of the hut. Nearby points of interest include Star Lake and the Parapet, a crag overlooking Madison Gulf. For current information, contact the AMC's Reservations Office (603-466-2727) or visit www.outdoors.org/lodging.

CAMPING

Great Gulf Wilderness

Wilderness regulations, intended to protect Wilderness resources and promote opportunities for challenge and solitude, prohibit use of motorized equipment or mechanical means of transportation of any sort. In accordance with USFS Wilderness policy, the trails in the Great Gulf area are in general maintained to a lower standard than trails outside Wilderness. They may be rough, overgrown, or essentially unmarked with minimal signage, and considerable care may be required to follow them. No camping is allowed within 200 ft. of any trail except at designated campsites (of which there are several marked by tentsite symbols between the Bluff and the Sphinx Trail), and wood or charcoal fires are not permitted at any place in the Great Gulf Wilderness. Camping is prohibited within 0.25 mi. of the Great Gulf Trail south of its junction with the Sphinx Trail, including Spaulding Lake and its vicinity. Hiking and camping group size must be no larger than 10 people. Camping and fires are also prohibited above the treeline (where trees are less than 8 ft. tall), except in winter, when camping is permitted above the treeline in places where snow cover is at least 2 ft. deep, but not on any frozen body of water. All former shelters have been removed.

Forest Protection Areas

The WMNF has established a number of Forest Protection Areas (FPAs)—formerly known as Restricted Use Areas—where camping and wood or charcoal fires are prohibited throughout the year. The specific areas are under continual review, and areas are added to or subtracted from the list in order to provide the greatest amount of protection to areas subject to damage by excessive camping, while imposing the lowest level of restrictions possible. A general list of FPAs in this section follows, but because there are often major changes from year to year, one should obtain current information on FPAs from the WMNF.

(1) No camping is permitted above treeline (where trees are less than 8 ft. tall) except in winter, and then only where there is at least 2 ft. of snow cover on the ground—but not on any frozen body of water. The point where the above-treeline restricted area begins is marked on most trails with small signs, but the absence of such signs should not be construed as proof of the legality of a site.

(2) No camping is permitted within 0.25 mi. of any trailhead, picnic area, or any facility for overnight accommodation such as a hut, cabin, shelter, tentsite, or campground, except as designated at the facility itself.

(3) No camping is permitted within 200 ft. of certain trails. In 2002, designated trails included the Valley Way south of its junction with the Scar Trail, from that junction up to Madison Hut.

(4) No camping is permitted on WMNF land within 0.25 mi. of certain roads (camping on private roadside land is illegal except by permission of the landowner). In 2006, these roads included NH 16 north of the Dana Place Inn, Jefferson Notch Rd. from the Cog Railway Base Rd. to the Caps Ridge Trail trailhead, and the Pinkham B Rd. (also known as Dolly Copp Rd.).

Established Trailside Campsites

The Log Cabin (RMC), first built about 1890 and totally rebuilt in 1985, is located at a spring at 3,300 ft. elevation, beside Lowe's Path at the junction with the Cabin-Cascades Trail. The cabin is partly enclosed and has room for about 10 guests. A fee is charged. There is no stove, and no wood fires are permitted in the area. Guests are requested to leave the cabin clean and are required to carry out all trash.

The Perch (RMC) is an open log shelter located at about 4,300 ft. on the Perch Path between the Randolph Path and Israel Ridge Path, but much closer to the former. It accommodates eight, and there are four tent platforms at the site. The caretaker at Gray Knob often visits to collect the overnight fee. Wood fires are not allowed in the area, and all trash must be carried out.

Crag Camp (RMC) is situated at the edge of King Ravine near the Spur Trail at about 4,200 ft. It is an enclosed cabin with room for about 20 guests. A fee is charged at all times. During July and August, it is maintained by a caretaker. Hikers are required to limit groups to 10 people. Wood fires are not allowed in the area, and all trash must be carried out.

Gray Knob (RMC) is an enclosed, winterized cabin on Gray Knob Trail at its junction with Hincks Trail, near Lowe's Path, at about 4,400 ft. It is staffed by a caretaker year-round, and a fee is charged at all times. Gray Knob has room for about 15 guests and is supplied with cooking utensils. Hikers are required to limit groups to 10 people. Wood fires are not allowed in the area, and all trash must be carried out.

These RMC shelters are all in Forest Protection Areas, and no camping is allowed within 0.25 mi. of them, except in the shelters and on the tent platforms themselves. Fees should be mailed to the RMC if not collected by the caretakers. Any infraction of rules or acts of vandalism should be reported to the above address.

Osgood Campsite (WMNF), consisting of tent platforms, is located near the junction of the Osgood Trail and Osgood Cutoff (which is on the AT).

Valley Way Campsite (WMNF), consisting of two tent platforms, is located on a short spur path off the Valley Way 3.1 mi. from Appalachia.

TRAIL DESCRIPTIONS

Gulfside Trail (WMNF)

This trail, the main route along the Northern Presidential ridge crest, leads from Madison Hut to the summit of Mt. Washington. It threads its way through the principal cols, avoiding the summits of the Northern Peaks, and offers extensive, ever-changing views. Its elevations range from about 4,800 ft. close to the hut to 6,288 ft. on the summit of Mt. Washington. The name Gulfside was given by J. Rayner Edmands who, starting in 1892, located and constructed the greater part of the trail, sometimes following trails that had existed before. All but about 0.8 mi. of the trail was once a graded path, and parts were paved with carefully placed stones—a work cut short by Edmands's death in 1910. The whole trail is part of the AT, except for a very short segment at the south end. For its entire distance, it forms the northwestern boundary of the Great Gulf Wilderness, though the path itself is not within the Wilderness.

The trail is well marked with large cairns, each topped with a yellow-painted stone, and, though care must be used, it can often be followed even in dense fog. Always carry a compass and study the map before starting, so you will be aware of your alternatives if a storm strikes suddenly. The trail is continuously exposed to the weather; dangerously high winds and low temperatures may occur with little warning at any season of the year. If such storms threaten serious trouble on the Gulfside Trail, do not attempt to ascend the summit cone of Mt. Washington, where conditions are usually far worse. If you are not close to either of the huts (at Madison Spring or Lakes of the Clouds), descend into one of the ravines on a trail if possible, or without trail if necessary. A night of discomfort in the woods is better than exposure to the weather on the heights, which may prove fatal. Slopes on the Great Gulf (southeast) side are more sheltered but generally steeper and farther from highways. It is particularly important not to head toward Edmands Col in deteriorating conditions; there is no easy trail out of this isolated mountain pass (which often acts like a natural wind tunnel) in bad weather, and hikers have sometimes been trapped in this desolate and isolated place by a storm. The emergency refuge shelter that was once located here was removed in 1982 after years of misuse and abuse (including illegal camping) by thoughtless visitors. In order to enjoy a safe trip through this spectacular but often dangerous area, there is no substitute for studying the map carefully and understanding the hazards and options before setting out on the ridge.

The following description of the path is in the southbound direction (toward Mt. Washington). See later for a description of the path in the reverse direction.

Part I. Madison Hut–Edmands Col

The trail begins about 30 yd. from Madison Hut at a junction with the Valley Way and Star Lake Trail and leads southwest through a patch of scrub. It then aims to the right (north) of Mt. Quincy Adams and ascends its steep, open north slope. At the top of this slope, on the high plateau between King Ravine and Mt. Quincy Adams, it is joined from the right by the Air Line, which has just been joined by the King Ravine Trail. Here there are striking views back to Mt. Madison, and into King Ravine at the Gateway a short distance down on the right. The Gulfside and Air Line coincide for less than 100 yd., then the Air Line branches left toward the summit of Mt. Adams. Much of the Gulfside Trail for about the next 0.5 mi. is paved with carefully placed stones. It rises moderately southwest, then becomes steeper, and at 0.9 mi. from the hut reaches a grassy lawn in the saddle (5,490 ft.) between Mt. Adams and Mt. Sam Adams. Here several trails intersect at a spot called Thunderstorm Junction, where a massive cairn once stood about 10 ft. tall. Entering the junction on the right is the Great Gully Trail, coming up across the slope from the southwest corner of King Ravine. Here, also, the Gulfside is crossed by Lowe's Path, ascending from Lowe's Store on US 2 to the summit of Mt. Adams. About 100 yd. down Lowe's Path, the Spur Trail branches right for Crag Camp. The summit of Mt. Adams is about 0.3 mi. from the junction (left) via Lowe's Path; a round trip to the summit requires about 25 min.

Continuing southwest from Thunderstorm Junction and beginning to descend, the Gulfside Trail passes a junction on the left with the Israel Ridge Path, which ascends a short distance to Lowe's Path and thence to the summit of Mt. Adams. For about 0.5 mi., the Gulfside Trail and Israel Ridge Path coincide, passing Peabody Spring (unreliable) just to the right in a small, grassy flat; more-reliable water is located a short distance beyond at the base of a conspicuous boulder just to the left of the path. Soon the trail climbs easily across a small ridge, where the Israel Ridge Path diverges right at a point 1.5 mi. from Madison Hut. Near this junction in wet weather there is a small pool called Storm Lake. The Gulfside bears a bit left toward the edge of Jefferson Ravine, and, always leading toward Mt. Jefferson, descends southwest along the narrow ridge that divides Jefferson Ravine from Castle Ravine, near the edge of the southeast cliffs, from which there are fine views into the Great Gulf. This part of the Gulfside was never graded. At the end of this descent, the trail reaches Edmands Col at 2.2 mi. from the hut, with 3.8 mi. to go to Mt. Washington.

At Edmands Col (4,938 ft.), there is a bronze tablet in memory of J. Rayner Edmands, who made most of the graded paths on the Northern Peaks. Gulfside Spring is 50 yd. south of the col on the Edmands Col Cutoff, and Spaulding Spring (reliable) is about 0.2 mi. north near the Castle Ravine Trail. The emergency shelter once located at this col has been dismantled, and none of the trails leaving this area is an entirely satisfactory escape route in bad weather. From the col, the Edmands Col Cutoff leads south, entering scrub almost immediately, affording the quickest route to this rough form of shelter in dangerous weather; it then continues about 0.5 mi. to the Six Husbands Trail leading down into the Great Gulf, but it is very rough and the Six Husbands Trail is fairly difficult to descend, making it a far less than ideal escape route unless the severity of the weather leaves no choice. The Randolph Path leads north into the Randolph Valley, running above treeline with great exposure to northwest winds for more than 0.5 mi. It is nevertheless probably the fastest, safest route to civilization unless high winds make it too dangerous to cross through Edmands Col. Branching from this path about 0.1 mi. north of the col are the Cornice, a very rough trail leading west entirely above treeline to the Castle Trail, and the Castle Ravine Trail, which descends steeply over very loose talus and may be hard to follow.

Part II. Edmands Col–Sphinx Col

South of Edmands Col, the Gulfside Trail ascends steeply over rough rocks, with Jefferson Ravine on the left. It passes flat-topped Dingmaul Rock, from which there is a good view down the ravine, with Mt. Adams on the left. This rock is named for a legendary alpine beast to which it is reputed to bear a remarkable resemblance—the more remarkable because there has never been a verified sighting of the beast. About 100 yd. beyond, the Mt. Jefferson Loop branches right and leads 0.4 mi. to the summit of Mt. Jefferson (5,716 ft.). The views from the summit are excellent, and the Mt. Jefferson Loop is only slightly longer than the parallel section of the Gulfside, though it requires about 300 ft. of extra climbing and about 10 min. more hiking time.

The path now rises less steeply. It crosses the Six Husbands Trail and soon reaches its greatest height on Mt. Jefferson, about 5,400 ft. Curving southwest and descending a little, it crosses Monticello Lawn, a comparatively smooth, grassy plateau. Here the Mt. Jefferson Loop rejoins the Gulfside about 0.3 mi. from the summit. A short distance beyond the edge of the lawn, the Cornice enters right from the Caps Ridge Trail. The Gulfside descends to the south, and from one point, there is a view of the Sphinx down the slope to the left. A few yards north of the low point in Sphinx Col, the Sphinx Trail branches left (east) into the Great Gulf through a grassy passage between ledges. Sphinx Col is 3.7 mi. from Madison Hut, with 2.3 mi. left to the summit of Mt. Washington. In bad weather, a fairly quick descent to sheltering scrub can be made via the Sphinx Trail, though once the treeline is reached this trail becomes rather steep and difficult.

Part III. Sphinx Col–Mount Washington

From Sphinx Col the path leads toward Mt. Washington, and soon the Mt. Clay Loop diverges left to climb over the summits of Mt. Clay, with impressive views into the Great Gulf. The Mt. Clay Loop adds about 300 ft. of climbing and 10 min.; the distance is about the same. The Gulfside Trail is slightly easier and passes close to a spring, but misses the best views. It bears right from the junction with the Mt. Clay Loop, runs south, and climbs moderately, angling up the west side of Mt. Clay. About 0.3 mi. above Sphinx Col, a loop leads to water a few steps down to the right. The side path continues about 30 yd. farther to Greenough Spring (more reliable), then rejoins the Gulfside about 100 yd. above its exit point. The Gulfside continues its moderate ascent, and the Jewell Trail from the Cog Railway Base Rd. enters from the right at 4.6 mi. From this junction, the ridge crest of Mt. Clay can be reached in good weather by a short scramble up the rocks without trail. The Gulfside swings southeast and soon descends slightly to a point near the Clay-Washington col (5,391 ft.), where the Mt. Clay Loop rejoins it from the left. A little to the east is the edge of the Great Gulf, with fine views, especially of the east cliffs of Mt. Clay.

The path continues southeast, rising gradually on Mt. Washington. About 0.1 mi. above the col, the Westside Trail branches right, crosses under the Cog Railway, and leads to the Crawford Path and Lakes of the Clouds Hut. The Gulfside continues southeast between the Cog Railway on the right and the edge of the gulf on the left. If the path is lost, the railway can be followed to the summit. At the extreme south corner of the gulf, the Great Gulf Trail joins the Gulfside from the left, 5.5 mi. from Madison Hut. Here the Gulfside turns sharp right, crosses the railroad, and continues south to the plateau just west of the summit. Here it passes a junction with the Trinity Heights Connector, a link in the AT, which branches left and climbs for 0.2 mi. to the true summit of Mt. Washington. In another 0.1 mi., the Gulfside joins the Crawford Path just below (north of) the old corral, and the two trails turn left and coincide to the summit.

Gulfside Trail (map 1:F9)

Distances from Madison Hut (4,825 ft.)

- to Air Line (5,125 ft.): 0.3 mi., 300 ft., 20 min.
- to Thunderstorm Junction (5,490 ft.): 0.9 mi., 650 ft., 45 min.
- to Israel Ridge Path, north junction (5,475 ft.): 1.0 mi., 650 ft., 50 min.   ▶

- to Israel Ridge Path, south junction (5,250 ft.): 1.5 mi., 650 ft., 1 hr. 5 min.
- to Edmands Col (4,938 ft.): 2.2 mi., 650 ft., 1 hr. 25 min.
- to Jefferson Loop, north end (5,125 ft.): 2.4 mi., 850 ft., 1 hr. 40 min.
- to Six Husbands Trail (5,325 ft.): 2.7 mi., 1,050 ft., 1 hr. 55 min.
- for Mt. Jefferson Loop, south end (5,375 ft.): 3.1 mi., 1,100 ft., 2 hr. 5 min.
- to The Cornice (5,325 ft.): 3.2 mi., 1,100 ft., 2 hr. 10 min.
- to Sphinx Trail (4,975 ft.): 3.7 mi., 1,100 ft., 2 hr. 25 min.
- for Mt. Clay Loop, north end (5,025 ft.): 3.8 mi., 1,150 ft., 2 hr. 30 min.
- to Jewell Trail (5,400 ft.): 4.6 mi., 1,550 ft., 3 hr. 5 min.
- for Mt. Clay Loop, south end (5,400 ft.): 4.9 mi., 1,600 ft., 3 hr. 15 min.
- to Westside Trail (5,500 ft.): 5.0 mi., 1,700 ft., 3 hr. 20 min.
- to Great Gulf Trail (5,925 ft.): 5.5 mi., 2,150 ft., 3 hr. 50 min.
- to Trinity Heights Connector (6,100 ft.): 5.7 mi., 2,300 ft., 4 hr.
- to Crawford Path (6,150 ft.): 5.8 mi., 2,350 ft., 4 hr. 5 min.
- to Mt. Washington summit (6,288 ft.) via Crawford Path: 6.0 mi., 2,500 ft., 4 hr. 15 min.
- to Lakes of the Clouds Hut (5,012 ft.) via Westside Trail and Crawford Path: 6.8 mi., 1,850 ft., 4 hr. 20 min.

Gulfside Trail (WMNF) [In Reverse]

Part I. Mount Washington–Sphinx Col

Descending from the summit of Mt. Washington, coinciding with the Crawford Path, the trail is on the right (west) side of the railroad track. After passing between the buildings, it leads generally northwest; avoid random side paths toward the south. Shortly it reaches its point of departure from the Crawford Path, just below the remains of an old corral, and turns sharp right. In 0.1 mi., it passes a junction with the Trinity Heights Connector, a link in the AT, which branches right and climbs for 0.2 mi. to the true summit of Mt. Washington. The Gulfside Trail then descends steadily, crossing the railroad, and at 0.5 mi., as the Gulfside turns sharp left at the extreme south corner of the Great Gulf, the Great Gulf Trail joins on the right. The Gulfside continues northwest between the Cog Railway on the left and the edge of the gulf on the right. At 1.0 mi., the Westside Trail branches left, crosses under the Cog Railway, and leads to the Crawford Path and Lakes of the Clouds Hut. The Gulfside descends gradually to a point near the Clay-Washington col (5,391 ft.), where the Mt. Clay Loop diverges right to traverse the summits of Mt. Clay, with impressive views into the Great Gulf. The Mt. Clay Loop adds about 300 ft. of climbing and 10 min.; the distance is about the same. The Gulf-side Trail is slightly easier and passes close to a spring, but misses the best views. A little to the east at this col is the edge of the Great Gulf, with fine views, especially of the east cliffs of Mt. Clay.

After a slight ascent, the Gulfside begins to angle down the west side of Mt. Clay, and the Jewell Trail from the Cog Railway Base Rd. enters from the left at 1.4 mi. From this junction, the ridge crest of Mt. Clay can be reached by a short scramble up the rocks without a trail. At about 0.5 mi. beyond this junction, a loop leads left to Greenough Spring (reliable), then rejoins the Gulfside about 100 yd. below its exit point. As the grade levels approaching Sphinx Col, the Mt. Clay Loop rejoins on the right. At Sphinx Col, it is 2.3 mi. from Mt. Washington and 3.7 mi. to Madison Hut. In bad weather, a fairly quick descent to sheltering scrub can be made via the Sphinx Trail, though once the treeline is reached this trail becomes rather steep and difficult.

Part II. Sphinx Col–Edmands Col

A few yards north of the low point in Sphinx Col, the Sphinx Trail branches right (east) into the Great Gulf through a grassy passage between ledges. The Gulfside ascends to the north, and from one point, there is a view of the Sphinx down the slope to the right. The Cornice enters left from the Caps Ridge Trail a short distance before the Gulfside begins to cross Monticello Lawn, a comparatively smooth, grassy plateau. Here the Mt. Jefferson Loop branches left and leads 0.3 mi. to the summit of Mt. Jefferson (5,716 ft.). The views from the summit are excellent, and the Mt. Jefferson Loop is only slightly longer than the parallel section of the Gulfside, though it requires about 300 ft. of extra climbing and about 10 min. more hiking time.

The path now turns northeast and rises less steeply. It crosses the Six Husbands Trail soon after reaching its greatest height on Mt. Jefferson, about 5,400 ft., then descends moderately to the point where the Mt. Jefferson Loop rejoins on the left about 0.4 mi. from the summit. The trail now descends steeply north over rough rocks, with Jefferson Ravine on the right, and about 100 yd. beyond the junction, it passes flat-topped Dingmaul Rock, from which there is a good view down the ravine, with Mt. Adams on the left. The trail reaches Edmands Col at 3.8 mi. from Mt. Washington, with 2.2 mi. to go to Madison Hut.

At Edmands Col (4,938 ft.), there is a bronze tablet in memory of J. Rayner Edmands, who made most of the graded paths on the Northern Peaks. Gulfside Spring (unreliable in dry seasons) is 50 yd. south of the col, and Spaulding Spring (reliable) is about 0.2 mi. north near the Castle Ravine Trail. The emergency shelter once located at this col has been dismantled, and none of the trails leaving this area is a particularly satisfactory escape route in bad weather. From the col, the Edmands Col Cutoff leads south, entering scrub almost immediately, affording the quickest route to this rough form of shelter in dangerous weather; it then continues about 0.5 mi. to the Six Husbands Trail leading down to the Great Gulf, but it is very rough and the Six Husbands Trail is fairly difficult to descend, making it a far less than ideal escape route unless the severity of the weather leaves no choice. The Randolph Path leads north into the Randolph Valley, running above treeline with great exposure to northwest winds for more than 0.5 mi. It is nevertheless probably the fastest, safest route to civilization unless high winds make it too dangerous to cross through Edmands Col. Branching from this path about 0.1 mi. north of the col are the Cornice, a very rough trail leading west entirely above the treeline to the Castle Trail, and the Castle Ravine Trail, which descends steeply over very loose talus and may be hard to follow.

Part III. Edmands Col–Madison Spring Hut

Leaving Edmands Col, the Gulfside climbs moderately along the edge of Jefferson Ravine, ascending northeast along the narrow ridge that divides Jefferson Ravine from Castle Ravine near the edge of the southeast cliffs, from which there are fine views into the Great Gulf. This part of the Gulfside was never graded. About 0.7 mi. above Edmands Col the trail reaches the crest of a small ridge, where the Israel Ridge Path enters left. Near this junction in wet weather, there is a small pool called Storm Lake. For about 0.5 mi., the Gulfside Trail and Israel Ridge Path coincide, passing reliable water at the base of a conspicuous boulder just to the right of the path; Peabody Spring (unreliable) is just beyond on the left in a small, grassy flat. The Gulfside Trail continues to ascend and, as it levels out on a grassy lawn in the saddle (5,490 ft.) between Mt. Adams and Mt. Sam Adams, the Israel Ridge Path diverges right and ascends a short distance to Lowe's Path and thence to the summit of Mt. Adams.

In another 0.1 mi., several trails intersect at a spot called Thunderstorm Junction, where a massive cairn once stood about 10 ft. tall. Entering the junction on the left is the Great Gully Trail, coming up across the slope from the southwest corner of King Ravine. Here, also, the Gulfside is crossed by Lowe's Path, ascending from Lowe's Store on US 2 to the summit of Mt. Adams. About 100 yd. down Lowe's Path, the Spur Trail branches right for Crag Camp. The summit of Mt. Adams is about 0.3 mi. from the junction (right) via Lowe's Path; a round trip to the summit requires about 25 min.

From Thunderstorm Junction, the Gulfside descends northeast, gradually at first, and enters a section about 0.5 mi. long that is paved with carefully placed stones. At the end of this section, on the high plateau between King Ravine and Mt. Quincy Adams, the Air Line enters on the right, descending from Mt. Adams, and the trails coincide for less than 100 yd. Then the Air Line branches left at the top of the steep, open north slope of Mt. Quincy Adams, and just below this junction, the King Ravine Trail branches left from the Air Line. Here there are striking views ahead to Mt. Madison, and into King Ravine at the Gateway a short distance down on the left. The Gulfside then descends the slope and passes through a patch of scrub to a junction with the Valley Way and Star Lake Trail about 30 yd. from Madison Hut.

Gulfside Trail [In Reverse] (map 1:F9)

Distances from the summit of Mt. Washington (6,288 ft.) to
- Crawford Path junction (6,150 ft. ft.): 0.2 mi., 0 ft., 5 min.
- Trinity Heights Connector (6,100 ft.): 0.3 mi., 0 ft., 10 min.
- Great Gulf Trail (5,925 ft.): 0.5 mi., 0 ft., 15 min.
- Westside Trail (5,500 ft.): 1.0 mi., 0 ft., 30 min.
- Mt. Clay Loop, south end (5,400 ft.): 1.1 mi., 0 ft., 35 min.
- Jewell Trail (5,400 ft.): 1.4 mi., 50 ft., 45 min.
- Mt. Clay Loop, north end (5,025 ft.): 2.2 mi., 50 ft., 1 hr. 5 min.
- Sphinx Trail (4,975 ft.): 2.3 mi., 50 ft., 1 hr. 10 min.
- The Cornice (5,325 ft.): 2.8 mi., 400 ft., 1 hr. 35 min.
- Mt. Jefferson Loop, south end (5,375 ft.): 2.9 mi., 450 ft., 1 hr. 40 min.
- Six Husbands Trail (5,325 ft.): 3.3 mi., 450 ft., 1 hr. 55 min.
- Mt. Jefferson Loop, north end (5,125 ft.): 3.6 mi., 450 ft., 2 hr.
- Edmands Col (4,938 ft.): 3.8 mi., 450 ft., 2 hr. 10 min. ▶

- Israel Ridge Path, south junction (5,250 ft.): 4.5 mi., 750 ft., 2 hr. 40 min.
- Israel Ridge Path, north junction (5,475 ft.): 5.0 mi., 1,000 ft., 3 hr.
- Thunderstorm Junction (5,490 ft.): 5.1 mi., 1,000 ft., 3 hr. 5 min.
- Air Line (5,125 ft.): 5.6 mi., 1,000 ft., 3 hr. 20 min.
- Madison Hut (4,825 ft.): 6.0 mi., 1,000 ft., 3 hr. 30 min.

Distance from Lakes of the Clouds Hut (5,012 ft.) to
- Madison Hut (4,825 ft.) via Westside Trail, Crawford Path, and Gulfside Trail: 6.8 mi. , 1,650 ft., 4 hr. 15 min.

Mount Jefferson Loop (AMC)

This trail provides access to the summit of Mt. Jefferson from the Gulfside Trail. It diverges right (west) from the Gulfside, 0.2 mi. south of Edmands Col, and climbs steeply almost straight up the slope. Just below the summit, the Six Husbands Trail enters on the left, then the Castle Trail enters on the right, and soon the junction with Caps Ridge Trail is reached at the base of the summit crag. The true summit is 40 yd. right (west) on the Caps Ridge Trail. The Mt. Jefferson Loop then descends to rejoin the Gulfside Trail on Monticello Lawn.

Mount Jefferson Loop (map 1:F9)

Distances from north junction with Gulfside Trail (5,125 ft.) to
- Mt. Jefferson summit (5,716 ft.): 0.4 mi., 600 ft., 30 min.
- south junction with Gulfside Trail (5,375 ft.): 0.7 mi., 600 ft. (rev. 350 ft.), 40 min.

Mount Clay Loop (AMC)

This trail traverses the summit ridge of Mt. Clay roughly parallel to the Gulfside Trail, providing access to the superb views into the Great Gulf from Clay's east cliffs. The entire trail (except for its end points) is within the Great Gulf Wilderness.

The trail diverges left (east) from the Gulfside Trail about 0.1 mi. south of Sphinx Col, and ascends a somewhat steep, rough slope to the ragged ridge crest. After crossing the summit and passing over several slightly lower knobs, the trail descends easily to the flat col between Mt. Clay and Mt. Washington, where it rejoins the Gulfside Trail.

Mount Clay Loop (map 1:F9)

Distances from north junction with Gulfside Trail (5,025 ft.) to
- summit of Mt. Clay (5,533 ft.): 0.5 mi., 500 ft., 30 min.
- south junction with Gulfside Trail (5,400 ft.): 1.2 mi., 650 ft. (rev. 300 ft.), 55 min.

Edmands Col Cutoff (RMC)

This important link, connecting the Gulfside Trail and Randolph Path at Edmands Col with the Six Husbands Trail, makes possible a quick escape from Edmands Col into plentiful sheltering scrub on the lee side of Mt. Jefferson; it also provides a route to civilization through the Great Gulf via the Six Husbands Trail, and although this route is long, with a steep, rough, and rather difficult descent, it may be the safest escape route from the vicinity of Edmands Col in severe weather. Footing on this trail is very rough and rocky. It is almost entirely within the Great Gulf Wilderness.

Leaving Edmands Col, the trail passes Gulfside Spring in 50 yd., then begins a rough scramble over rockslides and through scrub, marked by cairns. The trail is generally almost level but has many small rises and falls over minor ridges and gullies, with good views to the Great Gulf and out to the east. It ends at the Six Husbands Trail 0.3 mi. below that trail's junction with the Gulfside Trail.

Edmands Col Cutoff (map 1:F9)

Distance from Edmands Col (4,938 ft.) to
- Six Husbands Trail (4,925 ft.): 0.5 mi., 100 ft. (rev 100 ft.), 20 min.

The Cornice (RMC)

This trail circles the west slope of Mt. Jefferson, running completely above the treeline, with many interesting views. It starts near Edmands Col, crosses the Castle Trail and the Caps Ridge Trail, and returns to the Gulfside at Monticello Lawn, linking the trails on the west and northwest slopes of Jefferson. Its southern segment, which has relatively good footing, provides an excellent shortcut from the Caps Ridge Trail to the Gulfside on Monticello Lawn south of Mt. Jefferson. However, the section leading from Edmands Col to the Caps Ridge Trail is extremely rough, with a large amount of tedious and strenuous rock-hopping, which is very hard on knees and ankles. This section of the trail, therefore, may take considerably more time than the estimates that follow. As a route between Edmands Col and the Caps Ridge Trail, the Cornice saves a little climbing compared to the route over the summit of Jefferson, but it is much longer, requires more exertion, and is just as exposed to the weather. This makes its value as a route to avoid Jefferson's summit in bad weather very questionable.

The Cornice diverges west from the Randolph Path near Spaulding Spring, 0.1 mi. north of the Gulfside Trail in Edmands Col, where the Castle Ravine Trail also diverges from the Randolph Path. It crosses a small grassy depression where there may be no perceptible footway until it climbs the rocky bank on the other side. It then ascends moderately over large rocks, passing above a rock formation that resembles a petrified cousin of the Loch Ness monster, and circles around the north and west sides of Mt. Jefferson, crossing the Castle Trail above the Upper Castle. It continues across the rocky slope, intersects the Caps Ridge Trail above the Upper Cap, and turns left (east) up the Caps Ridge Trail for about 20 yd., then diverges right (south) and climbs gradually with improved footing to the Gulfside Trail just below Monticello Lawn.

The Cornice (map 1:F9)

Distances from Randolph Path (4,900 ft.) to
- Castle Trail (5,100 ft.): 0.6 mi., 200 ft., 25 min.
- Caps Ridge Trail (5,025 ft.): 1.3 mi., 200 ft. (rev. 100 ft.), 45 min.
- Gulfside Trail junction (5,325 ft.): 1.8 mi., 500 ft., 1 hr. 10 min.

Randolph Path (RMC)

This graded path extends southwest from the Pinkham B (Dolly Copp) Rd. near Randolph village, ascending diagonally up the slopes of Mt. Madison and Mt. Adams to the Gulfside Trail in Edmands Col between Mt. Adams and Mt. Jefferson. In addition to providing a route from Randolph to Edmands Col, it crosses numerous other trails along the way and thus constitutes an important linking trail between them. Some sections are heavily used and well beaten, while others bear very little traffic and, though well cleared and marked, have a less obvious footway. J. Rayner Edmands made the Randolph Path from 1893 to 1899. Parts of it were reconstructed in 1978 as a memorial to Christopher Goetze, an active RMC member and former editor of *Appalachia,* the AMC's mountaineering and conservation journal.

The path begins at the parking space known as Randolph East, located on the Pinkham B Rd. 0.2 mi. south of US 2. Coinciding with the Howker Ridge Trail, it quickly crosses the Presidential Range Rail Trail, and 30 yd. beyond turns right (west) where the Howker Ridge Trail diverges left (southeast). The Randolph Path runs along the south edge of the power-line clearing for about 0.3 mi., then swings southwest and ascends to a brushy logged area, where it bears right—follow markings carefully. Entering mature woods, it ascends moderately to cross the Sylvan Way at 0.7 mi., and at 1.4 mi., it reaches Snyder Brook, where the Inlook Trail and Brookside join on the left. The Brookside and the Randolph Path cross the brook together on large stepping-stones (the former bridge at this crossing was washed out in 2005 and will not be replaced), then the Brookside diverges right and leads down to the Valley Way. After a short climb, the Randolph Path crosses the Valley Way, and soon after that joins the Air Line, coincides with it for 20 yd., then leaves it on the right.

At 1.9 mi., the Short Line enters right; by this shortcut route, it is 1.3 mi. to US 2 at Appalachia. The Short Line coincides with the Randolph Path for 0.4 mi., then branches left for King Ravine. The Randolph Path descends slightly and crosses Cold Brook on Sanders Bridge, and the Cliffway diverges right just beyond. At 3.1 mi., the King Ravine Trail is crossed at its junction with the Amphibrach, an intersection called the Pentadoi. The Randolph Path continues across Spur Brook on ledges just below some interesting pools and cascades, and just beyond the brook, the Spur Trail diverges left. The Randolph Path climbs around the nose of a minor ridge and becomes steeper and rougher. Soon the Log Cabin Cutoff diverges right and runs, nearly level but with rough footing, 0.2 mi. to the Log Cabin.

At 3.9 mi. from Randolph East, Lowe's Path is crossed and the grade moderates as the trail angles up the steep west side of Nowell Ridge, though the footing is rocky. At 4.7 mi., good outlooks begin to appear, providing particularly notable views of the Castles nearby and Mt. Lafayette in the distance to the southwest. At 4.9 mi., the Perch Path crosses, leading left (north) to the Gray Knob Trail and right (south) to the Perch and

Israel Ridge Path; a small brook runs across the Perch Path about 60 yd. south of the Randolph Path. Above this junction, the Randolph Path rises due south through high scrub. At 5.4 mi., the Gray Knob Trail from Crag Camp and Gray Knob enters left at about the point where the Randolph Path rises out of the high scrub. In another 70 yd., the Israel Ridge Path enters right (west), ascending from US 2, and the trails coincide for about 150 yd.; then the Israel Ridge Path branches left for Mt. Adams in an area where views to Jefferson and the Castles are particularly fine. From this point, the Randolph Path is nearly level to its end at Edmands Col, curving around the head of Castle Ravine, offering continuous excellent views. It is above treeline, much exposed to the weather, and its footway is visible for a long distance ahead. Near Edmands Col is Spaulding Spring (reliable water), in a small grassy valley on the right where two trails enter the Randolph Path from the right at nearly the same point: the Castle Ravine Trail from US 2 comes up through the length of this little valley, and the Cornice leading to the Caps and Castles runs across it. In 0.1 mi. more the Randolph Path joins the Gulfside Trail in Edmands Col.

Randolph Path (map 1:E9–F9)

Distances from Randolph East parking area (1,225 ft.) to
- Valley Way (1,953 ft.): 1.5 mi., 750 ft., 1 hr. 5 min.
- Air Line (2,000 ft.): 1.6 mi., 800 ft., 1 hr. 10 min.
- Short Line, north junction (2,275 ft.): 1.9 mi., 1,050 ft., 1 hr. 30 min.
- King Ravine Trail and Amphibrach (2,925 ft.): 3.1 mi., 1,700 ft., 2 hr. 25 min.
- Lowe's Path (3,600 ft.): 3.9 mi., 2,400 ft., 3 hr. 10 min.
- Perch Path (4,325 ft.): 4.9 mi., 3,100 ft., 4 hr.
- Israel Ridge Path, north junction (4,825 ft.): 5.4 mi., 3,600 ft., 4 hr. 30 min.
- Edmands Col and Gulfside Trail (4,938 ft.): 6.1 mi., 3,700 ft., 4 hr. 55 min.
- Mt. Washington summit (6,288 ft.) via Gulfside Trail and Crawford Path: 9.9 mi., 5,550 ft. (rev. 450 ft.), 7 hr. 45 min.

The Link (RMC)

This path links the Appalachia parking area and the trails to Mt. Madison with the trails ascending Mt. Adams and Mt. Jefferson, connecting with the Amphibrach, Cliffway, Lowe's Path, and Israel Ridge Path, and the Castle Ravine, Emerald, Castle, and Caps Ridge trails. It is graded as far as Cascade Brook. The section between the Caps Ridge and Castle trails, although very rough, makes possible a circuit of the Caps and the Castles from Jefferson Notch Rd. Though some sections are heavily used, much of the trail is very lightly used and, though well cleared and marked, may have little evident footway.

The Link diverges right from the Air Line 100 yd. south of Appalachia, just after entering the woods beyond the power-line clearing, and runs west, fairly close to the edge of this clearing. At 0.6 mi., it enters a logging road and bears left; then Beechwood Way diverges left, and, just east of Cold Brook, Sylvan Way enters left. Cold Brook is crossed at 0.7 mi. on the Memorial Bridge, where there is a fine view upstream to Cold Brook Fall, which can be reached in less than 100 yd. by Sylvan Way or by a spur from the Amphibrach. Memorial Bridge is a memorial to J. Rayner Edmands, Eugene B. Cook, and other pioneer path makers: Thomas Starr King, James Gordon, Charles E. Lowe, Laban M. Watson, William H. Peek, Hubbard Hunt, William G. Nowell, and William Sargent.

Just west of the brook, the Amphibrach diverges left and the Link continues straight ahead. The Link then follows old logging roads southwest with gradually increasing grades and occasional wet footing. At 2.0 mi., the Cliffway leads left (east) to White Cliff, a fine viewpoint on Nowell Ridge, and the Link swings to the south and climbs at easy grades, crossing Lowe's Path at 2.7 mi. It crosses the north branch of the Mystic Stream at 3.1 mi. and the main Mystic Stream, in a region of small cascades, at 3.3 mi. It soon curves left, rounds the western buttress of Nowell Ridge, and becomes rougher, running southeast nearly level and entering Cascade Ravine on the mountainside high above the stream. At 4.0 mi., it joins the Israel Ridge Path coming up on the right from US 2; the two trails coincide for 50 yd., then the Israel Ridge Path diverges sharp left for Mt. Adams, passing the Cabin-Cascades Trail in about 60 yd. The Link continues straight from this junction, descending sharply to Cascade Brook, which it crosses on a large flat ledge at the top of the largest cascade, where there is a view of Mt. Bowman. This crossing may be difficult at high water. The trail makes a steep and very rough climb up the bank of the brook, then swings right and crosses an old landslide (follow markings carefully). The grade now eases and the footing gradually improves as it rounds the tip of Israel Ridge and runs generally south into Castle Ravine.

At 5.1 mi., the Link joins the Castle Ravine Trail, with which it co-incides while the two trails pass the Emerald Trail and cross Castle Brook, then at 5.4 mi., the Link diverges sharp right and ascends steeply west, angling up the very rough southwest wall of Castle Ravine. At 6.0 mi., it crosses the Castle Trail below the first Castle at about 4,025 ft., then runs south, generally descending gradually, over a very rough pathway with countless treacherous roots, rocks, and hollows that are very tricky and tedious to negotiate. At 6.5 mi., the trail crosses a gravelly slide with good views, and at 7.0 mi., it crosses a fair-sized brook flowing over mossy ledges. At 7.6 mi., it turns sharp left uphill and in 50 yd. reaches the Caps Ridge Trail 1.1 mi. above the Jefferson Notch Rd., about 100 yd. above the famous ledge with the potholes and the fine view up to Jefferson.

The Link (map 1:E9–F8)

Distances from Appalachia parking area (1,306 ft.) to
- Memorial Bridge (1,425 ft.): 0.7 mi., 100 ft., 25 min.
- Cliffway (2,170 ft.): 2.0 mi., 850 ft., 1 hr. 25 min.
- Lowe's Path (2,475 ft.): 2.7 mi., 1,150 ft., 1 hr. 55 min.
- Israel Ridge Path (2,800 ft.): 4.0 mi., 1,500 ft., 2 hr. 45 min.
- Castle Ravine Trail, lower junction (3,125 ft.): 5.1 mi., 1,800 ft., 3 hr. 25 min.
- Castle Trail (4,025 ft.): 6.0 mi., 2,700 ft., 4 hr. 20 min.
- Caps Ridge Trail (3,800 ft.): 7.6 mi., 2,850 ft. (rev. 400 ft.), 5 hr. 15 min.

Presidential Range Rail Trail

This multi-use trail follows the roadbed of the former railroad right-of-way (tracks removed in 1997) that runs for 18.3 mi. from Gorham to Waumbek Junction near Cherry Pond. It is open to a variety of non-motorized uses, including walking, snowshoeing, cross-country skiing, bicycling, and dog-sled travel. In its own right, it has little interest for hikers, but—running roughly parallel to US 2—it is useful as a connecting link between the trails on the northern edge of the Presidential Range. It provides an easy and also pleasant and safe (compared with the alternative of walking along high-speed US 2) pedestrian route between the Randolph East and Appalachia trailheads, Lowe's Path, and the Bowman trailhead—even at night. As the trail is always obvious and unvarying in nature and difficulty, no detailed description is necessary. While this trail will also be encountered near Cherry Pond in Section Twelve, only the small part that is useful to Northern Presidential hikers is mentioned here. As it is assumed that hikers will use only segments as required rather than the Northern Presidential section as a whole, segment distances and times rather than cumulative ones are given.

Presidential Range Rail Trail (map 1: E9-E8)
- Randolph East (1,250 ft.) to Appalachia (1,310 ft.): 0.9 mi., 60 ft., 30 min.
- Appalachia (1,310 ft.) to Lowe's Path (1,450 ft.): 2.2 mi., 140 ft., 1 hr. 10 min.
- Lowe's Store (1,450 ft.) to Bowman (1,500 ft.): 0.9 mi., 50 ft., 30 min.

Great Gulf Trail (WMNF)

This trail begins at the parking area on the west side of NH 16, about 1.5 mi. south of its junction with Pinkham B (Dolly Copp) Rd. near Dolly Copp Campground. It follows the West Branch of the Peabody River through the Great Gulf, climbs up the headwall, and ends at a junction with the Gulfside Trail 0.5 mi. below the summit of Mt. Washington. Some of the brook crossings may be difficult or dangerous in moderate to high water conditions, and brooks can rise very quickly in heavy rains in this deep, steep-walled valley. Ascent on the headwall is steep and rough. Except for first 1.6 mi., this trail is in the Great Gulf Wilderness; camping is prohibited within 0.25 mi. of the trail above the junction with the Sphinx Trail, and below that point, it is limited to designated trailside sites or sites at least 200 ft. away from the trail.

Leaving the parking lot, the trail leads north on an old road then turns left and descends slightly to cross the Peabody River on a suspension bridge. It then ascends to a junction at 0.3 mi. with the former route from Dolly Copp Campground, now called the Great Gulf Link Trail. The Great Gulf Trail turns sharp left here and follows a logging road along the northwest bank of the West Branch of the Peabody River, at first close to the stream and later some distance away from it. An alternate route of the trail for skiing diverges right at 0.6 mi. and rejoins at 1.0 mi., where the main trail turns sharp left. At 1.6 mi., the Hayes Copp Ski Trail diverges right, the Great Gulf Trail soon crosses into the Great Gulf Wilderness, and the Osgood Trail diverges right at 1.8 mi.; Osgood Campsite is 0.9 mi. from here via the Osgood Trail. The Great Gulf Trail returns to the West Branch and follows it fairly closely for 0.7 mi., then climbs to the high gravelly bank called the Bluff, where there is a good view of the gulf and the mountains around it. The trail follows the edge of the Bluff, then at 2.7 mi., the Osgood Cutoff (which is part of the AT) continues straight ahead while the Great Gulf Trail descends sharp left; for a short distance this trail is also part of the AT. In 50 yd., it crosses Parapet Brook (no bridge), then climbs to the crest of the little ridge that separates Parapet Brook from the West Branch, where the Madison Gulf Trail enters right, coming down from the vicinity of Madison Hut through Madison Gulf. The two trails coincide for a short distance, descending to cross the West Branch on a suspension bridge and ascending the steep bank on the south side. Here, the Madison Gulf Trail branches left, taking the AT designation with it, while the Great Gulf Trail turns right, leading up the south bank of the river past Clam Rock, a huge boulder on the left, at 3.1 mi.

At 3.9 mi., the Great Gulf Trail crosses Chandler Brook, and on the far bank, the Chandler Brook Trail diverges left and ascends to the Mt. Washington Auto Rd. The Great Gulf Trail continues close to the river, passing in sight of the mouth of the stream that issues from Jefferson Ravine on the north, to join the Six Husbands Trail (right) and Wamsutta Trail (left) at 4.5 mi. At 5.2 mi., the trail climbs up ledges beside a cascade and continues past numerous other attractive cascades in the next 0.2 mi. After crossing over to the northwest bank of the West Branch (may be difficult), it soon crosses the brook that descends from Sphinx Col and, at 5.6 mi., reaches the junction where the Sphinx Trail, leading to the Gulfside Trail, diverges right. Camping is prohibited within 0.25 mi. of the trail above this junction. The Great Gulf Trail soon crosses again to the southeast bank of the West Branch, passing waterfalls, including Weetamoo Falls, the finest in the gulf. There are remarkable views up to Mt. Adams and Mt. Madison. The trail crosses an eastern tributary and, after a slight ascent, reaches Spaulding Lake (4,228 ft.) at 6.5 mi. from NH 16 and about 1.4 mi. by trail from the summit of Mt. Washington.

The Great Gulf Trail continues on the east side of the lake, and a little beyond begins to ascend the steep headwall. The trail runs south and then southeast, rising 1,600 ft. in about 0.8 mi. over fragments of stone, many of which are loose. The way may be poorly marked, because snow slides may sweep away cairns. The trail generally curves a little to the left until within a few yards of the top of the headwall; then, bearing slightly right, it emerges from the gulf and ends at the Gulfside Trail near the Cog Railway. It is 0.4 mi. from here to the summit of Mt. Washington by the Gulfside Trail and Trinity Heights Connector.

Great Gulf Trail (map 1:F10–F9)

Distances from parking area on NH 16 (1,350 ft.) to
- Osgood Trail (1,850 ft.): 1.8 mi., 500 ft., 1 hr. 10 min.
- Osgood Cutoff (2,300 ft.): 2.7 mi., 950 ft., 1 hr. 50 min.
- Madison Gulf Trail, south junction (2,300 ft.): 2.8 mi., 1,000 ft. (rev. 50 ft.), 1 hr. 55 min.
- Six Husbands and Wamsutta trails (3,100 ft.): 4.5 mi., 1,800 ft., 3 hr. 10 min.
- Sphinx Trail (3,625 ft.): 5.6 mi., 2,350 ft., 4 hr.
- Spaulding Lake (4,228 ft.): 6.5 mi., 2,950 ft., 4 hr. 45 min.
- Gulfside Trail junction (5,925 ft.): 7.4 mi., 4,650 ft., 6 hr. 5 min.
- Mt. Washington summit (6,288 ft.) via Gulfside Trail and Trinity Heights Connector: 7.8 mi., 5,000 ft., 6 hr. 25 min.

Great Gulf Link Trail (WMNF)

This trail was formerly a segment of the Great Gulf Trail. It leaves Dolly Copp Campground at the south end of the main camp road, which is a dead end. The trail enters the woods, and turns sharp left in 0.1 mi. onto an old logging road that has cross-country ski markers in both directions. It follows the logging road south along the west bank of the Peabody River, passing some interesting pools, and at 0.7 mi., it passes a junction with a branch of the Hayes Copp Ski Trail on the right. It ends at a junction with the Great Gulf Trail, which comes in on the left from the parking lot on NH 16 and continues straight ahead into the gulf.

Great Gulf Link Trail (map 1:F10)

Distance from Dolly Copp Campground (1,250 ft.) to
- Great Gulf Trail (1,375 ft.): 1.0 mi., 150 ft., 35 min.

Madison Gulf Trail (AMC)

This trail begins on the Mt. Washington Auto Rd. a little more than 2 mi. from the Glen House site, opposite the Old Jackson Rd. It first crosses a low ridge then descends gently to the West Branch, where it meets the Great Gulf Trail, then ascends along Parapet Brook to the Parapet, where it ends at a point 0.3 mi. from Madison Hut. It is almost entirely within the Great Gulf Wilderness. From the Auto Rd. to its departure from the Great Gulf Trail, the Madison Gulf Trail is part of the AT, but because it is in Wilderness, paint blazes (including the familiar white AT blazes) are not used.

Caution: The section of this trail on the headwall of Madison Gulf is one of the most difficult in the White Mountains, going over several ledge outcrops, bouldery areas, and a chimney with loose rock. The steep slabs may be slippery when wet, and several ledges require scrambling and the use of handholds—hikers with short arms may have a particular problem reaching the handholds. Stream crossings may be very difficult in wet weather. The trail is not recommended for the descent, for hikers with heavy packs, or in wet weather. Allow extra time, and do not start up the headwall late in the day. The ascent of the headwall may require several hours more than the estimated time; parties frequently fail to reach the hut before dark because of slowness on the headwall.

This trail is well protected from storms and has plenty of water. Combined with the Old Jackson Rd., it is the shortest route (7.0 mi.) from Pinkham Notch Visitor Center to Madison Hut via the Great Gulf, but not usually the easiest; there are several reasonable alternative routes, though none of them is without drawbacks. The route via the Osgood Cutoff and Osgood Trail, 7.5 mi. long, is steep in parts but has no hard brook crossings or difficult scrambles; however, it is very exposed to weather in the upper part, even if the rough but more sheltered Parapet Trail is used to bypass Mt. Madison's summit. The route via the Buttress Trail is 8.4 mi. long, and has two significant brook crossings and somewhat more weather exposure than the Madison Gulf Trail, though substantially less than the Osgood-Parapet route. In any event, for parties traveling to the hut from the Great Gulf side, there is no way to avoid the 0.3-mi. walk to Madison Hut across the windswept col between Madison and Adams, except by going over the summit of Madison where conditions may well be much worse. Therefore choice of route comes down to a trade-off among the factors of distance, weather exposure, brook crossings, and rock scrambles; hikers must consider which factors they feel better prepared to deal with, taking current and expected conditions into account. The main advantage that the Madison Gulf Trail has in bad weather, compared with the Buttress Trail, is that the brook crossings on the Madison Gulf Trail, even though they may be difficult, are unlikely to be impassable, whereas those on the Buttress Trail may be impossible to cross without an unacceptable risk of drowning. However, in rainy conditions the deep streams and steep slippery ledges on the Madison Gulf Trail would pose great difficulty. In sum, hikers who are not prepared for this level of challenge would be well advised to change their plans rather than attempt any of the direct routes between Pinkham Notch Visitor Center and Madison Hut in adverse conditions, and even in favorable conditions the Madison Gulf Trail must be treated with serious caution and vigilance.

The Madison Gulf Trail leaves the Auto Rd. above the 2-mi. mark, opposite the Old Jackson Rd. junction, and enters the Great Gulf Wilderness. In 0.2 mi., a side path branches right in a little pass west of Low's Bald Spot and climbs 0.1 mi. to this little ledgy knob, an excellent viewpoint. The Madison Gulf Trail bears left and ascends over a ledge with a limited view, then descends, first rapidly for a short distance, then easily, crossing many small brooks. The trail curves into the valley of the West Branch of the Peabody River and continues descending gently until it meets the Great Gulf Trail on the south bank at 2.1 mi. The two trails now run together, descending the steep bank to the West Branch, crossing a suspension bridge to the north bank, and climbing to the crest of the little ridge that divides Parapet Brook from the West Branch. Here the Great Gulf Trail continues straight ahead, leading to NH 16 or (via the Osgood Cutoff) to the Osgood Trail for Mt. Madison and Madison Hut. The Madison Gulf Trail turns left up the narrow ridge and continues between the two streams until it enters its former route near the bank of Parapet Brook at 2.5 mi. At 2.8 mi., it crosses one channel of the divided brook, runs between the two for 0.1 mi., then crosses the other to the northeast bank. It follows the brook bank for a little way; then it turns right, away from the brook, then turns left and ascends along the valley wall at a moderate grade, coming back to the brook at the mouth of the branch stream from Osgood Ridge. From here, it follows Parapet Brook rather closely, and at 3.5 mi., crosses the brook for the first of three times in less than 0.5 mi., ascending to the lower floor of the gulf where it reaches Sylvan Cascade, a fine waterfall, at 4.1 mi.

The Madison Gulf Trail then ascends to the upper floor of the gulf, where it crosses numerous small brooks. From the floor, it rises gradually to Mossy Slide at the foot of the headwall, then ascends very rapidly alongside a stream, which becomes partly hidden among the rocks as the trail rises. The trail then reaches the headwall of the gulf and climbs very steeply, with some difficult scrambles on the ledges. As it emerges on the rocks at treeline, it bears right and the grade moderates, and soon it ends at the Parapet Trail. For the Parapet (0.1 mi.) and Madison Hut (0.3 mi.), turn left; for the Osgood Trail via the Parapet Trail, turn right.

Madison Gulf Trail (map 1:F9)

Distances from Mt. Washington Auto Rd. (2,675 ft.) to
- Great Gulf Trail (2,300 ft.): 2.1 mi., 250 ft. (rev. 600 ft.), 1 hr. 10 min.
- foot of Madison Gulf headwall at Sylvan Cascade (3,900 ft.): 4.1 mi., 1,850 ft., 3 hr.
- Parapet Trail (4,850 ft.): 4.8 mi., 2,800 ft., 3 hr. 50 min.
- Madison Hut (4,825 ft.) via Parapet and Star Lake trails: 5.1 mi., 2,850 ft., 4 hr.

Distance from Pinkham Notch Visitor Center (2,032 ft.) to
- Madison Hut (4,825 ft.) via Old Jackson Rd. and Madison Gulf, Parapet, and Star Lake trails: 7.0 mi., 3,550 ft., 5 hr. 20 min.

Chandler Brook Trail (AMC)

This steep and rough but wild and beautiful trail passes many cascades as it climbs from the Great Gulf Trail to the Auto Rd. just above the 4-mi. post. Lying on a very steep slope, its brook crossings can quickly become difficult in rainy weather. It is almost entirely within the Great Gulf Wilderness.

The trail diverges south from the Great Gulf Trail 3.9 mi. from NH 16, just above its crossing of Chandler Brook, and follows the brook rather closely, crossing three times, passing fine waterfalls that can be seen from the trail. From the last crossing, it runs southeast, rising over a jumbled mass of stones and keeping west of interesting rock formations. The trail enters the Auto Rd. near a ledge of white quartz at the Horn, 0.3 mi. above the 4-mi. post. (Descending, look for this white ledge, which is close to the Auto Rd. The trail is marked by cairns here and is visible from the road.)

Chandler Brook Trail (map 1:F9)

Distance from Great Gulf Trail (2,800 ft.) to
- Mt. Washington Auto Rd. (4,125 ft.): 0.9 mi., 1,300 ft., 1 hr. 5 min.

Wamsutta Trail (AMC)

This steep and rough but wild and beautiful trail begins on the Great Gulf Trail and ascends to the Auto Rd. just above the 6-mi. marker and opposite the Alpine Garden Trail, with which it provides routes to Tuckerman Junction, Lakes of the Clouds Hut, and other points to the south. It is almost entirely within the Great Gulf Wilderness. The trail was named for Wamsutta, the first of six successive husbands of Weetamoo, a queen of the Pocasset tribe, for whom a beautiful waterfall in the Great Gulf is named.

Leaving the Great Gulf Trail opposite the Six Husbands Trail, 4.5 mi. from NH 16, the trail crosses a small stream, then ascends gradually. Soon it climbs the very steep and rough northerly spur of Chandler Ridge. Passing to the left of a quartz ledge, the trail continues steeply to a small, open promontory on the crest of the spur, which offers a good view, at 0.9 mi. It then ascends gradually through woods, passing a spring on the right side of the trail. Continuing along the ridge crest at a moderate grade, the trail emerges at the treeline and climbs to a point near the top end of the winter shortcut of the Auto Rd. After turning right along this road, it ends in another 100 yd. at the Auto Rd., just above the 6-mi. post.

Wamsutta Trail (map 1:F9)

Distances from Great Gulf Trail (3,100 ft.) to
- outlook on promontory (4,350 ft.): 0.9 mi., 1,250 ft., 1 hr. 5 min.
- Mt. Washington Auto Rd. (5,305 ft.): 1.7 mi., 2,200 ft., 1 hr. 55 min.

Sphinx Trail (AMC)

This steep and very rough but wild and beautiful trail runs from the Great Gulf Trail below Spaulding Lake to the Gulfside Trail in Sphinx Col, between Mt. Jefferson and Mt. Clay. This trail is particularly important because it affords the quickest escape route for anyone overtaken by storm in the vicinity of Sphinx Col. It diverges east from the Gulfside Trail 40 yd. north of the lowest point in the col, running through a grassy, rock-walled corridor, and descends to the Great Gulf Trail. Once below the col, the hiker is quickly protected from the rigor of west and northwest winds. For a considerable part of its length, this trail climbs very steeply; there is a long section of very slippery rocks in a brook bed, very tedious particularly on the descent, and some of the scrambles on the ledges in the upper part are challenging. The trail's name is derived from the profile of a rock formation seen from just below the meadow where water is found. This trail is almost entirely within the Great Gulf Wilderness.

The trail branches northwest from the Great Gulf Trail 5.6 mi. from NH 16, near the crossing of the brook that flows down from Sphinx Col through the minor ravine between Mt. Clay and Mt. Jefferson. It soon turns due west and ascends close to the brook, first gradually, then very steeply, passing several attractive cascades and pools. For about 100 yd., it runs directly in the brook bed, where the rocks are extremely slippery. At 0.6 mi., at the foot of a broken ledge with several small streams cascading over it, the trail turns left away from the brook and angles up across two more small brooks. It climbs a small chimney where views out from the scrubby slope start to appear, then scrambles up ledges with several rock pitches of some difficulty. About 100 yd. above the chimney, after a slight descent, the trail crosses a small meadow where there is usually water under a rock just downhill to the north of the trail. The trail then climbs steeply up a rocky cleft, ascends easily over the crest of a small rocky ridge, and descends into a slight sag. It finally climbs to the ridge crest and traverses a grassy passage at the base of a rock wall to the Gulfside just north of Sphinx Col.

Sphinx Trail (map 1:F9)

Distance from Great Gulf Trail (3,625 ft.) to
• Gulfside Trail (4,975 ft.): 1.1 mi., 1,350 ft., 1 hr. 15 min.

Six Husbands Trail (AMC)

This steep and very rough but wild and beautiful trail provides magnificent views of the inner part of the Great Gulf. It diverges from the Great Gulf Trail 4.5 mi. from NH 16, opposite the Wamsutta Trail, and climbs up the north knee of Jefferson, crosses the Gulfside Trail, and ends at the

Mt. Jefferson Loop a short distance northeast of the summit. It is very steep and is not recommended for descent except to escape bad conditions above treeline. Up to the Gulfside Trail junction, it is entirely within the Great Gulf Wilderness. The name honors the six successive husbands of Weetamoo, queen of the Pocasset tribe.

Leaving the Great Gulf Trail, it descends directly across the West Branch, avoiding side paths along the stream. In times of high water, this crossing may be very difficult, but there may be a better crossing upstream. The trail climbs easily northward across a low ridge to join Jefferson Brook, the stream that flows from Jefferson Ravine, and ascends along its southwest bank. At 0.5 mi., the Buttress Trail branches right and crosses the stream. The Six Husbands Trail swings away from the brook (last sure water) and runs through an area containing many large boulders. Soon it begins to attack the very steep main buttress, the north knee of Jefferson, passing by one boulder cave and through another. At 1.0 mi., it ascends a steep ledge on a pair of ladders, then climbs under an overhanging ledge on a second pair, with a tricky spot at the top that might be dangerous if wet or icy. In another 100 yd., it reaches a promontory with a fine view, and begins a moderately difficult scramble up the crest of a rocky ridge.

At 1.3 mi., the trail reaches the top of the knee approximately at treeline, and the grade moderates. Across the bare stretches, the trail is marked by cairns. At 1.7 mi., the Edmands Col Cutoff branches right, leading in 0.5 mi. to Edmands Col, and the trail becomes steeper as it begins to climb the cone of Mt. Jefferson. Soon it passes over a talus slope that is usually covered well into July by a great drift of snow, conspicuous for a considerable distance from viewpoints to the east. Marked by cairns, the trail crosses the Gulfside Trail and continues west toward the summit of Mt. Jefferson, joining the Mt. Jefferson Loop 0.1 mi. below the summit.

Six Husbands Trail (map 1:F9)

Distances from Great Gulf Trail junction (3,100 ft.)
- to Buttress Trail (3,350 ft.): 0.5 mi., 250 ft., 25 min.
- to Edmands Col Cutoff (4,925 ft.): 1.7 mi., 1,850 ft., 1 hr. 45 min.
- to Gulfside Trail (5,325 ft.): 2.0 mi., 2,250 ft., 2 hr. 10 min.
- for Mt. Jefferson Loop (5,625 ft.): 2.3 mi., 2,550 ft., 2 hr. 25 min.

Buttress Trail (AMC)

This trail leads from the Six Husbands Trail to the Star Lake Trail near Madison Hut, and is the most direct route from the upper part of the Great Gulf to Madison Hut. It is mostly well sheltered until it nears the hut, and grades are moderate; while the footing is rough in the upper section, overall this trail is easier than most other Great Gulf trails. In bad weather, or for hikers with heavy packs, or for descending, it is probably the best route from the lower part of the Great Gulf to the hut, in spite of the somewhat greater distance. (See Madison Gulf Trail, the principal alternative, for a discussion of the options.) The trail is almost entirely within the Great Gulf Wilderness.

The trail diverges north from the Six Husbands Trail 0.5 mi. from the Great Gulf Trail, and immediately crosses Jefferson Brook (last sure water), the brook that flows out of Jefferson Ravine. On the far side of the brook, it bears left through a wet area on bog bridges; avoid several beaten paths that diverge right into a camping area.

After 0.1 mi., the trail bears right (east) and, ascending moderately, climbs diagonally across a steep slope of large, loose, angular fragments of rock (care must be taken not to dislodge the loose rocks). At the top of this talus slope, there is a spectacular view up the Great Gulf, and to the steep buttress of Jefferson's north knee rising nearby across a small valley. The trail continues east, rising steadily along a steep, wooded slope, then at 0.5 mi., it reaches a ridge corner and swings left (north) and runs at easy grades across a gently sloping upland covered with trees, passing to the right of a spring (reliable water) at 1.0 mi. At 1.2 mi., the trail passes through a boulder cave formed by a large boulder across the path, then reaches the foot of a steep ledge, swings left, and climbs it. At 1.4 mi., the trail swings right after passing between two ledges; the ledge on the right provides a fine view. The trail now ascends less steeply (but with rough footing) on open rocks above the scrub line, with an excellent view across Madison Gulf to Mt. Madison. It crosses a minor ridge and descends moderately. After passing under an overhanging rock, it reenters high scrub that provides shelter almost all the way to the junction with the Star Lake Trail, which is reached in the gap between the Parapet and Mt. Quincy Adams, just southwest of Star Lake and 0.3 mi. from Madison Hut.

Buttress Trail (map 1:F9)

Distances from Six Husbands Trail junction (3,350 ft.) to
- Star Lake Trail (4,900 ft.): 1.9 mi., 1,600 ft. (rev. 50 ft.), 1 hr. 45 min.
- Madison Hut (4,825 ft.) via Star Lake Trail: 2.2 mi., 1,600 ft., 1 hr. 55 min.

Osgood Trail (AMC)

This trail runs from the Great Gulf Trail, 1.8 mi. from the Great Gulf Wilderness parking area on NH 16, up the southeast ridge of Mt. Madison to the summit, then down to Madison Hut. The upper 1.7 mi. is very exposed to the weather and has very rough footing. Made by Benjamin F. Osgood in 1878, this is the oldest trail now in use to the summit of Mt. Madison. Above the Osgood Cutoff, it is part of the AT. The section of the trail that formerly ran from the Great Gulf Trail to the Mt. Washington Auto Rd. has been abandoned. The Osgood Trail begins in the Great Gulf Wilderness, but for most of its length it is just outside the boundary (in fact, it constitutes the northern section of the eastern boundary of the Great Gulf Wilderness).

This trail leaves the Great Gulf Trail and ascends at an easy to moderate grade. At 0.3 mi., it crosses a small brook, follows it, recrosses, and bears away from it to the left. At 0.8 mi., the Osgood Cutoff comes in from the left, and a spur path leads right over a small brook (last sure water) and continues about 100 yd. to Osgood Campsite. From this junction to Madison Hut, the Osgood Trail is part of the AT.

At 1.4 mi., the trail begins to climb a very steep and rough section, then at about 1.6 mi., it gradually but steadily becomes less steep, and the grade is easy by the time the trail emerges on the crest of Osgood Ridge at the treeline at 2.1 mi. Ahead, on the crest of the ridge, 10 or 12 small, rocky peaks curve to the left in a crescent toward the summit of Mt. Madison; the trail, marked by cairns, follows this ridge crest with rough footing. At 2.8 mi. from the Great Gulf Trail, the Osgood Trail reaches Osgood Junction in a small hollow. Here, the Daniel Webster–Scout Trail enters on the right, ascending from Dolly Copp Campground, and the Parapet Trail diverges left on a level path marked by cairns and passes around the south side of the cone of Madison with little change of elevation, making a very rough but comparatively sheltered route to Madison Hut.

From Osgood Junction the Osgood Trail climbs over a prominent crag, crosses a shallow sag, and starts up the east ridge of Madison's summit cone, where it is soon joined on the right by the Howker Ridge Trail. Hikers planning to descend on the Howker Ridge Trail must take care to distinguish that trail from beaten side paths that lead back to the Osgood Trail. The Osgood Trail ascends to the summit of Mt. Madison at 3.3 mi., where the Watson Path enters on the right, then follows the crest of the ridge past several large cairns, drops off to the left (south), and continues to descend westward just below the ridge crest and above the steep slopes falling off into Madison Gulf on the left. Soon it crosses to the north side of the ridge and descends steeply, and, 30 yd. before it reaches Madison Hut, the Pine Link joins on the right.

Osgood Trail (map 1:F10–F9)

Distances from Great Gulf Trail (1,850 ft.) to
- Osgood Cutoff (2,486 ft.): 0.8 mi., 650 ft., 45 min.
- Osgood Junction (4,822 ft.): 2.8 mi., 3,000 ft., 2 hr. 55 min.
- Mt. Madison summit (5,366 ft.): 3.3 mi., 3,550 ft., 3 hr. 25 min.
- Madison Hut (4,825 ft.): 3.8 mi., 3,550 ft. (rev. 550 ft.), 3 hr. 40 min.

Osgood Cutoff (AMC)

This link trail, a part of the AT, provides a convenient shortcut from the Great Gulf and Madison Gulf trails to the Osgood Trail. It is entirely within the Great Gulf Wilderness. This trail leaves the Great Gulf Trail on the Bluff, continuing straight ahead where the Great Gulf Trail turns sharp left to descend to Parapet Brook. The Osgood Cutoff climbs moderately for 0.2 mi. to its former junction with the Madison Gulf Trail, then turns sharp right and runs nearly on contour east across several small brooks to the Osgood Trail at its junction with the spur path to Osgood Campsite, where there is reliable water.

Osgood Cutoff (map 1:F9)

Distance from Madison Gulf Trail (2,300 ft.) to
- Osgood Trail (2,486 ft.): 0.6 mi., 200 ft., 25 min.

Daniel Webster–Scout Trail (WMNF)

This trail, cut in 1933 by Boy Scouts from the Daniel Webster Council, leads from Dolly Copp Campground to the Osgood Trail at Osgood Junction, 0.5 mi. below the summit of Mt. Madison. It begins on the main campground road 0.9 mi. south of the campground entrance on the Pinkham B (Dolly Copp) Rd., with adequate parking available on the left in another 0.1 mi. For most of its length, the trail's grades are moderate and its footing is somewhat rocky but not unusually rough; however, the upper part of this trail is very steep and very exposed to the weather.

The trail starts out through a section of open woods with some very large trees, soon crosses the Hayes Copp Ski Trail (here a grassy logging road), and swings northwest almost to the bank of Culhane Brook. Veering away from the brook just before reaching it, the trail climbs moderately up the east slope of Madison, mostly angling upward and carefully avoiding a more direct assault on the steeper parts of the mountainside. At 2.0 mi., it reaches the base of a little buttress, where the forest changes rather abruptly from hardwoods to evergreens. It winds steeply up this buttress to its top, switchbacks upward a bit farther, then resumes its moderate ascent, angling northwest across the steep slope, becoming steeper and rockier. At 2.9 mi., it begins a very steep and rough climb nearly straight up the slope with ever-increasing amounts of talus and decreasing amounts of scrub, where views begin to appear and improve. At 3.2 mi., the trail reaches the treeline and moderates somewhat, though it is still steep. As it approaches the ridge crest, it turns left and directly ascends the slope for the last 100 yd. to Osgood Junction and the Osgood Trail.

Daniel Webster–Scout Trail (map 1:F10–F9)

Distances from Dolly Copp Campground (1,250 ft.) to
- foot of little buttress (2,800 ft.): 2.0 mi., 1,550 ft., 1 hr. 45 min.
- Osgood Junction (4,822 ft.): 3.5 mi., 3,600 ft., 3 hr. 35 min.
- Mt. Madison summit (5,366 ft.) via Osgood Trail: 4.1 mi., 4,100 ft., 4 hr. 5 min.

Parapet Trail (AMC)

This trail, marked with cairns and blue paint, runs at a roughly constant elevation around the south side of the cone of Mt. Madison, from the

Osgood and Daniel Webster–Scout trails at Osgood Junction to the Star Lake Trail between the Parapet and Madison Hut. Although above timberline and extremely rough, particularly in its eastern half, in bad weather the Parapet Trail is mostly sheltered from the northwest winds. The rocks can be very slippery, the trail may be hard to follow if visibility is poor, and the extra effort of rock-hopping more than expends the energy saved by avoiding the climb of about 500 ft. over the summit of Mt. Madison. Therefore, it is probably a useful bad-weather route only if strong northwest or west winds are a major part of the problem.

From Osgood Junction, the trail rises very slightly, marked by cairns across the open rocks; at the start care must be taken to distinguish its cairns from those ascending the ridge crest on the right, which belong to the Osgood Trail. At 0.8 mi., the Madison Gulf Trail enters left at the bottom of a little gully, and the Parapet Trail ascends a ledge and then makes a sharp right turn at 0.9 mi., where a spur path leads left 30 yd. onto the Parapet, a ledge that commands excellent views over the Great Gulf and Madison Gulf to the mountains beyond. The Parapet Trail then runs north, passing above Star Lake, and joins the Star Lake Trail 0.1 mi. south of Madison Hut.

Parapet Trail (map 1:F9)

Distances from Osgood Junction (4,822 ft.) to

- Madison Gulf Trail (4,850 ft.): 0.8 mi., 150 ft. (rev. 100 ft.), 30 min.
- Star Lake Trail (4,900 ft.): 1.0 mi., 200 ft., 35 min.
- Madison Hut (4,825 ft.) via Star Lake Trail: 1.1 mi., 200 ft., 40 min.

Pine Link (AMC)

The Pine Link ascends Mt. Madison from the highest point of the Pinkham B (Dolly Copp) Rd., almost directly opposite the private road to the Horton Center on Pine Mountain, 2.4 mi. from US 2 at the foot of the big hill west of Gorham and 1.9 mi. from NH 16 near Dolly Copp Campground. This interesting trail provides an unusual variety of views from its outlook ledges and from the section above the treeline on Madison's northwest slope. Combined with the upper part of the Howker Ridge Trail, Pine Link provides a very scenic loop. In general, it is not unusually steep, but the footing is often rough and consumes an unusual amount of attention and energy in comparison to most trails of similar steepness. The part above the treeline is continuously exposed to the full force of northwest winds for about 0.7 mi. and might be difficult to follow if visibility is poor, and also requires a considerable amount of fairly strenuous rock-hopping. The result is that the trail generally proves more challenging than its statistical details might indicate.

The trail first ascends the northwest slope of a spur of Howker Ridge, climbing by a series of short steep pitches interspersed with level sections. At 1.0 mi., it crosses a flat, swampy area and ascends another steep pitch, then climbs to the ridge crest of the spur and follows it. At 1.7 mi., it passes an overgrown outlook with restricted views from the south side of the trail, the result of a 1968 fire. At 1.9 mi., just before the trail descends into a sag, a spur path leads left 20 yd. to a bare crag with fine views up to Madison and out to the Carters. At 2.4 mi., after a fairly long section of trail that has a brook running in and out of it, the Pine Link turns right and joins the Howker Ridge Trail in a shady little glen. Turning left at this junction, the Pine Link coincides with the Howker Ridge Trail. The two trails pass over a ledgy minor knob (a "howk") that offers a good view and then descend from the ledge down a steep cleft to a wet sag. After passing a small cave on the right side of the trail, the Pine Link branches right at 2.8 mi. at the foot of the most prominent howk. The fine viewpoint at the top of this crag is only about 0.1 mi. above the junction and is well worth a visit. From the junction the Pine Link runs nearly level across a wet area, then rises moderately on the slope above Bumpus Basin, crossing several small brooks. Climbing out of the scrub at 3.3 mi., it runs above the treeline with fine views and great exposure to the weather. After crossing the Watson Path at 3.5 mi. (0.3 mi. below the summit of Mt. Madison), the Pine Link descends gradually, frequently crossing jumbles of large rocks that require strenuous rock-hopping, to the Osgood Trail 30 yd. from Madison Hut.

Pine Link (map 1:E10–F9)

Distances from Pinkham B (Dolly Copp) Rd. (1,650 ft.) to

- Howker Ridge Trail, lower junction (3,850 ft.): 2.4 mi., 2,300 ft. (rev. 100 ft.), 2 hr. 20 min.
- Watson Path (4,950 ft.): 3.5 mi., 3,500 ft. (rev. 100 ft.), 3 hr. 30 min.
- Madison Hut (4,825 ft.): 4.0 mi., 3,500 ft. (rev. 150 ft.), 3 hr. 45 min.

Howker Ridge Trail (RMC)

This wild, rough, very scenic trail was built by Eugene B. Cook and William H. Peek, although the lower part no longer follows the original route. It leads from the Pinkham B (Dolly Copp) Rd. at the Randolph East parking area, 0.2 mi. south of US 2, to the Osgood Trail near the summit of Mt. Madison. It is an interesting trail with a great variety of attractive scenery and woods, passing three fine cascades in the lower part of the trail and offering excellent outlooks at different altitudes higher up. Howker Ridge is the long, curving northeast ridge of Mt. Madison that partly encloses the deep, bowl-shaped valley called Bumpus Basin. The trail follows the crest of the ridge, on which there are four little peaks called the Howks. The ridge gets its name from family named Howker that once had a farm at its base.

Coinciding with the Randolph Path, the trail quickly crosses the Presidential Range Rail Trail, and 30 yd. beyond diverges left (southeast) where the Randolph Path turns right (west). (Logging activity has disrupted this part of the trail somewhat in recent years, and trail markings must be observed and followed with great care.) It crosses a recent logging road near a yarding area, then enters a shallow gully and turns right, going up through it. At 0.4 mi., it reaches the bank of Bumpus Brook and follows it, passing Stairs Fall, a cascade on a tributary that enters Bumpus Brook directly across from the viewpoint. The trail continues along the brook, enters the WMNF, and passes a small rocky gorge called the Devil's Kitchen and other interesting pools and cascades. At Coosauk Fall (currently dry because of changes in stream flow) the Sylvan Way enters on the right, and in less than 0.1 mi., the Kelton Trail diverges right. At 1.0 mi., the Howker Ridge Trail crosses Bumpus Brook at the foot of Hitchcock Fall, then climbs steeply up the bank on the other side, levels off, descends slightly, and reaches a junction with a spur trail that leads right 40 yd. to the Bear Pit, a natural cleft in the ledge that forms a traplike box. The main trail climbs steeply through conifer woods, then moderates, reaching a rocky shoulder and descending into a slight sag. It resumes climbing and passes over a ledgy ridge crest called Blueberry Ledge—now far too overgrown to produce many blueberries—then continues up the ridge. It continues to climb, steeply at first and then moderately as it approaches the crest of the first howk, a long, narrow, densely wooded ridge capped by a number of small peaks. Following the ridge at easy grades, it crosses the ledgy but viewless summit of the first howk at 2.3 mi., passes a limited outlook ahead to Mt. Madison, then descends steeply for a short distance. After crossing through a long, fairly level sag, the trail climbs seriously again, and at 3.0 mi., it passes over the ledgy summit of the second howk, where there are fine views up to Mt. Madison and out to the Carter Range to the east and the Crescent and Pliny ranges to the north and northwest. Descending into the woods again rather steeply with one ledgy scramble, it passes through the shady glen where the Pine Link enters on the left; there is water down this trail in less than 100 yd.

From this junction, the two trails coincide for 0.3 mi., ascending over one of a group of several small, ledgy knobs that constitute the third howk, affording another good view. Descending a steep cleft to a wet sag, the trail passes a small cave to the right of the path and then ascends to a junction where the Pine Link branches right. Bearing slightly left, the Howker Ridge Trail climbs rather steeply up ledges to the open summit of the highest, most prominent howk (4,315 ft.) at 3.6 mi., where there are fine views in all directions. The trail descends back into the scrub, climbs over another minor crag, and passes through one last patch of high scrub before breaking out above treeline for good. The ensuing section of trail is very exposed to northwest winds and may be difficult to follow in poor visibility; however, if the trail is lost in conditions that do not dictate a retreat below the treeline, it is easy enough to reach the Osgood Trail simply by climbing up to the ridge crest, as the Osgood Trail follows that crest closely. From the treeline the trail climbs steeply up the rocks, generally angling a bit to the left and aiming for the notch between the most prominent visible crag and the lower crag to its left. As it approaches the ridge crest, it turns more to the right, heading for the most prominent visible crag, and enters the Osgood Trail about 100 yd. above a small sag and 0.2 mi. below the summit of Mt. Madison.

On the descent, at the junction of the Howker Ridge and Osgood trails, care must be taken to avoid beaten paths that lead back into the Osgood Trail. On leaving the junction one should keep well to the left, descending only slightly, until the RMC sign a short distance down the path has been sighted.

Howker Ridge Trail (map 1:E9–F9)

Distances from Pinkham B (Dolly Copp) Rd. (1,225 ft.) to
- Hitchcock Fall (1,875 ft.): 1.0 mi., 650 ft., 50 min.
- first howk (3,450 ft.): 2.3 mi., 2,200 ft., 2 hr. 15 min.
- Pine Link, lower junction (3,850 ft.): 3.1 mi., 2,800 ft. (rev. 200 ft.), 2 hr. 55 min.
- Osgood Trail (5,100 ft.): 4.2 mi., 4,200 ft. (rev. 100 ft.), 4 hr. 10 min.
- Mt. Madison summit (5,366 ft.) via Osgood Trail: 4.5 mi., 4,450 ft., 4 hr. 30 min.

Kelton Trail (RMC)

This path runs from the Howker Ridge Trail just above Coosauk Fall (currently dry) to the Brookside just below Salmacis Fall, from which the Watson Path and Valley Way can be quickly reached. It passes two fine viewpoints, the Overlook and the Upper Inlook.

The trail branches right from the Howker Ridge Trail 0.8 mi. from the Pinkham B (Dolly Copp) Rd. It climbs steeply with some slippery sections to Kelton Crag, then ascends toward the fingerlike north spur of Gordon Ridge, reaching an upper crag at the edge of a very old burn. From both these crags, there are restricted views; there is usually water on the right between them. Ascending, the trail reaches the Overlook at the edge of the old burn, where there are good views north and east. It then runs west to the Upper Inlook (outlook to the west) at 0.9 mi., where the Inlook Trail enters right from Dome Rock. The Kelton Trail then runs south nearly level through dense woods. It crosses Gordon Rill (reliable water) and traverses a section where extensive trail work has made travel across a rough slope easier. At 1.7 mi., it crosses Snyder Brook, climbs a very steep pitch up the bank, and ends at the Brookside 0.1 mi. below the foot of Salmacis Fall.

Kelton Trail (map 1:E9)

Distances from Howker Ridge Trail (1,700 ft.) to
- Kelton Crag (2,075 ft.): 0.3 mi., 400 ft., 25 min.
- Inlook Trail (2,732 ft.): 0.9 mi., 1,050 ft., 1 hr.
- The Brookside (2,750 ft.): 1.7 mi., 1,100 ft., 1 hr. 25 min.

Inlook Trail (RMC)

This path ascends the ridge that leads northwest from the end of the finger-like north spur of Gordon Ridge, offering excellent views from the brink of the line of cliffs that overlook Snyder Brook and culminate in Dome Rock. It begins at the junction of the Randolph Path and the Brookside on the east bank of Snyder Brook. It ascends, steeply at the start, soon reaching the first of several "inlooks" up the valley of Snyder Brook to Mt. Madison, Mt. John Quincy Adams, and Mt. Adams. It then ascends alternately over open ledges and through the woods, steeply at times. After passing Dome Rock, which offers an excellent view north from the tip of the finger, the trail swings right, leaving from the back of the ledge (sign), and continues up to the Upper Inlook (good view west) near the crest of the finger, where it ends at its junction with the Kelton Trail.

Inlook Trail (map 1:E9)

Distances from Randolph Path (1,900 ft.) to
- Dome Rock (2,662 ft.): 0.6 mi., 750 ft., 40 min.
- Kelton Trail (2,732 ft.): 0.7 mi., 850 ft., 45 min.

The Brookside (RMC)

This trail follows Snyder Brook, offering views of many cascades and pools. The upper part is fairly steep and rough. It begins at the junction with the Valley Way, at the point where the Valley Way leaves the edge of the brook 0.9 mi. from the Appalachia parking area, and climbs along the brook to the Watson Path a short distance north of Bruin Rock.

The Brookside leaves the Valley Way about 30 yd. above the Valley Way's junction with the Beechwood Way, continuing straight where the Valley Way turns uphill to the right. After a short washed-out section, the Randolph Path joins on the right, and the two trails cross Snyder Brook together on large stepping-stones (the former bridge at this crossing was washed out in 2005 and will not be replaced). Here the Randolph Path turns left, the Inlook Trail leaves straight ahead, and the Brookside turns right, continuing up the bank of the brook. At 0.3 mi., the Brookside re-crosses the brook and climbs along the west bank at a moderate grade with good footing, rising well above the brook through a fine birch forest, with occasional views through the trees to cliffs on the valley wall on the other side of the brook. Returning gradually to brook level, it comes to the junction with the Kelton Trail, which enters from the left at 1.2 mi. Above this point, the Brookside becomes steeper and rougher (though recent intensive trail work has significantly improved the footing), and again runs close to the brook, passing Salmacis Fall (limited view north from the top). It continues along a wild and beautiful part of the brook, with cascades and mossy rocks in a fine forest. It then climbs away from the brook and finally ascends sharply to the Watson Path a short distance north of Bruin Rock.

The Brookside (map 1:E9)
Distance from the Valley Way (1,900 ft.) to
• Watson Path (3,250 ft.): 1.7 mi, 1,350 ft., 1 hr. 30 min.

Watson Path (RMC)

The original Watson Path, completed by Laban M. Watson in 1882, led from the Ravine House to the summit of Mt. Madison. The present path begins at the Scar Trail, leads across the Valley Way to Bruin Rock, and then follows the original route to the summit. It is an interesting route to Mt. Madison, but it is very steep and rough, and, on the slopes above treeline, exposed to the full fury of northwest winds in a storm. The cairns above treeline are not very prominent, and the trail may be hard to follow when visibility is poor. Therefore, in bad weather it is potentially one of the most dangerous routes on the Northern Peaks.

Branching from the Scar Trail 0.3 mi. from the Valley Way, it runs level, turning sharp left at 0.1 mi. and crossing the Valley Way at 0.2 mi., at a point on that trail 2.4 mi. from the Appalachia parking area. This first section is seldom used and is rather difficult to follow. After crossing the Valley Way, the trail continues at an easy grade (but with one rough scramble around a large boulder), passing the junction with the Brookside on the left just before reaching Bruin Rock—a large, flat-topped boulder on the west bank of Snyder Brook. In another 80 yd., the Lower Bruin branches to the right toward the Valley Way, and the Watson Path crosses the brook at the foot of Duck Fall. The trail soon attacks the steep flank of Gordon Ridge on a very steep and rough footway. At 1.0 mi., it emerges from the scrub onto the grassy, stony back of the ridge, crosses the Pine Link at 1.4 mi., and ascends to the summit of Mt. Madison over rough and shelving stones.

Watson Path (map 1:E9–F9)

Distances from Scar Trail (3,175 ft.) to
- Valley Way (3,175 ft.): 0.2 mi., 0 ft., 5 min.
- Pine Link (4,950 ft.): 1.4 mi., 1,750 ft., 1 hr. 35 min.
- Mt. Madison summit (5,366 ft.): 1.7 mi., 2,200 ft., 1 hr. 55 min.

Distance from Appalachia parking area (1,306 ft.) to
- Mt. Madison summit (5,366 ft.) via Valley Way and Watson Path: 3.9 mi., 4,050 ft., 4 hr.

Valley Way (WMNF)

This is the most direct and easiest route from the Appalachia parking area to Madison Hut, well sheltered almost to the door of the hut. Note that the parking area is a stop of the AMC's Hiker Shuttle. In bad weather, it is the safest route to or from the hut. J. R. Edmands constructed it in his unmistakable style in 1895 to 1897, using parts of earlier trails constructed by Laban Watson and Eugene Cook.

The trail, in common with the Air Line, begins at Appalachia and crosses the Presidential Range Rail Trail to a fork, where the Valley Way leads to the left and the Air Line to the right across the power-line clearing into the woods. Just into the woods, the Maple Walk diverges left, and at 0.2 mi., Sylvan Way crosses. The trail soon enters the WMNF, and at 0.5 mi., the Fallsway comes in on the left, soon departs on the left for Tama Fall and the Brookbank, then reenters the Valley Way in a few yards—a short but worthwhile loop.

The Valley Way leads nearer Snyder Brook and is soon joined from the right by the Beechwood Way. About 30 yd. above this junction the Brookside continues straight, while the Valley Way turns right and climbs 100 yd. to the crossing of the Randolph Path at 0.9 mi., then climbs at a comfortable grade high above Snyder Brook. At 2.1 mi., the Scar Trail branches right, leading to the Air Line via Durand Scar, an excellent outlook on the Scar Loop only about 0.2 mi. above the Valley Way, well worth the small effort required to visit it. At 2.4 mi., the Watson Path crosses, leading left to the summit of Mt. Madison. The Valley Way angles up the rather steep slopes of Durand Ridge at a moderate grade considerably above the stream. At 2.8 mi., the Lower Bruin enters left, coming up from Bruin Rock and Duck Fall. At 3.1 mi., a short side path on the right leads to the recently reopened Valley Way Campsite. Soon the trail passes a spring to the right of the trail. At 3.3 mi., the Upper Bruin branches steeply right, leading in 0.2 mi. to the Air Line at the lower end of the knife-edge.

Now the Valley Way becomes steeper and approaches nearer to Snyder Brook. High up in the scrub, the path swings to the right, away from the brook, then swings back toward the stream and emerges from the scrub close to the stream, reaching a junction with the Air Line Cutoff 50 yd. below the hut. It ends in another 10 yd. at a junction with the Gulfside and Star Lake trails.

Valley Way (map 1:E9–F9)

Distances from Appalachia parking area (1,306 ft.) to

- Randolph Path crossing (1,953 ft.): 0.9 mi., 650 ft., 45 min.
- Watson Path crossing (3,175 ft.): 2.4 mi., 1,900 ft., 2 hr. 10 min.
- Upper Bruin junction (4,150 ft.): 3.3 mi., 2,900 ft., 3 hr. 5 min.
- Madison Hut (4,825 ft.): 3.8 mi., 3,550 ft., 3 hr. 40 min.
- Mt. Madison summit (5,366 ft.) via Osgood Trail: 4.2 mi., 4,100 ft., 4 hr. 10 min.

Lower Bruin (RMC)

This short trail branches right from the Watson Path on the west bank of Snyder Brook, where the Watson Path crosses the brook at Duck Fall. It ascends rapidly with rough footing, passes through a campsite area, and turns right uphill away from the brook. It soon turns left and continues to climb rather steeply, then becomes gradual and ends at the Valley Way. In the reverse direction, care should be taken to turn left into the campsite area rather than following a beaten path down to the brook.

Lower Bruin (map 1:E9)

Distance from Watson Path (3,325 ft.) to

- Valley Way (3,584 ft.): 0.2 mi., 250 ft., 15 min.

Upper Bruin (RMC)

This short but steep trail and its companion, the Lower Bruin, are the remnants of the original trail to Mt. Adams from Randolph. It branches to the right from the Valley Way 3.3 mi. from Appalachia and climbs to the Air Line near the treeline, 3.1 mi. from Appalachia.

Upper Bruin (map 1:F9)

Distance from Valley Way (4,150 ft.) to
* Air Line (4,400 ft.): 0.2 mi., 250 ft., 15 min.

Air Line (AMC)

This trail, completed in 1885, is the shortest route to Mt. Adams from a highway. It runs from the Appalachia parking area up Durand Ridge to the summit. The middle section is rather steep, and the sections on the knife-edged crest of Durand Ridge and above treeline are very exposed to weather but afford magnificent views.

The trail, in common with the Valley Way, begins at Appalachia and crosses the Presidential Range Rail Trail to a fork near the edge of the power-line clearing, where the Air Line leads right and Valley Way left. In 40 yd., just after the Air Line enters the woods, the Link diverges right. The Air Line crosses the Sylvan Way at 0.2 mi. and the Beechwood Way and Beechwood Brook at 0.6 mi. At 0.8 mi. from Appalachia, the Short Line diverges right, and at 0.9 mi., the Air Line enters the Randolph Path, co-incides with it for 20 yd., then diverges left uphill. At 1.6 mi., there may be water in a spring 30 yd. left (east) of the path (sign). From here the path becomes steeper for 0.5 mi., then eases up and reaches an old and now completely overgrown clearing known as Camp Placid Stream (water unreliable) at 2.4 mi., where the Scar Trail enters on the left, coming up from the Valley Way.

At 3.0 mi., the Air Line emerges from the scrub, and at 3.1 mi., the Upper Bruin comes up left from the Valley Way. The Air Line now ascends over the bare, ledgy crest of Durand Ridge known as the Knife-edge, passing over crags that drop off sharply into King Ravine on the right and descend steeply but not precipitously into Snyder Glen on the left. At 3.2 mi., just south of the little peak called Needle Rock, the Chemin des

Dames comes up from King Ravine. The Air Line now climbs steadily up the ridge toward Mt. Adams. From several outlooks along the upper part of this ridge, one can look back down the ridge for a fine demonstration of the difference between the U-shaped glacial cirque of King Ravine on the left (west), and the ordinary V-shaped brook valley of Snyder Glen on the right (east). At 3.5 mi., the Air Line Cutoff diverges left (southeast) to Madison Hut, which is visible from this junction in clear weather.

Air Line Cutoff (AMC). This short branch path provides a direct route 0.2 mi. (10 min.) long, fully sheltered by scrub, from the Air Line high on Durand Ridge to the Valley Way just below Madison Hut. Water can be obtained on this trail not far from the Air Line.

The Air Line now departs a little from the edge of the ravine, going left of the jutting crags at the ravine's southeast corner, and rises steeply. There is no single well-beaten footway in this section, so following the trail in poor visibility requires great care. At 3.7 mi., it passes the Gateway of King Ravine, where the King Ravine Trail diverges right and plunges between two crags into that gulf. Here there is a striking view of Mt. Madison. In 60 yd., the path enters the Gulfside Trail, turns right, and coincides with it for 70 yd. on the high plateau at the head of the ravine. Then the Air Line diverges to the left (southwest), passing northwest of Mt. Quincy Adams, up a rough way over large, angular stones to the summit of Mt. Adams, where it meets Lowe's Path and the Star Lake Trail.

Air Line (map 1:E9–F9)

Distances from Appalachia parking area (1,306 ft.) to

- Randolph Path (2,000 ft.): 0.9 mi., 700 ft., 50 min.
- Scar Trail (3,700 ft.): 2.4 mi., 2,400 ft., 2 hr. 25 min.
- Chemin des Dames (4,475 ft.): 3.2 mi., 3,150 ft., 3 hr. 10 min.
- Air Line Cutoff (4,800 ft.): 3.5 mi., 3,500 ft., 3 hr. 30 min.
- Gulfside Trail (5,125 ft.): 3.7 mi., 3,850 ft., 3 hr. 45 min.
- Mt. Adams summit (5,799 ft.): 4.3 mi., 4,500 ft., 4 hr. 25 min.
- Madison Hut (4,825 ft.) via Air Line Cutoff: 3.7 mi., 3,550 ft., 3 hr. 40 min.

Scar Trail (RMC)

This trail runs from the Valley Way 2.1 mi. from Appalachia to the Air Line at Camp Placid Stream, an old overgrown clearing 2.4 mi. from Appalachia. It provides a route to Mt. Adams that includes the spectacular views from Durand Ridge while avoiding the steepest section of the Air Line, and it also has excellent outlooks of its own from Durand Scar, reached by the Scar Loop.

The trail ascends moderately and divides 0.2 mi. above the Valley Way. The Scar Loop, an alternative route to the right, climbs up a natural ramp between two sections of rock face, turns sharp left, and 40 yd. above the loop junction reaches Durand Scar, which commands excellent views both up and down the valley of Snyder Brook; those up to Adams and Madison are especially fine. The Scar Loop then scrambles up the ledge, climbs steeply, passes a restricted outlook on the left up the Snyder Brook valley toward Mt. Madison, and descends slightly to rejoin the main path 0.4 mi. above the Valley Way.

The main Scar Trail, which is easier but misses the best views, bears left at the loop junction. In 0.1 mi., it turns sharp right as the Watson Path diverges left, then climbs across a small brook to the upper loop junction where the Scar Loop reenters. From here, the trail winds its way up the mountainside to the Air Line with mostly moderate grades and good footing.

Scar Trail (map 1:E9)

Distances from Valley Way (2,811 ft.) to
- Durand Scar (3,150 ft.) via Scar Loop: 0.2 mi., 350 ft., 15 min.
- Watson Path (3,175 ft.) via main trail: 0.3 mi., 350 ft., 20 min.
- Air Line (3,700 ft.) via either main trail or loop: 1.0 mi., 900 ft., 55 min.

Distance from Appalachia parking area (1,306 ft.) to
- Mt. Adams summit (5,799 ft.) via Valley Way, Scar Trail or Scar Loop, and Air Line: 5.1 mi., 4,500 ft., 4 hr. 50 min.

Star Lake Trail (AMC)

This trail leads from Madison Hut to the summit of Mt. Adams, much of the way angling up the steep southeast side of Mt. John Quincy Adams. It is often more sheltered from the wind than the Air Line, but it is steep and rough, especially in the upper part where it rock-hops a great deal of large talus and then tackles some fairly challenging rock scrambles on the steep section just below the summit ridge. It may also be difficult to follow when descending.

The trail runs south from the hut, rising gently, and at 0.2 mi., the Parapet Trail branches to the left, passing east of Star Lake and leading to the Parapet and to the Madison Gulf and Osgood trails. The Star Lake Trail passes along the west shore of the lake, and beyond it at 0.3 mi., the Buttress Trail diverges left and descends into the Great Gulf. The Star Lake Trail ascends southwest on the steep southeast slope of Mt. Quincy Adams, leaving the scrub and passing a good spring below the trail. It becomes progressively steeper and rougher as it angles up the steep, rocky slope, and the rocks become larger and require more strenuous hopping. Approaching the crest of a minor easterly ridge, it turns right and climbs very steeply with some fairly difficult scrambles to the top of the shoulder, then ascends moderately along the ridge crest to the summit of Adams, where it meets Lowe's Path and the Air Line.

Star Lake Trail (map 1:F9)

Distances from Madison Hut (4,825 ft.) to

- Buttress Trail (4,900 ft.): 0.3 mi., 100 ft., 10 min.
- Mt. Adams summit (5,799 ft.): 1.0 mi., 1,000 ft., 1 hr.

Short Line (RMC)

This graded path, leading from the Air Line to the King Ravine Trail below Mossy Fall, was made in 1899–1901 by J. Rayner Edmands. It offers direct access to the Randolph Path and to King Ravine from the Appalachia parking area.

The Short Line branches right from the Air Line 0.8 mi. from Appalachia. At 0.5 mi., it unites with the Randolph Path, coincides with it for 0.4 mi., then branches left and leads south up the valley of Cold Brook toward King Ravine, keeping a short distance east of the stream. At 2.7 mi. from Appalachia, the path joins the King Ravine Trail just below Mossy Fall.

Short Line (map 1:E9)

Distances from Air Line junction (1,825 ft.) to

- Randolph Path, lower junction (2,275 ft.): 0.5 mi., 450 ft., 30 min.
- Randolph Path, upper junction (2,500 ft.): 0.9 mi., 700 ft., 50 min.
- King Ravine Trail (3,150 ft.): 1.9 mi., 1,350 ft., 1 hr. 40 min.

King Ravine Trail (RMC)

This trail through King Ravine was constructed as a branch of Lowe's Path by Charles E. Lowe in 1876. It is very steep and rough on the headwall of the ravine, but it is one of the most spectacular trails in the White Mountains, offering an overwhelming variety of wild and magnificent scenery. It is not a good trail to descend because of steep, rough, slippery footing, and extra time should be allowed in either direction because of the roughness—and the views. The trip to the floor of the ravine is well worth the effort even if you do not choose to ascend the headwall. Though the King Ravine Trail begins on Lowe's Path, a more direct route to the most scenic part of the trail leads from Appalachia via the Air Line and Short Line.

The King Ravine Trail diverges left from Lowe's Path 1.8 mi. from US 2 and rises over a low swell of Nowell Ridge. It then descends gradually, and at 0.8 mi., it crosses Spur Brook below some cascades known as Canyon Fall, and in another 0.2 mi., it crosses the Randolph Path at its junction with the Amphibrach, a spot called the Pentadoi. Skirting the east spur of Nowell Ridge, it enters King Ravine and descends slightly, crosses a western branch of Cold Brook, goes across the lower floor of the ravine, and crosses the main stream. At 1.8 mi., near the foot of Mossy Fall (last sure water), it is joined by the Short Line, the usual route of access from the Appalachia parking area. Just above this fall, Cold Brook, already a good-sized stream, gushes from beneath the boulders that have fallen into the ravine.

So far, the path has been fairly gradual, but in the next 0.3 mi., it rises about 500 ft. and gains the upper floor of the ravine (about 3,700 ft.). The grandeur of the views of the ravine from the jumbled rocks that the trail passes around amply rewards the trip to this area, even if one does not continue up the headwall. The Chemin des Dames, leading very steeply up to the Air Line, branches sharp left at 2.2 mi. The King Ravine Trail turns sharp right here and then divides in another 10 yd. An alternate route called the Subway—more interesting but very strenuous—leads to the right from this junction; it is one of the celebrated features of White Mountain trails, winding through boulder caves over and under boulders ranging up to the size of a small house. The main path, called the Elevated, leads to the left avoiding many of the boulder caves, and is thus much easier; it also offers some good views of the ravine. The paths rejoin after 220 yd. on the Subway or 140 yd. on the Elevated, and soon the Great Gully Trail diverges right, then the King Ravine Trail divides again. The left fork is the main trail and the right is a loop path, about 30 yd. shorter than the main trail, that leads to boulder caves near the foot of the headwall; these caves have ice that remains throughout the year. After the paths rejoin at about 0.7 mi. from the Short Line junction, the ascent of the headwall begins. It is very steep and rough, rising about 1,100 ft. in 0.5 mi. over large blocks of rock marked with cairns and paint. It climbs to the Gateway, where the trail emerges from the ravine between two crags and immediately joins the Air Line just below its junction with the Gulfside Trail. From the Gateway, there is a striking view of Mt. Madison. Madison Hut is in sight and can be reached by taking the Gulfside Trail left. The summit of Mt. Adams is 0.6 mi. away via the Air Line.

King Ravine Trail (map 1:E9–F9)

Distances from Lowe's Path (2,575 ft.) to
- Randolph Path and the Amphibrach (2,925 ft.): 1.0 mi., 450 ft. (rev. 100 ft.), 45 min.
- Short Line (3,150 ft.): 1.8 mi., 700 ft. (rev. 100 ft.), 1 hr. 15 min.
- foot of King Ravine headwall (3,825 ft.): 2.5 mi., 1,450 ft., 2 hr.
- Air Line (5,100 ft.): 3.1 mi., 2,700 ft., 2 hr. 55 min.

Distance from Appalachia parking area (1,306 ft.) to
- summit of Mt. Adams (5,799 ft.) via Air Line, Short Line, King Ravine Trail, and Air Line: 4.6 mi., 4,500 ft., 4 hr. 35 min.

Chemin des Dames (RMC)

This trail leads from the floor of King Ravine up its east wall and joins the Air Line just above the treeline. It is the shortest route out of the ravine, but is nevertheless very steep and rough, climbing about 800 ft. in 0.4 mi. over gravel and talus, some of which is loose; it is also a difficult trail to descend.

Leaving the King Ravine Trail just before the point where the Subway and Elevated divide, it winds through scrub and boulders to the east side of the ravine, where it climbs steeply over talus through varying amounts of scrub, permitting plentiful though not constant views. About halfway up the steep slope, it passes through a boulder cave called Tunnel Rock. Above this, there are many fine views out across King Ravine and up to the towering crags of Durand Ridge. High up, the trail angles to the right across the top of a small slide and along the base of a rock face, reaching the Air Line in a little col.

Chemin des Dames (map 1:F9)
Distance from King Ravine Trail (3,700 ft.) to
• Air Line junction (4,475 ft.): 0.4 mi., 800 ft., 35 min.

Great Gully Trail (RMC)

This remarkably wild and beautiful trail provides an alternative route between the floor of King Ravine and the Gulfside Trail, reaching the latter at Thunderstorm Junction. It is extremely steep and rough, and, like the other trails in the ravine, especially difficult to descend. It is well marked but lightly used, and must be followed with some care. It has one particularly difficult scramble, and should not be attempted in wet or icy conditions. On this shady north slope, large snowdrifts may cover the trail well into June.

Leaving the King Ravine Trail just past the point where the Subway and Elevated rejoin, the Great Gully Trail runs across the floor of the ravine at easy grades, then ascends steadily through scrubby birches in a region damaged by an avalanche, and at 0.3 mi., it reaches (but does not cross) the brook that flows down the gully. At the base of an attractive high cascade, the trail turns right, away from the brook, and climbs up rocks to the spine of a narrow ridge and to a promontory with a spectacular view. The trail then passes under an overhanging rock on a ledge with a high sheer drop close by on the left, forcing the faint of heart to crawl on their bellies, possibly dragging their packs behind them. After negotiating this pitch, the climber is rewarded with a fine view of the cascade. Here the trail turns sharp right and climbs past a sheer dropoff to another viewpoint, then crosses the brook above the cascade at a spot where *Arnica mollis,* an herb of the Aster family sought by Thoreau on his trips to the mountains, grows in profusion. The trail continues to climb steeply to the treeline, with several more scrambles, ascends over a talus slope, then exits left from the rocks (watch for cairns marking this turn). It then begins to moderate as it runs almost due south across a grassy area marked by cairns that might be hard to follow in poor visibility, and finally meets the Gulfside and Lowe's Path at Thunderstorm Junction.

Great Gully Trail (map 1:F9)

Distance from King Ravine Trail (3,775 ft.) to
- Gulfside Trail (5,490 ft.): 1.0 mi., 1,700 ft., 1 hr. 20 min.

The Amphibrach (RMC)

This trail begins on the Link at the west end of Memorial Bridge, 0.7 mi. from the Appalachia parking area, then runs south near Cold Brook and its tributary Spur Brook to the five-way junction with the Randolph Path and King Ravine Trail known as the Pentadoi. The trail takes its unusual name from the marking that was used when it was first made, about 1883: three blazes—short, long, and short—arranged vertically. It is a good alternative approach to King Ravine or to any point reached via the Randolph Path or the Link—and, via the Beechwood Way, to points reached by the Short Line, the Air Line, or the Valley Way. Its moderate grade and relative smoothness make it comparatively less difficult when descent after dark is necessary. It is, in fact, one of the kindest trails to the feet in this region.

From the Link at Memorial Bridge, the Amphibrach follows the course of Cold Brook, ascending west of the stream but generally not in sight of the water. In 20 yd. from the junction, a side trail branches left 50 yd. to the foot of Cold Brook Fall. Soon the Amphibrach enters the WMNF. At 1.1 mi., the Monaway crosses, leading right to the Cliffway and left to Coldspur Ledges, pleasant flat ledges at the confluence of Cold and Spur brooks reached about 80 yd. from this junction. The Amphibrach soon crosses Spur Brook on the rocks and then bears away to the left (east), ascending the tongue of land between the two brooks, climbing moderately. At 1.5 mi., it crosses the Cliffway, which leads right (west) less than 0.2 mi. to picturesque Spur Brook Fall. Becoming a bit rougher, the Amphibrach continues upward to join the King Ravine Trail a few steps below the Pentadoi.

The Amphibrach (map 1:E9)

Distances from Memorial Bridge (1,425) to

- Monaway (2,200 ft.): 1.1 mi., 800 ft., 55 min.
- Randolph Path and King Ravine Trail (2,925 ft.): 1.9 mi., 1,500 ft., 1 hr. 40 min.

Cliffway (RMC)

This path begins on the Link, 2.0 mi. from the Appalachia parking area, and runs across the Amphibrach to the Randolph Path, 2.1 mi. from Appalachia via Air Line and Short Line. Many of its former viewpoints from the cliffs and ledges of the low swell of Nowell Ridge are now overgrown, but White Cliff still offers an excellent view of the Randolph Valley and the Pliny and Crescent ranges to the north. The trail has generally easy grades, but though well marked it is very lightly used, and care may be required to follow it.

Leaving the Link, the Cliffway climbs gradually with several turns to the fine viewpoint at White Cliff, where it turns sharp right. Here the Ladderback Trail diverges left along the cliff top.

Ladderback Trail (RMC). This short link trail—named for Ladderback Rock, a large boulder in the woods—connects the Monaway to the Cliffway at White Cliff, permitting a short loop hike including White Cliff and the overgrown Bog Ledge and King Cliff. The trail is rough and must be followed with great care. It leaves White Cliff and in a short distance, as it turns sharp right, it is joined from the left by Along the Brink, a path only 20 yd. long that parallels the Ladderback Trail a few steps closer to the brink of White Cliff. The Ladderback Trail then descends past Ladderback Rock to the Monaway 0.2 mi. (5 min.) from White Cliff.

At 1.0 mi., after ascending a zigzag course, the Cliffway crosses Bog Ledge, where there is a cleared view of King Ravine and Mts. Adams and Madison, then descends sharply for a short distance and turns left through a boggy area. It then turns sharp left again, passes overgrown King Cliff, and in another 0.1 mi. meets the Monaway. The Monaway continues straight, while the Cliffway turns sharp right and drops down a small broken ledge that resembles a ruined stairway, then runs nearly level across a moist area to Spur Brook at the base of picturesque Spur

Brook Fall. It then climbs beside the fall, crosses Spur Brook above the fall, and runs across the Amphibrach to the Randolph Path at the west end of Sanders Bridge over Cold Brook.

Cliffway (map 1:E9)

Distances from the Link (2,170 ft.) to
- White Cliff (2,484 ft.): 0.7 mi., 300 ft., 30 min.
- Spur Brook Fall (2,550 ft.): 1.7 mi., 500 ft. (rev 100 ft.), 1 hr. 5 min.
- Randolph Path (2,575 ft.): 2.1 mi., 500 ft., 1 hr. 20 min.

Monaway (RMC)

This short link trail affords the shortest route from the Randolph area to the Cliffway at White Cliff or King Cliff. It begins on the Amphibrach just below that trail's crossing of Spur Brook. At this junction, a short segment of the Monaway leads downhill (east) about 80 yd. to pleasant Coldspur Ledges at the confluence of Cold and Spur brooks. The main part of the Monaway runs uphill (west) from the Amphibrach at a moderate grade, passes a junction on the right at 0.3 mi. with the Ladderback Trail to White Cliff, then swings south and meets the Cliffway about 0.1 mi. east of overgrown King Cliff. Turn left here for Spur Brook Fall or continue straight to Bog Ledge and White Cliff.

Monaway (map 1:E9)

Distance from the Amphibrach (2,200 ft.) to
- Cliffway (2,550 ft.): 0.4 mi., 350 ft., 25 min.

Spur Trail (RMC)

This trail leads from the Randolph Path, just above its junction with the King Ravine Trail, to Lowe's Path just below Thunderstorm Junction. It ascends the east spur of Nowell Ridge near the west edge of King Ravine, passing Crag Camp (cabin). At several points below the treeline, there are fine outlooks into King Ravine, and above the treeline, views into King Ravine and up to Madison and Adams are continuous and excellent. The lower part is steep and rough, while the upper part runs completely in the open, very exposed to weather.

The Spur Trail diverges south from the Randolph Path about 100 yd. west of its junction with the King Ravine Trail, on the west bank of Spur Brook, and climbs rather steeply along Spur Brook past attractive cascades and pools. At 0.2 mi., a short branch path leads left 90 yd. to Chandler Fall, where the brook runs down a steep, smooth slab of rock; from the base of the fall, there is a view north. At 0.3 mi., the Hincks Trail to Gray Knob cabin diverges right, and the Spur Trail crosses to the east side of the brook, the last water until Crag Camp. It ascends the spur that forms the west wall of King Ravine, passing a side path that leads left 10 yd. to the Lower Crag, a good outlook to the ravine and Mts. Madison and Adams. At 0.9 mi., it reaches the Upper Crag, where it passes Crag Camp and soon reaches the junction on the right with the Gray Knob Trail, which leads west 0.4 mi. to Gray Knob cabin.

The trail continues to climb quite steeply up the ridge, but not so near the edge of the ravine. At 1.1 mi., a side path (sign, hard to see on the descent) leads left 100 yd. to Knight's Castle, a spectacular perch high up on the ravine wall. Here the Spur Trail passes into high scrub, and in another 0.2 mi., it breaks out above the treeline, commanding excellent views; those to King Ravine are better in the lower portion, while those to Madison and Adams are better higher up. The grade moderates as it joins Nowell Ridge, ascending well to the east of the crest. It finally merges with Lowe's Path 100 yd. below the Gulfside Trail at Thunderstorm Junction.

Spur Trail (map 1:E9–F9)

Distances from Randolph Path (2,950 ft.) to
- Crag Camp (4,247 ft.): 0.9 mi., 1,300 ft., 1 hr. 5 min.
- Lowe's Path (5,425 ft.): 2.0 mi., 2,500 ft., 2 hr. 15 min.
- Mt. Adams summit (5,799 ft.) via Lowe's Path: 2.4 mi., 2,850 ft., 2 hr. 40 min.

Hincks Trail (RMC)

This short link trail connects the Spur Trail and Randolph Path to Gray Knob cabin. It is fairly steep and rough. It diverges right from the Spur Trail immediately before the crossing of Spur Brook, about 0.3 mi. above the Randolph Path. Soon it comes to the edge of Spur Brook near a pleasant little cascade over mossy rocks, then winds rather steeply up the valley, passing through several patches of woods damaged by wind, to Gray Knob.

Hincks Trail (map 1:E9–F9)

Distance from Spur Trail (3,450 ft.) to
• Gray Knob cabin (4,375 ft.): 0.7 mi., 950 ft., 50 min.

Gray Knob Trail (RMC)

This trail connects three of the four RMC camps (Crag Camp, Gray Knob, and the Perch) with each other. It also links the upper parts of the Spur Trail and Lowe's, Randolph, and Israel Ridge paths, affording in particular a route from Crag Camp and Gray Knob to Edmands Col without loss of elevation. Grades are mostly easy but the footing is frequently rough, and south of Lowe's Path, it has substantial weather exposure, although some sheltering scrub is usually close by.

Leaving the Spur Trail 25 yd. west of Crag Camp, it climbs over a knoll with limited views, then passes a side path on the right leading down 25 yd. to a good piped spring. It traverses a rough slope nearly on the level; then, soon after passing a spring (left), it ascends a short pitch to Gray Knob cabin (left) at 0.4 mi., where the Hincks Trail enters on the right. The Gray Knob Trail then runs almost level, passing the Quay Path, a shortcut on the right that runs 50 yd. to Lowe's Path at a fine outlook ledge called the Quay. The Gray Knob Trail crosses Lowe's Path at 0.5 mi. and almost immediately enters scrub of variable height, offering a mixture of shelter and weather exposure with nearly constant views, and begins to climb moderately. At 0.8 mi., the Perch Path diverges right. The Gray Knob Trail continues to climb moderately up the slope, then levels off and runs nearly on contour to the Randolph Path just before its junction with the Israel Ridge Path.

Gray Knob Trail (map 1:F9)

Distances from Spur Trail (4,250 ft.) to
• Lowe's Path (4,400 ft.): 0.5 mi., 150 ft., 20 min.
• Randolph Path (4,825 ft.): 1.7 mi., 600 ft., 1 hr. 10 min.

Perch Path (RMC)

This path runs from the Gray Knob Trail across the Randolph Path and past the Perch (lean-to) to the Israel Ridge Path. It diverges right from the Gray Knob

Trail 0.3 mi. south of Lowe's Path, then descends moderately and crosses the Randolph Path at 0.3 mi. It soon passes a small brook, then the Perch and its tent platforms, and runs nearly level to the Israel Ridge Path at a sharp curve.

Perch Path (map 1:F9)

Distances from Gray Knob Trail (4,550 ft.) to
- The Perch (4,313 ft.): 0.4 mi., 0 ft. (rev. 250 ft.), 10 min.
- Israel Ridge Path junction (4,300 ft.): 0.5 mi., 0 ft., 15 min.

Lowe's Path (RMC)

This trail, cut from 1875 to 1876 by Charles E. Lowe and Dr. William G. Nowell from Lowe's house in Randolph to the summit of Mt. Adams, is the oldest of the mountain trails that ascend the peaks from the Randolph Valley. It begins on the south side of US 2, 100 yd. west of Lowe's Store, at which cars may be parked (small fee). It is perhaps the easiest way to climb Mt. Adams, with moderate grades (except for the steep middle section), good footing, and excellent views, but it still has considerable exposure to weather in the part above the treeline.

Leaving US 2, Lowe's Path follows a broad woods road for 100 yd., then diverges right at a sign giving the history of the trail. It crosses a snow-mobile trail, the Presidential Range Rail Trail, and then the power lines, and ascends through woods at a moderate grade, heading at first southwest and then southeast, and crossing several small brooks. At 1.7 mi., the Link crosses, and at 1.8 mi., the King Ravine Trail branches left. Lowe's Path continues to ascend, becoming steeper and rougher, and at 2.4 mi., it passes just to the right of the Log Cabin. Here the Log Cabin Cutoff, nearly level but rough, runs left 0.2 mi. to the Randolph Path, and the very rough Cabin-Cascades Trail to the Israel Ridge Path in Cascade Ravine leaves on the right. Water (reliable) is found at the Log Cabin. The path now begins to ascend more seriously and crosses the Randolph Path at 2.7 mi. At this junction, the Randolph Path, angling up to the right, is more obvious than Lowe's Path, which climbs straight ahead up some rocks. Lowe's Path climbs steeply up to the crest of Nowell Ridge, then moderates. At a fine outlook ledge called the Quay at 3.2 mi., the very short Quay Path diverges left to Gray Knob Trail, and 30 yd. farther the Gray Knob Trail crosses. The cabin at Gray Knob is 0.1 mi. left (east) by either route.

Soon the trail breaks out of the scrub, and from here onward it is above treeline and completely exposed to wind. Views are very fine. At 4.1 mi., after the steady ascent up Nowell Ridge, the trail reaches the crag known as Adams 4 (5,355 ft.), descends into a little sag, then rises moderately again, keeping to the left (east) of Mt. Sam Adams. The Spur Trail joins on the left 100 yd. below Thunderstorm Junction, the major intersection with the Gulfside at 4.4 mi., where the Great Gully Trail also enters on the left. Lowe's Path climbs moderately up the jumbled rocks of the cone of Mt. Adams, passing the junction where the Israel Ridge Path enters right at 4.5 mi. Climbing almost due east, it reaches the summit of Mt. Adams at 4.7 mi., where it meets the Air Line and Star Lake Trail.

Lowe's Path (map 1:E9–F9)

Distances from US 2 near Lowe's Store (1,375 ft.) to

- The Link (2,475 ft.): 1.7 mi., 1,100 ft., 1 hr. 25 min.
- King Ravine Trail (2,575 ft.): 1.8 mi., 1,200 ft., 1 hr. 30 min.
- Log Cabin (3,263 ft.): 2.4 mi., 1,900 ft., 2 hr. 10 min.
- Randolph Path (3,600 ft.): 2.7 mi., 2,250 ft., 2 hr. 30 min.
- Gray Knob Trail (4,400 ft.): 3.2 mi., 3,050 ft., 3 hr. 10 min.
- Adams 4 summit (5,355 ft.): 4.1 mi., 4,000 ft., 4 hr. 5 min.
- Gulfside Trail (5,490 ft.): 4.4 mi., 4,150 ft., 4 hr. 15 min.
- Mt. Adams summit (5,799 ft.): 4.7 mi., 4,450 ft., 4 hr. 35 min.

Cabin-Cascades Trail (RMC)

One of the earliest trails constructed by the AMC (1881), the Cabin-Cascades Trail leads from the Log Cabin on Lowe's Path to the Israel Ridge Path near the cascades on Cascade Brook, descending almost all the way. It is generally rough with one rather steep, very rough section.

The trail begins at Lowe's Path 2.4 mi. from US 2, opposite the Log Cabin. It runs gradually downhill, with minor ups and downs, crossing the Mystic Stream at 0.3 mi. At 0.7 mi., it enters Cascade Ravine and descends a steep pitch, passing a limited outlook to the Castles and Mt. Bowman rising over Israel Ridge. It then begins the final steep, rough descent to Cascade Brook, ending at the Israel Ridge Path just above its upper junction with the Link. The first and highest cascade can be reached by descending on the Israel Ridge Path 60 yd. to the Link, then following it downward to the left another 60 yd. to the ledges at the top of the cascade.

The second cascade can be seen by following the Israel Ridge Path about 150 yd. upward.

Cabin-Cascades Trail (map 1:E9–F9)

Distance from Lowe's Path (3,263 ft.) to
* Israel Ridge Path (2,825 ft.): 1.0 mi., 0 ft. (rev. 450 ft.), 30 min.

Israel Ridge Path (RMC)

This trail runs to the summit of Mt. Adams from the Castle Trail, 1.3 mi. from US 2 at Bowman (which is 1.0 mi. west of Lowe's Store). Beginning in 1892, J. Rayner Edmands constructed it as a graded path. Although hurricanes and slides have severely damaged the original trail, and there have been many relocations, the upper part is still one of the finest and most beautiful of the Randolph trails. Some brook crossings may be difficult in high water, and parts of the trail are steep and rough.

From Bowman follow the Castle Trail for 1.3 mi. Here, the Israel Ridge Path branches left, and at 0.1 mi., the path crosses to the east bank of the Israel River. It follows the river, then turns left up the bank at 0.4 mi., where the Castle Ravine Trail diverges right and continues along the river. Becoming steeper and rougher, the Israel Ridge Path bears southeast up the slope of Nowell Ridge into Cascade Ravine, and at 1.2 mi., the Link enters left. The trails coincide for 50 yd., and then the Link diverges right to cross Cascade Brook. The highest of the cascades can be reached by following the Link 60 yd. downhill to the right. In another 60 yd., the Cabin-Cascades Trail enters left from the Log Cabin. The Israel Ridge Path now enters virgin growth. From this point to the treeline, the forest has never been disturbed by lumbering, though slides and windstorms have done much damage.

The path ascends steeply on the north side of Cascade Brook, climbing one steep ledge on ladders. It passes sloping ledges beside the second cascade, where there is a view to the northwest, then crosses the brook at the head of this cascade at 1.4 mi., turns right downstream for a short distance, then turns left and climbs. It ascends steeply up Israel Ridge, sometimes also called the Emerald Tongue, which rises between Cascade and Castle Ravines. At 2.2 mi., after a long sidehill section along the east side of the ridge with two more ladders up steep ledges, the path turns sharp left (east) where the Emerald Trail diverges right to descend steeply into Castle Ravine. Emerald Bluff, a remarkable outlook to the Castles and Castle Ravine that is well worth a visit, can be reached from this junction in less than 0.2 mi. by following the Emerald Trail and a spur path that turns right before the main trail begins its steep descent. The Israel Ridge Path angles up a rather steep slope, then turns right at 2.4 mi. where the Perch Path enters left (east), 0.1 mi. from the Perch. The main path ascends south to the treeline, where it joins the Randolph Path at 2.8 mi. The junction of the Gray Knob Trail with the Randolph Path is 70 yd. to the left (north) at this point. For 0.1 mi., the Israel Ridge and Randolph Paths coincide, then the Israel Ridge Path branches to the left and, curving east, ascends the southwest ridge of Mt. Adams and joins the Gulfside Trail at 3.3 mi., near Storm Lake. It coincides with the Gulfside for 0.5 mi., running northeast past Peabody Spring to the Adams–Sam Adams col. At 3.8 mi., with the cairn at Thunderstorm Junction in sight ahead, the Israel Ridge Path branches right from the Gulfside Trail, and enters Lowe's Path at 3.9 mi., which leads to the summit of Mt. Adams at 4.1 mi. The cairns between the Gulfside Trail and Lowe's Path are rather sketchy, so in poor visibility it might be better to follow Lowe's Path from Thunderstorm Junction to the summit.

Israel Ridge Path (map 1:E8–F9)

Distances from Castle Trail (1,900 ft.) to
- Castle Ravine Trail (2,100 ft.): 0.4 mi., 200 ft., 20 min.
- The Link (2,800 ft.): 1.2 mi., 900 ft., 1 hr. 5 min.
- Perch Path (4,300 ft.): 2.4 mi., 2,400 ft., 2 hr. 25 min.
- Randolph Path, lower junction (4,825 ft.): 2.8 mi., 2,950 ft., 2 hr. 55 min.
- Gulfside Trail (5,250 ft.): 3.3 mi., 3,350 ft., 3 hr. 20 min.
- Mt. Adams summit (5,799 ft.) via Lowe's Path: 4.1 mi., 3,900 ft., 4 hr.
- Edmands Col (4,938 ft.) via Randolph Path: 3.5 mi., 3,050 ft., 3 hr. 15 min.

Emerald Trail (RMC)

This steep, rough, wild trail connects the Israel Ridge Path with the Castle Ravine Trail, passing Emerald Bluff, a fine viewpoint to the Castles and Castle Ravine. The short section between the Israel Ridge Path and Emerald Bluff is uncharacteristically gradual and easy. The path is lightly used and must be followed with some care. Emerald Bluff can be visited from US 2 by a wild, scenic loop hike using the Castle Ravine Trail, Emerald Trail, and Israel Ridge Path.

This trail leaves the combined Castle Ravine Trail and Link 0.2 mi. from their lower junction and descends slightly across a channel of Castle Brook, then climbs a very steep and rough slope. As the trail levels off on the crest of Israel Ridge just south of Emerald Bluff, it turns sharp right. Here a side path turns left and leads 50 yd. to the viewpoint on Emerald Bluff. The main trail runs at easy grades to the Israel Ridge Path 0.2 mi. below its junction with the Perch Path.

Emerald Trail (map 1:F9)

Distances from Castle Ravine Trail and the Link (3,225 ft.) to
- Emerald Bluff (4,025 ft.): 0.5 mi., 800 ft., 40 min.
- Israel Ridge Path (4,050 ft.): 0.6 mi., 850 ft., 45 min.

Castle Ravine Trail (RMC)

This scenic, challenging trail diverges from the Israel Ridge Path 1.7 mi. from US 2 at Bowman and leads through wild and beautiful Castle Ravine to the Randolph Path near Edmands Col. Although it is reasonably well sheltered except for the highest section, parts of the trail are very rough, especially where it crosses a great deal of unstable talus on the headwall, which makes footing extremely poor for descending or when the rocks are wet. It is well marked but lightly used, and must be followed with some care—particularly on the headwall, where winter avalanches may remove the markings. Some of the brook crossings may be very difficult at moderate to high water, and the ravine walls are very steep, making rapid flooding likely during heavy rain. Except for very experienced hikers, it would almost certainly prove to be a very difficult escape route from Edmands Col in bad-weather conditions.

From Bowman follow the Castle Trail and then the Israel Ridge Path to a point 1.7 mi. from Bowman. Here the Israel Ridge Path turns left up a slope, while the Castle Ravine Trail leads straight ahead near the river. It crosses to the west bank (difficult at high water and not easy at other times) and soon reaches a point abreast of the Forks of Israel, where Cascade and Castle brooks unite to form the Israel River. The trail crosses to the east bank of Castle Brook, passes a fine cascade, and recrosses to the west bank. In general, it follows the route of an old logging road, now almost imperceptible. After entering Castle Ravine, the trail crosses to the east bank and climbs at a moderate grade well above the brook. At 1.5 mi., the Link enters from the left, and the two trails coincide, passing at 1.7 mi. the junction with the Emerald Trail left (north) from Israel Ridge. After crossing to the southwest side of the brook in a tract of enchanted cool virgin forest beloved of *Musca nigra,* the Link diverges right for the Castle Trail at 1.8 mi., while the Castle Ravine Trail continues up the ravine close to the brook, crossing it several times and once using its bed for a short distance. It recrosses Castle Brook near the foot of the headwall, close to where the stream emerges from under the mossy boulders that have fallen into the ravine, then winds through a rocky area where water can often be heard running underground. The trail then turns left and mounts the steep slope, and at 2.1 mi., it passes under Roof Rock, a large flat-bottomed boulder that would provide some shelter in a rainstorm.

Rising very steeply southeast with very rough footing, the trail soon winds up a patch of bare rocks marked by small cairns and dashes of paint, where there are good views up to the Castles and down the valley northward to the Pliny Range. It reenters the scrub at a large cairn, and in 100 yd., it reemerges from the scrub at the foot of a steep slope of very loose rock (use extreme care, particularly when descending). It climbs very steeply to the top of the headwall, marked by cairns and paint on rocks, then ascends gradually in a grassy little valley with little evident footway and sparsely placed cairns, passing Spaulding Spring and joining the Randolph Path (sign) on the rocks to the left of the grassy valley, 0.1 mi. north of Edmands Col.

Descending, follow the Randolph Path north from Edmands Col to the small grassy valley, then descend along it until the line of cairns is found leading down the headwall.

Castle Ravine Trail (map 1:E8–F9)

Distances from Israel Ridge Path (2,100 ft.) to
- The Link, lower junction (3,125 ft.): 1.5 mi., 1,050 ft., 1 hr. 15 min.
- Roof Rock (3,600 ft.): 2.1 mi., 1,500 ft., 1 hr. 50 min.
- Randolph Path (4,900 ft.): 2.8 mi., 2,800 ft., 2 hr. 50 min.

Castle Trail (AMC)

This trail follows the narrow, serrated ridge that runs northwest from Mt. Jefferson, providing magnificent views in a spectacular setting. The part that traverses the Castles is rough with some difficult rock scrambles. In bad weather, it can be a dangerous trail because of long and continuous exposure to the northwest winds at and above the Castles. The path was first cut in 1883 to 1884, but most of it has since been relocated.

The Castle Trail begins at Bowman on US 2, 3 mi. west of the Appalachia parking area and 4.2 mi. east of the junction of US 2 and NH 115. Park on the north side of the former railroad grade (now the Presidential Range Rail Trail).

The trail follows the Presidential Range Rail Trail to the right for 100 yd. and turns left into the woods just past a gate. It crosses a pipeline clearing and then traverses an open logged area where the footway may be obscured by brush. At 0.3 mi., it enters the WMNF, crosses a power line, and soon reaches the bank of the Israel River. Here the trail turns sharp left and runs along the bank for 60 yd., then crosses the river (may be difficult at high water) at 0.4 mi. On the far side, the trail turns left and parallels the stream for 100 yd., then bears right up a bank and rises at an easy grade through a hardwood forest.

At 1.3 mi., the Israel Ridge Path branches left (east) toward the brook. The last sure water is a short distance along this trail. The Castle Trail continues to rise above the brook on the northeast flank of Mt. Bowman, and at 1.5 mi., it turns sharp right away from the brook. Now climbing up the slope at a steeper angle, it ascends a long series of rock steps, passes to the right of a very large boulder at 2.2 mi., and becomes much steeper for the next 0.3 mi. At 2.5 mi., it enters a blowdown area near the crest of the ridge connecting Mt. Bowman and the Castellated Ridge and becomes almost level. Soon it ascends easily with excellent footing through open woods with abundant ferns, and gradually becomes steeper again as it climbs the main ridge below the Castles to a densely wooded shoulder with a sharp, ragged crest. Here it winds along the steep slopes near the ridge crest to a little gap at 3.5 mi., where the Link crosses, coming up from Castle Ravine on the left and leading off to the Caps Ridge Trail on the right.

The ridge becomes very narrow and the trail becomes steep and rough with some fairly difficult scrambles. After passing over two ledges with a good outlook from each, it reaches treeline and climbs to the foot of the first and most impressive Castle, a pair of 20-ft. pillars, at 3.8 mi. The view is very fine. The trail leads on past a slightly higher but less impressive Castle, runs through a small col filled with scrub that would provide reasonable shelter in a storm, and continues to ascend over several higher but lesser crags as the Castellated Ridge blends into the main mass of Mt. Jefferson. At 4.5 mi., the Cornice crosses, leading northeast to the Randolph Path near Edmands Col and south to the Caps Ridge and Gulfside trails. The Castle Trail ascends moderately over the rocks and joins the Mt. Jefferson Loop in a small flat area just north of the summit crag.

Castle Trail (map 1:E8–F9)

Distances from Bowman (1,500 ft.) to

- Israel Ridge Path (1,900 ft.): 1.3 mi., 400 ft., 50 min.
- The Link junction (4,025 ft.): 3.5 mi., 2,550 ft., 3 hr.
- first Castle (4,450 ft.): 3.8 mi., 2,950 ft., 3 hr. 20 min.
- Mt. Jefferson summit (5,716 ft.): 5.0 mi., 4,200 ft., 4 hr. 35 min.

Caps Ridge Trail (AMC)

The Caps Ridge Trail makes a direct ascent of Mt. Jefferson from the height-of-land (3,008 ft.) on the road through Jefferson Notch, the pass between Mt. Jefferson and the Dartmouth Range. This is the highest trailhead on a public through-road in the White Mountains, making it possible to ascend Mt. Jefferson with much less elevation gain than on any other trail to a Presidential peak over 5,000 ft., except for a few trails that begin high on the Mt. Washington Auto Rd. However, the Caps Ridge Trail is steep and rough with numerous ledges that require rock scrambling and are slippery when wet, and the upper part is very exposed to weather. Therefore, the route is more strenuous than might be anticipated from the relatively small distance and elevation gain. (One should take note that it is not easier to ascend Mt. Washington via the Caps Ridge Trail than via the Jewell Trail because the descent from Monticello Lawn to Sphinx Col mostly cancels out the advantage of the higher start.)

The south end of Jefferson Notch Rd. is located directly opposite Mt. Clinton Rd. at a crossroads on Base Rd. (the road that runs from

US 302 to the Cog Railway). The north end is on Valley Rd. in Jefferson (which runs between US 2 and NH 115). The high point in the notch is about 5.5 mi. from Valley Rd. on the north and 3.4 mi. from Base Rd. on the south. Jefferson Notch Rd. is a good gravel road, open in summer and early fall, but because of the high elevation it reaches, snow and mud disappear late in spring and ice returns early. Drive with care because it is winding and narrow in places, and watch out for logging trucks. The southern half is usually in better condition than the northern half, which is often very rough (but still sound).

The trail leaves the parking area and crosses a wet section on log bridges, then ascends steadily up the lower part of the ridge. At 1.0 mi., there is an outcrop of granite on the right that provides a fine view, particularly of the summit of Jefferson and the Caps Ridge ahead. There are several potholes in this outcrop; such potholes are normally formed only by torrential streams, and such streams occur on high ridges like the Ridge of the Caps only during the melting of a glacier, so these potholes indicate to geologists that the continental ice sheet once covered this area.

About 100 yd. beyond this outcrop, the Link enters from the left, providing a nearly level but rough path that runs 1.6 mi. to the Castle Trail just below the Castles, making possible a very scenic though strenuous loop over the Caps and Castles. The Caps Ridge Trail follows the narrow crest of the ridge, becoming steeper and rougher as it climbs up into scrub, and views become increasingly frequent. At 1.5 mi., the trail reaches the lowest Cap after a steep scramble up ledges, and it runs entirely in the open from here on. The trail ascends very steeply up the ridge to the highest Cap at 1.9 mi., then continues to climb steeply as the ridge blends into the summit mass. At 2.1 mi., the Cornice enters left, providing a very rough route to the Castle Trail and Edmands Col, and then diverges right in 20 yd., providing an easy shortcut to Monticello Lawn and points to the south. The Caps Ridge Trail continues east, keeping a little south of the crest of the ridge, to the summit of Mt. Jefferson, then descends east 40 yd. to the base of the little conical summit crag, where it meets the Mt. Jefferson Loop just above its junctions with the Castle and Six Husbands trails.

Caps Ridge Trail (map 1:F8–F9)

Distances from Jefferson Notch Rd. (3,008 ft.)
- to The Link (3,800 ft.): 1.1 mi., 800 ft., 55 min.
- to Lower Cap (4,422 ft.): 1.5 mi., 1,400 ft., 1 hr. 25 min.
- to Upper Cap (4,830 ft.): 1.9 mi., 1,800 ft., 1 hr. 50 min.
- to The Cornice (5,025 ft.): 2.1 mi., 2,000 ft., 2 hr. 5 min.
- to Mt. Jefferson summit (5,716 ft.): 2.5 mi., 2,700 ft., 2 hr. 35 min.
- to junction with Mt. Jefferson Loop (5,700 ft.): 2.6 mi., 2,700 ft., 2 hr. 40 min.
- to Gulfside Trail (5,325 ft.) via Cornice: 2.5 mi., 2,300 ft., 2 hr. 25 min.
- to Mt. Washington summit (6,288 ft.) via Cornice, Gulfside Trail, and Crawford Path: 5.2 mi., 3,700 ft. (rev. 400 ft.), 4 hr. 25 min.
- for loop over Caps and Castles (via Caps Ridge Trail, Castle Trail, Link, and Caps Ridge Trail): 6.7 mi., 2,850 ft., 4 hr. 45 min.

Boundary Line Trail (WMNF)

This trail connects the Jefferson Notch Rd., 1.4 mi. south of the Caps Ridge Trail, to the hikers' parking area on the Cog Railway Base Rd., 1.1 mi. from its junction with the Jefferson Notch Rd. It thus provides a shortcut between the trailheads of the Caps Ridge Trail and the Jewell Trail or the Ammonoosuc Ravine Trail (Section One), though it is lightly used and often poorly marked (and, in 2006, obscured by blowdowns), and must be followed with care. It diverges left (north) from the Jewell Trail 0.4 mi. from the Base Rd. parking lot and runs north, nearly level, closely following the straight boundary line between two unincorporated townships. At 0.5 mi., it crosses Clay Brook, then continues to its end at the Jefferson Notch Rd.

Boundary Line Trail (map 1:F8)

Distance from Jewell Trail (2,525 ft.) to
- Jefferson Notch Rd. (2,525 ft.): 0.9 mi., 50 ft. (rev. 50 ft.), 30 min.

Distance from Cog Railway Base Rd. parking area (2,500 ft.) to
- Caps Ridge Trail (3,008 ft.) via Jewell Trail, Boundary Line Trail, and Jefferson Notch Rd.: 2.7 mi., 550 ft., 1 hr. 40 min.

Jewell Trail (WMNF)

This trail begins at a parking area on the Cog Railway Base Rd., 1.1 mi. from its junction with Jefferson Notch Rd. and Mt. Clinton Rd. Base Rd. is the road that leads from US 302 to the Cog Railway Base Station at Marshfield. The trail ascends the unnamed ridge that leads west from Mt. Clay and ends at the Gulfside Trail high on the west slope of Mt. Clay, 0.3 mi. north of the Clay-Washington col and 1.4 mi. north of the summit of Mt. Washington. The grade is constant but seldom steep, there are no rock scrambles, and the footing is generally very good below the treeline and only moderately rough and rocky in the last section below the Gulfside. It provides the easiest route to Mt. Washington from the west, featuring a great length of ridge walking above the treeline with fine views, but this part is also greatly exposed to the weather and offers no shelter between the summit and treeline. In bad weather, or if afternoon thunderstorms threaten, it is safer to descend from Mt. Washington via Lakes of the Clouds Hut and the Ammonoosuc Ravine Trail, despite the steep and slippery footing on the latter trail; descent by the Jewell Trail offers much easier footing and thus may be preferred when the weather cooperates. The trail is named for Sergeant Winfield S. Jewell, once an observer for the Army Signal Corps on Mt. Washington, who perished on the Greeley expedition to the Arctic in 1884.

The Jewell Trail enters the woods directly across the road from the parking area, crosses the Ammonoosuc River at 0.1 mi., then swings northeast and ascends at an easy grade. At 0.4 mi., the Boundary Line Trail diverges left, while the Jewell Trail ascends the crest of the low ridge between the Ammonoosuc River and Clay Brook, joining the old route of the trail at 1.0 mi. The old path (sign) can be followed right 0.4 mi. to the Base Station. From the junction the main trail descends slightly to Clay Brook, crosses on a footbridge, then climbs northeast by long switchbacks. At 2.0 mi., it passes through a blowdown patch at the edge of the steep wall of Burt Ravine, where there are interesting though limited views. It then swings somewhat to the north side of the ridge and climbs east, staying well below the ridge crest until near the treeline. Reaching treeline at about 3.0 mi., it zigzags at a moderate grade with rough, rocky footing up the ridge crest, which quickly becomes less prominent and blends into the slope of Mt. Clay. At 3.5 mi., the trail swings to the right away from what remains of the ridge and angles up the slope at an easy grade to the Gulfside Trail. For Mt. Washington, follow the Gulfside right. In good weather, the fine views from the cliffs of Mt. Clay can be reached fairly easily by a scramble directly up the rocks above the junction.

Jewell Trail (map 1:F8–F9)

Distances from Cog Railway Base Rd. parking area (2,500 ft.) to

- Clay Brook crossing (2,850 ft.): 1.1 mi., 400 ft. (rev. 50 ft.), 45 min.
- Gulfside Trail (5,400 ft.): 3.7 mi., 2,950 ft., 3 hr. 20 min.
- Mt. Washington summit (6,288 ft.) via Gulfside Trail: 5.1 mi., 3,900 ft. (rev. 50 ft.), 4 hr. 30 min.

Pine Mountain Trail (WMNF)

This trail was reopened in the 1990s to restore an abandoned section of the Pine Link that once linked an old route of the AT in Gorham with the Northern Presidentials via Pine Mountain. The trailhead can be reached by turning west onto Promenade St. from NH 16 at a point 0.2 mi. south of its junction with US 2 at the eastern edge of the Gorham business district. Follow this road past a small cemetery on the right side and an equipment shed on the left side at 0.5 mi., then a larger cemetery on the right side. The road becomes gravel at 0.6 mi. and continues to a gravel pit at 0.7 mi. from NH 16, where cars may be parked (sign).

The trail first follows an old gravel road that starts on the left side of the pit, 25 yd. beyond the trail sign, then swings right and then left uphill above and behind the open pit, passing through an overgrown section of the pit. At 0.2 mi., it crosses a snowmobile trail that follows the natural gas pipeline clearing. The trail enters the woods on the far side of the clearing (sign) and follows an old road (also a snowmobile trail) for 0.3 mi., bearing left twice. The trail turns right off this road (sign) and passes through a logged area, then swings left onto a small ridge (arrow) and ascends. At 1.3 mi., the trail descends briefly to a swampy saddle, enters the WMNF, and angles up the northwest slope of Pine Mountain, crossing several old logging roads. At 2.1 mi., there is a spur path leading 50 yd. left to a limited view to the north. At 2.3 mi., the grade eases and the trail swings left under utility lines; here an unmarked but well-trodden path ascends to the left and in 0.1 mi. reaches the north summit and the Horton Center worship area, where there is an excellent view from a rocky pinnacle called Chapel Rock. Hikers are welcome to enjoy the views and meditate, but are requested to avoid disturbing religious activities that may be in progress there. The main trail follows the utility lines for 60 yd., then bears right and ascends to a T-intersection with the old tractor road at 2.4 mi.; a right turn here leads to the Pine Mountain Rd. in 0.1 mi. Turning left here, the main trail ascends to the summit of Pine Mountain, passing two side paths left to eastern outlooks. From the viewless summit, where footings from an old fire tower remain, the Ledge Trail leads 0.1 mi. ahead to the south cliffs and excellent views.

Pine Mountain Trail (map 5:E10)

Distance from gravel pit on Promenade Rd. (825 ft.) to
- Pine Mountain summit (2,405 ft.): 2.7 mi., 1,650 ft. (rev. 50 ft.), 2 hr. 10 min.

Pine Mountain Road

This trail uses the private automobile road to the Horton Center on Pine Mountain most of the way to the summit of Pine Mountain. The road begins a little northwest of the highest point of the Pinkham B (Dolly Copp) Rd., opposite the Pine Link trailhead (where parking is available), 2.4 mi. from US 2 at the foot of the big hill west of Gorham and 1.9 mi. from NH 16 near Dolly Copp Campground. It is closed to public vehicular use and has a locked gate, but is open to the public as a foot trail to the summit; hikers should watch out for automobiles. The Ledge Trail, a foot trail over the top of the south cliff, diverges from the road and runs to the summit; it is frequently used to make a loop over the summit. The views from the summit area are fine, both to the much higher surrounding peaks and to the valleys of the Androscoggin, Moose, and Peabody rivers. The Douglas Horton Center, a center for renewal and education operated by the New Hampshire Conference of the United Church of Christ (Congregational), occupies a tract of 100 acres on the summit. The center consists of six buildings and an outdoor chapel on the more precipitous northeast peak (which has excellent views and can be reached by a spur path from the Pine Mountain Trail). Although camping is not permitted on this mountain, day-hikers are welcome to use the trails and appreciate the views but should be careful to avoid disturbing religious activities that may be in progress there.

The road runs northeast from Pinkham B Rd. across the col and winds its way up the south and west flanks of the mountain. At 0.9 mi., the Ledge

Trail branches right to climb to the summit by way of the south cliff. The road now climbs more steadily, and at 1.6 mi. from Pinkham B Rd., opposite the Spirit Lodge of the Horton Center, the trail turns to the right off the gravel road and follows the old tractor road, which joins the Pine Mountain Trail in 0.1 mi. The trail turns right here and ascends easily for 0.3 mi. to the summit, passing two spur paths leading to eastern outlooks. From the summit, the Ledge Trail continues ahead 0.1 mi. to the south cliff viewpoints.

Pine Mountain Road (map 1:E10)

Distances from Pinkham B (Dolly Copp) Rd. (1,650 ft.)
- to Ledge Trail (1,800 ft.): 0.9 mi., 200 ft. (rev. 50 ft.), 35 min.
- to Pine Mountain summit (2,405 ft.) via Pine Mountain Trail: 2.0 mi., 800 ft., 1 hr. 25 min.
- for loop to Pine Mountain via Ledge Trail with return via Pine Mountain Trail and Pine Mountain Road: 3.5 mi., 850 ft., 2 hr. 10 min.

Ledge Trail (WMNF)

This trail runs to the summit of Pine Mountain from the Pine Mountain Rd. (a private road, closed to public vehicles), making possible an attractive loop with a sporty ascent past excellent views and an easy return. It diverges from the Pine Mountain Rd. 0.9 mi. from the Pinkham B (Dolly Copp) Rd., ascends through woods to the base of the south cliff, then swings left and climbs steeply to the east of the cliff to its top, with beautiful views to the south and west. It then ascends gradually through woods, passing two side paths to outlooks on the right, and meets the Pine Mountain Trail at the wooded summit.

Ledge Trail (map 1:E10)

Distance from Pine Mountain Rd. (1,800 ft.) to
- summit (2,405 ft.): 0.6 mi., 600 ft., 35 min.

Town Line Brook Trail (RMC)

This good but steep path gives access to Triple Falls from Pinkham B (Dolly Copp) Rd., 1.9 mi. southeast of US 2. Triple Falls are beautiful cascades on Town Line Brook named Proteus, Erebus, and Evans. The watershed is steep and the rainwater runs off very rapidly, so the falls should be visited during or immediately after a rainfall.

Town Line Brook Trail (map 1:E10)

Distance from Pinkham B (Dolly Copp) Rd. (1,475 ft.) to
• the end of the path above Triple Falls (1,725 ft.): 0.2 mi., 250 ft., 15 min.

Sylvan Way (RMC)

The Sylvan Way departs from the Link at the east end of Memorial Bridge, 0.7 mi. from the Appalachia parking area, and leads over Snyder Brook to the Howker Ridge Trail just above Coosauk Fall (currently dry). Leaving Memorial Bridge, after 80 yd. it turns left away from Cold Brook at the base of Cold Brook Fall, where a beaten path continues ahead up the brook. The Sylvan Way crosses the Beechwood Way at 0.1 mi., the Air Line at 0.6 mi., and the Valley Way 100 yd. farther. At 0.7 mi., within a space of 30 yd., the Maple Walk enters left, the Fallsway crosses, the Sylvan Way crosses Snyder Brook on ledges 60 yd. above Gordon Fall, and the Brookbank crosses. From here, the Sylvan Way ascends gradually, crossing the Randolph Path at 1.1 mi. It then passes through a recently logged area, then enters the WMNF and continues to the Howker Ridge Trail.

Sylvan Way (map 1:E9)

Distance from Memorial Bridge (1,425 ft.) to
• Howker Ridge Trail (1,625 ft.): 1.7 mi., 250 ft. (rev. 50 ft.), 1 hr.

Fallsway (RMC)

The Fallsway is an alternative route to the first 0.6 mi. of the Valley Way, following close to Snyder Brook and passing several falls. From the east end of the Appalachia parking area it goes east for 60 yd., then turns right on a gravel road and crosses the Presidential Range Rail Trail and the power lines. Here the Brookbank diverges left as the Fallsway enters the woods and continues straight ahead. At 0.2 mi. from Appalachia, the path reaches Snyder Brook and soon passes Gordon Fall. In 60 yd., the Sylvan Way crosses and the Maple Walk enters right as the trail continues up the brook in hemlock woods. Lower and Upper Salroc Falls are passed, and soon the

Fallsway enters the Valley Way at 0.6 mi., below Tama Fall. In 30 yd., the Fallsway leaves the Valley Way and passes Tama Fall, where the Brookbank enters, and in another 60 yd., the Fallsway ends at the Valley Way.

Fallsway (map 1:E9)

Distance from Appalachia parking area (1,306 ft.) to
• Valley Way junction above Tama Fall (1,700 ft.): 0.7 mi., 400 ft., 35 min.

Brookbank (RMC)

The Brookbank follows the lower part of Snyder Brook on the opposite side from the Fallsway. It leaves the Fallsway on the left, 100 yd. from Appalachia, and follows the Presdential Range Rail Trail east for 0.1 mi. to a bridge over Snyder Brook. Across the bridge it turns right and in 70 yd. reaches a powerline. Here it turns right again and then in 20 yd. swings left and enters the woods. It runs up the east side of the brook, passing Gordon Fall, Sylvan Way, Lower and Upper Salroc Falls, and Tama Fall. Above Tama Fall, it recrosses the brook and reenters the Fallsway.

Brookbank (map 1:E9)

Distance from lower junction with Fallsway (1,310 ft.) to
• upper junction with Fallsway (1,675 ft.): 0.7 mi., 350 ft., 30 min.

Maple Walk (RMC)

The Maple Walk diverges left from the Valley Way, a few yards from the Appalachia parking area, and runs at easy grades to the junction of the Fallsway and the Sylvan Way just above Gordon Fall.

Maple Walk (map 1:E9)

Distance from Valley Way (1,310 ft.) to
• Sylvan Way and Fallsway (1,400 ft.): 0.2 mi., 100 ft., 10 min.

Beechwood Way (RMC)

This path runs from the Link 0.6 mi. from Appalachia to the Valley Way 0.9 mi. from Appalachia, just below its junctions with the Brookside and the Randolph Path. It follows a good logging road with moderate grades. It leaves the Link, crosses the Sylvan Way in 100 yd. and then the Air Line at 0.6 mi., and ends at the Valley Way.

Beechwood Way (map 1:E9)

Distance from Link (1,400 ft.) to
• Valley Way (1,850 ft.): 0.8 mi., 450 ft., 40 min.

SUGGESTED HIKES

For more information on suggested hikes, see p. ix.

Easy Hikes

Waterfall Hikes. On the north side of the Presidentials the RMC trail system provides access to a number of waterfalls and cascades. Although all these falls are essentially small, unspectacular cascades, they do provide pleasant walks along the banks of sparkling, splashing brooks. The dense trail network makes an almost infinite variety of walks possible—it is quite feasible to simply wander until one's capacity for the day is reached. Several easy trips are described here, and more possibilities are listed under Moderate Hikes.

Triple Falls [rt: 0.4 mi., 250 ft., 0:20]. These cascades on Town Line Brook can be visited in a very short trip on the fairly steep Town Line Brook Trail.

Fallsway Loop [lp: 1.5 mi., 400 ft., 0:55]. This easy loop via the Fallsway and Brookbank passes Gordon, Salroc, and Tama Falls.

Lower Howker Ridge Trail [rt: 2.0 mi., 650 ft., 1:20]. The lower part of this trail passes Stairs and Hitchcock Falls, as well as some smaller falls and the interesting little gorge called Devil's Kitchen.

Moderate Hikes

Pine Mountain. This small ledgy peak at the northeast end of the Presidential Range offers perhaps the best views in the region for the effort required. The main trail is a good gravel road, closed to public vehicular use but open to hiking. From the viewless summit, one should continue on the Ledge Trail 0.1 mi. to the south cliff outlooks [rt: 4.2 mi., 900 ft., 2:30]. This is an asset for people looking for smooth footing. Still, many hikers will prefer a shorter and more sporty ascent on the Ledge Trail to the south ledges [lp: 3.5 mi., 850 ft., 2:10].

The Bluff [rt: 5.4 mi., 950 ft., 3:10]. This fairly easy trip follows the Great Gulf Trail along the West Branch of the Peabody River to a viewpoint in the lower gulf.

Dome Rock Loop [lp: 4.0 mi., 1,500 ft., 2:45]. This fairly rugged trip offers good views from Dome Rock and several other open ledges. Follow Maple Walk and Sylvan Way to Howker Ridge Trail near Coosauk Fall, ascend the Kelton Trail, then descend the Inlook Trail past Dome Rock and return via Brookside, Valley Way, and either Fallsway or Brookbank. The Kelton and Inlook trails both have fairly steep sections with rough footing.

Waterfall Hikes. A good trip involving many waterfalls can be made by taking the Link and Amphibrach past Cold Brook Fall, and then making the side trips to the pleasant, broad Coldspur Ledges via the short eastern extension of the Monaway and to Spur Brook Falls via the Cliffway. One can return by the same route [rt: 4.8 mi., 1,300 ft., 3:05] or lengthen the trip by continuing to the end of the Amphibrach at the junction called the Pentadoi, then following the Randolph Path down to Valley Way, and soon diverging on either the Fallsway or Brookbank [lp: 5.3 mi., 1,700 ft., 3:30].

King Ravine [rt: 6.2 mi., 2400 ft., 4:20]. Although usually regarded as a route to the summit of Mt. Adams, this wild ravine, with its rugged scenery and its fascinating boulders and boulder caves, is a completely worthy objective in its own right. The shortest, easiest route to the ravine floor is via the Air Line, Short Line, and King Ravine Trail. It is also feasible to visit King Ravine as an extension of the waterfalls trip described earlier, following the Amphibrach to the Pentadoi and the King Ravine Trail from there to the floor of the ravine, then descending on the Short Line to the Randolph Path, Valley Way, and Fallsway or Brookbank [lp: 7.0 mi, 2,500 ft., 4:45].

The Howks [rt: 5.8 mi., 2,900 ft., 4:20]. This rugged trip affords excellent views from several ledges on the northern ridges of Mt. Madison. Take Pine Link to the Howker Ridge Trail and continue to the open summit of the highest Howk.

Mt. Jefferson via Caps Ridge Trail [rt: 5.0 mi., 2,700 ft., 3:50]. The Caps Ridge Trail has some fairly steep, rough sections, but the relatively short distance and elevation gain make this the route of choice to Mt. Jefferson for most hikers.

Strenuous Hikes

Note: On ascents of the Northern Peaks, one should never underestimate the potential severity of above-treeline weather, or the strenuousness of the usual elevation gain of more than 4,000 ft. Possible routes of ascent are nearly limitless, considering all the side trails and the variations and linkings they permit.

Mt. Madison. The easiest route to Madison is probably via Madison Spring Hut, using the Valley Way and Osgood Trail [rt: 8.4 mi., 4,100 ft., 6:15]. The Daniel Webster-Scout Trail [rt: 8.2 mi., 4,100 ft., 6:10] and the Osgood Trail [rt: 10.2 mi., 4,100 ft., 7:10] offer routes of somewhat greater difficulty, rougher, and much more exposed to weather. The Howker Ridge Trail is a beautiful, wild route, but is much rougher and requires some care to follow, particularly above treeline [rt: 9.0 mi., 4,750 ft., 6:55].

Mt. Adams. There are numerous direct routes to Mt. Adams, such as Lowe's Path [ow: 4.7 mi., 4,450 ft., 4:35] and the Air Line [ow: 4.3 mi., 4,500 ft., 4:25], not to mention the routes via Madison Hut; the most popular route via the hut combines the Valley Way, Gulfside Trail, and Lowe's Path [ow: 5.0 mi., 4,500 ft., 4:45]. The King Ravine Trail (including the variations afforded by the Great Gully Trail and the Chemin des Dames–Air Line combination) provides what are possibly the most scenic routes to the summit, but these are all extremely strenuous. One attractive route that is no more strenuous than the direct trails follows the Valley Way, the Scar Trail and Loop, and the Air Line, thereby including the fine ledge outlook called the Scar and the long, open knife-edged section of Durand Ridge [ow: 5.0 mi., 4,500 ft., 4:45]. Another route, perhaps a bit steeper and rougher than the direct routes, follows the Link, Amphibrach, Randolph Path, and Spur Trail to Thunderstorm Junction, passing the Knight's Castle, an unusual and spectacular viewpoint on the brink of King Ravine's cliffs [ow: 5.2 mi., 4,500 ft., 4:50].

Mt. Jefferson via Castle Trail [rt: 10:0 mi., 4,200 ft., 7:05]. This is a beautiful but strenuous route requiring some fairly difficult ledge scrambling on the spectacular Castles. The loop involving the Caps Ridge and Castle trails and the Link is scenic and very entertaining, but one must take into account the roughness of the Link with its numerous ankle-twisting holes between rocks and roots, requiring an adequate supply of energy and daylight [lp: 6.7 mi., 2,850 ft., 4:45].

Spaulding Lake [rt: 13.0 mi., 3,000 ft., 8:00]. This trip follows the Great Gulf Trail past cascades and pools to a tiny pond enclosed by high mountain walls.

SECTION THREE
The Franconia, Twin, and Willey Ranges

2

The central region of the White Mountains is a great wooded area studded with fine peaks, with no through-highways and only a few gravel roads near the edges. The vast expanses of unbroken forest compensate for mountains that are, except for the Franconia Range and the cliffs of Mt. Bond, generally less rugged than the Presidentials. The region is bordered on the west and northwest by US 3 (and I-93), on the north by US 302, on the east by NH 16, and on the south by the Kancamagus Highway (NH 112). Section Three includes the west and northwest portion of this central region, including the Franconia Range, Twin Range, and Willey Range. Most of the Pemigewasset Wilderness is also covered here. Please note that in this book the term Pemigewasset Wilderness is used strictly to refer to the officially designated Wilderness Area, not to the somewhat broader but less clearly defined area that has traditionally borne this name. Section Three is divided from Section Four, which covers the eastern portion of the central region, by the Wilderness Trail (described in Section Three), and by a continuation of the line of the Wilderness Trail east from its terminus at Stillwater Junction, over the plateau between Mt. Bemis and Mt. Willey, to US 302 in Crawford Notch. There are only two points of contact between trails described in Section Three and those described in Section Four: first, where the Cedar Brook Trail (Section Four) meets the Wilderness Trail, just east of the latter's crossing of the East Branch of the Pemigewasset River on a suspension bridge; and second, where the Carrigain Notch Trail (Section Four) meets the Wilderness Trail and Shoal Pond Trail at Stillwater Junction. All of Section Three is covered by the AMC's *Franconia–Pemigewasset Map* (map 2).

In this section, the Appalachian Trail (AT) follows the Liberty Spring Trail and the Franconia Ridge Trail over Little Haystack Mountain and Mt. Lincoln to Mt. Lafayette. It then runs along the Garfield Ridge Trail to Galehead Hut, passing close to the summit of Mt. Garfield along the way. After following the Twinway over South Twin Mountain and Mt. Guyot and passing near the summit of Zealand Mountain, it reaches Zealand Falls Hut, then takes the Ethan Pond Trail to US 302 in Crawford Notch.

FRANCONIA NOTCH AND THE FLUME

Franconia Notch lies between the Franconia Range on the east and the Kinsman Range and Cannon Mountain on the west. The region includes many interesting and accessible natural features such as Indian Head; Profile, Echo, and Lonesome lakes; and the Flume, the Pool, and the Basin. The most famous of all Franconia Notch features—the Profile (Old Man of the Mountain)—was destroyed by the natural forces that created it, gravity and erosion, in May 2003. The Flume and the Pool are described later; the others, which are west of US 3, are discussed in Section Five. From the Flume area north to Echo Lake, the valley bottom and lower slopes on both sides lie within Franconia Notch State Park. Information regarding trails and other facilities is available during the summer and fall tourist season at the Flume Visitor Center at the south end of the park, and throughout the year (except for the late-fall and early-spring "off-seasons") at the Cannon Mountain Tramway. Information is also available from the information center in Lincoln, located opposite the I-93 exit ramp. Hiker parking is available at the Flume Visitor Center, Basin, Lafayette Place, Old Man, Cannon Mountain Tramway, and Echo Lake parking lots. There is no parking at the AT crossing near the former Whitehouse Bridge site, which is now reached by the Whitehouse Trail from the hikers' parking lot on US 3 just north of the Flume Visitor Center. A paved bike path runs the entire length of the notch from the parking area at the Flume to the Skookumchuck Trail and is available for pedestrian use, though those on foot should be careful not to impede bicycle traffic unnecessarily. Concord Trailways has bus service from Boston at Logan Airport and South Station to Lincoln and Franconia, which may operate only on weekends. In summer, connections to trailheads can be made by using the AMC's Hiker Shuttle.

The Flume, one of the best-known features in the Franconia region, is a narrow gorge that can be reached from the Flume Visitor Center by graded trails or by an NHDP bus. A network of graded trails connects points of interest, and a boardwalk runs up through the Flume itself. It is open to visitors from about May 15 to October 15; there is an admission fee for the Flume and the Pool during this time. In the Flume, one can see broad ledges worn smooth by the action of the water and scoured by an avalanche in June 1883 that swept away the once famous suspended boulder. Avalanche Falls at the upper end is also worth visiting. The Pool is an interesting pothole formation in the Pemigewasset River, more than 100 ft. in diameter and 40 ft. deep; it can be reached by a path of about 0.5 mi.

from the visitor center. The Flume Path, Rim Path, Ridge Path, and Wildwood Path can be used to make a 2-mi. loop walk from the visitor center that visits the Flume, Liberty Gorge and Cascade, the Pool, and a view of Mt. Liberty and Mt. Flume. In winter, this is an easy, popular, and beautiful area to walk in, and there is no admission fee; however, several of the boardwalks are removed for the season, restricting access to some parts of the Flume.

GEOGRAPHY

The Pemigewasset Wilderness is a vast forested area surrounded by tall mountains and drained by the East Branch of the Pemigewasset River. A bit more than a century ago it was an untracked wilderness, but lumber operations in the period from about 1890 to 1940 left it a virtual wasteland, logged and burned almost to total destruction, often referred to as the "so-called Pemigewasset Wilderness." Though the birch forests that clothe its slopes in many areas still testify subtly to the devastation of the not-so-distant past, the beauty of the area is almost completely restored, and the act of Congress establishing the Pemigewasset Wilderness has once again officially entitled it to the name of Wilderness. The history of the logging, and of the railroads that made it possible, is recounted in C. Francis Belcher's *Logging Railroads of the White Mountains,* published by AMC Books, and *J. E. Henry's Logging Railroads* by Bill Gove, both out of print as of 2006.

The main part of the Pemigewasset Wilderness, north of the East Branch, is divided into two lobes by the long ridge of Mt. Bond.

The Franconia Range and the Twin Range are the two high ridges that form a great horseshoe enclosing the western lobe of the Pemigewasset Wilderness. This lobe is drained by Franconia and Lincoln brooks, which almost encircle the long wooded ridge called Owl's Head Mountain. Starting at the southwest end of the horseshoe and running almost due north, the main ridge rises over several lower mountains to the high peaks of the Franconia Range: Mts. Flume, Liberty, Little Haystack, Lincoln, and Lafayette, the high point on the ridge. Swinging around to the east, the ridge crosses Mt. Garfield, Galehead Mountain, and South Twin Mountain, passing its lowest point (other than the ends), about 3,400 ft., between Garfield and Galehead. Rising again to South Twin

Mountain, where a major spur ridge leads north to North Twin Mountain, the main ridge runs southeast to Mt. Guyot. Here another major spur, Zealand Ridge, runs east. Before Zealand Ridge comes to an abrupt end at Zealand Notch, another ridge runs north from it over the Little River Mountains, which consist of Mt. Hale and the Sugarloaves. From Mt. Guyot, the main ridge runs south over Mt. Bond and Bondcliff before dropping to the East Branch. To the east of the great horseshoe lies the Willey Range, forming the west wall of Crawford Notch and the east wall of the broad, flat eastern lobe of the Pemigewasset Wilderness. The Rosebrook Range is a lower northwest spur of the Willey Range. Running south from the Willey Range is the broad plateau that connects the Willey Range to the Nancy Range and Mt. Carrigain. Slopes rise steeply to this plateau from Crawford Notch, bearing the highest waterfalls in the White Mountains, then incline gradually westward into the Pemigewasset Wilderness.

The Franconia Range ranks second among the ranges of the White Mountains only in elevation. Its sharp, narrow ridge contrasts strikingly with the broad, massive Presidential Range. Once called "Great Haystack" on Carrigain's map of 1816, Mt. Lafayette (5,260 ft.) was renamed in honor of the Marquis de Lafayette in gratitude for his assistance in the War of Independence. The highest part of the ridge, from Mt. Lafayette over Mt. Lincoln (5,089 ft.) to Little Haystack Mountain (4,780 ft.), rises well above the treeline. This part of the ridge is a Gothic masterpiece. Especially when seen from the west (particularly from North Kinsman), it suggests the ruins of a gigantic medieval cathedral. The peaks along the high, serrated ridge are like towers supported by soaring buttresses that rise from the floor of the notch. Part of the ridge between Lincoln and Little Haystack is a knife-edge with interesting rock formations. To the south rise the sharp, ledgy peaks of Mt. Liberty (4,459 ft.) and Mt. Flume (4,328 ft.), which are connected to each other and to Little Haystack Mountain by long, graceful parabolic ridges. Both these peaks have very fine views in all directions, particularly to the east to rugged Mt. Bond and over the vast expanse of the Pemigewasset Wilderness. Eagle Cliff (3,420 ft.), a northwesterly spur of Mt. Lafayette, is remarkable for its sheer cliffs and for the "Eaglet," a detached finger of rock that can be seen best from the vicinity of the Cannon Mountain Tramway parking area. At the south end of the range, the ledges of Little Coolidge Mountain (2,421 ft.) overlook the town of Lincoln. There is no maintained trail to these ledges, but they can be reached by bushwhacking from Lincoln village.

The Twin Range is connected to the Franconia Range by the Garfield Ridge. This jumbled, mostly densely wooded ridge runs north from Lafayette, then swings to the east and culminates in the fine rocky peak of Mt. Garfield (4,500 ft.), which rises like a sphinx watching over the valleys of Franconia and Lincoln brooks to the south and provides one of the finest views in the White Mountains, including a spectacular panorama of the higher Franconias to the south. After passing Galehead Mountain (4,024 ft.), a wooded hump with an outlook over the Twin Brook valley from near the edge of its summit plateau, the ridge reaches South Twin Mountain (4,902 ft.), where the views from the open summit are similar to Garfield's and equally fine, but from a different perspective. The summit of North Twin Mountain (4,761 ft.) is densely wooded, but a ledge almost at the summit on the west and another a short distance northeast provide magnificent views. Haystack Mountain (2,713 ft.), also sometimes called the Nubble, is a small but very prominent rocky peak that rises sharply from the lower end of North Twin's north ridge; it has no maintained trail.

The main ridge now swings southeast, then south, crossing the bare summits of Mt. Guyot (4,580 ft.) and Mt. Bond (4,698 ft.), and then Bondcliff (4,265 ft.), the fine series of crags and ledges southwest of Mt. Bond. These three peaks, in addition to the spur of Bond called West Bond (4,540 ft.), command views unequaled in the White Mountains for their expansive vistas of forests and mountains with virtually no sign of roads or buildings. For example, from the summit of Mt. Bond only the summit buildings on Mt. Washington and the Loon Mountain ski slopes give visible evidence of human intrusion. Arnold Guyot was the geographer who made the first accurate map of the White Mountains, supplanting the previous best map, the work of Professor G. P. Bond of Harvard; thus, the most remote set of peaks in the White Mountains bear the names of these two pioneer mapmakers. Guyot himself named several important White Mountain peaks, including Mt. Tripyramid. Wherever there were mountains to be explored, Guyot could be found—there are also mountains named for him in several other ranges, including the Great Smoky

Mountains, the Colorado Rockies, and the Sierra Nevada of California. Even a crater on the moon bears his name.

The interior of the western lobe is a relatively narrow valley surrounded by steep slopes and occupied mainly by the long wooded ridge of Owl's Head Mountain (4,025 ft.), one of the more remote major peaks in the White Mountains, named for the shape of its south end. The summit is wooded, but the great western slide provides some very fine views up to the Franconia Ridge and the isolated valley of Lincoln Brook.

The high point of the Zealand Ridge, Zealand Mountain (4,260 ft.), is wooded and viewless, but there is a magnificent outlook from Zeacliff, which overlooks Zealand Notch and the eastern part of the Pemigewasset Wilderness from the east end of the ridge. Originally called the New Zealand Valley, presumably owing to its remoteness, the name was shortened to Zealand for the convenience of the railroad and post office. Much of Zealand Notch and the area to the north was reduced to a jumble of seared rock and sterile soil by a series of intensely hot fires around 1900. It has now made a reasonably complete recovery, a remarkable and outstanding testimony to the infinite healing powers of nature. Nowhere else in New England is there a better example of regeneration after disaster. At the height-of-land in Zealand Notch is Zealand Pond, which has beaver dams as well as outlets at both ends; its waters eventually flow to the sea in both the Merrimack and the Connecticut rivers.

The Little River Mountains, lying between the Zealand River and Little River, offer excellent and easily attained panoramas of the surrounding summits from Middle Sugarloaf (2,539 ft.) and North Sugarloaf (2,310 ft.). The steady growth of a fringe of trees around the summit of Mt. Hale (4,054 ft.) has been progressively obscuring what was once an extensive view from this peak—the highest summit of the range—which was named for the Rev. Edward Everett Hale, author of the well-known patriotic tale "The Man without a Country."

The Willey Range is a high ridge that rises sharply out of Crawford Notch. The ridge is rather narrow with steep sides, giving it a rugged appearance from many viewpoints, but its crest undulates gently for about 2.5 mi. with relatively broad summits and shallow cols. The main peaks (from south to north) are Mt. Willey (4,285 ft.), named for the family whose members were all killed by a landslide that swept down its east face in 1826; Mt. Field

(4,340 ft.), named for Darby Field, leader of the first recorded ascent of Mt. Washington; and Mt. Tom (4,051 ft.), named for Thomas Crawford, younger brother of Ethan Allen Crawford and fellow White Mountain innkeeper. All these peaks are wooded to the top, but Willey has fine outlooks to the east over Crawford Notch and to the south into the eastern lobe of the Pemigewasset Wilderness. Tom temporarily offers good views from two blowdown patches at the summit; a similar blowdown patch on Field is now completely grown up, though there is an outlook to the northeast. A westerly spur of the Willey Range ends abruptly at Zealand Notch with the cliffs of Whitewall Mountain (3,405 ft.). Easterly spurs Mt. Avalon (3,442 ft.) and Mt. Willard (2,865 ft.) offer fine views for relatively little exertion; actually, probably no other spot in the White Mountains affords so grand a view as Mt. Willard for so little effort. The Rosebrook Range continues northwest from Mt. Tom over Mt. Echo (3,084 ft.), Mt. Stickney (3,043 ft.), Mt. Rosebrook (3,004 ft.), and Mt. Oscar (2,746 ft.). There are no hiking trails on these peaks, but the summit ledges of Mt. Oscar, with magnificent views over the Zealand Valley, can be reached by following ski slopes of the West Mountain section of Bretton Woods Ski Area to a point near the summit of Mt. Oscar; the ledges are a short distance behind the top of the ski slopes.

Arethusa Falls and Ripley Falls are situated on brooks that flow down the steep west side of Crawford Notch; in times of high water, these waterfalls can be quite spectacular. Between them stands Frankenstein Cliff, named for Godfrey N. Frankenstein, an artist whose work in the White Mountains was once well known. A network of trails connects these features and affords the opportunity for a variety of shorter day hikes.

The interior of the eastern lobe is broad and relatively flat, with no important mountains, but Thoreau Falls, Ethan Pond, and Shoal Pond are interesting features. This region was the site of the most extensive logging in the White Mountains; in the wake of the devastation that resulted, part of the eastern lobe was commonly referred to as the Desolation region.

HUTS

For information concerning the AMC's huts or the Highland Center at Crawford Notch, including opening and closing schedules, contact the AMC's Reservations Office (603-466-2727) or visit www.outdoors.org/lodging.

Greenleaf Hut (AMC)

Greenleaf Hut was built in 1929 and is located at about 4,200 ft. at the junction of the Old Bridle Path and Greenleaf Trail on Mt. Lafayette, overlooking Eagle Lake. It is reached from US 3 via the Greenleaf Trail (2.7 mi.) or Old Bridle Path (2.9 mi.), and is 1.1 mi. from the summit of Mt. Lafayette and 7.7 mi. from Galehead Hut. The hut accommodates 48 guests and is open to the public from mid-May to mid-October (caretaker basis in May). Pets are not permitted in the hut.

Galehead Hut (AMC)

Galehead Hut, built in 1932 and completely rebuilt in between 1999 and 2000, is located at about 3,800 ft. on a little hump on the Garfield Ridge, near the Twinway and the Garfield Ridge, Frost, and Twin Brook trails. It is reached in 4.6 mi. from the Gale River Loop Rd. (FR 25 and FR 92) via the Gale River and Garfield Ridge trails. It accommodates 38 guests and is open to the public from mid-May to mid-October (caretaker basis in May). Pets are not permitted in the hut.

Zealand Falls Hut (AMC)

This hut, built in 1932, is located at 2,630 ft. beside Zealand Falls on Whitewall Brook, at the north end of Zealand Notch, near the Twinway and the Zealand and Ethan Pond trails. It is reached from the Zealand Rd. via the Zealand Trail and Twinway in 2.7 mi.; in winter Zealand Rd. is closed, which increases the approach walk to 6.5 mi. The hut accommodates 36 guests and is open to the public from early June to mid-October on a full-service basis, and on a caretaker basis for the rest of the year. Pets are not permitted in the hut.

The Highland Center at Crawford Notch (AMC)

Located on 26-acres of private land at the head of Crawford Notch, the Highland Center, opened in 2003, is a lodging and education center open to the public year-round. It is located at the site of the former Crawford House grand hotel on US 302, about 20 mi. west of North Conway and 8.5 mi. east of the traffic lights in Twin Mountain village. The Highland Center is a stop on the AMC's Hiker Shuttle routes during summer and fall.

The Highland Lodge contains 34 lodging rooms accommodating a total of 122 beds, including shared rooms with shared baths and private rooms with private baths. The adjacent Shapleigh Bunk House includes 16 beds in two bunkrooms, as well as a common room and pantry with refrigerator and microwave. Reservations are encouraged and may be made through the AMC's Reservations Office (603-466-2727). The center's construction uses energy-efficient materials and is designed to complement the landscape while paying tribute to the intriguing human history in Crawford Notch. Meals consisting of hearty mountain fare are served in a family-style setting.

A wide variety of educational programs and skills training for children, teens, and adults are offered at the Highland Center, aiming to help participants increase their understanding of the natural environment and gain proficiency in outdoor skills such as map and compass use or wilderness first aid. Day-hikers, backpackers, and other visitors can access trail and weather information at the center.

The Macomber Family Information Center, open during summer and fall, is located in the historic Crawford Depot, a former train station renovated by the AMC, and houses interpretive displays, an information desk, and a small store that stocks last-minute hiker supplies, guidebooks, the AMC's publications, and souvenir items. It is also a major stop and transfer point for the AMC's Hiker Shuttle, which operates during the summer and early fall, and serves as a depot for the excursion trains that run on the Crawford Notch line during the tourist season.

From the AMC's Crawford Notch property, many trails can be accessed, including the Mt. Willard Trail and the Avalon Trail. Parking next to the Macomber Family Information Center is limited to 30 minutes. Parking for overnight guests is located on the Highland Center property near the main building. Parking for the Crawford Path is available in the USFS lot (recreational permit required) located just off Mt. Clinton Rd. near its junction with US 302. Other trails easily accessed from the Highland Center include the Around-the-Lake Trail, Red Bench Trail, Saco Lake Trail, and Webster-Jackson Trail.

CAMPING

Pemigewasset Wilderness

Wilderness regulations, intended to protect Wilderness resources and promote opportunities for challenge and solitude, prohibit use of motorized equipment or mechanical means of transportation of any sort. In accordance with USFS Wilderness policy, the trails in the Pemigewasset Wilderness are in general maintained to a lower standard than trails outside Wilderness. They may be rough, overgrown, or essentially unmarked with minimal signage, and considerable care may be required to follow them. Camping and wood or charcoal fires are not allowed within 200 ft. of any trail except at designated campsites. Camping is prohibited within 0.25 mi. of the Lincoln Woods Trail and the East Branch of the Pemigewasset River (including islands) from the Kancamagus Highway up to the Wilderness boundary, and within 200 ft. of the East Branch from the Wilderness boundary up to the Thoreau Falls Trail crossing (including islands). Camping and fires are also prohibited within 0.25 mi. of 13 Falls Campsite, the former Franconia Brook Campsite, Thoreau Falls, Galehead Hut, Garfield Ridge Campsite, and Guyot Campsite (the last three facilities are outside, but less than 0.25 mi. from, the Wilderness boundary). Hiking and camping group size must be no larger than 10 people. Camping and fires are also prohibited above the treeline (where trees are less than 8 ft. tall), except in winter, when camping is permitted above the treeline in places where snow cover is at least 2 ft. deep, but not on any frozen body of water.

Forest Protection Areas

The WMNF has established a number of Forest Protection Areas (FPAs)—formerly known as Restricted Use Areas—where camping and wood or charcoal fires are prohibited throughout the year. The specific areas are under continual review, and areas are added to or subtracted from the list in order to provide the greatest amount of protection to areas subject to damage by excessive camping, while imposing the lowest level of restrictions possible. A general list of FPAs in this section follows, but because there are often major changes from year to year, one should obtain current information on FPAs from the WMNF.

(1) No camping is permitted above treeline (where trees are less than 8 ft. tall), except in winter, and then only in places where there is at least 2 ft. of snow cover on the ground—but not on any frozen body of water. The point where the restricted area begins is marked on most trails with small signs, but the absence of such signs should not be construed as proof of the legality of a site.

(2) No camping is permitted within 0.25 mi. of any trailhead, picnic area, or any facility for overnight accommodation such as a hut, cabin, shelter, tentsite, or campground, except as designated at the facility itself. In the area covered by Section Three, camping is also forbidden within 0.25 mi. of Thoreau Falls or within 200 ft. of Black Pond.

(3) No camping is permitted within 200 ft. of certain trails, except at designated sites. In 2006, designated trails included those portions of the Old Bridle Path, Falling Waters Trail, and Liberty Spring Trail that are not in Franconia Notch State Park (where trailside camping is absolutely prohibited); also the Bondcliff Trail from its junction with the Wilderness Trail to its second crossing of Black Brook. No camping is permitted within 0.25 mi. of the Lincoln Woods Trail or the East Branch of the Pemigewasset River (including islands) from the Kancamagus Highway up to the Wilderness boundary near the Franconia Brook Trail junction, or along Franconia Brook from its confluence with the East Branch to the second island (including islands). The one former exception to this rule, the Franconia Brook Campsite, has been moved to the east side of the East Branch, on the East Side Trail; it is dangerous to cross to the trails on the west side of the river at times of high water.

(4) No camping is permitted on WMNF land within 0.25 mi. of certain roads (camping on private roadside land is illegal except by permission of the landowner). In 2006, these roads included US 302 west of Bartlett, New Hampshire, the Zealand Rd. (FR 16), the Kancamagus Highway (NH 112), and the south branch of the Gale River Rd. (FR 92) from US 3 to the Garfield Trail trailhead.

Franconia Notch State Park

Camping and fires are prohibited in Franconia Notch State Park, except at Lafayette Place Campground (fee charged).

Established Trailside Campsites

During peak summer and fall periods, groups of six or more planning to use AMC-managed backcountry campsites are asked to use the AMC's group notification system. For more information, visit http://www.outdoors.org/lodging/campsites/campsites-notification.cfm.

Camp 16 Campsite (WMNF), located at the junction of the Wilderness and Bondcliff trails, has been closed, and camping within 200 ft. of either of the two trails is prohibited.

13 Falls Tentsite (AMC), located at the junction of the Franconia Brook, Lincoln Brook, and Twin Brook trails, has nine tent pads. A caretaker is present during the summer months, and a fee is charged. The former shelter has been removed.

Franconia Brook Tentsite (WMNF) is now located on the East Side Trail 2.6 mi. from the Kancamagus Highway. There are 24 tentsites; reservations can be made in advance or at the site itself. Stepping-stones cross the East Branch here, but this route to the trails on the west side of the river is dangerous at times of high water.

Guyot Campsite (AMC), located on a spur path that diverges from the Bondcliff Trail between its junction with the Twinway and the summit of Mt. Bond, has an open log shelter accommodating 12, with six tent platforms in addition. There is a fine spring that is reliable in summer but may not always flow in the cold seasons. A caretaker is in charge during the summer months, and there is a fee. This site is often crowded, with an overflow area in use, for much of the summer, particularly weekends.

Liberty Spring Tentsite (AMC), located near a fine spring on the Liberty Spring Trail 0.3 mi. below its junction with the Franconia Ridge Trail, has 10 tent platforms. A caretaker is in charge during the summer months, and there is a fee. The former shelter was removed in 1970.

Garfield Ridge Campsite (AMC), located near a fine spring on a short spur path from the Garfield Ridge Trail 0.4 mi. east of Mt. Garfield, has seven 4-person tent platforms and one 12-person shelter. A caretaker is in charge during the summer months, and there is a fee.

Ethan Pond Campsite (AMC) is located near the shore of Ethan Pond, about 2.8 mi. from the Willey House Station. There is a shelter (capacity 8) and five tent platforms (capacity 20). Water (which is not fit to drink without treatment) may be obtained where the side path crosses the inlet brook. A caretaker is in charge during the summer months, and there is a fee.

TRAIL DESCRIPTIONS

Franconia Ridge Trail (AMC)

This trail follows the backbone of the ridge that runs south from Mt. Lafayette, beginning on the summit of Lafayette at the junction of the Garfield Ridge and Greenleaf trails; passing over Mt. Lincoln, Little Haystack Mountain, Mt. Liberty, and Mt. Flume; and ending at a junction with the Flume Slide Trail and the Osseo Trail just south of Mt. Flume. Much work has been done to define and stabilize the trail and to reduce erosion; the late Guy Waterman and Laura Waterman, authors of many books on hiking and backcountry ethics in the Northeast, spent many hours observing each step taken by passing hikers to determine the best placement of individual rocks. Hikers are urged to stay on the trail to save the thin alpine soils and fragile vegetation. From Mt. Lafayette to the Liberty Spring Trail, this trail is part of the AT.

Caution: The portion of the Franconia Ridge above the treeline from Lafayette to Little Haystack does not involve any unusually difficult or hazardous climbing, but it is almost constantly exposed to the full force of any storms and is dangerous in bad weather or high winds. In particular, because of the sharpness, narrowness, and complete exposure to weather of the ridge crest on Lafayette, Lincoln, and Little Haystack, the danger from lightning is unusually great, and this portion of the ridge should be avoided when electrical storms appear to be brewing.

The following description of the path is in the southbound direction (away from Mt. Lafayette). See later for a description of the path in the reverse direction.

Leaving the summit of Mt. Lafayette, the trail descends at a moderate grade to the first sag, where it passes through a small scrub patch that might provide some shelter in bad weather. It then climbs across a prominent hump, descends to another sag, and climbs again to the summit of Mt. Lincoln at 1.0 mi. From there, it descends sharply, keeping mostly just to the east of the crest of the knife-edged ridge between Mt. Lincoln and Little Haystack Mountain, which has steep slopes on both sides. At the base of this knife-edged section, the ridge becomes nearly level and much broader, and the trail continues on the ridge crest in the open to the junction with the Falling Waters Trail on the right at 1.7 mi., just under the summit rock of Little Haystack Mountain

The Franconia Ridge Trail continues to the south end of the Little Haystack summit ridge, enters the scrub and descends steeply over ledges for a short distance, then moderates and follows the long, fairly gradual ridge to a junction with the Liberty Spring Trail on the right at 3.5 mi. There is water at Liberty Spring Campsite, 0.3 mi. down this trail. The Franconia Ridge Trail ascends over ledges to the rocky summit of Mt. Liberty at 3.8 mi., reaching the summit from the east, then makes a hairpin turn and descends to the east just a few yards south of its ascent route. The descent is steep at first, then moderates. The trail passes through two small sags and ascends to the open summit of Mt. Flume, then descends along the edge of the west-facing cliff (use extra caution in windy or slippery conditions) and enters the woods. It ends 0.1 mi. south of the summit of Flume in a little col, at the junction with the Osseo Trail straight ahead and the Flume Slide Trail on the right.

Franconia Ridge Trail (map 2:H5)

Distances from Mt. Lafayette summit (5,260 ft.) to
- Mt. Lincoln summit (5,089 ft.): 1.0 mi., 300 ft., 40 min.
- Falling Waters Trail (4,760 ft.): 1.7 mi., 350 ft., 1 hr.
- Liberty Spring Trail (4,260 ft.): 3.5 mi., 550 ft., 2 hr.
- Mt. Liberty summit (4,459 ft.): 3.8 mi., 750 ft., 2 hr. 15 min.
- Mt. Flume summit (4,328 ft.): 4.9 mi., 1,200 ft., 3 hr. 5 min.
- Flume Slide Trail–Osseo Trail junction (4,240 ft.): 5.0 mi., 1,200 ft., 3 hr. 5 min.

Franconia Ridge Trail (AMC) [In Reverse]

The trail begins 0.1 mi. south of the summit of Mt. Flume in a little col, at the junction with the Osseo Trail and the Flume Slide Trail. It climbs out of the scrub and ascends along the edge of the west-facing cliff (use extra caution in windy or slippery conditions). From Mt. Flume, it descends across a lesser knob, crosses two small sags, and climbs at a progressively steeper grade to the open summit of Mt. Liberty at 1.2 mi., reaching the summit from the east, then makes a hairpin turn and descends to the east just a few yards north of its ascent route. It then continues to descend across ledges into the woods and passes a junction with the Liberty Spring Trail on the left at 1.5 mi. There is water at Liberty Spring Campsite, 0.3 mi. down this trail. The trail continues down and then up the long, gradual ridge, becoming rather steep over ledges as it approaches the treeline on Little Haystack. At 3.4 mi., it reaches the junction with the Falling Waters Trail on the left, just under the summit rock of Little Haystack Mountain.

From Little Haystack the trail follows a broad, nearly level ridge crest in the open to the foot of Mt. Lincoln, then ascends sharply, keeping mostly just to the east of the crest of the knife-edged ridge between Mt. Lincoln and Little Haystack Mountain, which has steep slopes on both sides. After passing over the summit of Mt. Lincoln at 4.1 mi., the trail descends to a sag, climbs across a prominent hump, then descends to another sag, where it passes through a small scrub patch that might provide some shelter in bad weather. The trail then climbs at a moderate grade to the summit of Mt. Lafayette, where it meets the Greenleaf Trail on the left (west) and the Garfield Ridge Trail, which continues straight ahead along the north ridge.

Franconia Ridge Trail [In Reverse] (map 2:H5)

Distances from Flume Slide Trail–Osseo Trail junction (4,240 ft.) to
- Mt. Flume summit (4,328 ft.): 0.1 mi., 100 ft., 5 min.
- Mt. Liberty summit (4,459 ft.): 1.2 mi., 650 ft., 55 min.
- Liberty Spring Trail (4,260 ft.): 1.5 mi., 650 ft., 1 hr. 5 min.
- Falling Waters Trail (4,760 ft.): 3.4 mi., 1,350 ft., 2 hr. 25 min.
- Mt. Lincoln summit (5,089 ft.): 4.1 mi., 1,750 ft., 2 hr. 55 min.
- Mt. Lafayette summit (5,260 ft.): 5.0 mi., 2,200 ft., 3 hr. 35 min.

Flume Slide Trail (AMC)

This trail runs from the Liberty Spring Trail, 0.6 mi. from its junction with the Cascade Brook and Whitehouse trails, to the Franconia Ridge Trail 0.1 mi. south of the summit of Mt. Flume. It is an extremely steep, rough trail, with polished rock slabs that are extremely slippery when wet (and they are nearly always wet because of the many seep springs on these steep slopes). It is not recommended for descent, and its use is discouraged in wet weather when the ledges are more than ordinarily dangerous. Views from the trail itself are very limited, as it ascends a part of the old slide that is almost completely overgrown. The route over the slide is marked by paint on the ledges.

The trail leaves the Liberty Spring Trail on an old logging road that contours to the right (south). Soon the trail swings left off the logging road in a more easterly direction and begins a gradual ascent on the southwest shoulder of Mt. Liberty, with occasional slight descents. At 0.3 mi., it crosses a small brook, and about 0.1 mi. farther on, it crosses a large brook on stepping-stones. After rising from the brook bed, the trail climbs gradually, crossing several more small brooks. At 1.5 mi., the trail crosses a small brook, bears right after 40 yd., then turns left in another 20 yd., avoiding a beaten path straight ahead. At 1.9 mi., it crosses Flume Brook for the first time and follows it closely, making several more crossings of the main brook and its branches. In this region, the trail should be followed carefully; in general, it keeps close to the brook. As the trail ascends, it leaves the remnants of the brook behind, and slide gravel becomes more prominent underfoot. At 2.6 mi., there is a restricted view up to the summit crags of Mt. Flume. Now the climbing begins in earnest, and the first ledges are soon reached. (Beaten side paths run through the woods alongside the ledges and bypass some of the worst spots.) While on the slide, be careful not to dislodge stones that might endanger climbers below, and beware of rockfall from above. After struggling up the smooth, wet ledges with occasional outlooks, the trail turns left at 3.1 mi. and continues on a steep, rocky, rooty path through the woods to the main ridge crest, where the Franconia Ridge Trail leads left (north) and the Osseo Trail leads right (south). A few steps before this junction is reached, a rough beaten path (which may not be easy to discern and follow) leads 30 yd. right (south) to a small crag with an excellent view.

Flume Slide Trail (map 2:H4–H5)

Distances from Liberty Spring Trail (1,800 ft.) to
- foot of slide (2,850 ft.): 2.6 mi., 1,050 ft., 1 hr. 50 min.
- Franconia Ridge Trail (4,240 ft.): 3.3 mi., 2,450 ft., 2 hr. 55 min.

Liberty Spring Trail (AMC)

This trail climbs past Liberty Spring Campsite to the Franconia Ridge Trail 0.3 mi. north of Mt. Liberty. It begins on the Franconia Notch bike path just north of the bridge over the Pemigewasset River, near the site of the former Whitehouse Bridge (parking no longer available); the Cascade Brook Trail (Section Five) begins just south of this bridge. This trailhead is reached from the hikers' parking lot on US 3 just north of the Flume Visitor Center by the Whitehouse Trail and the parking area is a stop for the AMC's Hiker Shuttle. or from the Flume or Basin parking areas by the paved bike path. The trail ascends steadily and rather steeply at times, with some moderately rough footing. This trail is part of the AT.

From the bike path, the trail climbs moderately northeast through hardwood growth. At 0.4 mi., it turns sharp right, joining the old main logging road from the former Whitehouse mill, and soon levels off. At 0.6 mi., the Flume Slide Trail leaves right (south). The Liberty Spring Trail bears left, ascending gradually, and crosses a fairly large brook at 1.1 mi. It then climbs moderately, turns sharp left off the logging road at 1.4 mi., then turns sharp right at 2.2 mi. and climbs more steeply by switchbacks. In places the footing is rough. At 2.6 mi., the trail reaches Liberty Spring Campsite (3,800 ft.) on the left and the spring (last sure water) on the right. The path then ascends fairly steeply through conifers and ends in 0.3 mi. at the Franconia Ridge Trail; turn left (north) for Mt. Lafayette, right (south) for Mt. Liberty.

Liberty Spring Trail (map 2:H4–H5)

Distances from Whitehouse Trail (1,400 ft.) to
- sharp left turn (2,350 ft.): 1.4 mi., 950 ft., 1 hr. 10 min.
- Liberty Spring Campsite (3,870 ft.): 2.6 mi., 2,450 ft., 2 hr. 30 min.
- Franconia Ridge Trail (4,260 ft.): 2.9 mi., 2,850 ft., 2 hr. 55 min.
- Mt. Liberty summit (4,459 ft.) via Franconia Ridge Trail: 3.2 mi., 3,050 ft., 3 hr. 10 min.

Whitehouse Trail (AMC)

This trail connects the hikers' parking lot off US 3 just north of the Flume Visitor Center with the Liberty Spring Trail and the Cascade Brook Trail (Section Five), near the former parking area site at Whitehouse Bridge (where parking is no longer available). Thus, it is the usual route to these trails for hikers who arrive in the area by automobile.

The trail leaves the parking lot and runs north parallel to the main highway, passing over a minor ridge. It descends to the bike path at 0.6 mi. and follows it left to the junction with the Cascade Brook Trail, which diverges left just before (south of) the bridge over the Pemigewasset River. The Whitehouse Trail continues across the bridge and officially ends in another 50 yd. where the Liberty Spring Trail diverges right off the bike path.

Whitehouse Trail (map 2:H4)

Distance from Flume hikers' parking area (1,400 ft.) to
* Liberty Spring Trail (1,400 ft.): 0.8 mi., 100 ft. (rev. 100 ft.), 25 min.

Falling Waters Trail (AMC)

This trail begins at the Lafayette Place parking lots (located on each side of the Franconia Notch Parkway) and climbs to the Franconia Ridge Trail at the summit of Little Haystack Mountain, passing numerous waterfalls in its lower part. It is steep and rough in parts and better for ascent than descent, but not normally dangerous unless there is ice on the ledgy sections near the brook.

The trail leaves the parking lot on the east side of the parkway (reached from the west side by a paved path 0.1 mi. long) near the hiker information kiosk, in common with the Old Bridle Path, and passes through a clearing into the woods. In 0.2 mi., it turns sharp right from the Old Bridle Path and immediately crosses Walker Brook on a bridge, then leads away from the brook heading east, then turns south. At 0.7 mi., it crosses Dry Brook (use care if the water is high), turns left, and follows up the south bank to a beautiful cascade known as Stairs Falls. Above the falls, the trail passes beneath Sawteeth Ledges and crosses the brook to the north bank just below Swiftwater Falls, which descends 60 ft. in a shady glen, then climbs a steep rock staircase to the north bank and follows an old logging road that rises gradually in the narrow gorge of Dry Brook. The trail leaves the old road at a steep embankment and ascends more roughly to Cloudland Falls (80 ft.) at 1.3 mi. It then climbs steeply up the steep bank of the brook with a ledgy scramble to the top of the falls. Here there is a viewpoint looking out over the valley toward Mt. Moosilauke on the skyline.

At the head of Cloudland Falls are two small (25 ft.) falls practically facing each other. The one to the south, which emerges from the woods, is on the branch of Dry Brook that runs down from Little Haystack, while the other is on the Mt. Lincoln branch. The trail continues steeply on the north bank of the Mt. Lincoln branch, soon crosses to the south bank, crosses back to the north side, climbs to and follows an old logging road, and recrosses to the south bank at 1.6 mi. Here it swings to the right, away from the brook, and angles uphill on an old logging road. Soon the trail takes the left fork of the old road, then diverges to the left off the road and ascends the ridge via a series of switchbacks.

At the south end of the last switchback, at 2.8 mi., a side trail leads south downhill about 100 yd. to the northeast corner of Shining Rock, where there are fine views south and west over Franconia Notch. This steep granite ledge, more than 200 ft. tall and nearly 800 ft. long, is usually covered with water from springs in the woods above and, seen from the mountains across the notch, shines like a mirror in the sunlight. *Caution:* Climbing Shining Rock without rock-climbing equipment and training is extremely dangerous. This steep ledge is wet and very slippery; several accidents involving serious injuries have occurred here to hikers who tried to scramble up the rock.

From the Shining Rock spur junction, the main trail continues north for a short distance, then turns right and climbs in a nearly straight line to the Franconia Ridge Trail at the summit of Little Haystack.

Falling Waters Trail (map 2:H4–H5)

Distances from Lafayette Place parking area (1,780 ft.) to
- Dry Brook (2,000 ft.): 0.7 mi., 200 ft., 25 min.
- highest crossing of Dry Brook (2,860 ft.): 1.6 mi., 1,100 ft., 1 hr. 20 min.
- Shining Rock side path (4,130 ft.): 2.8 mi., 2,350 ft., 2 hr. 35 min.
- Franconia Ridge Trail (4,760 ft.): 3.2 mi., 3,000 ft., 3 hr. 5 min.

Old Bridle Path (AMC)

This trail runs from the Lafayette Place parking lots (located on each side of the Franconia Notch Parkway) to Greenleaf Hut, where it joins the Greenleaf Trail. It affords fine views, particularly down into and across Walker Ravine, from many outlooks in the upper half of the trail. For much of its length it follows the route of a former bridle path.

The trail leaves the parking lot (which is a stop for the AMC's Hiker Shuttle) on the east side of the parkway (reached from the west side by a paved path 0.1 mi. long) near the hiker information kiosk, in common with the Falling Waters Trail, and passes through a clearing into the woods. In 0.2 mi., the Falling Waters Trail turns sharp right and immediately crosses Walker Brook on a bridge, while the Old Bridle Path continues along the brook for 50 yd., then swings left away from the brook and starts to climb at a moderate grade. Old Bridle Path swings back to the right, and at 1.1 mi., it enters the WMNF (sign) and soon comes to the edge of the bank high above Walker Brook, then swings away again. At 1.6 mi., it makes a sharp left turn with rock steps at the edge of the ravine, where there is a glimpse of Mt. Lincoln through the trees, then turns right and soon gains the ridge. At 1.9 mi., the first of the spectacular outlooks from the brink of the ravine is reached, and several more are passed in the next 0.1 mi. The trail then begins to ascend the steep part of the ridge, sometimes called Agony Ridge (a name that originated with hut people who had to pack heavy loads up this steep section). In one pitch, the trail struggles up a steep basalt dike with somewhat slippery footing. At 2.4 mi., an unmarked side path diverges right, passes two fine outlooks, and rejoins the main trail 40 yd. above the lower junction. Still climbing, the main trail passes a view to Cannon Mountain, Kinsman Mountain, and Mt. Moosilauke from a grassy spot, then crosses a small sag through a patch of dead trees and soon reaches Greenleaf Hut.

Old Bridle Path (map 2:H4–H5)

Distances from Lafayette Place parking area (1,780 ft.) to
- sharp turn with rock steps (3,020 ft.): 1.6 mi., 1,250 ft., 1 hr. 25 min.
- Greenleaf Hut (4,220 ft.): 2.9 mi., 2,450 ft., 2 hr. 40 min.
- Mt. Lafayette summit (5,260 ft.) via Greenleaf Trail: 4.0 mi., 3,550 ft. (rev. 50 ft.), 3 hr. 45 min.

Greenleaf Trail (AMC)

This trail runs from the Cannon Mountain Tramway parking lot on the west side of the Franconia Notch Parkway to Greenleaf Hut, where the Old Bridle Path joins, and thence to the summit of Mt. Lafayette, where it ends at the junction of the Franconia Ridge and Garfield Ridge trails.

Until it reaches the hut, the trail is almost completely in the woods with few views, except when it traverses Eagle Pass, a wild, narrow cleft between Eagle Cliff and the west buttress of Mt. Lafayette that has many interesting cliff and rock formations.

From the parking lot, the trail follows a sidewalk through the parkway underpass, turns left and follows the northbound ramp for 25 yd., then turns right across a ditch into the woods (sign). It runs southeast roughly parallel to the parkway, crosses the gravel outwash of a slide at 0.7 mi., then climbs moderately by numerous switchbacks to Eagle Pass at 1.5 mi. The path leads east nearly on the level through the pass, where a boulder on the right offers a unique view of Cannon Cliff. It crosses a small overgrown gravel slide, then swings more to the south and rises by long switchbacks, angling up a northwest shoulder over loose stones that are slippery in wet weather. It finally reaches the top of the shoulder, passes a side path that descends on the right 100 yd. to a ledge with a view northwest, and continues a short distance to reach Greenleaf Hut at 2.7 mi.

At the hut, the Old Bridle Path enters on the right from Lafayette Place. The Greenleaf Trail heads toward Lafayette, enters the scrub, and dips slightly, passing south of the Eagle Lakes, two picturesque shallow tarns (though the upper lake is rapidly becoming a bog). The trail rises, passing over several minor knobs, and at 3.2 mi., swings left after passing an open, sandy area on the right. The trail soon climbs above the scrub into the open and ascends at a moderate grade, sometimes on rock steps between stone walls. At 3.6 mi., the trail bears left around a ledge on the right side of the trail from which a remarkable spring issues, very small but fairly reliable. Now the trail turns right and soon reaches the summit of Mt. Lafayette. Here the Garfield Ridge Trail leads north and then northeast to Mt. Garfield, Garfield Ridge Campsite, Galehead Hut, and the Twin Range. To the south, the Franconia Ridge Trail leads to Liberty Spring Campsite and the Franconia Notch Parkway via the Liberty Spring Trail, or to the Kancamagus Highway via the Osseo Trail.

Greenleaf Trail (map 2:G4–H5)

Distances from Cannon Mountain Tramway parking area (1,980 ft.) to

- Eagle Pass (2,980 ft.): 1.5 mi., 1,000 ft., 1 hr. 15 min.
- Greenleaf Hut (4,220 ft.): 2.7 mi., 2,250 ft., 2 hr. 30 min.
- Mt. Lafayette summit (5,260 ft.): 3.8 mi., 3,300 ft., 3 hr. 35 min.

Skookumchuck Trail (WMNF)

This is an attractive and less frequently used route from the Franconia Notch area to the north ridge of Mt. Lafayette, 0.8 mi. below the summit. It begins on US 3 at a parking lot that also serves the north end of the Franconia Notch bike path, located 0.3 mi. south of the junction of US 3 and NH 141 and just north of the point where US 3 divides at its northern junction with I-93 and the Franconia Notch Parkway.

Leaving the parking lot, the trail climbs away from the highway, crosses a snowmobile trail, and runs generally south, crossing a small brook at 0.6 mi. At 1.1 mi., it reaches the old route at the edge of Skookumchuck Brook and follows the brook upstream. At 1.8 mi., it crosses a small tributary on a rock bridge, climbs steeply away from the brook on rock steps, then continues up the valley well above the brook at a moderate grade through a fine stand of birch. At 2.5 mi., it passes a small brook (unreliable) and continues to a shoulder at 3.6 mi., where there is a glimpse ahead to Lafayette's north peak. After a short, gradual descent, the trail angles to the north at mostly easy grades, then emerges above the treeline just before reaching its junction with the Garfield Ridge Trail.

Skookumchuck Trail (map 2:G4–G5)

Distances from US 3 (1,700 ft.) to
- Garfield Ridge Trail (4,680 ft.): 4.3 mi., 3,000 ft., 3 hr. 40 min.
- Mt. Lafayette summit (5,260 ft.) via Garfield Ridge Trail: 5.1 mi., 3,550 ft., 4 hr. 20 min.

Garfield Ridge Trail (AMC)

This trail runs from the junction with the Franconia Ridge and Greenleaf trails at the summit of Mt. Lafayette to the Twinway near Galehead Hut, traversing the high ridge that joins the Franconia Range to South Twin Mountain and passing near the summit of Mt. Garfield on the way. The footway is rough, and there are numerous minor gains and losses of elevation, so the trail is more difficult than one might gather from a glance at the map. Extra time should be allowed, particularly by those carrying heavy packs.

The following description of the path is in the northbound direction (away from Mt. Lafayette). See later description of the path in the reverse direction.

The trail leaves the summit of Mt. Lafayette and runs north along the open ridge over the north peak, then descends steeply to a junction on the left with the Skookumchuck Trail on a shoulder at 0.8 mi. Swinging northeast, the Garfield Ridge Trail then drops steeply to timberline and continues to descend at a moderate grade near the crest of the ridge to a sag at 1.7 mi. From here, the trail passes over a series of knobs (one of which has a short but rather faint side path on the right that leads to a fine outlook over the Pemigewasset Wilderness on a large wooded hump). It descends the rough end of the hump to a tangled col at 2.5 mi., then climbs gradually toward Mt. Garfield. At 3.0 mi., near the foot of Garfield's cone, it passes to the right (south) of Garfield Pond, then climbs steeply, with many rock steps, to its high point on Mt. Garfield at 3.5 mi.; the bare summit and its old fire tower foundation, with magnificent views, is 60 yd. to the right (south) over open ledges. The trail then descends steeply, bearing right at 3.7 mi. at the junction where the Garfield Trail enters on the left from US 3. At 3.9 mi., where there is a small brook beside the trail, a side path runs left 200 yd. to the AMC's Garfield Ridge Campsite, passing a fine outlook over the Franconia Brook valley on the way. The main trail continues to descend steeply with one tricky section of wet ledge. It crosses a small brook and reaches a major col at 4.4 mi., where the Franconia Brook Trail leaves right and descends to 13 Falls. From this junction, the Garfield Ridge Trail runs along the bumpy ridge, sometimes north and sometimes south of the crest, with many ups and downs. After passing an outlook to Owl's Head Mountain and descending a steep pitch, it reaches the junction where the Gale River Trail enters from the left at 6.0 mi. The Garfield Ridge Trail now contours around the steep slope of Galehead Mountain, passing an outlook north, then turns right and climbs to a junction with the Twinway and the Frost Trail 40 yd. from Galehead Hut; turn right for the hut.

Garfield Ridge Trail (map 2:H5–G6)

Distances from Mt. Lafayette summit (5,260 ft.) to
- Skookumchuck Trail (4,680 ft.): 0.8 mi., 0 ft., 25 min.
- high point on Mt. Garfield (4,460 ft.): 3.5 mi., 1,000 ft., 2 hr. 15 min.
- Garfield Ridge Campsite spur path (3,900 ft.): 3.9 mi., 1,000 ft., 2 hr. 25 min.
- Franconia Brook Trail (3,420 ft.): 4.4 mi., 1,000 ft., 2 hr. 40 min.
- Gale River Trail (3,390 ft.): 6.0 mi., 1,300 ft., 3 hr. 40 min.
- Galehead Hut (3,780 ft.): 6.6 mi., 1,700 ft., 4 hr. 10 min.

Garfield Ridge Trail (AMC) [In Reverse]

From its junction with the Twinway and the Frost Trail 40 yd. from Gale-head Hut, the Garfield Ridge Trail descends moderately, then swings left and contours around the steep slope of Galehead Mountain, passing an outlook north, to the junction where the Gale River Trail enters from the right at 0.6 mi. From there, the Garfield Ridge Trail climbs a steep pitch to an outlook to Owl's Head Mountain, then runs along the bumpy ridge, sometimes north and sometimes south of the crest, with many ups and downs, to a major col at 2.2 mi. where the Franconia Brook Trail leaves left and descends to 13 Falls. From this junction the Garfield Ridge Trail ascends moderately, crosses a small brook, and soon becomes much steeper with one tricky section of wet ledge. At 2.7 mi., where there is a small brook beside the trail, a side path runs right 200 yd. to the AMC's Garfield Ridge Campsite, passing a fine outlook over the Franconia Brook valley on the way. The main trail continues to climb steeply past a junction at 2.9 mi. where the Garfield Trail enters on the right from US 3, and then reaches its high point on Mt. Garfield at 3.1 mi.; the bare summit and its old fire tower foundation, with magnificent views, is 60 yd. left (south) over open ledges. The trail then descends steeply, with many rock steps, and passes to the left (south) of Garfield Pond at 3.6 mi., near the foot of Garfield's cone. After descending gradually to a tangled col at 4.1 mi., it ascends the rough end of a large wooded hump and passes over a series of knobs (one of which has a short but rather faint side path on the left that leads to a fine outlook over the Pemigewasset Wilderness). It reaches a sag at 4.9 mi., ascends near the crest of the ridge at a moderate grade, then climbs steeply past the timberline to a junction on the right with the Skookumchuck Trail on a shoulder at 5.9 mi. It continues to climb steeply, following the open crest of the ridge to the north peak of Mt. Lafayette, then runs with easier grades to the main summit, where the Greenleaf Trail enters on the right and the Franconia Ridge Trail continues straight ahead.

Garfield Ridge Trail [In Reverse] (map 2:H5–G6)

Distances from Galehead Hut (3,780 ft.) to
- Gale River Trail (3,390 ft.): 0.6 mi., 0 ft., 20 min.
- Franconia Brook Trail (3,420 ft.): 2.2 mi., 350 ft., 1 hr. 20 min.
- Garfield Ridge Campsite spur path (3,900 ft.): 2.7 mi., 850 ft., 1 hr. 50 min. ▶

- high point on Mt. Garfield (4,460 ft.): 3.1 mi., 1,400 ft., 2 hr. 20 min.
- Skookumchuck Trail (4,680 ft.): 5.9 mi., 2,600 ft., 4 hr. 10 min.
- Mt. Lafayette summit (5,260 ft.): 6.6 mi., 3,200 ft., 4 hr. 55 min.

Garfield Trail (WMNF)

This trail runs from the Gale River Loop Rd. (FR 92) to the Garfield Ridge Trail 0.2 mi. east of the summit of Mt. Garfield, which is bare rock with magnificent views. Most of the way the trail follows an old road used for access to the former fire tower, and its grades are easy to moderate all the way to Garfield except for the short steep pitch on the Garfield Ridge Trail just below the summit. The trailhead is reached by leaving US 3 at a small picnic area 0.3 mi. south of its intersection with Trudeau Rd.; this intersection, often called Five Corners, has signs for Trudeau Rd. and for the Ammonoosuc District Ranger Station (which will be closed at some future date). Avoiding a right fork, follow the Gale River Loop Rd. south for 1.2 mi., then swing left and cross a bridge to a parking lot on the right. (Straight ahead on this road, it is 1.6 mi. to the trailhead for the Gale River Trail.) This trail lies within the watershed of a municipal water supply, and hikers and campers should take care not to pollute any of the streams in this watershed.

The trail begins at the parking lot, climbing an embankment and following the top of the north bank of the South Branch of the Gale River through fine woods with many large hemlocks. At 0.7 mi., it descends and swings to the right toward the river, meets the old fire tower access road, and turns left on it. The trail now climbs slowly away from the river heading generally south. It crosses Thompson and Spruce brooks and a snowmobile trail (which has bridges across the two brooks that flow close by on either side of the main trail in this area, potentially useful for avoiding some of these brook crossings in high-water conditions). The Garfield Trail then recrosses Spruce Brook at 1.2 mi.

At 2.8 mi., the trail crosses a ridge (once completely burned over and known as Burnt Knoll) and descends slightly. There is a fine birch forest in this vicinity that has grown up in the old burned area, particularly below the trail; above the trail, the growth is mostly coniferous, indicating that the trail may follow the approximate upper boundary of the old burn. Soon the trail re-

sumes its moderate ascent by several sweeping switchbacks in the mostly coniferous woods above the old burned area, and reaches a blowdown patch at
4.1 mi. Here it turns sharp left and climbs easily through an area of large conifers and then around the east side of the cone of Mt. Garfield to a junction
with the Garfield Ridge Trail, which enters from the left, ascending from Garfield Ridge Campsite. The summit of Garfield is reached in 0.2 mi. by turning
right and following the steep, rocky section of the Garfield Ridge Trail to its
high point, then scrambling over the ledges on the left for another 60 yd. to the
foundation of the old fire tower.

Garfield Trail (map 2:G5)

Distances from Gale River Loop Rd. (FR 92) (1,500 ft.) to
- Garfield Ridge Trail (4,180 ft.): 4.8 mi., 2,700 ft., 3 hr. 45 min.
- Mt. Garfield summit (4,500 ft.) via Garfield Ridge Trail: 5.0 mi., 3,000 ft.,
  4 hr.
- Garfield Ridge Campsite (3,900 ft.) via Garfield Ridge Trail: 5.0 mi., 2,700 ft.,
  3 hr. 50 min.

Gale River Trail (WMNF)

This trail runs from the Gale River Loop Rd. (FR 92) to the Garfield
Ridge Trail 0.6 mi. west of Galehead Hut. The trailhead is reached by leav-
ing US 3 at its intersection with Trudeau Rd.; this intersection, often called
Five Corners, has signs for Trudeau Rd. and for the Ammonoosuc District
Ranger Station (which will be closed at some future date). Follow the Gale
River Rd. (FR 25) southeast, bearing left at 0.6 mi., then turn sharp right
at 1.3 mi. on the Gale River Loop Rd. and continue to the parking area on
the left at 1.6 mi. (Straight ahead on the road it is 1.6 mi. from here to the
Garfield Trail parking lot.) The parking area is a stop for the AMC's Hiker
Shuttle. This trail lies within the watershed of a municipal water supply,
and hikers and campers should take care not to pollute any of the streams
in this watershed.

The trail enters the woods, soon descends a bank and crosses a tributary brook, then turns right on an old logging road that climbs easily along
the west side of the North Branch of the Gale River, some distance away
from the stream. At 1.4 mi., it comes to the edge of the stream, crosses it
at 1.7 mi. on large rocks near the site of a bridge that was washed away in

2005. It then becomes somewhat rougher, with several bypasses of muddy sections and washouts. The trail passes through an old logging-camp site, crosses a major tributary, and recrosses to the west side of the North Branch at 2.5 mi. on stepping-stones (difficult only in very high water). After passing the gravel outwash of an overgrown slide, the trail emerges at 3.1 mi. on a gravel bank above the stream at the base of a slide, where there are fine views up the valley and toward the Twins. The trail now becomes significantly steeper and rougher, and ends with a fairly steep climb to the Garfield Ridge Trail.

Gale River Trail (map 2:G5–G6)

Distances from Gale River Loop Rd. (FR 92) (1,600 ft.) to
- Garfield Ridge Trail (3,390 ft.): 4.0 mi., 1,800 ft., 2 hr. 55 min.
- Galehead Hut (3,780 ft.) via Garfield Ridge Trail: 4.6 mi., 2,200 ft., 3 hr. 25 min.

Frost Trail (AMC)

This short trail leads from Galehead Hut to the summit of Galehead Mountain. Leaving the hut clearing, it descends into a sag, then turns sharp right at a junction where the Twin Brook Trail enters left. After a short distance, the Frost Trail ascends a steep pitch, at the top of which a side path leads left 30 yd. to an excellent outlook over the Twin Brook valley. The main trail continues at a moderate grade to the rather flat and nearly viewless summit.

Frost Trail (map 2:G6)

Distance from Galehead Hut (3,780 ft.) to
- Galehead Mountain summit (4,024 ft.): 0.5 mi., 250 ft., 25 min.

Twinway (AMC)

This trail extends from Galehead Hut to a junction with the Zealand Trail and the Ethan Pond Trail 0.2 mi. beyond Zealand Falls Hut, forming a very important ridge crest link along the north edge of the Pemigewasset Wilderness that connects the mountains of the western part of the region—the Franconia Range, Garfield, and the Twins—to the Bonds, the Zealand-Hale region, the Willey Range, and the northern parts of the Pemigewasset Wilderness. The trail offers magnificent views from the summits of South Twin Mountain and Mt. Guyot and from the outlook at Zeacliff, and connecting trails lead to a number of other superb outlooks. For its entire length, it is part of the AT.

The following description of the path is in the eastbound direction (from Galehead Hut to Zealand Falls Hut). See later description of the path in the reverse direction.

From the junction of the Frost and Garfield Ridge trails 40 yd. from Galehead Hut, the Twinway passes over a ledgy hump, descends to a sag, then climbs steadily and steeply up the cone of South Twin to the south knob of the open summit at 0.8 mi. The North Twin Spur begins here, running straight ahead 40 yd. to the north knob and then on to North Twin, and the Twinway turns right (south), enters the woods, and descends along the broad ridge toward Mt. Guyot, with easy to moderate grades after an initial steep pitch below the summit. At 1.8 mi., the trail crosses a ledgy hump with views ahead to Guyot and Carrigain and back to South Twin. It descends easily to the main col between South Twin and Guyot, then climbs out of the scrub to open rocks on the side of Guyot and passes the junction with the Bondcliff Trail on the right at 2.8 mi. Guyot Campsite is 0.8 mi. from this junction via the Bondcliff Trail and a spur path.

The Twinway now turns left and ascends in the open to the flat northeast summit of Guyot at 2.9 mi., and, reentering the woods, descends at a moderate grade with some rough footing on the long ridge toward Zealand Mountain, reaching the col at 3.9 mi. It then climbs rather steeply, and at 4.1 mi., a few yards before reaching the height-of-land, passes a small cairn marking a side path on the left that runs nearly level 0.1 mi. to the true summit of Zealand Mountain. The main trail continues at mostly easy grades down the ridge, passes a ledge overlooking Zeacliff Pond at 5.1 mi., then descends a rather steep pitch with a ladder, and in a sag at 5.3 mi. passes a side path that leads off to the right and descends to the shore of Zeacliff Pond in 0.1 mi. The main trail ascends over a number of ledgy humps, passing the junction right with the Zeacliff Trail at 5.7 mi. It soon reaches a loop side path that leads to the right over the magnificent Zeacliff outlook and rejoins the main trail 50 yd. east of its point of departure.

Between the loop junctions, the Twinway climbs over a ledge with views that are good but greatly inferior to those from the Zeacliff outlook. At the farther loop junction, the Twinway turns left and descends moderately through a fine forest of birches. At 6.9 mi., the trail crosses two branches of Whitewall Brook on ledges, and the Lend-a-Hand Trail immediately enters on the left. The Twinway passes Zealand Falls Hut at 7.0 mi., where a short side path leads right to scenic ledges on Whitewall Brook. The main trail then descends steeply on rock steps for a short distance, passing a side path right to a viewpoint for Zealand Falls, then crosses the outlet of Zealand Pond and reaches the grade of the old logging railroad. Here the Zealand Trail turns left and the Ethan Pond Trail turns right, both on the railroad grade.

Twinway (map 2:G6–G7)

Distances from Galehead Hut (3,780 ft.) to

- South Twin summit (4,902 ft.): 0.8 mi., 1,150 ft., 1 hr.
- Bondcliff Trail (4,508 ft.): 2.8 mi., 1,350 ft., 2 hr. 5 min.
- Zealand Mountain summit spur (4,250 ft.): 4.1 mi., 1,650 ft., 2 hr. 55 min.
- Zeacliff Trail (3,700 ft.): 5.7 mi., 1,750 ft., 3 hr. 45 min.
- Zealand Falls Hut (2,630 ft.): 7.0 mi., 1,750 ft., 4 hr. 25 min.
- Ethan Pond Trail–Zealand Trail junction (2,460 ft.): 7.2 mi., 1,750 ft., 4 hr. 30 min.

Twinway (AMC) [In Reverse]

From the junction of the Zealand and Ethan Pond trails, the Twinway crosses the outlet of Zealand Pond, then climbs steeply on rock steps to Zealand Falls Hut at 0.2 mi., passing a side path left to a viewpoint for Zealand Falls. At the hut a short side path leads left to open ledges on Whitewall Brook. The Twinway then ascends moderately, passing a junction on the right with the Lend-a-Hand Trail just before it crosses two branches of Whitewall Brook on ledges, and continues to climb steadily through a fine forest of birches toward the crest of Zealand Ridge. At 1.4 mi., where the trail levels off and swings right, a loop side path continues straight ahead, passing over the magnificent Zeacliff outlook and rejoining the main trail 50 yd. west of its point of departure. Between the loop junctions, the Twinway climbs over a ledge with views that are good but greatly inferior to those from the

Zeacliff outlook. The Twinway passes a junction with the Zeacliff Trail on the left, then ascends over several ledgy humps and crosses a sag at 1.9 mi., where a side path leads off to the left and descends to the shore of Zeacliff Pond in 0.1 mi. The main trail ascends a rather steep pitch with a ladder to a ledge overlooking the pond, then continues along the crest of the ridge at mostly easy grades over several wooded knobs. At 3.1 mi., just after crossing the height-of-land on the last of these knobs, it reaches a small cairn marking a side path on the right that runs nearly level 0.1 mi. to the true summit of Zealand Mountain. The main trail descends sharply to a col, then climbs moderately up with some rough footing the long ridge to Mt. Guyot, breaking into the open just as it reaches that peak's flat northeast summit. It then descends a short distance over open rocks to the junction with the Bondcliff Trail on the left at 4.4 mi. Guyot Campsite is 0.8 mi. from this junction via the Bondcliff Trail and a spur path.

From this junction, the Twinway swings right and descends into the scrub, passes through the main col between Guyot and South Twin, and then begins the long, fairly gradual climb toward South Twin. At 5.5 mi., the trail crosses a ledgy hump with views ahead to South Twin and back to Guyot and Carrigain. After ascending a short steep pitch up the cone of South Twin, it reaches the south knob of the open summit at 6.4 mi. The North Twin Spur begins here, turning right and running 40 yd. to the north knob and then on to North Twin, while the Twinway turns left (west) and begins a steady steep descent toward Galehead Hut. At the bottom of this descent, it crosses a small sag, passes over a ledgy hump, and soon reaches a junction 40 yd. from the hut, where the Garfield Ridge Trail enters on the right and the Frost Trail continues straight ahead to the hut.

Twinway [In Reverse] (map 2:G6–G7)

Distances from Ethan Pond Trail/Zealand Trail junction (2,460 ft.) to
- Zealand Falls Hut (2,630 ft.): 0.2 mi., 150 ft., 10 min.
- Zeacliff Trail (3,700 ft.): 1.5 mi., 1,200 ft., 1 hr. 20 min.
- Zealand Mountain summit spur (4,250 ft.): 3.1 mi., 1,850 ft., 2 hr. 30 min.
- Bondcliff Trail (4,508 ft.): 4.4 mi., 2,400 ft., 3 hr. 25 min.
- South Twin summit (4,902 ft.): 6.4 mi., 2,950 ft., 4 hr. 40 min.
- Galehead Hut (3,780 ft.): 7.2 mi., 3,000 ft., 5 hr. 5 min.

North Twin Spur (AMC)

This trail connects the Twinway on the summit of South Twin with the North Twin Trail on the bare summit of North Twin. It leaves the Twinway at the south knob of South Twin, crosses the north knob in 40 yd., traverses an open shoulder, then descends moderately to the fern-filled col at 0.8 mi. Then it ascends to the summit of North Twin, where the North Twin Trail continues straight ahead and a spur path leads left 60 yd. to a fine outlook from the western edge of the summit area.

North Twin Spur (map 2:G6)

Distance from South Twin Mountain summit (4,902 ft.) to
  • North Twin Mountain summit (4,761 ft.): 1.3 mi., 300 ft. (rev. 450 ft.), 50 min.

North Twin Trail (WMNF)

This trail ascends to the summit of North Twin from Haystack Rd. (FR 304), which begins on US 3 about 2.3 mi. west of Twin Mountain village, just west of a large WMNF boundary sign, and runs south 2.5 mi. to a parking area just past its crossing of the Little River. *Caution:* The three crossings of the Little River on this trail are very difficult or impassable at high water; the third is the least difficult, and the first two can be avoided by staying on the east bank and bushwhacking along the river. This trail is in the watershed of a municipal water supply, and hikers and campers should take care not to pollute the streams.

The trail leaves the parking area and crosses the river three times, at 0.8 mi., 1.3 mi., and 1.9 mi., ascending easily on an old railroad grade with occasional bypasses. After the third crossing, the trail begins to climb away from the river and railroad grade, crossing and recrossing a tributary brook. The long, steady climb continues, and at 3.5 mi., the trail becomes quite steep, reaching the ledgy end of the ridge at 4.0 mi. The trail now climbs easily, passes a superb outlook ledge at 4.2 mi., and reaches the summit of North Twin at 4.3 mi. The North Twin Spur continues straight ahead to South Twin, and a side path leads right 60 yd. to a fine outlook from the western edge of the summit area.

North Twin Trail (map 2:G6)

Distances from Haystack Rd. (1,800 ft.) to
- third crossing of Little River (2,350 ft.): 1.9 mi., 550 ft., 1 hr. 15 min.
- North Twin summit (4,761 ft.): 4.3 mi., 2,950 ft., 3 hr. 40 min.

Zeacliff Trail (AMC)

This trail runs from the Ethan Pond Trail 1.3 mi. south of its junction with Zealand Pond to the Twinway 0.1 mi. west of the Zeacliff outlook. It is an attractive trail, much less frequently used than most trails in this area, but extremely steep and rough in parts and not recommended for hikers with heavy packs. Practically all of it is in the Pemigewasset Wilderness.

The trail leaves the Ethan Pond Trail and descends west over open talus, soon bearing right (northwest)—here the trail must be followed with care. It then bears left and drops very steeply through the woods to cross Whitewall Brook at 0.2 mi. It then climbs to the west very steeply, up an old slide at first. The grade eases at 0.6 mi., and soon the trail reaches the top of the ridge, where it ascends northwest gradually through a beautiful birch forest. It then angles along the left edge of the ridge crest, descends slightly, and scrambles up to the left of a ledge. It winds upward to the northwest through rough, ledgy terrain, then at 1.4 mi., it turns right and scrambles up steep ledges, with a view of Mt. Bond at the top. Above this point, the trail ascends moderately to the ridge crest and the Twinway. To reach the Zeacliff outlook, turn right at this junction.

Zeacliff Trail (map 2:G7)

Distance from Ethan Pond Trail (2,448 ft.) to
- Twinway (3,700 ft.): 1.4 mi., 1,450 ft. (rev. 200 ft.), 1 hr. 25 min.

Zealand Trail (WMNF)

The Zealand Trail runs from the end of Zealand Rd. to a junction with the Ethan Pond Trail and the Twinway just below Zealand Falls Hut. It is reached by following Zealand Rd. (FR 16), which leaves US 302 at Zealand Campground about 2.3 mi. east of Twin Mountain village, to a parking area on the left 3.5 mi. from US 302, just before a gate. The parking area is a stop for the AMC's Hiker Shuttle. Zealand Rd. is closed to public vehicular use from mid-November to mid-May, and at those times hikers and skiers must not park at the gate or along the highway, but must use the parking area across US 302 0.2 mi. east of Zealand Rd. The Zealand Trail is relatively easy, following an old railroad grade much of the way, and passing through an area of beaver swamps, meadows, and ponds, with views of the surrounding mountains. All major brook crossings have bridges, but the trip can be a very wet one in wet weather, and some of the bridges occasionally float away in floods.

Leaving the parking area, the trail follows the railroad grade for 0.2 mi., then a bypass that is somewhat rough. It then returns to the grade and approaches the Zealand River at 0.8 mi., near some ledges in the stream. Here it diverges right from the grade and continues on the west bank, then rejoins the grade and makes the first of several brook crossings at 1.5 mi. The trail now passes through an area of beaver activity, with a boardwalk at 1.8 mi. but otherwise staying mostly on the railroad grade, and at 2.3 mi., the A–Z Trail enters from the left. The Zealand Trail crosses the outlet brook and skirts Zealand Pond, ending at 2.5 mi., where the Ethan Pond Trail continues straight ahead on the old railroad grade and the Twinway turns right to Zealand Falls Hut, 0.2 mi. away.

Zealand Trail (map 2:G7)

Distances from end of Zealand Rd. (2,000 ft.) to

- A–Z Trail (2,450 ft.): 2.3 mi., 450 ft., 1 hr. 25 min.
- Ethan Pond Trail–Twinway junction (2,460 ft.): 2.5 mi., 450 ft., 1 hr. 30 min.
- Zealand Falls Hut (2,630 ft.) via Twinway: 2.8 mi., 650 ft., 1 hr. 45 min.

Lend-a-Hand Trail (AMC)

This trail connects Zealand Falls Hut with the summit of Mt. Hale, which offers some restricted views over trees that are steadily growing taller. The grade is fairly easy but the footing is rather rough for a good part of its distance, particularly for those trying to balance heavy packs, because there are a great many plank walkways across a very wet section. The trail takes its name from a journal for charitable organizations that was edited by Edward Everett Hale, the Boston pastor and author for whom Mt. Hale was named.

This trail diverges right (north) from the Twinway 0.1 mi. above Zealand Falls Hut and climbs steadily, crossing a small brook three times. After about 0.5 mi., the grade becomes easy in a long section with numerous plank walkways, where small brooks flow in and through the trail. At 1.5 mi., the trail enters a scrubby, ledgy area and ascends moderately. In a rocky area at 1.9 mi., an opening 30 yd. right of the trail offers a good outlook toward Carrigain Notch. At 2.4 mi., the trail climbs another rocky pitch and continues in dense conifers to the summit clearing, where the Hale Brook Trail leaves east (right). Many of the rocks around the former fire tower site are reputed to be strongly magnetic.

Lend-a-Hand Trail (map 2:G7–G6)

Distance from Twinway (2,730 ft.) to
- Mt. Hale summit (4,054 ft.): 2.7 mi., 1,300 ft., 2 hr.

Hale Brook Trail (WMNF)

This trail climbs from Zealand Rd. (FR 16), at a parking area 2.5 mi. from US 302, to the clearing at the summit of Mt. Hale, where there are restricted views over trees that have been steadily reclaiming the formerly bare summit in the more than 40 years since the fire tower was removed. The trail is relatively easy, with moderate grades and good footing, and passes through a very fine birch forest much of the way.

The trail leaves the parking area, crosses a cross-country ski trail, then ascends steadily to cross Hale Brook at 0.8 mi. The trail continues the steady climb, then swings left at 1.1 mi. and ascends gradually across the steep slope above Hale Brook, recrossing the brook in its rocky bed at 1.3 mi. Now the trail ascends by several switchbacks, crossing a small brook at 1.7 mi. Still ascending and curving gradually to the right, it enters the conifers and attains the summit from the east.

Hale Brook Trail (map 2:G7–G6)

Distance from Zealand Rd. (1,770 ft.) to
- Mt. Hale summit (4,054 ft.): 2.2 mi., 2,300 ft., 2 hr. 15 min.

Sugarloaf Trail (WMNF)

This trail ascends both North Sugarloaf and Middle Sugarloaf from Zealand Rd. (FR 16), just south of the bridge over the Zealand River 1.0 mi. from US 302. Parking is just north of the bridge. These two little peaks offer excellent views from their open, ledgy summits for a relatively small effort.

Leaving the road, the Sugarloaf Trail follows the river for 0.2 mi., coinciding with the Trestle Trail, then swings left as the Trestle Trail continues straight ahead along the river. After this junction, the Sugarloaf Trail immediately crosses a snowmobile trail and a logging road and climbs gradually, passing a few large boulders, where it turns sharp right (arrow). At 0.7 mi., it makes an abrupt ascent toward the notch between North and Middle Sugarloaf. In this notch, at 0.9 mi., the trail divides. The left branch traverses the flat ridge between the peaks for 0.2 mi., then turns sharp right and climbs by switchbacks to the summit of Middle Sugarloaf at 0.5 mi. from the notch, becoming very steep in the last ledgy section, which includes a ladder. The right branch descends slightly, circles the west side of North Sugarloaf, and then climbs to the ridge crest. Here, with an outlook to the left, the trail turns right and leads through scrub to open ledges at the south edge of the summit of North Sugarloaf at 0.3 mi. from the notch.

Sugarloaf Trail (map 2:F6)

Distances from Zealand Rd. (1,644 ft.)
- to Middle Sugarloaf (2,539 ft.): 1.4 mi., 900 ft., 1 hr. 10 min.
- to North Sugarloaf (2,310 ft.): 1.2 mi., 700 ft. (rev 50 ft.), 55 min.
- for round trip to both summits: 3.4 mi., 1,100 ft., 2 hr. 15 min.

Trestle Trail (WMNF)

This short loop trail begins and ends at the bridge over the Zealand River on Zealand Rd. (FR 16), 1.0 mi. from US 302. (Parking is at the north end of the bridge.) The trail leaves the road at the south end of the bridge and follows the river, coinciding with the Sugarloaf Trail for 0.2 mi. After the Sugarloaf Trail diverges left, the Trestle Trail leads away from the river, crosses a snowmobile trail, then turns sharp right at a large boulder to join and follow the snowmobile trail for a short distance. Then the trail turns sharp right on an old railroad grade, crosses the Zealand River at 0.6 mi. (may be very difficult or dangerous; the bridge at this crossing was washed out in 2005), and soon enters Sugarloaf II Campground. After following the campground road for 0.1 mi., it reenters the woods and returns to Zealand Rd. at the north end of the bridge.

Trestle Trail (map 2:F6)
Distance from Zealand Rd. (1,644 ft.) for
  • complete loop: 1.0 mi., 100 ft., 35 min.

Around-the-Lake Trail (AMC)

This trail provides an easy, scenic loop hike around Ammonoosuc Lake, a small, secluded alpine tarn located near the AMC's Highland Center at Crawford Notch and almost hidden unexpectedly close to the other more conspicuous and better-known Crawford Notch attractions. This short loop walk can be combined with other walks in the area or explored by itself for its natural beauty and its many historical reminders of the Crawford House, which epitomized the grand-hotel era of the 19th century.

The trail starts opposite the Highland Center at the turnaround and follows an old paved road downhill in a northerly direction. It turns left onto an old drive (sign), then bears right into the woods on an old grassy road. It then bears left onto a blazed trail, enters the WMNF, and reaches the loop junction at 0.3 mi. Taking the left (west) branch, the path crosses a brook on a plank bridge, dips past Merrill Spring (which often flows in winter), and runs along the west shore of the lake. At 0.6 mi., the Red Bench Trail, a spur path 0.3 mi. long, departs on the left (north) and runs parallel to the railroad, ascending gradually, then crosses the tracks diagonally and leads to a bench with an exceptional view of the Southern Presidentials. From the junction with this spur, the Around-the-Lake Trail bears right, passing the Down to the Lake Spur, a side path to a view of the Gateway of Crawford Notch, the deep cleft between Mts. Webster and Willard, from the north shore of the lake at the site of the former hotel's boat dock. The trail swings around the northeast shore, crosses a small dam and field at the outlet, follows an old road across a bridge and uphill away from the lake, and finally bears right into the woods back to the loop junction.

Around-the-Lake Trail (map 2:G8–G7)

Distances from Highland Center at Crawford Notch (1,900 ft.) for
- complete loop around Ammonoosuc Lake: 1.2 mi., 100 ft., 40 min.
- complete loop including Red Bench viewpoint: 1.8 mi., 150 ft., 1 hr.

Mount Willard Trail (NHDP)

This path runs from the AMC's Macomber Family Information Center (Crawford Depot), on the west side of US 302 across from Saco Lake, to the ledges above the cliffs overlooking Crawford Notch. The upper part was formerly a carriage road, and the trail has easy to moderate grades, good footing, and magnificent views from the ledges, offering perhaps the finest views in the White Mountains for effort required.

From the Macomber Family Information Center at Crawford Depot this trail coincides with the Avalon Trail for 0.1 mi., where it diverges to the left and runs on the level, crosses a small brook, then soon turns right to begin the ascent. In another 100 yd., the trail bears right, bypassing to the west a severely washed-out portion of the old carriage road. At 0.5 mi., the trail passes to the left of Centennial Pool, then bears left and at 0.7 mi. turns right, rejoining the old carriage road, which it follows the rest of the way to the ledges just east of the true summit.

Mt. Willard Trail (map 2:G8)

Distance from Macomber Family Information Center (Crawford Depot) (1,900 ft.) to
- Mt. Willard summit (2,800 ft.): 1.6 mi., 900 ft., 1 hr. 15 min.

Avalon Trail (AMC)

This trail runs from the AMC's Macomber Family Information Center (Crawford Depot) on the west side of US 302 to the Willey Range Trail 90 yd. north of the summit of Mt. Field, passing a short spur path to the fine outlook on Mt. Avalon along the way. Some parts of this trail are moderately steep and rough.

After 0.1 mi. from the information center, the Mt. Willard Trail leaves left, and the Avalon Trail ascends gradually and soon crosses Crawford Brook. Just beyond this crossing, a loop path diverges left, passes by Beecher and Pearl Cascades, and shortly rejoins the main trail. The Avalon Trail continues at an easy grade, recrosses the brook at 0.8 mi., and begins a moderate ascent. At 1.3 mi., the A–Z Trail to Zealand Falls Hut diverges right. The Avalon Trail soon begins to climb a steep, rocky slope, and at 1.8 mi., in the small col just below Mt. Avalon's summit, a short side path diverges left and climbs steeply 100 yd. to this fine viewpoint. The main trail passes through a flat, ledgy area, then climbs steadily, with restricted views to the northeast, then continues with easier grades to the Willey Range Trail. For the summit of Mt. Field, go left (south) 90 yd.

Avalon Trail (map 2:G8–G7)

Distances from Macomber Family Information Center (Crawford Depot) (1,900 ft.) to
- A–Z Trail (2,700 ft.): 1.3 mi., 800 ft., 1 hr. 5 min.
- Mt. Avalon spur path (3,350 ft.): 1.8 mi., 1,450 ft., 1 hr. 40 min.
- Willey Range Trail (4,280 ft.): 2.8 mi., 2,400 ft., 2 hr. 35 min.

A–Z Trail (AMC)

This trail runs to the Zealand Trail from the Avalon Trail 1.3 mi. from the Macomber Family Information Center (Crawford Depot), crossing the Willey Range at the Field-Tom col, and thus provides a route between Zealand Falls Hut and US 302 at the high point of Crawford Notch and access to the north end of the Willey Range from either starting point.

The A–Z Trail diverges right from the Avalon Trail and soon descends to cross a steep-walled gully, then climbs steadily, angling up along the side of the brook valley that has its head at the Field-Tom col. At 0.6 mi., the trail crosses the brook, swings right, and soon begins to climb more steeply. It bears left to reach the height-of-land at 1.0 mi., where the Mt. Tom Spur diverges right. The trail starts to descend gradually, and in 80 yd., the Willey Range Trail enters on the left. The trail now descends more steeply with rougher footing for 0.5 mi., then the grade eases. It crosses a snowmobile trail and two branches of Mt. Field Brook, traverses a long easy section with a slight ascent, and recrosses the snowmobile trail at 2.4 mi. It descends moderately through a beautiful birch forest, crossing several small brooks, then more steeply to cross a larger brook at 3.0 mi. It climbs over a low ridge and continues down at easy grades, skirting a beaver pond, and reaches the Zealand Trail 2.3 mi. from the end of Zealand Rd.; Zealand Falls Hut is 0.5 mi. left via the Zealand Trail and Twinway.

A–Z Trail (map 2:G7)

Distances from Avalon Trail (2,700 ft.) to

- Willey Range Trail (3,700 ft.): 1.0 mi., 1,000 ft., 1 hr.
- Zealand Trail (2,450 ft.): 3.7 mi., 1,100 ft. (rev. 1,350 ft.), 2 hr. 25 min.
- Zealand Falls Hut (2,630 ft.) via Zealand Trail and Twinway: 4.2 mi., 1,300 ft., 2 hr. 40 min.

Ethan Pond Trail (AMC)

This trail begins at the Willey House Station site in a parking area just below the railroad tracks, reached by a paved road 0.3 mi. long that leaves the west side of US 302 directly opposite the Webster Cliff Trail, about 1 mi. south of the Willey House site. It ends at the junction of the Zealand Trail and the Twinway, 0.2 mi. below Zealand Falls Hut. It is part of the AT.

The trail crosses the tracks and ascends on an old logging road, and the Arethusa–Ripley Falls Trail diverges left in 0.2 mi. The Ethan Pond Trail climbs steadily, then becomes more gradual, and at 1.3 mi., the Kedron Flume Trail enters on the right. At 1.6 mi., the Willey Range Trail leaves straight ahead, and the Ethan Pond Trail turns left and climbs steadily to the height-of-land at 2.1 mi., passing from Crawford Notch State Park into the WMNF. It enters and follows an old logging road down to a point close to the southeast corner of Ethan Pond, which however is not visible from the trail. This pond is named for its discoverer, Ethan Allen Crawford. Here, at 2.6 mi. from Willey House Station, a side trail on the right leads past the inlet of Ethan Pond, where there is a view of the Twin Range over the pond, then reaches Ethan Pond Campsite in 250 yd.

The Ethan Pond Trail now descends gradually with many plank walkways, passing through semi-open bogs and beautiful spruce forest. At 3.3 mi., it bears right onto a relocated section to the north, then rejoins the old route at 3.9 mi. At 4.4 mi., it bears right, then left onto a spur of the old Zealand Valley railroad, and follows it to the main line at 4.6 mi., where the Shoal Pond Trail enters from the left. At 4.9 mi., the Ethan

Pond Trail crosses the North Fork on a wooden bridge, and at 5.1 mi., the Thoreau Falls Trail diverges left to continue down the North Fork. The Ethan Pond Trail follows the old railroad grade on a gradual curve into Zealand Notch, with its steep, fire-scarred walls. As the trail crosses the talus slopes of Whitewall Mountain, it comes into the open with fine views, and at 5.9 mi., in the middle of this section, the Zeacliff Trail diverges left. The Ethan Pond Trail soon reenters the woods and continues on the remains of the railroad grade (which is badly washed out in places) to the junction with the Zealand Trail and the Twinway. For Zealand Falls Hut, turn sharp left onto the Twinway and follow it for 0.2 mi.

Ethan Pond Trail (map 2:H8–G7)

Distances from Willey House Station site (1,440 ft.) to
- Willey Range Trail (2,680 ft.): 1.6 mi., 1,250 ft., 1 hr. 25 min.
- side trail to Ethan Pond Campsite (2,860 ft.): 2.6 mi., 1,450 ft. (rev. 50 ft.), 2 hr.
- Shoal Pond Trail (2,500 ft.): 4.6 mi., 1,450 ft. (rev. 350 ft.), 3 hr.
- Thoreau Falls Trail (2,460 ft.): 5.1 mi., 1,450 ft. (rev. 50 ft.), 3 hr. 15 min.
- Zeacliff Trail (2,448 ft.): 5.9 mi., 1,450 ft., 3 hr. 40 min.
- Zealand Trail–Twinway junction (2,460 ft.): 7.2 mi., 1,500 ft., 4 hr. 20 min.
- Zealand Falls Hut (2,630 ft.) via Twinway: 7.4 mi., 1,700 ft., 4 hr. 35 min.

Kedron Flume Trail (AMC)

This trail runs from the Willey House site on US 302 to the Ethan Pond Trail 0.3 mi. south of its junction with the Willey Range Trail, passing Kedron Flume, an interesting cascade. As far as Kedron Flume, the trail has easy to moderate grades with good footing, but past the flume, it is very steep and rough.

Leaving US 302 south of the buildings at the Willey House site, the trail passes through a picnic area and enters the woods, climbing by switchbacks. At 0.4 mi., it crosses the railroad tracks, where there is a fine view of Mt. Willard. At 1.0 mi., after a short descent, it crosses Kedron Brook. Above is an interesting flume and below is a waterfall where there is an excellent outlook; use care on slippery rocks. Above here, the trail makes a very steep and rough climb, following a small brook part of the way, then becomes easier as it approaches the Ethan Pond Trail.

Kedron Flume Trail (map 2:G8)

Distances from Willey House site (1,300 ft.) to
- Kedron Flume (2,000 ft.): 1.0 mi., 700 ft., 50 min.
- Ethan Pond Trail (2,450 ft.): 1.3 mi., 1,150 ft., 1 hr. 15 min.

Willey Range Trail (AMC)

This trail begins on the Ethan Pond Trail 1.6 mi. from the Willey House Station site, then runs over the summits of Mt. Willey and Mt. Field to the A–Z Trail in the Field-Tom col. In combination with the Ethan Pond, A–Z, and Avalon trails, it makes possible various trips over the Willey Range to or from the Willey House Station site, Macomber Family Information Center (Crawford Depot), and Zealand Falls Hut. The section on the south slope of Mt. Willey is very steep and rough.

This trail continues straight ahead where the Ethan Pond Trail turns left, crosses Kedron Brook in 100 yd., and at 0.2 mi., turns sharp left and crosses a smaller brook. At 0.4 mi., it crosses another small brook, then climbs a very steep and rough slope with several new ladders, offering occasional restricted outlooks. The best view is from the east outlook, just before the summit of Mt. Willey, reached by an unsigned side path that leaves on the right 40 yd. below the summit cairn. The main trail reaches the summit at 1.1 mi. and circles around to the south outlook, which affords a sweeping view over the northeastern part of the Pemigewasset Wilderness. It then descends gradually, keeping mostly to the west side of the ridge and losing only 300 ft. in altitude at its low point, then climbs to the summit of Mt. Field, where there is an outlook to the northeast, at 2.5 mi. About 90 yd. north of this summit the Avalon Trail diverges right, and the Willey Range Trail climbs over a small knob and descends gradually northwest to the A–Z Trail just below the Field-Tom col at 3.4 mi. Turn left for Zealand Falls Hut, or right for the Mt. Tom Spur, Macomber Family Information Center (Crawford Depot), and US 302.

Willey Range Trail (map 2:G8–G7)

Distances from Ethan Pond Trail (2,680 ft.) to
- Mt. Willey summit (4,285 ft.): 1.1 mi., 1,600 ft., 1 hr. 20 min.
- Mt. Field summit (4,340 ft.): 2.5 mi., 1,950 ft. (rev. 300 ft.), 2 hr. 15 min.
- A–Z Trail (3,700 ft.): 3.4 mi., 1,950 ft. (rev. 650 ft.), 2 hr. 40 min.

Mount Tom Spur (AMC)

This short trail runs from the A–Z Trail to the summit of Mt. Tom. It leaves the A–Z Trail at the height-of-land, 80 yd. east of the Willey Range Trail junction, and climbs at easy grades with one somewhat steeper pitch to a false summit, where a side path on the right leads 70 yd. to an open blowdown area with views east and south. Here the main path swings left and reaches the true summit in another 60 yd. A blowdown patch near the summit will permit interesting views west and south into the Pemigewasset Wilderness for a few years.

Mount Tom Spur (map 2:G7)

Distance from A–Z Trail (3,700 ft.) to

- Mt. Tom summit (4,051 ft.): 0.6 mi., 350 ft., 30 min.

Arethusa Falls Trail (NHDP)

This trail is the direct route to Arethusa Falls, which is nearly 200 ft. high, the highest in New Hampshire. It begins at the Arethusa Falls parking lot, located on a spur road off the west side of US 302, 3.4 mi. south of the Willey House site in Crawford Notch State Park. (There is plenty of parking space in the lot just off US 302 if the upper lot spaces are full.)

The trail crosses the railroad and leads left (south) for 50 yd., then turns right into the woods. It soon passes a spur path left to some cascades, then follows old roads above the north bank of Bemis Brook. The Bemis Brook Trail, which diverges left at 0.1 mi. and rejoins at 0.5 mi., provides an attractive but rougher alternative route closer to the brook. Here the Arethusa Falls Trail turns right onto a relocated section, and in 50 yd. the new route swings left and climbs moderately on a well-constructed footway, following an old logging road. At 1.0 mi., it crosses the first of two bridges over tributary brooks. After the second bridge, it climbs steadily and swings right to meet the Arethusa-Ripley Falls Trail, 0.2 mi. above Arethusa Falls. Turn left and descend more than 100 ft. on a spur trail to reach the falls; for the best views, one must cross Bemis Brook, which is potentially difficult in the high-water conditions when the falls are most impressive.

Arethusa Falls Trail (map 2:H8)

Distance from Arethusa Falls parking area (1,240 ft.) to
- Arethusa-Ripley Falls Trail (2,120 ft.): 1.3 mi., 900 ft., 1 hr. 5 min.
- Arethusa Falls (2,000 ft.) via spur trail: 1.5 mi., 900 ft. (rev. 100 ft.), 1 hr. 10 min.

Bemis Brook Trail (NHDP)

This is a slightly longer and somewhat rougher alternative route to the lower part of the Arethusa Falls Trail, running closer to Bemis Brook. It departs to the left from the Arethusa Falls Trail 0.1 mi. from its start at the railroad, angles toward the brook, and then follows close to the brook, passing spur paths leading left to Fawn Pool, Coliseum Falls, and Bemis Brook Falls. It then climbs steeply up the bank to rejoin the Arethusa Falls Trail.

Bemis Brook Trail (map 2:H8)

Distance from leaving Arethusa Falls Trail (1,300 ft.) to
- rejoin Arethusa Falls Trail (1,700 ft.): 0.5 mi., 400 ft., 25 min.

Arethusa–Ripley Falls Trail (AMC/NHDP)

These two spectacular waterfalls in Crawford Notch are connected by a trail that starts at the upper end of the relocated Arethusa Falls Trail. From this junction a graded spur path angles southwest down the side of the valley 0.2 mi. to the base of Arethusa Falls; the best view of the falls is obtained by crossing Bemis Brook, which may be difficult at high water when falls viewing is best.

From the upper end of the Arethusa Falls Trail, the Arethusa–Ripley Falls Trail climbs to the west on the south side of a brook, which it soon crosses. Becoming rougher, it leads northeast across several small watercourses to the plateau behind Frankenstein Cliff. Turning east, the trail passes a southeast outlook and then the junction on the right with the Frankenstein Cliff Trail at 1.1 mi., where it turns sharp left and heads northwest across the plateau. The trail drops gradually and then more steeply, crossing a small brook, and follows a narrow rooty path across a steep slope to the top of Ripley Falls, which are about 100 ft. high. In dry weather, the water flow is rather low. The rocks just off the path near the falls are dangerously slippery and should be avoided. The trail descends a steep slope by switchbacks to cross Avalanche Brook at the foot of the falls at 2.3 mi. It climbs a short steep pitch, then descends gradually to the east with fairly rough footing to join the Ethan Pond Trail 0.2 mi. above the Willey House Station site, which is reached by continuing straight ahead.

Arethusa–Ripley Falls Trail (map 2:H8)

Distances from Arethusa Falls Trail (2,120 ft.) to

- Frankenstein Cliff Trail (2,420 ft.): 1.1 mi., 300 ft., 40 min.
- Ripley Falls (1,750 ft.): 2.3 mi., 400 ft. (rev. 750 ft.), 1 hr. 20 min.
- Ethan Pond Trail (1,600 ft.): 2.6 mi., 450 ft. (rev. 200 ft.), 1 hr. 30 min.
- Willey House Station site (1,440 ft.) via Ethan Pond Trail: 2.8 mi., 450 ft. (rev. 150 ft.), 1 hr. 35 min.

Frankenstein Cliff Trail (NHDP)

This trail provides access to Frankenstein Cliff, a prominent bluff that juts out from the tableland south of Mt. Willey and affords excellent views of the lower part of Crawford Notch. It begins at a spur road (prominently signed for Arethusa Falls) off the west side of US 302, 3.4 mi. south of the Willey House site in Crawford Notch State Park. There is plenty of parking space in the lot just off US 302 if the upper lot spaces are full.

Leaving the upper parking area, the trail runs north below and roughly parallel to the railroad grade with many minor ups and downs. At 0.1 mi., a green-blazed shortcut path 0.1 mi. long leading from the lower parking lot enters on the right. At 0.6 mi., the trail reaches the junction with a former route coming up directly from US 302, where the present trail turns sharp left and passes under the Frankenstein railroad trestle near the south abutment. (Trespassing on the railroad right of way, including the use of its bed as a footway, is extremely dangerous and is prohibited; the tracks are now actively used by excursion trains from May through October.) The trail ascends by switchbacks, steeply in places, with gravelly footing that is especially slippery on the descent. At 0.8 mi., it traverses below two cliff faces (use caution); when descending, avoid a beaten path leading left down a rocky gully beneath the lower cliff. The trail continues ascending through open hardwood forest, crossing a streambed where there is usually water. At

1.2 mi., after a scramble up a ledgy slot, the trail turns sharp left and continues through a fine forest of spruce and balsam to a cliff-top outlook similar to that on Mt. Willard, with a view south along the notch, at 1.3 mi.

Leaving the outlook, the trail ascends gradually through a fine stand of spruce in a west-northwest direction, skirting the top of the cliffs, with views of the valley and Mt. Bemis. At 1.5 mi., a spur path called the Falcon Cliff Trail diverges right and ascends north, first easily then more steeply, through a brushy hardwood area; then it turns sharp right, runs along the edge of a wooded bluff, and makes a short descent at 0.2 mi. to a partially open south-facing viewpoint on the top of a crag called Falcon Cliff, with a 200-ft. climb from the main trail. The main trail continues to ascend and passes just south of the summit of a small knob. At one point, there is a view of Arethusa Falls far up at the head of the valley. Near the height-of-land the trail levels off, passes an outlook to Mt. Washington over the Dry River Valley at 1.8 mi., then descends the ridge for a short distance and winds gradually downward to meet the Arethusa–Ripley Falls Trail.

Frankenstein Cliff Trail (map 2:H8)

Distances from the Arethusa Falls parking area (1,240 ft.) to

- Frankenstein Cliff outlook (2,150 ft.): 1.3 mi., 900 ft., 1 hr. 5 min.
- Arethusa–Ripley Falls Trail (2,420 ft.): 2.1 mi., 1,300 ft. (rev. 100 ft.), 1 hr. 40 min.

Lincoln Woods Trail/Wilderness Trail (WMNF)

The Lincoln Woods Trail runs for 2.9 mi. and the Wilderness Trail continues another 6.0 mi. along the East Branch of the Pemigewasset River, from the Kancamagus Highway (NH 112) to Stillwater Junction, forming the central artery from which numerous trails diverge and lead to various parts of the Pemigewasset Wilderness and to the adjoining mountains. Originally, the entire 8.9-mi. trail was called the Wilderness Trail, but the USFS changed the name of the first 2.9-mi. segment to Lincoln Woods Trail because that part of the trail lies outside the Pemigewasset Wilderness; for convenience the two trails are treated as one in the following description. For most of its length, the trail follows the bed of a logging railroad that last operated in 1948. It begins at a large parking area (Lincoln Woods) just east of the highway bridge over the East Branch, 5.6 mi. from the information center at the

I-93 exit in Lincoln and about 0.3 mi. beyond the Hancock Campground. This trail receives extremely heavy use, particularly in the few miles nearest the highway, and camping is strictly regulated. Details concerning such restrictions can be obtained at the Lincoln Woods Information Center, located next to the parking area, or from other USFS sources.

Leaving the parking lot, the Lincoln Woods Trail runs across the porch of the information center and descends a wooden stairway, swings left past a kiosk and crosses the East Branch on a suspension bridge, then turns right and follows the railroad bed, climbing almost imperceptibly. At 1.4 mi., the Osseo Trail diverges left. Soon the Lincoln Woods Trail comes close to the river's edge, and a fine view upstream to Mt. Bond can be obtained from the rocks just off the trail. At 2.6 mi., the Black Pond Trail leaves left. The former Franconia Brook Campsite (permanently closed to all camping) is situated on the left at 2.8 mi.; a new campsite, Franconia Brook East, has been constructed on the opposite side of the East Branch. Just before the bridge across Franconia Brook, a side trail leads north up the west bank 0.4 mi. to Franconia Falls, where the brook falls over broad ledges with many fine cascades and pools. Hikers wishing to visit Franconia Falls must obtain free permits (whose number will be limited) at the Lincoln Woods information center; these permits can also be reserved in advance.

The Lincoln Woods Trail crosses Franconia Brook on a footbridge. On the north bank a sign indicates a rough path leading to the right to a rock-hop crossing of the East Branch to the Pemi East Side Trail and the new Franconia Brook Campsite; this crossing is dangerous at times of high water and may require some wading at other times. About 50 yd. beyond the Franconia Brook footbridge, at 2.9 mi., the Franconia Brook Trail climbs the bank on the left (north). Here, at the Pemigewasset Wilderness boundary, the Lincoln Woods Trail ends and the Wilderness Trail begins. From this junction the trail bears right, bypassing a wet section of the railroad grade, then rejoins the grade and continues to swing to the east. It crosses a brook at 3.9 mi. and reaches the Camp 16 clearing (where camping is no longer permitted) at 4.7 mi. Here the Bondcliff Trail diverges left (north), and the Wilderness Trail crosses Black Brook on a footbridge to the left of the old railroad bridge. This bridge, the last railroad trestle of the East Branch line still standing, is the subject of a thorny administrative debate because it is both a nonconforming artificial structure in Wilderness, which by law must be removed, and an important historical artifact, which by law must be preserved. At 5.4 mi., the Wilderness Trail crosses to the south bank of the East Branch on a 180-ft. suspension bridge. On the far side, the Cedar Brook Trail (see Section Four) branches to the right (southwest).

Continuing upstream from the bridge, the Wilderness Trail now skirts the end of the long north ridge of Mt. Hancock, and just after crossing a small slide it reaches North Fork Junction at 6.3 mi., where the Thoreau Falls Trail diverges left (north) and the Wilderness Trail continues straight ahead. At 7.2 mi., the trail diverges from the railroad grade (which crossed the river here), crosses Crystal Brook, and soon rejoins the grade, which has crossed back to this bank. After passing through the clearing of Camp 18, the trail leaves the railroad for the last time at 8.0 mi., following a path along the bank that crosses a low, piney ridge and then descends to cross the Carrigain Branch (which may be difficult at high water) at 8.7 mi. Soon it reaches Stillwater Junction, coming into the junction at a right angle to the stream. Here the Carrigain Notch Trail (Section Four) leads right (southeast) to the Sawyer River Rd., and the Shoal Pond Trail crosses the stream directly ahead at an old dam (no bridge). (Avoid the path angling left down to the stream, which is an abandoned section of the Wilderness Trail.) Desolation Shelter, formerly located on the Carrigain Notch Trail 0.6 mi. from Stillwater Junction, was removed in 1997.

Lincoln Woods Trail/Wilderness Trail (map 2:I5–H7)

Distances from Kancamagus Highway (1,160 ft.) to
- Franconia Brook Trail and Pemigewasset Wilderness boundary (1,440 ft.): 2.9 mi., 300 ft., 1 hr. 35 min.
- Bondcliff Trail (1,600 ft.): 4.7 mi., 450 ft., 2 hr. 35 min.
- Cedar Brook Trail (1,640 ft.): 5.4 mi., 500 ft., 2 hr. 55 min.
- Thoreau Falls Trail (1,743 ft.): 6.3 mi., 600 ft., 3 hr. 25 min.
- Stillwater Junction (2,050 ft.): 8.9 mi., 900 ft., 4 hr. 55 min.

Pemi East Side Trail (WMNF)

This trail, a former truck road used to haul timber out of the Pemigewasset Wilderness in the 1940s, provides easy, scenic walking along the east and south sides of the East Branch of the Pemigewasset River. Hikers need to be aware that if they wish to cross the East Branch at any point other than on one of the two suspension bridges (the one near the start of the Lincoln Woods Trail or the one on the Wilderness Trail 5.4 mi. from the same point) or the rock-hop crossing near the Franconia Brook Campsite, they will probably have to ford the brook, which will often involve at least some easy swimming in the most favorable conditions but will undoubtedly prove dangerous or impossible at high water or in cold seasons. The trail begins at the Lincoln Woods parking area off NH 112 (the Kancamagus Highway), just east of the highway bridge over the East Branch and 5.6 mi. from the information center at the I-93 exit in Lincoln, and leads into the Pemigewasset Wilderness, ending at the Cedar Brook Trail, 0.6 mi. above the suspension bridge on the Wilderness Trail.

The first 2.8 mi. of this trail (also known as the East Branch Truck Rd., FR 87), up to a gate marking the Wilderness boundary, is a narrow gravel road occasionally used by USFS vehicles for administrative purposes but not open to public vehicular use. This section provides hikers access to the Franconia Brook East Campsite (24 sites) at 2.6 mi. The entire trail receives far less use than the parallel Lincoln Woods Trail and Wilderness Trail on the opposite side of the East Branch. An easy 11.1-mi. lowland loop can be made using the Pemi East Side Trail, Cedar Brook Trail, Wilderness Trail, and Lincoln Woods Trail.

Leaving the parking area, the trail runs across the deck of the Lincoln Woods information center and descends a short path to the gravel road, where it turns right. The road ascends gently, passing a spur logging road on the right at 0.2 mi. and a short side path left to the edge of the East Branch at 0.5 mi. At 0.6 mi., the Pine Island Trail diverges left and the Pemi East Side Trail makes a short, steep climb. It descends briefly at 1.0 mi. and meanders past small beaver meadows, passing the north junction with the Pine Island Trail at 1.4 mi.

The trail climbs over a knoll, and at 2.5 mi., a clearing on a bank above the river provides a view of the mountains to the west. After passing through the Franconia Brook Campsite area it reaches the gate and the Pemigewasset Wilderness boundary at 2.8 mi. Just before the gate a spur road descends left to a rock-hop crossing of the East Branch, and on the far bank of the river a rough path continues a short distance to the Wilderness Trail by the north end of the footbridge over Franconia Brook; this crossing is dangerous in high water and should not be attempted at such times.

Beyond the gate, the Pemi East Side Trail enters the Wilderness, swings east, and narrows to a footway. At 3.1 mi., a side path descends 25 yd. left to an attractive pool and cascade. The trail follows the East Branch closely, passing flat ledges fringing a pool at 3.4 mi., then pulls away from the river. The trail crosses Cedar Brook (difficult in high water) at 3.9 mi. and makes a sharp right turn at 4.0 mi. where an obscure trail joins from the left. The trail continues at easy grades through the woods, with occasional glimpses of the river, then bears right at 4.9 mi. and climbs moderately to the Cedar Brook Trail. To reach the Wilderness Trail and suspension bridge in 0.6 mi., turn left.

Pemi East Side Trail (map 2:I5-H6)

Distances from Kancamagus Highway (1,160 ft.) to

- gate at Wilderness boundary (1,420 ft.): 2.8 mi., 300 ft. (rev. 50 ft.), 1 hr. 35 min.
- Cedar Brook Trail (1,716 ft.): 5.1 mi., 600 ft., 2 hr. 50 min.

Pine Island Trail (WMNF)

This short trail provides pleasant walking along the East Branch of the Pemigewasset River, making possible an easy loop hike in combination with the Pemi East Side Trail. It leaves the Pemi East Side Trail on the left, 0.6 mi. from the Lincoln Woods parking area. It briefly follows an old logging road, then bears left to cross Pine Island Brook (may be difficult in high water) and a second, smaller brook. The trail soon swings right (north) and follows the wide, rocky river. After passing through a red pine grove it bears left, then right, and crosses a rocky brook bed at 0.6 mi.; a few steps left is a view upstream to West Bond and Bondcliff. The trail enters coniferous woods and continues along the river, then turns right and soon ends at the Pemi East Side Trail, 1.4 mi. from the Lincoln Woods parking area.

Pine Island Trail (map 2:I6)

Distance from south junction with Pemi East Side Trail (1,220 ft.) to

- north junction with Pemi East Side Trail (1,260 ft.): 0.9 mi., 50 ft., 30 min.

Distance from Lincoln Woods parking area (1,160 ft.) for

- loop via Pemi East Side Trail and Pine Island Trail: 2.9 mi., 100 ft., 1 hr. 30 min

Osseo Trail (AMC)

This trail connects the Lincoln Woods Trail with the south end of the Franconia Ridge, near the summit of Mt. Flume. It begins on the west side of the Lincoln Woods Trail, 1.4 mi. north of the parking area on the Kancamagus Highway. It heads west, following a brook in a flat area, then climbs the bank to the right and soon enters a section of an old incline logging railroad grade at one of its switchbacks. It continues up the valley on this grade and then on old logging roads not far above the brook. At 2.1 mi., it turns right and climbs by switchbacks to the top of the ridge above the valley to the north, then ascends the ridge—winding about at first, then climbing by zigzags as the ridge becomes steeper. At the top of this section are several wooden staircases, and at 3.2 mi., a side path (sign) leads right to a "downlook" with a very fine view of Mt. Bond.

Soon the trail reaches the top of the ridge, and its grade becomes easy until it reaches the crest of the Franconia Ridge in an unusually flat area at 3.7 mi. The trail turns sharp right here and ascends near the crest of a narrow ridge to a junction with the Flume Slide Trail on the left and the Franconia Ridge Trail straight ahead.

> **Osseo Trail (map 2:I6–H5)**
> Distance from Lincoln Woods Trail (1,300 ft.) to
> • Flume Slide Trail–Franconia Ridge Trail junction (4,240 ft): 4.1 mi., 2,950 ft., 3 hr. 30 min.
> Distance from Kancamagus Highway (1,160 ft.) to
> • Mt. Flume summit (4,328 ft.) via Lincoln Woods Trail, Osseo Trail, and Franconia Ridge Trail: 5.6 mi., 3,150 ft., 4 hr. 25 min.

Black Pond Trail (WMNF)

This short, easy spur trail leaves the Lincoln Woods Trail 2.6 mi. from the Kancamagus Highway and ends at Black Pond, where there is a view of the southwest slopes and ridges of Mt. Bond from the western shore. Diverging left (west) from the Lincoln Woods Trail, it first follows a former logging railroad spur, then leaves it on the left after 150 yd. and skirts the north shore of an old ice pond, which is in sight but not actually reached. Beyond the boggy pond, it skirts a beaver-flooded area and joins an old logging road, crosses the Camp 7 clearing (now overgrown by raspberries), and approaches Birch Island Brook, then bears slightly right away from it up a moderate incline. At 0.5 mi., it makes a short but sharp descent to cross the outlet brook from Black Pond, then recrosses it at a boggy spot. Soon it crosses the outlet brook for the third time and follows it to Black Pond, then skirts the southwest side of the pond and ends at the viewpoint.

Black Pond Trail (map 2:H6)

Distance from Lincoln Woods Trail (1,410 ft.) to
• Black Pond (1,590 ft.): 0.8 mi., 200 ft., 30 min.

Franconia Brook Trail (WMNF)

This trail runs from the Wilderness Trail 2.9 mi. from the Kancamagus Highway to the Garfield Ridge Trail 0.9 mi. east of the summit of Mt. Garfield, thus connecting the Pemigewasset East Branch valley with the Franconia-Garfield ridge crest. Practically the entire trail is in the Pemigewasset Wilderness. The many significant brook crossings might be difficult at high water.

It diverges north from the Wilderness Trail at a point about 50 yd. beyond the footbridge across Franconia Brook, at the boundary of the Pemigewasset Wilderness, and climbs up a steep bank to an old railroad grade, which it follows. It crosses Camp 9 Brook twice, and swings right at 1.0 mi. off the railroad grade to bypass a section flooded by an enthusiastic beaver colony. The trail crosses Camp 9 Brook again, turns sharp left back along the brook (avoid the beaten path leading ahead into the swamp) and climbs its bank, and soon rejoins the railroad grade, turning sharp right on it. In the reverse direction, take care to make the left turn off the railroad grade and the right turn, at the brook crossing. The trail continues to the junction with the Lincoln Brook Trail, which diverges left (west) at 1.7 mi.

The Franconia Brook Trail next passes to the left of several small beaver ponds and open swamps, with views of lower ridges of Mt. Bond to the east; in 2006, one short section of the trail was flooded by beaver activity, making necessary a bypass to the left across a beaver dam. It continues to ascend gradually on the old railroad grade, crossing Hellgate Brook at 2.6 mi., Redrock Brook at 3.6 mi., and Twin Brook at 4.7 mi., and passing through clearings at the sites of Camps 10, 12, and 13. At 5.2 mi., the trail reaches 13 Falls, a series of beautiful waterfalls and cascades, and turns right, leaving the old railroad grade on an old logging road. In 100 yd., the Lincoln Brook Trail reenters from the left (west), and in quick succession, a spur path leads right to 13 Falls Campsite and the Twin Brook Trail branches off to the right. The Franconia Brook Trail continues on an old logging road and crosses a branch of Franconia Brook at 6.2 mi., then climbs somewhat more steeply along old logging roads, often rather rough and muddy, to the top of the ridge, where it ends at the Garfield Ridge Trail in the deep col east of Mt. Garfield. Garfield Ridge Campsite is 0.6 mi. to the left (west) by the Garfield Ridge Trail and spur path; Galehead Hut is 2.2 mi. to the right.

Franconia Brook Trail (map 2:H6–G5)
Distances from Wilderness Trail (1,440 ft.) to
- Lincoln Brook Trail, south junction (1,760 ft.): 1.7 mi., 300 ft., 1 hr.
- 13 Falls Campsite (2,196 ft.): 5.2 mi., 750 ft., 3 hr.
- Garfield Ridge Trail (3,420 ft.): 7.4 mi., 2,000 ft., 4 hr. 40 min.

Lincoln Brook Trail (WMNF)

This trail begins and ends on the Franconia Brook Trail, and together these two trails make a complete circuit around the base of Owl's Head Mountain. The south junction is 1.7 mi. north of the Wilderness Trail, and the north junction is near 13 Falls Campsite, 5.2 mi. from the Wilderness Trail. *Caution:* Several of the brook crossings on this trail may be very difficult at high water. The entire trail is in the Pemigewasset Wilderness.

Turning left (west) off the Franconia Brook Trail, the Lincoln Brook Trail leads southwest through the woods above an area flooded by beavers, then descends slightly to join an old railroad bed just before the crossing of Franconia Brook at 0.5 mi. In another 0.4 mi., it crosses Lincoln Brook from the north to the south side.

These crossings, which are not easy even at moderate water levels and are particularly difficult at high water, can be avoided by bushwhacking along the west banks of Franconia and Lincoln brooks from Franconia Brook Falls, following old logging roads and anglers' paths part of the way. Another possible route involves bushwhacking due north from the end of the Black Pond Trail; this route rises easily through open woods, then descends a rather steep bank just before reaching the Lincoln Brook Trail. The Franconia Brook route merely requires one to follow the brook bank, while the Black Pond route requires some careful use of map and compass—although it is fairly easy to navigate going north toward Owl's Head (where it is relatively hard to miss the Lincoln Brook Trail entirely), it is somewhat more difficult to return to the pond (which is easily missed unless one follows the bearing very carefully).

Beyond the Lincoln Brook crossing, the Lincoln Brook Trail follows the brook upstream on a long northward curve, passing several small but attractive cascades. It crosses a small brook at 2.2 mi., soon joins an old railroad grade that is muddy in places, and then crosses the larger Liberty Brook at 2.8 mi. Soon it enters the Camp 12 clearing, climbs left to avoid a mudhole, rejoins the road, and crosses Lincoln Brook (sometimes difficult) to the east side at 3.0 mi. At 3.4 mi., it traverses the base of an old slide from Owl's Head (the principal access route to that remote summit), beyond which the Lincoln Brook Trail receives much less use. It crosses Lincoln Brook again at 4.3 mi. and continues north, crossing a divide into the Franconia Brook drainage with some glimpses of the northern Franconia Range behind (west) and Mt. Garfield to the north. Parts of the trail through and north of the divide may be rough and, in some seasons, quite wet, and considerable care may be required to follow it in this area. From the divide, the trail descends moderately to cross a west branch of Franconia Brook at 6.6 mi., then turns sharp right and follows a logging road down the north bank of this tributary past cascades and pools. It then swings to the right off the old road, passes waterfalls, crosses the main stream at an open ledgy area just above the confluence with the western tributary, and rejoins the Franconia Brook Trail near 13 Falls Campsite.

Lincoln Brook Trail (map 2:H6–H5)

Distances from Franconia Brook Trail, south junction (1,760 ft.) to
- Owl's Head slide (2,560 ft.): 3.4 mi., 800 ft., 2 hr. 5 min.
- height-of-land (3,200 ft.): 4.8 mi., 1,450 ft., 3 hr. 10 min.
- Franconia Brook Trail near 13 Falls Campsite (2,180 ft.): 6.9 mi., 1,450 ft. (rev. 1,000 ft.), 4 hr. 10 min.

Owl's Head Path

This unofficial, unmaintained path ascends the slide on the west side of this remote mountain, starting from the Lincoln Brook Trail 3.4 mi. from its south junction with the Franconia Brook Trail and 0.4 mi. beyond the second crossing of Lincoln Brook. (*Note:* Hikers often mistake Liberty Brook for Lincoln Brook, and thus think they have already passed the Owl's Head slide path when they arrive at the Lincoln Brook crossing that is about 0.2 mi. beyond Liberty Brook but still 0.4 mi. before the Owl's Head Path. At the slide, the main brook is nearby on the west and the steep mountainside rises immediately to the east.) At times, there have been cairns marking this junction, but USFS regulations prohibit the marking of unofficial paths in Wilderness, so hikers should be prepared to find the beginning of the path—and the path itself—without signs or other markings.

The path begins about 30 yd. before (south of) a mossy rock slide in the woods to the right. *Caution:* The slide is very steep and rough, and though considerably overgrown it is still potentially dangerous because of loose rock and smooth ledges, especially when wet. Great care should be taken both ascending and descending. Hikers who find the slide unappealing may be able to bushwhack up or down the steep slope to the north, parallel to the slide, through mostly open woods.

Leaving the Lincoln Brook Trail, the path climbs through dense evergreens, quickly reaching the open part of the slide, which provides good views of the Lincoln Brook valley and the Franconia Range. There is no well-defined path on the slide, but one or several routes may be marked by cairns of varying size, visibility, and usefulness. Open ledges more than halfway up the slide offer the best views and a convenient spot for a rest stop. At the top of the slide, 0.3 mi. and 700 ft. above the Lincoln Brook Trail, just after the trail enters the woods there is a small spring spurting from the rock like a fountain, which unfortunately is not completely reliable. After a steep and rough pitch on an old section of the slide track that trees have reclaimed, the trail exits to the left from the track. Above here, the well-trodden but very rough unmaintained path is frequently blocked for short distances by blowdowns; be careful to return to the path after passing these obstructions. The path climbs rather steeply up to the ridge, which is reached at 0.8 mi., then swings left and runs near the crest with minor ups and downs until it finally climbs a short pitch and abruptly reaches a tiny clearing at the wooded summit. This point, which has been regarded as the true summit for more than 40 years, has been proved in the past year or two to be slightly lower than several less peak-like points about 0.2 mi. farther north along the ridge. At present (fall 2006), there is no continuous path leading to the newly-established true summit, so hikers who wish to visit it must be prepared to bushwhack through dense growth and blowdown. For the present time, the AMC's Four Thousand Footer Committee will continue to recognize the knob where the well-beaten path currently ends as the official summit of Owl's Head. Excellent views are sometimes obtained from the summit area by ambitious tree climbers—if this summit were not densely wooded it would afford one of the finest views in the mountains because of its strategic location in the center of the great horseshoe formed by the ridge running from the Franconias to the Bonds.

Owl's Head Path (map 2:H5)

Distance from Lincoln Brook Trail (2,560 ft.) to
- Owl's Head summit (4,025 ft.): 1.0 mi., 1,500 ft., 1 hr. 15 min.

Distance from Kancamagus Highway (1,160 ft.) to
- Owl's Head (4,025 ft.) via Lincoln Woods Trail, Franconia Brook Trail, Lincoln Brook Trail, and Owl's Head slide path: 9.0 mi., 2,850 ft., 5 hr. 55 min.

Twin Brook Trail (AMC)

This trail connects 13 Falls Campsite to Galehead Hut, running almost entirely within the Pemigewasset Wilderness. It diverges from the Franconia Brook Trail near the campsite and rises gradually east-northeast, soon entering beautiful birch woods. At the start, take care to identify the trail at sharp bends, avoiding several old logging roads. After 0.4 mi. the trail swings to the northeast and heads up the valley of Twin Brook, keeping to the left (west) of the brook, which is occasionally audible but not visible. After traversing four distinct minor ridges of Galehead Mountain in the next mile, the trail eventually climbs more steeply to its terminus on the Frost Trail 0.1 mi. from Galehead Hut. For the hut, make a right turn onto the Frost Trail.

Twin Brook Trail (map 2:H5–G6)

Distances from 13 Falls Campsite (2,196 ft.) to
- Frost Trail (3,750 ft.): 2.6 mi., 1,550 ft., 2 hr. 5 min.
- Galehead Hut (3,780 ft.) via Frost Trail: 2.7 mi., 1,550 ft., 2 hr. 10 min.

Bondcliff Trail (AMC)

This trail begins on the Wilderness Trail at the site of Camp 16, 4.7 mi. from the Kancamagus Highway, ascends over Bondcliff and Mt. Bond, and ends at the Twinway just west of the summit of Mt. Guyot. It connects the Pemigewasset East Branch Valley with the high summits of the Twin Range, and the entire trail is in the Pemigewasset Wilderness except for a short segment at the north end. The long section on Bondcliff and one shorter section on Guyot are above the treeline, with great exposure to the weather. The views from this trail are unsurpassed in the White Mountains.

Leaving the Wilderness Trail at Camp 16, the Bondcliff Trail runs level for 100 yd., then turns sharp left just before a phantom crossing of Black Brook and climbs a bank to an old logging road. Soon it enters a relocated section (this relocation has eliminated four crossings of Black Brook). At 1.1 mi., after a slight descent, it bears left to rejoin the logging road along the brook and ascends easily, though parts of the road are severely eroded. It then crosses the brook four times; the second crossing, at 1.9 mi., provides the last sure water. At the third crossing, at 2.5 mi., the trail turns right and crosses the brook bed (often dry). In 40 yd.—a tricky spot—the trail reaches another brook bed (usually dry), descends along it to the right for 20 yd., then swings sharp left out of the brook bed and climbs a steep slope on rock steps. (Descending, the trail swings right at the bottom of the steps into the brook bed, ascends along it for 20 yd., then turns sharp left out of it.) The trail then swings left to another old logging road and crosses a gravel bank where one can look almost straight up to the summit of Bondcliff. In a short distance, it makes the last brook crossing in a steep, south-facing ravine; if the brook is dry here, water can often be found a short distance farther up in the streambed. The trail winds up a small, prow-shaped, "hanging" ridge that protrudes into the main ravine, then swings left at 3.2 mi. and begins a long sidehill ascent up the steep slope on a logging road, heading back to the southwest. At 4.1 mi., the trail reaches the crest of Bondcliff's south ridge, swings north, and ascends the ridge to a short, rather difficult scramble up a ledge. Soon it breaks out of the scrub and climbs along the edge of the cliffs, with spectacular views, reaching the summit of Bondcliff at 4.4 mi. *Caution:* The trail runs above the treeline for about a mile and is potentially dangerous in bad weather, particularly high winds. When visibility is poor, stay well to the right (east) of the edge of the precipices.

The trail now descends the open ridge into a long, flat col, then ascends the steep slope of Mt. Bond, reentering scrubby woods about halfway up. At 5.6 mi., the trail passes just west of the summit of Mt. Bond, which commands a magnificent unrestricted view of the surrounding wilderness and mountains. Here the trail bears left (northwest); in the reverse direction, it bears right (southwest) off the summit area. The trail descends north, crossing a minor knob, then drops down rather steeply past the spur path to West Bond at 6.1 mi., and leaves the Pemigewasset Wilderness. It reaches the Bond-Guyot col at 6.3 mi., where a spur path descends right (east) 0.2 mi. and 250 ft. to Guyot Campsite and its spring. The Bondcliff Trail then ascends to the bare south summit of Mt. Guyot and continues in the open 0.2 mi. to its junction with the Twinway 0.1 mi. west of the higher, but less open, north summit of Guyot. Go straight ahead here for the Twins and Galehead Hut, or turn right for Zealand Mountain and Zealand Falls Hut.

Bondcliff Trail (map 2:H6)

Distances from Wilderness Trail (1,600 ft.) to
- Bondcliff summit (4,265 ft.): 4.4 mi., 2,750 ft. (rev. 100 ft.), 3 hr. 35 min.
- Mt. Bond summit (4,698 ft.): 5.6 mi., 3,400 ft. (rev. 200 ft.), 4 hr. 30 min.
- Guyot Campsite spur (4,360 ft.): 6.3 mi., 3,450 ft. (rev. 400 ft.), 4 hr. 50 min.
- Twinway (4,508 ft.): 6.9 mi., 3,650 ft. (rev. 50 ft.), 5 hr. 15 min.

West Bond Spur (AMC)

This short path provides access to the sharp rocky summit of the West Peak of Mt. Bond, which is perched high above the deep valleys of an extensive wilderness area, commanding magnificent views. The entire trail is in the Pemigewasset Wilderness. It leaves the Bondcliff Trail 0.6 mi. north of the summit of Mt. Bond and 0.2 mi. south of the spur to Guyot Campsite, descends moderately for 0.3 mi. to the col at the foot of West Bond, and ascends moderately for a short distance. It then climbs the steep cone to the summit, which is the most easterly of several small peaks on a ridge running east and west.

West Bond Spur (map 2:H6)
Distance from Bondcliff Trail (4,500 ft.) to
• West Bond summit (4,540 ft.): 0.5 mi., 200 ft. (rev. 150 ft.), 20 min.

Thoreau Falls Trail (WMNF)

This trail runs from the Wilderness Trail at North Fork Junction, 6.3 mi. from the Kancamagus Highway, past Thoreau Falls to the Ethan Pond Trail roughly halfway between Ethan Pond Campsite and Zealand Falls Hut. Much of it follows an old railroad grade, but there are a few rather steep and rough sections. Practically the entire trail is in the Pemigewasset Wilderness.

The trail diverges left (north) from the Wilderness Trail on a railroad bed, which it leaves after 0.4 mi. to cross the East Branch of the Pemigewasset on a 60-ft. bridge, then the trail returns to the railroad bed and follows it along the North Fork. At 2.1 mi., the trail leaves the railroad grade for good and soon turns right and climbs, using a bypass that avoids two former crossings of the North Fork. Descending to rejoin the old route at 2.9 mi., it follows a logging road, then leaves it on the left at 3.6 mi. and soon becomes rougher and steeper, reaching a ledge next to the North Fork at 4.0 mi. The trail approaches Thoreau Falls and climbs steeply on a rough footpath to the right of the falls, which are beautiful when there is a good flow of water. It crosses the North Fork at the top of the falls (use caution) at 5.0 mi., where there is a fine view up to Mts. Bond and Guyot. (In high water, there may be a better and safer brook crossing just upstream from the trail.) Leaving the stream, the trail soon ends at the Ethan Pond Trail, about 0.2 mi. west of the latter's bridge over the North Fork. Turn left for Zealand Falls Hut or right for Ethan Pond Shelter.

Thoreau Falls Trail (map 2:H6–G7)
Distance from Wilderness Trail (1,743 ft.) to
• Ethan Pond Trail (2,460 ft.): 5.1 mi., 750 ft. (rev. 50 ft.), 2 hr. 55 min.

Shoal Pond Trail (AMC)

This trail runs through remote, wild country from its junction with the Wilderness Trail and the Carrigain Notch Trail (see Section Four) at Stillwater Junction to the Ethan Pond Trail between Zealand Falls Hut and Ethan Pond Campsite. Practically the entire trail is in the Pemigewasset Wilderness.

At Stillwater Junction, the trail leads across the East Branch at the site of an old dam (no bridge; may be difficult in moderate water and dangerous in high water), turns left on a railroad bed and almost immediately leaves it on the right, then soon bears right onto another railroad bed. Leaving the railroad temporarily, the trail crosses Shoal Pond Brook at 0.6 mi.; this crossing may be difficult if the water is high. The trail regains the railroad bed and passes a spur path on the right at 1.0 mi. that leads to a pleasant pool in the brook. At 1.2 mi., it bears left off the railroad bed and follows logging roads, crossing Shoal Pond Brook from west to east at 1.4 mi. It crosses a tributary at 1.7 mi. and recrosses Shoal Pond Brook at 2.4 mi. At 3.2 mi., the trail crosses the brook for the last time, from west to east, and soon reaches Shoal Pond. Because of bogginess caused by beaver activity, the trail runs a short distance to the east of the pond, keeping away from its immediate vicinity, but a short side path at 3.5 mi. leads to the south shore of the pond and a view of Zealand Notch. The trail passes another short side path to the shore and continues on an old railroad grade to the Ethan Pond Trail.

Shoal Pond Trail (map 2:H7–G7)

Distances from Stillwater Junction (2,050 ft.) to
- Shoal Pond (2,550 ft.): 3.3 mi., 500 ft., 1 hr. 55 min.
- Ethan Pond Trail (2,500 ft.): 4.0 mi., 500 ft. (rev. 50 ft.), 2 hr. 15 min.

SUGGESTED HIKES

For more information on suggested hikes, see p. ix.

Easy Hikes

Mt. Willard [rt: 3.2 mi., 900 ft., 2:05]. This low peak has long been celebrated for the view of Crawford Notch from the brink of its impressive cliffs; it is easily reached by the Mt. Willard Trail.

Arethusa Falls Area. Arethusa Falls and Ripley Falls are the two highest waterfalls in NH. Arethusa Falls [rt: 3.0 mi., 1,000 ft., 2:00] is somewhat more demanding than Ripley Falls [rt: 1.0 mi., 400 ft., 0:40]. On a visit to Arethusa Falls, the Bemis Brook Trail can be used either ascending or descending to obtain additional views of other falls in Bemis Brook. With a car spot, both of the big falls can be visited in one trip via the Arethusa–Ripley Falls Trail [lp: 4.5 mi., 1,450 ft., 3:00]. It is also possible to use the Frankenstein Cliff Trail to make a loop that includes Arethusa Falls and Frankenstein Cliff [lp: 4.9 mi., 1,500 ft., 3:10].

Lincoln Woods Trails. From the Lincoln Woods parking area on the Kancamagus Highway, trails on either side of the East Branch of the Pemigewasset River provide easy, scenic walks. On the east side, the Pemi East Side Trail and Pine Island Trail offer a pleasant loop [lp: 2.9 mi., 100 ft., 1:30]. On the west side, the Lincoln Woods Trail can be followed to a riverside viewpoint [rt: 3.2 mi., 150 ft., 1:40], or can be used to access side trails to Black Pond [rt: 6.8 mi., 450 ft., 3:35] or Franconia Falls [rt: 6.4 mi., 350 ft., 3:20; free permit required].

Falling Waters Trail [rt: 2.6 mi., 800 ft., 1:40]. The lower part of this trail leads past three waterfalls; the highest, Cloudland Falls, is a good turnaround point.

Eagle Pass [rt: 3.0 mi., 1,000 ft., 2:00]. This narrow, rocky cleft between Mt. Lafayette and Eagle Cliff merits exploration; it is reached by the Greenleaf Trail.

Moderate Hikes

The Sugarloaves [rt: 3.4 mi., 1,100 ft., 2:15]. These two open summits near the village of Twin Mountain offer excellent views for modest effort via the Sugarloaf Trail.

Zealand Falls [rt: 5.4 mi., 650 ft., 3:00]. This easy walk on the Zealand Trail leads past beaver ponds and meadows and ends with a short, steep climb on the Twinway to a waterfall and AMC hut. As longer alternatives to visiting the hut, one can follow the Ethan Pond Trail out into spectacular Zealand Notch [rt: 7.6 mi., 450 ft., 4:00] or continue through the notch and down a short distance on Thoreau Falls Trail to the view ledge atop Thoreau Falls [rt: 9.4 mi., 500 ft., 4:55].

Ethan Pond [rt: 5.4 mi., 1,550 ft., 3:30]. A moderate climb up the Ethan Pond Trail leads to this attractive backcountry pond with a view of the Twin Range.

Mt. Avalon [rt. 3.6 mi., 1,550 ft., 2:35]. The best view available from the Willey Range is found on this little crag, reached by the steep Avalon Trail and the spur path to the summit; visitors should make the short side trip on the loop to Beecher and Pearl Cascades on the way.

Old Bridle Path Outlooks [rt: 4.0 mi., 1,600 ft., 2:50]. A series of ledges partway up Old Bridle Path offer spectacular views of Franconia Ridge.

Mt. Tom [rt: 5.8 mi., 2,150 ft., 4:00]. Open blowdown areas offer good views atop this Willey Range peak, reached by the Avalon Trail, A–Z Trail, and Mt. Tom Spur. Using the Willey Range and Avalon trails, this trip can be extended to include Mt. Field [lp: 7.2 mi., 2,800 ft., 5:00] or Mts. Field and Willey [lp: 10.0 mi., 3,450 ft., 6:45].

Mt. Hale. This partially wooded summit can be climbed by Hale Brook Trail [rt: 4.4 mi., 2,300 ft., 3:20] or by an interesting longer loop by following the Lend-a-Hand Trail from the summit to Zealand Falls Hut, then following the Twinway and Zealand Trail back out to Zealand Rd. [lp: 8.7 mi., 2,300 ft., 5:30].

Strenuous Hikes

Zeacliff [rt: 7.8 mi., 1,600 ft., 4:40]. This perch at the northern end of the Pemigewasset Wilderness commands one of the finest outlooks in the Whites; it is reached by the Zealand Trail and Twinway.

South Twin Mountain [rt: 10.8 mi., 3,400 ft., 7:05]. This high, open peak affords panoramic views. It can be ascended directly via the Gale River Trail, Garfield Ridge Trail, and Twinway, passing the renovated Galehead Hut en route.

Mt. Garfield [rt: 10:0 mi., 3,000 ft., 6:30]. The summit ledges of this peak are perched high above the Pemigewasset Wilderness and offer one of the best views in the Whites. The Garfield Trail, though long, is easier than most mountain trails, with generally good footing and moderate grades. The last 0.2 mi. to the summit, via the Garfield Ridge Trail, is fairly steep and rough with some rather easy scrambling.

Franconia Ridge [lp: 8.9 mi., 3,850 ft., 6:25]. Though virtually every-one agrees that there is too much traffic on Franconia Ridge, it is hard to imagine a serious hiker with enough resolve to forego one of the most spectacular walks in the East. The usual loop over Mt. Lafayette and Mt. Lincoln follows the Old Bridle Path, Greenleaf Trail, Franconia Ridge Trail, and Falling Waters Trail. It is a good trip in either direction, but many hikers will prefer the excuse to rest while ascending that is of-fered by the excellent outlook ledges on the Bridle Path, and appreciate the cold brooks for soaking heads and feet on the descent of the Fall-ing Waters Trail. A less crowded alternative is to climb Mt. Lafayette via the Skookumchuck and Garfield Ridge trails, including a traverse of the mountain's open north ridge [rt: 10.2 mi., 3,550 ft., 6:50].

Mt. Liberty [rt: 8.0 mi., 3,250 ft., 5:35]. This rocky, open summit offers excellent views; it is most easily climbed by the Whitehouse and Liberty Springs trails. Mt. Flume can be added to this trip, with a return over Mt. Liberty [rt: 10.2 mi., 4,250 ft., 7:15]; the Flume Slide Trail is not rec-ommended for descent. The separate ascent of Mt. Flume via the Osseo Trail [rt: 11.2 mi., 3,150 ft., 7:10] is another good option.

SECTION FOUR
THE CARRIGAIN AND MOAT REGIONS

This section covers the eastern portion of the central region of the White Mountains (that part not included in Section Three), consisting of the areas bounded on the north by US 302, on the east by NH 16, and on the south by the Kancamagus Highway (NH 112); at its western edge it includes all areas and trails south and east of the Wilderness Trail. For a more precise description of the western boundary of Section Four, see the first paragraph of Section Three. Section Four includes Mt. Carrigain and Mt. Hancock, the lesser mountains that surround them, and the lower but interesting mountains that rise to the east between the Saco and Swift rivers, principally Mt. Tremont and the Moat Range. The area is covered by the AMC's *Crawford Notch–Sandwich Range Map* (map 3).

Important access roads in this area include the Kancamagus Highway (NH 112), which connects I-93 and US 3 in Lincoln to NH 16 in Conway and is a regular state highway that is paved and well maintained, open in winter except during the worst storms. Bear Notch Rd. runs 9.3 mi. from US 302 at the crossroads in Bartlett village to the Kancamagus Highway in Albany Intervale about 13 mi. west of Conway. It is paved, but not plowed in winter except for the 2-mi. section immediately north of the Kancamagus Highway. North of Bear Notch, it closely follows the line of an old railroad, and excellent outlooks have been cleared. The gravel Sawyer River Rd. (FR 34) begins on US 302 0.1 mi. north of the major bridge over the Sawyer River, 1.6 mi. north of the Sawyer Rock picnic area or 7.9 mi. south of the Willey House site in Crawford Notch State Park. There may not be a road sign except for a brown post with FR 34 on it, and it is usually closed by a locked gate during the snow season.

The Appalachian Trail (AT) does not pass through this section.

GEOGRAPHY

Mt. Carrigain (4,700 ft.) is the central and highest point of a mass of jumbled ridges that divides the watershed of the East Branch of the Pemigewasset River from that of the Saco River and its tributary, the Swift River. It was named for Philip Carrigain, New Hampshire secretary of state from 1805 to 1810. Carrigain made a map of the whole state in 1816, which included an early attempt to portray the White Mountains region that can best be described as imaginative. He was one of the party that named Mts. Adams, Jefferson, Madison, and Monroe from the summit of Mt. Washington in 1820. The view from the observation tower on Mt. Carrigain takes in a wide area and includes most of the important peaks of the White Mountains, making this peak one of the competitors for the title of the finest viewpoint in the White Mountains. The view from Signal Ridge, Carrigain's southeasterly spur, is also magnificent. The northeasterly spur, Vose Spur (3,862 ft.), forms the west wall of the deep cleft of Carrigain Notch, facing Mt. Lowell on the east. Vose Spur has no trails, and therefore the climb up its steep slopes through dense woods (or across the mostly pathless scrubby ridge from the summit of Carrigain) is one of the most challenging bushwhack ascents in the White Mountains.

To the west of Mt. Carrigain, Mt. Hancock rises. It is a long ridge with several summits, of which the most important are the North Peak (4,420 ft.) and the South Peak (4,319 ft.). Both peaks are wooded to the top, but there is an excellent outlook ledge near the summit of the North Peak and a good but restricted outlook from the South Peak. At one time, this was one of the most inaccessible mountains in the White Mountains, remote and trailless with slopes devastated by logging, but it is now routinely ascended via the Hancock Loop Trail.

The ridge between Mt. Carrigain and Mt. Hancock has no trail, and travel along it is extremely difficult; the line along this ridge shown on many maps is part of the Lincoln-Livermore town boundary. Carrigain Pond, a beautiful and remote mountain pond that is one of the higher sources of the Pemigewasset River, lies just north of the ridge between Carrigain and Hancock at an elevation of about 3,200 ft. The Captain (3,540 ft.), located only 0.3 mi. from Carrigain Pond, is a striking little peak, a miniature Half Dome with sheer cliffs overlooking the Sawyer River valley; however, it is well hidden at the end of this isolated valley and can be seen from only a few viewpoints, most notably the summit of Mt. Tremont.

The group of peaks northeast of Carrigain Notch that rise along the ridge that forms the watershed divide between the Saco and the East Branch of the Pemigewasset include Mt. Lowell (3,740 ft.), Mt. Anderson (3,740 ft.), Mt. Nancy (3,926 ft.), and Mt. Bemis (3,725 ft.). None of these peaks is reached by an officially maintained trail. The region is remarkable for its four picturesque ponds—Nancy Pond, Norcross Pond, Little Norcross Pond, and Duck Pond—which lie at the unusually high altitude of about 3,100 ft. There is also a stand of virgin spruce just south of Nancy Pond on the north slopes of Duck Pond Mountain, said to be one of the two largest remaining areas of virgin forest in the state, though the hurricane of 1938 did great damage, felling many of the older trees. In October 1964, the USFS established in this region the 460-acre Nancy Brook Scenic Area, to be maintained as nearly as possible in an undisturbed condition.

The tallest of several lesser peaks that rise in the region around Sawyer Pond, west of Bear Notch Rd. is Mt. Tremont (3,371 ft.). Tremont lies south of the big bend in the Saco River above Bartlett; it is a narrow ridge that runs north and south, with three conspicuous summits of which the southernmost is the highest. Still farther south is a high shoulder, Owl's Cliff (2,940 ft.). The main summit of Tremont has spectacular views to the south, west, and north; Owl's Cliff has a fine outlook to the south. Southwest of both Mt. Tremont and Sawyer Pond is Green's Cliff (2,926 ft.), with cliffs on its south and east faces; it is very prominent from the overlooks on the eastern half of the Kancamagus Highway. Ledges near its summit provide views, but there is no trail. Sawyer Pond, which lies in a steep-walled basin on the southwest side of Mt. Tremont, and Church Pond, which lies in a flat area north of the Kancamagus Highway and southeast of Green's Cliff, are attractive objectives reached by relatively short, easy trails.

Bear Notch, crossed by the scenic Bear Notch Rd. from Bartlett village to the Kancamagus Highway in Albany Intervale, lies between Bartlett Haystack and Bear Mountain. The WMNF Bartlett Experimental Forest occupies a large area on the north slopes of these mountains. Bartlett Haystack (2,980 ft.), an aptly named mountain that was sometimes called Mt. Silver Spring in the days when hazy elegance was preferred to plain and effective description, is another interesting peak with no trails that rises east of Mt. Tremont. A ledge just a few feet west of the summit, shaped like the prow of a ship, affords a magnificent view to the south, west, and north. Bartlett Haystack is a relatively easy bushwhack from Haystacks Rd. (FR 44), and is one of the more rewarding objectives available to experienced hikers who wish to begin to acquire the skills of off-trail navigation by map and compass. The USGS Bartlett 7.5-minute quad, now available in provisional format, is very useful for the ascent of this peak (previous maps were highly inaccurate in their location of FR 44). Leave FR 44 at any convenient point less than 0.5 mi. from its junction with the Bear Notch Rd. near the height-of-land in Bear Notch, climb roughly northwest to the crest of the peak's east ridge, then follow the ridge crest to the summit. (Although a compass bearing is useful for confirmation of the proper direction, you should follow the ridge crest, heading for the highest ground you can find rather than attempting to follow a precise compass bearing. This route illustrates one of the complexities of off-trail navigation in the Whites: in this case the mountain will lead you to its summit if you let it, while an attempt to follow a precise bearing on the ascent can pull you off the ridge crest and into steep, difficult terrain. The compass is essential to the off-trail navigator, but following a bearing is often more difficult than following a feature of terrain—a ridge or a brook, for example—using the compass to confirm the correct approximate direction.) For the descent (which, as is often the case, may involve more sophisticated navigation than the ascent), you can follow the ridge you ascended east down to FR 44, or you can descend into the brook valley just to the north of this ridge and follow the brook out to the road (a somewhat easier route to navigate, as again the compass bearing is not necessary once the brook is reached and confirmed to be heading in the approximate correct direction). It is also possible to descend somewhat more to the south, more directly toward Bear Notch, but take care not to leave the ridge too quickly, because the slope directly below the summit on the south is steep and rough.

Moat Mountain is a long ridge that rises impressively to the west of the Saco River nearly opposite North Conway. The whole ridge was burned over many decades ago, and all the major summits are still bare, with magnificent views; there are also numerous scattered outlooks along the wooded parts of the ridge. There has been some uncertainty about the names of the summits in the range, but in this guide, the peaks are called North Moat Mountain (3,196 ft.), Middle Moat Mountain (2,805 ft.), and South Moat Mountain (2,770 ft.). The peak at the apex of the Red Ridge (2,785 ft.) has sometimes also been called Middle Moat. From North Moat a ridge runs west to densely wooded Big Attitash Mountain (2,910 ft.), sometimes called West Moat, then the ridge passes over the lesser summits of Big Attitash and swings southwest to Table Mountain

(2,675 ft.), which has fine views to the south from several open ledges just below the summit. Next, the ridge swings west again to the trailless Bear Mountain (3,220 ft.), which forms the east side of Bear Notch. South of Bear Mountain and very close to the Kancamagus Highway are the picturesque Rocky Gorge on the Saco River and nearby Falls Pond, a small scenic body of water reached by a short, easy trail from the highway. An unnamed rocky southern spur of the Moat group, which affords excellent views, is ascended by the Boulder Loop Trail—a moderately strenuous nature trail with numbered stations keyed to an information leaflet. On the east side of the Moat Range are White Horse Ledge (1,450 ft.) and Cathedral Ledge (1,159 ft.), two detached bluffs that present impressive cliffs to the Saco Valley. An auto road ascends to the summit of Cathedral Ledge. Farther to the north, Little Attitash Mountain (2,504 ft.) is a trailless peak on a long, curving ridge that extends northeast from Big Attitash to end in Humphrey's Ledge (1,510 ft.). Pitman's Arch, a shallow cave in the face of Humphrey's Ledge, was once reached by a toll path that is now completely overgrown. Diana's Baths is a set of very scenic cascades, located on the Moat Mountain Trail near West Side Rd., where Lucy Brook runs over ledges and through large potholes

CAMPING

Pemigewasset Wilderness

Wilderness regulations, intended to protect Wilderness resources and promote opportunities for challenge and solitude, prohibit use of motorized equipment or mechanical means of transportation of any sort. In accordance with USFS Wilderness policy, the trails in the Pemigewasset Wilderness are in general maintained to a lower standard than trails outside Wilderness. They may be rough, overgrown, or essentially unmarked with minimal signage, and considerable care may be required to follow them. Camping and wood or charcoal fires are not allowed within 200 ft. of any trail except at designated campsites. Camping is prohibited within 0.25 mi. of the Wilderness Trail and the East Branch of the Pemigewasset River (including islands), from the Kancamagus Highway up to the Wilderness boundary, and within 200 ft. of the East Branch from the Wilderness Boundary up to the Thoreau Falls Trail crossing (including islands). Camping and fires are also prohibited within 0.25 mi. of 13 Falls Campsite, Thoreau Falls, Galehead Hut, Garfield Ridge Campsite, and Guyot Campsite (the last three facilities are outside, but less than 0.25 mi. from, the Wilderness boundary). Hiking and camping group size must be no larger than 10 people. Camping and fires are also prohibited above the treeline (where trees are less than 8 ft. tall), except in winter, when camping is permitted above the treeline in places where snow cover is at least 2 ft. deep, but not on any frozen body of water.

Forest Protection Areas

The WMNF has established a number of Forest Protection Areas (FPAs)—formerly known as Restricted Use Areas—where camping and wood or charcoal fires are prohibited throughout the year. The specific areas are under continual review, and areas are added to or subtracted from the list in order to provide the greatest amount of protection to areas subject to damage by excessive camping, while imposing the lowest level of restrictions possible. A general list of FPAs in this section follows, but because there are often major changes from year to year, one should obtain current information on FPAs from the WMNF.

(1) No camping is permitted above treeline (where trees are less than 8 ft. tall), except in winter, and then only in places where there is at least 2 ft. of snow cover on the ground—but not on any frozen body of water. The point where the restricted area begins is marked on most trails with small signs, but the absence of such signs should not be construed as proof of the legality of a site.

(2) No camping is permitted within 0.25 mi. of any trailhead, picnic area, or any facility for overnight accommodation such as a hut, cabin, shelter, tentsite, or campground, except as designated at the facility itself. In the area covered by Section Four, camping and fires are also prohibited within 0.25 mi. of the Big and Little Sawyer Ponds, and Diana's Baths (located on the Moat Mountain Trail). Camping is also not permitted in the Bartlett Experimental Forest.

(3) No camping is permitted within 200 ft. of certain trails. In 2006, designated trails included the Sawyer Pond Trail from the end of the 0.25-mi. FPA along the Sawyer River Rd. to the beginning of the 0.25-mi.

FPA around Sawyer Pond, and the Cedar Brook Trail between its junctions with the Hancock Notch and Hancock Loop trails.

(4) No camping is permitted on WMNF land within 0.25 mi. of certain roads (camping on private roadside land is illegal except by permission of the landowner). In 2002, these roads included US 302 west of Bartlett, New Hampshire, the Sawyer River Rd., the Kancamagus Highway, the Bear Notch Rd., and the Dugway Rd. from the Kancamagus Highway to the picnic area.

Established Trailside Campsites

Sawyer Pond Campsite (WMNF) is located on Sawyer Pond, reached by the Sawyer Pond Trail. There are six tent platforms on the northwest side of the pond, and a shelter that accommodates eight.

TRAIL DESCRIPTIONS

Signal Ridge Trail (WMNF)

This trail ascends to the summit of Mt. Carrigain by way of Signal Ridge, starting from Sawyer River Rd. (FR 34) 2.0 mi. from its junction with US 302, which is 1.6 mi. north of the Sawyer Rock picnic area. The trail begins on the right just before the bridge over Whiteface Brook; there is a parking lot on the left, just beyond the bridge. A crossing of Whiteface Brook less than 0.2 mi. from the road may be difficult at high water; at such times it may be best to avoid the crossing by bushwhacking up the south bank of the brook from the parking lot. The trail climbs moderately for most of its distance, using old roads that once provided access to the fire warden's cabin. The views from the observation tower on the summit and from Signal Ridge are magnificent. The loop back to Sawyer River Rd. via the Desolation and Carrigain Notch trails is interesting but much longer, rougher, and more strenuous.

Leaving the road, the Signal Ridge Trail soon reaches and follows an old logging road that crosses Whiteface Brook at 0.2 mi., then follows the south bank of the attractive brook, passing small cascades and pools. At 0.8 mi., it begins to climb steadily away from the brook, then levels and crosses a flat divide. At 1.4 mi., the Carrigain Brook Rd., a grass-grown logging road, crosses the trail at a right angle. (This road is not passable by vehicles, but it can be followed south 1.6 mi. to Sawyer River Rd. about 0.3 mi. before the gate at the end of that road. However, there is a difficult brook crossing just before Sawyer River Rd. is reached, and parts of the road are becoming overgrown.) At 1.7 mi., the Carrigain Notch Trail diverges right toward the Pemigewasset Wilderness via scenic Carrigain Notch, and the Signal Ridge Trail soon crosses Carrigain Brook, which may be difficult at high water. The trail passes an area of beaver activity, crosses a brook, and begins to ascend, gradually at first. At 2.4 mi., it turns sharp left where an old road continues straight up the valley. The trail angles up the end of a ridge, turns right to climb, then makes another sharp left turn (arrow) at the site of an old camp and angles up again.

At 2.8 mi., the Signal Ridge Trail turns sharp right into a birch-lined straight section 1.0 mi. long with rocky footing that rises steadily at an angle up the steep side of the valley, with occasional views to the cliffs of Mt. Lowell across Carrigain Notch. At the end of this section, the trail turns sharp left and zigzags up the nose of Signal Ridge through several areas that were damaged by the windstorm of December 1980, reaching the high point of the bare crest of the ridge at 4.5 mi. Views are excellent, particularly to the cliffs of Mt. Lowell across Carrigain Notch. The trail descends slightly, then angles left around to the south slope of the summit cone, climbing gradually to the site of the old fire warden's cabin, where there is a well (water unsafe to drink without treatment). Bearing left from the small clearing, the trail soon swings right and climbs steeply to the small sag between Carrigain's two summit knobs, then turns right and soon reaches the summit. Here the Desolation Trail enters from the Pemigewasset Wilderness.

Signal Ridge Trail (map 3:I8–H7)

Distances from Sawyer River Rd. (1,480 ft.) to

- Carrigain Notch Trail (1,900 ft.): 1.7 mi., 400 ft., 1 hr. 5 min.
- Signal Ridge (4,420 ft.): 4.5 mi., 2,950 ft., 3 hr. 45 min.
- Mt. Carrigain summit (4,700 ft.): 5.0 mi., 3,250 ft. (rev. 50 ft.), 4 hr. 10 min.

Distance from US 302 (897 ft.) to

- Mt. Carrigain summit (4,700 ft.): 7.0 mi., 3,850 ft. (rev. 50 ft.), 5 hr. 25 min.

Carrigain Notch Trail (AMC)

This trail begins on the Signal Ridge Trail at a point 1.7 mi. from Sawyer River Rd., runs through Carrigain Notch and ends at Stillwater Junction, where it meets the Wilderness and Shoal Pond trails (see Section Three). The section of this trail northwest of Carrigain Notch lies within the Pemigewasset Wilderness.

It diverges right (north) from the Signal Ridge Trail and crosses Carrigain Brook in 60 yd.; care is required to find the trail on the opposite bank at this crossing, going either way. Continuing on logging roads at easy grades, it passes through an area of beaver activity, then several stony areas, and at 1.6 mi., turns left off the road to bypass a muddy section. Here, just off to the right of the trail, there is a view of the ledges of Vose Spur, which form the west side of Carrigain Notch. Soon returning to the road, the trail climbs more steeply, and at 2.3 mi., reaches its height-of-land well up on the west wall of the notch and enters the Pemigewasset Wilderness. Very soon, it strikes and follows an old logging road on the north side of the notch, descending moderately. At 3.1 mi., it turns left off the logging road and follows a path through the woods that avoids the wet sections of the old road while continuing to use some of the dry parts. At 4.1 mi., the trail enters an old railroad grade and turns sharp left on it; the Nancy Pond Trail follows the grade to the right from this point. At 4.9 mi., the trail bears left off the railroad grade, then soon turns sharp right where the Desolation Trail continues straight across the brook. At 5.1 mi., it bears to the right, away from the Carrigain Branch, and reaches Stillwater Junction on the East Branch; here the Wilderness Trail turns sharp left, and the Shoal Pond Trail turns right and immediately crosses the East Branch of the Pemigewasset.

Carrigain Notch Trail (map 3:I8–H7)

Distances from Signal Ridge Trail (1,900 ft.) to
- Carrigain Notch (2,637 ft.): 2.3 mi., 750 ft., 1 hr. 30 min.
- Nancy Pond Trail (2,140 ft.): 4.1 mi., 750 ft. (rev. 500 ft.), 2 hr. 25 min.
- Desolation Trail (2,180 ft.): 4.9 mi., 800 ft., 2 hr. 50 min.
- Stillwater Junction (2,050 ft.): 5.7 mi., 800 ft. (rev. 150 ft.), 3 hr. 15 min.

Desolation Trail (AMC)

This trail ascends to the summit of Mt. Carrigain from the Carrigain Notch Trail about 0.8 mi. southeast of Stillwater Junction. The upper part of the trail is very steep and rough and requires great care, particularly on the descent or with heavy packs; substantial extra time may be required in either direction. Practically the entire trail is in the Pemigewasset Wilderness.

The trail leaves the Carrigain Notch Trail at a sharp turn near the edge of a tributary of the Carrigain Branch and crosses the brook. It follows a railroad grade for 60 yd., then diverges left and climbs moderately, at times on old logging roads. It climbs into a fine stand of birches and merges into an unusually straight old logging road on the west side of the ridge crest. (For a long section of this road, there is old telephone wire at the left edge of the trail that hikers need to watch for, as it may trip an unwary individual.) The old road crosses to the east side of the ridge, deteriorates, and ends at 1.3 mi. The trail crosses a short section of slippery rock blocks and continues through an area where many rock steps have been built, then swings directly up the slope into virgin woods and climbs a very steep and rough section. The grade gradually eases up and the footing slowly improves as the trail reaches the crest of the steep ridge. At 1.8 mi., the trail abruptly reaches the top of the steep section, swings left, and angles around the cone at an easy grade until it reaches and climbs the last short steep pitch to the summit observation tower, where it meets the Signal Ridge Trail.

Desolation Trail (map 3:H7)

Distances from Carrigain Notch Trail (2,180 ft.) to
- upper end of old logging road (3,530 ft.): 1.3 mi., 1,350 ft., 1 hr. 20 min.
- Mt. Carrigain summit (4,700 ft.): 1.9 mi., 2,500 ft., 2 hr. 10 min.

Nancy Pond Trail (Camp Pasquaney/WMNF)

This trail begins on the west side of US 302, 2.8 mi. north of the Sawyer Rock picnic area and 6.7 mi. south of the Willey House site in Crawford Notch State Park. It passes Nancy Cascades and Nancy and Norcross ponds, and ends on the Carrigain Notch Trail 0.8 mi. east of the junction with the Desolation Trail. The section of the trail west of Norcross Pond lies within the Pemigewasset Wilderness. Deep snow or ice may remain in the shady ravine above Nancy Cascades quite late in spring.

Leaving US 302, the trail follows an assortment of paths and old roads but is well marked with yellow paint and signs. It first follows a logging road for 250 yd., diverges left and crosses a small brook, then joins a logging road along Halfway Brook, and soon turns right off the road and crosses Halfway Brook. It enters the Nancy Pond Scenic Area, and then a woods road joins from the right (descending, bear right here). The trail continues to the WMNF boundary, marked by a large pile of red-painted stones, at 0.8 mi. Here the trail enters and follows an old logging road along Nancy Brook, crossing the brook on the rocks at 1.6 mi. (may be difficult at high water). It turns left and continues upstream on the road, passing the remains of the Lucy Mill at 1.8 mi. Above here, the old road virtually disappears, and the trail ascends through a rough area of landslides, recrosses Nancy Brook, and soon reaches the foot of Nancy Cascades at 2.4 mi., where the stream falls over a high, steep ledge into a beautiful pool.

The trail turns sharp left at the pool and ascends the steep slope by switchbacks, providing another outlook at the middle of the cascades, and passes near the top of the cascades, which are several hundred feet high, at 2.8 mi. From the top of the cascades, the trail winds through the moss-carpeted virgin spruce forest past a small overgrown tarn to the northeast shore of Nancy Pond (4 acres in area) at 3.4 mi. Continuing along the north shore, the trail crosses the swamp at the upper end, then passes over the almost imperceptible height-of-land that divides the Saco from the Pemigewasset drainage and reaches Little Norcross Pond. Skirting the north shore, it then climbs over another small rise to Norcross Pond (7 acres in area). Again hugging the north shore (where beaver flooding may occur), and crossing into the Pemigewasset Wilderness, the trail enters a logging road 25 yd. before reaching the ledgy natural dam at the west end of Norcross Pond at 4.3 mi. (In the reverse direction, turn right off the logging road 25 yd. from the ledgy dam and follow a path along the shore of the pond.) At the ledges, there is a commanding outlook to Mt. Bond and the Twin Range, with the Franconias in the distance.

After crossing the stream at the outlet of Norcross Pond, the Nancy Pond Trail descends gradually west on a logging road, passing a spring (iron pipe) on the south side of the trail at 5.5 mi. At 6.0 mi., the trail veers right, crosses Norcross Brook (may be difficult in high water), then shortly reaches an old railroad bed and swings left onto it. At 6.4 mi., it crosses Anderson Brook (may be difficult in high water), then passes along the south side of the Camp 19 clearing. At 6.8 mi., it turns left off the railroad grade and crosses the East Branch of the Pemigewasset River on a bridge, just a short distance below the point where the East Branch begins at the confluence of Norcross and Anderson brooks. On the other side, it follows another railroad grade, bearing right at a fork. It then crosses Notch Brook and ends 25 yd. beyond, where the Carrigain Notch Trail enters sharp left from Sawyer River Rd. and continues straight ahead on the railroad grade to the Desolation Trail and Stillwater Junction.

Nancy Pond Trail (map 3:H8–H7)

Distances from US 302 (940 ft.) to
- foot of Nancy Cascades (2,400 ft.): 2.4 mi., 1,450 ft., 1 hr. 55 min.
- Nancy Pond (3,100 ft.): 3.5 mi., 2,150 ft., 2 hr. 50 min.
- Norcross Pond outlet (3,120 ft.): 4.3 mi., 2,150 ft., 3 hr. 15 min.
- Carrigain Notch Trail (2,140 ft.): 7.1 mi., 2,200 ft. (rev. 1,000 ft.), 4 hr. 40 min.
- Stillwater Junction (2,050 ft.) via Carrigain Notch Trail: 8.7 mi., 2,200 ft. (rev. 100 ft.), 5 hr. 25 min.

Cedar Brook Trail (WMNF)

This trail runs from the Hancock Notch Trail, 1.8 mi. from the Kancamagus Highway, to the Wilderness Trail at the east end of the suspension bridge, 5.4 mi. from the Kancamagus Highway. In combination with the Hancock Notch and Hancock Loop trails, the southern portion of this trail affords the most direct route to Mt. Hancock. The five crossings of the North Fork of the Hancock Branch between the Hancock Notch Trail and the Hancock Loop Trail are difficult in high water, but the first two are easily bypassed and the others can be avoided by bushwhacking along the east bank to the Hancock Loop Trail (which makes a sixth crossing soon after its divergence from the Cedar Brook Trail).

Leaving the Hancock Notch Trail, the Cedar Brook Trail immediately crosses a small brook and climbs moderately on an old logging road for about 0.2 mi., then crosses the North Fork of the Hancock Branch five times in 0.4 mi. The first two crossings are only 40 yd. apart and can be avoided by following a well-beaten path on the near bank. The beginning of the Hancock Loop Trail is reached on the right at 0.7 mi., 150 yd. beyond the fifth crossing.

The Cedar Brook Trail soon passes into the Pemigewasset Wilderness, climbing moderately on a somewhat rough footway that occasionally must be carefully distinguished from miscellaneous brooks and muddy abandoned routes of the trail. It reaches the height-of-land between Mt. Hancock and Mt. Hitchcock at 1.4 mi. and descends on logging roads, swinging out to the west then back to the northeast side of the valley, crossing several brooks. It reaches the site of Camp 24A (sign) at 2.9 mi., then continues to descend on old roads, and at 4.1 mi., it drops down a bank to the old logging railroad at the edge of Cedar Brook and turns sharp right on the railroad grade. (In the reverse direction, bear left off the grade where the trail comes to the edge of the brook.)

Soon it passes through the extensive clearings of Camp 24 and continues down toward the East Branch of the Pemigewasset. At 5.5 mi., the Pemi East Side Trail enters on the left; this trail, an old truck road, follows the south and east banks of the East Branch to the Lincoln Woods parking lot. The Cedar Brook Trail swings to the east, paralleling the East Branch, and joins the Wilderness Trail at the east end of the suspension bridge.

Cedar Brook Trail (map 3:I6–H6)

Distances from Hancock Notch Trail (2,520 ft.) to
- Hancock Loop Trail (2,720 ft.): 0.7 mi., 200 ft., 25 min.
- height-of-land (3,100 ft.): 1.4 mi., 600 ft., 1 hr.
- Camp 24A (2,400 ft.): 2.9 mi., 600 ft. (rev. 700 ft.), 1 hr. 45 min.
- Camp 24 (1,940 ft.): 4.3 mi., 600 ft. (rev. 450 ft.), 2 hr. 25 min.
- Wilderness Trail (1,640 ft.): 6.1 mi., 600 ft. (rev. 300 ft.), 3 hr. 20 min.

Hancock Notch Trail (WMNF)

This trail begins at the Kancamagus Highway at the hairpin turn, passes through Hancock Notch between Mt. Hancock and Mt. Huntington, then descends along the Sawyer River to the Sawyer River Trail. At the Kancamagus Highway terminus, parking is available at the Hancock Overlook just above the trailhead. With the Cedar Brook and Hancock Loop trails, this trail provides the easiest and most popular route to Mt. Hancock. From the Kancamagus Highway to the Cedar Brook Trail, the Hancock Notch Trail is heavily used, wide, and easily followed; from the Cedar Brook Trail to the Sawyer River Trail, it is very lightly used, often overgrown, wet and rough, and in places requires care to follow.

The trail begins across the Kancamagus Highway from the parking area. Leaving the highway at the hairpin, it follows an old railroad bed, crossing a brook at 0.6 mi., and gradually approaching the North Fork of the Hancock Branch. It stays on the same side of the North Fork, swinging right slightly uphill at 1.5 mi. to enter a logging road at the point where the railroad grade crossed the river; take care not to follow the remains of the railroad grade across the river here. The trail follows the logging road at an easy grade, then descends slightly, crosses three brooks in less than 0.1 mi., and soon reaches the junction with the Cedar Brook Trail at 1.8 mi. (For Mt. Hancock, turn left on this trail across a small brook.)

The Hancock Notch Trail now rises somewhat more steeply and bears left (northeast) on a relocation at 2.0 mi. It climbs over a rise and descends gradually southeast, crossing four small brooks and rejoining the original route at 2.4 mi. The trail now climbs gradually again, reaching the broad, flat floor of Hancock Notch at 2.7 mi. For 0.2 mi., it runs nearly level through spruce woods, becoming quite wet at the east end of this section, passing an open spot with a glimpse of the talus slopes on Mt. Huntington.

East of the notch, the trail may be overgrown and difficult to follow. It passes through a dense stand of spruce on a rougher footway, descending quite rapidly at times. The grade soon moderates and the trail crosses to the north side of the Sawyer River at 3.6 mi., then back to the south side at 4.2 mi. Soon the trail diverges from the river, passes by a beaver pond, and follows logging roads across a south branch of the river. Continuing to descend easily, it crosses the Sawyer River twice more, at 5.5 mi. and 6.0 mi. (both crossings may be difficult at high water), and follows newer logging roads to its end at the Sawyer River Trail in Hayshed Field, an overgrown clearing 1.2 mi. from Sawyer River Rd.

Hancock Notch Trail (map 3:I6–I7)

Distances from Kancamagus Highway (2,129 ft.) to
- Cedar Brook Trail (2,520 ft.): 1.8 mi., 400 ft., 1 hr. 5 min.
- Hancock Notch (2,800 ft.): 2.7 mi., 800 ft., 1 hr. 45 min.
- Sawyer River Trail (1,780 ft.): 6.9 mi., 800 ft. (rev. 1,000 ft.), 3 hr. 50 min.

Hancock Loop Trail (AMC)

This trail makes a loop over both the major summits of Mt. Hancock. The trail is steep and rough but well trodden and easy to follow, though the part on the ridge between the peaks is subject to blowdowns. It is most easily reached from the hairpin turn on the Kancamagus Highway by following the Hancock Notch and Cedar Brook trails for 2.5 mi. There are five brook crossings on the Cedar Brook Trail that may be difficult at high water.

Leaving the Cedar Brook Trail on the right (east), 150 yd. north of the fifth crossing of the North Branch of the Hancock Branch, the trail follows an old logging road and soon recrosses the main brook, then passes over a steep, rocky brook bed and a wet area. Keeping south of the main brook, some distance away from it and considerably higher, the trail continues its gradual ascent and reaches the loop junction at 1.1 mi. from the start. From this point the circuit over the two main summits of Mt. Hancock can be made in either direction, so for convenience of description the trail is divided into three segments: North Link, Ridge Link, and South Link.

The *North Link* diverges left from the logging road at the loop junction and descends moderately at an angle. Soon it crosses a flat gravel area, usually dry but often with water flowing into it from the brook bed above and disappearing into the sand, where the foot of the Arrow Slide is visible about 50 yd. to the left. The trail then climbs roughly parallel to the slide, first at a moderate grade angling across the hillside, then straight up, very steep and rough, though recent reconstruction by the AMC's trail crew has greatly improved the footway. Near the top, the trail veers left and becomes less steep. At the wooded summit of North Hancock, a side path leads left 40 yd. to a fine view south to the Sandwich Range and Osceola, while the Ridge Link turns right.

The *South Link* continues along the logging road from the loop junction for another 0.1 mi., then swings right up the mountainside. The climb to South Hancock is unrelievedly steep, crossing numerous old logging roads. (These are some of the roads that are so prominent as light green lines across the dark slope when seen from other peaks.) At the summit, the Ridge Link enters on the left (north), and a short path descends straight ahead (east) to a viewpoint overlooking the Sawyer River valley.

The *Ridge Link* connects the summits of North and South Hancock. From the summit of North Hancock, it starts almost due north and curves to the right (east, then south), traversing the generally broad, bumpy ridge with several minor ups and downs, then climbs the final narrow section of ridge to the south peak at 1.4 mi., where the South Link enters on the right (west).

Hancock Loop Trail (map 3:16–17)

Distances from Cedar Brook Trail (2,720 ft.) to
- loop junction (3,400 ft.): 1.1 mi., 700 ft., 55 min.
- North Hancock (4,420 ft.) via North Link: 1.8 mi., 1,800 ft. (rev. 100 ft.), 1 hr. 50 min.
- South Hancock (4,319 ft.) via South Link: 1.6 mi., 1,600 ft., 1 hr. 35 min.

Distances of loop over both summits from
- Cedar Brook Trail (2,720 ft.) in either direction: 4.8 mi., 2,100 ft., 3 hr. 25 min.
- Kancamagus Highway (2,129 ft.): 9.8 mi., 2,700 ft., 6 hr. 15 min.

Forest Discovery Trail (WMNF)

This graded gravel path provides an easy loop hike on the north side of the Kancamagus Highway, starting at a parking area 2.2 mi. east of the Lincoln Woods trailhead and 0.1 mi. east of Big Rock Campground. Interpretive panels along the trail explain the various forest management techniques utilized on the WMNF. From the parking area the trail angles to the right for 80 yd., then turns left at an arrow and left again at a T-intersection. It ascends easily, swings to the right through a wildlife opening, and continues to a clear-cut area at 0.6 mi., where there is a view of Mt. Osceola. It descends by switchbacks to a junction at 0.8 mi., where the main trail turns right, while a spur path (sign: Riparian Area & Softwood Groups) diverges left. The spur path crosses a bridge over a small brook and quickly reaches a loop junction. The left fork of the spur loop ascends and descends slightly, makes a hairpin turn to the right, and turns right again to return to the spur loop junction. Continue ahead across the bridge to return to the main trail; distance for the spur path, including the loop and return, is 0.3 mi. From the junction with the spur, the main trail descends gradually for 0.2 mi., passing a connecting path on the right, then turns right and returns to the parking area.

Forest Discovery Trail (map 3:16)

Distance from parking area on Kancamagus Highway (1,500 ft.) for
- complete loop, including spur path: 1.4 mi., 150 ft., 45 min.

Sawyer River Trail (WMNF)

This trail leads from Sawyer River Rd. (FR 34), at the end of the section open to public vehicular use about 4.0 mi. from US 302, to the Kancamagus Highway 3.1 mi. west of the Sabbaday Falls parking area and 0.6 mi. east of Lily Pond. Almost all the way, it follows the bed of an old logging railroad at easy grades.

The trail follows the gravel road past the gate, and in 100 yd., the Sawyer Pond Trail turns left to cross the Sawyer River on a footbridge. The Sawyer River Trail continues, taking the left of two gravel roads at a fork, crosses the Sawyer River on the logging-road bridge, and diverges right onto the old railroad grade 100 yd. beyond the bridge. (The gravel road can be followed 1.1 mi. to the junction of the Sawyer River Trail and Hancock Notch Trail, where it enters the Sawyer River Trail at a right angle; there are excellent views of Mt. Tremont and Mt. Carrigain from this road.) The railroad grade continues along the Sawyer River for 0.7 mi., then begins to swing to the south. It crosses a washed-out area and two brooks, and reaches a junction at 1.2 mi., where the Hancock Notch Trail turns sharp right and the gravel road described earlier enters on the left. The Sawyer River Trail follows the old railroad bed across an imperceptible divide in the flat region west of Green's Cliff, passing several beaver swamps, and crosses Meadow Brook on a bridge at 2.5 mi. It follows the west bank of this stream for some distance, passing a junction where the Nanamocomuck (X-C) Ski Trail enters on the left at 3.2 mi., then swings southwest. The ski trail diverges right just before the Sawyer River Trail crosses the Swift River (which can be very difficult in high water) at 3.5 mi. The trail now ascends easily upstream along the river, passing a fine cascade and pool, then climbs up the bank, bearing left twice, to the Kancamagus Highway.

Sawyer River Trail (map 3:I8–I7)

Distances from Sawyer River Rd. (1,610 ft.) to
- Hancock Notch Trail (1,780 ft.): 1.2 mi., 150 ft., 40 min.
- Kancamagus Highway (1,806 ft.): 3.8 mi., 350 ft. (rev. 150 ft.), 2 hr. 5 min

Church Pond Loop Trail (WMNF)

This loop trail provides an interesting short, level walk to Church Pond and the adjacent Church Pond Bog. It passes through an extensive, very flat and poorly drained region of pine and spruce swamps and bogs, providing access to a kind of terrain and forest that trails in the White Mountains seldom visit. It is a very wet trip at times, with several sections likely to be very muddy. *Caution*: The crossing of the Swift River near the trailhead usually requires wading and can be dangerous at high water. The trail begins in Passaconaway Campground just off the Kancamagus Highway, at the far end of the west loop road near Site 19. Parking at the trailhead is limited and the campground is closed much of the year, so it may be necessary to use the Downes Brook Trail parking lot on the south side of the highway.

The path descends slightly and fords the Swift River to the north side, where it follows a normally dry streambed left for 20 yd., then turns to the right into the woods, and soon crosses another channel of the Swift River that is usually not as difficult as the main channel. On the far bank the trail, angles left through dense, fast-growing streamside vegetation and may require considerable care to follow. At 0.3 mi., the loop junction is reached; it is 0.8 mi. to the pond by the left-hand path (which has more log bridges over wet sections), or 1.4 mi. by the right-hand path (which has one very muddy unbridged section). The Nanamocomuck (X-C) Ski Trail uses the first part of each branch.

From the loop junction, the walk is described in the clockwise direction. Taking the left-hand branch, the trail follows an old logging road for 0.4 mi. to the junction where the ski trail diverges left. The Church Pond Loop soon bears left and becomes a footpath, crossing a boggy area on log bridges (many of which were rotten and loose in 2006). Swinging right, it emerges at 1.1 mi. on a knoll covered with red pines, overlooking Church Pond, providing fine views. (In the reverse direction, at the foot of the short descent from the knoll, bear right at an arrow where a beaten path runs straight ahead into a swamp.) From the knoll, the trail turns sharp right and runs above the shore of the pond for about 250 yd., then turns right again and starts back to the loop junction, first traversing a very muddy area with no log bridges, then running on mostly drier ground, repeatedly bearing right as it skirts the extensive Church Pond Bog. The ski trail enters on the left 0.2 mi. before the loop junction.

Church Pond Loop Trail (map 3:J8–I8)

Distance from Passaconaway Campground (1,251 ft.) for
  • complete loop: 2.8 mi., 50 ft., 1 hr. 25 min.

Sawyer Pond Trail (WMNF)

This trail (which has easy grades throughout its length) begins at a parking area 0.2 mi. in on a side road that leaves the north side of the Kancamagus Highway 0.6 mi. east of Passaconaway Campground and 1.4 mi. west of Bear Notch Rd. After passing Sawyer Pond and its campsite, the trail ends at Sawyer River Rd. (FR 34), near the gate that marks the end of public vehicular access at 4.0 mi. *Caution:* The crossing of the Swift River near the Kancamagus Highway usually requires wading and can be dangerous at high water.

From the parking area, the trail passes through a clearing, angles right to the bank of the Swift River, and fords the stream to a sandbar. It soon enters the woods, where the Nanamocomuck (X-C) Ski Trail joins on the right, and runs through a beautiful pine grove. At 0.7 mi., the ski trail diverges on the left, and at 1.1 mi., the Brunel Trail diverges right. At 1.7 mi., the Sawyer Pond Trail crosses a gravel logging road, then skirts the west slope of Birch Hill, descends gently, and crosses a grass-grown logging road (used and marked as a snowmobile trail) diagonally at 2.6 mi. It then comes close to a small brook, bears left away from it, passes over a flat divide, and descends to Sawyer Pond. As the pond is approached, there are a number of conflicting side paths; use care to stay on the correct path. At a point 15 yd. from the pond, the trail turns left and crosses the outlet brook at 4.5 mi. Here a path leads along the shore, with good views up to Mt. Tremont and Owl's Cliff, and reaches the shelter in 0.2 mi. The main trail passes to the left of the tent platforms of the Sawyer Pond Campsite, and in 0.1 mi., it passes another side path that leads right 0.2 mi. to the shelter. It then descends gradually on an old logging road, and turns sharp left off the road at 5.7 mi. and recrosses the Sawyer Pond outlet brook on a bridge. From there, it runs to the bank of the Sawyer River, turns right to cross the river on a footbridge, then turns right again on the gravel extension of Sawyer River Rd. and continues about 100 yd. to the gate.

Sawyer Pond Trail (map 3:J8–I8)

Distances from Kancamagus Highway (1,237 ft.) to
- Brunel Trail (1,330 ft.): 1.1 mi., 100 ft., 35 min.
- Sawyer Pond (1,940 ft.): 4.5 mi., 900 ft. (rev. 200 ft.), 2 hr. 40 min.
- Sawyer River Rd. (1,610 ft.): 6.0 mi., 900 ft. (rev 350 ft.), 3 hr. 25 min.

Rail 'N River Trail (WMNF)

This graded path provides a short, easy loop through attractive pine and spruce woods near the Swift River with interpretive panels describing the farming and logging history of the area. It starts at the parking lot for the Passaconaway Historic Site, which includes the nearby Russell-Colbath House (open in summer and fall), on the north side of the Kancamagus Highway, 0.5 mi. west of its junction with Bear Notch Rd. From the parking area, it runs briefly west past a barn, then swings right to the loop junction. The east end of the loop continues ahead, briefly follows the bed of an old logging railroad, bears left at 0.1 mi., and turns left again on the bank of the Swift River at 0.2 mi. It runs alongside the river for 60 yd., with a view back to Bear Mountain, then bears left and continues through several more turns back to the loop junction. To return to the parking lot, bear right.

Rail 'N River Trail (map 3:J8)

Distance from Passaconaway Historic Site parking lot (1,240 ft) for
- complete loop: 0.6 mi., 0 ft., 20 min.

Rob Brook Trail (WMNF)

This nearly level trail follows old roads and a logging railroad grade through an area of attractive ponds and swamps, with some good views and much beaver activity (which may cause flooding of some trail sections). It parallels the Rob Brook Rd. (FR 35), beginning and ending on that road, which leaves Bear Notch Rd. about 0.8 mi. north of the Kancamagus Highway, opposite the trailhead of the Lower Nanamocomuck (X-C) Ski Trail. It is far more interesting and scenic but somewhat more difficult than the parallel section of road, traversing kinds of terrain not often visited by trails in the White Mountains. Most of the trail is dry, but some brook crossings (including several made on beaver dams) are extremely difficult at high water and wet (requiring wading in a significant depth of water) even in normal conditions. Two bridges near the north end of the trail have been washed out in recent years and will not be replaced.

At the start, it follows Rob Brook Rd., coinciding with the Upper Nanamocomuck (X-C) Ski Trail for the first mile. It diverges off the road to the right 0.2 mi. from Bear Notch Rd., then crosses back over Rob Brook Rd. at 0.7 mi., and descends easily on an old road. It crosses an area of open bogs on a boardwalk with a glimpse of Mt. Carrigain on the right and Mt. Chocorua on the left, then takes the right branch at a fork where the Upper Nanamocomuck Ski Trail continues straight. At 1.3 mi., the Rob Brook Trail reaches an old railroad grade and turns sharp right onto it. Soon it joins Rob Brook and crosses it five times. At the third crossing, which is made at a long beaver dam (usually requiring wading), there is a fine view of Mt. Tremont and Owl's Cliff. The Rob Brook Trail then continues on the railroad grade until it reaches the Rob Brook Rd., which at this point is also the route of the Brunel Trail. To the right, following this road, it is 0.3 mi. to the point where the Brunel Trail turns off the road and 2.9 mi. to the Bear Notch Rd.

Rob Brook Trail (map 3:I9–I8)

Distance from Bear Notch Rd. (1,338 ft.) to
- Rob Brook Rd./Brunel Trail (1,320 ft.): 2.8 mi., 100 ft. (rev. 100 ft.), 1 hr. 25 min.

Brunel Trail (WMNF)

This little-used trail runs from the Sawyer Pond Trail 1.1 mi. north of the Kancamagus Highway to the summit of Mt. Tremont. However, the most frequently used approach to this trail is the WMNF Rob Brook Rd. (FR 35), which leaves Bear Notch Rd. about 0.8 mi. north of the Kancamagus Highway. Rob Brook Rd. is closed to public vehicular travel, but it provides the easiest route to the point where the Brunel Trail departs from it, 2.6 mi. from Bear Notch Rd. The remainder of the Brunel Trail south of this point to the Kancamagus Highway is seldom used, largely because the ford of the Swift River near the start of the Sawyer Pond Trail is frequently difficult. The Rob Brook Trail provides a much more attractive alternative to this road walk but is apt to make a hiker's boots and other clothing rather soggy. Parts of the Brunel Trail are very steep and rough; the footway may be obscure in some areas, so the yellow blazes must be followed with care. The views to the west from Mt. Tremont, and to the south from Owl's Cliff, are excellent.

The trail diverges right (northeast) from the Sawyer Pond Trail, and it enters the extension of Rob Brook Rd. in 0.3 mi, turns right, and follows this road past the junction with the Rob Brook Trail on the right at 0.9 mi. to the Albany-Bartlett town line (sign) at 1.2 mi., where the trail (sign) turns left off the road. This point is 2.6 mi. from Bear Notch Rd. via Rob Brook Rd.

Leaving Rob Brook Rd., the Brunel Trail passes through a stand of large conifers, then rises moderately through hardwoods. At 2.5 mi., it crosses a small brook and soon passes several large boulders that announce the approach to the east end of Owl's Cliff. At 2.8 mi., the trail swings left and climbs a very steep section, then turns sharp right (arrow). The grade moderates and finally becomes easy as the height-of-land is reached. At 3.1 mi. (1.9 mi. from Rob Brook Rd.), a spur path (sign) diverges left and climbs to a point just below the summit of Owl's Cliff, then descends over a steep ledge to a fine outlook (use caution if wet or icy) 0.2 mi. from the main trail. From the junction, the Brunel Trail descends at a moderate grade into the sag, passes through a section where the footway is very overgrown and obscure (watch carefully for blazes), and then ascends very steeply; sections running straight up the slope alternate with old logging roads angling to the left. At 3.9 mi. (2.7 mi. from Rob Brook Rd.), the trail scrambles up a ledge and reaches the summit ledges of Mt. Tremont, where the Mt. Tremont Trail enters from the north.

Brunel Trail (map 3:I8)

Distances from Sawyer Pond Trail (1,330 ft.) to

- departure from Rob Brook Rd. at Albany-Bartlett town line (1,330 ft.): 1.2 mi., 0 ft., 35 min.
- Owl's Cliff spur (2,800 ft.): 3.1 mi., 1,500 ft., 2 hr. 20 min.
- Mt. Tremont summit (3,371 ft.): 3.9 mi., 2,300 ft. (rev. 250 ft.), 3 hr. 5 min. ▶

Distances from Bear Notch Rd. (1,338 ft.) to
- departure from Rob Brook Rd. at Albany-Bartlett town line (1,330 ft.) via Rob Brook Rd.: 2.6 mi., 100 ft. (rev. 100 ft.), 1 hr. 20 min.
- Mt. Tremont summit: 5.3 mi., 2,400 ft. (rev. 250 ft.), 3 hr. 50 min.

Mount Tremont Trail (WMNF)

This trail begins on the south side of US 302, 0.5 mi. west of the Sawyer Rock picnic area and 0.1 mi. west of the bridge over Stony Brook, and climbs, steeply at times, to the summit of Mt. Tremont, where there are fine views.

Leaving US 302, it soon reaches and follows the west side of Stony Brook, passing several cascades. At 0.7 mi., it swings right and climbs steadily for 0.3 mi. to the top of the ridge (watch for a sharp right turn up a steep bank). It then levels off and crosses a recent logging road. For the next 0.25 mi. there is still some lingering evidence of the extensive blowdown caused by the windstorm of December 1980; follow markings carefully.

At 1.5 mi., the trail swings right onto a relocated section and makes a slight descent to cross a branch of Stony Brook, then zigzags up the steep northeast side of the mountain at a moderate grade, crossing a sharp boundary between birch woods and virgin conifers at 2.4 mi. It climbs a steep, rough section with many switchbacks to the ridge top, passes an outlook on the right, and continues to the ledgy summit.

Mount Tremont Trail (map 3:I8)

Distance from US 302 (820 ft.) to
- Mt. Tremont summit (3,371 ft.): 2.8 mi., 2,600 ft. (rev. 50 ft.), 2 hr. 40 min.

Lovequist Loop (WMNF)

This short, easy loop path provides access to scenic little Falls Pond from the popular Rocky Gorge Picnic Area, which is located on the Kancamagus Highway 8.4 mi. west of NH 16 and 3.4 mi. east of its junction with the Bear Notch Rd. From the parking area at Rocky Gorge, follow the paved walkway 0.1 mi. to the bridge across the gorge. About 125 yd. past the bridge, the loop junction is reached; here a 35-yd. side path descends to the shore of Falls Pond, where there is a good view of the lower ridges of Bear Mountain. The section of the loop on the east shore of the pond is also part of the Lower Nanamocomuck (X-C) Ski Trail. Turning left, to follow the loop in a clockwise direction, the trails coincide for about 100 yd., then the pond loop turns right at the south end of the pond and swings around its west shore. After traveling 0.4 mi. from the ski trail junction, the pond loop rejoins the ski trail at the north end of the pond and returns to the loop junction near the bridge across the Swift River.

Lovequist Loop (map 3:19)

Distance from Rocky Gorge Picnic Area (1,120 ft.) for
• complete loop: 1.0 mi., 50 ft., 30 min.

Boulder Loop Trail (WMNF)

This is a loop trail to ledges on a southwest spur of the Moat Range, starting from the north side of Passaconaway Rd. just west of the entrance to the WMNF Covered Bridge Campground. There is a parking area on the south side of the road. (The west part of Passaconaway Rd. is closed to vehicles from November to May, requiring a short extra walk at these times for hikers approaching this trailhead from the Kancamagus Highway.) It offers excellent views for a relatively modest effort, though it does involve about 1,000 ft. of climbing. An interpretive leaflet, keyed to numbered stations along the trail, can be obtained at the Saco Ranger District Office on the Kancamagus Highway near NH 16, and is sometimes available at the trailhead.

The trail leaves Passaconaway Rd. and reaches the loop junction at 0.2 mi. From here, the loop is described in the clockwise direction. Taking the left-hand branch, the trail shortly passes a large rock face (left), where it turns right and climbs moderately past an outlook to Chocorua, then soon turns sharp left. At 1.3 mi., at the main trail's high point, a spur path leads right (south) 0.1 mi. to ledges that afford a fine view of Mt. Passaconaway, Mt. Chocorua, and Middle Sister. The main trail continues around the ledges and descends fairly steeply toward Big Brook, then turns right below the ledges and, running at an easier grade, crosses a stream, and passes an overhanging boulder (left) at 2.3 mi. It then returns to the loop junction at 2.6 mi., 0.2 mi. from Passaconaway Rd.

Boulder Loop Trail (map 3:I10)

Distances from Passaconaway Rd. (860 ft.)
- to loop junction (910 ft.): 0.2 mi., 50 ft., 10 min.
- to spur path to ledges (1,750 ft.): 1.3 mi., 900 ft., 1 hr. 5 min.
- for complete loop including spur to ledges: 3.1 mi., 950 ft., 2 hr.

Moat Mountain Trail (WMNF)

This trail traverses the main ridge of Moat Mountain, providing magnificent views from numerous outlooks. Parts of the ridge are very exposed to weather, particularly the section that crosses Middle Moat and South Moat. The trail can be hard to follow along the open ridge sections in poor visibility conditions—look carefully for blazes, which may be faded.

The south terminus of the trail is located on Passaconaway Rd. At the lights in Conway village, turn north (directly opposite NH 153) onto Washington St., which becomes West Side Rd. Go left at a fork, then at 0.9 mi., turn left on Passaconaway Rd. The Moat Mountain Trail (sign) leaves Passaconaway Rd. at a new trailhead parking area on the right, 4.1 mi. from Conway. Passaconaway Rd. continues and joins the Kancamagus Highway near Blackberry Crossing Campground (but the west part of Passaconaway Rd. is closed to vehicles from November to May).

The northeast terminus of the trail is reached from Conway village via Washington St. and West Side Rd., or from North Conway (at a point just north of the Eastern Slope Inn) by following River Rd. west for 1.0 mi. across the Saco River to West Side Rd. Once on West Side Rd., drive north for another 1.4 mi. to a large parking lot on the west side of the road.

Starting from the northeast terminus, a wide, graded, handicapped-accessible path descends slightly then turns left and winds through coniferous woods for 0.6 mi., intersecting the former route (a gravel road) at the clearing just below the mill site at Diana's Baths, a series of scenic cascades where Lucy Brook runs over ledges and through large potholes. The Moat Mountain Trail leaves the upper end of the clearing, close to the baths, by a logging road that follows the north bank of Lucy Brook to a fork (sign) at 1.2 mi. Here the Red Ridge Trail turns left across the brook, eventually rejoining the Moat Mountain Trail at the apex of Red Ridge, making possible a fine loop hike. The Moat Mountain Trail crosses Lucy Brook (difficult at high water) at 1.4 mi., and follows the south bank, then at 2.4 mi., turns abruptly left up-hill, away from the stream (last sure water), at the point where the Attitash Trail continues straight ahead along the stream toward Big Attitash Mountain. The Moat Mountain Trail ascends through the woods, and at 2.8 mi., begins to pass over ledgy areas, reaching the first good outlook at 3.6 mi. It reaches a shoulder at 4.0 mi. and runs nearly level through a patch of larger trees, then climbs fairly steeply through decreasing scrub and increasing bare ledge to the summit of North Moat at 4.3 mi., where there is an unobstructed view in all directions.

From the summit of North Moat, the trail descends sharply to the base of the cone, then easily along a shoulder with occasional views. At the end of the shoulder it drops steeply, passing over several ledges that require some scrambling, traverses another shoulder where there is a fine outlook to the right in a ledgy area, then descends to a col in a fine spruce forest. Ascending again, it passes the junction with the Red Ridge Trail left (east) at 5.4 mi., just below several large rocks that provide good views. The trail descends to the major col on the ridge, then climbs up to low scrub followed by open ledges with continuous views, and passes east of the summit of Middle Moat (which can be reached in 80 yd. over open ledges) at 6.4 mi. The trail descends to a minor col with a patch of woods that would provide some shelter in a storm, then ascends to the summit of South Moat at 7.0 mi.

The trail then descends into scrub and gradually increasing numbers of beautiful red pines, with views decreasing in frequency. At 7.6 mi., the trail passes an outlook to Mt. Chocorua (on the ascent from the south terminus, this is the first good outlook reached), and the trail becomes steep with rough footing. Below this section, the grade eases considerably, and at 8.4 mi., the trail turns right onto a wide, well-constructed relocation. It runs generally west at easy grades, crosses Dry Brook on a bridge at 8.7 mi., swings left and then right over a small ridge, and crosses a small brook at 9.4 mi. It climbs over another low ridge, then turns sharp left onto a logging road and leads past a gate to the parking area on Passaconaway Rd.

Moat Mountain Trail (map 3:I11–J10)

Distances from West Side Rd. (550 ft.) to
- Red Ridge Trail, lower junction (750 ft.): 1.2 mi., 200 ft., 40 min.
- Attitash Trail (1,080 ft.): 2.4 mi., 550 ft., 1 hr. 30 min. ▶

- North Moat summit (3,196 ft.): 4.3 mi., 2,650 ft., 3 hr. 30 min.
- Red Ridge Trail, upper junction (2,760 ft.): 5.4 mi., 2,800 ft., 4 hr. 5 min.
- Middle Moat summit area (2,800 ft.): 6.4 mi., 3,150 ft., 4 hr. 45 min.
- South Moat summit (2,770 ft.): 7.0 mi., 3,250 ft., 5 hr. 10 min.
- Passaconaway Rd. (650 ft.): 9.7 mi., 3,350 ft., 6 hr. 30 min.

Distances from Passaconaway Rd. (650 ft.) to

- South Moat summit (2,770 ft.): 2.7 mi., 2,200 ft., 2 hr. 25 min.
- Middle Moat summit area (2,800 ft.): 3.3 mi., 2,350 ft., 2 hr. 50 min.
- Red Ridge Trail, upper junction (2,760 ft.): 4.2 mi., 2,650 ft., 3 hr. 25 min.
- North Moat summit (3,196 ft.): 5.3 mi., 3,250 ft., 4 hr. 15 min.
- Attitash Trail (1,080 ft.): 7.2 mi., 3,250 ft., 5 hr. 15 min.
- Red Ridge Trail, lower junction (750 ft.): 8.5 mi., 3,250 ft., 5 hr. 50 min.
- West Side Rd. (550 ft.): 9.7 mi., 3,250 ft., 6 hr. 30 min.

Red Ridge Trail (WMNF)

This trail ascends Red Ridge, with magnificent views, leaving the Moat Mountain Trail 1.2 mi. from West Side Rd. and rejoining it at the unnamed peak at the apex of Red Ridge, 1.1 mi. south of the summit of North Moat. With the Moat Mountain Trail, the Red Ridge Trail provides a very attractive loop over the open summit of North Moat.

This trail branches left (south) from the Moat Mountain Trail and immediately crosses Lucy Brook, a difficult crossing in high water. It ascends generally south at a gentle grade, crossing an area of active logging where it must be followed with care. The Red Ridge Link leaves on the left for White Horse Ledge at 0.8 mi., and the Red Ridge Trail generally descends gradually until it crosses the gravel Red Ridge Rd. (FR 379) at 1.5 mi. The trail soon turns sharp right, approaches Moat Brook and follows it, then crosses it at 2.0 mi., and zigzags steeply upward, climbing to a gravel bank (use caution here, particularly on the descent) where there are good views. Continuing upward rather steeply, it ascends a steep ledge by means of an eroded trap dike and soon attains the crest of Red Ridge, where the grade moderates. Passing alternately through scrub and over ledges with good views, it reaches the bottom of an extensive open ledge section with magnificent views at 3.0 mi. At 3.4 mi., it reenters scrub and soon rejoins the Moat Mountain Trail at the foot of several little rock knobs on the top of a small peak on the main ridge crest between North Moat and Middle Moat.

> **Red Ridge Trail (map 3:I10)**
> Distances from Moat Mountain Trail, lower junction (750 ft.) to
> - Red Ridge Link (950 ft.): 0.8 mi., 200 ft., 30 min.
> - crossing of Moat Brook (1,160 ft.): 2.0 mi., 500 ft. (rev. 100 ft.), 1 hr. 15 min.
> - Moat Mountain Trail, upper junction (2,760 ft.): 3.6 mi., 2,100 ft., 2 hr. 50 min.

Red Ridge Link (NHDP)

This short path links the Red Ridge Trail with the White Horse Ledge Trail, connecting the trails on Moat Mountain with those on White Horse and Cathedral Ledges. It leaves the Red Ridge Trail on the left (east) 0.8 mi. from the Moat Mountain Trail, just past the top of a small rise. It ascends through open hemlock forest and then younger growth at a moderate grade, turning sharp left, then sharp right 60 yd. farther, at the tops of two wooded ledges. These turns may be difficult to see, particularly descending, if the trail blazes are faded. It ends at the White Horse Ledge Trail 0.2 mi. below the summit ledges.

> **Red Ridge Link (map 3:I10)**
> Distance from Red Ridge Trail (950 ft.) to
> - White Horse Ledge Trail (1,370 ft.): 0.4 mi., 400 ft., 25 min.

Attitash Trail (WMNF)

This trail runs from Bear Notch Rd., 2.7 mi. south of its junction with US 302 in Bartlett village, to the Moat Mountain Trail 2.3 mi. west of West Side Rd. The trail is well trodden from Bear Notch Rd. to the ledges of Table Mountain, where there are good views from an area burned by a small forest fire in October 1984. Except for these ledges, the trail is in the woods all the way, and the section east of Table Mountain is wild, rough, and very lightly used. In the past this part of the trail has not been cleared on a regular basis, and some sections may be (and in 2006 were) severely overgrown, obstructed by blowdowns, and very difficult to follow.

Leaving the small parking area on Bear Notch Rd., the trail follows a grass-grown gravel logging road that crosses a major branch of Louisville

Brook in about 120 yd. At 0.3 mi., the trail bears right on an older road as the gravel road bears left into a clear-cut area. At 0.6 mi., the trail comes to the edge of Louisville Brook at a small, ledgy cascade, and follows near the brook. In less than 0.1 mi., it crosses a branch of the brook then turns left (arrow) at a logging road fork and ascends moderately to the col between Bear Mountain and Table Mountain at 1.3 mi. It turns sharp left here and climbs more steeply; loose gravel on ledges makes for frequently slippery footing, particularly on the descent. Soon reaching the edge of the burned area, the trail crosses two ledges with excellent views to the south and southwest. At 1.9 mi., it reaches its high point on Table Mountain, and passes somewhat south of the summit, with views available a short distance to the right from the edge of the south cliff.

From this point, the trail appears to be used more by moose than by humans, and some sections are often very difficult to follow. It descends easily, then steadily into a col at 2.5 mi., where there is a brook (unreliable), passes a ledgy spot with a glimpse back to Table Mountain, and soon climbs a very steep pitch to the main ridge of Big Attitash. From here, the trail runs along the north side of the ridge, crossing the west and middle knobs of Big Attitash with short intervening descents, and finally passes very close to the summit of Big Attitash at 4.7 mi. Then it descends, steeply and roughly at times, into the valley of Lucy Brook, which is crossed at 5.9 mi., where it may be dry. The trail soon turns right onto a relocated section, climbs and descends, crosses a side stream and two branches of the main brook, then follows a logging road and crosses back over Lucy Brook just before reaching the junction with the Moat Mountain Trail at 7.2 mi. (These crossings may be difficult in high water.) The Moat Mountain Trail can be followed to the right to North Moat or straight ahead to Diana's Baths and West Side Rd.

Attitash Trail (map 3:I9–I10)

Distances from Bear Notch Rd. (1,260 ft.) to
- high point on Table Mountain (2,610 ft.): 1.9 mi., 1,350 ft., 1 hr. 40 min.
- Big Attitash Mountain summit (2,910 ft.): 4.7 mi., 2,350 ft. (rev. 700 ft.), 3 hr. 30 min.
- Moat Mountain Trail (1,080 ft.): 7.2 mi., 2,450 ft. (rev. 1,950 ft.), 4 hr. 50 min.

Paths on White Horse Ledge and Cathedral Ledge (NHDP)

These two bluffs on an eastern spur of the Moat Range afford interesting views and are reached by trails from Echo Lake State Park. An automobile road also ascends Cathedral Ledge. The cliffs on both bluffs are very popular with rock climbers but cannot be safely ascended without proper equipment and training. The two principal trails are the White Horse Ledge Trail and the Bryce Path. The Bryce Path is named for James Bryce (later Viscount Bryce), a British statesman and author of many books on the theory of government, including *The American Commonwealth,* an important study of the U.S. government from a British perspective. Bryce laid out this trail, which originally consisted of the path up the slope between the two cliffs and the branches to both summits, in 1907 when he was British ambassador to the United States. Construction on private land between Echo Lake and the foot of White Horse Ledge compelled a major relocation of the southern part of the White Horse Ledge Trail in 2001; this relocation is well constructed and clearly marked. For the sake of simplicity, and in order to describe the trails in the sequence in which they are usually followed, the two trails are described here as a single loop trail over White Horse Ledge, with a spur path to Cathedral Ledge. There are two routes available from public roads to the loop junction:

(1) Leave Main St. in North Conway just north of the Eastern Slope Inn and take River Rd., which runs west across the Saco River. Turn left at 1.0 mi. onto West Side Rd., then right at 1.4 mi. onto Echo Lake Rd., following signs for Echo Lake State Park, and reach the park gate at 1.5 mi. If the park is closed, parking is available on an old segment of road to the left, and the park road can be followed on foot from the gate to the trailhead (signs). From here the path (the Echo Lake Trail) descends 60 yd. nearly to the edge of Echo Lake, then bears left and runs along the lake, some distance away but mostly in sight of it. At 0.4 mi., the trail to the ledges turns sharp left, whereas the Echo Lake Trail continues around the lake and returns to the trailhead at the parking area in another 0.5 mi.; it is poorly marked and its footway is not always well defined, particularly in the vicinity of the main beach, but its route along the shore is fairly obvious, and there are good views of the cliffs from the east shore. From its junction with the Echo Lake Trail,

the trail to the ledges runs almost perfectly straight through attractive woods, crossing two unsigned but fairly well beaten paths, and reaches a crossroads, which is the loop junction, at 0.7 mi.

(2) Continue straight at 1.0 mi. from North Conway's Main St. instead of turning left for Echo Lake State Park, then turn left onto Cathedral Ledge Rd. at 1.5 mi. from Main St. Follow Cathedral Ledge Rd. (which ends in 1.8 mi. just below the summit of Cathedral Ledge) for 0.3 mi., then park on the left just beyond a dirt road closed off by a chain gate. Follow the dirt road on foot for 0.3 mi., passing the former parking area, avoiding branching roads to the right and a footpath to the left, to the loop junction at the crossroads. This route is shorter (saving a bit less than 0.4 mi. and about 10 min. each way) and avoids park admission fees, but is less attractive. It has sometimes been called the Bryce Link.

At the crossroads, where there is a fine view of the impressive slabs of White Horse Ledge, one road leads south up into a clearing. Facing this road, access route 1 is on your left, access route 2 is behind you, and on your right is the Bryce Path, which ascends to the sag between the two summits and gives access to either. Just to the left of and parallel to the road you are facing is the beginning of the south part of the White Horse Ledge Trail, which runs from the loop junction along the east side of White Horse Ledge and then climbs its south ridge to the Red Ridge Link junction near the summit of White Horse Ledge. The loop is described here in the counterclockwise direction. However, for those who merely wish to view the climbing ledges, the beginning of the south part of the White Horse Ledge Trail can be followed for 0.2 mi. to the point where the rock climbers' path to the base of White Horse Ledge leaves on the right; the steep slab, whose base is 80 yd. from this junction, is worth a visit, but its ascent is a technical climb that must be left to properly trained and equipped rock climbers.

From the loop junction, the Bryce Path passes near the foundation of an old sugarhouse and the clearing, then reaches a rock slab in the woods and climbs directly uphill steeply with rough footing and two wooden stairways for about 0.1 mi. It then bears right and runs almost level to a junction at 0.3 mi. from the loop junction.

Here the path to Cathedral Ledge continues almost straight across a flat, wooded upland for 0.2 mi., then turns sharp right and climbs rather steeply for another 0.2 mi. to a T intersection, where it turns left and reaches the turnaround at the top of Cathedral Ledge Rd. in another 40 yd. A right at the T leads to the south outlook in 80 yd. (The summit area is interlaced with countless beaten paths.) The true summit is a wooded ledge, but there are several fine viewpoints from the rim of the summit area, including the fenced east outlook at the top of the main cliff.

From the junction with the path to Cathedral Ledge, the White Horse Ledge Trail turns left uphill. It then turns right at a group of large boulders and climbs steeply for a short distance, then swings left and climbs moderately, and at 0.5 mi. from the loop junction, it reaches an open ledge that provides a fine vista east across the valley to Kearsarge North and the Green Hills, the best view available from the White Horse Ledge Trail. The trail soon reenters the woods and climbs moderately, then turns left and runs at easy grades near the crest of the ridge. At 0.9 mi., it emerges on a large wooded ledge and turns right, following the crest of the ledge to the summit, where there is a view east to the Green Hills. A few steps beyond the high point the trail turns right into the woods (follow yellow blazes on the rocks); a ledge 25 yd. to the left at this turn provides a fine view of Moat Mountain. The trail descends easily northwest and then west, then turns sharp left where the Red Ridge Link enters on the right at 1.1 mi. The White Horse Ledge Trail descends moderately to the south by switchbacks, then swings left through a logged area, and bears left onto the relocated section of trail at 1.5 mi., angling down along the south slope of the ridge. It turns left at a red-blazed birch, climbs briefly, then descends and turns sharp right where a climbers' path diverges left to the cliffs. The trail descends by switchbacks, then swings north and weaves through large boulders at the base of the cliffs, with minor ups and downs. It dips right to a low point, then climbs and turns sharp left near the edge of a green on a private golf course. It runs through a narrow strip of woods behind the White Mountain Hotel, and at 2.5 mi., the rock climbers' path to the base of White Horse Ledge enters on the left. From here, the trail continues at easy grades to the loop junction.

White Horse Ledge Trail and Bryce Path (map 3:I11–I10)

Distances from Echo Lake parking area (490 ft.)
- to loop junction (570 ft.): 0.7 mi., 100 ft., 20 min.
- to White Horse Ledge–Cathedral Ledge fork (900 ft.): 1.0 mi., 400 ft., 40 min.
- to White Horse Ledge (1,450 ft.): 1.6 mi., 950 ft., 1 hr. 15 min.
- to loop junction (570 ft.): 3.4 mi., 1,050 ft. (rev. 950 ft.), 2 hr. 15 min.
- for a complete loop: 4.1 mi., 1,050 ft., 2 hr. 35 min.

Distances from Echo Lake parking area (490 ft.) to
- Cathedral Ledge (1,159 ft.) via Cathedral Ledge branch: 1.4 mi., 700 ft. (rev. 50 ft.), 1 hr.
- White Horse Ledge and Cathedral Ledge (returning to trail fork from each): 4.0 mi., 1,300 ft., 2 hr. 40 min.
- White Horse Ledge and Cathedral Ledge (making side trip to Cathedral Ledge and loop over White Horse Ledge): 4.9 mi., 1,400 ft., 3 hr. 10 min.

SUGGESTED HIKES

For more information on suggested hikes, see p. ix.

Easy Hikes

Lovequist Loop [lp: 1.0 mi., 50 ft., 0:30]. A short hike from the Rocky Gorge picnic area around Falls Pond.

Sawyer Pond [rt: 3.0 mi., 350 ft., 1:40]. This attractive and popular mountain pond situated at the base of Mt. Tremont is easily reached by the Sawyer Pond Trail from Sawyer River Rd.

Church Pond [lp: 2.8 mi., 50 ft., 1:25]. An attractive but less popular pond reached by a loop path from the Kancamagus Highway. The Swift River must be forded at the start, and the pond lies in a flat region of swamps and poorly drained woodlands, very different from the terrain usually crossed by hiking trails—visitors should expect wet feet.

Boulder Loop Trail [lp: 3.1 mi., 950 ft., 2:00]. This interpretive nature trail ascends a low spur of the Moat group and offers fine views from open ledges.

Moderate Hikes

Table Mountain [rt: 3.8 mi., 1,350 ft., 2:35]. This less visited peak offers good views from its south ledges; use the Attitash Trail from Bear Notch Rd.

South Moat Mountain [rt: 5.4 mi., 2,300 ft., 3:50]. This bare summit, accessed via the south end of the Moat Mountain Trail, has excellent views in all directions.

Mt. Tremont [rt: 5.6 mi., 2,650 ft., 4:05]. This infrequently climbed peak offers fine views; the Mt. Tremont Trail is steep in places and must be followed with care.

Strenuous Hikes

Nancy Pond Trail. The trip to Nancy Cascades [rt: 4.8 mi., 1,450 ft., 3:10] is attractive in itself, but it is worth the effort to continue to the unusual ledge that dams Norcross Pond and affords a fine view into the Pemigewasset Wilderness [rt: 8.6 mi., 2,150 ft., 5:20].

Mt. Carrigain [rt: 10.0 mi., 3,300 ft., 6:35]. The tower on this peak, accessed by the Signal Ridge Trail, offers what many people believe is the best view of all in the Whites.

Mt. Hancock [lp: 9.8 mi., 2,700 ft., 6:15]. The Hancock Notch, Cedar Brook, and Hancock Loop trails provide an interesting loop over this remote mountain, with outlooks from the north and south summits.

North Moat Loop [lp: 10.2 mi., 2,900 ft., 6:35]. The circuit over this mountain via the Red Ridge and Moat Mountain trails is one of the most beautiful trips in this region, traversing large amounts of open ledge.

SECTION FIVE

CANNON AND KINSMAN

This section covers the trails on Kinsman Mountain, Cannon Mountain, and the lower peaks in the same range, principally Mt. Wolf, the Cannon Balls, and Mt. Pemigewasset. It also covers trails on several smaller mountains to the west and north, including Bald Mountain and Artist's Bluff, Cooley Hill, Mt. Agassiz, and Kilburn Crags. The area is bounded on the east by I-93, US 3, and the Franconia Notch Parkway, and on the south by NH 112 (Lost River Rd.). The entire section (except for the outlying Kilburn Crags Trail) is covered by the AMC's *Moosilauke–Kinsman Map* (map 4). In addition, all the trails in this section except the Cobble Hill, Jericho Rd., and Kilburn Crags trails are also shown on the AMC's *Franconia–Pemigewasset Map* (map 2).

A paved bike path runs the entire length of the notch from the parking area at the Flume to the Skookumchuck Trail and is available for pedestrian use, though those on foot should be careful not to impede bicycle traffic unnecessarily. Information regarding trails and other facilities is available during the summer and fall tourist season at the Flume Visitor Center at the south end of the park, and throughout the year (except for the late-fall and early-spring "off-seasons") at the Cannon Mountain Tramway. Information is also available from the information center in Lincoln, located opposite the I-93 exit ramp. Concord Trailways has bus service from Boston at Logan Airport and South Station to Lincoln and Franconia, which may operate only on weekends. In summer, connections to trailheads can be made by using the AMC's Hiker Shuttle.

In this section, the Appalachian Trail (AT) follows the Kinsman Ridge Trail from Kinsman Notch to Kinsman Junction (near Kinsman Pond), the Fishin' Jimmy Trail from Kinsman Junction to Lonesome Lake Hut, and the Cascade Brook Trail from Lonesome Lake Hut to a trail junction near the former Whitehouse Bridge site, which is reached by the Whitehouse Trail from the hikers' parking area just north of the Flume Visitor Center or by the bike path from the Basin parking lots.

GEOGRAPHY

The heart of this region is the Cannon-Kinsman Range. The northern half of the range is a high, well-defined ridge, of which Cannon Mountain and the two peaks of Kinsman Mountain are the most important summits.

The southern half of the range is broad, with only one significant summit, Mt. Wolf.

At the north end of the range is Cannon Mountain (4,100 ft.). This dome-shaped mountain was long famous for its magnificent profile, the Old Man of the Mountain, which fell in May 2003 because of the natural forces of weathering and erosion, and for its imposing east cliff. The mountain, also sometimes known as Profile Mountain, takes its officially recognized name from a natural stone table resting on a boulder that resembles a cannon when seen from Profile Clearing. The Great Stone Face (the name by which the Old Man was immortalized in a story by Nathaniel Hawthorne) was formed by three ledges at the north end of the east cliff that were not in a vertical line and only appeared to be a profile when viewed from the vicinity of Profile Lake. For many years, state park personnel protected the Old Man from the otherwise inexorable forces of ice and gravity by filling cracks with cement and maintaining a system of cables and turnbuckles, but on the night of May 3, 2003, the forces of nature finally prevailed. Cannon Mountain has a major ski area operated by the state of New Hampshire, with an aerial tramway (the successor to the first such passenger tramway in North America) that extends from a valley station (1,970 ft.) just off the parkway to a mountain station (4,000 ft.) just below the main summit. The tramway is operated throughout the year for tourists and for skiers in the winter. Hiking is not permitted on ski trails.

On the ridge southwest of Cannon Mountain are three humps called the Cannon Balls (east to west: 3,769 ft., 3,660 ft., and 3,693 ft.). All are wooded, but the highest, the northeast Cannon Ball, has several restricted outlooks. Bridal Veil Falls, one of the more attractive falls in the White Mountains, is located on Coppermine Brook in the ravine between Cannon Mountain and the Cannon Balls on the northwest side of the ridge. Lonesome Lake (2,740 ft.) is located on the high plateau that forms the floor of the ravine south of the ridge between Cannon Mountain and the Cannon Balls. Trails completely encircle the lake, which has excellent views from its shores. The whole area around the lake is in Franconia Notch State Park, and camping is not permitted.

Kinsman Mountain rises to the south of the Cannon Balls, and its two peaks are the highest points on the ridge. North Kinsman (4,293 ft.) is wooded, and its true summit is actually a pointed boulder in the woods beside the trail, but ledges just to the east of the summit command magnificent views. The view of Mt. Lafayette and Mt. Lincoln across Franconia Notch is particularly impressive. South Kinsman (4,358 ft.) has a broad, flat summit with two knobs of nearly equal height. The USGS Lincoln quad puts the summit elevation on the north knob, which is just off the main trail, but the south knob bears the cairn and is preferred by most hikers. Views are fine, but one must wander around the summit plateau to obtain the best outlooks. Kinsman Mountain shelters two very beautiful small ponds: Kinsman Pond under the east cliffs of North Kinsman, and Harrington Pond under the bluff at the end of South Kinsman's south ridge.

Two spurs of the Kinsman group are especially notable. On the west, Bald Peak (2,470 ft.) is a flat, ledgy knob with good views, reached by a short spur path from the Mt. Kinsman Trail. On the east, lying below the massive southeast ridge of South Kinsman, is Mt. Pemigewasset (2,557 ft.), with its famous natural rock profile, the Indian Head; the ledgy summit affords excellent views and its ascent requires only a modest effort.

South of Kinsman Mountain, only Mt. Wolf has much claim to prominence. Its summit bears a ledge with an excellent view to the east and northeast. Although lacking in impressive peaks, the southern part of the range does have several interesting aquatic attractions, including Lost River, Gordon Pond, Gordon Falls, Georgiana Falls, and Harvard Falls. The Lost River Reservation, property of the Society for the Protection of New Hampshire Forests (SPNHF), lies about 6 mi. west of North Woodstock on NH 112 (Lost River Rd.). Here Lost River, one of the tributaries of Moosilauke Brook, flows for nearly 0.5 mi. through a series of caves and large potholes, for the most part underground. At one place, it falls 20 ft. within one of the caves, and at another, known as Paradise Falls, it falls 30 ft. in the open. Trails, walks, and ladders make the caves accessible. To protect the forest and caves, the SPNHF began to acquire the surrounding land in 1911, and it now owns about 770 acres bordering the highway on both sides. The SPNHF maintains a nature garden containing more than 300 indigenous plants and an Ecology Trail that circles the inner parking lot area and provides information at numbered and marked sites described in a brochure provided by the SPNHF. The reservation is open from May through October; an admission fee is charged.

This section also includes several scattered peaks and trails. Just northeast of Cannon Mountain are Bald Mountain (2,340 ft.) and Artist's Bluff (2,340 ft.), two small but very interesting peaks at the north end of Franconia Notch that offer excellent views for little exertion. Bald Mountain is a striking miniature mountain with a bold, bare, rocky cone, whereas Artist's Bluff is a wooded dome that bears the fine cliff for which it is named on its southeast face. Between the villages of Franconia and Bethlehem, Mt. Agassiz (2,369 ft.) is reached by a paved road 0.8 mi. long (formerly an auto toll road) that leaves NH 142 1.0 mi. south of its junction with US 302 in Bethlehem village. There is an excellent and extensive view from the summit. The former restaurant and observation tower are now a private residence, so hikers, who are currently welcome to enjoy the views from the summit (on foot only), should exercise great care to respect the rights of the property owner by staying away from all buildings. Cooley Hill (2,485 ft.) is a wooded, viewless peak, but a trail built to its former fire tower has survived the loss of its principal reason for existence. The Kilburn Crags above the town of Littleton provide an easily visited viewpoint with an excellent view of the White Mountain high peaks.

HUTS

Lonesome Lake Hut (AMC)

Lonesome Lake Hut, at about 2,760 ft., is located on the southwest shore of Lonesome Lake, with superb views of the Franconia Range. The hut was built in 1964, replacing cabins on the northeast shore. It accommodates 48 guests and is open to the public year-round (full-service June, July, and August, and on a caretaker basis from September to mid-May). Pets are not permitted in the hut. The hut can be reached by the Lonesome Lake Trail, or by the Cascade Brook Trail (via the Whitehouse Trail or the Basin-Cascades Trail) from the Franconia Notch Parkway, by the Fishin' Jimmy Trail from Kinsman Junction, or by the Dodge Cutoff from the Hi-Cannon Trail. Camping is not permitted around the hut or the lake, or anywhere else in Franconia Notch State Park except at Lafayette Campground. For schedules and information, contact the AMC's Reservations Office (603-466-2727) or visit www.outdoors.org/lodging.

CAMPING

Forest Protection Areas

The WMNF has established a number of Forest Protection Areas (FPAs)—formerly known as Restricted Use Areas—where camping and wood or charcoal fires are prohibited throughout the year. The specific areas are under continual review, and areas are added to or subtracted from the list in order to provide the greatest amount of protection to areas subject to damage by excessive camping, while imposing the lowest level of restrictions possible. A general list of FPAs in this section follows, but because there are often major changes from year to year, one should obtain current information on FPAs from the WMNF.

(1) No camping is permitted above treeline (where trees are less than 8 ft. tall), except in winter, and then only in places where there is at least 2 ft. of snow cover on the ground—but not on any frozen body of water. The point where the restricted area begins is marked on most trails with small signs, but the absence of such signs should not be construed as proof of the legality of a site.

(2) No camping is permitted within 0.25 mi. of any trailhead, picnic area, or any facility for overnight accommodation such as a hut, cabin, shelter, tentsite, or campground, except as designated at the facility itself. In this section, camping is also forbidden within 200 ft. of the Woodsville water supply dam on the Wild Ammonoosuc River.

(3) No camping is permitted on WMNF land within 0.25 mi. of certain roads (camping on private roadside land is illegal except by permission of the landowner). In 2006, these roads included NH 112 (Lost River Rd.) between Lincoln and Woodsville.

Franconia Notch State Park

No camping is permitted in Franconia Notch State Park except at Lafayette Campground (fee charged). In this section, the areas included in the park consist mostly of the northeast slopes of Cannon Mountain and the regions surrounding Lonesome Lake and extending east from the lake to the Franconia Notch Parkway.

Established Trailside Campsites

During peak summer and fall periods, groups of six or more planning to use AMC-managed backcountry campsites are asked to use the AMC's group notification system. For more information, visit http://www.outdoors .org/lodging/campsites/campsites-notification.cfm.

Eliza Brook Shelter (AMC) is located on the Kinsman Ridge Trail at its crossing of Eliza Brook, between Mt. Wolf and Mt. Kinsman.

Kinsman Pond Campsite (AMC), with a shelter honoring Michael Tenney and three tent platforms, is located on Kinsman Pond near Kinsman Junction, where the Kinsman Ridge, Kinsman Pond, and Fishin' Jimmy trails meet. There is a caretaker in summer, and a fee is charged. Water is available from the pond but is not potable without treatment.

Coppermine Shelter (WMNF) is located on the Coppermine Trail just west of Bridal Veil Falls.

TRAIL DESCRIPTIONS

Kinsman Ridge Trail (AMC)

This trail follows the crest of the main ridge from the height-of-land on NH 112 in Kinsman Notch to the Cannon Mountain Tramway parking lot just off the Franconia Notch Parkway (look for the trail sign on a post in the lot and park nearby). At the south end, the trail leaves NH 112 just to the north of the height-of-land, 0.5 mi. north of the Lost River entrance and almost directly opposite the parking area at the north terminus of the Beaver Brook Trail. From NH 112 to Kinsman Junction, it is part of the AT. For much of its length, it is a more difficult route than one might infer from the map—footing is often rough and there are many minor ups and downs. Hikers with heavy packs should allow considerable extra time for many parts of the trail. There is little water on or near several long sections of the trail, and none that a cautious hiker will drink without treatment.

The following description of the path is in the northbound direction (from Kinsman Notch to the Cannon Mountain Tramway parking lot). See the description of the path in the reverse direction that follows.

The trail leaves NH 112 and climbs a steep sidehill bearing gradually away from the road for 0.1 mi., then swings right and climbs very steeply northeast through a part of the SPNHF Lost River Reservation. At 0.4 mi., the grade relaxes, and the trail soon crosses a swampy sag on log bridges and reaches a junction on the right at 0.6 mi. with the Dilly Trail from Lost River. At 0.9 mi., the Kinsman Ridge Trail crosses the summit of a wooded knob, passes a southeast outlook, and descends steeply by zigzags, soon passes a small stream (unreliable), and follows the ridge over several minor humps. At 2.4 mi., it passes an outlook to the east, then crosses a larger wooded hump and descends steadily. At 3.3 mi., it reaches its low point south of Mt. Wolf, crossing a stagnant brook in a ravine, then ascends 30 yd. to the junction where the Gordon Pond Trail enters on the right, 0.3 mi. from Gordon Pond.

The trail now climbs by short, steep sections alternating with easy sections and occasional minor descents, crossing a small brook (reliable water) at 3.9 mi., and ascends to a point just below the summit of the west knob of Mt. Wolf. Then it descends slightly into a shallow sag and climbs to a point near the summit of the east knob of Mt. Wolf at 4.6 mi., where it makes a sharp left turn. Here a side path leads to the right 60 yd. to the summit of the east knob, where there is a fine view of the Franconias and the peaks to the east and southeast. The main trail then descends the east side of Mt. Wolf's north ridge at a moderate grade, but with a rough footway and two significant ascents along the way. At 5.4 mi., where the trail turns left for the second of these ascents, a side path descends 20 yd. right to the edge of a bog known as Failing Water Pond, where there is a view of South Kinsman. At 6.0 mi., the trail turns left, runs almost level, then descends and meets the Reel Brook Trail, which enters left at 6.5 mi., just south of the col between Mt. Wolf and Kinsman Mountain (this was the original Kinsman Notch). The Kinsman Ridge Trail continues along the ridge top, crosses under power lines at 7.0 mi., and descends to the bank of Eliza Brook at 7.5 mi., where a side path runs left 55 yd. to Eliza Brook Shelter.

The Kinsman Ridge Trail crosses Eliza Brook and in 50 yd. intersects a grass-grown, gravel, logging road and follows it to the left. (Watch carefully for the point where the trail turns off this road, going in either direction.) The trail follows the road for 0.3 mi., then turns left off it and follows a very scenic section of Eliza Brook, with several attractive cascades and pools. At 8.6 mi., the trail recrosses Eliza Brook and soon climbs rather steeply to cross the bog at the east end of Harrington Pond on log bridges. Here, at 8.9 mi., there is an interesting view of the shoulder of South Kinsman rising above the beautiful pond. (*Note:* The section of the trail between Harrington Pond and South Kinsman may require much extra time, particularly for those with heavy packs, and is also somewhat exposed to weather.) The trail continues at a moderate grade for 0.3 mi., then climbs a steep pitch, crosses a minor hump and a blowdown patch, then struggles up a very steep and rough pitch to an outlook where the climbing becomes somewhat easier. It continues to the bare south knob of South Kinsman's summit, which is very exposed to the weather, at 9.9 mi.

From here the Kinsman Ridge Trail crosses a scrub-filled sag, passes 15 yd. to the west of the north knob of South Kinsman at 10.0 mi., and descends relatively easily to the col between South and North Kinsman at 10.5 mi. The trail then climbs steadily to a side path (sign) that leads to the right at 10.9 mi.; this side path runs 25 yd. to a fine outlook to the Franconias and continues, descending steeply, another 70 yd. to a ledge that looks directly down on Kinsman Pond. The true summit of North Kinsman is a pointed boulder on the right (east) side of the main trail, 30 yd. north of the outlook spur. The Kinsman Ridge Trail now descends steeply to the junction with the Mt. Kinsman Trail on the left at 11.3 mi., then continues to Kinsman Junction at 11.5 mi. Here the Fishin' Jimmy Trail continues the AT to Lonesome Lake, and the Kinsman Pond Trail bears right, leading in 0.1 mi. to Kinsman Pond and Kinsman Pond Shelter.

The Kinsman Ridge Trail turns sharp left at Kinsman Junction, and soon rises abruptly 100 ft. to a hump (3,812 ft.) on the ridge. It then continues over the Cannon Balls, the three humps that make up the ridge leading to Cannon Mountain. After passing near the top of the first (west) Cannon Ball at 12.5 mi., it descends sharply to a deep ravine where a small, sluggish brook usually contains some water. The trail circles to the north of the second (middle) Cannon Ball and enters the next col with very little descent. After passing several scattered viewpoints while climbing over the third (northeast) Cannon Ball at 13.7 mi., it descends rather steeply and roughly to the junction at 13.9 mi. with the Lonesome Lake Trail, which leads southeast 1.0 mi. to Lonesome Lake Hut (water can be found 0.2 mi. down this trail).

In a few yards, the trail reaches the low point in Coppermine Col, at the base of Cannon Mountain, then climbs a very steep and rough slope among huge boulders. At 14.3 mi., the Hi-Cannon Trail enters right, and the Kinsman Ridge Trail swings left and climbs gradually to the gravel Rim Trail at 14.7 mi., where it encounters the maze of trails in the summit area. The true summit, with its observation platform and lookout tower, is reached in 120 yd. by following the gravel path straight ahead from this junction; a path continues from the tower down to the Cannon Mountain Tramway summit station.

The Kinsman Ridge Trail bears right at the junction and coincides with the Rim Trail for about 0.2 mi. around the edge of the summit plateau, affording excellent views, then turns sharp right downhill (sign) as the Rim Trail continues on toward the tramway terminal. Descending the semi-open east flank of the main peak over rocks and ledges, then through scrub, it crosses a moist sag and ascends slightly to the east summit. At the point where it makes a right-angle turn left (north), a side trail turns sharp right and descends easily southeast for 60 yd., emerging on ledges where there is a magnificent view across the notch to the Franconia Range. The main trail descends steadily, and at 15.7 mi., it turns right onto a ski trail and descends along its right edge. Soon the trail descends steeply through a semi-open area of ski glades, with rough and rocky footing including some slippery ledges. The hiking trail crosses the ski route four times, with occasional views north; follow markings carefully. At 16.1 mi., it continues steeply down into the woods as the ski trail descends to the left. The descent remains steep down through eroded gravelly sections with slippery footing. Finally, it emerges in a field at the base of a steep slope and follows a service road left for 150 yd. to its end at the Cannon Mountain Tramway parking lot.

Kinsman Ridge Trail (map 4:I3–G4)

Distances from NH 112 in Kinsman Notch (1,870 ft.) to

- Dilly Trail (2,650 ft.): 0.6 mi., 800 ft., 40 min.
- Gordon Pond Trail (2,700 ft.): 3.3 mi., 1,450 ft., 2 hr. 25 min.
- Reel Brook Trail (2,600 ft.): 6.5 mi., 2,500 ft., 4 hr. 30 min.
- Eliza Brook Shelter spur (2,400 ft.): 7.5 mi., 2,550 ft., 5 hr.
- Harrington Pond (3,400 ft.): 8.9 mi., 3,550 ft., 6 hr. 15 min.
- South Kinsman summit (4,358 ft.): 10.0 mi., 4,500 ft., 7 hr. 15 min. ▶

- North Kinsman summit (4,293 ft.): 10.9 mi., 4,800 ft., 7 hr. 50 min.
- Mt. Kinsman Trail (3,900 ft.): 11.3 mi., 4,800 ft., 8 hr. 5 min.
- Kinsman Junction (3,750 ft.): 11.5 mi., 4,800 ft., 8 hr. 10 min.
- Lonesome Lake Trail (3,400 ft.): 13.9 mi., 5,500 ft., 9 hr. 40 min.
- Hi-Cannon Trail (3,850 ft.): 14.3 mi., 5,950 ft., 10 hr. 5 min.
- Rim Trail junction near Cannon Mountain summit (4,050 ft.): 14.7 mi., 6,150 ft., 10 hr. 25 min.
- side path to ledges (3,800 ft.): 15.4 mi., 6,200 ft., 10 hr. 50 min.
- Cannon Mountain Tramway parking area (1,980 ft.): 16.9 mi., 6,200 ft., 11 hr. 35 min.

Kinsman Ridge Trail (AMC) [In Reverse]

From the Cannon Mountain Tramway parking area near the main buildings, the trail turns left and follows a gravel road to a picnic area (sign) for 150 yd., then turns right and follows the left edge of a field for 80 yd. to the bottom of a steep slope. Turning left (sign) into the woods, the trail climbs moderately and then steeply by switchbacks, with some gravel sections that are severely eroded. At 0.8 mi., it enters a semi-open area of ski glades and climbs steeply with rough and rocky footing, including some slippery ledges. The hiking trail crosses the ski route four times, with occasional views north; follow markings carefully. From the top of the glades, it ascends along the left edge of a ski trail, and at 1.2 mi., it turns left off the ski trail (signs), enters the woods, and climbs moderately, then easily. In a level area at 1.5 mi., a side path diverges from the left side of the trail (straight ahead) and descends easily southeast for 60 yd., emerging on ledges where there is a magnificent view across the notch to the Franconia Range. Here the main trail turns sharp right (west) to cross over the east summit and pass through a moist sag, after which it climbs rather steeply up through rocks and scrub to the gravel Rim Trail at 2.0 mi. It turns left here (right leads to the tramway terminal) and coincides with the Rim Trail for 0.2 mi., affording excellent views. Then the Kinsman Ridge Trail continues straight ahead on an ordinary dirt footpath at the point where the gravel path turns sharp right to reach the summit observation platform and lookout tower in 120 yd. and then continues to the tramway summit station.

From this junction with the tourist paths, the Kinsman Ridge Trail descends gradually to the junction at 2.5 mi. with the Hi-Cannon Trail, which continues straight where the Kinsman Ridge Trail turns right, and soon drops very steeply down a rough path among huge boulders to Coppermine Col. It then climbs for a few yards to the junction on the left at 3.0 mi. with the Lonesome Lake Trail, which leads southeast 1.0 mi. to Lonesome Lake Hut (water can be found 0.2 mi. down this trail). The Kinsman Ridge Trail now begins the traverse of the Cannon Balls, the three humps that make up the ridge leading to Kinsman Mountain. It ascends a steep and rough section above the Lonesome Lake Trail junction and passes several scattered viewpoints while climbing over the first (northeast) Cannon Ball at 3.2 mi., then descends to a col. The trail circles to the north of the second (middle) Cannon Ball and descends moderately to a deep ravine where a small, sluggish brook usually contains some water, then ascends sharply and passes near the top of the third (west) Cannon Ball at 4.4 mi. After crossing another hump (3,812 ft.) and dropping to a flat region, it reaches Kinsman Junction at 5.4 mi. Here the Fishin' Jimmy Trail (a part of the AT) enters on the left from Lonesome Lake, and the Kinsman Pond Trail runs straight ahead, leading in 0.1 mi. to Kinsman Pond and Kinsman Pond Shelter.

From Kinsman Junction, the Kinsman Ridge Trail (now part of the AT for the rest of its length) turns right and climbs up ledges to the junction where the Mt. Kinsman Trail enters on the right at 5.6 mi., then continues to climb steeply to the summit of North Kinsman at 6.0 mi. Here a side path (sign) leads to the left 25 yd. to a fine outlook to the Franconias and continues, descending steeply, another 70 yd. to a ledge that looks directly down on Kinsman Pond. The true summit of North Kinsman is a pointed boulder on the left (east) side of the main trail, 30 yd. north of the outlook spur. The main trail descends steadily to the col between North and South Kinsman at 6.4 mi., then ascends relatively easily and passes 15 yd. to the west of the north knob of South Kinsman's summit at 6.9 mi.

The Kinsman Ridge Trail then crosses a scrub-filled sag to the bare south knob of South Kinsman, which is very exposed to the weather, at 7.0 mi. (*Note:* The section of the trail between South Kinsman and Harrington Pond may require much extra time, particularly for those with heavy packs, and is also somewhat exposed to weather.) From South Kinsman the trail descends moderately, then drops down a very steep and rough pitch, crosses a blowdown patch and a minor hump, then descends another steep pitch. It continues to descend at a moderate grade for 0.3 mi., then crosses the bog at the east end of Harrington Pond on log bridges. Here, at 8.0 mi., there is an interesting view of the shoulder of South Kinsman rising above the beautiful pond. The trail resumes a rather steep descent, then crosses Eliza Brook at 8.3 mi. and follows a very scenic section of the brook, with several attractive cascades and pools. At 9.1 mi., the trail intersects a grass-grown, gravel, logging road and follows it to the right. (Watch carefully for the point where the trail turns off this road, going in either direction.) The trail follows the road for 0.3 mi., then turns right off it and in 50 yd. recrosses Eliza Brook, reaching a junction at 9.4 mi., where a side path runs right 55 yd. to Eliza Brook Shelter.

From here, the Kinsman Ridge Trail crosses under power lines at 9.9 mi. and continues along a ridge crest to the junction with Reel Brook Trail, which enters right at 10.4 mi., just south of the col between Mt. Wolf and Kinsman Mountain (this was the original Kinsman Notch). The Kinsman Ridge Trail now ascends moderately then runs almost level, then turns right and ascends the east side of Mt. Wolf's north ridge at a moderate grade, but with a rough footway and two significant descents along the way. At 11.5 mi., where the trail turns right at the bottom of the first descent, a side path descends 20 yd. left to the edge of a bog known as Failing Water Pond, where there is a view of South Kinsman. The main trail continues to ascend to a point near the summit of the east knob of Mt. Wolf at 12.3 mi., where it makes a sharp right turn. A side path here leads left 60 yd. to the summit of the east knob, where there is a fine view of the Franconias and the peaks to the east and southeast. The main trail descends slightly into a shallow sag, then ascends slightly to a point just below the summit of the west knob of Mt. Wolf. Here it turns left, descending by short, steep sections alternating with easy sections and occasional minor ascents across a small brook (reliable water) at 13.0 mi. to the junction with the Gordon Pond Trail on the left at 13.6 mi., 0.3 mi. from Gordon Pond.

The Kinsman Ridge Trail descends another 30 yd. to its low point south of Mt. Wolf, crosses a stagnant brook in a ravine, then ascends moderately. It runs to the left of the summit of a large wooded hump, passes an outlook to the east, and follows the ridge crest over several minor humps, finally ascending steeply by zigzags past a southeast outlook to the summit of a wooded knob at 16.0 mi. The trail now descends moderately to a junction with the Dilly Trail from Lost River on the left at 16.2 mi. The Kinsman Ridge Trail soon crosses a swampy sag on log bridges and begins a very steep descent southwest through a part of the SPNHF Lost River Reservation toward Kinsman Notch, swinging to the left with NH 112 visible below on the right for the last part of the descent.

Kinsman Ridge Trail [In Reverse] (map 4:I3–G4)

Distances from Cannon Mountain Tramway parking area (1,980 ft.) to
- side path to ledges (3,800 ft.): 1.5 mi., 1,800 ft., 1 hr. 40 min.
- Rim Trail junction near tramway terminal (4,050 ft.): 2.0 mi., 2,100 ft., 2 hr. 5 min.
- Hi-Cannon Trail (3,850 ft.): 2.5 mi., 2,100 ft., 2 hr. 20 min.
- Lonesome Lake Trail (3,400 ft.): 3.0 mi., 2,100 ft., 2 hr. 35 min.
- Kinsman Junction (3,750 ft.): 5.4 mi., 3,150 ft., 4 hr. 15 min.
- Mt. Kinsman Trail (3,900 ft.): 5.6 mi., 3,300 ft., 4 hr. 25 min.
- North Kinsman summit (4,293 ft.): 6.0 mi., 3,700 ft., 4 hr. 50 min.
- South Kinsman summit (4,358 ft.): 6.9 mi., 4,050 ft., 5 hr. 30 min.
- Harrington Pond (3,400 ft.): 8.0 mi., 4,050 ft., 6 hr.
- Eliza Brook Shelter spur (2,400 ft.): 9.4 mi., 4,050 ft., 6 hr. 45 min.
- Reel Brook Trail (2,600 ft.): 10.4 mi., 4,300 ft., 7 hr. 20 min.
- Gordon Pond Trail (2,700 ft.): 13.6 mi., 5,450 ft., 9 hr. 30 min.
- Dilly Trail (2,650 ft.): 16.2 mi., 6,050 ft., 11 hr. 5 min.
- NH 112 in Kinsman Notch (1,870 ft.): 16.9 mi., 6,050 ft., 11 hr. 30 min.

Bald Mountain–Artist's Bluff Path (NHDP)

Artist's Bluff and the summit of Bald Mountain provide fine views for very little effort. The trail begins and ends on NH 18 just west of its junction with the Franconia Notch Parkway, north of Echo Lake. The west trailhead is located at the edge of the large parking lot for the Roland Peabody Memorial Slope section of the Cannon Mountain Ski Area, on the north side of NH 18 about 0.4 mi. from the parkway. This parking lot is closed when the ski area is not open, and cars must be parked just off the highway (sign). The east trailhead (no parking—the nearest parking is at the beach parking lot or the west trailhead) is on NH 18 a short distance east of the Echo Lake beach parking area.

Cross the Peabody Slopes parking lot to the trail sign. The red-blazed trail follows an old carriage road that climbs steadily to the top of the ridge at 0.3 mi. At this point, a spur path diverges left and climbs through the woods, with one scramble up a ledge, then ascends steeply up the open rocky cone of Bald Mountain, reaching the top in another 0.1 mi. About 25 yd. beyond the junction with the trail to Bald Mountain, the main trail turns right from the old road and runs over the wooded hump that bears the Artist's Bluff cliff on its east end, passing two outlook ledges. It then descends to the top of a steep, gravelly gully at 0.7 mi., where a path whose sign has been repeatedly pilfered leads left 50 yd. to the top of Artist's Bluff. The main trail continues steeply down the gully to NH 18, which can be followed 0.3 mi. back to the starting point.

Bald Mountain–Artist's Bluff Path (map 4:G4)

Distances from Peabody Slopes parking area (2,000 ft.)

- to fork in trail (2,180 ft.): 0.3 mi., 200 ft., 15 min.
- to Bald Mountain (2,340 ft.) via spur path: 0.4 mi., 350 ft., 25 min.
- to Echo Lake beach parking area (1,960 ft.) direct via Artist's Bluff: 0.9 mi., 350 ft., 40 min.
- to Echo Lake beach parking area (1,960 ft.) via side trip to Bald Mountain and Artist's Bluff: 1.2 mi., 500 ft., 50 min.
- for complete loop, including side trip to Bald Mountain, via NH 18: 1.5 mi., 550 ft., 1 hr.

Lonesome Lake Trail (AMC)

This yellow-blazed trail begins on the west side of the Franconia Notch Parkway, at the picnic area at the end of the south parking lot at Lafayette Campground (the parking area is a stop for the AMC's Hiker Shuttle), and runs past Lonesome Lake to the Kinsman Ridge Trail at Coppermine Col. It follows the route of an old bridle path much of the way to Lonesome Lake, with good footing and easy to moderate grades; beyond the lake it becomes frequently fairly steep and quite rough with poor footing.

The trail leaves the parking lot at a large trail sign, crosses the Pemigewasset River on a footbridge and then crosses the Pemi Trail, and follows a yellow-blazed path through the campground, climbing at a moderate grade. At 0.3 mi., a bridge crosses a small brook at a sharp left turn in the trail, and at 0.4 mi., the Hi-Cannon Trail leaves right. From this point, the trail ascends by three long switchbacks, then descends slightly to a junction at 1.2 mi. near the shore of Lonesome Lake, where the old bridle path ends; here the Cascade Brook Trail enters left and the Dodge Cutoff diverges right. A few steps ahead, there is a fine view of North and South Kinsman rising from the far side of the lake. For the shortest route to Lonesome Lake Hut follow the Cascade Brook and Fishin' Jimmy trails. The Lonesome Lake Trail becomes a footpath that continues along the north shore, coinciding with the Around-Lonesome-Lake Trail, which diverges left after 0.2 mi. and leads to Lonesome Lake Hut in another 0.3 mi. The Lonesome Lake Trail continues northwest, soon begins to rise more steeply, and ends at the Kinsman Ridge Trail in Coppermine Col, 0.8 mi. southwest of the summit of Cannon Mountain.

Lonesome Lake Trail (map 4:H4)

Distances from Lafayette Campground west side parking area (1,770 ft.) to
- Hi-Cannon Trail (1,925 ft.): 0.4 mi., 150 ft., 20 min.
- Cascade Brook Trail/Dodge Cutoff (2,740 ft.): 1.2 mi., 950 ft., 1 hr. 5 min.
- Kinsman Ridge Trail (3,400 ft.): 2.3 mi., 1,650 ft., 2 hr.
- Lonesome Lake Hut (2,740 ft.) via Cascade Brook Trail and Fishin' Jimmy Trail: 1.6 mi., 950 ft., 1 hr. 15 min.

Around-Lonesome-Lake Trail (AMC)

This trail, composed mostly of portions of other trails, encircles Lonesome Lake and affords fine views, especially of the Franconia Range. The part on the west shore of the lake is subject to flooding in wet seasons, though log bridges cross most of the boggy places.

Starting at the junction of the Dodge Cutoff and the Lonesome Lake and Cascade Brook trails, this trail follows the Cascade Brook Trail south along the east shore. It then turns west and, following the Fishin' Jimmy Trail, crosses the outlet of the lake and continues across the open beach area as the Fishin' Jimmy Trail bears left to ascend to the hut. The trail continues north through the bogs along the west side of the lake (the only section not shared with another trail), crosses several inlet brooks, and meets the Lonesome Lake Trail shortly after entering the woods. Here it turns right on the Lonesome Lake Trail and continues to the junction with Dodge Cutoff and the Cascade Brook Trail, completing the circuit.

Around-Lonesome-Lake Trail (map 4:H4)

Distance from any starting point (2,740 ft.) for
- complete loop: 0.8 mi., 0 ft., 25 min.

Hi-Cannon Trail (NHDP)

This trail begins at the Lonesome Lake Trail 0.4 mi. from the parking area at Lafayette Campground, and ends on the Kinsman Ridge Trail 0.4 mi. south of the summit of Cannon Mountain. It is steep near Cliff House, somewhat rough at times, and potentially dangerous if there is ice on the ledges above Cliff House. It passes several fine viewpoints, particularly the ledges overlooking Lonesome Lake.

The trail diverges right (west) from the Lonesome Lake Trail and begins to ascend steadily by switchbacks. Watch carefully for a sharp right switchback at 0.1 mi., where an old logging road continues straight and rejoins the Lonesome Lake Trail. At 0.8 mi., the Dodge Cutoff from Lonesome Lake enters on the left at the top of a ridge. Soon the Hi-Cannon Trail becomes significantly steeper and rougher. At 1.2 mi., there is a fine outlook to the area around Lafayette Campground and across Franconia Notch. The trail turns left here, and 100 yd. farther, passes Cliff House (right)—a natural rock shelter—and ascends a ladder with a tricky ledge at the top (dangerous if icy). It then passes through woods along a cliff edge with three fine outlooks over Lonesome Lake in the next 0.2 mi. (use caution on the ledges, as cliffs drop off sharply from them). Then the trail ascends moderately with much rough footing to the top of the ridge, turns right, and ends at its junction with the Kinsman Ridge Trail at 2.0 mi. For the summit of Cannon Mountain, follow the Kinsman Ridge Trail straight uphill for 0.4 mi.

Hi-Cannon Trail (map 4:H4)

Distances from Lonesome Lake Trail (1,925 ft.) to

- Dodge Cutoff (2,850 ft.): 0.8 mi., 900 ft., 50 min.
- Kinsman Ridge Trail (3,850 ft.): 2.0 mi., 1,900 ft., 1 hr. 55 min.

Distance from Lafayette Place (1,770 ft.) to

- Cannon Mountain summit (4,100 ft.) via Lonesome Lake, Hi-Cannon, and Kinsman Ridge trails: 2.8 mi., 2,350 ft., 2 hr. 35 min.

Dodge Cutoff (NHDP)

This short link between the Lonesome Lake and Hi-Cannon trails provides a shortcut between Lonesome Lake and Cannon Mountain. It is lightly used and in places requires care to follow. It was named in honor of Joe Dodge, a legendary, highly respected and cherished White Mountain character who was best known as the longtime manager of the AMC hut system.

It leads northeast from the junction of the Lonesome Lake and Cascade Brook trails on the east shore of the lake, 0.3 mi. from Lonesome Lake Hut. After climbing over a low ridge and crossing a moist sag, it ascends by switchbacks, rather steeply for a while, to the Hi-Cannon Trail 0.8 mi. above the junction of the Lonesome Lake and Hi-Cannon trails and 1.5 mi. below the summit of Cannon Mountain.

Dodge Cutoff (map 4:H4)

Distance from Lonesome Lake Trail (2,740 ft.) to
• Hi-Cannon Trail (2,850 ft.): 0.3 mi., 100 ft., 15 min.

Distance from Lafayette Campground (1,770 ft.) to
• summit of Cannon Mountain (4,100 ft.) via Lonesome Lake Trail, Dodge Cutoff, Hi-Cannon Trail, and Kinsman Ridge Trail: 3.0 mi., 2,350 ft., 2 hr. 40 min.

Pemi Trail (NHDP)

This trail extends from a parking lot near Profile Lake to the hikers' parking area just north of the Flume Visitor Center, providing pedestrians a fairly easy footpath that is an alternative route to the bike path along the central part of Franconia Notch. The markings are not always obvious and signs are not always present at intersections with roads and the bike path, so following it requires a bit of care, particularly at points where it diverges from these other routes. It has incorporated almost all of the former Profile Lake Trail, a name now applied to a short paved tourist path. The crossings of Cascade Brook and Whitehouse Brook near the south end may be difficult in high water conditions.

The Pemi Trail leaves the southwest corner of the Old Man site parking area on the west side of the Franconia Notch Parkway, ascends granite steps into the woods, then turns sharp left and descends to the west shore of Profile Lake. It skirts along the west shore of the Lake, with views of Eagle Cliff rising above the parkway. In this first section, the trail passes several unmarked paths used by rock climbers. It crosses a wet area south of the lake on log bridges, and at 0.7 mi., it enters the bike path, follows it right for 50 yd., then turns left and reenters the woods. It runs close to the parkway, passing two short alternate routes for cross-country skiers on the right, then crosses the Pemigewasset on a bridge at 1.2 mi. It continues down the valley, with occasional short ascents, then runs above an extensive beaver wetland. At 1.8 mi., a side path diverges sharp right and leads in 25 yd. to a fine view of Cannon Cliff. In another 60 yd., the main trail crosses through an area of beaver activity, where it must be followed with care; here a bypass path diverges left around the beaver area, rejoining the main trail at 1.9 mi., just before recrossing the Pemigewasset on another bridge. In another 100 yd., the trail crosses the bike path, then soon bears right onto a gravel road that leads into Lafayette Campground just below the headquarters buildings.

It continues south on the campground road that follows most closely along the west bank of the river, crosses the Lonesome Lake Trail, and enters the woods between Campsites 67 and 68. It continues for 1.7 mi. fairly close to the river until it intersects the Basin-Cascades Trail, 50 yd. west of the Basin.

It turns left here onto the Basin-Cascades Trail, then in 20 yd., it diverges to the right off the Basin-Cascades Trail; in another 40 yd., it turns left (sign), then right, descends easily along the river, passing some cascades, and crosses Cascade Brook (may be difficult at high water) at 4.3 mi. The trail soon begins to swing away from the river, crosses Whitehouse Brook (may be difficult at high water), then joins the Cascade Brook Trail and follows it to the left, passing under both lanes of I-93 to the bike path. From there, it follows the Whitehouse Trail to the hikers' parking lot just north of the Flume.

Pemi Trail (map 4:H4)

Distances from Old Man parking area on west side of parkway (1,960 ft.) to
- Lafayette Campground (1,770 ft.): 2.0 mi., 100 ft. (rev. 300 ft.), 1 hr. 5 min.
- Basin-Cascades Trail (1,520 ft.): 3.9 mi., 100 ft. (rev. 250 ft.), 2 hr.
- Cascade Brook Trail (1,520 ft.): 4.7 mi., 100 ft., 2 hr. 25 min.
- Whitehouse Trail (1,400 ft.) via Cascade Brook Trail: 4.9 mi., 100 ft. (rev. 100 ft.), 2 hr. 30 min.
- Flume hikers' parking lot (1,400 ft.) via Whitehouse Trail: 5.6 mi., 200 ft. (rev. 100 ft.), 2 hr. 55 min.

Basin-Cascades Trail (NHDP)

This trail starts at the Basin (parking areas on either side of Franconia Notch Parkway) and ascends along the beautiful lower half of Cascade Brook to the Cascade Brook Trail. The brook is extremely scenic and trail grades are mostly moderate, but the footing is often fairly rough. From the parking areas on either side of the parkway, follow the tourist paths past the Basin and on to the west bank of the Pemigewasset, about 0.2 mi. from either starting point, where the trailhead is situated at the western edge of the maze of paths that surrounds the Basin.

From the trailhead (sign) at the junction with the Pemi Trail, the path leads northwest, angling toward Cascade Brook, then climbs along the brook past cascades, small falls, and ledges with views of the Franconia Range across the notch, reached by numerous unmarked side paths. At 0.4 mi., the trail passes a rough side path (sign) that leads down to a good view of Kinsman Falls, and 50 yd. farther up, as the main trail comes out on the bank of the brook, a ledge on the left provides a viewpoint at the top of these falls. In another 100 yd., the trail crosses Cascade Brook (no bridge; may be difficult in high water) and continues with rough footing along the brook past more cascades and pools. It passes Rocky Glen Falls (sign) at 0.9 mi., then swings sharp left up through a small box canyon and soon ends at the Cascade Brook Trail on the south bank of the brook. For a good view of Rocky Glen Falls from above, return cautiously about 60 yd. down the brook bank.

Basin-Cascades Trail (map 4:H4)

Distance from trailhead near the Basin (1,520 ft.) to
• Cascade Brook Trail (2,084 ft.): 1.0 mi., 550 ft., 45 min.

Cascade Brook Trail (AMC)

This relatively easy trail, a link in the AT, leads to Lonesome Lake from the bike path at the former Whitehouse Bridge site, just south of the bike path's bridge over the Pemigewasset (the Liberty Spring Trail begins just north of the bridge). There is no parking at the Whitehouse Bridge site, which is reached in 0.8 mi. from the hikers' parking area just north of the Flume Visitor Center via the Whitehouse Trail (see Section Three) or in 0.7 mi. via the bike path from the Basin parking lot on the northbound side of the parkway.

From the junction with the bike path, the trail crosses under the parkway (coinciding with the Pemi Trail), then turns right at the edge of the parkway clearing and enters the woods; after 0.2 mi., the Pemi Trail leaves on the right. The Cascade Brook Trail climbs at a moderate grade and crosses Whitehouse Brook at 0.4 mi., just above a fine cascade. It continues generally northwest, reaching a junction at 1.5 mi. at the edge of Cascade Brook, where the Basin-Cascades Trail enters right. For a good view of Rocky Glen Falls from above, walk cautiously about 60 yd. down the brook bank. The Cascade Brook Trail immediately crosses Cascade Brook on a new footbridge and continues to climb along the northeast bank. At 2.0 mi., the Kinsman Pond Trail diverges left and crosses the brook, and from this point, the Cascade Brook Trail follows an old logging road, becoming rougher and rockier, to the junction with Fishin' Jimmy Trail at the outlet of Lonesome Lake at 2.8 mi. From here, Lonesome Lake Hut is 150 yd. to the left. The Cascade Brook Trail continues along the east side of the lake and ends at a junction with the Lonesome Lake Trail and the Dodge Cutoff at 3.1 mi.

Cascade Brook Trail (map 4:H4)

Distances from Whitehouse Trail junction (1,400 ft.) to

- Basin-Cascades Trail (2,084 ft.): 1.5 mi., 700 ft., 1 hr. 5 min.
- Kinsman Pond Trail (2,294 ft.): 2.0 mi., 900 ft., 1 hr. 25 min.
- Fishin' Jimmy Trail (2,740 ft.): 2.8 mi., 1,350 ft., 2 hr. 5 min.
- Lonesome Lake Trail and Dodge Cutoff (2,740 ft.): 3.1 mi., 1,350 ft., 2 hr. 15 min.

Fishin' Jimmy Trail (AMC)

This trail, a link in the AT, leads from Lonesome Lake to the Kinsman Ridge Trail at Kinsman Junction, near Kinsman Pond. Parts of it are steep and rough, with wooden steps on ledges. It received its peculiar name from a well-known local character called Fishin' Jimmy—his real name was James Whitcher—who lived in the Franconia area and was featured in a story by Annie Trumbull Slosson, once a popular New England author.

Diverging from the Cascade Brook Trail at the south end of Lonesome Lake, this trail crosses the outlet brook on a bridge, passes the junction with the Around-Lonesome-Lake Trail near the beach at the southwest corner of the lake, and reaches Lonesome Lake Hut at 0.1 mi. It runs around the lower end of a ridge coming down from the Middle Cannon Ball, making several ascents and descents and passing over a ledgy ridge crest at 0.6 mi. It then crosses several small brooks, with the last reliable water source in a small mossy, ledgy brook at 1.1 mi., and soon begins to climb, at times steeply but with occasional minor descents as well. At 1.7 mi., it curls around a large boulder on the left and passes through a fairly flat area. At 1.9 mi., it reaches the top of the serious climbing and ascends gradually to Kinsman Junction and the Kinsman Ridge Trail at 2.0 mi., 0.1 mi. north of Kinsman Pond Shelter on the Kinsman Pond Trail.

Fishin' Jimmy Trail (map 4:H4)

Distances from Cascade Brook Trail (2,740 ft.) to

- Lonesome Lake Hut (2,740 ft.): 0.1 mi., 0 ft., 5 min.
- Kinsman Junction (3,750 ft.): 2.0 mi., 1,200 ft. (rev. 200 ft.), 1 hr. 35 min.

Kinsman Pond Trail (AMC)

This trail leads to Kinsman Pond and Kinsman Junction from the Cascade Brook Trail, 2.0 mi. from its beginning on the bike path at the Whitehouse Bridge site, which is reached by following the Whitehouse Trail (Section Three) 0.8 mi. north from the hikers' parking lot just north of the Flume Visitor Center. The lower half of the trail has reasonably good footing, but the upper part is wet, steep, rocky, and very rough, and at times it shares the footway with small brooks, making rocks slippery; it may also be difficult to follow for short stretches.

Leaving the Cascade Brook Trail, this trail immediately crosses to the southwest side of the brook and proceeds west on old logging roads. Soon it crosses a small brook and begins to rise moderately, following a brook past several small but attractive cascades and passing into dense boreal forest. At 1.3 mi., the trail crosses the brook and soon runs in its bed for 0.1 mi. From here on, the trail is very rough and eroded. At 1.6 mi., the grade becomes easy, and the trail crosses the outlet brook from the pond at 1.9 mi., passes a water source left (sign), and reaches the foot of the pond at 2.1 mi. The trail climbs up and down on the ledgy east shore of the pond, with the impressive bulk of North Kinsman rising from the opposite shore, and passes Kinsman Pond Shelter (which accommodates 12) and then several tentsites. Water in this area is unsafe to drink unless treated. Kinsman Junction, where the Kinsman Pond Trail meets the Kinsman Ridge and Fishin' Jimmy trails, is 0.1 mi. beyond the shelter.

Kinsman Pond Trail (map 4:H4)

Distance from Cascade Brook Trail (2,294 ft.) to
• Kinsman Junction (3,750 ft.): 2.5 mi., 1,500 ft. (rev 50 ft.), 2 hr.

Mount Pemigewasset Trail (NHDP)

This trail runs from the Flume Visitor Center parking area to the summit of Mt. Pemigewasset (Indian Head), where excellent views can be obtained with modest effort. Grades and footing are mostly easy. The trail reaches the vertical summit cliffs very abruptly, so care should be exercised, particularly with small children or in slippery conditions.

The trail follows the bike path north from the parking lot for 150 yd., turns left on a gravel path and passes under old US 3 in a tunnel, then turns left and crosses a brook on a bridge. It descends a short distance, then turns sharp right and ascends under both lanes of the Franconia Notch Parkway. It enters the woods at 0.4 mi. and ascends northwest, crossing several small brooks on log bridges. It swings to the left, then turns right and then left along a small brook, climbing moderately. At 1.3 mi., it squeezes around a large boulder and swings left uphill, climbing a bit more steeply to the ridge crest, which it follows to the left (south). It passes the junction with the Indian Head Trail on the right at 1.7 mi. and reaches the summit ledges at 1.8 mi. At the true summit, which is just beyond the first ledges and a bit to the left, there is a fine northeast view.

Mount Pemigewasset Trail (map 4:H4)

Distance from Flume Visitor Center parking area (1,350 ft.) to
• Mt. Pemigewasset summit (2,557 ft.): 1.8 mi., 1,250 ft. (rev. 50 ft.), 1 hr. 30 min.

Indian Head Trail (AMC)

This trail runs to the summit of Mt. Pemigewasset (Indian Head), where open ledges afford excellent views. It begins on the west side of US 3 south of the Indian Head Resort at a small parking area, reached by a short gravel road marked with a Trailhead Parking sign. This trail is much less heavily used than the Mt. Pemigewasset Trail; the footway may be wet and obscure in places, and markings should be followed with care.

The trail leaves the parking area and crosses a small field. It turns left and accompanies a small brook under the parkway, then ascends by easy grades through hardwoods on an old logging road along the brook. At 1.1 mi., it turns to the right onto another old woods road, then soon leaves it and climbs moderately, circling well around under the south side of the cliffs that form the Indian Head. It then ascends steeply for a short distance, and at 1.8 mi., just below the summit ledges, it joins the Mt. Pemigewasset Trail and follows it to the right to the summit.

Indian Head Trail (map 4:I4–H4)

Distance from US 3 (1,000 ft.) to
  • Mt. Pemigewasset summit (2,557 ft.): 1.9 mi., 1,550 ft., 1 hr. 45 min.

Georgiana Falls Path

Georgiana Falls is a series of cascades on Harvard Brook that end in a pool. Above Georgiana Falls, there are more cascades terminating in the more imposing Harvard Falls about 0.4 mi. farther up the brook. These falls are also known as Upper and Lower Georgiana Falls, nomenclature that may in fact be more historically correct. The path is on private land and not officially maintained. From US 3 about 2.5 mi. north of North Woodstock, opposite the Longhorn Restaurant, turn west onto Hanson Farm Rd. Where Hanson Farm Rd. turns right, continue across Hanson Brook on a bridge to a parking area at the end of the pavement, 0.1 mi. from US 3.

Follow a dirt road through a tunnel under the northbound lanes of I-93, then bear right at a fork (snowmobile trail signs), then swing left through the tunnel under the southbound lanes. At 0.5 mi., where the road bears right and becomes overgrown, the trail (blazed yellow at first, then red) turns left into the woods and follows the north side of Harvard Brook. At 0.7 mi., it crosses a rocky brook bed, climbs on sloping ledges beside cascades, briefly reenters the woods on the right, and emerges on ledges at the base of Georgiana Falls. Above these falls, the trail is minimally maintained and marked; it reenters the woods and follows a steep, sometimes slippery route on a network of interlacing beaten paths, with no single well-defined trail, to Harvard Falls. It is often possible to follow broad ledges in the brook partway up from Georgiana Falls. From the ledges at the top of Harvard Falls, there are good views of the Pemigewasset Valley and Loon Mountain.

Georgiana Falls Path (map 4:I4)

Distances from Hanson Farm Rd. (900 ft.) to
- Georgiana Falls (1,150 ft.): 0.7 mi., 250 ft., 30 min.
- Harvard Falls (1,650 ft.): 1.2 mi., 750 ft., 1 hr.

Gordon Pond Trail (WMNF)

This trail runs from NH 112 1.7 mi. west of its junction with US 3 in North Woodstock to the Kinsman Ridge Trail south of Mt. Wolf, passing Gordon Fall and Gordon Pond. It is lightly used and may be overgrown in places, and cannot be recommended for inexperienced hikers; it may be abandoned in the near future. The trailhead on NH 112 (where the WMNF trail sign may be missing) is located at a private driveway opposite Govoni's Restaurant and Agassiz Basin (see Section Six); there are signs here for the restaurant and Agassiz Basin in summer but not at other times. Park just west of the buildings.

This trail follows the driveway between the buildings on the north side of NH 112 (No Trespassing signs do not apply to hikers who stay on the trail), and at 0.1 mi., it turns right at a crossroads and follows an old railroad grade. At 0.6 mi., it reaches the power lines, turns left and follows the power-line clearing for 0.2 mi., then turns right and crosses under the lines into the woods, reaching the old railroad grade at 1.0 mi. and turning left onto it. At 1.3 mi., turn left off the railroad grade where another road enters on the right. (In the opposite direction, bear right here; there may be an arrow pointing to the wrong branch.) At 1.8 mi., the trail approaches Gordon Pond Brook and a logging road crosses the brook, but the trail remains on the southwest bank and swings to the northwest to recross the power lines at 2.0 mi. The trail finally crosses Gordon Pond Brook (may be difficult at high water) at 2.2 mi. and continues along the north bank, crossing a tributary at 2.8 mi., then swings left to recross the main brook at 3.5 mi. It continues on an old road, becoming somewhat steeper, and crosses a minor ridge to the southerly branch of Gordon Pond

Brook where it passes Gordon Fall. Crossing the brook on a ledge at the top of the fall at 3.9 mi., it soon recrosses, passes a very wet section of trail, then crosses Gordon Pond Brook at 4.6 mi. Just before it recrosses the main brook at 4.7 mi., unsigned paths lead right to the shore of the pond, where there is an interesting view of the steep face of Mt. Wolf. The main trail does not come within sight of the pond but continues at a level grade, bears left where an unsigned path enters right, and climbs easily to the Kinsman Ridge Trail.

Gordon Pond Trail (map 4:I4–I3)

Distances from NH 112 (900 ft.) to
- Gordon Fall (2,300 ft.): 3.9 mi., 1,400 ft., 2 hr. 40 min.
- Kinsman Ridge Trail (2,700 ft.): 5.0 mi., 1,800 ft., 3 hr. 25 min.

Dilly Trail (SPNHF)

This short but challenging trail runs from Lost River Reservation to the Kinsman Ridge Trail 0.6 mi. from NH 112. It is open only during the hours and season (summer and fall, daytime) when Lost River is open, and closed to the public at all other times. It is extremely steep and rough but offers an interesting outlook across the valley. Its trailhead, shared with the Ecology Trail, is on a parking area access road directly across from a gazebo. In 25 yd. from the road, the Ecology Trail leaves on the left, and the Dilly Trail soon begins to ascend by short switchbacks a very steep, badly eroded gully with very loose footing, requiring caution, particularly when descending. At 0.4 mi., where the trail reaches the top rim of the steep slope, a side path leads sharp right 40 yd. to a fine outlook from the rim. The main trail turns sharp left, and continues at moderate grades to the Kinsman Ridge Trail; because of ice storm damage, this section may be overgrown.

Dilly Trail (map 4:I3)

Distances from Lost River Reservation parking lot (1,820 ft.) to
- lookout over Lost River (2,520 ft.): 0.4 mi., 700 ft., 35 min.
- Kinsman Ridge Trail (2,650 ft.): 0.5 mi., 850 ft., 45 min.

Coppermine Trail (WMNF)

This trail to Bridal Veil Falls begins on Coppermine Rd., which leaves the east side of NH 116 3.4 mi. south of NH 18 in Franconia (and 1.0 mi. south of the Franconia Airport) or 7.7 mi. north of NH 112 at Bungay Corner. Park near NH 116 and follow the road. Avoid a new development road (Beechwood Lane) on the left, and beware of other complications that may be caused by such development. At 0.4 mi., the trail bears left on an older road (hiker logo sign and yellow blazes). At 1.0 mi., the trail joins Coppermine Brook and follows along the north side, climbing at easy to moderate grades, then crosses to the south side on a bridge at 2.3 mi., passes the WMNF Coppermine Shelter, and ends at the base of Bridal Veil Falls.

Coppermine Trail (map 4:G3–H4)

Distance from NH 116 (994 ft.) to
- Bridal Veil Falls (2,100 ft.): 2.5 mi., 1,100 ft., 1 hr. 50 min.

Mount Kinsman Trail (WMNF)

This trail climbs to the Kinsman Ridge Trail 0.4 mi. north of North Kinsman from the east side of NH 116 at the Franconia-Easton town line, about 4.4 mi. south of NH 18 in Franconia village and 2.0 mi. north of the Easton town hall. There is limited roadside parking; do not block driveways. There is a sign for the town line a few yards north of the trail, but most of the time, there has not been a sign for the trail itself, which follows a logging road closed by a chain gate between two granite pillars opposite a house. The trail climbs at moderate grades, is well trodden, and has been recently blazed in blue, but some care is required to follow it, particularly in the lower section where there are many intersecting woods roads.

From the gate, the trail follows a sandy logging road that ascends moderately under tall pines, swinging to the right, always taking the right at forks where several other roads diverge to the left. It bears right again at the edge of a grass-grown log yard at 0.5 mi. Ascending easily, at times level, it swings left, passes an old sugarhouse that stands on the left at 0.6 mi., and swings right again. It makes a short bypass to the left of a wet section of road at 0.9 mi., enters the WMNF at 1.1 mi. and turns right off the road (cairn and arrow), then in 30 yd., turns left onto another road.

This road, distinctly older and steeper, crosses a substantial brook at 1.5 mi. near the site of the former Kinsman Cabin. At 1.8 mi., the trail crosses a small brook that falls over a mossy ledge to the left of the trail, then crosses Flume Brook at 2.1 mi. Just over Flume Brook, a side path on the right descends close to the brook bank for 150 yd. to small, steep-walled Kinsman Flume, a classic eroded dike with an overhanging boulder at the top that presents a reasonable facsimile of a profile. The main trail continues on the road for another 70 yd., then turns sharp left at the point where a spur path 0.2 mi. long diverges sharp right, descends briefly, then makes an easy ascent to Bald Peak, a bare ledgy dome with fine views that crowns a western spur of Kinsman Mountain.

The ax-blazed trail now joins and follows Flume Brook, winding up the mountainside at easy to moderate grades, with good footing except for short, scattered steep pitches with rough footing. It crosses several small brooks and at 3.5 mi., it swings right and angles upward, then swings left and climbs straight up to the ridge top, where it meets the Kinsman Ridge Trail. For North and South Kinsman, turn right; for Kinsman Pond and Kinsman Junction, turn left.

Mount Kinsman Trail (map 4:G3–H4)

Distances from NH 116 (1,030 ft.) to
- Bald Peak spur trail (2,400 ft.): 2.1 mi., 1,350 ft., 1 hr. 45 min.
- Kinsman Ridge Trail (3,900 ft.): 3.7 mi., 2,900 ft., 3 hr. 20 min.

Reel Brook Trail (WMNF)

This lightly used trail ascends to the Kinsman Ridge Trail in the col between Mt. Wolf and South Kinsman (the original Kinsman Notch), 1.0 mi. south of Eliza Brook Shelter. It begins on a gravel road that leaves NH 116 3.7 mi. north of the junction with NH 112 at Bungay Corner and 1.1 mi. south of the Easton town hall. The road, which is not plowed in winter, is rough but passable for cars to a fork (hiker logo on post) at 0.6 mi. from NH 116, where the left branch leads to an open field (parking). The grades on this trail are moderate, but the footing is often very muddy.

The trail enters the woods (sign) and follows a logging road southeast, parallel to but some distance northwest of Reel Brook, crossing several small brooks. At 1.2 mi., the road bears right and descends, and very shortly the trail diverges left, crosses a small brook, and turns left onto a wide log-ging road at 1.3 mi. (In the opposite direction, this turn, though there is a sign, could easily be missed; be sure to turn sharp right off the wide logging road 100 yd. after leaving the power-line clearing.) In 100 yd., the trail en-ters the power-line clearing, crosses it on a diagonal (avoid a path diverg-ing left up along the lines), and reenters the woods. The old road crosses a tributary, then Reel Brook itself twice, and enters a newer logging road that descends from the left just before the third and last crossing of Reel Brook at 1.9 mi. Here the trail turns right and follows the logging road away from the brook. The road is periodically bulldozed for maintenance access to the power lines, and as a result, it is often very muddy, with numerous loose stones; when such conditions prevail, care must be taken, especially descending. It climbs moderately to a fork at 2.4 mi., where the main road swings left to the power lines, while the trail, with improved footing, forks right on another old logging road. In another 100 yd., the trail diverges right off this road, which swings left. From here, the trail climbs gradually to the junction with the Kinsman Ridge Trail on the ridge crest.

Reel Brook Trail (map 4:H3)

Distance from road fork near field (1,400 ft.) to
• Kinsman Ridge Trail (2,600 ft.): 2.9 mi., 1,300 ft. (rev 100 ft.), 2 hr. 5 min.

Jericho Road Trail (WMNF)

This trail ascends to the site of the Cooley Hill fire tower from a point just north of the height-of-land on the west side of NH 116, 1.9 mi. north of its junction with NH 112 at Bungay Corner, starting on a gated gravel logging road (FR 480). It was originally constructed as a horse trail and mostly follows logging roads of varying ages. There are no views, but some sections, particularly in the upper half, are quite pleasant for walking.

The trail follows the gravel road uphill, swings to the right (north), and then continues straight (marked by a hiker logo and arrow) on an older, somewhat overgrown road (FR 480A) at 0.3 mi., where the newer road bears right. After passing through an overgrown log yard at 1.3 mi., the road crosses a ditch where the newer section ends abruptly. The trail swings around the west side of a hump and descends into a sag, where it comes to a WMNF boundary corner distinctively marked with a pile of red-painted stones at 2.3 mi. Here the trail turns right off the road and, marked by flagging and ax blazes, continues to descend gradually, then climbs moderately. At 2.6 mi., it turns sharp left onto another old road that ascends from the right, and follows the road up the crest of the ridge to a small wooded ledge near the concrete piers of the old fire tower. The trailless true summit of Cooley Hill, about 100 yd. north of the tower remains, has been recently logged, providing some limited views. From the end of the official hiking trail, an unofficial trail-bike track continues down the northwest side of the mountain.

Jericho Rd. Trail (map 4:H3)

Distance from NH 116 (1,385 ft.) to
• Cooley Hill (2,480 ft.): 3.2 mi., 1,250 ft. (rev. 150 ft.), 2 hr. 15 min.

Cobble Hill Trail (WMNF)

This trail begins on NH 112 at a point 0.1 mi. west of the Woodsville Reservoir, and follows a gated gravel road (FR 310) and older woods roads along the west side of Dearth Brook to the WMNF boundary at the height-of-land between Cobble Hill and Moody Ledge. The old road continues north of the height-of-land for another 1.4 mi. down across private land to Mill Brook Rd. south of Landaff Center village, passing through woods much disrupted by logging. There are no views from this trail, but there is a small cascade in the brook on the right about 100 yd. from NH 112 that is interesting when there is a good flow of water. At 0.7 mi., from NH 112, the abandoned South Landaff Rd. leaves left, leading in about 2 mi. to an extensive area of old ruined farms where there are many interesting stone walls, cellar holes, and other remnants of the hill farm culture that once flourished in this part of New England. This culture declined severely during the second half of the 19th century and mostly died out in the first decades of the 20th century, and was the subject—or at least the setting—of much of Robert Frost's poetry.

Cobble Hill Trail (map 4:H2)

Distance from NH 112 (1,017 ft.) to
• WMNF boundary (1,800 ft.): 2.1 mi., 800 ft., 1 hr. 25 min.

Kilburn Crags Trail (LCC)

This trail, maintained by the Littleton Conservation Commission, offers easy access to a ledge with a fine view over the town of Littleton to the Presidential and Franconia ranges. Take I-93 to Exit 43 and proceed to the junction of NH 18 and NH 135, just south of the exit. Turn right (west) onto the combined NH 18/135, also called St. Johnsbury Rd. A sign and small parking area are on the left (south) side of the road, 0.5 mi. from the junction. Please stay on the designated trail, which is partly on private land.

From the parking area, the trail climbs up along the left edge of a field; the footway may be obscure in tall grass. The trail enters the woods on a well-defined road at the upper left corner of the field, and at 0.2 mi., another old road joins from the left. (Bear left here on the descent.) The trail climbs moderately, passing a bench, then levels at 0.4 mi. It bears left at a fork at 0.5 mi. and again at 0.6 mi., passes another bench, then swings left (east) at 0.7 mi., and climbs to a high point on a north spur of Walker Mountain. The trail then descends slightly to the ledge.

Kilburn Crags Trail (USGS Littleton quad)

Distance from NH 18/135 (1,050 ft.) to
* Kilburn Crags viewpoint (1,350 ft.): 0.9 mi., 350 ft. (rev. 50 ft.), 40 min.

SUGGESTED HIKES

For more information on suggested hikes, see p. ix.

Easy Hikes

Bald Mountain and Artist's Bluff. Bald Mountain is a scale-model mountain; very impressive in appearance, with excellent views, it can be easily climbed, with a bit of ledge scrambling at the top [rt: 0.8 mi., 350 ft., 0:35]. Additional views, though marred by the interchanges of the Franconia Notch Parkway, can be enjoyed from Artist's Bluff [lp: 1.5 mi., 550 ft., 1:00].

Basin-Cascades Trail [rt: 2.4 mi., 600 ft., 1:30]. This trail follows Cascade Brook from the Basin area to the Cascade Brook Trail; there are many broad ledges and small cascades, and one can stop, enjoy, and turn back at any point or continue all the way to Rocky Glen Falls.

Kilburn Crags [rt: 1.8 mi., 400 ft., 1:05]. An easy trip to a viewpoint overlooking the town of Littleton and many high peaks.

Lonesome Lake [rt: 3.2 mi., 1,000 ft., 2:05]. This very popular objective offers fine views of the Franconia Range; use the Lonesome Lake Trail and short sections of the Cascade Brook, Fishin' Jimmy, and Around-Lonesome-Lake trails.

Moderate Hikes

Mt. Pemigewasset [rt: 3.6 mi., 1,300 ft., 2:25]. The Mt. Pemigewasset Trail provides access from the Flume Visitor Center to an excellent outlook from a prowlike cliff atop the Indian Head.

Bridal Veil Falls [rt: 5.0 mi., 1,100 ft., 3:05]. This attractive waterfall is easily reached by the Coppermine Trail.

Bald Peak [rt: 4.6 mi., 1,450 ft., 3:00]. This rocky spur of Kinsman Mountain has fine views; it is accessed by a side path off the Mt. Kinsman Trail.

Cannon Mountain. The rocky Kinsman Ridge Trail provides access to a fine broad ledge on the east peak of Cannon that commands a spectacular view across Franconia Notch [rt: 3.0 mi., 1,800 ft., 2:25]; one can easily extend the trip to the tramway-accessible summit [rt: 4.4 mi., 2,100 ft., 3:15]. Another good route to the summit is the Hi-Cannon Trail, with a bird's-eye view of Lonesome Lake en route [rt: 5.6 mi., 2,350 ft., 4:00].

Strenuous Hikes

Kinsman Mountain. North Kinsman has a spectacular view out to the Franconia Range and almost straight down to picturesque Kinsman Pond at the foot of its cliffs; an interesting and varied trip can be made using the Mt. Kinsman Trail from NH 116 and including the spur paths to Kinsman Flume and Bald Peak and a side trip to Kinsman Pond [rt: 9.4 mi., 3,600 ft., 6:30]. South Kinsman, with its fine views, particularly to the south, can be added to this trip [rt: 11.2 mi., 4,250 ft., 7:45].

SECTION SIX
THE MOOSILAUKE REGION

This section covers Mt. Moosilauke and several lower ranges and peaks, including the Benton Range, the Stinson-Carr-Kineo area, and the chain of medium-sized mountains that rise east of and roughly parallel to the Connecticut River between Hanover and Glencliff. The area is bordered on the east by the Connecticut River, on the north by NH 112, on the east by US 3 (and I-93), and on the south by NH 25, NH 118, and US 4. Most of this section is covered by the AMC's *Moosilauke–Kinsman Map* (map 4).

Many of the trails on the east side of Moosilauke begin at a trailhead at the end of Ravine Lodge Rd., the access road to the Dartmouth Outing Club (DOC) Ravine Lodge (which is now open to the public). The road (not plowed in winter) leaves NH 118 on the north, 5.8 mi. east of its northerly junction with NH 25 and 7.2 mi. west of its junction with NH 112. From NH 118, it is 1.6 mi. to the turnaround at the end of the road, where the trails begin. There have been a number of changes to names of important roads in this section: North and South Rd. is now Long Pond Rd., Cummins Pond Rd. is now Lyme-Dorchester Rd., Jacobs Brook Rd. is now Quinttown Rd., and Atwell Hill Rd. is now Cape Moonshine Rd.

In this section, the Appalachian Trail (AT), maintained by the DOC, begins at the New Hampshire boundary at the bridge over the Connecticut River, close to the western edge of both the town of Hanover and the campus of Dartmouth College. It follows the Velvet Rocks Trail, Hanover Center Trail, and Moose Mountain Trail over Moose Mountain; the Holts Ledge Trail over Holts Ledge; and, after a short section parallel to the Lyme-Dorchester Rd., the Lambert Ridge Trail to the summit of Smarts Mountain. From there it follows the J Trail and Kodak Trail to Mt. Cube, and the Mt. Cube Trail, Atwell Hill Trail, Ore Hill Trail, and Wachipauka Pond Trail to NH 25. It leaves NH 25 on the Town Line Trail, runs along Long Pond Rd. (formerly North and South Rd.) and High St. (formerly Sanatorium Rd.) for short distances, then follows the Glencliff Trail and Moosilauke Carriage Rd. to the summit of Mt. Moosilauke and descends on the Beaver Brook Trail to Kinsman Notch.

GEOGRAPHY

The farthest west of White Mountain peaks more than 4,000 ft. tall is Mt. Moosilauke (4,802 ft.), which is the dominating peak of the region between Franconia Notch and the Connecticut River. There is disagreement whether the name should be pronounced to rhyme with "rock" or with "rocky"; at one time Moosilauke was commonly corrupted to "Moose-hillock," but the name actually means "a bald place" and has no reference to large, antlered beasts. The bare summit, once the site of a stone lodge called the Tip-Top House, commands an extremely fine view over ridge after ridge of the White Mountains to the east, and across the Connecticut Valley to the west. It has several minor summits, the most important being the South Peak (4,523 ft.), an excellent viewpoint with fine views that are denied to the main summit into Tunnel Ravine, the deep ravine that lies between Moosilauke and its trailless western neighbor, Mt. Clough (3,561 ft.). To the north are two prominent wooded humps, the trailless Mt. Blue (4,529 ft.), and Mt. Jim (4,172 ft.), which form the ridge that encloses Jobildunk Ravine, a glacial cirque on the east side of the mountain, through which the headwaters of the Baker River flow from their source in a bog that was once Deer Lake. The summit of Moosilauke is very exposed to weather, and there is no longer any shelter near the summit. *A Trail Guide to Mount Moosilauke,* containing much information on the human and natural history of the mountain, has been published by the Environmental Studies Division of the DOC but is currently out of print.

The Benton Range, which rises to the west of Mt. Clough, is composed of Black Mountain (2,830 ft.), Sugarloaf Mountain (2,609 ft.), the Hogsback (2,810 ft.), Jeffers Mountain (2,994 ft.), Blueberry Mountain (2,662 ft.), and Owls Head (1,967 ft.). Of these peaks, all but Jeffers provide excellent views, though only Black and Blueberry have maintained trails.

Stinson Mountain (2,900 ft.), Carr Mountain (3,453 ft.), Rattlesnake Mountain (1,594 ft.), and trailless Mt. Kineo (3,313 ft.) rise in the angle formed by the Pemigewasset and Baker rivers. Stinson Mountain and Carr Mountain offer good views from summits that once bore fire towers. In the northern part of the area is the site of the village of Peeling, a hill community that was the original settlement in the town of Woodstock but was deserted about the time of the Civil War. Most of the area has grown up, and only traces of the village remain. Those interested in visiting this region should contact the Pemigewasset Ranger District office in Plymouth for information.

Agassiz Basin is an interesting series of potholes on Moosilauke Brook next to NH 112, 1.6 mi. west of North Woodstock. The basin is next to Govoni's Restaurant, and there are signs during the summer season. Two bridges cross the gorge, connected by a short path on the south bank; the upper one reaches NH 112 on the porch of the restaurant. The entire loop is about 250 yd. long.

The chain of medium-sized mountains that rise east of and roughly parallel to the Connecticut River between Hanover and Glencliff—sometimes called the Middle Connecticut River Mountains—begins at the Hanover (south) end with a region of low hills, then finally reaches Moose Mountain, the southernmost mountain of consequence in the chain. From here northward, the AT is never far from the divide between the Connecticut and Pemigewasset drainages, but the mountains that it passes over do not really form a range because they are mostly clearly separate peaks rising from a hilly upland with no significant connecting ridges between them. Velvet Rocks (1,243 ft.) is a low ridge in Hanover named for its moss-covered ledges; its western knob has an outlook southeast. Moose Mountain (North Peak, 2,313 ft.; South Peak, 2,293 ft.), is located in Hanover; the Moose Mountain Trail crosses the South Peak and passes near the summit of the North Peak. There are views to the southeast from the South Peak, southwest from the north knob of the North Peak, and northeast from a ledge along the north ridge. Passing through the notch between the two peaks is the old Province Rd. (known in the Hanover area as Wolfeboro Rd.), laid out in 1772 to connect Governor Wentworth's residence in Wolfeboro with the Connecticut Valley towns, where the residents were becoming disaffected with the royal government in New Hampshire. Holts Ledge (2,110 ft.) has good views to the east and southeast, though access to the outlook is often restricted during the season when peregrine falcons, which nest on the cliffs below the ledge in most years, are raising their young. Smarts Mountain (3,238 ft.), located in Lyme, affords interesting views of a lesser-known country from its abandoned fire tower. Its southwest spur, Lambert Ridge, is ledgy with good views. Located in Orford, Mt. Cube (2,909 ft.) has several fine viewpoints and is one of the more rewarding small mountains in this part of New Hampshire. Webster Slide Mountain (2,184 ft.) rises steeply above Wachipauka Pond, with excellent views from the top of the ledge that plunges toward the shore of the pond, while nearby Mt. Mist (2,230 ft.) is wooded but has a fine outlook. The chain is traversed by the AT and the network of side trails maintained by the DOC. The northeastern part of this region, including all the trails described in this section that are located north of NH 25A, is shown on the AMC's *Moosilauke–Kinsman Map* (map 4). The region south of NH 25A is covered by USGS quads, but the most useful maps for this section are the *National Geographic Trails Illustrated Franconia Notch/Lincoln Map* (#740, NGTI), the Appalachian Trail Conservancy's (ATC) map of the AT from Hanover to Glencliff, and a map published by the DOC showing the DOC trail network, which consists of the AT and its side trails from Pomfret, Vermont, to Kinsman Notch in New Hampshire, which may be obtained from Director of Trails and Shelters, Box 9, Robinson Hall, Dartmouth College, Hanover, NH 03755. All three maps cover all trails described in this chain. Unless otherwise noted, all sections of the AT between Hanover and Glencliff are described from south to north.

CAMPING

Most of this section south of NH 25A is private land, where camping and fires are permitted only at official campsites. On the publicly owned lands of the AT corridor—all the way from Hanover to Glencliff—camping is permitted, but not within 200 ft. of the AT itself except at the official campsites. The part of this section north of NH 25A is mostly in the WMNF, where camping is permitted in accordance with the usual restrictions. Much of the land on Moosilauke itself is owned by Dartmouth College. No camping or fires are permitted on Dartmouth College land, which lies east and south of the summit of Moosilauke, roughly bounded by a line starting just south of Hurricane Mountain and following the ridge crest over South Peak, Mt. Moosilauke, Mt. Blue, Mt. Jim, and Mt. Waternomee, and then south from Waternomee to NH 118.

Forest Protection Areas

The WMNF has established a number of Forest Protection Areas (FPAs)—formerly known as Restricted Use Areas—where camping and wood or charcoal fires are prohibited throughout the year. The specific areas are under continual review, and areas are added to or subtracted from the list to provide the greatest amount of protection to areas subject to damage by excessive camping, while imposing the lowest level of restrictions possible. A general list of FPAs in this section follows, but because there are often major changes from year to year, one should obtain current information on FPAs from the WMNF.

(1) No camping is permitted above treeline (where trees are less than 8 ft. tall), except in winter, and then only in places where there is at least 2 ft. of snow cover on the ground—but not on any frozen body of water. The point where the restricted area begins is marked on most trails with small signs, but the absence of such signs should not be construed as proof of the legality of a site.

(2) No camping is permitted within 0.25 mi. of any trailhead, picnic area, or any facility for overnight accommodation such as a hut, cabin, shelter, tentsite, or campground, except as designated at the facility itself. In the area covered by Section Six, camping is also prohibited within 0.25 mi. of Long Pond (including islands), the site of the former Beaver Brook Shelter (not the new shelter), and Stinson Lake Rd. where it crosses Brown Brook.

(3) No camping is permitted within 200 ft. of certain trails. In 2006, designated trails included the entire AT from NH 25A to Kinsman Notch.

No camping is permitted on WMNF land within 0.25 mi. of certain roads (camping on private roadside land is illegal except by permission of the landowner). In 2006, these roads included Breezy Point Rd., Buffalo Rd., Noxon Rd. (FR 62), NH 112 (Kinsman Notch Rd.) between Lincoln and Bath, and Tunnel Brook Rd. (FR 700).

Established Trailside Campsites

Velvet Rocks Shelter (DOC) is located 1.8 mi. north of the center of Hanover on a spur path 0.2 mi. from the Velvet Rocks Trail (AT). It was rebuilt in 2006.

Moose Mountain Shelter (DOC), with two nearby tentsites, has been relocated to a point on the ridge of Moose Mountain, on a loop path off the

Moose Mountain Trail (AT) 0.1 mi. north of the crossing of Old Wolfe-boro (Province) Rd.

Trapper John Shelter (DOC) is near Holts Ledge, 1.1 mi. from Lyme-Dorchester Rd. via the Holts Ledge Trail (AT) and a spur path.

Smarts Campsite (DOC) is near the summit of Smarts Mountain. The former fire warden's cabin is also maintained as a shelter by the DOC.

Hexacuba Shelter (DOC) is an innovative hexagonal shelter for 10 people on a spur path 0.2 mi. off the Kodak Trail (AT), 1.6 mi. south of the south peak of Mt. Cube. The former Mt. Cube Shelter, 0.2 mi. from Baker Rd. via the Mt. Cube Section, no longer exists.

Ore Hill Shelter (DOC) is on a short spur path off the Ore Hill Trail, 0.6 mi. north of Atwell Hill Rd.

Jeffers Brook Shelter (DOC) is located just off the Town Line Trail, which is a part of the AT.

Beaver Brook Shelter (DOC) is located on the Beaver Brook Trail (a part of the AT), 1.5 mi. from NH 112 in Kinsman Notch. Camping is pro-hibited at the former shelter site near NH 112.

Three Ponds Shelter (WMNF) is located on a knoll above the middle pond on a side trail from the Three Ponds Trail.

TRAIL DESCRIPTIONS

Beaver Brook Trail (DOC)

This trail, which climbs to the summit of Moosilauke from NH 112 at a large parking area near the height-of-land in Kinsman Notch, is a link in the AT. It passes the beautiful Beaver Brook Cascades, but the section along the cascades is extremely steep and rough, making this trail the most arduous route to Moosilauke despite its relatively short distance. *Caution:* In icy conditions this part of the trail may be dangerous. The upper part of the trail has been completely relocated and now coincides with the Ben-ton Trail for the last 0.4 mi. to Moosilauke's summit. As a result, it now ascends Moosilauke's open north ridge, where it is much more exposed to weather than the former route (which was quite well sheltered); conse-quently, this part may be dangerous in bad weather.

Leaving NH 112 almost directly opposite the Kinsman Ridge Trail, this trail crosses a bridge over Beaver Brook, swings to the left, and recrosses the brook on a bridge. The trail soon begins the climb along Beaver Brook, rising very steeply past Beaver Brook Cascades with many rock steps, wooden steps, and hand rungs. At 1.1 mi., the cascades end, and the trail bears left along a tributary and becomes progressively easier, following old logging roads. At 1.5 mi., it passes a side path that leads right in 80 yd. to Beaver Brook Shelter (DOC). Here there is an excellent view to the northeast, and a small stream 60 yd. farther along provides water (may not be reliable). The main trail continues to climb, and at a junction in a flat area at 1.9 mi., the Asquam-Ridge Trail turns sharp left. Here the Beaver Brook Trail bears right and ascends easily toward the edge of Jobildunk Ravine, passing a viewpoint over the valley. The old trail skirted the edge of this ravine, but the new trail turns sharp right uphill on the relocated route at 2.5 mi., then immediately turns sharp left and climbs fairly steeply to a point high up on the side of the highest knob of Mt. Blue. It then descends to a col, climbs over another knob with several restricted outlooks, descends to a second col, and climbs to the junction with the Benton Trail just below the treeline, at 3.4 mi. From this point, the two trails coincide, soon reaching the treeline and ascending the open, very exposed ridge crest to the summit.

Beaver Brook Trail (map 4:I3)

Distances from NH 112 (1,870 ft.) to
- Beaver Brook Shelter (3,750 ft.): 1.5 mi., 1,900 ft., 1 hr. 40 min.
- Asquam-Ridge Trail (4,050 ft.): 1.9 mi., 2,200 ft., 2 hr. 5 min.
- Benton Trail (4,550 ft.): 3.4 mi., 2,850 ft. (rev. 150 ft.), 3 hr. 10 min.
- Mt. Moosilauke summit (4,802 ft.): 3.8 mi., 3,100 ft., 3 hr. 25 min.

Tunnel Brook Trail (WMNF)

This trail runs between Tunnel Brook Rd. (FR 700) and Long Pond Rd. (FR 19; formerly North and South Rd.) through the deep valley (the "tunnel") between Mt. Moosilauke and Mt. Clough. To reach the north trailhead, follow the road that leaves NH 112 at a point 0.3 mi. east of its eastern junction with NH 116 and 1.9 mi. west of the WMNF Wildwood Campground. Turn left (south) at a junction 1.4 mi. from NH 112 and continue to the trailhead at the end of the maintained section, 3.8 mi. from NH 112. The south trailhead is located on Long Pond Rd., 0.4 mi. north of the point where it leaves High St. (formerly Sanatorium Rd.) 1.0 mi. from NH 25 in Glencliff. The central portion is subject to disruption by beaver activity, and, though the trail is currently well maintained and clear, short sections could become very wet or obscure. There are good views of beaver ponds and the slides on Mt. Clough, and grades are mostly easy.

Leaving the parking area at the end of Tunnel Brook Rd., the trail continues south on an old logging road (sign); avoid a newer logging road that bears to the left. After passing a beaver meadow, it crosses Tunnel Brook at 0.8 mi., becomes rougher in an area of old landslides, descends slightly to recross at 1.3 mi., and soon reaches an outlook to a beaver pond and the slides on Mt. Clough. It skirts several beaver ponds with more views, then at 1.6 mi., it swings right near a campsite and recrosses Tunnel Brook on a beaver dam; this spot may be obscure. At 1.9 mi., it reaches an open spot on the shore of Mud Pond, with a view up to the South Peak of Moosilauke. Soon it crosses the outwash from a slide and begins to descend on a logging road along Slide Brook, passing a reservoir at 3.3 mi. and crossing and recrossing the brook. Care should be taken not to pollute Slide Brook, the water supply for the New Hampshire Home for the Elderly in Glencliff. At 4.2 mi., the trail crosses Jeffers Brook, passes a camp, and ends at Long Pond Rd.

Tunnel Brook Trail (map 4:I2)

Distances from end of Tunnel Brook Rd. (1,880 ft.) to
- Mud Pond (2,280 ft.): 1.9 mi., 400 ft., 1 hr. 10 min.
- Long Pond Rd. (1,393 ft.): 4.4 mi., 400 ft. (rev. 900 ft.), 2 hr. 25 min.

Benton Trail (WMNF)

This trail climbs to the summit of Mt. Moosilauke from Tunnel Brook Rd. (FR 700). To reach the trailhead, follow the road that leaves NH 112 at a point 0.3 mi. east of its eastern junction with NH 116 and 1.9 mi. west of the WMNF Wildwood Campground. Turn left (south) at a junction 1.4 mi. from NH 112, then continue to the trailhead 3.0 mi. from NH 112. The trail follows the route of an old bridle path with moderate grades and good footing, making this a very pleasant and fairly easy route to the magnificent views from Moosilauke's summit, though the brook crossing at about 0.2 mi. from the start is difficult when the water level is high. For the last 0.3 mi., the Benton Trail ascends the open north ridge of Moosilauke, where it is greatly exposed to the elements, so this section may be dangerous in bad weather.

The trail descends slightly from the parking lot to an old logging road, follows the road along Tunnel Brook for 0.2 mi., then crosses the brook (may be difficult at high water) and bears right on an old logging road, crossing a newer logging road and then ascending the wooded spur that forms the south wall of Little Tunnel Ravine. At 1.3 mi., there is a splendid view to the left into the ravine. The trail passes a spring (sign) on the right at 2.2 mi., then soon turns sharp right and climbs at moderate grades through a beautiful evergreen forest to the treeline, passing an outlook west. The Beaver Brook Trail (a part of the AT) enters from the left at 3.2 mi. just before the Benton Trail breaks out from the scrubby trees, and the two trails together ascend the bare north ridge, marked by cairns, to the summit.

Benton Trail (map 4:I2–I3)

Distances from Tunnel Brook Rd. (1,700 ft.) to
- Little Tunnel Ravine outlook (2,800 ft.): 1.3 mi., 1,100 ft., 1 hr. 10 min.
- Beaver Brook Trail junction (4,550 ft.): 3.2 mi., 2,850 ft., 3 hr.
- Mt. Moosilauke summit (4,802 ft.): 3.6 mi., 3,100 ft., 3 hr. 20 min.

Glencliff Trail (DOC)

This trail runs from High St. (formerly Sanatorium Rd.), 1.2 mi. from its junction with NH 25 in Glencliff village, to the Moosilauke Carriage Rd. in a sag just north of Moosilauke's South Peak. It is part of the AT. There is only one steep section, and the footing is generally good. The trailhead parking area is on the right a short distance past the trail sign; from here, one may follow an old farm road past a gate, joining the trail in about 0.1 mi.

The trail leaves the road, passes a gate and enters a pasture, and soon crosses a small brook on a bridge. It joins a farm road that ascends from the parking area, then crosses a brook, follows a cart track along the left edge of a field, and enters the woods at 0.4 mi., where the Hurricane Trail immediately diverges right (east). The Glencliff Trail ascends moderately on a logging road that gradually fades away, crosses several small brooks, and passes a restricted outlook from a blowdown patch at 2.0 mi. Soon the trail swings right, going straight up the slope, and at 2.5 mi., it becomes quite steep, passing a talus slope that offers good views to the west. At the top of the ridge, it levels and reaches the junction with a spur path (sign) that leads right 0.2 mi. to the open summit of South Peak. In a few more steps, it enters the Moosilauke Carriage Rd.; for the summit, turn left.

Glencliff Trail (map 4:J2–I2)

Distances from High St. (formerly Sanatorium Rd.) (1,480 ft.) to
- Moosilauke Carriage Rd. (4,460 ft.): 3.0 mi., 3,000 ft., 3 hr.
- Mt. Moosilauke summit (4,802 ft.) via Moosilauke Carriage Rd.: 3.9 mi., 3,300 ft., 3 hr. 35 min.

Town Line Trail (DOC)

This trail, a short link in the AT constructed mainly to eliminate a road walk for AT hikers, runs from the northeast side of NH 25, just southeast of the Warren-Benton town line (parking 100 yd. farther southeast on the southwest side of NH 25), to Long Pond Rd. (formerly North and South Rd.) 0.1 mi. north of the point where it leaves High St. (formerly Sanatorium Rd.) 1.0 mi. from NH 25 in Glencliff. In times of high water, the crossing of Oliverian Brook next to NH 25 is dangerous, and in such conditions hikers traveling between Mt. Moosilauke and points to the south on the AT should follow High St. and NH 25 rather than attempting to use this trail.

The trail drops down a steep bank and crosses Oliverian Brook (fairly difficult even at moderate water levels) and follows the bank of the brook downstream, then swings left away from the brook, climbs moderately over a narrow ridge crest, and continues across low ridges and shallow sags. At 0.9 mi., the trail crosses a good-sized brook on a bridge, and in another 90 yd. a side path leaves left and runs north 0.1 mi. to Jeffers Brook Shelter. The main trail passes an unmarked path that leads 40 yd. right to cascades on Jeffers Brook, then passes another side path that leads 70 yd. left to the shelter, and continues to Long Pond Rd.

Town Line Trail (map 4:J2)

Distance from NH 25 (1,000 ft.) to
- Long Pond Rd. (1,330 ft.): 1.1 mi., 450 ft. (rev. 100 ft.), 45 min.

Hurricane Trail (DOC)

This trail runs around the lower south end of Moosilauke, making possible a number of loop trips by linking the lower end of the Glencliff Trail, the lower part of the Moosilauke Carriage Rd., and the complex of trails that leave Ravine Lodge Rd. East of the Moosilauke Carriage Rd., the Hurricane Trail is level and clear; some parts to the west are moderately steep and rough.

The Hurricane Trail continues straight where the Gorge Brook Trail turns right, 0.2 mi. from Ravine Lodge Rd. It crosses Gorge Brook on a log bridge and descends to the bank of Baker River, where it picks up a logging road and follows it on a long curve away from the river. At 1.0 mi., it reaches the Moosilauke Carriage Rd. and turns left (downhill). The two trails coincide for 0.3 mi., crossing Big Brook on a bridge, then the Hurricane Trail turns right (west) off the Carriage Rd. and follows a logging road into a small, moist clearing. Here it turns sharp left, follows Little Brook for a while, and climbs to the height-of-land at 2.6 mi. It continues nearly level for 0.2 mi., passing north of the little hump called Hurricane Mountain, then descends, rather steeply at times with rough footing for about 0.3 mi., then the footing improves. At 3.3 mi., the grade eases on a plateau, and the descent is easy to moderate to the Glencliff Trail 0.4 mi. from High St. (formerly Sanatorium Rd.).

Hurricane Trail (map 4:I3–I2)

Distances from Gorge Brook Trail (2,460 ft.) to
- Moosilauke Carriage Rd., upper junction (2,380 ft.): 1.0 mi., 50 ft. (rev. 100 ft.), 30 min.
- height-of-land (2,980 ft.): 2.6 mi., 900 ft. (rev. 250 ft.), 1 hr. 45 min.
- Glencliff Trail (1,680 ft.): 4.3 mi., 900 ft. (rev. 1,300 ft.), 2 hr. 35 min.

Moosilauke Carriage Road (WMNF/DOC)

This former carriage road climbs to the summit of Moosilauke from Breezy Point, a large clearing with good views, the site of the Moosilauke Inn. The road to Breezy Point leaves NH 118 2.5 mi. north of its junction with NH 25 (which is 1.0 mi. north of Warren village). Follow the road for 1.6 mi., just past the left-branching driveway to the former inn, and park where the road descends slightly (sign). (The road may be impassable before this point, in which case hikers will have to park on the shoulder of the road and walk a short extra distance.) Grades are easy to moderate and the footing is in general very good; marking is light in the first part, after which the trail becomes unmistakable. The upper part is above the treeline and greatly exposed to the elements, so it can be dangerous in bad weather. The lower part, up to a barricade at 4.1 mi., receives heavy snowmobile use in winter.

Continuing on the grassy road, the trail crosses Merrill Brook on a bridge, then enters a clearing at 0.3 mi., where it passes straight through and continues on a logging road with DOC markings. The Hurricane Trail enters left at 1.3 mi., and the two trails cross Big Brook together on a bridge. The Hurricane Trail diverges right to Ravine Lodge Rd. at 1.6 mi., and the old carriage road begins to climb by a series of switchbacks through a beautiful mature hardwood forest, with easy to moderate grades and excellent footing. At 3.0 mi., the Snapper Trail enters right. The next section of the road has been widened and improved, eliminating what was formerly a washed-out section with poor footing. Starting at 3.5 mi., there are occasional views back to the south and east. At 4.1 mi., the old road is blocked by a row of boulders to prevent further vehicular use. At 4.2 mi., the Glencliff Trail enters from the left; a few steps along the Glencliff Trail, a spur trail leads left 0.2 mi. to South Peak, a fine viewpoint. The old road, now part of the AT, continues along the ridge, with a narrow fringe of trees on each side. At 4.9 mi., it reaches the treeline and ascends the windswept ridge to the summit.

Moosilauke Carriage Road (map 4:J3–I3)

Distances from Breezy Point trailhead (1,720 ft.) to

- Snapper Trail (3,360 ft.): 3.0 mi., 1,650 ft., 2 hr. 20 min.
- Glencliff Trail (4,460 ft.): 4.2 mi., 2,750 ft., 3 hr. 30 min.
- Mt. Moosilauke summit (4,802 ft.): 5.1 mi., 3,100 ft., 4 hr. 5 min.

Gorge Brook Trail (DOC)

This trail runs from the end of Ravine Lodge Rd. to the summit of Moosilauke. The upper part has been completely relocated, making the trail substantially longer but eliminating the steep grades and rough footing of the former route. It is now a relatively easy trail that affords some interesting views as it climbs.

Leaving the turnaround at the end of Ravine Lodge Rd., it follows the gravel logging road for 100 yd., then turns left, descends to Baker River and crosses it on a footbridge, and immediately turns left at 0.2 mi. where the Asquam-Ridge Trail diverges right. In a short distance, the Hurricane Trail continues straight ahead, whereas the Gorge Brook Trail turns sharp right uphill and follows Gorge Brook, then crosses it on a bridge at 0.6 mi. The relocated Snapper Trail diverges on the left just past this bridge, while the Gorge Brook Trail continues close to the brook and recrosses it at 1.3 mi. on another bridge. At 1.6 mi., it passes the memorial plaque for the Ross McKenney Forest; here the new route begins and swings well to the right of the former route. At 2.1 mi., it turns left onto an old logging road, passes a cleared outlook to the south, then turns left off the road and winds uphill at moderate grades, passing more outlooks to the south and east. At 3.3 mi., it reaches a shoulder covered with low scrub that affords a view to the summit ahead and soon breaks into the open on the grassy ridge crest. It continues to the base of the summit rocks, then clambers up the last rocky 50 yd. to the summit.

On the descent, though the trails are fairly well signed, the maze of beaten paths (including several abandoned trails) in this area might prove confusing in poor visibility. From the summit, the Gorge Brook Trail descends eastward down the rocks and then runs southeast along a grassy shoulder until it reaches the scrub.

Gorge Brook Trail (map 4:J3–I3)

Distances from Ravine Lodge Rd. (2,460 ft.) to
- Snapper Trail (2,620 ft.): 0.6 mi., 250 ft. (rev. 100 ft.), 25 min.
- McKenney Forest plaque (3,250 ft.): 1.6 mi., 900 ft., 1 hr. 15 min.
- Mt. Moosilauke summit (4,802 ft.): 3.7 mi., 2,450 ft., 3 hr. 5 min.

Snapper Trail (DOC)

This trail was originally cut as a downhill ski trail, but it has been almost completely relocated and now features less steep grades and drier footing than before. It runs from the Gorge Brook Trail 0.6 mi. from Ravine Lodge Rd. to the Moosilauke Carriage Rd. 2.1 mi. below the summit of Moosilauke. It makes possible a number of loop hikes from Ravine Lodge Rd.; particularly attractive is the circuit over the summit of Moosilauke that combines the Snapper

Trail–Moosilauke Carriage Rd. route with the Gorge Brook Trail—these two routes are now approximately equal in distance and difficulty.

Leaving the Gorge Brook Trail just after its first crossing of Gorge Brook, it ascends northwest along a tributary and crosses it at 0.3 mi. The trail swings left, then right, crosses another tributary, then angles up the slope in a southwest direction at a moderate grade. At 0.9 mi., it crosses the old trail route and continues to its junction with the Moosilauke Carriage Rd.

Snapper Trail (map 4:J3–J2)

Distance from Gorge Brook Trail (2,620 ft.) to
- Moosilauke Carriage Rd. (3,360 ft.): 1.1 mi., 750 ft., 55 min.

Distance from Ravine Lodge Rd. (2,460 ft.) to
- Mt. Moosilauke summit (4,802 ft.) via Gorge Brook Trail, Snapper Trail, and Moosilauke Carriage Rd.: 3.8 mi., 2,450 ft. (rev. 100 ft.), 3 hr. 5 min.

Asquam-Ridge Trail (DOC)

This trail runs from the Gorge Brook Trail 0.2 mi. from Ravine Lodge Rd. to the Beaver Brook Trail on top of the Blue Ridge, providing a long but rather easy route to Moosilauke's summit.

It leaves the Gorge Brook Trail just across the Baker River footbridge, where it turns sharp right and follows the west bank of the river. At 0.5 mi., it merges with a logging road that comes in from the right; this road ascends 0.5 mi. from the end of Ravine Lodge Rd. and crosses the river on a bridge before it reaches this intersection. The Asquam-Ridge Trail continues along the river, then crosses it on a footbridge at 1.5 mi. and turns sharp right to ascend gradually away from the river. At 1.9 mi., the trail turns sharp left where the Al Merrill Loop from Ravine Lodge Rd. enters straight ahead, and then follows another logging road very gradually upward. Eventually it encounters some steeper pitches, passes a few yards left of the wooded summit of Mt. Jim, then descends easily to the Beaver Brook Trail.

Asquam-Ridge Trail (map 4:J3–I3)

Distances from Gorge Brook Trail (2,360 ft.) to
- Beaver Brook Trail (4,050 ft.): 3.9 mi., 1,800 ft. (rev. 100 ft.), 2 hr. 50 min.
- Mt. Moosilauke summit (4,802 ft.) via Beaver Brook Trail: 5.8 mi., 2,700 ft. (rev. 150 ft.), 4 hr. 10 min.

Al Merrill Loop (DOC)

This trail follows logging roads for its entire length from the end of Ravine Lodge Rd. to the Asquam-Ridge Trail and, while it was originally intended mostly as a ski trail, it is excellent for hiking. Up to the height-of-land (just past the fine 10th Mountain Division memorial outlook), it provides easy grades and footing, affording a hike of less than 5 mi. while rising only about 900 ft. to a fine viewpoint. A loop hike that is a bit longer with slightly rougher footing can be made by continuing to the junction with the Asquam-Ridge Trail and following that trail back to the starting point. This loop is perhaps a bit easier in the opposite direction (up by the Asquam-Ridge Trail, down by the Al Merrill Loop).

Leaving the turnaround at the end of Ravine Lodge Rd., this trail continues on the gravel logging road past the junction where the Gorge Brook Trail diverges from the road on the left. It takes the right fork of the road at 0.1 mi., where the left fork leads to a bridge across the stream and continues to join the Asquam-Ridge Trail. It continues past a spur path that leads left to John Rand Cabin (not open to the public) at 0.5 mi., and climbs to a fork in a clearing at 1.2 mi., where it bears left as a dead-end ski trail goes to the right. Still ascending easily by long switchbacks, at 2.4 mi., it reaches the 10th Mountain Division memorial outlook, where there is a fine view up to the summit of Moosilauke. Soon the trail crosses the height-of-land and descends with somewhat less easy footing to the junction where it enters the Asquam-Ridge Trail at a switchback; left (downhill) leads down toward Ravine Lodge Rd., whereas right (uphill) leads toward Mt. Jim and the summit of Moosilauke.

Al Merrill Loop (map 4:J3–I3)

Distances from Ravine Lodge Rd. (2,460 ft.)
- to 10th Mountain Division outlook (3,350 ft.): 2.4 mi., 900 ft., 1 hr. 40 min.
- to Asquam-Ridge Trail (3,100 ft.): 3.2 mi., 950 ft. (rev. 300 ft.), 2 hr. 5 min.
- for complete loop via Asquam-Ridge Trail and extension of Ravine Lodge Rd.: 5.1 mi., 1,050 ft., 3 hr. 10 min.

Blueberry Mountain Trail (WMNF)

This trail crosses the ridge of Blueberry Mountain, affording interesting views from scattered ledges on both sides of the crest. The east terminus is reached by following High St. (formerly Sanatorium Rd.) for 1.0 mi. from NH 25 in Glencliff, then turning left (north) on Long Pond Rd. (formerly North and South Rd.) and following it for 0.8 mi. to a small parking area on the left. The west terminus is reached by taking Lime Kiln Rd. from NH 25 in East Haverhill, 5.2 mi. north of Glencliff and 0.4 mi. north of a power-line crossing where there is an interesting view of the Benton Range to the north. Keep straight ahead on Page Rd. at a junction at 1.4 mi. where Lime Kiln Rd. turns left, and continue to the trail sign on Blueberry Mountain Rd., which leaves left at 2.4 mi. Parking is available 0.1 mi. up this road, just before a gate that one should not drive past even if it is open. The western section of the trail is lightly used, but the footway is fairly easy to follow for experienced hikers.

Starting at Long Pond Rd., the trail follows a relatively new logging road for 0.2 mi., then turns sharp right up a short, steep bank and follows old logging roads, crossing a newer grassy road at 0.4 mi. It ascends through hardwoods then enters coniferous woods and begins to climb ledges with restricted views, then turns sharp right at 1.2 mi. and continues to climb. Soon it reaches ledges that are more open, with outlooks to the east and south, including an unusual and interesting view into the slide-scarred ravine of Slide Brook on Moosilauke; the best outlook is on the right at 1.6 mi.. At 1.7 mi., it reaches the crest of the main ridge, where a side path leads right (north) 0.1 mi. to the ledges of the true summit, which offers restricted views over trees.

The trail (this part receives much less use but is well marked) then descends gradually across the broad ridge crest through scrubby trees and ledges with limited views, passing to the left of a boggy depression and crossing a small moist glen, then turns sharp right at a cairn and soon reaches a fine view of Black Mountain, Sugarloaf, and the Hogsback. Other views to Sugarloaf and to the Connecticut Valley are passed as the trail descends on ledges. The trail drops below the ledges, passes through a short area of moss-carpeted coniferous woods, and enters the upper end of a system of logging roads that it follows the rest of the way. It crosses many small brooks and one rather wet stretch. At 3.2 mi., after leaving an extensive section of birch woods, it crosses a stone wall and enters a region of abandoned farms where many stone walls and cellar holes remain, and mint that escaped from a farm garden many decades ago still grows among the corduroy logs in the old road. At 4.0 mi., the trail enters a newer grass-grown road and turns sharp left on it, crossing the WMNF boundary in 125 yd. The newer road leads past a gate, passes a field with a good view up to Sugarloaf, and ends at the junction of Blueberry Mountain Rd. and Page Rd.

Blueberry Mountain Trail (map 4:I2–I1)

Distances from Long Pond Rd. (1,558 ft.) to
- ridge crest near Blueberry Mountain summit (2,600 ft.): 1.7 mi., 1,050 ft., 1 hr. 25 min.
- junction of Blueberry Mountain Rd. and Page Rd. (1,176 ft.): 4.5 mi., 1,050 ft. (rev. 1,400 ft.), 2 hr. 45 min.

Black Mountain Trail (WMNF)

This trail ascends Black Mountain from the north, using old logging roads and the old tractor road to the former fire tower. It is a fairly easy way to ascend this attractive small mountain, but is much less interesting and only slightly easier than the Chippewa Trail. From the four-way intersection on NH 116 in Benton village, 2.9 mi. west of the western junction of NH 112 and NH 116, follow Howe Hill Rd., which runs uphill approximately south. The road changes to gravel at 0.6 mi., and the maintained section ends at 0.8 mi., where a much rougher, often muddy section continues ahead. Vehicles with low clearance should park here to the left of the trail sign, taking care not to block driveways. High-clearance vehicles may be able to drive another 0.2 mi. to a designated parking area on the right.

From the end of the maintained section of Howe Hill Rd., the trail follows the rougher road through logged areas, bearing left at a junction at 0.5 mi. (arrow). The road soon narrows and bears slightly left in a log yard, then takes the right branch at a fork and winds steadily uphill, passing near several more logged areas. It then swings right (southwest) and angles up the slope at easier grades. At 2.4 mi., the Chippewa Trail joins from the right, and the open, ledgy ridge crest at the old fire tower site is another 40 yd. ahead. There are good views from the ridge crest both east and west of the tower site; Tipping Rock, where there are more good views, is 150 yd. to the east via a faint path over ledges and through scrubby areas.

Black Mountain Trail (map 4:H2–I1)

Distance from end of maintained section of Howe Hill Rd. (1,550 ft.) to
• Black Mountain summit (2,830 ft.): 2.4 mi., 1,300 ft., 1 hr. 50 min.

Chippewa Trail (WMNF)

This very scenic trail ascends Black Mountain from Lime Kiln Rd., which leaves NH 25 in East Haverhill, 5.2 mi. north of Glencliff and 0.4 mi. north of a power-line crossing. Bear left at a major fork at 1.4 mi., and continue to the trailhead at a point 3.1 mi. from NH 25, just past a sharp turn in the road. In the other direction, the trailhead is 1.8 mi. from the junction of Lime Kiln Rd. and NH 116. The trail, well blazed with yellow paint, begins on the east side of the road at a small parking area; at times, there has been a trail sign at the edge of the woods.

The trail descends a short, fairly steep pitch through a logged area, crosses two small brooks, and skirts a beaver pond with a view of Sugarloaf Mtn. It turns left up a bank and in 40 yd. crosses a larger brook on logs next to a beaver dam, then climbs to a logging road and turns right on it; the Lime Kilns are located on a side trail that begins a short distance left on this road (sign). In another 60 yd., the trail diverges left from this road on a much older road and begins the ascent of the mountain. At 0.6 mi., it passes to the left of a cellar hole in an overgrown pasture and, after passing through a shallow sag, begins to climb more steeply. It passes a state forest boundary sign and then turns sharp left just before a rock outcrop on the ridge crest, continuing to climb among ledges in woods dominated by red pines and passing two side paths leading 50 yd. right to ledges with good views. At 1.1 mi., the main trail turns sharp left where a side path leads right 25 yd. to a ledge that affords fine views south and west. In this area, the blue blazes of a property line must not be confused with trail blazes. After 1.3 mi., the trail climbs mostly on ledges past excellent outlooks scattered along the way until it reaches a knob with an interesting view of the summit rocks ahead, then crosses a shallow, moist sag and reaches the junction with the Black Mountain Trail from Benton village.

The open ridge crest at the old fire tower site is 40 yd. to the right, with good outlook points on the ridge crest both east and west of the tower site. Tipping Rock, on a ledge with good views, is 150 yd. east of the tower site via a faint path over ledges and through scrubby areas.

Chippewa Trail (map 4:I1)

Distance from parking area off Lime Kiln Rd. (1,320 ft.) to
- Black Mountain summit (2,830 ft.): 1.8 mi., 1,550 ft. (rev. 50 ft.), 1 hr. 40 min.

Stinson Mountain Trail (WMNF)

The fire tower on this small, relatively easy mountain has been dismantled, but fine views are still available in several directions, and metamorphosed strata make the summit ledge geologically interesting. The trail is reached by following Main St., which becomes Stinson Lake Rd., north from NH 25 in Rumney. Main St. leaves NH 25 7.3 mi. west of Exit 26 on I-93. At the foot of the lake, 5.0 mi. from NH 25 and 0.1 mi. south of the Stinson Lake General Store and Post Office, turn right uphill on Cross Rd. for 0.8 mi., then turn right again on Lower Doe Town Rd., bearing left to a parking lot at 0.3 mi. on the left.

The trail leaves the parking lot and soon enters and follows an old farm road between stone walls. After passing a cellar hole on the left side of the trail, it becomes steeper, and at 0.9 mi., it bears left, joining a logging road that comes up from the right (descending, make sure to turn right here). At 1.1 mi., the trail takes the right fork at a junction; left is the old tractor road (now a snowmobile trail) to the summit; it is slightly longer and has one very wet stretch on the ridge crest. The trail climbs by switchbacks and rejoins the old tractor road just below the summit (note the left turn here for the descent). From here, either of two routes, which make a very short loop, climb to the summit ledges. From the northwest base of the summit ledges, a spur path leads southwest about 80 yd. to a view over Stinson Lake.

Stinson Mountain Trail (map 4:K3)

Distance from parking lot (1,495 ft.) to
- Stinson Mountain summit (2,900 ft.): 1.8 mi., 1,400 ft., 1 hr. 35 min.

Rattlesnake Mountain Trail (WMNF)

This trail climbs moderately to a loop over the ledges of Rattlesnake Mountain with their fine views over the Baker River valley, providing excellent views for a very modest effort. It begins on Buffalo Rd., the road along the north bank of Baker River, 2.5 mi. west from the crossroads in Rumney village; or, from NH 25, 6.4 mi. west of the West Plymouth traffic circle, follow Sand Hill Rd. across Baker River, then turn right after 0.3 mi. and follow Buffalo Rd. 1.2 mi. to a small parking area just before the Nathan Clifford Birthplace historical marker.

The trail follows a logging road that soon becomes rather steep, then levels out on the ridge crest and passes the west end of the summit loop on the right at 0.8 mi. In another 80 yd., the east end of the summit loop turns right off the old road, meanders through the woods, and ascends over ledges with many fine views, bearing right and reaching the summit at 1.3 mi. It descends and then turns sharp right at the base of the summit ledge, where a faint spur path leads to a view west, and returns over a rocky knob to the old road at 1.7 mi. Turn left here to return to the parking area. Part of the summit area was burned by a forest fire in 2008.

Rattlesnake Mountain Trail (map 4:L2)

Distances from Buffalo Rd. (630 ft.)

- to Rattlesnake Mountain summit (1,594 ft.): 1.3 mi., 950 ft., 1 hr. 10 min.
- for complete loop: 2.5 mi., 1,000 ft., 1 hr. 45 min.

Carr Mountain Trail (WMNF)

This trail provides access to the summit of Carr Mountain, where several rounded rock knobs provide good though somewhat restricted views. It begins on the Three Ponds Trail 0.5 mi. from the parking area on Stinson Lake Rd., ascends to the ridge crest where a short spur trail leads to the summit of Carr Mountain, and descends to the old Warren-Wentworth highway. Maintenance has recently resumed on the western half of the trail, which for some time had been very obscure. For the west trailhead, turn off NH 25 into the Warren Fish Hatchery and Wildlife Center, follow a paved road south for 0.1 mi., then turn left on Clifford Brook Rd. where there is a trail sign. This gravel road may be driven for 0.7 mi. to a marked grassy parking area on the right; do not park near the house at the end of the road.

The trail diverges sharp left (south) from the Three Ponds Trail and descends to cross Sucker Brook at 0.2 mi. on flat ledges that are submerged when water flow is above average, then crosses an old road on the south bank of the brook. (The Sucker Brook crossing is difficult at high water, and the trail section between Three Ponds Trail and the brook receives little use. Some use of the Carr Mountain Trail is by local residents who enter the trail from Stinson Lake Rd. by this old road along the south bank of Sucker Brook. This is private land, however, and the landowner objects strongly to hikers' cars being parked in this area rather than at the official trailhead parking lot. The brook crossing can also be avoided by following the Three Ponds Trail to its bridge over Sucker Brook, then returning back southeast along the brook on the old logging road to the Carr Mountain Trail. This route is about 0.8 mi. longer than the direct trail route.)

Once across Sucker Brook, the trail climbs easily to meet its former route (an old woods road) and continues a moderate ascent through a fine hardwood forest. It swings sharp right at 1.4 mi. (avoid a snowmobile trail that diverges left) and then swings back to the left at 1.7 mi., then winds upward near the crest of a ridge close to a small brook. Higher up it approaches and then crosses a very small mossy brook, then zigzags upward with some rough footing and soon comes close to the crest of the main ridge. The ascent becomes gradual through dense, moist coniferous woods, and at 2.9 mi., a side path turns left to the summit area. The best view is probably from the top of the first knob encountered on the left side of this spur, which ends in about 70 yd. at the remnants of the former fire tower.

The main trail descends, reaching a small brook that it crosses twice. It continues to descend moderately on logging roads that gradually become more and more discernible. At 4.8 mi., it turns sharp left onto a newer woods road; leading right from this junction (straight ahead, ascending) is a signed but obscure footpath that runs to a small waterfall at 0.1 mi. and, after crossing this waterfall's brook and passing over a low ridge, Waternomee Falls at 0.2 mi. At 5.5 mi., the road crosses a long meadow (follow yellow blazes on posts), passes to the left of a house, and becomes a clear gravel road that passes the parking spot on the left at 5.8 mi. and continues to the old Warren-Wentworth highway opposite a small cemetery, near the old fish hatchery. In the reverse direction, from the end of the gravel road by the house ascend through the meadow, following yellow-blazed posts to the point where the trail joins the old logging road in the woods.

Carr Mountain Trail (map 4:K3–K2)

Distances from Three Ponds Trail (1,450 ft.) to

- Carr Mountain summit side path (3,420 ft.): 2.9 mi., 2,100 ft. (rev 150 ft.), 2 hr. 30 min.
- Old Warren-Wentworth highway (700 ft.): 6.5 mi., 2,100 ft. (rev. 2,700 ft.), 4 hr. 20 min.

Three Ponds Trail (WMNF)

This trail starts on Stinson Lake Rd. at a parking lot 6.9 mi. north of NH 25 and 1.8 mi. north of the Stinson Lake General Store and Post Office. It passes the attractive ponds with several interesting outlooks to Carr Mountain and Mt. Kineo, crosses a low ridge, and descends to the gravel road used by the Hubbard Brook Trail, 0.2 mi. from NH 118. This gravel road (FR 211; a sign reads "922") leaves NH 118 4.4 mi. northeast of the junction of NH 118 and NH 25, which is about 1 mi. north of Warren village. Drive in 0.1 mi. and park on the right in a cleared area before a gate. South of the ridge, this trail mostly coincides with a snowmobile trail. The northern part of this trail, between the ponds and NH 118, is lightly used and may require care to follow; it is not recommended for inexperienced hikers.

Leaving the parking lot, it rises moderately and passes junctions with the Mt. Kineo Trail right at 0.1 mi. and the Carr Mountain Trail left at 0.5 mi., then descends gently. At 1.0 mi., it crosses Sucker Brook on a bridge and turns right upstream along the brook, following an old logging road. After a relocation through the woods to the right it returns to the road, crosses a tributary on a snowmobile bridge, then crosses the main brook three times without bridges; all of these crossings may be difficult at high water, but the upper two can be avoided by following a snowmobile bypass on the right. After the last crossing, the trail follows another relocation to the right, then returns to the old route before reaching the middle pond. At 2.2 mi., on the shore of the middle pond, a side path diverges right, passes Three Ponds Shelter on a knoll overlooking the pond, and rejoins the main trail.

At 2.5 mi., the Donkey Hill Cutoff diverges right, whereas the Three Ponds Trail turns left across a brook on a beaver dam (this area may be flooded), passes the northeast corner of the middle pond, then picks up a logging road and follows it to a point 80 yd. from the upper pond. Here the road continues to the edge of the pond (interesting views), but the trail turns sharp left and starts to ascend. From here on it is much less heavily used and must be followed with care. The trail enters an old logging road (where the snowmobile trail joins from the left), leaves it on a bypass around the swamp at Foxglove Pond, and crosses Brown Brook for the first of three times at 3.8 mi. At 4.0 mi., the snowmobile trail diverges left and the Three Ponds Trail ascends to a high plateau on the side of Whitcher Hill. The trail crosses the height-of-land at 5.1 mi., then descends steadily. At the bottom of the slope the trail turns right and runs through an area of recent logging, crossing two skid roads and briefly coinciding with the new Warren-Woodstock snowmobile trail. It crosses two branches of Blodgett Brook on new snowmobile bridges, turns left (in the reverse direction bear right here) and continues to the Hubbard Brook Trail, 0.1 mi. east of the gate on FR 211.

Three Ponds Trail (map 4:K3–J3)

Distances from Stinson Lake Rd. (1,310 ft.) to

- Three Ponds Shelter (1,750 ft.): 2.3 mi., 450 ft., 1 hr. 20 min.
- height-of-land (2,380 ft.): 5.1 mi., 1,100 ft., 3 hr. 5 min.
- Hubbard Brook Trail (1,430 ft.): 7.2 mi., 1,100 ft. (rev. 950 ft.), 4 hr. 10 min.

Donkey Hill Cutoff (WMNF)

This trail links the Three Ponds Trail 2.5 mi. from the Stinson Lake Rd. parking area to the Mt. Kineo Trail 1.7 mi. from the parking area, making possible a loop hike. Leaving the Three Ponds Trail, it skirts an area flooded by beaver activity and leads northeast, crossing a low ridge dividing the drainages of Sucker Brook and Brown Brook. At 0.6 mi., it swings southeast, crossing several small ridges as it follows the edge of an extensive beaver swamp with views of Mt. Kineo. It ends at a point where the Mt. Kineo Trail crosses Brown Brook.

Donkey Hill Cutoff (map 4:K3)
Distance from Three Ponds Trail (1,730 ft.) to
• Mt. Kineo Trail (1,680 ft.): 1.1 mi., 50 ft. (rev. 100 ft.), 35 min.

Mount Kineo Trail (WMNF)

This trail begins on the Three Ponds Trail 0.1 mi. from the parking lot on Stinson Lake Rd., crosses the ridge of Mt. Kineo almost a mile east of the true summit, and descends to a spur road off Hubbard Brook Rd. (FR 22) 6.3 mi. from US 3 in West Thornton. An easy loop can be made using the south part of this trail, the Donkey Hill Cutoff, and the Three Ponds Trail. The part of this trail beyond the Donkey Hill Cutoff and south of the Mt. Kineo ridge crest is an attractive woods walk, lightly used and possibly not easy to follow, so not appropriate for inexperienced hikers.

Leaving the Three Ponds Trail, it proceeds north over several minor ups and downs and enters the old route of the trail (a logging road along Brown Brook) at 1.0 mi.; in the reverse direction, bear right here. The trail climbs along the attractive brook, passing a fine cascade and crossing a branch brook twice. At 1.6 mi., where the Donkey Hill Cutoff diverges left, the Mt. Kineo Trail crosses the brook on ledges (difficult in high water). It runs north nearly level along the edge of a large swamp; markings are sparse and the footway is indistinct in places and subject to beaver flooding. At 2.2 mi., it turns right on an unmarked bypass, crosses a brook, and skirts a swampy area, soon rejoining the original route. In 0.1 mi., it swings right, away from the swamp, and crosses a small brook twice. It makes a short loop to the south, heads north for 0.2 mi., then makes a long eastward traverse across the slope through hardwood forest badly damaged by the 1998 ice storm. Higher up, the trail leaves the ice-damaged area, alternately angling up on old logging roads and climbing straight up on steep, rough sections. At 3.9 mi., it crosses the ridge in a small col, then descends to an old logging road, which it follows steadily downward through several muddy stretches to a gravel spur road passable by cars, about 0.5 mi. from its junction with Hubbard Brook Rd. (sign).

Mount Kineo Trail (map 4:K3–J3)

Distances from Three Ponds Trail (1,340 ft.) to
- Donkey Hill Cutoff (1,680 ft.): 1.6 mi., 450 ft. (rev. 100 ft.), 1 hr.
- height-of-land (2,850 ft.): 3.9 mi., 1,600 ft., 2 hr. 45 min.
- Hubbard Brook Rd. spur (1,930 ft.): 5.1 mi., 1,600 ft. (rev. 900 ft.), 3 hr. 20 min.

Hubbard Brook Trail (WMNF)

This trail leaves Hubbard Brook Rd. (FR 22) at a hairpin turn across Hubbard Brook, 7.6 mi. from US 3 in West Thornton, and runs to a gate on a gravel logging road (FR 211) 0.1 mi. from NH 118. The entrance to FR 211 (the sign reads "922") is 4.4 mi. northeast of the junction of NH 118 with NH 25 (this junction is 1.0 mi. north of Warren village). Park on the right before the gate. The trail provides a woods walk through the notch between Mt. Cushman and Mt. Kineo, passing several beaver ponds. It receives little use, but is well blazed and easy for experienced hikers to follow.

Leaving FR 22, it runs nearly level to a beaver pond at 0.5 mi. where the trail might be subject to disruption by flooding because of beaver activity; many new bog bridges have been installed here. It enters the woods just above the north end of the pond, continues alongside beaver swamps with some muddy footing, crosses a height-of-land at 0.9 mi., and descends for about 0.5 mi. It follows an assortment of logging roads and paths, crossing a beaver dam between two meadows and a brook beyond. At 1.9 mi., it crosses a small brook, turns right, and in 0.1 mi., turns left onto a gravel logging road (sign) that passes Three Ponds Trail on the left at 2.3 mi. and continues 100 yd. to a bridge over the East Branch of Baker River and the gate and parking space beyond.

Hubbard Brook Trail (map 4:J3)

Distance from Hubbard Brook Rd. (1,860 ft.) to
- gate on FR 211 (1,420 ft.): 2.4 mi., 100 ft. (rev. 550 ft.), 1 hr. 15 min

Peaked Hill Pond Trail (WMNF)

This trail follows a logging road to Peaked Hill Pond from US 3, 2.1 mi. north of exit 29 of I-93, at the Shamrock Motel. The trail is easy, and there is a pleasant view of Peaked Hill from the shore of the pond, which is partly private property. From US 3, follow Peaked Hill Rd. west under I-93, then turn right at 0.4 mi., and park on the left just before a steel gate at 0.6 mi. (do not block gate). The road bears left and ascends gradually, and at 0.5 mi. from the gate, a woods road bears to the right off the road to bypass an old pasture, then returns to the main road and follows it to the right. The road bears left at 0.9 mi. and crosses a logging clearing at 1.4 mi. At 1.5 mi., the trail leaves the road on the right and descends to the shore of the pond, where it ends.

Peaked Hill Pond Trail (map 4:K4)

Distance from gate (820 ft.) to
- Peaked Hill Pond (1,200 ft.): 1.7 mi., 400 ft., 1 hr. 5 min.

Velvet Rocks Trail (DOC)

This section of the AT passes through the town of Hanover, climbs over the interesting low ridge called Velvet Rocks, passing a loop path to Velvet Rocks Shelter, and ends on Trescott Rd. opposite the western terminus of the Hanover Center Trail, 0.9 mi north of the junction of Trescott Rd. and Hanover Center Rd. The main purpose of the Velvet Rocks Trail and Hanover Center Trail is to take the AT across the Connecticut Valley and connect the mountains of Vermont and New Hampshire. This part of the AT passes through a moderately populated area, but over the years relocations have eliminated road walks except for the 1.4 mi. section from the Connecticut River bridge to the official west end of the Velvet Rocks Trail. There is no parking at or near the official west terminus of the Velvet Rocks Trail; hikers must find legal parking in downtown Hanover (inquire at the DOC office in Robinson Hall at the town common). For directions to the east terminus, see Hanover Center Trail (west terminus); one can also follow East Wheelock St. and its continuation, Trescott Rd., 3.0 mi. from NH 120 at the north edge of the Dartmouth athletic complex.

Beginning at the state line on the Connecticut River bridge between Hanover, New Hampshire, and Norwich, Vermont, the AT follows West Wheelock St. to the square at the town common in Hanover. Turning right on North Main St., it soon turns left onto Lebanon St., which merges into

NH 120 at 1.2 mi. It crosses here to the east side of NH 120 and, in 100 yd. it turns left (signs) and runs along a hedge, traversing the south end of Chase Field, then enters the woods at 1.4 mi.

At this point, the segment officially known as the Velvet Rocks Trail (sign) begins. The trail swings left, then right, and ascends moderately. At 2.1 mi., the blue-blazed Velvet Rocks Shelter Loop Trail diverges left.

Velvet Rocks Shelter Loop Trail: The trail climbs easily 0.2 mi. to Velvet Rocks Shelter, then continues up a ridge passing an outlook southeast at 0.3 mi., just beyond its high point. It then descends to a junction at 0.4 mi., where a spur trail on the left descends 0.3 mi. to East Wheelock St. just west of Balch Hill Lane. Here the loop trail turns right and descends a short, steep pitch to rejoin the Velvet Rocks Trail in a sag at 0.5 mi.; 15 yd. before the junction a blue-blazed spur diverges left, leading 0.2 mi. to Ledyard Spring. (From the spring, a blue-blazed, lightly used path descends easily to Trescott Rd.—the continuation of East Wheelock St.—just east of its junction with Grasse Rd.) Velvet Rocks Shelter Loop Trail ascent is 100 ft. (rev. 150 ft.).

From its lower junction with the shelter loop trail, the Velvet Rocks Trail descends, swings left, and ascends easily to its upper junction with the shelter loop trail in a sag at 2.6 mi. It climbs over a knoll, then ascends steeply through a hemlock forest to the highest knob (no views) on the Velvet Rocks ridge at 3.3 mi.; a short distance before the high point, the Trescott Rd. spur (no sign, blue blazed) diverges left and descends 0.4 mi. to Trescott Rd., 0.3 mi. east of Grasse Rd. The main trail descends moderately with several switchbacks, passing by a series of beautiful mossy ledges that provide the name "velvet rocks." At 4.5 mi., it crosses a cattail marsh on a footbridge, then climbs over a knoll and rises gently to Trescott Rd.; there is a hiker's parking lot 50 yd. to the left on the east side of the road.

Velvet Rocks Trail (ATC/NGTI maps)

Distances from Connecticut River bridge (390 ft.) to
- Velvet Rocks Trail, official west end (530 ft.): 1.4 mi., 150 ft., 45 min.
- Velvet Rocks Shelter Loop Trail (975 ft.): 2.1 mi., 600 ft., 1 hr. 20 min.
- high point on Velvet Rocks ridge (1,243 ft.): 3.3 mi., 1,000 ft. (rev. 150 ft.), 2 hr. 10 min.
- Trescott Rd. (915 ft.): 5.2 mi., 1,200 ft. (rev. 550 ft.), 3 hr. 10 min.

Hanover Center Trail (DOC)

This is the section of the AT between Trescott Rd. and Three Mile Rd. Parking is available at both ends of the trail. For the west terminus, follow Greensboro Rd. east from NH 120 at the traffic lights at bottom of the hill south of downtown Hanover (this is 3.5 mi. north of I-91 Exit 18). At 1.9 mi. from NH 120, at a T-intersection, turn left on Etna Rd, then turn left on Trescott Rd. at 2.6 mi., just before reaching the center of Etna village. The trailhead is at 3.5 mi. For the crossing of Hanover Center Rd. in the middle of this section, continue on Etna Rd. through Etna village and the Hanover Center Rd. to the trail crossing just before a cemetery at 3.6 mi. For the east terminus, continue on Etna Rd. through Etna village; at 3.3 mi., turn right onto Ruddsboro Rd., and at 4.8 mi., turn left onto unpaved Three Mile Rd. and continue to the trailhead at 6.1 mi.

From Trescott Rd., the trail passes a spur on the left from the parking area, ascends gradually through a pine plantation, runs along the edge of a field, and swings left into the woods. It descends, passes through a stone wall, and climbs briefly. At 0.7 mi., it turns left on an old logging road, follows it for 90 yd., then turns right and descends. It crosses a brook, a field, and another brook, and reaches Hanover Center Rd. (limited parking) at 1.3 mi. It crosses the road and ascends moderately, then gradually through old pasture pines, passing through a stone wall. At 1.9 mi., it enters a large open field with a view southwest, then reenters the woods in 0.2 mi. It continues an easy to moderate ascent, with occasional short descents, and at 3.4 mi., it turns right onto an old trail segment. It crosses a woods road, passes through a wet section, then bears right at 3.7 mi., and soon reaches Three Mile Rd.

Hanover Center Trail (ATC/NGTI maps)

Distances from Trescott Rd. (915 ft.) to
- Hanover Center Rd. (845 ft.): 1.3 mi., 100 ft. (rev. 150 ft.), 40 min.
- Three Mile Rd. (1,400 ft.): 3.8 mi., 800 ft. (rev. 150 ft.), 2 hr. 20 min.

Moose Mountain Trail (DOC)

This is the AT section that crosses over Moose Mountain. The southern terminus is on Three Mile Rd.; follow Greensboro Rd. east from NH 120 at the traffic lights at bottom of the hill south of downtown Hanover (this is

3.5 mi. north of I-91 Exit 18). At 1.9 mi. from NH 120, at a T-intersection, turn left on Etna Rd. and continue through Etna village; at 3.3 mi., turn right onto Ruddsboro Rd., and at 4.8 mi., turn left onto unpaved Three Mile Rd. and continue to the trailhead at 6.1 mi., with parking available on the west side of the road. The northern terminus is on Goose Pond Rd., 3.7 mi. from NH 10, with parking available on the north side of the road at the south end of the Holts Ledge Trail.

Leaving Three Mile Rd., the trail descends across Mink Brook and ascends to a junction at 0.4 mi., where the abandoned Fred Harris Trail leaves left on an old road. The Moose Mountain Trail climbs moderately past a clearing with views to the southeast and reaches the wooded summit of the South Peak of Moose Mountain at 1.9 mi. It then descends to the notch between the two peaks of Moose Mountain, where it crosses the historic Old Wolfeboro Rd. (Province Rd.) at 2.4 mi.

The trail now ascends moderately, a side path 0.1 mi. long diverges right, passing the new Moose Mountain Shelter in 75 yd. and continuing past side paths to the privy and two tent sites, and rejoins the main trail. The main trail climbs over a knob, swings right below wooded cliffs, and reaches the north end of the shelter loop path at 2.7 mi. In 50 yd., it crosses a small brook, then ascends easily along the ridge. It passes over the southern knob of the North Peak, descends slightly, and reaches its high point on the North Peak of Moose Mountain at 3.9 mi. Here there is a view to the southwest from quartzite ledges on the left. The trail then descends past a fine northeast outlook toward Smarts Mountain (the best viewpoint on the mountain), continues down the ridge, then descends steadily by long switchbacks. It crosses a branch of Hewes Brook at 5.2 mi., and continues to Goose Pond Rd.

Moose Mountain Trail (ATC/NGTI maps)

Distances from Three Mile Rd. (1,400 ft.) to
- Old Wolfeboro Rd. (2,000 ft.): 2.4 mi., 1,000 ft. (rev. 400 ft.), 1 hr. 40 min.
- Goose Pond Rd. (950 ft.): 5.6 mi., 1,400 ft. (rev. 1,450 ft.), 3 hr. 30 min.

Holts Ledge Trail (DOC)

This is the segment of the AT that crosses between Goose Pond Rd. and Lyme-Dorchester Rd., passing over Holts Ledge. The endangered peregrine falcon has nested there in recent years, and portions of the ledge may be closed during the nesting season to prevent disturbance to the birds. The northern terminus is on Lyme-Dorchester Rd., just west of the Dartmouth Skiway, and the south terminus is on Goose Pond Rd., 3.7 mi. east of NH 10. Because Holts Ledge is more frequently ascended from the north, this trail is described in the north to south direction.

Note: For AT through-hikers or others interested in a walking route between the north trailhead of the Holts Ledge Trail and the south trailhead of the Lambert Ridge Trail, a 1.9-mi. long section of the AT runs roughly parallel to Lyme-Dorchester Rd. At the fork in the Lyme-Dorchester Rd. 3.2 mi. east of NH 10, near the base of the Dartmouth Skiway, the trail follows the left (northeast) fork for 0.2 mi. to the edge of an overgrown field, which it enters, marked by a blazed post, and crosses a snowmobile trail. It ascends gradually, crosses a brook, then descends gradually until it enters an old road at a granite AT mileage post. It follows this old road to Lyme-Dorchester Rd., where it turns left and crosses a bridge to the trailhead for the Lambert Ridge Trail (AT) and Ranger Trail.

Leaving Lyme-Dorchester Rd., the Holts Ledge Trail ascends moderately through hardwoods. At 0.7 mi., it crosses a ski area access road, and at 0.8 mi., a side path to the right descends 0.3 mi. to Trapper John Shelter. The main trail climbs, turning right to cross a small brook and then left to cross a tributary. At 1.4 mi., the trail reaches the brink of the cliff and turns sharp right; to the left a side path leads 70 yd. to a clearing behind a fence that protects the falcon nesting area, with excellent views to the east. The main trail ascends through woods along the edge of the cliffs, passing two more outlooks, and reaches the wooded crest of Holts Ledge at 1.7 mi. The trail descends, turns sharp right at 1.9 mi., and continues down the east side of a ridge. It crosses a snowmobile trail and at the bottom of the descent, it follows a woods road, swinging east and then south past a beaver flowage before ascending gradually for 0.3 mi. to Goose Pond Rd.

Holts Ledge Trail (ATC/NGTI maps)

Distances from Lyme-Dorchester Rd. (870 ft.) to
- side trail to outlook (1,930 ft.): 1.4 mi., 1,050 ft., 1 hr. 15 min.
- crest of Holts Ledge (2,100 ft.): 1.7 mi., 1,250 ft., 1 hr. 30 min.
- Goose Pond Rd. (950 ft.): 3.7 mi., 1,350 ft. (rev. 1,250 ft.), 2 hr. 30 min.

Lambert Ridge Trail (DOC)

This scenic trail, with several viewpoints, is the segment of the AT between Lyme-Dorchester Rd., 5.1 mi. east of NH 10, and the summit of Smarts Mountain. Ascending from the road moderately by switchbacks, it passes a side path right to a ledge with a southwest view and reaches a ledge with a view east at 0.8 mi. Here it makes a sharp left turn at the edge of a cliff (use caution) and continues climbing along the ledgy ridge with occasional views. At 1.8 mi., there is a fine view of the summit ahead, and the trail passes more outlooks and descends into a sag with a small stream at 2.3 mi. It then swings right (east) and ascends again to join the Ranger Trail at 3.3 mi. At 3.7 mi., a spur leads right 50 yd. to a tentsite with a restricted view south, and at 3.9 mi., the J Trail diverges right and carries the AT northward. The Ranger Trail continues another 50 yd. to the fire tower, passing a spur 30 yd. right to the warden's cabin. Water is often available in a spring 0.2 mi. north of the summit on the blue-blazed Daniel Doan Trail, which descends to Quinttown Rd.

Lambert Ridge Trail (ATC/NGTI maps)

Distances from Lyme-Dorchester Rd. (1,110 ft.) to
- Ranger Trail (2,600 ft.): 3.3 mi., 1,800 ft. (rev. 300 ft.), 2 hr. 35 min.
- J Trail/Daniel Doan Trail (3,230 ft.): 3.9 mi., 2,400 ft., 3 hr. 10 min.

Ranger Trail (DOC)

This trail, the old fire warden's trail to the fire tower on Smarts Mountain, ascends to the summit from Lyme-Dorchester Rd. 5.1 mi. east of NH 10 (the same place where the Lambert Ridge Trail begins). The upper 0.6 mi. coincides with the Lambert Ridge Trail and is part of the AT. The lower part of this trail is not officially maintained but is still signed, and because it is significantly easier than the parallel section of the Lambert Ridge Trail, and provides the opportunity for a partial loop hike in combination with that trail, it will probably continue to receive enough use to keep it easy to follow.

The trail starts up a woods road and ascends at mostly easy grades, with Grant Brook on the right (east). The road ends at a garage at 1.9 mi., and the trail turns right across the brook. The brook is recrossed at 2.3 mi.

(last reliable water), and the grade becomes steeper as the trail becomes rough, eroded, and slippery in places. At 3.0 mi., the Lambert Ridge Trail (AT) enters on the left, and the Ranger Trail coincides with it from here to the summit. At 3.5 mi., a spur leads right 50 yd. to a tentsite with a restricted view south, and at 3.6 mi., the J Trail diverges right and carries the AT northward. The Ranger Trail continues another 50 yd. to the fire tower, passing a spur 30 yd. right to the warden's cabin, where the Daniel Doan Trail descends to Mousley Brook Rd.

Ranger Trail (ATC/NGTI maps)

Distances from Lyme-Dorchester Rd. (1,110 ft.) to
- Lambert Ridge Trail (2,600 ft.): 3.0 mi., 1,500 ft., 2 hr. 15 min.
- Smarts Mountain summit (3,238 ft.): 3.6 mi., 2,100 ft., 2 hr. 50 min.

Daniel Doan Trail (DOC)

This trail follows the route of the former Mousley Brook Trail (once the AT route north of Smarts Mountain) ascends Smarts Mountain from the northwest along the valley of Mousley Brook. It is named in honor of Daniel Doan, the author of the first of the popular *50 Hikes* series, who was a Dartmouth alumnus and spent his adolescent years in nearby Orford. Doan also wrote a novel, *Amos Jackman,* in which most of the action takes place within a short distance of this trail's Quinttown trailhead. The trail uses old logging roads for most of its length and is fairly easy to follow on the descent, but has several poorly marked junctions where care must be used to follow the trail when ascending. From NH 25A 3.9 mi. east of its junction with NH 10 (where there are signs for Quinttown Rd. and Thomson Tree Farm), follow Quinttown Rd. 1.8 mi. east to a crossroads at a nearly deserted farming village called Quinttown. Quinttown Rd. continues east (straight ahead) from Quinttown past a locked gate to the J Trail (AT south) and Kodak Trail (AT north). For the Daniel Doan Trail, follow Mousley Brook Rd. south from Quinttown for 0.8 mi., past Marsh Rd. (which diverges left), a large farm (right), and several small camps (left), to a cable gate at the end of the maintained section of road, where there is a parking spot on the left. The road may not be passable in winter, so it may be necessary to walk at least part of the way from Quinttown.

Continue on foot up the road past the cable, taking the right fork where two parallel bridges cross Mousley Brook, to the trail sign at 0.2 mi. Here there is a camp on the left and the former DOC Quinttown Trail (now a gravel road) diverges right. The Daniel Doan Trail continues ahead up an old woods road, passing a driveway diverging sharp left to the camp, then bears right (sign) at 0.1 mi. just before the road reaches a gate and bridge. It ascends easily up an old farm road, wet and eroded in places, crossing a logging road leading from a log yard on the right. At 1.5 mi., it bears left to bypass a wet, eroded section of the old trail, then rejoins the old route just before crossing Mousley Brook at 1.9 mi. It ascends along the south bank of the brook, then veers away to the right and becomes steeper, narrowing to a footpath as it ascends over scattered ledges. At 2.9 mi., the grade eases, and the trail passes several springs (left) and the old warden's cabin (right) before reaching the summit and the renovated fire tower, which provides fine views. Here the J Trail turns left and the Lambert Ridge Trail (along with the coinciding Ranger Trail) continues straight.

Daniel Doan Trail (ATC/NGTI maps)

Distances from parking spot on Mousley Brook Rd. (1,350 ft.) to
- Mousley Brook crossing (2,200 ft.): 1.9 mi., 850 ft., 1 hr. 25 min.
- Smarts Mountain summit (3,238 ft.): 3.2 mi., 1,900 ft., 2 hr. 35 min.

J Trail (DOC)

This is the segment of the AT from the summit of Smarts Mountain to Quinttown Rd. 2.9 mi. from NH 25A. Quinttown Rd. leaves NH 25A 3.9 mi. east of its junction with NH 10 (where there are signs for Quinttown Rd. and Thomson Tree Farm); at 1.8 mi., at the crossroads called Quinttown where Mousley Brook Rd. diverges right (south), Quinttown Rd. continues straight through the crossroads and reaches a locked gate at 2.4 mi. Park on the left before the gate, taking care not to block the road. The trailhead is 0.5 mi. past the gate; in winter or mud season, it may be necessary to walk the entire 1.1 mi. from Quinttown. This trail is described from north to south; mileages are given from the gate.

The trail descends gradually and crosses the South Branch of Jacobs Brook on rocks (the former bridge here was washed out in 2005) and ascends through hardwood forest. It reaches evergreen woods as the grade becomes easier on the J-shaped ridge at 2.3 mi. At 4.0 mi., the trail swings right (west) and descends slightly, passes a spring located on the left and the junction on the left with the abandoned DOC Clark Pond Loop (which descends southeast to the Lyme-Dorchester Rd.), then continues to the coinciding Lambert Ridge and Ranger trails at 4.3 mi. The Ranger Trail continues another 50 yd. to the fire tower, passing a spur that leads to the right 30 yd. to the warden's cabin. Water is often available in a spring 0.2 mi. north of the summit on the blue-blazed Daniel Doan Trail, which descends to Mousley Brook Rd. and offers an alternative return route to the J Trail trailhead.

J Trail (ATC/NGTI maps)
Distance from Quinttown Rd. at locked gate (1,300 ft.) to
• Lambert Ridge Trail (3,230 ft.): 4.3 mi., 1,950 ft., 3 hr. 10 min.

Kodak Trail (DOC)

This is the segment of the AT from Quinttown Rd. 2.4 mi. from NH 25A to the main (south) peak of Mt. Cube. Quinttown Rd. leaves NH 25A 3.9 mi. east of its junction with NH 10 (where there are signs for Quinttown Rd. and Thomson Tree Farm); at 1.8 mi., at the crossroads called Quinttown where Mousley Brook Rd. diverges right (south), Quinttown Rd. continues straight through the crossroads and reaches a locked gate at 2.4 mi. Park on the left before the gate, taking care not to block the road. The trailhead is 0.5 mi. past the gate; in winter or mud season, it may be necessary to walk the entire 1.1 mi. from Quinttown. Mileages are given from the gate.

The trail ascends moderately from the road, swinging right as it climbs to the top of Eastman Ledges at 1.1 mi., where there is a fine view of Smarts Mountain. The trail then swings to the north, passing over a low ridge and descending to cross the North Branch of Jacobs Brook at 1.6 mi. At 2.0 mi., a spur path leads right uphill 0.2 mi. to hexagonal Hexacuba Shelter; the water source for the shelter is the brook at the spur path junction. The main trail crosses the brook and soon ascends roughly by switchbacks to the southwest ridge of Mt. Cube and reaches ledges with southwest views. It descends into a sag at 3.1 mi. and then climbs on scattered ledges to the bare summit of Mt. Cube, where the Mt. Cube Section enters from the left and the Mt. Cube Trail from the right.

Kodak Trail (ATC/NGTI maps)

Distance from Quinttown Rd. at locked gate (1,300 ft.) to
• Mt. Cube summit (2,909 ft.): 3.5 mi., 1,800 ft. (rev. 200 ft.), 2 hr. 40 min.

Mount Cube Trail (DOC)

This is the segment of the AT from the main (south) summit of Mt. Cube to NH 25A at a point 4.6 mi. west of its junction with NH 25 and 1.9 mi. east of its high point near Mt. Cube Farm. It is described here from north to south.

Leaving NH 25A, the trail ascends gradually on an old woods road past stone walls and a cellar hole, then crosses a gravel road at 0.5 mi. and swings right and narrows. At 1.5 mi., it descends, soon turns left onto an old logging road that it follows for 50 yd., then turns right off the road and descends again, soon crossing Brackett Brook. It rises easily through open hardwoods, then ascends by long switchbacks, passing a stone chair on the right at 2.5 mi. At 3.3 mi., the trail reaches the old route of the AT along the ridge between the two peaks of Mt. Cube. Here a somewhat obscure spur path follows a segment of the old AT to the right 0.3 mi. from the junction to the open ledges of the north peak, where there is a wide view to the north and east prominently featuring Moosilauke. The Mt. Cube Trail turns left at this junction and follows the old route to the summit of the bare south peak, where it meets the Kodak Trail and the Mt. Cube Section.

Mount Cube Trail (ATC/NGTI maps)

Distance from NH 25A (900 ft.) to
• Mt. Cube summit (2,909 ft.): 3.4 mi., 2,000 ft., 2 hr. 40 min.

Mount Cube Section (DOC/RTC)

This extensively relocated former route of the AT to the main (south) summit of Mt. Cube, also formerly known as the South Cube Trail, is now being maintained as a section of the planned Cross Rivendell Trail, which is projected to traverse the Rivendell Interstate School District (composed of Orford, New Hampshire, and Fairlee, Thetford, and Vershire, Vermont) to Flagpole Hill in Vershire VT. Formerly rather steep and eroded, it now provides a pleasant route to Mt. Cube with moderate grades and two viewpoints along the way. It is mostly on private land.

The trailhead is on Baker Rd., a gravel road that runs south from NH 25A 8.3 mi. west of NH 25 in Wentworth and 7.1 mi. east of NH 10 in Orford. The trailhead (sign) is on the east side of the road 0.9 mi. from NH 25A; park north of the trailhead on the west side of the road. The trail leaves Baker Rd. on an old logging road at first. At 0.1 mi., it swings left onto the first relocated section, then ascends by many switchbacks. After entering a beautiful spruce forest, it ascends past a cleared outlook west at 1.2 mi. and climbs short switchbacks with many rock steps to a ledge with a view west at 1.5 mi. It turns left here and descends slightly for 0.2 mi., then resumes the ascent, reaching quartzite ledges 100 yd. below the bare summit. From the summit, the Kodak Trail runs south and the Mt. Cube Trail north; the fine northeast outlook from the north peak can be reached by following the Mt. Cube Trail and a spur path (part of the former AT) north for 0.4 mi.

Mount Cube Section (ATC/NGTI maps)

Distance from Baker Rd. (1,400 ft.) to
  • Mt. Cube summit (2,909 ft.): 2.1 mi., 1,500 ft., 1 hr. 50 min.

Atwell Hill Trail (DOC)

This is the segment of the AT from NH 25A to Cape Moonshine Rd. opposite the Ore Hill Trail, 3.3 mi. south of NH 25C and 2.1 mi. north of NH 25A. The trailhead on NH 25A is 4.5 mi. west of NH 25 and 0.1 mi. east of the Mt. Cube Trail. The trail ascends gradually from NH 25A and bears left onto an old woods road at 0.2 mi. At 1.2 mi., it bears right (east) off the woods road, crosses an extensive swampy area with many stepping-stones, and ascends to Cape Moonshine Rd.

Atwell Hill Trail (map 4:K1)

Distance from NH 25A (900 ft.) to
  • Cape Moonshine Rd. (1,400 ft.): 1.7 mi., 500 ft., 1 hr. 5 min.

Ore Hill Trail (DOC)

This is the segment of the AT from Cape Moonshine Rd. opposite the At-well Hill Trail, 3.3 mi. south of NH 25C and 2.1 mi. north of NH 25A, to NH 25C at a point 3.5 mi. west of NH 25 and 0.1 mi. west of the Wachi-pauka Pond Trail. It passes under power lines and ascends through a part of Sentinel State Forest, and at 0.6 mi., a spur path leads right 100 yd. to Ore Hill Shelter; water is available by following a path 150 yd. south from the shelter. The main trail crosses the height-of-land on Sentinel Mountain at 0.8 mi., then descends. At 2.0 mi., it crosses a small stream and soon passes a beaver pond on the right. It swings right (east) on an old woods road for 0.1 mi., then leaves it left (north) and ascends to its high point on Ore Hill in a fine stand of sugar maples at 2.8 mi., where it bears right and descends to NH 25C.

Ore Hill Trail (map 4:K1–J1)

Distance from Cape Moonshine Rd. (1,400 ft.) to
- NH 25C (1,550 ft.): 3.4 mi., 800 ft. (rev. 650 ft.), 2 hr. 5 min.

Wachipauka Pond Trail (DOC)

This segment of the AT, which runs from NH 25C to NH 25, leaves NH 25C at a point 3.4 mi. west of NH 25 and 0.1 mi. east of the Ore Hill Trail. Its trailhead on NH 25 is 4.4 mi. west of the junction of NH 25 and NH 118 and 0.6 mi. west of the Glencliff Post Office, and 150 yd. south of the western terminus of the Town Line Trail. It also provides access to Wachipauka Pond and the Webster Slide Trail, and because the north trailhead is used most often to reach these features, it is described here from north to south.

Leaving NH 25, it crosses an old railroad grade and climbs easily, then turns sharp right at 0.5 mi. and ascends steadily to its high point on Wyatt Hill at 1.2 mi. It descends west gradually to a swampy area, then contours along the base of Webster Slide Mountain above the west shore of Wachipauka Pond. At 2.3 mi., the Webster Slide Trail leaves right for the spectacular summit ledges of Webster Slide Mountain, while an un-marked but obvious side path descends 0.2 mi. and 150 ft. left to a clear-ing at the northwest corner of the pond. The main trail passes Hairy Root

Spring, then climbs gradually, passing a short spur path left to an excellent east outlook. It crosses the wooded summit of Mt. Mist at 3.1 mi. and descends gradually, then rises slightly as it passes around a low hill and continues across Ore Hill Brook to NH 25C.

Wachipauka Pond Trail (map 4:J1-J2)

Distances from NH 25 (1,050 ft.) to
- Webster Slide Trail (1,650 ft.): 2.3 mi., 850 ft. (rev. 250 ft.), 1 hr. 35 min.
- NH 25C (1,500 ft.): 4.9 mi., 1,550 ft. (rev. 850 ft.), 3 hr. 15 min.

Webster Slide Trail (DOC)

The spectacular outlook from this mountain's east ledges, which look straight down onto Wachipauka Pond, is reached by a spur trail that leaves the Wachipauka Pond Trail (AT) right (west) 2.3 mi. from NH 25. It follows an old woods road (a former route of AT) for 0.2 mi., then turns sharp right and climbs rather steeply to the summit at 0.6 mi. and continues down past the site of the former shelter to the ledgy viewpoint (use caution).

Webster Slide Trail (map 4:J1)

Distance from Wachipauka Pond Trail (1,650 ft.) to
- Webster Slide Mountain ledge outlook (2,180 ft.): 0.7 mi., 550 ft., 40 min.

SUGGESTED HIKES

For more information on suggested hikes, see p. ix.

Easy Hikes

Rattlesnake Mountain [lp: 2.5 mi., 1,000 ft., 1:45]. The loop trail over this small ledgy mountain offers good views of the Baker River valley.

Three Ponds Loop [lp: 5.3 mi., 600 ft., 2:55]. An interesting loop through a region of ponds and swamps via the Three Ponds Trail,

Mt. Kineo Trail, and Donkey Hill Cutoff; add 0.4 mi. rt for a side trip to the upper pond.

Holts Ledge [rt: 2.8 mi., 1,050 ft., 1:55]. Ascend the Holts Ledge Trail from the north to a short side path leading to excellent eastern views; stay behind the fence to avoid disturbing nesting peregrine falcons (April 1 through August 1).

Tunnel Brook Notch [rt: 3.8 mi., 400 ft., 2:05]. The north end of Tunnel Brook Trail from Tunnel Brook Rd. provides easy access to this scenic area of slides and beaver ponds.

Moderate Hikes

Stinson Mountain [rt: 3.6 mi., 1,400 ft., 2:30]. A fairly easy climb up the Stinson Mountain Trail leads to good views south and northwest from this former fire tower peak.

Blueberry Mountain [rt: 3.6 mi., 1,100 ft., 2:20]. A pleasant hike up the east end of the Blueberry Mountain Trail, with open ledges looking east and south.

Black Mountain [rt: 3.6 mi., 1,600 ft., 2:35]. This fine viewpoint in the Benton Range is reached by the steep but attractive Chippewa Trail.

Al Merrill Loop [lp: 5.1 mi., 1,050 ft., 3:05]. An easy loop via the Al Merrill Loop, Asquam-Ridge Trail, and an extension of Ravine Lodge Rd., passing an excellent outlook toward Mt. Moosilauke.

Moose Mountain, North Peak [rt: 3.4 mi., 1,350 ft., 2:25]. There are two viewpoints on this hike along the north section of the Moose Mountain Trail from Goose Pond Rd. to the north knob of the North Peak. The trip can easily be extended to the South Peak and another view [rt: 7.4 mi., 2,150 ft., 4:45].

Lambert Ridge [rt: 3.8 mi., 1,200 ft., 2:30]. Take the Lambert Ridge Trail to the north end of the ledgy ridge with several good views.

Mt. Cube [rt: 5.0 mi., 1,600 ft., 3:20]. Enjoy expansive views from both the south and north summits. Use the Mt. Cube Section, a short section of the Mt. Cube Trail, and a spur path to the north peak.

Wachipauka Pond and Webster Slide Mountain [rt: 6.4 mi., 1,800 ft., 4:05]. Visit the attractive pond via the Wachipauka Pond Trail and a spur path, then climb the Webster Slide Trail for a bird's eye view.

Strenuous Hikes

Smarts Mountain [lp: 7.5 mi., 2,400 ft., 4:55]. Enjoy the open ledges of the Lambert Ridge Trail on the way up to the summit fire tower and descend via the Ranger Trail.

Mt. Moosilauke. This bald dome is the dominating peak of the region. Unless the brook at the start is high, the Benton Trail on the west side is a very attractive and less used route [rt: 7.2 mi., 3,100 ft., 5:10]. An interesting loop from the east side, including a short side trip to unusual views from the South Peak, can be made via the Gorge Brook Trail, Moosilauke Carriage Rd., and Snapper Trail [lp: 7.9 mi., 2,600 ft., 5:15]. A good long loop with a wide variety of scenery can be made via the Glencliff, Tunnel Brook, and Benton trails, with some road walking [lp: 13.3 mi., 4,000 ft., 8:40].

SECTION SEVEN
THE WATERVILLE VALLEY AND SQUAM LAKE REGIONS

This section covers the mountains that surround the valley of the Mad River, commonly called the Waterville Valley, including Mt. Tecumseh, Mt. Osceola, Mt. Tripyramid, Sandwich Mountain, and their subordinate peaks. The section also covers the lower ranges to the south and southwest, including the mountains in the vicinity of Squam Lake: the Squam Range, the Rattlesnakes, and Red Hill. This region is bounded on the west by the Pemigewasset River (and I-93, which follows the river fairly closely), on the north by the Kancamagus Highway (NH 112), and on the south by NH 25. This is the western part of a larger mountainous region bounded on the east by NH 16; it extends nearly 30 mi. from Lincoln to Conway without being crossed from north to south by any road. This western part of the larger region consists of a jumble of relatively disorganized shorter ridges and isolated peaks, while the eastern part (covered in Section Eight, Mt. Chocorua and the Eastern Sandwich Range) is dominated by the prominent and well-defined ridge crest of the eastern Sandwich Range formed by Mts. Whiteface, Passaconaway, Paugus, and Chocorua. This division of the larger region into two sections places Mt. Tripyramid and Sandwich Mountain in Section Seven and Mt. Whiteface and the Sleeper Ridge in Section Eight, although all these mountains have traditionally been considered part of the Sandwich Range (the rest of the mountains covered in Section Seven have not customarily been considered as belonging to the Sandwich Range). At the boundary between Section Seven and Section Eight, the only points of contact between trails are at the junction of the Mt. Tripyramid Trail (Section Seven) with the Kate Sleeper Trail (Section Eight), and at the junction of the Flat Mountain Pond Trail (Section Seven) with the McCrillis Trail (Section Eight).

Almost the entire section is covered by the AMC's *Crawford Notch–Sandwich Range Map* (map 3). On Red Hill, the Red Hill Trail and the southern end of the Eagle Cliff Trail are not covered by any of the AMC's maps, but are shown on the USGS Center Sandwich and Center Harbor quads. The southern part of the Squam Range (Mt. Livermore and points to the south) is covered better by the AMC's *Moosilauke–Kinsman Map* (map 4), but this map does not extend all the way to the southern ends of the Crawford-Ridgepole Trail and the Old Highway. The area containing these trails is shown on the USGS Holderness quad, though the Crawford-Ridgepole Trail up to the southeast summit of Cotton Mountain is not shown, and the Old Highway is shown but not titled. The Squam Lakes Association (SLA), which maintains most of the trails on Squam Range, publishes a trail guide to the paths they maintain. The trail guide, which has a map that covers the entire area (including Red Hill), can be ordered from the SLA. Bradford Washburn's detailed map of the Squam Range (scale 1:15,000) offers much greater detail than the AMC's maps, but omits the same areas; it is also available from the SLA.

GEOGRAPHY

Waterville Valley, the town, must be carefully distinguished from the Waterville Valley (the valley of the Mad River); a significant part of the Waterville Valley lies in the town of Thornton, while the town of Waterville Valley includes the summits of Mts. Whiteface and Passaconaway, which are not considered part of the Waterville Valley by even the broadest definition. Therefore, some features are in the Waterville Valley but not in Waterville Valley, and vice versa. In fact, the original name of the town was plain Waterville; it was changed to Waterville Valley in 1967 to share in the publicity that the major ski area of that name had generated. *The Waterville Valley*, by Nathaniel Goodrich (who participated in the scouting and building of many White Mountain trails and also was the first person to suggest the creation of a Four Thousand Footer Club), recounts the history of the Waterville Valley from its first settlers up to a time just before the modern major tourist development started, and gives a fascinating picture not only of this particular place when it was a rustic backwater known only to a few people—who, however, loved it passionately—but of a period of history and a way of life that, among other things, produced a large portion of the hiking trails that we enjoy today.

From I-93 near Campton, NH 49 (Mad River Rd.) runs northeast beside the Mad River for more than 11 mi. into the center of Waterville Valley, passing a group of lodges and condominiums and ending near the Waterville Valley library, the Golf and Tennis Club, the ski-touring center, and the Snows Mountain Ski Area. At 10.6 mi. from I-93, Tripoli Rd. (FR 30) turns sharp left, continues ahead where the road to the Mt. Tecumseh Ski Area (a more prominent road at this point) diverges left at 1.3 mi., and soon after that begins to follow the West Branch of the Mad River northwest to the height-of-land west of Waterville Valley (Thornton Gap, 2,300 ft., the pass between Mts. Osceola and Tecumseh). It then continues westward to its end at NH 175 (East Side Rd.) and I-93 near Woodstock. The road is gravel except for paved sections on each end, and much of it is narrow and winding; drive slowly and with caution. This road has not been plowed during the winter (except from NH 49 to the junction with the side road to the Livermore Rd. parking area) and is usually gated from late fall through the spring; there is also a gate at the height-of-land, which may be closed to prevent use of the road by through traffic when the gates at the ends are open. There is a town road (West Branch Rd.) that runs from Waterville Valley at the town library about 0.8 mi. west to Tripoli Rd. at a point north of the ski area, crossing a bridge over the West Branch of the Mad River just before it reaches Tripoli Rd. Livermore Rd. (FR 53) and its trailhead parking area are reached from Tripoli Rd. by following this road a short distance across the bridge to a fork where Livermore Rd. bears left and the road to Waterville Valley village turns right.

The Waterville Valley Athletic and Improvement Association (WVAIA) maintains a system of local trails to points of interest. Trail information and a WVAIA trail map may be obtained at the Town Square retail complex. Some of these trails intersect or coincide with ski-touring trails that may have the same name as a hiking trail but follow a somewhat different route. A separate map of the extensive ski-touring network is available locally.

Named for the Shawnee leader, Mt. Tecumseh (4,003 ft.) is the highest and northernmost summit of the ridges that form the west wall of the Waterville Valley, beneath which the Mad River flows. There are outlooks at its summit and better ones (cleared) on the Sosman Trail along its south ridge. Thornton Gap, at the head of the northwestern branch of the Mad River, separates Mt. Tecumseh from Mt. Osceola to the northeast; to the west, southwest, and south, several ridges run out from Tecumseh toward Woodstock and Thornton. On the end of the south ridge, the fine rocky peak of Welch Mountain (2,605 ft.) overlooks the Campton meadows and forms the impressive northwest wall of the narrow south gateway to the upper Waterville Valley. The views from Welch's open summit are excellent. Dickey Mountain (2,734 ft.) is close to Welch on the northwest, with many fine outlooks.

The tallest peak in the region, Mt. Osceola (4,340 ft.), lies north of the valley. It was named for the great chief of the Seminole people. It is a

narrow, steep-sided ridge with a number of slides in its valleys, and is particularly impressive when seen from the outlooks along the western half
of the Kancamagus Highway. Although there is no longer a fire tower on
its summit, it still commands magnificent views. Osceola has two subordinate peaks, the wooded East Peak (4,156 ft.) and the trailless West Peak
(4,114 ft.). Continuing the ridge of Osceola to the west is trailless Scar
Ridge (3,774 ft.), which runs northwest parallel to the Hancock Branch
and the Kancamagus Highway and ends with a group of lower peaks above
Lincoln village, of which the most important is Loon Mountain (3,065 ft.),
which can be ascended via the major ski area on its north slope. At the
far west end of the Loon group is Russell Crag (1,926 ft.), rising directly
above I-93 just north of the Tripoli Rd. exit, with interesting ledges but
no trails; north of the crag is Russell Pond, with a WMNF campground
reached by a paved side road (closed in winter) off Tripoli Rd. To the east
of Osceola is Mad River Notch, in which the Greeley Ponds are located,
and across that notch is Mt. Kancamagus (3,763 ft.), a trailless mass of
rounded, wooded ridges named for a Penacook chieftain.

The rugged and very picturesque mountain that forms the east wall
of the Waterville Valley, Mt. Tripyramid also overlooks Albany Intervale,
which lies to the north and east. Most of it is within the Sandwich Range
Wilderness. It was named by the illustrious cartographer Arnold Guyot
for the three pyramidal peaks that cap the narrow, steep-sided ridge. North
Peak (4,180 ft.) once afforded a sweeping view to the north that is now
mostly overgrown. Middle Peak (4,140 ft.), the most nearly symmetrical
pyramid of the three, provides a view toward Passaconaway and Chocorua
from the summit; a fine outlook over the Waterville Valley toward Tecumseh and Osceola is located to the west of the trail near the summit. South
Peak (4,100 ft.) is viewless. From South Peak, the tall, rolling Sleeper
Ridge (covered in Section Eight) connects Tripyramid with Mt. Whiteface
and the eastern part of the Sandwich Range. Scaur Peak (3,605 ft.) caps
the prominent northern spur of Tripyramid. Livermore Pass (2,900 ft.) lies
between Mt. Tripyramid and Mt. Kancamagus. A major east spur of Tripyramid is called the Fool Killer (3,548 ft.) because it blends into the main
mass so well, when viewed from a distance, that incautious parties attempting to climb Tripyramid from the east before the construction of the trails
often found themselves on top of the Fool Killer instead, separated from

their goal by a long, scrubby ridge with deep valleys on either side from which the ascent to the summits of Tripyramid would require a lengthy and very difficult battle with the dense, wind-wracked small trees.

Tripyramid is best known for its slides, great scars that are visible from long distances, which provide excellent views. The North Slide, which occurred during heavy rains in August 1885, is located on the northwest slope of North Peak. This slide exposed a great deal of bedrock that is geologically interesting, and is ascended mainly on steep ledges. The South Slide, located on the southwest face of the South Peak, fell in 1869 and is mostly gravel. Two smaller slides descend into the valley of Sabbaday Brook from the east face of Middle Peak. Tripyramid is steep and rugged, and all routes to its summits have at least one rough section; consequently, the mountain is more difficult to climb than a casual assessment of the altitude, distance, and elevation gain might suggest.

Sabbaday Falls, a picturesque small waterfall and pool formed by an eroded trap rock dike, is reached from Sabbaday Falls Picnic Area on the Kancamagus Highway by a gravel pathway section of the Sabbaday Brook Trail.

Sandwich Mountain (3,980 ft.), sometimes called Sandwich Dome, is the western-most major summit of the Sandwich Range; its western ridge forms the south wall of the Waterville Valley. It is mostly within the Sandwich Range Wilderness. It looks over the lower Mad River to the west, and Sandwich Notch separates it from the Campton and Holderness mountains on the south and southwest. Sandwich Mountain was once called Black Mountain, a name that has also been applied to its southwest spur (3,500 ft.), which is ledgy with many fine outlooks, and to a nubble (2,732 ft.) at the end of this spur. According to the USGS, it is the nubble that is currently officially entitled to the name of Black Mountain, but the southwest spur is also commonly referred to as Black Mountain. To the northeast, a high pass separates Sandwich Mountain from the long ridge of the Flat Mountain (3,334 ft.) in Waterville; Pond Brook has cut a deep ravine between its east shoulder and the rounded Flat Mountain (2,940 ft.) in Sandwich. The Flat Mountain Ponds (2,320 ft.) lie east of Sandwich Mountain and west of Mt. Whiteface, between the two Flat Mountains; originally two separate ponds, they have been united by the dam at their south end, making one larger pond. The area is still recovering from lumbering begun in 1920 and an extensive fire in 1923. In the flat region south of Sandwich Mountain lie a number of attractive ponds, including Guinea Pond and Black Mountain Pond. South of these ponds is Mt. Israel (2,630 ft.), which provides a fine panorama of the Sandwich Range from its north ledge and offers great rewards for the modest effort required to reach it.

Jennings Peak (3,460 ft.) and Noon Peak (2,976 ft.) form a ridge running north from Sandwich Mountain toward Waterville Valley. Sandwich Mountain has fine views north over the valley, but the views from the cliffs that drop from the summit of Jennings Peak into the valley of Smarts Brook are even better. Acteon Ridge runs from Jennings Peak to the west over sharp, bare Sachem Peak (2,860 ft.) and ends in the open rocky humps of Bald Knob (2,300 ft.), which faces Welch Mountain across the Mad River Valley and forms the other half of the gateway; this ridge is occasionally traversed, although there is no path.

Sandwich Notch is crossed by the Sandwich Notch Rd., a rough, interesting gravel road that passes through a former farming region that has almost completely reverted to forest and is now a part of the WMNF. The road, which runs northwest from Center Sandwich to NH 49 between Campton and Waterville Valley, is sound but narrow, steep and rough, and very slow going; it is maintained this way to protect it from becoming an attractive route for through traffic. Unlike other White Mountain notches, Sandwich Notch is a complex notch, made up of two distinct mountain passes: the one on the south (1,470 ft.), between Mt. Israel and the eastern end of the Squam Range, separates the watershed of the Bearcamp River (a Saco tributary) from the valley of the Beebe River (a Pemigewasset tributary); the one on the north (1,770 ft.), between Sandwich Mountain and Campton Mountain, separates the valley of the Beebe River from the Waterville Valley—the valley of the Mad River (another Pemigewasset tributary). Beede Falls and nearby Cow Cave (reached in a short distance by the Bearcamp River Trail), in the Sandwich town park 3.4 mi. from Center Sandwich, are worth a visit; the town park parking area is also a Bearcamp River Trail trailhead. From NH 113 in Center Sandwich, take Grove St. northwest from the village, bear left at 0.4 mi. onto Diamond Ledge Rd., and keep left at 2.4 mi., where the right-hand road leads to Mead Base (a WODC/SLA trail-crew camp), the trailhead for the Wentworth Trail to Mt. Israel; the Bearcamp River Trail passes through this trailhead. The road continues past trailheads for the Crawford-Ridgepole Trail at 3.9 mi., the Guinea Pond Trail at 5.7 mi., and the Algonquin Trail at 7.3 mi., and ends at NH 49 at 11.0 mi.

The Squam Range begins at Sandwich Notch across from Mt. Israel and runs roughly southwest toward Holderness. This area is almost entirely private property, open to day-hikers by the gracious permission of the landowners, but camping is not permitted. Its peaks, from northeast to southwest, are an unnamed knob (2,218 ft.), Mt. Doublehead (2,158 ft.), Mt. Squam (2,223 ft.), Mt. Percival (2,212 ft.), a knob sometimes called the Sawtooth (2,260 ft.) that is the actual high point of the range, Mt. Morgan (2,220 ft.), Mt. Webster (2,076 ft.), Mt. Livermore (1,500 ft.), and Cotton Mountain (1,270 ft.). The Crawford-Ridgepole Trail crosses over or near all of these summits except for Cotton Mountain, and several trails ascend the ridge from NH 113; curiously, the Sawtooth, the high point of the range, is bypassed by the trail. By far the most popular hike on the range, often fairly crowded, is the loop over Mts. Morgan and Percival, which offer superb views south over the lake and hill country and north to the higher mountains; the rest of the range is lightly visited and the trails, including the Crawford-Ridgepole Trail, often require some care to follow, though the rewards of pleasant walks to several excellent viewpoints are great.

The Rattlesnakes—West Rattlesnake (1,260 ft.) and East Rattlesnake (1,289 ft.)—are a pair of hills that rise just across the highway from Mts. Morgan and Percival and offer excellent lake views for little effort. West Rattlesnake has fine views to the south and west from its southwest cliff. East Rattlesnake has a more limited but still excellent view over Squam Lake. Five Finger Point, which lies southeast of the Rattlesnakes and has a perimeter trail connected to the Rattlesnakes' trail network, offers attractive lakeside walking on undeveloped rocky shores.

Red Hill (2,030 ft.) and its ledgy northern spur, Eagle Cliff (1,410 ft.), rise between Squam Lake and Lake Winnipesaukee. The summit of Red Hill (which has a fire tower) offers excellent views in all directions for very modest effort; Eagle Cliff offers interesting but much less extensive views and a somewhat more challenging trail to ascend.

A number of public and quasi-public reservations in this region offer the opportunity for pleasant walking; some have trails. The Bearcamp River Trail from Sandwich Notch to South Tamworth, nearly 17 mi. long, offers a variety of walks through woods, farmlands, and wetlands along or near the Bearcamp River, linking several reservations and parcels of land protected by conservation easements. A map of this trail is available at local stores. Of particular interest is the western end of the trail, which passes by Beede Falls, Cow Cave, the Cook Farm, and several unnamed cascades. The Alice Bemis Thompson Wildlife Refuge offers a loop path 2 mi. long through interesting wetlands drained by Atwood Brook, which flows into Bearcamp Pond, with views of the Sandwich Range.

CAMPING

Sandwich Range Wilderness

Wilderness regulations, intended to protect Wilderness resources and promote opportunities for challenge and solitude, prohibit use of motorized equipment or mechanical means of transportation of any sort. In accordance with USFS Wilderness policy, the trails in the Sandwich Range Wilderness are in general maintained to a lower standard than trails outside Wilderness. They may be rough, overgrown, or essentially unmarked with minimal signage, and considerable care may be required to follow them. Hiking and camping group size must be no larger than 10 people. Camping and fires are also prohibited above the treeline (where trees are less than 8 ft. tall) except in winter, when camping is permitted above the treeline in places where snow cover is at least 2 ft. deep, but not on any frozen body of water. Many shelters have been removed, and the remaining ones will be dismantled when major maintenance is required; one should not count on using any of these shelters.

Squam Lakes Region

The trails described in this guide on the Squam Range, the Rattlesnakes, and Red Hill are almost entirely on private land, and while the owners welcome hikers for day use, camping is not allowed.

Forest Protection Areas

The WMNF has established a number of Forest Protection Areas (FPAs)—formerly known as Restricted Use Areas—where camping and wood or charcoal fires are prohibited throughout the year. The specific areas are under continual review, and areas are added to or subtracted from the list in order to provide the greatest amount of protection to areas subject to damage by excessive camping, while imposing the lowest level of restrictions possible. A general list of FPAs in this section follows, but because there are often major changes from year to year, one should obtain current information on FPAs from the WMNF.

(1) No camping is permitted above treeline (where trees are less than 8 ft. tall), except in winter, and then only in places where there is at least 2 ft. of snow cover on the ground—but not on any frozen body of water. The point where the above-treeline restricted area begins is marked on most trails with small signs, but the absence of such signs should not be construed as proof of the legality of a site.

(2) No camping is permitted within 0.25 mi. of any trailhead, picnic area, or any facility for overnight accommodation such as a hut, cabin, shelter, tentsite, or campground, except as designated at the facility itself. In the area covered by Section Seven, camping is also forbidden within 0.25 mi. of Sabbaday Falls, East Pond, and Kiah Pond, within 0.25 mi. of the Greeley Ponds Trail between the Kancamagus Highway and the first stream crossing, and at any point within the Greeley Ponds Scenic Area.

(3) No camping is permitted within 200 ft. of Black Mountain Pond or Smarts Brook (along which the Smarts Brook Trail runs) from NH 49 to the Beaver Pond.

(4) No camping is permitted on WMNF land within 0.25 mi. of certain roads (camping on private roadside land is illegal except by permission of the landowner). In 2006, these roads included the Kancamagus Highway, NH 49 (Mad River Rd.), Beebe River Rd. (FR 400), Kiah Pond Rd. (FR 418), Sandwich Notch Rd., Upper Hall Pond Rd. (FR 422), Lower Hall Pond Rd. (FR 417), and the Hix Mountain Rd. for the first 0.25 mi. east from the Tripoli Rd. Camping is permitted along the Tripoli Rd.

(fee charged), but not within 200 ft. of any trail or along the 0.5-mi. section east of the crossing of the West Branch of the Mad River (BM 1949)—an area where the stream runs close by the north side of the road.

Established Trailside Campsites

Flat Mountain Pond Shelter (WMNF) is located on the shore of Flat Mountain Pond on the Flat Mountain Pond Trail. This area is in the Sandwich Range Wilderness.

Black Mountain Pond Shelter (WMNF), formerly located on the shore of Black Mountain Pond on the Black Mountain Pond Trail, has been removed. This area is in the Sandwich Range Wilderness. Tent camping is permitted in the area, but not within 200 ft. of the pond.

TRAIL DESCRIPTIONS

Mount Tecumseh Trail (WMNF)

This trail ascends Mt. Tecumseh, starting at the Waterville Valley Ski Area at the top edge of the parking area well to the right of the main lodge (as you face it). It climbs the east slope of Tecumseh, then descends the northwest ridge to a parking area just off Tripoli Rd. (FR 30), 1.2 mi. west of the Mt. Osceola Trail parking area. The eastern part of the trail was relocated in 1991 to eliminate the former sections that used the ski slopes.

Starting at a trail sign at the edge of the ski area parking lot, the trail crosses a small brook and follows the south side of Tecumseh Brook for 0.3 mi., then crosses the brook and follows a section of trail along a small ridge above the north side. At 1.1 mi., the trail drops down and recrosses the brook, then climbs to intersect the former route, an old logging road, about 20 yd. from the edge of the ski slope; good views can be obtained by following the old trail left to the edge of the open slope. The main trail turns right and follows the rocky old road, angling upward along the south side of the Tecumseh Brook valley, then climbs steadily to the main ridge crest south of Tecumseh, where it turns right in a flat area. Here, at 2.2 mi., the Sosman Trail from the top of the ski area enters from the left. In another 120 yd., the Sosman Trail forks left to ascend the summit from the west. The Mt. Tecumseh Trail swings right, descends slightly to circle the base of the steep cone, and finally climbs steeply to reach the summit from the north at 2.5 mi. The summit offers views over and between trees, particularly to Mt. Osceola and Mt. Tripyramid. The trail junctions at the summit have not always been well signed; the Mt. Tecumseh Trail leaves north (about 15 degrees magnetic) for the ski area and west-northwest (about 310 degrees magnetic) for Tripoli Rd., while the Sosman Trail runs almost due south (about 190 degrees magnetic) along the ridge crest, then turns sharp right (west) off the ridge and descends.

From the summit of Tecumseh, the Mt. Tecumseh Trail descends west, then swings northwest past a restricted north outlook and descends steeply, then moderately to a broad saddle. It ascends to the summit of the west ridge at 3.2 mi. and passes over three knobs; on the third, westernmost knob a side path leads left 30 yd. to a view of Moosilauke from a blowdown patch. The trail then descends steadily to another saddle at 4.2 mi. Here it turns right and angles down the north slope of the ridge on an old logging road. Near the bottom of the slope, it turns left, then right, crosses Eastman Brook (difficult at high water), and ends at Tripoli Rd.

Mount Tecumseh Trail (map 3:J6)

Distances from Mt. Tecumseh Ski Area parking lot (1,840 ft.) to
- Mt. Tecumseh summit (4,003 ft.): 2.5 mi., 2,200 ft. (rev. 50 ft.), 2 hr. 20 min.
- Tripoli Rd. (1,820 ft.): 5.6 mi., 2,400 ft. (rev. 2,400 ft.), 4 hr.

Sosman Trail (WVAIA)

This trail connects the summit of Tecumseh with the top of the ski slopes. It can be followed easily from the peak to the slopes (the direction in which it is usually followed), but it can be difficult to find the beginning at the top of the ski slopes. It leaves the summit of Tecumseh along the ridge to the south (sign may be absent), then turns to the west and switchbacks with rough footing down the slope and around the rocky nose of the ridge, with restricted views to the west. It turns to the right onto the Mt. Tecumseh Trail at 0.2 mi., then after 120 yd., it diverges right and follows the ridge south. At 0.4 mi., it climbs a rocky hump with an interesting view of Tecumseh's summit cone, and just beyond are an excellent outlook to the west and one to the northeast with a rustic wooden bench. The trail runs south nearly level along the ridge, bearing left at 0.8 mi. and emerging beneath a transmission tower. Here the trail, with an obscure footway, bears left, then right, coming out at the top of a chairlift. From the clearing next to the tower, it is possible to follow a grassy road 100 yd. to the top of the ski slopes at the site of a former chairlift. From either point, it is about 1.8 mi. to the base lodge via ski trails. To find the trail at the top of the ski area, where there is no sign, it is easiest to follow the grassy road to the transmission tower, where the trail enters the woods on its right.

Sosman Trail (map 3:J6)

Distances from summit of Mt. Tecumseh (4,003 ft.) to
- top of ski area (3,850 ft.): 0.8 mi., 100 ft. (rev. 250 ft.), 25 min.
- ski area base lodge (1,840 ft.) via ski trails: 2.6 mi., 100 ft. (rev. 2,000 ft.), 1 hr. 20 min.

Welch-Dickey Loop Trail (WVAIA)

This loop trail affords excellent views for a modest effort, with nearly 2 mi. of partly open walking at relatively low elevations. On the south ledges of Welch Mountain it runs through the southernmost of one of the few stands of jack pine *(Pinus banksiana)* that occur in New Hampshire; this is a tree that commonly occurs much farther north and benefits from fires because it releases its seeds most readily after its cones have been scorched (when, presumably, most of its competitors have been killed by the fire). The section that ascends Welch Mountain is often one of the first trails to be clear of snow in spring. However, some of the ledges provide mildly challenging rock scrambles and may be slippery when wet and dangerous in icy conditions, so they must be ascended with caution. From NH 49, about 4.5 mi. from its junction with NH 175, turn left onto Upper Mad River Rd., which runs northwest across the Mad River. In 0.7 mi., turn right on Orris Rd. (Welch Mountain sign) and follow this road for 0.6 mi., then take a short fork to the right into a large new parking area, where the trail begins. If the parking area is full, roadside parking is permitted about 0.2 mi. south of the trailhead—take care not to block driveways.

In 15 yd. from the parking area, the trail forks. This description follows the counterclockwise direction, first taking the right-hand fork leading toward Welch Mountain—the ledges are steeper on this side and easier to ascend than descend for most hikers. This branch soon crosses a brook and follows its east side for about 0.5 mi., then turns sharp right and angles up southeastward to reach the large, flat open ledges on the south ridge of Welch Mountain at 1.3 mi. from the start. There are fine views east across the valley to Mt. Tripyramid and Sandwich Mountain and its rocky Acteon Ridge. Then the trail climbs, steeply at times with several short scrambles, over open ledges interspersed with jack pines and dwarf birches to the ledgy summit of Welch Mountain at 1.9 mi.

From here, the loop drops steeply to a wooded notch (use caution, staying left of the blazes along the top of the cliff), then rises, working to the left around a high rock slab. Just above this slab a poorly marked branch trail leads right 0.2 mi. to the north outlook from an open ledge. The main loop continues over the summit of Dickey Mountain at 2.4 mi. and descends another prominent ridge to the southwest, with many outlook ledges, entering the woods to stay at the base of a particularly interesting ledge with an impressive drop-off at 3.2 mi. It continues to descend, then turns left onto a logging road with a cellar hole on the right, and soon reaches the loop junction and the parking lot.

Welch-Dickey Loop Trail (map 3:K5)

Distances from Orris Rd. parking area (1,060 ft.)
- to Welch Mountain summit (2,605 ft.) via Welch branch: 1.9 mi., 1,550 ft., 1 hr. 45 min.
- to Dickey Mountain summit (2,734 ft.) via Dickey branch: 2.1 mi., 1,650 ft., 1 hr. 55 min.
- for complete loop: 4.4 mi., 1,800 ft., 3 hr. 5 min.

Timber Camp Trail (WVAIA)

This trail leaves the west side of the Greeley Ponds Trail, 1.1 mi. north of the Livermore Trail, and follows old logging roads into the high basin of Greeley Brook on the east side of Mt. Osceola. Two open areas at the upper end of the trail offer interesting views.

The trail leaves the Greeley Ponds Trail about 75 yd. south of the latter's bridged crossing of the Mad River. It leads north along a grassy logging road at easy grades, high above the river. At 0.3 mi., it bears left and reaches a fork at 0.6 mi. Taking the left fork, signed "To High Camp," the trail climbs to a hairpin turn left (south) at 0.8 mi., then loops back to the north. At 1.2 mi., it turns left along the base of a gravel bank, which provides views of **Mt.** Tri-pyramid, Mt. Kancamagus, and the Painted Cliff of Mt. Osceola.

The trail continues up the logging road, with the footway becoming overgrown in places, though the route of the road is obvious. After crossing two small brooks in a wet area, the trail emerges in a stony clearing with more views and continues another 125 yd. to its end at a sign marking the site of "High Camp."

Timber Camp Trail (map 3:J6)

Distances from Greeley Ponds Trail (1,720 ft.) to
- fork (2,060 ft.): 0.6 mi., 350 ft., 25 min.
- gravel bank (2,400 ft.): 1.2 mi., 700 ft., 55 min.
- High Camp (2,540 ft.): 1.5 mi., 800 ft., 1 hr., 10 min.

Goodrich Rock Trail (WVAIA)

This trail leads from the west side of the Greeley Ponds Trail, 0.9 mi. north of the Livermore Trail, to the Davis Boulders and Goodrich Rock (one of the largest glacial erratics in New Hampshire) on a shoulder of East Osceola. Leaving the Greeley Ponds Trail, it climbs steadily for 0.3 mi. on an old logging road, then swings left and meanders to the first boulders. It turns left across a small streambed and passes through a split boulder and a boulder cave. Beyond the boulders, the trail bears left across a flat area, then slabs easily before a short, rough pitch leads to the base of Goodrich Rock. Yellow blazes lead around the left side of the immense boulder and up to its back side, where a 20-ft. ladder provides access to its flat top and a view across the valley to Sandwich Dome. Use great caution ascending and descending the ladder.

Goodrich Rock Trail (map 3:J6)

Distance from Greeley Ponds Trail (1,700 ft.) to
- Goodrich Rock (2,325 ft.): 0.8 mi., 600 ft., 40 min.

Flume Brook Trail (WVAIA)

This trail provides an attractive walk up the valley of Flume Brook to a small rock flume and cascades. It leaves the east side of Greeley Ponds Trail, 1.2 mi. from the Livermore Trail and 0.1 north of the crossing of the

Mad River on Knight's Bridge. It climbs easily up an old logging road on the south side of Flume Brook. At 0.3 mi., the trail turns right off the road and climbs moderately, at times close beside the brook. At 1.2 mi., the Old Skidder Trail leaves on the right. The Flume Brook Trail continues ahead, bearing northeast and reaching the base of the Flume at 1.3 mi. The path continues on a rougher footway through the Flume to cascades at its upper end.

Flume Brook Trail (map 3:J7)

Distance from Greeley Ponds Trail (1,780 ft.) to
  • the Flume (2,500 ft.): 1.3 mi., 700 ft., 1 hr.

Old Skidder Trail (WVAIA)

This recently cut, lightly used trail links the Flume Brook Trail, 0.1 mi. below The Flume, with the Livermore Trail, 4.6 mi. from that trail's southern terminus at Depot Camp. It has little evident footway and is sparsely marked; thus, it is suitable only for experienced hikers comfortable with following obscure trails. It makes possible a pleasant 8.2 mi. loop hike in combination with the Livermore, Greeley Ponds, and Flume Brook trails.

Leaving the Flume Brook Trail, the Old Skidder Trail runs across a ferny clearing and climbs moderately northeast, following an obvious old road across the steep slope above Flume Brook. It passes under a rock face at 0.1 mi., and at 0.2 mi., after providing a glimpse of Mt. Osceola, the trail levels off. At 0.5 mi., at the end of a long straightaway, it turns right off the road (blazes) and climbs southeast up a much more obscure footway where saw-cuts help define the route. It makes several right and left turns, some of which are marked by blazes, passes over a knoll carpeted with birch and ferns, then swings east to the Livermore Trail. Turn right for Depot Camp.

Old Skidder Trail (map 3:J7)

Distance from Flume Brook Trail (2,400 ft.) to
  • Livermore Trail (2,820 ft.): 0.8 mi., 400 ft., 35 min.

Norway Rapids Trail (WVAIA)

This short trail links the Cascade Path with the Livermore Trail, providing access to Norway Rapids, a scenic ledgy area on Avalanche Brook. Coinciding at first with the wide Snows Mountain Ski Trail, it leaves the Cascade Path on the left, 1.2 mi. from the Snows Mountain Ski Area parking lot, and crosses Cascade Brook on a bridge. In 60 yd., the Norway Rapids Trail turns left off the ski trail and rises easily through hardwoods. It meanders across a plateau and dips slightly to Norway Rapids at 0.4 mi. (difficult crossing at high water). On the far side of the brook, the trail turns sharp left, runs along a relocated section on the bank with views down to the rapids, then swings right and climbs gently to the Livermore Trail, 1.8 mi. from the Depot Camp parking area.

Norway Rapids Trail (map 3:J7)

Distances from Cascade Path (1,725 ft.) to
- Norway Rapids (1,750 ft.): 0.4 mi., 100 ft. (rev. 50 ft.), 15 min.
- Livermore Trail (1,796 ft.): 0.5 mi., 150 ft., 20 min.

Cascade Path (WVAIA)

This trail provides easy access to a series of scenic waterfalls on Cascade Brook. It leaves the northeast corner of the large parking lot at the base of the Snows Mountain Ski Area, located off Boulder Way less than 0.1 mi. north of its junction with West Branch Rd. by the Osceola Library. From the parking area, it crosses Cascade Ridge Rd. and swings right up an old ski slope. It runs briefly beside the road, then continues up the ski trail, passing the junction with the Boulder Path on the left at 0.2 mi. Here the Cascade Path bears right off the ski trail, ascends through a patch of woods, crosses the development road, and then climbs up the continuation of the ski trail. At 0.3 mi., the Cascade Path bears left off the ski trail at a sign, enters the woods, ascends gently on a relocated section, then turns left onto the older route, passing the junction with Elephant Rock Trail on the right at 0.5 mi. The Cascade Path continues nearly level, then descends easily along the lower slopes of Snows Mountain.

At 1.2 mi., it reaches Cascade Brook and turns right on a wide ski trail. (In the reverse direction turn left off the ski trail just before a bridge over a small brook.) In 70 yd., the ski trail and Norway Rapids Trail turn left across a bridge over Cascade Brook. The Cascade Path continues up the west bank of the brook, climbing easily to the base of the first cascade at 1.4 mi. The main trail turns left here, crosses the brook, and climbs along the east bank, passing several more cascades and pools before ending at the gravel Snows Mountain service road at 1.7 mi. From the base of the first cascade, an alternate "Westside" path continues 0.3 mi. up the west bank of the brook to the service road; the main trail provides better views of the cascades. From the top of the Cascade Path the service road can be followed left 0.6 mi. to the Livermore Trail 2.2 mi. from the Livermore Rd. parking area, or right 0.8 mi. to the top of the Snows Mountain ski lift, making possible loop hikes with other WVAIA trails.

Cascade Path (map 3:J6-J7)

Distances from Snows Mountain Ski Area parking lot (1,540 ft.) to
- first cascade (1,780 ft.): 1.4 mi., 400 ft. (rev. 150 ft.), 55 min.
- service road (1,940 ft.): 1.7 mi., 550 ft., 1 hr., 10 min.

Boulder Path (WVAIA)

This trail leaves the Livermore Trail on the right, 0.6 mi. from the Livermore Rd. parking area, and runs 70 yd. to a crossing of Avalanche Brook (difficult at high water) just downstream from a huge boulder. After crossing the brook, it turns left and follows an old road along the brook for 0.1 mi., then turns right off the road (sign) and ascends moderately. At 0.3 mi., it turns right onto the wide Lower Snows Mountain X-C Trail, rises slightly, then descends gradually. At 0.6 mi., it leaves the WMNF (signs), crosses a private driveway, swings left, and continues to the Cascade Path, 0.2 mi. above the Snows Mountain Ski Area parking lot.

Boulder Path (map 3:J6)

Distance from Livermore Trail (1,580 ft.) to
- Cascade Path (1,700 ft.): 0.7 mi., 150 ft. (rev. 50 ft.), 35 min.

Big Pines Path (WVAIA)

This short path leads to a stand of impressive white pines near the bank of the Mad River. It leaves the Livermore Trail 0.7 mi. from the Depot Camp parking area, runs at easy grades, then makes two short, steep drops to the pines.

Big Pines Path (map 3:J6)

Distance from Livermore Trail (1,620 ft.) to
* Big Pines (1,580 ft.): 0.2 mi., 0 ft. (rev. 50 ft.), 5 min.

Elephant Rock Trail (WVAIA)

This short trail links the Cascade Path with the top of Snows Mountain Ski Area and Greeley Ledges Trail. It leaves Cascade Path on the right, 0.5 mi. from the Snows Mountain Ski Area parking lot. In 100 yd., it passes Elephant Rock, a large boulder; the tree that formed the elephant's "trunk" is no longer present. The trail rises at easy to moderate grades, emerging near the top of the Beanbender ski slope. Walk left 100 yd. up the slope to reach the top of the lift and Greeley Ledges Trail.

Elephant Rock Trail (map 3:J6-J7)

Distance from Cascade Path (1,840 ft.) to
* top of ski area (2,100 ft.): 0.4 mi., 250 ft., 20 min.

Greeley Ledges Trail (WVAIA)

This short trail connects the Snows Mountain hiking trail with the top of Snows Mountain Ski Area. It leaves the north loop of the Snows Mountain hiking trail on the left, 0.7 mi. from the parking area at the base of the ski slopes. It ascends through hardwoods, then climbs into a rocky area of spruces. After passing a ledge on the left with a limited view of Mt. Tecumseh, it rises a short distance to the top of the ski area behind the chairlift.

Greeley Ledges Trail (map 3:J7)

Distance from Snows Mountain hiking trail (1,950 ft.) to
* top of ski area (2,100 ft.): 0.2 mi., 150 ft., 15 min.

Kettles Path (WVAIA)

This trail links the Livermore Trail with the Scaur Trail near its upper end and provides part of the easiest route to the ledge outlook at The Scaur. The trail passes by several "kettles"—dry bowl-shaped hollows in the woods created at the end of the last ice age. Meltwater debris accumulated around ice blocks left by the retreating glacier. After the ice chunks melted, their kettle-shaped depressions remained. This type of formation is common in sandy outwash areas such as the Ossipee plains or Cape Cod but is unusual in the White Mountains.

The Kettles Path leaves the north side of Livermore Trail 0.9 mi. from the Depot Camp parking area. It runs nearly level for 0.3 mi., then ascends two short, steep pitches to The Kettles, seen on both sides of the trail at 0.4 mi. Beyond The Kettles, the trail climbs easily to meet the Scaur Trail at 0.9 mi. Turn right to reach The Scaur in 0.2 mi.

Kettles Path (map 3:J7-J6)

Distances from Livermore Trail (1,640 ft.) to
- The Kettles (1,750 ft.): 0.4 mi., 100 ft., 15 min.
- Scaur Trail (1,900 ft.): 0.9 mi., 250 ft., 35 min.

Scaur Trail (WVAIA)

This trail, steep in places, leads from Greeley Ponds Trail, 0.7 mi. north of the Livermore Trail, to The Scaur, a rocky outlook with a good view south. Leaving the Greeley Ponds Trail, it runs 30 yd. to a crossing of the Mad River (difficult at high water). It then climbs, steeply at times, to a junction with the Kettles Path on the right at 0.4 mi. The Scaur Trail climbs moderately to the east, then swings south on a steep ascent up the back side of the knob to the outlook.

Scaur Trail (map 3:J6-J7)

Distance from Greeley Ponds Trail (1,660 ft.) to
- The Scaur (2,230 ft.): 0.6 mi., 550 ft., 35 min.

Fletcher's Cascade Trail (WVAIA)

This trail leads from the Drakes Brook Trail, 0.4 mi. from the parking area off NH 49, to Fletcher's Cascades, a series of waterfalls on the lower slope of Flat Mountain. It bears left on a logging road (a ski trail in winter) where Drakes Brook Trail bears right off the road to cross Drakes Brook. The Fletcher's Cascade Trail follows the road for 100 yd., then turns right into the woods at a sign. It climbs easily along the north side of Drakes Brook, passing through logged areas with occasional views up to Noon Peak. At 0.8 mi., the trail crosses the north fork of Drakes Brook, entering the Sandwich Range Wilderness, and climbs steadily to the lower cascades at 1.1 mi. Above here, the trail becomes rougher, climbing another 0.1 mi. to the upper cascades.

Fletcher's Cascade Trail (map 3:J6-J7)

Distance from Drakes Brook Trail (1,540 ft.) to
- upper cascades (2,200 ft.): 1.2 mi., 650 ft., 55 min.

Snows Mountain Trail (WVAIA)

This loop trail follows the route of the former Woodbury Trail to the shoulder of Snows Mountain, ascends the ridge to a viewpoint spur path, then descends the west slope of the mountain. The trail is lightly used and in places requires care to follow, though it is well blazed in yellow.

The north end of the loop trail begins at the south end of a large parking lot at the base of the Snows Mountain Ski Area, located off Boulder Way less than 0.1 mi. north of its junction with West Branch Rd. by the Osceola Library. Climb up along the right (south) side of the ski trail beneath the chairlift. At 0.3 mi., the trail turns right into the woods at a sign and climbs for another 0.3 mi., then levels off. At 0.7 mi., the Greeley Ledge Trail leaves left. At 1.0 mi., a short connecting path diverges left to the Snows Mountain X-C Ski Trail, whereas the hiking trail continues ahead on an easy traverse. At 1.2 mi., the trail reaches the end of the old Woodbury Trail section and turns right, climbing steadily up the side of the ridge. The trail then ascends southeast along the ridge, winding back and forth across the crest. After a slight dip, it climbs steadily to a junction at a high point on the ridge, reached at 2.0 mi. Here a side trail leads left

0.1 mi. to a ledge with a view south to Sandwich Mountain and the Mad River Valley.

The south loop of the Snows Mountain Trail turns sharp right and descends, passing a short side path left to a southwest viewpoint at 2.1 mi. It drops steeply a short distance, then follows an old logging road along the mountain's west slope. Bearing left off the road, it descends through hardwood forest with many twists and turns. At 3.5 mi., it emerges at the driveway at 76 Snow's Mountain Rd. Follow the road downhill for 0.3 mi., then turn right on a paved path that leads 0.1 mi. north between tennis courts to the base of the chairlift and the parking area. (If ascending the south loop, the trail enters the woods at a sign at the upper end of the driveway at 46 Upper Greeley Hill Rd., located at a sharp left curve. Hikers should park in the designated area at the base of the ski slopes and walk up the road.)

Snows Mountain Trail (map 3:J6–J7)

Distances from Snows Mountain Ski Area parking lot (1,540 ft.)
- to Snows Mountain viewpoint spur (2,780 ft.): 2.0 mi., 1,250 ft., 1 hr. 40 min.
- for complete loop: 3.9 mi., 1,250 ft., 2 hr. 35 min.

Mount Osceola Trail (WMNF)

This trail begins at a parking area on Tripoli Rd. (FR 30), just west of the height-of-land in Thornton Gap 7.0 mi. from I-93, climbs over Mt. Osceola and East Osceola, and descends to the Greeley Ponds Trail at the height-of-land in Mad River Notch, 1.3 mi. south of the Kancamagus Highway. At the height-of-land on Tripoli Rd., there is a gate that is sometimes closed in spring and fall, so it may not be possible to reach the parking lot from the Waterville Valley side in a vehicle at such times. The trail from Thornton Gap to the summit of Osceola is relatively easy, with moderate grades and reasonably good footing, but the section between East Osceola and the Greeley Ponds Trail is extremely steep and rough.

The trail leaves Tripoli Rd. and climbs moderately with somewhat rocky footing, going east across the south slope of Breadtray Ridge. At 1.3 mi., it begins to climb by switchbacks toward the ridge top, and the footing improves. At 2.1 mi, a ledge on the left offers a view of Sandwich Mountain, and at 2.3 mi., it crosses a small brook (unreliable). The trail resumes its switchbacks, gains the summit ridge and turns right, and soon reaches the summit ledge at 3.2 mi., with excellent views. A good outlook to the north can be obtained from a small ledge on a short side path, which begins at the older fire tower site that is located in the woods just to the west of the open ledge.

The trail then turns left and descends from the summit, alternating flat stretches with steep, rocky descents. Just before reaching the main pass between Osceola and East Osceola, it descends a steep chimney, which can be avoided by a detour to the left (north). The trail crosses the pass at 3.8 mi. and climbs moderately with steep pitches past a fine outlook on the left, reaching the summit of East Osceola (marked by a small cairn) at 4.2 mi. The trail then crosses a lower knob and descends steeply, then moderately, to a shoulder. At the top of a gully, there is an outlook 25 yd. to the left on a side path. The main trail turns right and descends the steep, loose gully, then goes diagonally across a small, rocky slide with good views. It continues to descend very steeply past a sloping rock face, where it turns left. At 4.9 mi., it turns sharp left, with an abandoned route of the trail straight ahead, and descends moderately under the impressive cliffs of Osceola's north spur to the Greeley Ponds Trail.

Mount Osceola Trail (map 3:J6–I6)

Distances from Tripoli Rd. (2,280 ft.) to
- Mt. Osceola summit (4,340 ft.): 3.2 mi., 2,050 ft., 2 hr. 40 min.
- Mt. Osceola, East Peak (4,156 ft.): 4.2 mi., 2,400 ft. (rev. 550 ft.), 3 hr. 20 min.
- Greeley Ponds Trail (2,300 ft.): 5.7 mi., 2,400 ft. (rev. 1,850 ft.), 4 hr. 5 min.

Greeley Ponds Trail (WMNF)

This trail diverges from the Livermore Trail about 0.3 mi. from the parking area on Livermore Rd. (FR 53), leads past the Greeley Ponds and through Mad River Notch, and ends at the Kancamagus Highway 4.5 mi. east of the Lincoln Woods parking lot. The trail is crossed many times by a ski-touring trail marked with blue diamonds; the hiking trail is marked with yellow blazes. Grades are easy, and the ponds are beautiful.

The trail leaves the Livermore Trail sharp left just after the first bridge beyond the Depot Camp clearing, and follows an old truck road past the Scaur Trail right at 0.7 mi., the Goodrich Rock Trail left at 0.9 mi., and the Timber Camp Trail left at 1.1 mi. The truck road ends just beyond here, where the trail crosses the Mad River on Knight's Bridge. At 1.2 mi., the Flume Trail diverges right, and the trail soon crosses Flume Brook on a bridge and passes the site of an old logging camp, where the Kancamagus Ski-Touring Trail diverges right. It continues across several small brooks and enters the Greeley Ponds Scenic Area at 2.6 mi., and turns left to cross the Mad River; here a well-beaten path (ski-touring trail) continues straight for 0.2 mi. to a fine viewpoint on the southeast shore of the lower pond. The main trail reaches the southwest corner of the lower Greeley Pond at 2.9 mi., then the upper pond at 3.4 mi. Here an unmarked path crosses the upper pond outlet brook to a fine view on a small beach. The main trail ascends easily to Mad River Notch, passing a ski trail junction and then the Mt. Osceola Trail left at the height-of-land at 3.8 mi. It descends easily on an old logging road, bears right off it at 4.2 mi., and continues down at easy grades but with rough footing. At 4.8 mi., it crosses two branches of the South Fork of Hancock Branch and ends at the Kancamagus Highway.

Greeley Ponds Trail (map 3:J6–I6)

Distances from Livermore Trail (1,580 ft.) to

- lower Greeley Pond (2,180 ft.): 2.9 mi., 600 ft., 1 hr. 45 min.
- Mt. Osceola Trail (2,300 ft.): 3.8 mi., 700 ft., 2 hr. 15 min.
- Kancamagus Highway (1,940 ft.): 5.1 mi., 700 ft. (rev. 350 ft.), 2 hr. 55 min.

East Pond Trail (WMNF)

This trail passes scenic East Pond and climbs across the notch between Mt. Osceola and Scar Ridge, reaching an elevation of 3,100 ft. The southern trailhead is at a parking lot about 100 yd. up a gravel side road that leaves Tripoli Rd. (FR 30) 5.1 mi. east of its intersection with I-93. The northern trailhead is on the Kancamagus Highway at the bridge over the Hancock Branch, 3.7 mi. east of the Lincoln Woods parking lot.

From the southern trailhead, this trail follows the gravel road past a gate and continues straight on an older road where the gravel road swings right. At 0.4 mi., near the site of the old Tripoli Mill, the Little East Pond Trail turns left on an old railroad grade, whereas the East Pond Trail continues ahead on a logging road. At 0.8 mi., it crosses East Pond Brook, and at 1.4 mi., near the point where the East Pond Loop leaves left for Little East Pond, a side path leads right 40 yd. to the south shore of East Pond.

The trail swings to the left away from the pond and climbs moderately on old logging roads to the height-of-land at 2.2 mi., then descends steadily on logging roads, crossing Cheney Brook at 3.1 mi. and Pine Brook at 4.3 mi. Just after the latter crossing (which may be difficult at high water) the trail reaches an old logging railroad spur and follows it almost all the way to the Kancamagus Highway.

East Pond Trail (map 3:J5–I6)

Distances from Tripoli Rd. (1,800 ft.) to
- East Pond (2,600 ft.): 1.4 mi., 800 ft., 1 hr. 5 min.
- height-of-land (3,100 ft.): 2.2 mi., 1,300 ft., 1 hr. 45 min.
- Kancamagus Highway (1,760 ft.): 5.1 mi., 1,300 ft. (rev. 1,350 ft.), 3 hr. 10 min.

Little East Pond Trail (WMNF)

This trail leaves the East Pond Trail left (northwest) 0.4 mi. from Tripoli Rd. and follows an old railroad grade slightly uphill, passing through recently logged areas and crossing Clear Brook at 0.7 mi. Soon after that, the trail bears sharp right from the end of the railroad grade and climbs at a moderate grade to Little East Pond, where the East Pond Loop enters on the right. Recent beaver flooding may affect this junction.

Little East Pond Trail (map 3:J6–I5)

Distance from East Pond Trail (1,980 ft.) to
- Little East Pond (2,596 ft.): 1.7 mi., 600 ft., 1 hr. 10 min.

East Pond Loop (WMNF)

This trail runs between East Pond and Little East Pond, going up and down over several minor ridges at easy grades, making possible a loop trip that visits both ponds.

East Pond Loop (map 3:I6–I5)

Distance from East Pond (2,600 ft.) to
- Little East Pond (2,596 ft.): 1.5 mi., 200 ft. (rev. 200 ft.), 50 min.

Distance from Tripoli Rd. (1,800 ft.) for
- complete loop to both ponds: 5.0 mi., 1,000 ft., 3 hr.

Livermore Trail (WMNF)

This trail begins at a parking area at the beginning of Livermore Rd. near Waterville Valley and climbs through Livermore Pass (2,900 ft.) to the Kancamagus Highway across from Lily Pond. It once connected Waterville Valley to the Sawyer River logging railroad, which led to the now deserted village of Livermore on the Sawyer River. (The present Sawyer River Trail was a part of this Waterville-Livermore route.) The Livermore Trail consists of logging roads of various ages and conditions; the part through Livermore Pass is muddy and can be difficult to follow. The gravel southern section, from Tripoli Rd. to Flume Brook Camp, is also called Livermore Rd. (FR 53).

From the parking area on Livermore Rd., the trail follows the gated gravel road through an open field (site of Depot Camp) and across a bridge over a branch of the Mad River. The Greeley Ponds Trail, another gravel road, diverges sharp left at 0.3 mi., 40 yd. past the bridge. Soon the Livermore Trail crosses the main branch of the Mad River on another bridge. In the next 2.0 mi., several of the WVAIA local paths intersect the trail: the Boulder Path diverges right at 0.6 mi. from the parking area; the Big Pines Path diverges left at 0.6 mi.; the Kettles Path diverges left at 0.9 mi.; the Norway Rapids Trail diverges right at 1.8 mi.; and a service road diverges right at 2.2 mi. across a major logging road bridge, leading to the upper end of the Cascade Path at 0.6 mi. and the top of the Snows Mountain ski slopes at 1.4 mi.

At 2.6 mi., the Livermore Trail passes the south end of the Mt. Tripyramid Trail, which leads to the right across Avalanche Brook and provides access to the Tripyramid peaks via the South Slide. After passing the site of Avalanche Camp to the left of the trail at 3.1 mi., where the road becomes more grass-grown, the trail reaches a hairpin turn to the left at 3.6 mi.; here the northern part of the Mt. Tripyramid Trail diverges right toward the peaks via the difficult North Slide. At 3.8 mi., the Scaur Ridge Trail diverges right, offering a longer but safer and easier route to the summit of North Tripyramid. The Livermore Trail climbs steadily through another hairpin turn and reaches a minor height-of-land at 4.6 mi., where the Old Skidder Trail enters on the left, then descends gently and crosses a branch of Flume Brook at 4.8 mi. Soon it passes a trail sign on the left side of the trail and the clearing of Flume Brook Camp on the right, becoming wet and muddy at times.

At 5.0 mi., the gravel road ends in a grassy clearing; here the **Kancamagus Brook Ski Trail** (sign) diverges left (north) at the far end, whereas the Livermore Trail (sign) bears slightly right (northeast) into the woods on an older road. (In the reverse direction, the Livermore Trail continues south from the clearing.) From here the trail is rough, often very wet and muddy, sparsely marked, and must be followed with care. It climbs gradually into the very flat Livermore Pass at 5.6 mi. and descends from the pass, slowly at first. It runs in a dry brook bed for a while, then descends rather steeply, angling down the wall of a deep, wooded gorge; at 5.9 mi., it crosses the brook bed at the bottom of the gorge. The trail descends moderately, crossing several brooks, then bears left off the logging road at 6.7 mi. near an old logging camp located on the right and crosses a moist area to a clearing at 7.1 mi. It turns right here and follows a grassy gravel logging road (in the reverse direction, it turns left off the road at an arrow). It passes several restricted but interesting views, and reaches the Kancamagus Highway east of Kancamagus Pass across from Lily Pond.

Livermore Trail (map 3:J6–I7)

Distances from Livermore Rd. parking area (1,580 ft.) to

- south end, Mt. Tripyramid Trail (2,000 ft.): 2.6 mi., 400 ft., 1 hr. 30 min.
- north end, Mt. Tripyramid Trail (2,400 ft.): 3.6 mi., 800 ft., 2 hr. 10 min.
- crossing of branch of Flume Brook (2,780 ft.): 4.8 mi., 1,200 ft., 3 hr.
- Kancamagus Highway (2,060 ft.): 7.7 mi., 1,300 ft. (rev. 800 ft.), 4 hr. 30 min.

Mount Tripyramid Trail (WVAIA)

This trail makes a loop over the three summits of Tripyramid from the Livermore Trail, and is usually done from north to south in order to ascend the steep rock slabs of the North Slide and descend the loose gravel of the South Slide. Descent of the North Slide is more difficult than ascent and may be particularly daunting to hikers who have difficulty or lack experience on steep rock, whereas ascent of the South Slide can be very frustrating because of constant backsliding on the loose gravel. *Caution:* The steep rock slabs of the North Slide are difficult, and they are dangerous in wet or icy conditions. At all times—but particularly in adverse conditions, or for the descent—the

Scaur Ridge Trail is a much easier and safer route than the North Slide. The North Slide lies mostly in deep shade in seasons when the sun is low, so ice may form early in fall and remain late in spring. The loose footing on the South Slide may also be hazardous when wet or icy. Allow plenty of time for the steep, rough trip over the Tripyramids via the slides. This trail is almost entirely within the Sandwich Range Wilderness.

The north end of the loop leaves the Livermore Trail at a hairpin turn 3.6 mi. from the Livermore Rd. parking area (0.5 mi. beyond the Avalanche Camp clearing). The trail descends sharply for 50 yd. to cross Avalanche Brook (last reliable water), enters the Sandwich Range Wilderness, then ascends at a moderate grade, occasionally requiring some care to follow, and reaches the gravel outwash of the North Slide at about 0.5 mi. from the Livermore Trail. It now becomes extremely steep, climbing about 1,200 ft. in 0.5 mi. The lower part of the slide has the most difficult, slippery slabs; the upper part is more exposed but the rough, normally dry rock offers comparatively good traction. Follow paint blazes (often faint and sparse) on the rocks. Soon the trail reaches the first open slabs and views become steadily more extensive. Higher up, the trail ascends the right-hand track of the slide almost to its top, then turns sharp left into the woods at a cairn, and continues to climb steeply for 0.1 mi. to the junction where the Pine Bend Brook Trail enters from the left 20 yd. below the summit of North Peak.

The Mt. Tripyramid Trail and the Pine Bend Brook Trail now coincide. They cross over the summit of North Peak and descend at a moderate grade toward Middle Peak. Just north of the saddle between the North and Middle Peaks, the Sabbaday Brook Trail enters left from the Kancamagus Highway, and the Pine Bend Brook Trail ends. The Mt. Tripyramid Trail crosses the saddle and makes a steep ascent of the cone of Middle Peak. There is an outlook to the right of the trail near the true summit, which is a few yards left at the high point of the trail. The trail descends into the saddle between Middle and South Peaks, then climbs moderately to the wooded summit of South Peak. From this summit, the trail starts to descend steeply, and soon reaches the top of the South Slide. In another 60 yd., the Kate Sleeper Trail (Section Eight) to Mt. Whiteface diverges left at a sign. The descent to the foot of the slide at 3.0 mi. is steep, with loose gravel footing becoming more prevalent as one descends. From a small open area at the bottom of the slide, the trail turns right and follows logging roads, crossing several small brooks; Cold Brook, the first sure water, is crossed at 4.1 mi. Continuing on old roads, the trail eventually crosses Avalanche Brook, leaving the Sandwich Range Wilderness, and ends in another 25 yd. on the Livermore Trail, 2.6 mi. from the Livermore Rd. parking area.

Mount Tripyramid Trail (map 3:J7)

Distances from Livermore Trail (2,400 ft.) to
- summit of North Peak (4,180 ft.): 1.2 mi., 1,800 ft., 1 hr. 30 min.
- Sabbaday Brook Trail (3,850 ft.): 1.7 mi., 1,800 ft. (rev. 350 ft.), 1 hr. 45 min.
- summit of Middle Peak (4,140 ft.): 2.0 mi., 2,100 ft., 2 hr. 5 min.
- summit of South Peak (4,100 ft.): 2.4 mi., 2,200 ft. (rev. 150 ft.), 2 hr. 20 min.
- Kate Sleeper Trail (3,850 ft.): 2.6 mi., 2,200 ft. (rev. 250 ft.), 2 hr. 25 min.
- Livermore Trail (2,000 ft.): 4.9 mi., 2,200 ft. (rev. 1,850 ft.), 3 hr. 35 min.

Distance from Livermore Rd. parking area (1,580 ft.) for
- complete loop over Mt. Tripyramid via Livermore and Mt. Tripyramid trails: 11.0 mi., 3,000 ft., 7 hr.

Scaur Ridge Trail (WMNF)

This trail runs from the Livermore Trail to the Pine Bend Brook Trail, affording an easier, safer alternative route to the North Slide. It is almost entirely within the Sandwich Range Wilderness.

It diverges right (east) from the Livermore Trail at a point 3.8 mi. from the Livermore Rd. parking area. Following an old logging road at a moderate grade, it crosses a small brook at 0.9 mi., then soon bears left off the road. Now climbing somewhat more steeply, it turns right at 1.1 mi., then swings left and enters the Pine Bend Brook Trail at the top of a narrow ridge at 1.2 mi. The summit of North Tripyramid is 0.8 mi. to the right via the Pine Bend Brook Trail.

Scaur Ridge Trail (map 3:J7)

Distance from Livermore Trail (2,500 ft.) to
- Pine Bend Brook Trail (3,440 ft.): 1.2 mi., 950 ft., 1 hr. 5 min.

Distance from Livermore Rd. parking area (1,580 ft.) for
- complete loop over Mt. Tripyramid via Livermore, Scaur Ridge, and Mt. Tripyramid trails: 12.1 mi., 3,000 ft., 7 hr. 35 min.

Pine Bend Brook Trail (WMNF)

This trail ascends North Tripyramid from the Kancamagus Highway 1.0 mi. west of the Sabbaday Falls Picnic Area. Parts of it are steep and rough. The upper part of the trail is in the Sandwich Range Wilderness.

The trail leaves the highway and soon turns sharp right onto the grade of the old Swift River logging railroad, follows it for 0.1 mi., then turns sharp left off the railroad grade and follows a branch of Pine Bend Brook southwest on an old logging road, making three crossings of the brook. A relocation has been made to the right before the second crossing. After the third crossing, at 1.3 mi., the trail begins to swing more to the west and crosses several small tributaries. It then passes over a minor divide to a westerly branch of Pine Bend Brook, which it crosses and recrosses (last sure water), and enters the Sandwich Range Wilderness at 2.1 mi. After crossing the brook bed again in a rocky section at 2.2 mi., the trail becomes rough and steep as it ascends along the north bank of the brook valley, then turns left, recrosses the brook bed, and angles steeply with very poor footing up an even steeper slope. Soon it reaches and ascends a minor easterly ridge, with much less difficult climbing. Shortly after reaching this ridge, there is a restricted outlook to Mt. Washington and the cliffs of Mt. Lowell.

Eventually, the trail reaches the ridge running from Tripyramid north to Scaur Peak, crosses it and descends slightly to the west side, then turns left and continues almost level to the junction on the right at 3.2 mi. with the Scaur Ridge Trail. Rising gradually on the very narrow wooded ridge, the Pine Bend Brook Trail provides occasional glimpses of the North Slide, then descends slightly. Soon it attacks the final steep, rough, and rocky climb to North Peak with several scrambles over slippery ledges. The Mt. Tripyramid Trail enters from the North Slide on the right 20 yd. below this summit. (There are good views from the top of the slide, 0.1 mi. from this junction via the Mt. Tripyramid Trail.) The two trails then coincide, passing the summit of North Peak and descending at a moderate grade to the junction with the Sabbaday Brook Trail just north of the saddle between North and Middle Peaks.

Pine Bend Brook Trail (map 3:J8–J7)

Distances from Kancamagus Highway (1,370 ft.) to

- Scaur Ridge Trail (3,440 ft.): 3.2 mi., 2,050 ft., 2 hr. 40 min.
- summit of North Peak (4,180 ft.): 4.0 mi., 2,800 ft., 3 hr. 25 min.
- Sabbaday Brook Trail (3,850 ft.): 4.5 mi., 2,800 ft. (rev. 350 ft.), 3 hr. 40 min.

Sabbaday Brook Trail (WMNF)

This trail begins at the Sabbaday Falls Picnic Area and ascends to the saddle between North Tripyramid and Middle Tripyramid. There are numerous brook crossings, some of which may be difficult at high water. Except for the very steep, rough section just below the main ridge crest, grades are easy to moderate and the footing is mostly good. The upper part of the trail is in the Sandwich Range Wilderness.

From the parking area, follow a gravel tourist path along the brook. A side path bears left and passes several viewpoints over Sabbaday Falls, rejoining at 0.3 mi. where the gravel path ends, and from there the trail continues on an old logging road with easy grades. Shortly beyond the falls, footways diverge on either side of a rocky brook bed and then rejoin. At 0.7 mi., the trail makes the first of three crossings of Sabbaday Brook in 0.2 mi. (All three may be difficult in high water, but the first two can be avoided by bushwhacking along the west bank because they are only 0.1 mi. apart.) The trail follows the old logging road on the east bank of Sabbaday Brook for nearly 2.0 mi., entering the Sandwich Range Wilderness at 1.7 mi. (about halfway through this section), and then at 2.8 mi., it turns sharp right, descends briefly, and makes a fourth crossing of the brook. Above this point, both the brook and trail swing to the west, then northwest, up the narrow valley between Tripyramid and the Fool Killer, climbing more steadily and crossing the brook twice more. The trail passes the base of a small slide on the Fool Killer at 3.7 mi., crosses the brook for the seventh and last time (last water) at the head of the ravine at 4.1 mi., then swings back to the south, passes a restricted outlook to Mt. Passaconaway, and soon reenters the old route of the trail above the slide on the east slope of Tripyramid. It turns sharp right here and climbs steeply up slabs and broken rock, then becomes less steep but remains rough, with many rocks and roots. Finally, it levels off and meets the Pine Bend Brook Trail and the Mt. Tripyramid Trail just north of the saddle between North and

Middle Tripyramid; turn right for North Peak (0.5 mi.) or left for Middle Peak (0.3 mi.).

Sabbaday Brook Trail (map 3:J8–J7)

Distances from Sabbaday Falls Picnic Area (1,320 ft.) to
- fourth crossing of Sabbaday Brook (2,100 ft.): 2.8 mi., 800 ft., 1 hr. 50 min.
- Pine Bend Brook Trail/Mt. Tripyramid Trail (3,850 ft.): 4.9 mi., 2,550 ft., 3 hr. 45 min.

Sandwich Mountain Trail (WMNF)

This trail runs to the summit of Sandwich Mountain from a parking lot just off NH 49, 0.4 mi. southwest of its junction with Tripoli Rd. There are fine views from the trail at several different elevation levels. Almost the entire trail is in the Sandwich Range Wilderness.

The trail leaves the southwest corner of the parking lot, skirts left around a power station, and drops sharply to cross Drakes Brook. If the brook is very high and the crossing difficult, it is possible to reach the trail on the other side of the brook by bushwhacking up the west bank from where Drakes Brook crosses NH 49 just south of the parking lot. The trail turns east soon after crossing the brook and climbs moderately, then steeply at times to an outlook with excellent views north and east at 1.6 mi. It crosses the narrow ridge crest of Noon Peak, passes an outlook over the Drakes Brook valley, and descends gradually to a sag. It then follows a curving, gradual ridge covered with beautiful mosses and passes another outlook. There is a spring (unreliable) on the right (west) side of the trail, which soon skirts the east slope of Jennings Peak. The Drakes Brook Trail enters on the left at 2.7 mi., and at 2.8 mi., a spur path, steep at the top, leads right 0.2 mi. to the ledgy summit of Jennings Peak, which commands impressive views south and east. For the next 0.4 mi., the grades are easy across a shallow sag. The Smarts Brook Trail enters on the right at 3.3 mi., and the Sandwich Mountain Trail ascends moderately toward the summit of Sandwich Mountain. About 90 yd. below the summit, the Algonquin Trail enters on the right, and 15 yd. below the summit, the Bennett St. Trail enters on the right.

Sandwich Mountain Trail (map 3:J6–K7)

Distances from parking area off NH 49 (1,400 ft.) to
- outlook on Noon Peak (2,940 ft.): 1.6 mi., 1,550 ft., 1 hr. 35 min.
- Drakes Brook Trail, upper junction (3,240 ft.): 2.7 mi., 1,950 ft. (rev. 100 ft.), 2 hr. 20 min.
- Sandwich Mountain summit (3,980 ft.): 3.9 mi., 2,700 ft., 3 hr. 20 min.

Drakes Brook Trail (WMNF)

This trail leaves the same parking lot off NH 49 as the Sandwich Mountain Trail and rejoins that trail near Jennings Peak, providing an alternate route for ascent or descent of Sandwich Mountain as well as access to Fletcher's Cascades.

The trail leaves east from the north side of the parking lot and follows a logging road for 0.4 mi. At this point, the trail to Fletcher's Cascades continues up the road, and the Drakes Brook Trail diverges right and crosses Drakes Brook (difficult at high water). The trail follows an old logging road, climbing away from the brook and returning to its bank several times. At 2.6 mi., it leaves the logging road and climbs by switchbacks up the west side of the ravine to join the Sandwich Mountain Trail north of Jennings Peak, about 1.2 mi. from the summit of Sandwich Mountain.

Drakes Brook Trail (map 3:J6–K6)

Distances from parking area off NH 49 (1,400 ft.) to
- Sandwich Mountain Trail (3,240 ft.): 3.2 mi., 1,850 ft., 2 hr. 35 min.
- Sandwich Mountain summit (3,980 ft.) via Sandwich Mountain Trail: 4.4 mi., 2,600 ft., 3 hr. 30 min.

Smarts Brook Trail (WMNF)

This trail follows the valley of Smarts Brook from NH 49, 3.8 mi. east of its junction with NH 175, to the Sandwich Mountain Trail in the sag south of Jennings Peak. The upper part of the valley is in the Sandwich Range Wilderness and is wild and pleasant; below the Wilderness boundary there has been extensive logging.

The trail leaves the east side of NH 49 from the south end of a parking area just northeast of the Smarts Brook bridge, crosses the brook on the highway bridge, and immediately turns left. It climbs a short distance to a logging road, which it follows left. At 0.2 mi., where an alternate route continues ahead, it turns right, then soon turns left onto a recently improved logging road as the Tri-Town (X-C ski) Trail continues ahead. The Smarts Brook Trail follows the road past a fine cascade and pool on the left at 1.1 mi., and at 1.2 mi., the Tri-Town Trail enters from the right. At 1.3 mi., the Yellow Jacket (X-C ski) Trail diverges left across a bridge. (This trail and the Pine Flats Trail can be used as an attractive return route from this point to the trailhead. Follow the Yellow Jacket Trail, with minor ups and downs, to a junction on the left at 1.2 mi. from the Smarts Brook Trail. Turn sharp left here onto the Pine Flats Trail, which climbs to a pine-wooded plateau, then descends alongside a beautiful gorge on Smarts Brook, reaching the east side of the parking area at 1.9 mi.).

The Smarts Brook Trail passes to the left of Beaver Pond at 1.5 mi., and in another 125 yd., it crosses along the right side of a large logging yard; avoid skid roads diverging left. It then climbs easily through recently logged areas; blazes must be followed carefully where the trail intersects numerous skid roads. It enters the Sandwich Range Wilderness at 2.5 mi., soon crosses a tributary, and at 3.7 mi. passes several large boulders. It then crosses the brook and passes several more very large boulders in the next 0.4 mi. Soon it turns left and climbs by a long switchback to the ridge top, where it meets the Sandwich Mountain Trail.

Smarts Brook Trail (map 3:K6)

Distances from parking area on NH 49 (900 ft.) to

- pools in Smarts Brook (1,100 ft.): 1.1 mi., 200 ft., 40 min.
- Sandwich Mountain Trail (3,416 ft.): 5.1 mi., 2,500 ft., 3 hr. 50 min.
- Sandwich Mountain summit (3,980 ft.) via Sandwich Mountain Trail: 5.7 mi., 3,100 ft., 4 hr. 25 min.

Bennett Street Trail (WODC)

This trail runs to the summit of Sandwich Mountain from the Flat Mountain Pond Trail at a point 0.3 mi. past Jose's (rhymes with "doses") bridge and 0.5 mi. from the parking area on Bennett St. (which is 2.2 mi. from NH 113A; for trailhead access directions see Flat Mountain Pond Trail, p. 322). Its blue blazes should be followed with care. The upper part of the trail is in the Sandwich Range Wilderness.

From the parking area, go west on the Flat Mountain Pond Trail past the gate and Jose's bridge to a small clearing, where the Bennett St. Trail begins, turning right. It follows a logging road along the southwest bank of Pond Brook, crossing several small streams, and at 0.6 mi. from the Flat Mountain Pond Trail, the Gleason Trail diverges left. The Bennett St. Trail soon passes an unnamed cascade and then Great Falls, then bears away from Pond Brook and follows a tributary, crossing it twice. At 1.6 mi., it crosses the Flat Mountain Pond Trail, which at this point is an old railroad grade. The Bennett St. Trail ascends the bank above the grade, soon entering the Sandwich Range Wilderness. It climbs steadily, and at 2.3 mi., turns sharp right onto an old logging road. At 2.9 mi., it turns left off the logging road, and at 3.5 mi., the Gleason Trail rejoins on the left. The trail soon turns left onto another old road at a point where there is an unreliable spring on a side path right, and shortly passes a spur path left (sign) to another unreliable spring. It then climbs to a junction with the Sandwich Mountain Trail; the summit is 15 yd. to the right.

Bennett Street Trail (map 3:K7)

Distances from Flat Mountain Pond Trail (1,200 ft.) to
- crossing of Flat Mountain Pond Trail (1,850 ft.): 1.6 mi., 650 ft., 1 hr. 10 min.
- upper junction with Gleason Trail (3,650 ft.): 3.5 mi., 2,450 ft., 3 hr.
- Sandwich Mountain summit (3,980 ft.): 4.0 mi., 2,800 ft., 3 hr. 25 min.

Distance from Bennett St. parking area (1,060 ft.) to
- Sandwich Mountain summit (3,980 ft.) via Flat Mountain Pond and Bennett St. trails: 4.5 mi., 2,900 ft., 3 hr. 40 min.

Gleason Trail (AMC)

This trail begins and ends on the Bennett St. Trail, providing an alternative route to the summit of Sandwich Mountain that is 0.7 mi. shorter, but consequently steeper and rougher. The yellow blazes must be followed with care. The trail is rather steep, and footing may be poor when the trail is wet. The upper part of the trail is in the Sandwich Range Wilderness.

It diverges left from the Bennett St. Trail at 0.6 mi. (1.1 mi. from the Bennett St. parking area) and ascends across a ledgy brook to cross the Flat Mountain Pond Trail (an old railroad grade) at 0.5 mi. The trail enters the Sandwich Range Wilderness, soon turns left and climbs through a beautiful hardwood forest, then approaches a brook and turns right without crossing it at 1.0 mi. Soon the trail turns left onto a logging road, follows it for 40 yd., then turns off the road to the right. It continues rather steeply to the ridge top at 1.5 mi. and then levels off. It then ascends moderately to its upper junction with the Bennett St. Trail, 0.5 mi. below the summit of Sandwich Mountain.

Gleason Trail (map 3:K7)

Distance from Bennett St. Trail, lower junction (1,400 ft.) to
• Bennett St. Trail, upper junction (3,650 ft.): 2.2 mi., 2,250 ft., 2 hr. 15 min.
Distance from Bennett St. parking area (1,060 ft.) to
• summit of Sandwich Mountain (3,980 ft.) via Flat Mountain Pond, Bennett St., Gleason, and Bennett St. trails: 3.8 mi., 2,900 ft., 3 hr. 20 min.

Flat Mountain Pond Trail (WMNF)

This trail, with easy grades and footing for most of its distance, begins on Whiteface Intervale Rd. at a point 0.3 mi. north of its intersection with Bennett St., ascends to the Flat Mountain Ponds, then descends to Bennett St. at a parking area 2.2 mi. from NH 113A. To reach these trailheads, take Whiteface Intervale Rd., which leaves NH 113A about 3 mi. north of the western junction of NH 113 and NH 113A, where NH 113A bends from north-south to east-west. Bennett St. turns left from Whiteface Intervale Rd. 0.1 mi. from NH 113A, continues straight past a junction at 1.7 mi., where it becomes rougher, and is gated at 2.2 mi. at a parking lot 0.2 east of Jose's (rhymes with "doses") bridge. The upper section of the Flat Mountain Pond Trail, around and east of Flat Mountain Ponds, is in the Sandwich Range Wilderness.

The trail leaves Whiteface Intervale Rd. just before the bridge over the Whiteface River on a gated logging road, crosses a beaver pond outlet with good views, bears left at a fork, and turns sharp right off the road at 0.6 mi. Soon it reaches an older, grassy logging road and follows it left for 60 yd., then leaves this road to the right and passes an outlook to Mt. Whiteface at 0.9 mi. It ascends easily along a small ridge, then descends rather abruptly to Whiteface River. It crosses the river (no bridge; may be difficult at high water) at 1.6 mi., entering the Sandwich Range Wilderness, and immediately picks up the older route of the trail, a logging road that it follows to the left upstream along the east bank. At 1.7 mi., the McCrillis

Trail turns sharp right up the bank, and the Flat Mountain Pond Trail continues to ascend along the river at comfortable grades, crossing a major branch at 3.1 mi. (difficult at high water). Continuing the ascent, it passes over a small hump and descends to the edge of Flat Mountain Pond at 4.2 mi., where it enters the old Beebe River logging railroad grade. It follows the grade to a fork at the edge of the major inlet brook; the trail follows the left fork across the stream, while the right fork runs to the edge of a beaver pond with a view of Flat Mountain. Continuing along the shore of the long, narrow pond, the main trail soon diverges right on a rough footway to circle around an area in which the grade has been flooded. It passes a boulder with a view of Mt. Whiteface, and returns to the grade at the south end of the pond at 5.3 mi., leaving the Sandwich Range Wilderness. Here, 70 yd. straight ahead on a spur path, is the Flat Mountain Pond Shelter, worth visiting just for the view across the pond. The main trail turns right on the railroad grade and descends gradually into the valley of Pond Brook.

At 6.3 mi., the grade makes a hairpin turn to the left at a beaver pond, soon crosses a small brook, passes a logging-camp site, and crosses the brook twice more. At 7.6 mi., the trail crosses a major tributary and swings left, and at 7.7 mi., the Bennett St. Trail crosses. After a wet section where the railroad ties remain, the Gleason Trail crosses at 8.2 mi. (junction signed for the Gleason Trail only). Either the Bennett St. Trail or the Gleason Trail can be used as an attractive shortcut to Jose's bridge and the Bennett St. parking area. At 9.2 mi., the Guinea Pond Trail continues ahead on the railroad grade, while the Flat Mountain Pond Trail turns left and descends on a logging road, passes a gate, goes through a small clearing where the Bennett St. Trail enters on the left, and passes a second gate just before reaching the parking area 0.2 mi. past Jose's bridge.

Flat Mountain Pond Trail (map 3:K8–K7)

Distances from Whiteface Intervale Rd. (968 ft.) to

- McCrillis Trail (1,250 ft.): 1.7 mi., 400 ft. (rev. 100 ft.), 1 hr. 5 min.
- Flat Mountain Pond Shelter spur path (2,320 ft.): 5.3 mi., 1,450 ft., 3 hr. 25 min.
- Guinea Pond Trail (1,560 ft.): 9.2 mi., 1,450 ft. (rev. 750 ft.), 5 hr. 20 min.
- Bennett St. parking area (1,060 ft.): 10.3 mi., 1,450 ft. (rev. 500 ft.), 5 hr. 55 min.

Algonquin Trail (SLA)

This trail ascends Sandwich Dome from the north side of Sandwich Notch Rd. 1.5 mi. north of the power line along the Beebe River and 3.7 mi. south of NH 49. Trailhead parking is limited; a new parking area is in planning. This trail provides many extensive views from open ledges on the southwest shoulder, sometimes called Black Mountain. The trail is steep and rough in parts, with one fairly difficult rock scramble Almost the entire trail is in the Sandwich Range Wilderness.

The trail follows an old logging road across a brook and past a small meadow, and at 0.9 mi., in a small clearing, turns left off the road (watch carefully for yellow blazes). Soon it begins to climb steeply, then moderates and passes through a ledgy area with two small brooks, then climbs steeply again to a small pass at 2.1 mi. Here it turns right, descends slightly, then attacks the west end of the ridge, climbing steeply with one fairly difficult rock scramble. Two other rock pitches, formerly part of the main trail, are now bypassed by paths to the right; at the second, good views are missed unless one walks back to the ledges on the former route of the trail. The grade moderates as the trail climbs largely in the open, and at 2.8 mi. (elevation 3,300 ft.), the Black Mountain Pond Trail enters on the right. The Algonquin Trail continues to ascend moderately past several viewpoints, then descends steeply for a short distance into a sag at 3.5 mi. It ascends easily along the ridge with a few minor dips, then climbs moderately, passing an outlook south, and ends at the Sandwich Mountain Trail 90 yd. below the summit.

Algonquin Trail (map 3:K6–K7)

Distances from Sandwich Notch Rd. (1,420 ft.) to
- small pass (2,600 ft.): 2.1 mi., 1,200 ft., 1 hr. 40 min.
- Black Mountain Pond Trail (3,300 ft.): 2.8 mi., 1,900 ft., 2 hr. 20 min.
- Sandwich Mountain Trail (3,950 ft.): 4.5 mi., 2,650 ft. (rev. 100 ft.), 3 hr. 35 min.

Black Mountain Pond Trail (SLA)

This trail runs from the Guinea Pond Trail, 1.6 mi. from Sandwich Notch Rd., past Black Mountain Pond to the Algonquin Trail 1.8 mi. below the summit of Sandwich Mountain. Sections of the trail below Black Mountain Pond are wet, and the part from the pond to the ridge is very steep and rough with several fairly difficult scrambles. The former Black Mountain Pond Shelter has been removed. Nearly the entire trail is in the Sandwich Range Wilderness.

This trail leaves the north side of the Guinea Pond Trail almost directly opposite the Mead Trail, crosses the Beebe River on new rock stepping stones (may be difficult at very high water), continues generally north to the west bank of the Beebe River (which has turned to run north and south), then recrosses it at a beaver meadow. At 0.8 mi., it crosses an overgrown gravel road that crosses the brook on the left side of the trail. At 1.9 mi., a side path leads left 0.1 mi. to Mary Cary Falls. The main trail continues to ascend easily, recrosses the brook, and at 2.4 mi., it passes through an area heavily affected by camping (camping was still permitted at this site as of 2006, but not within 200 ft. of the pond or within marked revegetation areas). The trail can be difficult to follow here because of the ill-defined footway and sparse blazing; it turns left, then soon turns right and descends a short pitch to the west edge of Black Mountain Pond at the site of the former shelter. The trail winds around in the woods near the pond, passing through a small stand of virgin spruce, then turns right to bypass a beaver pond. It then begins the steep climb. About halfway up, it reaches the first of several outlook ledges with good views south; views to the west increase as the trail works around toward the west end of the shoulder. At 3.3 mi., it passes a boulder cave, turns sharp right, and continues to meet the Algonquin Trail at an elevation of 3,300 ft.

Black Mountain Pond Trail (map 3:K7–K6)

Distances from Guinea Pond Trail (1,450 ft.) to

- Black Mountain Pond (2,220 ft.): 2.4 mi., 750 ft., 1 hr. 35 min.
- Algonquin Trail (3,300 ft.): 3.5 mi., 1,850 ft., 2 hr. 40 min.

Guinea Pond Trail (WMNF)

This trail runs east from Sandwich Notch Rd. 5.7 mi. from Center Sandwich, just south of the bridge over the Beebe River, to the Flat Mountain Pond Trail 1.1 mi. from the Bennett St. parking area. The Sandwich Notch Rd. trailhead parking area has been relocated to the north side of the Beebe River Rd. (the road that runs west from the crossroads just north of the bridge), about 100 yd. west of the crossroads. There is no parking at the trail-head itself.

From Sandwich Notch Rd., the trail follows a gated road to the old railroad grade in a power-line clearing, then follows the grade along Beebe River past numerous ponds and swamps, with occasional views of Sandwich Mountain. At 1.2 mi., it passes a second gate, and soon the trail turns right, then left, on an old road in order to bypass a flooded section of the grade. It rejoins the railroad grade just before reaching the junctions with the Mead Trail on the right at 1.6 mi. and the Black Mountain Pond Trail on the left 10 yd. farther on. Continuing east, the trail crosses a brook twice; in high water, follow a beaten path along the south bank. The trail crosses another brook, and at 1.8 mi., a side path runs left 0.2 mi. to the shore of Guinea Pond. The trail continues on the railroad grade, then swings left off it to bypass a beaver swamp. At 2.8 mi., it crosses a branch of the Cold River and continues on the grade, crossing several small brooks, to the junction with the Flat Mountain Pond Trail, which enters right from Jose's bridge and follows the railroad grade ahead to Flat Mountain Pond.

Guinea Pond Trail (map 3:K6–K7)

Distances from Sandwich Notch Rd. (1,320 ft.) to
- Mead Trail/Black Mountain Pond Trail (1,450 ft.): 1.6 mi., 150 ft., 50 min.
- Flat Mountain Pond Trail (1,560 ft.): 4.0 mi., 250 ft., 2 hr. 10 min.

Mead Trail (SLA)

This trail ascends to the summit of Mt. Israel, where there are outstanding views (particularly to the higher peaks of the Sandwich Range close by on the north), from the Guinea Pond Trail 1.6 mi. from Sandwich Notch Rd.

It leaves the Guinea Pond Trail and crosses a small ridge, a sag, and the power lines; then it ascends along the ravine of a small brook, crossing it at 0.9 mi. It continues to ascend past a small spring (unreliable) to the Wentworth Trail; the summit ledge, with fine views, is 70 yd. left.

Mead Trail (map 3:K7)

Distance from Guinea Pond Trail (1,450 ft.) to
- Wentworth Trail (2,610 ft.): 1.7 mi., 1,150 ft., 1 hr. 25 min.

Wentworth Trail (SLA)

This trail ascends Mt. Israel from Mead Base (a WODC/SLA trail-crew camp), located 0.4 mi. up a side road off Sandwich Notch Rd. 2.4 mi. from Center Sandwich, and affords splendid views of the Lakes Region and the Sandwich Range. Park in the field below the camp buildings.

Bearcamp River Trail. The most interesting part of this 17-mi. long trail is the northernmost section, which runs 0.6 mi. from Mead Base to the Sandwich Town Park on Sandwich Notch Rd. 3.2 mi. from Center Sandwich. It can be hiked for its own sake or used as part of a very attractive and varied loop hike over Mt. Israel via the Wentworth Trail, Mead Trail, Guinea Pond Trail, a 2.5 mi. section of the Sandwich Notch Rd., and this segment. The following description is southbound from Sandwich Notch Rd. to Mead Base, as most hikers will probably use it in that direction. The yellow-blazed trail first descends gradually to the Bearcamp River at Beede Falls. The shallow pool at the foot of this beautiful cascade is a popular swimming hole in summer. Cross the river and descend along its northern bank, then bear left away from the river, and at 0.2 mi., pass Cow Cave (left), where legend says a lost cow safely spent a winter. Cross a small stream and bear right onto a grassy road, then pass a picnic area with restrooms (left) opposite an open field, and reach Mead Base at 0.6 mi.

The Wentworth Trail, blazed in yellow, enters the woods at the left rear of the main camp building (sign) and leads directly uphill, following an old cart path through an opening in a stone wall 0.3 mi. above the camp. It turns right and angles up the hillside above the wall, turns left, then turns right again at a brook bed at 0.8 mi. Soon it begins to switchback up the slope, and at 1.5 mi., it passes a rock face right and a fine outlook 10 yd. on the left across Squam Lake and Lake Winnipesaukee. The trail reaches the ridge 100 yd. farther up and climbing becomes easier, soon becoming almost level in a dense, shady coniferous forest. Then the trail turns right at a ledge (good view north) near the summit of the west knob and continues along the ridge, descending briefly before rising to the junction on the left with the Mead Trail; the summit is a ledge 70 yd. past the junction. Some cairns mark a lightly beaten path that leads about 100 yd. northeast from the summit to ledges with more views to the north and east.

Wentworth Trail (map 3:L7–K7)

Distance from Mead Base (930 ft.) to
- Mt. Israel summit (2,630 ft.): 2.1 mi., 1,700 ft., 1 hr. 55 min.

Distance from Mead Base (930 ft.), Sandwich Town Park (1,020 ft.), or Guinea Pond Trail parking area (1,320 ft.) for
- loop over Mt. Israel via Wentworth Trail, Mead Trail, Guinea Pond Trail, Sandwich Notch Rd., and Bearcamp River Trail: 8.5 mi., 1,850 ft., 5 hr. 10 min.

Crawford-Ridgepole Trail (SLA)

This trail follows the backbone of the Squam Range from Sandwich Notch Rd. to the south knob of Cotton Mountain. The trail starts on the Sandwich Notch Rd. 3.7 mi. from NH 113 in Center Sandwich and 0.5 mi. beyond Beede Falls (Sandwich town park parking area), and 2.0 mi. south of the power line along the Beebe River. There is parking space for one or two cars at the trailhead; other spaces may be found a short distance east along the road. Except for the very popular segment between Mt. Percival and Mt. Morgan, the trail is used infrequently, despite fine views in the Squam-Doublehead section.

From the road (sign), the trail ascends steeply, with one difficult ledge scramble. Higher up the grade eases and the trail passes southeast of the summit of an unnamed wooded peak (2,218 ft.), and continues along the ridge across a saddle to Doublehead Mountain (2,158 ft.), where there is a good view north just before the summit of East Doublehead. At 1.9 mi., 100 yd. beyond the summit of East Doublehead, the trail bears right and descends where the Doublehead Trail diverges left to NH 113. There is a very fine viewpoint, well worth the side trip, on the Doublehead Trail, 0.1 mi. from this junction. After passing over West Doublehead, where there is a limited outlook to the north, the Crawford-Ridgepole Trail continues along the ridge, much of the way over ledges that are slippery when wet. It climbs steeply out of a muddy col, with one fairly difficult ledge scramble, passes an excellent south outlook, then crosses an open ledge with fine views to the north. It crosses the east summit of Mt. Squam (2,223 ft.), where there is a restricted view, at 3.0 mi. The trail continues along the ledgy ridge, crossing the west summit of Mt. Squam, passing an outlook south and descending through a notch, then climbing to the Mt. Percival Trail and Mt. Percival's excellent views at 4.4 mi. Continuing along the ridge, it passes just west of the actual high point of the range (sometimes called the Sawtooth, it can be reached by a short but thick bushwhack and has a restricted view), and continues to a junction with the Mt. Morgan Trail at 5.2 mi. Here the Mt. Morgan Trail leads to the right 90 yd. to a fork; the left branch (almost straight ahead) leads another 50 yd. to a cliff-top viewpoint, whereas the right branch leads 50 yd. to the true summit of Mt. Morgan, where there is an interesting view north.

From this junction, the Crawford-Ridgepole Trail and the Mt. Morgan Trail coincide, descending a set of steps. Shortly a difficult spur path branches right, ascends three ladders, and climbs about 100 yd. through a boulder cave and up steep ledges to the cliff-top viewpoint. The main trail descends to a junction at 5.6 mi. where the Mt. Morgan Trail continues its descent to NH 113, and the Crawford-Ridgepole Trail turns right to climb at mostly easy grades towards Mt. Webster. At 7.1 mi. an umarked spur path leads left 50 yd. to a fine outlook over Squam Lake, and at 7.5 mi. another spur leads left a few steps to an eastern outlook.

The trail descends at moderate and easy grades, passing an outlook east at 8.1 mi., climbs slightly to the junction with the Old Mountain Rd. at 9.6 mi., then ascends to the summit of Mt. Livermore (view) at 10.0 mi. Coinciding with the Prescott Trail, it descends west from Mt. Livermore along a stone wall, then turns left on an old carriage road and descends by switchbacks. At 10.3 mi., the Prescott Trail branches left; the Crawford-Ridgepole Trail crosses two tiny streams near a low pass, then climbs through a rocky area in a beautiful hemlock grove to a south spur of Cotton Mountain. Here the Crawford-Ridgepole Trail ends because the Science Center of New Hampshire has closed the former connector to its trails because it requires an admission fee for use of its trails. From the spur of Cotton Mountain, descent can be made by following the Cotton Mountain Trail down to NH 113 near the Old Highway trailhead.

Crawford-Ridgepole Trail (maps 3/4:L6/USGS Holderness quad)

Distances from Sandwich Notch Rd. (1,220 ft.) to

- East Doublehead summit (2,158 ft.): 1.9 mi., 1,150 ft. (rev. 200 ft.), 1 hr. 30 min. ▶

- Mt. Squam, east summit (2,223 ft.): 3.0 mi., 1,450 ft. (rev. 250 ft.), 2 hr. 15 min.
- Mt. Percival summit (2,212 ft.): 4.4 mi., 1,700 ft. (rev. 250 ft.), 3 hr. 5 min.
- upper junction with Mt. Morgan Trail (2,200 ft.): 5.2 mi., 1,800 ft. (rev. 100 ft.), 3 hr. 30 min.
- Mt. Livermore summit (1,500 ft.): 10.0 mi., 2,300 ft. (rev. 1,200 ft.), 6 hr. 10 min.
- spur of Cotton Mountain (1,210 ft.): 11.3 mi., 2,600 ft. (rev. 600 ft.), 6 hr. 55 min.

Doublehead Trail (SLA)

This trail provides access to a ledge high on Doublehead Mountain that provides one of the finest views in the Squam Range. It begins on NH 113 at an SLA sign for "Old Highway" 3.5 mi. southwest of Center Sandwich, following the gravel Thompson Rd., (part of the old Holderness–Center Sandwich highway) which diverges right (west) at an angle past an old cemetery and a residence. Vehicles should be parked nearby on NH 113, with care taken not to block any roads.

Continue on foot on Thompson Rd., avoiding a new gated logging road on the right at 0.6 mi. The trail proper (sign, yellow blazes begin) leaves the old highway on the right 0.9 mi. from NH 113, across from a large clearing, and follows a recent skid road. At 1.2 mi., it bears right onto an older logging road and soon swings right, crossing a small brook. At 1.5 mi., the trail turns left onto a skidder road and enters an overgrown logged area where the footway is poorly defined and blazes must be followed with care. In another 100 yd., the trail turns sharp right (arrow) across a small brook, follows another skidder road, and joins a small brook. At the top of a steep pitch, it turns sharp left and soon crosses a stone wall, where it reenters mature woods. It crosses a skid road at 1.9 mi. and ascends with a bypass to the left, then swings right and climbs to a ledge at 2.2 mi. with excellent views to the south. It then turns left off the ledge and climbs to the Crawford-Ridgepole Trail 80 yd. west of the summit of East Doublehead.

Doublehead Trail (map 3:L6)

Distance from NH 113 (720 ft.) to
- Crawford-Ridgepole Trail (2,120 ft.): 2.3 mi., 1,450 ft. (rev. 50 ft.), 1 hr. 55 min.

Mount Percival Trail (SLA)

This trail provides access to the fine views and interesting boulder caves on Mt. Percival, and in combination with the Mt. Morgan Trail and Crawford-Ridgepole Trail, offers one of the most popular and scenic loop hikes on the southern fringe of the White Mountains. The trail begins on the north side of NH 113, 0.3 mi. northeast of the Mt. Morgan/Rattlesnake parking area. Parking for this trail is also available at the end of a short gravel road.

The trail follows a logging road past a chain gate and ascends at an easy grade. At 0.2 mi., the Morgan-Percival Connector diverges left for the Mt. Morgan Trail. The Mt. Percival Trail passes through a clearing, and at 0.4 mi., it turns left onto a relocated section, then loops back to rejoin the original route at 0.6 mi. At 0.9 mi., after a slight descent, it crosses a brook and climbs moderately. At 1.5 mi., it turns right (northeast) and traverses the south slope of Mt. Percival for 0.1 mi. The trail then swings left and climbs steeply to a fork at 1.9 mi. (From this fork an alternate route diverges left and ascends a difficult and very strenuous route through a boulder cave [not recommended in wet weather], then continues up ledges to the summit.) Here the main trail turns right, struggles up a steep, rough ledgy section, crosses a cliff top with a fine view of Squam Lake, and continues over ledges to join the Crawford-Ridgepole Trail at the summit.

Mount Percival Trail (map 3:L6)

Distances from NH 113 (800 ft.) to
- Mt. Percival summit (2,212 ft.): 2.0 mi., 1,450 ft., 1 hr. 45 min.

Mount Morgan Trail (SLA)

This trail leaves the west side of NH 113, 5.5 mi. northeast of its junction with US 3 in Holderness and 6.3 mi. southwest of its junction with NH 109 in Center Sandwich. From the small parking area, the trail follows a logging road, turning left off it almost immediately. At 0.1 mi., the Morgan-Percival Connector diverges right, leading 0.5 mi. to the Mt. Percival Trail. The trail climbs west at a moderate grade, then swings right and traverses to the north. At 1.4 mi., it swings left to begin the steeper ascent of the southeast slope of the mountain. At 1.7 mi., the Crawford-Ridgepole Trail enters left from Mt. Webster, and the two trails coincide, passing a spur path that branches left, ascends a ladder, and climbs about 100 yd. through a boulder cave to the cliff-top viewpoint. After climbing a set of steps, the main trails soon reach a junction where the Crawford-Ridgepole Trail diverges right for Mt. Percival. Here the Mt. Morgan Trail leads left to the cliff-top viewpoint; partway along, a short spur leaves it on the right and runs to the true summit.

Mount Morgan Trail (map 3:L6)

Distance from NH 113 (800 ft.) to
* Mt. Morgan summit (2,220 ft.): 2.1 mi., 1,450 ft., 1 hr. 45 min.

Morse Trail (SLA)

This trail links the lower ends of the Mt. Morgan and Mt. Percival trails, making possible an excellent loop hike without a road walk on NH 113. It diverges right from the Mt. Morgan Trail 0.1 mi. from NH 113 and descends easily to cross a small brook. It passes through a stone wall and ascends gradually, crosses a brook on a footbridge at 0.4 mi., passes through another stone wall, and bears right to meet the Mt. Percival Trail, 0.2 mi. from NH 113.

Morse Trail (map 3:L6)

Distance from Mt. Morgan Trail (820 ft.) to
* Mt. Percival Trail (850 ft.): 0.5 mi., 50 ft., 15 min.

Distance from Mt. Morgan parking area (800 ft.) for
* loop over Mts. Percival and Morgan via Mt. Morgan Trail, Morgan-Percival Connector, Mt. Percival Trail, Crawford-Ridgepole Trail, and Mt. Morgan Trail: 5.4 mi., 1,550 ft., 3 hr. 30 min.

Old Highway (SLA)

This trail, used for access to the lower ends of the Prescott Trail and Old Mountain Rd., continues straight where NH 113 turns right 1.3 mi. northeast of Holderness and 0.2 mi. beyond a gravel pit (the trailhead for the Cotton Mountain Trail) where parking is available on the shoulder of NH 113. A century ago, the old road followed by this trail was part of the main highway between Holderness and Center Sandwich. It leaves NH 113 at the same point as a paved driveway. It climbs at moderate, then easy grades through an area with many stone walls. At 0.8 mi., it turns left onto a newer road. The Prescott Trail diverges left (north) at the height-of-land at 0.9 mi., 100 yd. beyond the Prescott Cemetery, and after a short descent the Old Mountain Rd. diverges left at an acute angle at 1.1 mi. and runs near the edge of a large field. The Old Highway continues between two fields with a view east, then descends past a sugarhouse to a locked gate (no parking here) at the edge of Burleigh Farm Rd., which runs 0.6 mi. to NH 113 at a point 3.0 mi. from US 3. Parking is available on Burleigh Farm Rd. 0.2 mi. from NH 113, near the junction with Laurence Rd.

Old Highway (map 4:L6/USGS Holderness quad)

Distances from NH 113 (585 ft.) to

- Prescott Trail (900 ft.): 0.9 mi., 300 ft., 35 min.
- Burleigh Farm Rd. (750 ft.): 1.4 mi., 300 ft. (rev. 150 ft.), 50 min.

Prescott Trail (SLA)

This trail to Mt. Livermore (1,500 ft.) turns left off the Old Highway at the height-of-land 0.9 mi. from NH 113, 100 yd. beyond the Prescott Cemetery. It follows a logging road for 0.2 mi., turns sharp left off it and ascends gradually, then turns right uphill at 0.3 mi. The trail now climbs by switchbacks over a low ridge and descends gradually to the Crawford-Ridgepole Trail, which enters left at 1.0 mi. From this point, the two trails ascend together via switchbacks. Just below the summit, they turn sharp right and ascend steeply to the summit, where there is a view over Squam Lake.

Descending, the Crawford-Ridgepole Trail heading south and the Prescott Trail leave the summit together, turn sharp right (west) and descend along an old stone wall, then turn left onto an old bridle trail. After 0.4 mi., the Crawford-Ridgepole Trail leaves on the right.

Prescott Trail (map 4:L6)

Distances from Old Highway Trail (900 ft.) to

- Crawford-Ridgepole Trail (1,200 ft.): 1.0 mi., 350 ft. (rev. 50 ft.), 40 min.
- summit of Mt. Livermore (1,500 ft.): 1.4 mi., 650 ft., 1 hr.

Distance from NH 113 (585 ft.) for

- loop over Mt. Livermore (1,500 ft.) via Old Highway, Prescott Trail, Crawford-Ridgepole Trail, Old Mountain Rd., and Old Highway: 4.5 mi., 1,050 ft., 2 hr. 45 min.

Old Mountain Road (SLA-Webster)

This trail leaves sharp left from the Old Highway 1.1 mi. from its western end at NH 113. It ascends on an old road to the left of the field; at the top of the field, there is a view of Red Hill. The trail continues climbing at a moderate grade to the Crawford-Ridgepole Trail at the low point between Mt. Livermore and Mt. Webster. The old road continues from here descending to the north, but this section is not an official trail.

Old Mountain Road (map 4:L6)

Distance from Old Highway (800 ft.) to
* Crawford-Ridgepole Trail (1,300 ft.): 0.7 mi., 500 ft., 35 min.

Cotton Mountain Trail (SLA)

This trail provides access to a ledge with a fine view located on a south spur of Cotton Mountain and connects with the south end of the Crawford-Ridgepole Trail. It has been recently reconstructed by the SLA. The trail (sign) starts at a pull-off on the west side of NH 113, 1.1 mi. north of its junction with US 3 in Holderness. It follows a dirt road through a brushy gravel pit, curving right at 0.2 mi. into an open area, then left (cairns) to an SLA signpost, where the road bears left again and ends in 15 yd. at the top of the bank. Here the trail turns right into the woods (sign) and ascends, crossing an old road in 60 yd. It climbs rather steeply up the east slope of the mountain, circling around to the south side to reach the summit of the spur and the junction with the Crawford-Ridgepole Trail. A few yards before the junction, a spur path leads 20 yd. right to a ledge with a view over Squam Lake.

Cotton Mountain Trail (SLA map)

Distance from NH 113 (590 ft.) to
* summit of south spur of Cotton Mountain (1,210 ft.): 0.7 mi., 600 ft., 40 min.

Rattlesnake Paths (SLA)

Old Bridle Path. This is the easiest route to the West Rattlesnake outlooks. A very short and easy route to an excellent viewpoint, it receives very heavy use. It leaves the southeast side of NH 113 between Center Sandwich and Holderness, 5.5 mi. northeast of its junction with US 3 in Holderness and 6.3 mi. southwest of its junction with NH 109 in Center Sandwich, and about 70 yd. southwest of the entrance to the Mt. Morgan Trail (where there is a small parking area). It follows an old cart road 0.9 mi. with a 450-ft. ascent (40 min.) to the cliffs near the summit. Descending, this trail begins slightly northwest of the summit cliffs.

Ramsey Trail. This is a much steeper route to West Rattlesnake. It leaves Pinehurst Rd. (which begins on NH 113 0.5 mi. west of the Mt. Morgan/ Rattlesnake parking area) 0.7 mi. from NH 113 and 90 yd. east of the entrance to Rockywold and Deephaven camps, along with the Undercut Trail (sign), which has another entrance almost opposite the camp entrance. There is no parking at the trailhead; cars should be parked off the road before the gate 0.2 mi. farther east on Pinehurst Rd. In 0.1 mi., there is a crossroads, where the Ramsey Trail takes a sharp right and climbs steeply 600 ft. in 0.4 mi. more (0.7 mi. total, 40 min.) to a point just north of the summit cliffs, joining the Old Bridle Path. Left at the crossroads is the alternate route 0.1 mi. to Pinehurst Rd.; the Undercut Trail continues straight ahead from the crossroads and runs 0.9 mi. (follow markings very carefully) to NH 113 0.1 mi. west of the Old Bridle Path parking area.

Pasture Trail. This trail leads to West Rattlesnake from Pinehurst Rd. (which begins on NH 113 0.5 mi. west of the Mt. Morgan/Rattlesnake parking area) 0.9 mi. from NH 113. Park in the small area to the right before the first gate just past the junction with Bacon Rd. The trailhead (sign) is on the left 100 yd. past the gate. Start on a road to the left, then after 25 yd. turn right onto a footpath past Pinehurst Farm buildings. At 0.2 mi., the East Rattlesnake and Five Finger Point trails diverge right, and in 15 yd. the Pasture Trail bears left where the Col Trail continues straight ahead. The cliffs are reached at 0.6 mi. from the gate after a moderate ascent of 600 ft. (35 min.). Descending, the Pasture Trail leaves the east side of the lower (southern) of the two levels of ledge atop the cliffs.

Col Trail. This trail continues straight where the Pasture Trail bears left 0.2 mi. from the gate on Pinehurst Rd. Col Trail ascends moderately for 350 ft. in 0.3 mi. (20 min.) to the Ridge Trail, which follows it to the right for 30 yd. then diverges left. It passes over the height-of-land and descends about 250 ft. (follow with care) to the edge of a beaver swamp. It enters an old road and turns left, then bears right and reaches a woods road

0.7 mi. from the Ridge Trail junction. The trailhead on NH 113 is reached in another 0.2 mi. at a point 0.3 mi. east of the Holderness-Sandwich town line. To start from this trailhead, park near the highway and continue on foot on the woods road, continuing straight ahead (yellow blazes) at a fork where the better road bears right.

Ridge Trail. This trail connects West and East Rattlesnake. It begins just northeast of the cliffs of West Rattlesnake and descends gradually 250 ft. to a saddle at 0.4 mi., where the Col Trail comes in from the right and just beyond leaves again to the left. The Ridge Trail ascends, and the East Rattlesnake Trail enters right at 0.8 mi. The Ridge Trail reaches the ledge that overlooks Squam Lake at 0.9 mi. and continues to the summit and the Butterworth Trail at 1.0 mi. with a total ascent from the saddle of 300 ft.

East Rattlesnake Trail. This trail branches right from the Pasture Trail 0.2 mi. from the gate. In 25 yd., the Five Finger Point Trail continues straight ahead. The East Rattlesnake Trail turns left and ascends steadily 500 ft. in 0.4 mi. (0.6 mi. total, 35 min.) to the Ridge Trail, 0.1 mi. west of the East Rattlesnake outlook.

Five Finger Point Trail. This trail leaves the East Rattlesnake Trail and runs on a slight downgrade for 0.7 mi. to a loop path 1.3 mi. long that circles around the edge of Five Finger Point, with several interesting viewpoints and attractive small beaches where swimming is permitted (no lifeguards).

Butterworth Trail. This trail leads to East Rattlesnake from Metcalf Rd., which leaves NH 113 0.7 mi. east of the Holderness-Sandwich town line. The trail leaves Metcalf Rd. on the right, 0.5 mi. from NH 113 (no parking at trailhead; parking is available on the right 100 yd. beyond the trailhead) and climbs moderately 700 ft. in 0.7 mi. to the summit. The East Rattlesnake viewpoint is 0.1 mi. farther via the Ridge Trail.

Rattlesnake Paths (map 3:L6)

Red Hill Trail (SLA)

This trail follows an old jeep road and provides a fairly easy route to the fire tower on Red Hill, where there are fine views from the tower and some good outlooks from the summit ledges. In Center Harbor at the junction of NH 25 and NH 25B, go northwest on Bean Rd. for 1.4 mi., turn right (east) and follow Sibley Rd. (sign for fire lookout) for 1.1 mi., then turn left and continue 0.1 mi. to a new parking area on the right with a Lakes Region Conservation Trust (LRCT) kiosk (sign for fire lookout). The trail ascends on an eroded road, and at 0.1 mi. makes a right turn onto an older road, ascending steadily and crossing a brook on a bridge. At 0.3 mi., another old road joins from the right (bear right here on the descent). At 0.4 mi., the trail passes through a fence, joins the newer road for 20 yd., then turns left off it at an LRCT kiosk. Here it passes a cellar hole on the left, skirts a chain gate, and joins the old fire warden's road for a moderate, winding ascent to the summit. At 1.0 mi., there is a piped spring left. The Eagle Cliff Trail enters on the left just before the fire tower and fire warden's cabin on the summit of Red Hill.

Red Hill Trail (USGS Center Sandwich and Center Harbor quads)

Distance from parking area (680 ft.) to
- Red Hill summit (2,030 ft.): 1.7 mi., 1,350 ft., 1 hr. 30 min.

Eagle Cliff Trail (SLA)

This trail ascends Red Hill via Eagle Cliff, providing fine views. However, the part of this path that ascends to the best viewpoints is steep and rocky, much more difficult than the Red Hill Trail (though the upper part of this trail is fairly similar in difficulty), and may be hazardous in wet or icy conditions. A bypass path—recommended in adverse conditions, particularly for the descent—has been cut to avoid the most difficult and dangerous section. The Teedie Trail is also available as an alternative descent route in hazardous conditions. From the junction of NH 25 and NH 25B in Center Harbor, follow Bean Rd. for 5.2 mi. to a turnout at the edge of Squam Lake, about 0.4 mi. north of the Moultonborough-Sandwich town line. The trail (sign) leaves the highway on the opposite side, 200 yd. south of the turnout; limited parking may be available at the trailhead.

The trail begins by crossing a ditch in a thicket, then climbs through an overgrown field and enters more mature woods, ascending on a well-beaten path. At 0.5 mi., a newly cut bypass trail leaves on the right; it is about 0.1 mi. longer than the main trail, which becomes steep and rough with several rocky scrambles as it gets well up on the ledge. The bypass trail rejoins the main trail just below the best viewpoint on Eagle Cliff at 0.6 mi. From the upper ledge, the trail enters the woods and climbs over two knolls, then descends sharply to a small pass at 1.0 mi., where the Teedie Trail enters right.

Teedie Trail. This path descends by switchbacks in 0.7 mi. to a gravel driveway next to a private tennis court on Bean Rd. at the Moultonborough-Sandwich town line, about 0.4 mi. south of the beginning of the Eagle Cliff Trail. The trailhead (no parking here) is marked by a sign at the back edge of a small field, where the trail enters the woods. It is much less scenic than the Eagle Cliff Trail and, though it may not be well cleared and may take some care to follow, it should be considered as a way of avoiding the descent over the Eagle Cliff ledges in adverse conditions.

The Eagle Cliff Trail crosses another knoll and ascends steadily through a mixture of young growth in cutover areas and mature woods, and about a quarter mile below the summit it enters an area burned over by a fire set by an arsonist in April 1990. It finally levels out and meets the Red Hill Trail just below the summit of Red Hill. Descending, it diverges right from the Red Hill Trail (jeep road) just below the fire warden's cabin (sign).

Eagle Cliff Trail (map 3:L7/USGS Center Sandwich quad)

Distances from Bean Rd. (580 ft.) to
- Eagle Cliff viewpoint (1,270 ft.): 0.6 mi., 700 ft., 40 min.
- Red Hill fire tower (2,030 ft.): 2.7 mi., 1,650 ft. (rev. 200 ft.), 2 hr. 10 min.

SUGGESTED HIKES

For more information on suggested hikes, see p. ix.

Easy Hikes

West Rattlesnake [rt: 1.8 mi., 450 ft., 1:05]. The very popular Old Bridle Path provides an easy climb to ledges with beautiful views over Squam Lake. A good alternative to this busy route is the Pasture Trail [rt: 1.2 mi., 600 ft., 0:55].

Sabbaday Falls [rt: 0.6 mi., 100 ft., 0:20]. A gentle stroll up the graded lower part of Sabbaday Brook Trail and a side trail to an unusual waterfall.

Red Hill [rt: 3.4 mi, 1,350 ft., 2:20]. The Red Hill Trail follows an old jeep road to a tower with wide views of the Lakes Region.

Greeley Ponds [rt: 4.4 mi, 450 ft., 2:25]. The Greeley Ponds Trail from the Kancamagus Highway offers relatively easy access to these two remote ponds in beautiful Mad River Notch.

Moderate Hikes

East Ponds Loop [lp: 5.0 mi., 1,000 ft., 3:00]. A pleasant loop to two high mountain ponds via the East Pond Trail, Little East Pond Trail, and East Pond Loop.

Mt. Percival and Mt. Morgan [lp: 5.4 mi., 1,550 ft., 3:30]. This loop hike via the Mt. Percival Trail, Crawford-Ridgepole Trail, Mt. Morgan Trail, and Morgan-Percival Connector offers exceptional views for the effort required.

Mt. Israel. Located south of the main peaks of the Sandwich Range, this summit offers an impressive view of its higher neighbors. The most direct ascent is via the Wentworth Trail [rt: 4.2 mi., 1,700 ft., 2:55]; for a longer, more varied route ascend by the Guinea Pond and Mead trails. [rt: 6.6 mi., 1,300 ft., 3:55]. A particularly fine loop with a great variety of scenery—a ledgy summit, open swamps, interesting rock formations along a brook, and a walk on an historic road through long-abandoned farmland—can be made from Mead Base, the Sandwich Town Park, or the Guinea Pond Trail parking area via the Wentworth Trail, Mead Trail, Guinea Pond Trail, Sandwich Notch Rd., and the Bearcamp River Trail segment from Sandwich Notch Rd. to Mead Base (see Wentworth Trail). [lp: 8.5 mi., 1,850 ft., 5:10].

Welch and Dickey Mountains [lp: 4.4 mi., 1,800 ft., 3:05]. This loop offers a great deal of open ledge walking and is one of the finest half-day walks in the White Mountains, over fairly rugged terrain with excellent views for an unusually large portion of the way. The ledges are slippery when wet.

Mt. Osceola [rt: 6.4 mi., 2,050 ft., 4:15]. This high peak, with fine views, can be ascended fairly easily from the high point on Tripoli Rd., though the footing is rocky in the first mile. Hikers should be aware that the trail to Osceola from Greeley Ponds Trail is one of the steepest and roughest in the mountains.

Local Waterville Valley Trails. A variety of interesting objectives can be accessed via the fine network of trails in Waterville Valley. Among these are The Cascades via the Cascade Path [rt: 3.4 mi., 700 ft., 2:05], the Waterville Flume via the Livermore, Greeley Ponds, and Flume Brook trails [rt: 5.6 mi., 900 ft., 3:15], the ledgy outlook known as the Scaur via Livermore Trail, Kettles Path, and Scaur Trail [rt: 4.0 mi., 650 ft., 2:20] and two viewpoints in the upper valley of Greeley Brook via the Livermore, Greeley Ponds, and Timber Camp trails [rt: 5.8 mi., 1,000 ft., 3:25].

Flat Mountain Pond. This beautiful, remote pond in the Sandwich Range Wilderness can be accessed from the Bennett St. trailhead via the Flat Mountain Pond and Bennett St. trails [rt: 9.0 mi., 1,250 ft., 5:10] or from the Whiteface Intervale trailhead via the Flat Mountain Pond Trail [rt: 8.4 mi., 1,350 ft., 4:55]. Add 2.2 mi. round trip for a traverse along the western shore.

Strenuous Hikes

Jennings Peak Loop [lp: 6.5 mi., 2,150 ft., 4:20]. The fine views from this rocky spur of Sandwich Mountain can be enjoyed with a loop using the Sandwich Mountain and Drakes Brook trails. The partly open summit of Sandwich Mountain can also be included in this trip [lp: 8.7 mi., 2,850 ft., 5:45].

Sandwich Mountain via Algonquin Trail [rt: 9.0 mi., 2,750 ft., 5:55]. This is an extremely scenic route for a direct ascent of Sandwich from the south.

Tripyramid Slides Loop [lp: 11.0 mi., 3,000 ft., 7:00]. One of the most challenging and scenic trips in the Whites via the Livermore and Mt. Tripyramid trails. Steep slabs of the North Slide can be avoided (as when wet or icy) by using the Scaur Ridge Trail [lp: 12.1 mi., 3,000 ft., 7:35].

SECTION EIGHT

Mount Chocorua and the Eastern Sandwich Range

3

This section covers trails on Mts. Chocorua, Paugus, Passaconaway, and Whiteface, and on their subsidiary peaks and ridges. The region is bounded on the north by the Kancamagus Highway (NH 112), on the east by NH 16, on the south by NH 25, and on the west by Section Seven (Waterville Valley and Squam Lakes Region). This division places Mt. Tripyramid in Section Seven and Mt. Whiteface and the Sleeper Ridge in Section Eight. At the boundary between Sections Seven and Eight, the only points of contact between trails are at the junction of the Mt. Tripyramid Trail (Section Seven) with the Kate Sleeper Trail (Section Eight), and at the junction of the Flat Mountain Pond Trail (Section Seven) with the McCrillis Trail (Section Eight). The entire section is covered by the AMC's *Crawford Notch–Sandwich Range Map* (map 3). The Chocorua Mountain Club (CMC), Wonalancet Outdoor Club (WODC), and the WMNF maintain most of the trails in this area. The CMC marks its trails with yellow paint and signs, whereas the WODC trails have blue paint and signs; in the Sandwich Range Wilderness, most signs are unpainted wood and most paint blazing is being discontinued. The WODC publishes a contour map of the Sandwich Range Wilderness and the surrounding area, with short trail descriptions on the back, which covers most of Section Eight except for the east slopes of Mt. Chocorua; it can be obtained from the WODC. The CMC publishes a contour map of the Chocorua-Paugus region that includes a peak-identifying panorama of the view from the summit of Chocorua; it can be obtained from the CMC.

GEOGRAPHY

The Sandwich Range and the jumbled collection of ridges that rise to the west compose a mass of mountains that extend about 30 mi. from Conway on the Saco River to Campton on the Pemigewasset, with summits just over 4,000 ft. high rising abruptly about 3,000 ft. from the lake country to the south. Although the Sandwich Range is not outstanding for its elevation—the North Peak of Mt. Tripyramid, at 4,180 ft., is its highest point—the mountains are nevertheless quite rugged, and their viewpoints offer interesting combinations of mountain, forest, and lake scenery.

The picturesque rocky cone at the east end of the range, Mt. Chocorua (3,500 ft.), is reputedly one of the most frequently photographed mountains in the world—and certainly one of the most frequently ascended peaks in the White Mountains. It has a substantial network of trails; several trails are very heavily used, but it is usually possible to avoid crowds (until the summit is reached) by taking less popular trails. The Piper Trail, Champney Falls Trail, and Liberty Trail are probably the most popular. Confusion sometimes occurs from the fact that several trails are considered to extend all the way to the summit, although they converge below the summit, which is reached by only one path. Thus, a given segment of trail may bear several names at once—at least according to trail signs—although in this guide one trail is usually considered to end where two merge, and only two trails (the Piper Trail and the Brook Trail) are described as reaching the summit. In descending from the summit, go 50 yd. southwest on the only marked path, down a small gully to the first junction. The trails on the open rocks are marked with paint, and junctions are signed with WMNF signs or paint, or both. Camping on the upper slopes of Chocorua—a Forest Protection Area—is severely restricted to prevent damage to the mountain's natural qualities.

Caution: The extensive areas of open ledge that make Chocorua so attractive also pose a very real danger. Many of the trails have sections with many ledges that are dangerous when wet or icy, and the summit and upper ledges are severely exposed to lightning during electrical storms. Despite its comparatively modest elevation, Chocorua is one of the most dangerous peaks in the White Mountains in a thunderstorm. Although Chocorua is relatively low compared to other major White Mountain peaks, its trailheads are also located at low elevations, resulting in a substantial amount of elevation gain that makes Chocorua as strenuous a trip as many much higher peaks. The safety of any untreated water source in this heavily used area is very doubtful.

Three Sisters, which forms the northern ridge of Mt. Chocorua, is nearly as tall and has bare summits. First Sister (3,354 ft.) is the tallest of the three rocky knobs, and Middle Sister (3,340 ft.) bears the remains of an old stone fire tower. Carter Ledge (2,420 ft.) is a prominent ledgy spur just east of the Three Sisters. White Ledge (2,010 ft.) is a bluff farther east of the Three Sisters, with a ledgy top from which there is a good view east. The rocky south shoulder of Chocorua is called Bald Mountain (2,140 ft.). On the northwest side of the mountain is Champney Falls, named for Benjamin Champney (1817–1907), pioneer White Mountain artist. These falls are beautiful when there is a good flow of water but meager in dry seasons.

A low but rugged and shaggy mountain once aptly called "Old Shag," Mt. Paugus (3,198 ft.), was named by Lucy Larcom for the Pequawket chief who led the Abenaki forces at the battle of Lovewell's Pond. Because of its lumpy shape and scarred sides it has been given many different names; it may hold the record for having had the most different names—both common and unusual—of any peak in the White Mountains, including Bald Mountain, Moose Mountain, Ragged Mountain, Deer Mountain, Hunchback, Middle Mountain, and Frog Mountain. All trails end at an overgrown ledge 0.3 mi. south of the wooded true summit, which is not reached by any trail; good views can be obtained by descending a short distance down the west side of this ledge. Paugus Pass (2,220 ft.) is the lowest pass on the ridge that connects Mt. Paugus with Mt. Passaconaway and the Wonalancet Range on the west.

A graceful peak, Mt. Passaconaway (4,043 ft.) was named for the great and legendary sachem of the Penacooks (his name is thought to mean "child of the bear") who ruled at the time the first Europeans settled in New England. The mountain is densely wooded, with no view from the true summit, but a ledge on the Walden Trail a short distance from the summit offers a fine outlook to the east and north, and a ledge near the top of Dicey's Mill Trail offers a view to the northwest. Another outlook on the Walden Trail offers a fine view south. A side path diverges from the Walden Trail between the summit and the east outlook and descends 0.3 mi. to the splendid, secluded north outlook. A major ridge extends southeast to Paugus Pass over the two subpeaks that give the mountain its characteristic steplike profile when viewed from the lake country to the south. The first subpeak bears the unofficial name of Nanamocomuck Peak (3,340 ft.) after the eldest son of Passaconaway. Square Ledge (2,620 ft.) is a bold, rocky promontory that is a northeast spur of Nanamocomuck Peak. From the farther subpeak, which is sometimes called Mt. Hedgehog (3,140 ft.), the Wonalancet Range runs south, consisting of Hibbard Mountain (2,940 ft.) and Mt. Wonalancet (2,780 ft.); both peaks are wooded but have good outlook ledges. Wonalancet is named for a Penacook sachem who was a son of Passaconaway and succeeded him as senior chieftain.

Another Hedgehog Mountain (2,532 ft.) is located north of Mt. Passaconaway. This small but rugged mountain rises between Downes and Oliverian brooks and commands fine views over the Swift River Valley and up to Passaconaway; the best views are from ledges near the summit and on the east shoulder. Potash Mountain (2,700 ft.) lies to the west of Hedgehog, between Downes and Sabbaday brooks. The summit is open and ledgy and affords excellent views of the surrounding mountains and valleys in all directions.

The precipitous ledges south of its south summit doubtless gave Mt. Whiteface (4,020 ft.) its name. The true summit of the mountain is wooded, but the slightly lower south summit, 0.3 mi. south of the true summit, affords magnificent views from the bare ledge at the top of the precipices. Two lesser ridges run south on either side of the cliffs, while the backbone of the mountain runs north, then northeast, connecting it with Mt. Passaconaway. Sleeper Ridge on the northwest connects Whiteface to Mt. Tripyramid.

East of Mt. Whiteface lies the Bowl, a secluded valley of glacial origin encircled by the main ridge of Mt. Whiteface and the south ridge of Mt. Passaconaway. This area was never logged because of the efforts of many local people. The representative of the Kennett lumber interests in negotiating the sale of this land to the WMNF in a virgin state was Louis Tainter, whose ashes rest in a crypt cut into the ledge at the south summit of Mt. Whiteface. The Bowl was preserved for many decades as a special natural and research area and is now included within the Sandwich Range Wilderness.

West of Whiteface the range sprawls; one major ridge continues northwest over the high, rolling Sleeper Ridge—composed of West Sleeper (3,881 ft.) and East Sleeper (3,840 ft.)—to Tripyramid, then ends at Livermore Pass, the high notch (2,900 ft.) between Tripyramid and Mt. Kancamagus that is crossed by the Livermore Trail. Though Sleeper Ridge could have been named quite aptly for the sleepy appearance of its two rounded, rather gently sloping domes, it is actually named for Katherine Sleeper Walden, a civic-minded local innkeeper whose efforts in trail building (she founded the WODC), conservation, and public improvements were so energetic and pervasive that she earned the sobriquet of "matriarch of Wonalancet and the WODC." Walden was very active in preventing the Bowl from being logged. Two natural features (Sleeper Ridge and Mt. Katherine) and a trail (the Kate Sleeper Trail) have been named after her while the Walden Trail memorializes her husband, Arthur Walden, founder of the famous Chinook husky kennels in Wonalancet. West of the high Livermore Pass lies the mountain mass composed of peaks such as Kancamagus, Osceola, Scar Ridge, and Tecumseh; these have not been traditionally regarded as part of the Sandwich Range, although connected with it. Another major ridge runs southwest over Sandwich Dome and soon loses its definition as it descends across the Sandwich Notch Rd. to the Campton mountains and toward the Squam Range. Everything west of the Tripyramid–Sleeper Ridge col is covered in Section Seven.

Several public and quasi-public reservations in this region offer the opportunity for pleasant walking; some have trails. Of particular note is Hemenway State Forest, where fine views of the Sandwich Range can be obtained from the fire tower on Great Hill (1,300 ft.), which is reached in about 0.5 mi. by old roads that leave Great Hill Rd. at its junction with Hemenway Rd. On the northeast side of Hemenway State Forest is the Big Pines Natural Area; several trails reach this area from a trailhead on NH 113A, with a connecting path leading to Great Hill. Another network of trails is maintained in the Chocorua Conservation Lands south of Mt. Chocorua. This area, managed by the Chocorua Lake Conservation Foundation, contains several attractive natural features including Heron Pond (Lonely Lake), a glacial kettle pond. Access is from the Hammond Trail parking area on the north and from small parking areas on Fowler's Mill Rd. and Bolles Rd. on the south. There is also a network of short trails in this area maintained by the Tamworth Outing Club; most of these trails are multiuse, primarily maintained for cross-country skiing. The area can be reached from Tamworth village at the eastern junction of NH 113 and NH 113A by taking the road that leads west from the crossroads and bearing right (northwest) onto Great Hill Rd. At White Lake State Park, on the west side of NH 16 just north of West Ossipee, there is a 2-mi. trail around the lake and a branch loop that passes through the Pitch Pine National Natural Landmark.

Note: Confusion in finding trailheads on the southern side of the Sandwich Range sometimes results from the rather erratic behavior of NH 113 and NH 113A, the alternate routes between North Sandwich and Tamworth. Both roads change direction frequently, making directional designations almost meaningless, and NH 113 unites with and then diverges from NH 25 between its two junctions with NH 113A. It is therefore necessary to follow very carefully access directions for trailheads on the southeast slopes of the Sandwich Range—in particular, it is easy to end up on the wrong section of NH 113.

Whiteface Intervale Rd. leaves NH 113A about 3.0 mi. north of the western junction of NH 113 and NH 113A, where NH 113A bends from north–south to east–west. Bennett St. turns left from Whiteface Intervale Rd. 0.1 mi. from NH 113A, and continues straight past a junction at 1.7 mi., where it becomes rougher; it is gated at 2.2 mi. at a parking lot 0.2 mi. east of Jose's (rhymes with "doses") bridge.

Ferncroft Rd. leaves NH 113A at Wonalancet village, at a right-angle turn in the main highway; at 0.5 mi. from NH 113A, a gravel road (FR 337) turns right and reaches a parking area and kiosk in 0.1 mi. No parking is permitted on Ferncroft Rd. beyond this gravel road.

Fowler's Mill Rd. runs between NH 16 (at the bridge that crosses the south end of Chocorua Lake, about 1.5 mi. north of Chocorua village, where it is signed Chocorua Lake Rd.) and NH 113A (3.3 mi. north of the eastern junction of NH 113 and NH 113A in Tamworth, and just north of the bridge over Paugus Brook). Paugus Rd. (FR 68) branches north (sign) from Fowler's Mill Rd. 1.2 mi. east of NH 113A, and runs to a parking area at 0.8 mi., beyond which the road is closed to vehicles.

CAMPING

Sandwich Range Wilderness

The Sandwich Range Wilderness includes 35,000 acres on and around the principal peaks of the range, with 10,000 acres added in 2006. Wilderness regulations, intended to protect Wilderness resources and promote opportunities for challenge and solitude, prohibit use of motorized equipment or mechanical means of transportation of any sort. In accordance with USFS Wilderness policy, the trails in the Sandwich Range Wilderness are in general maintained to a lower standard than trails outside Wilderness. They may be rough, overgrown, or essentially unmarked with minimal signage, and considerable care may be required to follow them. Hiking and camping group size must be no larger than 10 people. Camping and fires are also prohibited above the treeline (where trees are less than 8 ft. tall) except in winter, when camping is permitted above the treeline in places where snow cover is at least 2 ft. deep, but not on any frozen body of water. Many shelters have been removed, and the remaining ones will be dismantled when major maintenance is required; one should not count on using any of these shelters.

Forest Protection Areas

The WMNF has established a number of Forest Protection Areas (FPAs)—formerly known as Restricted Use Areas—where camping and wood or charcoal fires are prohibited throughout the year. The specific areas are under continual review, and areas are added to or subtracted from the list to provide the greatest amount of protection to areas subject to damage by excessive camping, while imposing the lowest level of restrictions possible. A general list of FPAs in this section follows, but because there are often major changes from year to year, one should obtain current information on FPAs from the WMNF.

(1) No camping is permitted above treeline (where trees are less than 8 ft. tall), except in winter, and then only in places where there is at least 2 ft. of snow cover on the ground—but not on any frozen body of water. The point where the above-treeline restricted area begins is marked on most trails with small signs, but the absence of such signs should not be construed as proof of the legality of a site.

(2) No camping is permitted within 0.25 mi. of any trailhead, picnic area, or any facility for overnight accommodation such as a hut, cabin, shelter, tentsite, or campground, except as designated at the facility itself. In the area covered by Section Eight, camping is also forbidden within 0.25 mi. of Champney Falls and at any point within the Mt. Chocorua Scenic Area, except at Jim Liberty Cabin (overnight use allowed inside the cabin only) and Camp Penacook.

(3) No camping is permitted within 200 ft. of certain trails. In 2006, designated trails included the Champney Falls Trail from the edge of the Kancamagus Highway FPA to the edge of the Champney Falls FPA.

(4) No camping is permitted on WMNF land within 0.25 mi. of certain roads (camping on private roadside land is illegal except by permission of the landowner). In 2006, these roads included the Kancamagus Highway.

Established Trailside Campsites

Camp Penacook (WMNF), located on a spur path off the Piper Trail on Mt. Chocorua, is an open shelter that accommodates six to eight, with a tent platform that also accommodates six to eight. There is water nearby in a small stream.

Jim Liberty Cabin (WMNF) is located on a ledgy hump 0.5 mi. below the summit of Mt. Chocorua. Overnight use is allowed only inside the cabin, and fires are not allowed. The water source is scanty in dry weather.

Camp Rich (WODC), formerly located on the southwest side of Mt. Passaconaway on the Dicey's Mill Trail at about 3,500 ft. elevation, has been removed. The latrine at the site has been retained.

Camp Shehadi (WODC), at the junction of the Rollins and Kate Sleeper trails, 0.1 mi. north of the south summit of Mt. Whiteface, has been removed. Camping at the site (which has no convenient water source) is discouraged.

Camp Heermance (WODC), near the south summit of Mt. Whiteface, has been removed. Camping at the site (which has no convenient water source) is discouraged.

TRAIL DESCRIPTIONS

Champney Falls Trail (WMNF)

This heavily used trail runs from the Kancamagus Highway, at a point 11.5 mi. from NH 16 in Conway, to the Piper Trail in the flat saddle between Chocorua and the Three Sisters. Champney Falls is attractive, particularly when there is a good flow of water, and the trail has moderate grades all the way.

Leaving the parking area, the trail soon crosses Twin Brook on a footbridge, turns right, passes the junction at 0.1 mi., where the Bolles Trail diverges right, and proceeds south with easy grades, mostly on an old logging road, to Champney Brook. There it swings right to avoid an abandoned section of trail along the brook, then descends left and returns to the old road along the brook. At 1.4 mi., a loop path 0.4 mi. long diverges left to Pitcher Falls and Champney Falls, climbing steeply near the falls. *Caution:* Many of the ledges in the area around the falls are very slippery; there have been many serious accidents in this vicinity. The main trail passes a restricted outlook to the north, and the loop path rejoins it at 1.7 mi. The steady ascent continues. At 2.4 mi., the trail passes a good outlook to the north and reaches the first of several switchbacks, and at 3.0 mi., the Champney Falls Cutoff diverges left toward Middle Sister.

Champney Falls Cutoff (WMNF). This short trail—which has also been signed as the Middle Sister Cutoff in the past—leads from the Champney Falls Trail to the col between Middle Sister and First Sister, giving access to the fine views from the old tower site on Middle Sister. Leaving the Champney Falls Trail, it follows an old road past an outlook ledge, then swings to the right onto open ledges and soon reaches the Middle Sister Trail; total distance: 0.3 mi. (15 min.).

Soon after this junction, the Champney Falls Trail reaches the ledgy saddle—where there is an outlook on a side path to the right—then passes the junction on the left with the Middle Sister Trail, and in another 80 yd., ends at its junction with the Piper Trail, 0.6 mi. from the summit of Chocorua.

Champney Falls Trail (map 3:J9)

Distances from Kancamagus Highway (1,260 ft.) to

- Champney Falls loop, lower end (1,780 ft.): 1.4 mi., 500 ft., 55 min.
- Piper Trail (3,200 ft.): 3.2 mi., 1,950 ft., 2 hr. 35 min.
- Mt. Chocorua summit (3,500 ft.) via Piper Trail: 3.8 mi., 2,250 ft., 3 hr.

White Ledge Loop Trail (WMNF)

This loop trail to White Ledge has two entrance routes. The main access route is from White Ledge Campground; parking is available near the restrooms. The alternative access route (sign) leaves NH 16 opposite Pine Knoll Campground, about 0.5 mi. northeast of White Ledge Campground, and follows an old town road 0.5 mi. to the east branch of the trail, reaching it at a point 0.6 mi. from the campground; parking is available on the shoulder across the highway just north of the trail sign.

The main trail diverges right from the main campground road and reaches the loop junction at 0.3 mi. The loop is described here in a counterclockwise direction. Taking the east branch to the right across a small brook, the trail turns left and then right and runs past the junction with the alternative access route at 0.6 mi., then soon bears left and climbs steadily to the height-of-land east of the main bluff of White Ledge at 1.3 mi. The trail now descends gradually through a brushy logged area, and at 2.0 mi., it turns left near a clear-cut and climbs moderately up the east end of White Ledge, crossing ledges with outlooks to the north. It reaches the summit at 2.7 mi., where there is a restricted view east; a better view east is reached by an obscure side path that leaves the main trail 60 yd. north of the high point. The trail descends past an outlook to Mt. Chocorua, continues steadily down past an unmarked side path left to a fine southeast outlook, then turns sharp left at 3.7 mi. and reaches the loop junction at 4.1 mi.

White Ledge Loop Trail (map 3:J10)

Distances from White Ledge Campground (740 ft.)
- to loop junction (800 ft.): 0.3 mi., 50 ft., 10 min.
- to White Ledge summit (2,010 ft.) via east branch: 2.7 mi., 1,450 ft., 2 hr. 5 min.
- to White Ledge summit (2,010 ft.) via west branch: 1.7 mi., 1,300 ft., 1 hr. 30 min.
- for complete loop: 4.4 mi., 1,450 ft., 2 hr. 55 min.

Carter Ledge Trail (WMNF)

This trail provides an attractive route to Middle Sister from White Ledge Campground or (via Nickerson Ledge Trail) from the Piper Trail. Carter Ledge, an interesting objective in its own right, is a fine open ledge with views of Chocorua and one of only a few colonies of jack pine *(Pinus banksiana)* that exist in the White Mountains. The trailhead is located on the left branch of the campground road; park in the parking lot at the campground picnic area.

The trail diverges west from the left branch road 0.1 mi. south of the main fork. It climbs moderately to the long southeast ridge of Carter Ledge, passing the junction at 1.0 mi., where the Middle Sister Trail diverges to the right. The Carter Ledge Trail then continues to the junction with the Nickerson Ledge Trail, which enters on the left at 2.0 mi. After a short descent, the Carter Ledge Trail ascends a steep, gravelly slope with poor footing and turns right at an outlook to Mt. Chocorua. Continuing to climb steeply with many fine views from the ledges, the trail passes through the jack pine stand and reaches the summit of the ledge at 2.8 mi., where there is a good view north a few steps to the right of the trail. It passes through a sag, then works its way up the ledgy slope of Third Sister—steeply at times, with several outlooks and ledges that can be dangerous in wet or icy conditions, one of them a particularly tricky scramble on a potentially slippery, downward sloping ledge—and reaches the Middle Sister Trail 0.3 mi. northeast of Middle Sister.

Carter Ledge Trail (map 3:J10–J9)

Distances from White Ledge Campground (740 ft.) to

- Middle Sister Trail, lower junction (1,350 ft.): 1.0 mi., 600 ft., 50 min.
- Nickerson Ledge Trail (1,740 ft.): 2.0 mi., 1,000 ft., 1 hr. 30 min.
- Carter Ledge (2,420 ft.): 2.8 mi., 1,700 ft., 2 hr. 5 min.
- Middle Sister Trail, upper junction (3,150 ft.): 3.7 mi., 2,500 ft. (rev. 100 ft.), 3 hr. 5 min.

Middle Sister Trail (WMNF)

This trail begins on the Carter Ledge Trail 1.1 mi. from the WMNF White Ledge Campground, climbs over the Three Sisters, and ends at the Champney Falls Trail in the saddle between the Sisters and Chocorua. It provides good views.

Leaving the Carter Ledge Trail, this trail ascends gradually with occasional minor descents through mixed hardwoods and softwoods and crosses Hobbs Brook at 1.3 mi., then skirts an area severely damaged by the December 1980 windstorm. At 1.8 mi., it joins the former route of the trail and climbs more steeply to the col between the Three Sisters ridge and Blue Mountain at 2.4 mi., where the trail turns sharp left and ascends steadily along the northeast spur of the Third Sister, passing a good outlook north. At 3.3 mi., the Carter Ledge Trail enters on the left, and the Middle Sister Trail climbs steeply, with several ledge scrambles, crosses the ledgy summit of Third Sister and a small dip beyond, then reaches the summit of the Middle Sister at 3.6 mi. The trail descends across ledges marked by paint, passes the Champney Falls Cutoff (right), and climbs over the open ledges of First Sister to its terminus on the Champney Falls Trail. From here, it is 80 yd. (left) to the Piper Trail, then 0.6 mi. to the summit of Mt. Chocorua.

Middle Sister Trail (map 3:J10–J9)

Distances from Carter Ledge Trail (1,350 ft.) to

- Middle Sister summit (3,340 ft.): 3.6 mi., 2,000 ft., 2 hr. 50 min.
- Champney Falls Trail (3,200 ft.): 4.1 mi., 2,150 ft. (rev. 300 ft.), 3 hr. 10 min.

Piper Trail (WMNF)

This heavily used trail to Chocorua from NH 16, first blazed by Joshua Piper, begins behind Davies Campground and General Store, which is located 6.1 mi. south of the east terminus of the Kancamagus Highway (NH 112). It is one of the most heavily used trails in the White Mountains. To reach the new trailhead parking area, drive in on the dirt road to the right of the store (signs) for 0.2 mi.

The trail enters the woods at a kiosk, swings right across a stream and follows it for 0.3 mi., then turns first sharp left, then right to join a woods road that is the old route of the trail. (The section of the old route leading back from here to NH 16 is not open to the public.) The Weetamoo Trail diverges left at 0.6 mi., and the Nickerson Ledge Trail diverges right at 1.2 mi. After crossing the Chocorua River (a small brook at this point) at 1.8 mi., the trail ascends moderately, then climbs up a series of switchbacks with stone steps and paving. At 2.8 mi., a spur path diverges left and climbs 0.2 mi. and 200 ft. to Camp Penacook (open shelter, tent platform, water, view southeast). The main trail turns sharp right at this junction and ascends, with more stone steps and paving, soon reaching open ledges with spectacular views to the north, east, and south. After ascending past several outlooks, it reenters the woods and climbs to the ridge crest, where the Champney Falls Trail enters right at 3.6 mi., and in another 0.2 mi., the West Side Trail (part of the original Liberty Trail bridle path) enters on the right. The Piper Trail soon emerges from the woods and, marked with yellow paint, continues south along the ridge over open ledges, with occasional scrambles. It swings right and climbs over a rocky knob, ascends to the junction with the Brook Trail, then swings left and climbs the rock gully to the summit.

Piper Trail (map 3:J10–J9)

Distances from new WMNF parking area off NH 16 (780 ft.) to

- Nickerson Ledge Trail (1,320 ft.): 1.2 mi., 550 ft., 55 min.
- Chocorua River crossing (1,540 ft.): 1.8 mi., 750 ft., 1 hr. 15 min.   ▶

- Camp Penacook spur trail (2,500 ft.): 2.8 mi., 1,700 ft., 2 hr. 15 min.
- Champney Falls Trail (3,200 ft.): 3.6 mi., 2,400 ft., 3 hr.
- Mt. Chocorua summit (3,500 ft.): 4.3 mi., 2,700 ft., 3 hr. 30 min.

Nickerson Ledge Trail (WMNF)

This trail connects the Piper Trail with the Carter Ledge Trail and Middle Sister, making possible loop hikes that include the attractive ledges on the northeast part of the mountain. It leaves the Piper Trail 1.2 mi. from the parking lot off NH 16 and climbs rather steeply 0.2 mi. to Nickerson Ledge, which has a view south to the Ossipee Range, then continues along a broad ridge with a gradual ascent to the Carter Ledge Trail 2.0 mi. above White Ledge Campground.

Nickerson Ledge Trail (map 3:J10)

Distance from Piper Trail (1,320 ft.) to
- Carter Ledge Trail (1,740 ft.): 0.8 mi., 400 ft., 35 min.

Weetamoo Trail (CMC)

This attractive trail with moderate grades connects the lower part of the Piper Trail, 0.6 mi. from the parking lot off NH 16, with the Hammond Trail well up on Bald Mountain, and gives access to the open ledges of the south ridge of Chocorua from the Piper Trail.

The trail diverges left from the Piper Trail, ascends easily, and crosses the Chocorua River in a fine hemlock grove at 0.4 mi. It turns right and follows the river and then a tributary upstream, then swings left and climbs a long switchback. It ascends through young hardwood growth, enters spruce woods and passes a restricted outlook to Chocorua, then turns sharp left at 1.4 mi., and reaches Weetamoo Rock, an immense boulder, at 1.7 mi. The trail ends at the Hammond Trail, 2.0 mi. from the summit of Mt. Chocorua via the Hammond Trail, the Liberty Trail, and the Brook Trail.

Weetamoo Trail (map 3:J10–J9)

Distance from Piper Trail (960 ft.) to
- Hammond Trail (2,200 ft.): 1.9 mi., 1,250 ft., 1 hr. 35 min.

Hammond Trail (CMC)

This trail provides a route up Bald Mountain, the ledgy south shoulder of Mt. Chocorua. The trailhead is on Scott Rd., a dirt road (not plowed in winter) that leaves NH 16 on the left (west) directly opposite a large boulder, 3.0 mi. north of the junction with NH 113 in Chocorua village; parking is on the right 0.4 mi. from NH 16. Do not block access along Scott Rd.

The trail leaves the parking area, climbs over a small ridge, swings left and crosses Stony Brook, passes the WMNF boundary, then recrosses Stony Brook. At 0.8 mi., the trail crosses a logging road, then climbs steadily, passing a view to the southwest shortly before reaching the crest of Bald Mountain at 1.9 mi. It crosses a sag, then ascends along the ridge. At 2.1 mi., the Weetamoo Trail enters on the right, and the Hammond Trail ascends through fine spruce woods, crossing several ledgy humps and passing several outlooks to the right of the trail. From the last hump, where the summit of Mt. Chocorua is in sight ahead, the trail descends, then rises slightly to its end at the junction with the Liberty Trail, 1.1 mi. from the summit of Mt. Chocorua via the Liberty Trail and the Brook Trail.

Hammond Trail (map 3:J10–J9)

Distances from parking area on Scott Rd. (600 ft.) to

- Bald Mountain (2,140 ft.): 1.9 mi., 1,550 ft., 1 hr. 45 min.
- Liberty Trail (2,540 ft.): 3.0 mi., 2,000 ft. (rev. 50 ft.), 2 hr. 30 min.

Liberty Trail (WMNF)

This is the easiest route to Chocorua from the southwest (and probably the easiest of all the routes on the mountain), though there are some steep ledges in its upper part that are potentially dangerous if wet or icy. It begins at the parking area just before the gate on Paugus Rd. (FR 68). This is a very old path that was improved somewhat by James Liberty in 1887, and further developed as a toll bridle path by David Knowles and Newell Forrest in 1892. Knowles built the two-story Peak House in 1892, which was blown down in September 1915. The stone stable was rebuilt by the CMC in 1924 and named the Jim Liberty Shelter. This lasted until 1932, when spring winds blew off the roof, and in 1934, the WMNF replaced it with an enclosed cabin with bunks. Overnight use is allowed only inside the cabin, and fires are not allowed.

The Liberty Trail follows a gated side road that branches right just before the gate on the main road (which continues to the Bolles and Brook trails), and ascends at a steady, moderate grade, mostly along the route of the former bridle path. It descends slightly to cross Durrell Brook at 1.1 mi., then the moderate climb resumes and at 2.7 mi., it reaches the ridge top, where the Hammond Trail enters right. The Liberty Trail climbs a hump, passing a ledge on the left with a view west, descends into the sag beyond, then climbs past an outlook ledge on the right to Jim Liberty Cabin at 3.3 mi., where a side path on the right (sign) descends 0.1 mi. to a mediocre water source and a nearby ledge with a view east. The Liberty Trail swings to the left (west) at the foot of a ledge and follows the old bridle path, which was blasted out of the rock in many places. It circles around the southwest side of the cone, ascending moderately with some ledge scrambling (use caution if wet or icy), passing two outlooks to the south, and meets the Brook Trail on a ledge at 3.6 mi. The summit of Mt. Chocorua is 0.2 mi. farther via the Brook Trail; it can be avoided during bad weather by following the West Side Trail, which diverges to the left 35 yd. beyond the Brook Trail junction and runs north around the west side of the summit cone to the Piper Trail.

Liberty Trail (map 3:K9–J9)

Distances from Paugus Rd. parking area (900 ft.) to

- Hammond Trail (2,540 ft.): 2.7 mi., 1,700 ft. (rev. 50 ft.), 2 hr. 10 min.
- Jim Liberty Cabin (2,980 ft.): 3.3 mi., 2,200 ft. (rev. 50 ft.), 2 hr. 45 min.
- Brook Trail (3,200 ft.): 3.6 mi., 2,400 ft., 3 hr.
- Mt. Chocorua summit (3,500 ft.) via Brook Trail: 3.9 mi., 2,700 ft., 3 hr. 20 min.

West Side Trail (WMNF)

This trail runs from the Piper Trail 0.4 mi. north of the summit of Chocorua to the ledge where the Liberty and Brook trails join. It has easy grades and is well sheltered, and affords a route for avoiding the summit rocks in bad weather. It leaves the Piper Trail in a flat wooded area north of the summit and circles the west side of the cone to the Brook Trail, 35 yd. above its junction with the Liberty Trail.

West Side Trail (map 3:J9)

Distance from Piper Trail (3,200 ft.) to
* Brook Trail (3,200 ft.): 0.5 mi., 100 ft. (rev. 100 ft.), 20 min.

Brook Trail (CMC)

This trail runs from the parking area at the end of Paugus Rd. (FR 68) to the summit of Chocorua. The country people cut the trail to avoid paying a toll on the Liberty Trail. High up, it ascends steep ledges with excellent views; it is much more scenic but also more difficult than the Liberty Trail, and potentially dangerous in wet or icy conditions. An excellent loop trip can be made by ascending the Brook Trail and descending the Liberty Trail.

From the parking area on Paugus Rd., continue north on the gravel road (FR 68) past the gate. After 0.1 mi., the Bolles Trail diverges left, and at 0.4 mi., just before the bridge over Claybank Brook, the Brook Trail diverges to the right off the gravel road. It follows the south bank of the brook, soon turns right onto a relocated section and ascends, then swings left and descends back to the brook. It passes a junction on the left with the Bickford Trail at 0.9 mi., and climbs well above the brook. At 1.8 mi., the trail returns to the brook at a tiny waterfall, then finally crosses it at 2.5 mi. The trail becomes steeper, and the first ledge is reached at 3.0 mi.; just beyond here, the Bee Line Trail now enters from the left. From here, the trail climbs the steep, open ledges of Farlow Ridge, where it is marked with cairns and yellow paint; there is one fairly difficult scramble. At 3.4 mi., the Liberty Trail joins from the right on a ledge. In about 35 yd. from this junction the West Side Trail, a bad-weather summit bypass, turns left (north), and the Brook Trail climbs steeply east over the ledges, then swings left (northeast) to the junction where the Piper Trail enters left (sign). The two trails climb east to the summit through a small gully.

Brook Trail (map 3:K9–J9)

Distances from Paugus Rd. parking area (900 ft.) to
* Bickford Trail (1,140 ft.): 0.9 mi., 300 ft. (rev. 50 ft.), 35 min.
* Claybank Brook crossing (1,900 ft.): 2.5 mi., 1,050 ft., 1 hr. 45 min.
* Bee Line Trail (2,600 ft.): 3.0 mi., 1,750 ft., 2 hr. 25 min.
* Liberty Trail (3,200 ft.): 3.4 mi., 2,350 ft., 2 hr. 55 min.
* Mt. Chocorua summit (3,500 ft.): 3.6 mi., 2,650 ft., 3 hr. 10 min.

Bee Line Trail (CMC)

This trail runs from the Old Paugus Trail on the south ridge of Mt. Paugus to the Brook Trail on the upper west ledges of Mt. Chocorua, linking the two summits almost by a "bee line." It crosses the Bolles Trail well south of the height-of-land in the valley between the mountains, at a point 2.0 mi. north of the Paugus Rd. parking area and 3.8 mi. south of the Champney Falls Trail parking area on the Kancamagus Highway (NH 112). The upper end of the Chocorua section of this trail is now located 0.4 mi. below its former upper terminus; the former section of the Bee Line Trail above this point has been abandoned because of erosion and poor footing that resulted from the trail's steepness. Although the trail was originally designed to provide a direct route between the two summits, nowadays it is most frequently used to ascend to or descend from one of the peaks rather than as a connector between them—that is, from the middle to either end rather than from one end to the other—so it will be described in that manner. Most of the Paugus branch is in the Sandwich Range Wilderness, and the upper part of the Chocorua branch is in the Mt. Chocorua Forest Protection Area.

Chocorua Branch. The trail leaves the Bolles Trail and ascends gradually on an old logging road along the bank of a small brook that originates high on the western slope of Chocorua. After crossing this brook at 0.7 mi. and 1.1 mi., the trail enters the Mt. Chocorua Forest Protection Area (signs). It ascends moderately away from the brook, becoming gradually steeper as it enters a mixed softwood forest. At 1.4 mi., the trail bears right off the former route and traverses the wooded slope, climbing moderately, until it reaches its junction with the Brook Trail at 1.7 mi., just above its lowest semi-open ledge. From here, it is 0.4 mi. to the junction with the Liberty Trail and 0.6 mi. to the summit of Chocorua.

Paugus Branch. Leaving the Bolles Trail, the Bee Line Trail soon crosses Paugus Brook, enters the Sandwich Range Wilderness, and runs over a narrow ridge. At 0.2 mi., the Bee Line Cutoff departs left (southeast), providing a shortcut to Paugus Rd. The Bee Line Trail crosses a small brook and climbs by increasingly steep grades up the side of the mountain, making some use of old lumber roads, to the Old Paugus Trail near the top of the ridge, 1.1 mi. from the Bolles Trail and 0.7 mi. below the junction with the Lawrence Trail on the ledge near the summit of Paugus.

Bee Line Trail (map 3:J9)

Distances from Bolles Trail (1,300 ft.) to

- Brook Trail (2,600 ft.) via Chocorua Branch: 1.7 mi., 1,300 ft., 1 hr. 30 min.
- Old Paugus Trail (2,350 ft.) via Paugus Branch: 1.1 mi., 1,100 ft. (rev. 50 ft.), 1 hr. 5 min.

Distances from Paugus Rd. parking area (900 ft.) to

- Mt. Chocorua summit (3,500 ft.) via Bolles Trail, Bee Line Trail, and Brook Trail: 4.3 mi., 2,600 ft., 3 hr. 25 min.
- ledge near Mt. Paugus summit (3,100 ft.) via Bolles Trail, Bee Line Trail, and Old Paugus Trail: 3.8 mi., 2,250 ft. (rev. 50 ft.), 3 hr.

Bee Line Cutoff (CMC)

This trail provides a shortcut to the Bee Line Trail to Mt. Paugus from the Paugus Rd. parking area. It is almost entirely within the Sandwich Range Wilderness. It diverges northwest from the Bolles Trail 1.2 mi. from the parking area and follows an old lumber road. At 0.2 mi., it bears right, crosses a brook, and continues to the Bee Line Trail, 0.2 mi. west of the junction of the Bee Line and Bolles trails.

Bee Line Cutoff (map 3:J9)

Distance from Bolles Trail (1,100 ft.) to

- Bee Line Trail (1,300 ft.): 0.6 mi., 200 ft., 25 min.

Bolles Trail (WMNF)

This trail connects the Paugus Rd. (FR 68) parking lot with the Champney Falls Trail parking lot on the Kancamagus Highway, passing between Mt. Chocorua and Mt. Paugus and using old logging roads most of the way. It is named for Frank Bolles, who reopened a very old road approximately along the route of this trail in 1892 and called it the "Lost Trail." South of the height-of-land, most of the trail is in or near the Sandwich Range Wilderness.

The Bolles Trail diverges from the Brook Trail (which here is the gravel logging road extension of Paugus Rd.) 0.1 mi. north of the Paugus Rd. parking lot. At 0.2 mi., it crosses Paugus Brook on stepping-stones (may be difficult at high water), and at 0.5 mi., the Old Paugus Trail and

Bickford Trail enter left. In 90 yd., the Bickford Trail diverges right. Soon the Bolles Trail passes the huge Paugus Mill sawdust pile (left), and at 1.1 mi., the Bee Line Cutoff diverges left. The Bolles Trail now crosses two branches of Paugus Brook on snowmobile bridges. At 1.9 mi., it crosses the Bee Line Trail and a tributary brook. At 2.6 mi., it recrosses Paugus Brook, turns right in an old logging-camp site where berry bush growth often obscures the footway, and soon begins to climb more steeply through a sandy area to the height-of-land at 3.7 mi. The trail then descends steeply to Twin Brook, crosses it on a bridge, and swings left along the bank where an obscure snowmobile trail continues ahead. The Bolles Trail continues down the valley, crossing Twin Brook 10 more times and a tributary once; the last crossing is at 4.9 mi. The trail continues past a snowmobile trail diverging sharp right, bears right at 5.4 mi. where a former route of the trail crossed the brook to the left, and reaches the Champney Falls Trail 0.1 mi. south of its trailhead parking lot on the Kancamagus Highway.

Bolles Trail (map 3:J9)

Distances from Brook Trail (940 ft.) to
- Bickford Trail/Old Paugus Trail (1,000 ft.): 0.5 mi., 50 ft., 15 min.
- Bee Line Trail (1,300 ft.): 1.9 mi., 350 ft., 1 hr. 10 min.
- Kancamagus Highway (1,260 ft.): 5.7 mi., 1,300 ft. (rev. 1,000 ft.), 3 hr. 30 min.

Bickford Trail (WODC)

This trail runs from NH 113A 1.1 mi. east of Wonalancet to the lower part of the Brook Trail, offering a walking route from Wonalancet to the Old Paugus, Bolles, and Brook trails to Mt. Paugus and Mt. Chocorua. The trail's blue blazes must be followed with care because of lack of an obvious footway.

The trail leaves NH 113A and ascends easily on an old logging road, passes between several camps, crosses a driveway, and descends easily to a field with a private home at 0.7 mi. It bears left diagonally across the field between two sheds, reenters the woods at the east edge of the field, and soon enters the WMNF. It then climbs moderately to a ridge top, and descends on the other side, following and then crossing a brook. The Old Paugus Trail enters left 20 yd. west of Whitin Brook, and the two trails cross the brook and meet the Bolles Trail at 2.0 mi. The Bickford Trail turns left (north) on the Bolles Trail for 90 yd., then turns right (east), crosses Paugus Brook (may be difficult), climbs a steep pitch, and soon reaches a logging road (which can be followed to the right to the Paugus Rd. parking area). The Bickford Trail turns left and follows the road for 80 yd., then turns right (turns marked with arrows), ascends easily, then descends and crosses Claybank Brook to the Brook Trail, where the Bickford Trail ends.

Bickford Trail (map 3:K9–J9)

Distances from NH 113A (1,170 ft.) to
- Bolles Trail (1,000 ft.): 2.0 mi., 400 ft. (rev. 600 ft.), 1 hr. 10 min.
- Brook Trail (1,140 ft.): 2.7 mi., 550 ft., 1 hr. 40 min.

Old Paugus Trail (CMC)

This trail runs to the south knob of Mt. Paugus from the Bolles Trail 0.7 mi. from the Paugus Rd. parking area. It is almost entirely within the Sandwich Range Wilderness. Portions of the trail are very steep and rough, with poor footing, and may be dangerous in wet or icy conditions.

This trail leaves the Bolles Trail along with the Bickford Trail and the two trails cross Whitin Brook together, then the Bickford Trail diverges left 20 yd. beyond the brook. The Old Paugus Trail continues along Whitin Brook at easy grades, crosses it at 0.7 mi. (may be difficult at high water), then turns right at 1.0 mi. as the Whitin Brook Trail continues straight ahead along the brook. The trail now climbs steeply, passes a junction left with the Big Rock Cave Trail at 1.3 mi., climbs a steep gully, then swings right along the base of a rock face and climbs steadily through a spruce forest to the junction right with the Bee Line Trail at 2.1 mi. It ascends sharply with several short scrambles, passes an outlook south on the right (sign), ascends a wet, sloping ledge, then eases up and passes the site of the former Old Shag Camp. Soon it crosses a small brook and climbs steeply; at the top of the pitch, a short side path leads right to a ledge with a view of Mt. Chocorua while the main trail turns left and continues at easier grades to the ledgy south knob. Here the Old Paugus Trail ends and the Lawrence Trail continues ahead, leaving the clearing to the right (northwest). An excellent view to the west can be obtained by descending 50 yd. southwest over ledges and through a belt of scrub to a large open ledge.

Old Paugus Trail (map 3:J9)

Distances from Bolles Trail (1,000 ft.) to
- Bee Line Trail (2,350 ft.): 2.1 mi., 1,350 ft., 1 hr. 45 min.
- Lawrence Trail (3,100 ft.): 2.8 mi., 2,150 ft. (rev. 50 ft.), 2 hr. 30 min.

Whitin Brook Trail (CMC)

This trail runs from the Old Paugus Trail to the Cabin Trail and gives access to points in the vicinity of Paugus Pass from the Paugus Mill Rd. parking area. It must be followed with care, particularly at the crossings of Whitin Brook, which may be difficult at high water. It is almost entirely within the Sandwich Range Wilderness.

The trail continues along Whitin Brook where the Old Paugus Trail turns right, upslope, 1.0 mi. above the junction of the Old Paugus and Bolles trails. In 0.2 mi., the Big Rock Cave Trail crosses, then the Whitin Brook Trail crosses the brook three times. After the last crossing, at 0.7 mi., the trail continues up the valley at easy grades for 0.5 mi., then swings left away from the brook and climbs steadily through spruce woods, swinging to the right near the top, and ends at the Cabin Trail, 0.4 mi. south of its junction with the Lawrence Trail.

Whitin Brook Trail (map 3:J9–J8)

Distance from Old Paugus Trail (1,550 ft.) to
- Cabin Trail (2,150 ft.): 1.6 mi., 600 ft., 1 hr. 5 min.

Big Rock Cave Trail (WODC)

This trail runs from the Cabin Trail 0.3 mi. from NH 113A over the flat ridge of Mt. Mexico to the Whitin Brook and Old Paugus trails. It provides easy access to Big Rock Cave, a boulder cave that invites exploration.

Diverging right from the Cabin Trail, the Big Rock Cave Trail ascends moderately on a logging road that fades away to a trail, reaching the very flat summit of Mt. Mexico at 1.1 mi. and entering the Sandwich Range Wilderness. From here, it descends moderately, then steeply, and passes Big Rock Cave (right) at 1.6 mi. It continues down steeply, crosses Whitin Brook (may be difficult at high water) and the Whitin Brook Trail at 1.7 mi., and climbs to its end at the Old Paugus Trail.

Big Rock Cave Trail (map 3:K8–J9)

Distances from Cabin Trail (1,200 ft.) to
- Big Rock Cave (1,700 ft.): 1.6 mi., 800 ft. (rev. 300 ft.), 1 hr. 10 min.
- Old Paugus Trail (1,720 ft.): 2.1 mi., 900 ft. (rev. 100 ft.), 1 hr. 30 min.

Cabin Trail (WODC)

This trail runs from NH 113A 0.5 mi. east of Wonalancet to the Lawrence Trail 0.3 mi. east of Paugus Pass. Parking is available on the shoulder across from the trailhead; do not park on the driveway. The upper part of the trail is in the Sandwich Range Wilderness. The trail follows a private driveway for 60 yd., bears right onto another driveway and follows it for 120 yd., passing a house, then enters the woods on an older road. At 0.3 mi., the Big Rock Cave Trail diverges right, and soon the Cabin Trail bears right at a fork where an unmarked path diverges left. The Cabin Trail ascends easily along the west side of Whitin Ridge on a logging road, crossing several small brooks and entering the Sandwich Range Wilderness at 1.7 mi., At 2.2 mi., just after crossing to the east side of the ridge crest, it reaches a junction where the Whitin Brook Trail enters from the right. The Cabin Trail continues on the east side of Whitin Ridge, soon passes an outlook to Mt. Paugus, then climbs along a rough sidehill and descends slightly to its end at the Lawrence Trail.

Cabin Trail (map 3:K8–J8)

Distances from NH 113A (1,060 ft.) to
- Whitin Brook Trail (2,150 ft.): 2.2 mi., 1,100 ft., 1 hr. 40 min.
- Lawrence Trail (2,320 ft.): 2.6 mi., 1,250 ft., 1 hr. 55 min.

Lawrence Trail (WODC)

This trail runs from the four-way junction with the Old Mast Rd., Walden Trail, and Square Ledge Trail, 2.0 mi. from the Ferncroft Rd. parking area (via the Old Mast Rd.), to the junction with the Old Paugus Trail on the south knob of Mt. Paugus. The section on the west slope of Mt. Paugus is steep and rough, but a new relocation has bypassed a very steep and difficult section near the cliffs known as the Overhang. It is entirely within the Sandwich Range Wilderness.

The trail leaves the four-way junction at the north end of the Old Mast Rd. and descends slightly into Paugus Pass at 0.3 mi., where it is joined on the left (north) by the Oliverian Brook Trail from the Kancamagus Highway and on the right (south) by the Kelley Trail from Ferncroft. The Lawrence Trail climbs to a knob at 0.6 mi., where the Cabin Trail enters from the right. The Lawrence Trail next descends to the southeast side of the ridge at the base of the Overhang, and at 0.9 mi., it continues ahead on the relocated section on a gravelly footway where the old route turned left and uphill. It contours through dense hardwood growth well below the cliffs, with good footing, passing a limited view of the cliffs on Mt. Paugus, then swings left and climbs by easy switchbacks to join the old route in a hollow at 1.4 mi. Here it bears right, crosses two small brooks, enters spruce forest, and climbs a steep, eroded section where major trail work is planned, passing a view of Mt. Whiteface. At 1.7 mi., it swings right at an easier grade, crosses a small brook at 1.9 mi., and continues to the ledgy south knob of Mt. Paugus, where the Old Paugus Trail continues ahead. An excellent view to the west can be obtained by descending 50 yd. southwest over ledges and through a belt of scrub to a large open ledge. Descending, the Lawrence Trail leaves the northwest side of the ledge at the top of the knob; the trail sign is set back a few steps into the woods.

Lawrence Trail (map 3:J8–J9)

Distance from Old Mast Rd. (2,340 ft.) to
- the south knob of Mt. Paugus and the Old Paugus Trail (3,100 ft.): 2.1 mi., 1,100 ft. (rev. 350 ft.), 1 hr. 35 min.

Kelley Trail (WODC)

This trail runs from the Ferncroft Rd. parking area through an interesting ravine to a junction with the Lawrence and Oliverian Brook trails at Paugus Pass. The upper part of the trail, which is in the Sandwich Range Wilderness, is rough with poor footing and numerous slippery rocks.

For a short time during the retreat of the last continental glacier, this ravine was the outlet of glacial Lake Albany, which occupied the Albany Intervale, the broad valley to the north of the eastern Sandwich Range. This lake was contained by an ice dam at the east end, and until enough ice had melted from the ice dam to allow the meltwater to pass out by the present route of the Swift River, the water was forced through Paugus Pass and down this ravine in a torrential stream, which left evidence of significant carving by large and powerful waterfalls that the present small stream could not possibly have caused.

The trail leaves the Ferncroft Rd. parking area and follows a gated gravel logging road (FR 337), coinciding with the Old Mast Rd. and soon bearing left at a fork where the Gordon Path follows the road that runs straight ahead. After passing the junction with Wonalancet Range Trail on the left at 0.1 mi., the trails cross Spring Brook on a wooden bridge, and at 0.3 mi., the Kelley Trail turns off the Old Mast Rd. to the right and follows a woods road to a grassy logging road (FR 337) at 0.5 mi. Here the trail turns right and descends along this road 0.1 mi. to meet its former route at a culvert, where it turns left and ascends along the brook. Soon the trail begins to climb above the brook, then returns to the brook at the top of a small cascade. It now crosses the brook (or its dry bed) three times, briefly runs in the brook bed, then climbs steeply out of a small box ravine—one of the remnants of the outflow of glacial Lake Albany—and soon reaches Paugus Pass.

Kelley Trail (map 3:K8–J8)

Distance from Ferncroft Rd. parking area (1,140 ft.) to
 • Lawrence Trail and Oliverian Brook Trail (2,220 ft.): 2.3 mi., 1,100 ft., 1 hr. 40 min.

Oliverian Brook Trail (WMNF)

This trail runs from the Kancamagus Highway to the Lawrence and Kelley trails at Paugus Pass. It begins at a parking lot 0.1 mi. in from the Kancamagus Highway on a gravel road that begins on the south side of the highway 1.0 mi. west of the Bear Notch Rd. intersection. Parts of the trail, particularly south of the Passaconaway Cutoff, are wet, though recent relocations have improved the situation. Grades are mostly easy. The part of the trail south of the Passaconaway Cutoff is in the Sandwich Range Wilderness.

The trail follows the gravel road beyond the gate for 125 yd., turns sharp left (sign) on a cross-country ski trail that it follows for another 125 yd., then turns sharp right on the old route of the trail. It crosses an old railroad bed and a recent logging road, then bears right onto an old railroad grade along the west side of Oliverian Brook (in the reverse direction, bear left here) and follows it for nearly 0.5 mi., passing a beaver pond that sometimes floods the trail. At 1.1 mi., it turns left off the railroad grade, and at 1.9 mi., the Passaconaway Cutoff diverges right (southwest). The Oliverian Brook Trail continues south and crosses a major tributary at 2.2 mi., then the main brook at 2.7 mi. The trail now follows a relocated section on higher ground away from the brook to the east, then descends slightly to reach the junction with the Square Ledge Branch Trail, which leaves on the right and immediately crosses Oliverian Brook at 3.3 mi. The trail then rejoins the original route, crosses Oliverian Brook (no bridge), and continues to ascend along the brook to the multiple trail junction in Paugus Pass.

Oliverian Brook Trail (map 3:J8)

Distances from Kancamagus Highway (1,240 ft.) to

- Passaconaway Cutoff (1,500 ft.): 1.9 mi., 250 ft., 1 hr. 5 min.
- Square Ledge Branch Trail (1,750 ft.): 3.3 mi., 500 ft., 1 hr. 55 min.
- Paugus Pass (2,220 ft.): 4.4 mi., 1,000 ft., 2 hr. 40 min.

Old Mast Road (WODC)

This trail, which has easy to moderate grades and good footing throughout, runs from the Ferncroft Rd. parking area to the junction with the Walden, Square Ledge, and Lawrence trails 0.3 mi. west of Paugus Pass. The original road was reputedly built for hauling out the tallest timbers as masts for the British navy. The upper part of the trail is in the Sandwich Range Wilderness.

Leaving the parking area along with the Kelley Trail, the Old Mast Rd. follows the left-hand road at the first fork, where the Gordon Path follows the road that continues straight ahead. At 0.1 mi., the Wonalancet Range Trail diverges left, just before the bridge over Spring Brook, and at 0.3 mi., the Kelley Trail diverges right. Soon the Old Mast Rd. passes the WMNF boundary, then at 0.9 mi., it crosses an overgrown logging road, soon enters another old road, and follows it for 0.1 mi. The trail continues to climb, then levels, passes to the right of a small brook, and ends at the multiple trail junction.

Old Mast Rd. (map 3:K8–J8)
Distance from Ferncroft parking area (1,140 ft.) to
• Lawrence Trail/Walden Trail/Square Ledge Trail (2,340 ft.): 2.0 mi., 1,200 ft.,
  1 hr. 35 min.

Dicey's Mill Trail (WODC)

This trail ascends Mt. Passaconaway from the Ferncroft Rd. parking area, with moderate grades and good footing. It was the first trail to be built on the mountain. Most of it is in the Sandwich Range Wilderness.

From the parking area, return to Ferncroft Rd. and turn right, following the gravel road past Squirrel Bridge, where the Blueberry Ledge Trail turns left. Pass a gate (not intended to keep out hikers) and a house in a large clearing, and continue on the road, which becomes a logging road as it enters the woods. About 40 yd. before the trail enters the WMNF and Sandwich Range Wilderness at 0.8 mi., a marked path left crosses the Wonalancet River on a footbridge to the Blueberry Ledge Cutoff on the opposite bank. Soon the trail swings right and becomes steeper, then the grade becomes easy again and continues to the junction on the left with the Tom Wiggin Trail at 1.9 mi. At 2.3 mi., the Dicey's Mill Trail crosses the river at the site of Dicey's Mill—there are some remains of the old mill hidden in the woods nearby. Across the stream, the trail passes a large boulder and begins a long ascent, angling up the side of a ridge, following an old logging road at a moderate grade through hardwoods with occasional glimpses of the steep-sided Wonalancet Range rising on the opposite side of the valley. At the ridge top, at 3.7 mi., the Rollins Trail from Mt. Whiteface enters on the left. The Dicey's Mill Trail then climbs through a rough, wet section, crosses a small brook, and reaches the junction at 3.9 mi., where the East Loop bears right.

East Loop. This very short trail begins on the Dicey's Mill Trail near the small brook just below the site of Camp Rich, and runs nearly level for 0.2 mi. (5 min.) to the Walden Trail a short distance above the point where that trail makes a right turn at the base of its steep climb to the summit of Mt. Passaconaway. It is entirely within the Sandwich Range Wilderness.

From the East Loop junction, the Dicey's Mill Trail bears left, passes the site of the former Camp Rich (25 yd. left on a side trail), climbs moderately via wide switchbacks, then ascends steeply for 0.2 mi. to a northwest outlook. Here it turns right and meets the Walden Trail in another 20 yd. The summit is 40 yd. right on a spur path, while the Walden Trail leads ahead 90 yd. to the east outlook.

Dicey's Mill Trail (map 3:K8–J8)

Distances from Ferncroft Rd. parking area (1,140 ft.) to
- Tom Wiggin Trail (1,950 ft.): 1.9 mi., 850 ft. (rev. 50 ft.), 1 hr. 25 min.
- Rollins Trail (3,300 ft.): 3.7 mi., 2,200 ft., 2 hr. 55 min.
- Mt. Passaconaway summit (4,043 ft.): 4.6 mi., 2,950 ft., 3 hr. 45 min.

Walden Trail (WODC)

This trail ascends Mt. Passaconaway from the junction of the Old Mast Rd. and the Square Ledge and Lawrence trails via the southeast ridge. It is a more interesting but longer and rougher route to Mt. Passaconaway from Ferncroft Rd. (via the Old Mast Rd.) than the direct Dicey's Mill Trail. It has recently undergone one of the most intensive reconstruction programs to have been conducted anywhere in the White Mountains—sponsored by the WODC and Sandwich Conservation Association, under the leadership of Peter Smart and Chris Conrod and with the participation of countless others—to rectify the erosion and footing problems created by the steep grade. It is entirely within the Sandwich Range Wilderness. It was named for Arthur Walden, founder of the Chinook Kennels in Wonalancet and a widely known handler and breeder of husky sled dogs.

The trail runs northwest from the Old Mast Rd. up a very steep slope where much trail work has been done. There are several rock scrambles, including one especially tricky wet, broken ledge. At the top of the shoulder, the grade eases and the trail crosses a minor knob and a sag, then climbs steeply again and passes a side path that leads right 20 yd. to an outlook to the east and northeast, including Mts. Paugus and Chocorua. At 0.7 mi., it passes a side trail to the left (south) that leads about 100 yd. to a fine viewpoint to the south. The main trail passes just to the south of the large boulder that is the true summit of Mt. Hedgehog, and at 0.9 mi., the Wonalancet Range Trail enters left. The Walden Trail now descends steeply past an outlook to Mt. Washington to a col, descends to the left along a brook bed (possible water) for 50 yd., then swings right and climbs very steeply again over the next subpeak, locally called Nanamocomuck Peak in honor of the eldest son of Passaconaway. It then descends easily to a col, then climbs gradually to the junction right with the Square Ledge Trail at 2.1 mi. The trail now starts to angle upward around the south face of the mountain, and at 2.2 mi., it makes a right turn up the slope, soon passes the junction with the East Loop on the left, and climbs steeply over a recently reconstructed footway. At the top of a steep pitch, it swings left to a fine south outlook, then reaches the excellent east outlook. The junction with the Dicey's Mill Trail is 90 yd. beyond the outlook, and the true summit is 40 yd. left from that junction. Between the east outlook and the Dicey's Mill Trail a side path descends right 0.3 mi. and 200 ft. to a fine north outlook. (This side path is part of the long-abandoned Downes Brook Slide Trail, which was closed because of hazardous footing on steep slippery ledges below the outlook.)

Walden Trail (map 3:J8)

Distances from Old Mast Rd. (2,340 ft.) to

- Wonalancet Range Trail (3,100 ft.): 0.9 mi., 800 ft. (rev. 50 ft.), 50 min.
- Square Ledge Trail (3,300 ft.): 2.1 mi., 1,350 ft. (rev. 350 ft.), 1 hr. 45 min.
- Mt. Passaconaway summit (4,043 ft.): 2.8 mi., 2,100 ft., 2 hr. 25 min.

Wonalancet Range Trail (WODC)

This trail ascends from the Old Mast Rd., 0.1 mi. from the Ferncroft Rd. parking area, over the Wonalancet Range to the Walden Trail 0.2 mi. west of Mt. Hedgehog. There are good views from ledges on the way, and the trail offers an attractive but significantly longer and rougher alternative to the Dicey's Mill Trail, the most direct route to Mt. Passaconaway from Ferncroft. Most of this trail is within the Sandwich Range Wilderness.

The trail diverges left from the Old Mast Rd. just before the bridge over Spring Brook, soon turns left on a relocation, then left again to rejoin the older route. It climbs easily, entering the Sandwich Range Wilderness at 0.7 mi., then ascends more steeply with rocky footing. At 1.4 mi., after a very steep pitch, it passes a shortcut trail on the right that climbs 0.4 mi. to rejoin the main trail 0.4 mi. north of the summit of Mt. Wonalancet, avoiding ledges that provide good views but are slippery when wet or icy. The main trail turns left and climbs steeply, soon crossing a fine outlook ledge, then swings around to the south edge of Mt. Wonalancet and makes a hairpin turn north to pass over the flat summit at 1.8 mi. The trail passes the upper end of the shortcut in a sag at 2.2 mi., then climbs past a short spur on the right, which leads to an outlook to the south, and continues to ascend past an outlook to the west to the inconsequential summit of Mt. Hibbard at 2.7 mi. The trail continues to ascend moderately, then descends slightly to the junction with the Walden Trail.

Wonalancet Range Trail (map 3:K8–J8)

Distances from Old Mast Rd. (1,140 ft.) to
- Mt. Wonalancet summit (2,780 ft.): 1.8 mi., 1,650 ft., 1 hr. 45 min.
- Walden Trail (3,100 ft.): 3.2 mi., 2,150 ft. (rev. 200 ft.), 2 hr. 40 min.

Passaconaway Cutoff (WMNF)

This trail provides the shortest route to Mt. Passaconaway from the north, running from the Oliverian Brook Trail, 1.9 mi. from its parking lot off the Kancamagus Highway, to the Square Ledge Trail (and thence to the summit via the Walden Trail). The entire trail is in the Sandwich Range Wilderness. Leaving the Oliverian Brook Trail, the cutoff follows an old logging road at easy grades, crosses a brook at 0.5 mi., then runs above the brook. At 0.9 mi., it turns left and climbs steadily, with glimpses of Mt. Passaconaway across the valley. At 1.5 mi., it climbs over a ledge with a view north to Hedgehog Mountain and continues up to the junction with the Square Ledge Trail west of Square Ledge.

Passaconaway Cutoff (map 3:J8)

Distance from Oliverian Brook Trail (1,500 ft.) to
- Square Ledge Trail (2,550 ft.): 1.7 mi., 1,050 ft., 1 hr. 25 min.

Distance from Kancamagus Highway (1,240 ft.) to
- Mt. Passaconaway summit (4,043 ft.) via Oliverian Brook Trail, Passaconaway Cutoff, Square Ledge Trail, and Walden Trail: 5.1 mi., 2,800 ft., 3 hr. 55 min.

Square Ledge Trail (WODC)

This trail begins at the junction of the Old Mast Rd. and the Walden and Lawrence trails, climbs over Square Ledge, and ascends to the Walden Trail just below the summit cone of Mt. Passaconaway. It is entirely within the Sandwich Range Wilderness. In some recent years, peregrine falcons have nested on the cliff of Square Ledge, so access to the principal Square Ledge viewpoint may be restricted during the nesting season (April 1 to August 1).

From the junction at its southern end, it descends from the height-of-land, crossing two small brooks, and at 1.1 mi., just before the second brook, the Square Ledge Branch Trail diverges right (east) to join the Oliverian Brook Trail. A short distance farther, the main trail makes a sharp turn left (west) to ascend the ledge. It bears east for a short distance, then climbs very steeply to the shoulder. At 1.5 mi., at a sharp left turn, a spur leads right 20 yd. to Square Ledge outlook, where there is a fine view east across the valley. Leaving the ledge, the trail ascends to the wooded summit of the knob above the ledge. Just past this summit an unmarked side path climbs left up a steep ledge with a view of Mt. Passaconaway (use caution—the edge of the cliff is partly obscured by scrubby growth). The main trail descends alongside a rock face, then climbs steeply up a shoulder, turns sharp right, and descends to the junction with the Passaconaway Cutoff on the right at 2.1 mi. Here the Square Ledge Trail turns sharp left, crosses a dip, passes through an old logging-camp site, and crosses the base of a small slide; a view to Mt. Washington can be obtained by scrambling a short distance up this slide. The trail then becomes steep as it climbs to the Walden Trail.

Square Ledge Trail (map 3:J8)

Distances from Old Mast Rd./Lawrence Trail/Walden Trail (2,340 ft.) to
- Square Ledge outlook (2,550 ft.): 1.5 mi., 500 ft. (rev. 300 ft.), 1 hr.
- Passaconaway Cutoff (2,550 ft.): 2.1 mi., 650 ft. (rev. 150 ft.), 1 hr. 25 min.
- Walden Trail (3,300 ft.): 2.8 mi., 1,400 ft., 2 hr. 5 min.

Square Ledge Branch Trail (WMNF)

This short trail begins on the Oliverian Brook Trail 3.3 mi. from the Kancamagus Highway, immediately crosses Oliverian Brook, and ascends moderately to the Square Ledge Trail below the steep section that ascends the ledge. It is most frequently used to make a loop over Square Ledge from the Kancamagus Highway.

Square Ledge Branch Trail (map 3:J8)

Distance from Oliverian Brook Trail (1,750 ft.) to
- Square Ledge Trail (2,100 ft.): 0.5 mi., 350 ft., 25 min.

UNH Trail (WMNF)

This loop trail to the ledges of Hedgehog Mountain offers fine views from several viewpoints for a modest effort. It begins at the Downes Brook Trail parking lot, at the end of a short gravel road that leaves the south side of the Kancamagus Highway opposite the WMNF Passaconaway Campground. It was named for the University of New Hampshire Forestry Camp, formerly located nearby.

The trail leaves the Downes Brook Trail on the left 60 yd. from the edge of the parking lot and follows an old railroad grade 0.2 mi. to the loop junction; here the west branch of the loop turns right uphill, while the east branch continues straight on the old railroad grade. From this point, the loop will be described in the clockwise direction (east branch to summit, then west branch back), although the loop is equally good in the opposite direction.

From the loop junction, the east branch continues on the railroad grade, then turns off it on the right at 0.4 mi., and follows a logging road, climbing moderately, and swings right to cross White Brook at 1.3 mi. It crosses a small brook, climbs by switchbacks through spruce forest, and swings left to a northeast outlook. Here it bears right and climbs, swinging right again to the east ledges at 2.0 mi., where there are fine views south and east. The trail then runs along the top of the cliffs on the south face (follow blazes carefully) and enters the woods under the steep, ledgy south side of the main peak. It then bears gradually toward the north onto the west slope of the main peak of Hedgehog Mountain, which it climbs in a short series of ledgy switchbacks, reaching the summit at 2.9 mi., where ledges provide views to the north, west, and south. The trail then descends easily through an open area, with views to the north, then descends steadily and makes a left turn at 3.7 mi. Here a side path (sign) climbs steeply right 60 yd. to Allen's Ledge, swinging left along the base of a rock face; by descending carefully to a lower ledge perch, one can obtain a wide view to the east and northeast. The main trail descends to cross a small brook, then climbs a bank and turns right onto an old logging road (in the reverse direction, the trail descends left off the logging road) and follows it down to the loop junction.

UNH Trail (map 3:J8)

Distances from parking lot off Kancamagus Highway (1,250 ft.)
- to east ledges (2,300 ft.): 2.0 mi., 1,100 ft. (rev. 50 ft.), 1 hr. 35 min.

- to Hedgehog Mountain summit (2,532 ft.): 2.9 mi., 1,450 ft. (rev. 100 ft.), 2 hr. 10 min.
- for complete loop: 4.8 mi., 1,450 ft., 3 hr. 10 min.

Mount Potash Trail (WMNF)

This trail ascends to the open ledges of Potash Mountain, providing excellent views for relatively little effort. It begins on Downes Brook Trail, 0.3 mi. from the parking area on the road that leaves the Kancamagus Highway almost directly opposite the entrance to the Passaconaway Campground.

The trail turns sharp right off the Downes Brook Trail and heads generally southwest. After crossing Downes Brook (may be difficult) at 0.1 mi., the trail turns sharp left and soon crosses a gravel logging road. (This road provides an alternate approach to the trail that avoids the often difficult brook crossing; it begins on a gate on the Kancamagus Highway 0.6 mi. west of the trailhead—take care not to block the gate when parking.) After traversing a slope among hardwoods, the trail enters a beautiful hemlock forest, and at 0.9 mi., it turns sharp left and climbs, swinging left off the old route of the trail at 1.2 mi., then swinging right to rejoin the old route, which it now follows to the left. It crosses a southeast outlook and ascends moderately, then at 1.6 mi. leaves the old route again and angles up the east side of the mountain, circling clockwise with rough, rocky footing around the cone to avoid the steepest ledges. It crosses a ledge with excellent views up the valley of Downes Brook, then turns right and climbs steeply up open south-facing ledges to the summit.

Mount Potash Trail (map 3:J8)

Distance from Downes Brook Trail (1,300 ft.) to
- Potash Mountain summit (2,700 ft.): 1.9 mi., 1,400 ft., 1 hr. 40 min.

Rollins Trail (WODC)

This trail runs along the high ridge that connects Mt. Whiteface to Mt. Passaconaway. It begins at a junction with the Blueberry Ledge and McCrillis trails on the open ledges of the south knob of Mt. Whiteface and ends on the Dicey's Mill Trail 0.2 mi. below the site of the former Camp Rich. On the ridge of Mt. Whiteface, some sections are steep and rough. It is entirely within the Sandwich Range Wilderness.

Leaving the south ledges, the Rollins Trail passes over a wooded ledge with a glimpse ahead to the true summit, then descends sharply into the steep, narrow col between the true summit and the open south summit of Whiteface, passing the junction with the Kate Sleeper Trail at the site of the former Camp Shehadi on the left at 0.1 mi. From this col, it climbs north then runs along the ridge crest to the wooded true summit (no marking) of Mt. Whiteface at 0.3 mi. It continues along the narrow ridge, with outlooks to the east across the Bowl at 0.6 mi. and 1.4 mi., descending gradually with occasional steep pitches and two short ascents to the broad, deep pass between Whiteface and Passaconaway. The trail then angles slightly upward around the south face of Passaconaway to meet the Dicey's Mill Trail.

Rollins Trail (map 3:J8)

Distance from Blueberry Ledge Trail–McCrillis Trail junction (3,990 ft.) to
• Dicey's Mill Trail (3,300 ft.): 2.5 mi., 200 ft. (rev. 900 ft.), 1 hr. 20 min.

Blueberry Ledge Trail (WODC)

This trail, which was opened in 1899, ascends Mt. Whiteface from the Ferncroft Rd. parking area, ending at a junction with the McCrillis and Rollins trails on the wide ledges of the lower south summit. The trail is very scenic, but the upper part is steep and requires some rock scrambling. Though rock steps have been drilled out in the ledges at some difficult spots, the wooden steps that were also installed on the steepest ledge on this trail have been removed. This trail is still one of the more challenging climbs in the White Mountains. It is particularly difficult on the descent, and even more difficult when wet, and dangerous in icy conditions. Most of the trail is within the Sandwich Range Wilderness.

From the parking area, return to Ferncroft Rd. and follow it to Squirrel Bridge at 0.3 mi., where the Dicey's Mill Trail continues straight ahead. The Blueberry Ledge Trail turns left across the bridge and follows a private gravel road, avoiding driveways, then diverges left into the woods where the road curves right to the last house. Here, at 0.5 mi., the Pasture Path to Mt. Katherine leaves left. In 0.1 mi., the trail joins an old road, and soon the Blueberry Ledge Cutoff diverges right to follow the bank of the Wonalancet River. The trail crosses into the WMNF and the Sandwich Range Wilderness, and at 0.9 mi., it continues straight where the McCrillis Path to Whiteface Intervale Rd.—not to be confused with the McCrillis Trail to Mt. Whiteface—follows the old road sharp left. The Blueberry Ledge Trail now passes through a flat area, then ascends moderately. At 1.6 mi., it reaches the bottom of the ledges (where views are very limited) and climbs to the top of the ledges, where there is a view of the Ossipee Range. The Blueberry Ledge Cutoff rejoins on the right at a large cairn at 2.0 mi., and the Blueberry Ledge Trail reenters the woods.

The trail climbs gently through open hardwoods, then rises steeply past Wonalancet Outlook to the top of the ridge. It drops slightly into a hollow, then ascends slightly to a junction with the Tom Wiggin Trail on the right at 3.2 mi. Now the trail climbs moderately, then swings sharp right at an outlook at 3.6 mi., where it abruptly approaches the edge of a steep cliff and may be dangerous if slippery. Just beyond here, it climbs a steep ledge, then continues to scramble up the steep, rough, rocky ridge, with several excellent viewpoints, ending at the ledges of the lower south summit. The McCrillis Trail enters from the left, just north of the ledges, while the Rollins Trail continues north to the true summit of Mt. Whiteface and on toward Mt. Passaconaway.

Blueberry Ledge Trail (map 3:K8–J8)

Distances from Ferncroft Rd. parking area (1,140 ft.) to
- Blueberry Ledge Cutoff, upper junction (2,150 ft.): 2.0 mi., 1,000 ft., 1 hr. 30 min.
- south summit ledges of Mt. Whiteface (3,990 ft.): 3.9 mi., 2,850 ft., 3 hr. 25 min.

Blueberry Ledge Cutoff (WODC)

This trail begins and ends on the Blueberry Ledge Trail, providing a walk along the Wonalancet River as an alternative to the viewless ledges. It is equal in distance but somewhat rougher than the parallel section of the

Blueberry Ledge Trail. The upper part of the trail is in the Sandwich Range Wilderness.

It leaves the Blueberry Ledge Trail 0.6 mi. from the Ferncroft Rd. parking area, and descends slightly to the riverbank. At 0.3 mi., the Dicey's Mill Trail runs on the opposite bank quite near the river; an old logging road comes across the river over a footbridge from the Dicey's Mill Trail at this point, and the Blueberry Ledge Cutoff follows this road upstream into the Sandwich Range Wilderness. The trail soon climbs a small ridge and returns to the bank high above the brook. It swings away from the brook again, meets and follows a small tributary, then swings right and climbs steeply to the bottom of the upper ledge. Marked by cairns and paint, it climbs to meet the Blueberry Ledge Trail at the top of the ledge at a large cairn.

Blueberry Ledge Cutoff (map 3:K8)

Distance from Blueberry Ledge Trail, lower junction (1,300 ft.) to
- Blueberry Ledge Trail, upper junction (2,150 ft.): 1.4 mi., 850 ft., 1 hr. 10 min.

Tom Wiggin Trail (WODC)

This steep, rough, lightly used trail, cut by Thomas Wiggin in 1895 and nicknamed the "Fire Escape," connects the Dicey's Mill Trail 1.9 mi. from the Ferncroft Rd. parking area with the Blueberry Ledge Trail just below the upper ledges. It lies entirely within the Sandwich Range Wilderness.

Leaving the Dicey's Mill Trail, it descends to cross the Wonalancet River (may be difficult at high water), bears left and ascends a little knoll, crosses a small brook, and bears right. It tends to angle to the right as it climbs steeply up the mountainside, with many sections of loose, gravelly footing that are particularly tedious on the descent. Eventually, it reaches the Blueberry Ledge Trail just north of a small hollow.

Tom Wiggin Trail (map 3:J8)

Distance from Dicey's Mill Trail (1,950 ft.) to
- Blueberry Ledge Trail (3,350 ft.): 1.1 mi., 1,450 ft. (rev. 50 ft.), 1 hr. 15 min.

McCrillis Trail (WMNF)

This trail ascends Mt. Whiteface—ending at the lower south summit—from the Flat Mountain Pond Trail (see Section Seven), 1.7 mi. from Whiteface Intervale Rd. It is lightly used, and the lower part through hardwood forest requires care to follow, because of damage from the 1998 ice storm that has led to luxuriant undergrowth. The upper part is fairly steep and rough, but unlike the Blueberry Ledge Trail does not require rock scrambling (except for one ledge at the top that can be tricky in wet or icy conditions) and is more sheltered in bad weather. It is entirely within the Sandwich Range Wilderness. Be careful not to confuse this trail with the McCrillis Path, which runs from Whiteface Intervale Rd. to the Blueberry Ledge Trail.

Leaving the Flat Mountain Pond Trail on the east bank of the Whiteface River, the trail ascends a bank, then runs east nearly on the level to intersect the former route, an old logging road, at 0.4 mi. Turning left on this road, it climbs moderately through hardwoods, passes through a wet area, and at 2.0 mi., begins to climb steeply into a forest of conifers. At 2.6 mi., it passes the first of several outlooks, including one up on the left to the southwest, and others on the right, which provides good views out onto the "white face." The trail reenters the woods, climbs steeply again, and finally climbs along the edge of the southwest ledges (use caution) to a junction with the Rollins and Blueberry Ledge trails just north of the ledges of the lower south summit. The true summit is 0.3 mi. farther north via the Rollins Trail. (To descend on this trail, walk southwest from the highest rock of the south ledges along the southeast edge of the ledges. Once the first markings are found, it is easily followed.)

McCrillis Trail (map 3:K8–J8)

Distances from Flat Mountain Pond Trail (1,250 ft.) to
- base of steep climb (2,600 ft.): 2.0 mi., 1,350 ft., 1 hr. 40 min.
- Blueberry Ledge Trail/Rollins Trail (3,990 ft.): 3.2 mi., 2,750 ft., 3 hr.

Distance from Whiteface Intervale Rd. (968 ft.) to
- Blueberry Ledge Trail/Rollins Trail (3,990 ft.) via Flat Mountain Pond and McCrillis trails: 4.9 mi., 3,050 ft., 4 hr.

McCrillis Path (WODC)

This trail follows old roads with mostly easy grades from the Blueberry Ledge Trail, 0.9 mi. from the Ferncroft Rd. parking area, to the trailhead for the Flat Mountain Pond Trail on Whiteface Intervale Rd. Be careful not to confuse it with the McCrillis Trail to Mt. Whiteface. The eastern part of this trail, which is in the Sandwich Range Wilderness, gives access to a network of minor trails via the Tilton Spring Path, and passes through the remains of old farms that can be explored. Use of this trail west of the WMNF boundary, 1.1 mi. from the Blueberry Ledge Trail, is at present prohibited because of posting of the private land through which the western part of the trail passes. The WODC is working to reopen the trail; updates can be found on www.wodc.org.

The trail leaves the Blueberry Ledge Trail on the left and climbs to the height-of-land, following the old road that was once the main highway between Wonalancet and Whiteface Intervale. Tilton Spring Path leaves left at 0.2 mi., and there is a small cellar hole on the right at 0.8 mi. Beyond this point, the trail may be overgrown and obscure. It reaches the WMNF boundary at 1.1 mi.; beyond here, it passes through private land that is currently posted.

McCrillis Path (map 3:K8)

Distances from Blueberry Ledge Trail (1,400 ft.) to
- WMNF boundary (1,340 ft.): 1.1 mi., 50 ft. (rev. 100 ft.), 35 min.
- Flat Mountain Pond Trail trailhead (968 ft.): 2.9 mi., 50 ft. (rev. 500 ft.), 1 hr. 30 min.

Downes Brook Trail (WMNF)

This trail provides a route to the south summit ledges or the true summit of Mt. Whiteface in combination with the Kate Sleeper Trail and the Rollins Trail. (The trail segment between the Kate Sleeper Trail junction and the col between the summits of Mt. Whiteface, formerly a part of the Downes Brook Trail, is now part of the Kate Sleeper Trail.) The Downes Brook Trail begins at a parking area 0.1 mi. from the Kancamagus Highway on a gravel road that leaves on the south side of the highway almost directly opposite Passaconaway Campground. The trail crosses Downes

Brook 10 times, and several crossings may range from difficult to impassable at high water.

Leaving the parking area, the trail follows the edge of a gravel pit, and the UNH Trail diverges left on an old railroad grade in 60 yd. After a short climb, the Downes Brook Trail turns right, enters the woods, then turns left and follows an old logging road that runs along Downes Brook, at first some distance away and later mostly along the bank. At 0.3 mi., the Mt. Potash Trail diverges right, and at 0.7 mi., the Downes Brook Trail makes the first of four crossings of Downes Brook in a span of 0.6 mi. At 2.3 mi., it crosses an extensive gravel outwash, crosses the main brook twice more, and passes through an old logging camp at 3.0 mi. After three more crossings, there are views of the slides on the steep slope of Mt. Whiteface across the valley, and the trail crosses the brook for the last time in the flat pass between Sleeper Ridge and Mt. Whiteface. Here, at 5.2 mi., with a swampy area visible straight ahead, it ends at the junction with the Kate Sleeper Trail. To reach Mt. Whiteface, turn left on the Kate Sleeper Trail, which climbs moderately to the little col between the true summit and the bare south summit of Mt. Whiteface at 6.0 mi., where the former Camp Shehadi was located. To the left from this junction, the Rollins Trail climbs over the true summit of Whiteface at 0.2 mi. and continues toward Mt. Passaconaway; to the right it climbs a short, steep pitch and soon ends at the junction with the McCrillis and Blueberry Ledge trails at the edge of the broad, open ledges of the south summit.

Downes Brook Trail (map 3:J8)

Distances from Kancamagus Highway (1,250 ft.) to

- Sleeper Trail junction (3,400 ft.): 5.2 mi., 2,150 ft., 3 hr. 40 min.
- Rollins Trail junction (3,900 ft.) via Kate Sleeper Trail: 6.0 mi., 2,650 ft., 4 hr. 20 min.

Kate Sleeper Trail (WODC)

This trail connects Mt. Tripyramid with Mt. Whiteface and the eastern peaks of the Sandwich Range. It begins at the little col between the summits of Mt. Whiteface and runs over the high, double-domed Sleeper Ridge to the Mt. Tripyramid Trail high on the South Slide. A section of trail between Mt. Whiteface and the junction of the Downes Brook and

Kate Sleeper trails, formerly part of the Downes Brook Trail, has been annexed to the Kate Sleeper Trail to restore the historic extent of this trail. It is entirely within the Sandwich Range Wilderness. The only sure water on or near the Kate Sleeper Trail is on the Downes Brook Trail just north of the junction between the two trails in the sag between Whiteface and the Sleepers.

The trail leaves the col between the summits of Mt. Whiteface and descends at a moderate grade 0.8 mi. to its junction with the Downes Brook Trail. The Kate Sleeper Trail then skirts to the north of a swampy area and soon begins to ascend the East Sleeper; there are occasional glimpses to the east and north through the trees. Passing left (southwest) of the top of East Sleeper at 1.6 mi.—where a side path (sign) leads right 0.1 mi. to this viewless summit—the trail descends into the col between the Sleepers, then climbs to a point 30 yd. south of the summit of West Sleeper at 2.6 mi. After descending again and traversing a bit below the Tripyramid col, the trail bears west and contours along South Tripyramid until it enters the South Slide on the smaller eastern slide. Small cairns and blue blazes mark the winding route on the slide, as the trail climbs very steeply on loose gravel about 100 yd., then reenters the brush on the opposite side. After running about 50 yd. through this brushy area the trail enters the larger western slide, where it meets the Mt. Tripyramid Trail. To locate the beginning of the trail on the Tripyramid slide, look for a small sign at the extreme eastern edge of the western slide, 60 yd. below its top.

Kate Sleeper Trail (map 3:J7–J8)

Distances from Rollins Trail junction (3,900 ft.) to
- Downes Brook Trail (3,400 ft.): 0.8 mi., 0 ft. (rev. 500 ft.), 25 min.
- Mt. Tripyramid Trail (3,850 ft.): 3.3 mi., 900 ft. (rev. 450 ft.), 2 hr. 5 min.

Shorter Paths in the Ferncroft Area (WODC)

These trails are often not as well beaten as the more important paths, and signs and other markings may be sparse or absent, so they must be followed with care. They frequently cross private property, and landowner rights and privacy must be respected.

Brook Path. This trail, 2.0 mi. long, leaves NH 113A opposite the Cabin Trail trailhead and follows the north bank of the Wonalancet River for

0.9 mi., then crosses it on a bridge and ascends to a junction with a logging road, where it bears left and descends back near the brook. Becoming rougher, it passes an old dam and then Wonalancet Falls at 1.1 mi. It descends roughly a short distance past an old mill building, then follows an old woods road along the brook. At 1.8 mi., it climbs a steep bank, turns left onto a gravel road, and follows it for 0.2 mi. to a designated parking area on the left. This road leads another 0.1 mi. to NH 113A just south of the bridge across the Wonalancet River and 1.7 mi. east of the Cabin Trail trailhead.

Gordon Path. This trail, 1.2 mi. long, begins at the Ferncroft Rd. parking area, taking the right fork (almost straight ahead) where the Old Mast Rd. and Kelley Trail bear left; after 0.2 mi., it turns to the right off this road and climbs over a low ridge. It descends on old logging roads, crosses a branch of Spring Brook on a bridge, then emerges in a yard (private property). It then bears right on a gravel driveway that comes out onto NH 113A at a point 0.1 mi. east of its junction with Ferncroft Rd. and 0.3 mi. west of the Cabin Trail trailhead.

Pasture Path. This trail, 1.1 mi. long, diverges left from the Blueberry Ledge Trail 0.5 mi. from the Ferncroft Rd. parking area; ascending gradually, it leads past Tilton Spring at 0.6 mi., where it passes through an intersection with the Tilton Spring Path (right) and the Red Path (left). It continues ascending gently through logged areas and then bears left to the summit of Mt. Katherine (1,380 ft.), a broad ledge with good views of Wonalancet and the Sandwich Range.

Red Path. This trail, 0.7 mi. long, begins at the site of the former Wonalancet post office (on Ferncroft Rd. just west of its junction with NH 113A). It follows a gravel road past houses, then continues on a logging road, soon turns right onto an older road, and ascends to Tilton Spring, where it meets the Tilton Spring Path and the Pasture Path.

Tilton Spring Path. This trail, 0.9 mi. long, begins at Tilton Spring and ascends gradually, entering the WMNF at 0.2 mi. It swings right at 0.5 mi. and ascends easily to the McCrillis Path at a point 0.2 mi. from the Blueberry Ledge Trail.

Shorter Paths in the Ferncroft Area (map 3: K8–K9)

SUGGESTED HIKES

For more information on suggested hikes, see p. ix.

Easy Hikes

Champney and Pitcher Falls [rt: 3.2 mi., 600 ft., 1:55]. An easy-graded climb up Champney Falls Trail and a spur path to a pair of waterfalls, best viewed after a significant rainfall.

Allen's Ledge [rt: 2.2 mi., 650 ft., 1:25]. A moderate climb up the west loop of the UNH Trail to a good viewpoint.

Big Rock Cave [rt: 3.8 mi., 1,250 ft., 2:30]. This interesting boulder cave on a southern spur of Mt. Paugus, reached by the Cabin Trail and Big Rock Cave Trail, is a good objective for small children.

Moderate Hikes

White Ledge [lp: 4.4 mi., 1,450 ft., 2:55]. A loop over an eastern spur of Mt. Chocorua with several good views.

Mt. Potash [rt: 4.4 mi., 1,500 ft., 2:55]. A small, open peak on the north side of the Sandwich Range, reached by the Downes Brook and Mt. Potash trails.

Hedgehog Mountain [lp: 4.8 mi., 1,450 ft., 3:10]. The UNH Trail makes an excellent loop with three viewpoints on this low mountain north of Mt. Passaconaway.

Carter Ledge [rt: 5.6 mi., 1,650 ft., 3:40]. A scenic route up the Piper, Nickerson Ledge, and Carter Ledge trails leads to this magnificent open ledge; the climb is steep near the top. The trail can be followed onward to Middle Sister and Chocorua itself, but there is a very tricky ledge scramble along the way.

Strenuous Hikes

Mt. Chocorua. There are several attractive routes up one of the most popular peaks in the White Mountains. From the Kancamagus Highway a relatively easy route follows the Champney Falls and Piper trails [rt: 7.6 mi., 2,250 ft., 4:55]. The Brook and Liberty trails make a fine loop, but with significantly steeper and rougher climbing, from the southwest [lp: 7.5 mi., 2,750 ft., 5:05]. A longer and even more challenging route ascends via the Piper, Nickerson Ledge, Carter Ledge, Middle Sister, and Piper trails and descends by the Liberty, Hammond, Weetamoo, and Piper trails [lp: 9.6 mi., 3,200 ft., 6:25].

Mt. Passaconaway [rt: 10.2 mi., 2,800 ft., 6:30]. The route ascending this wooded peak from the Kancamagus Highway offers several views; use the Oliverian Brook Trail, Passaconaway Cutoff, Square Ledge, and Walden trails. Add 0.6 mi. rt and 200 ft. for a side trip to the spectacular north outlook.

Mt. Whiteface. The broad ledges of the south summit offer an excellent view over the lake country to the south; the ledges and the wooded summit can be reached by ascending the scenic and challenging Blueberry Ledge Trail [rt: 8.4 mi., 3,050 ft., 5:45] or the longer, more routine route via the Flat Mountain Pond and McCrillis trails [rt: 10.4 mi., 3,250 ft., 6:50].

SECTION NINE
THE CARTER AND BALDFACE RANGES

This section covers the Carter-Moriah Range and the Baldface Range, along with the broad valley of the Wild River that lies between these two high ranges as well as the lower mountains on the long subsidiary ridges that extend south from them. In the Carter-Moriah Range the major peaks are Wildcat Mountain, Carter Dome, Mt. Hight, South Carter Mountain, Middle Carter Mountain, Mt. Moriah, and Shelburne Moriah Mountain; in the Baldface Range, the major peaks are North Baldface, South Baldface, West Royce Mountain, and East Royce Mountain; and in the southern part, the major peaks are Black Mountain, North and South Doublehead, Kearsarge North, Black Cap, Peaked Mountain, and Middle Mountain. The area is bounded on the west by NH 16, on the north by US 2, and on the east and south by ME 113/NH 113 (which crosses the state line several times). Many trails in this section coincide with or intersect cross-country ski or snowmobile trails, and care often must be taken to distinguish the hiking trails from the others. The entire area is covered by the AMC's *Carter Range–Evans Notch Map* (map 5). In late 2006, the valley of the Wild River and surrounding slopes were officially designated as the new Wild River Wilderness.

In this section, the Appalachian Trail (AT) begins at NH 16 opposite Pinkham Notch Visitor Center and follows the Lost Pond, Wildcat Ridge, Nineteen-Mile Brook, Carter-Moriah, Kenduskeag, and Rattle River trails to US 2 east of Gorham. It crosses the summits of Wildcat Mountain, Carter Dome, Mt. Hight, South Carter Mountain, Middle Carter Mountain, and North Carter Mountain, and passes near the summit of Mt. Moriah.

GEOGRAPHY

The Carter-Moriah Range would be a great deal more prominent among White Mountain ranges were it not for those neighbors that rise 1,500 ft. higher across Pinkham Notch. On a ridge about 10 mi. long, there are eight significant peaks more than 4,000 ft. tall and wild, dramatic Carter Notch. The finest views in the range are commanded by Mt. Hight, which remains bare after having been swept by fire in 1903. Those from Shelburne Moriah Mountain, Carter Dome, and Mt. Moriah are also excellent, and there are several fine outlooks in various directions along the trails. To the east, the range overlooks the broad, forested valley of the Wild River and the rocky peaks of the Baldface group, and far beyond lies the Atlantic Ocean, which reflects the sun on the southeast horizon behind Sebago Lake on clear midmornings.

Wildcat Mountain rises at the south end of the range. Of its numerous summits, the highest is the one nearest to Carter Notch; its five most prominent summits are designated, from east to west, A Peak (4,422 ft.), B Peak (4,330 ft.), C Peak (4,298 ft.), D Peak (4,062 ft.), and E Peak (4,046 ft.). The mountain is heavily wooded, but there are magnificent outlook ledges on the Wildcat Ridge Trail west of E Peak, a lookout platform with extensive views on D Peak near the top of the Wildcat Ski Area, and fine views straight down into Carter Notch from A Peak.

Carter Notch, the deep cleft between Carter Dome and Wildcat Mountain, includes some of the finest scenery in this region, particularly the two small, beautiful Carter Lakes that lie in the secluded hollow in the deepest part of the notch. The actual pass (3,388 ft.) in the main ridge connecting Carter Dome to Wildcat Mountain is north of the lakes and 100 ft. higher than them, whereas the Rampart, a barrier of rocks that have fallen from the cliffs above on both Wildcat and Carter Dome, stretches across the floor of the notch, so that the lakes are totally enclosed by natural walls and their outlet brook on the south side is forced to run underground. Above the lakes, the impressive wooded cliffs of Wildcat Mountain rise vertically nearly 1,000 ft. to the west, and to the east, Carter Dome also rises steeply, with the immense boulder called Pulpit Rock jutting out above the notch. A rough trail leaves the Wildcat River Trail about 100 yd. south of Carter Notch Hut and runs east over the Rampart's huge rocks, where there is a good view toward Jackson, and the many boulder caves among the fallen rocks, where ice sometimes remains through the summer, invite exploration (use caution).

Carter Dome (4,832 ft.) once bore a fire tower on its flat, scrub-fringed top. There are good views west and north and limited views south from open areas in the vicinity of the summit; the bare southeast spur crossed by the Rainbow Trail is a much better viewpoint. A bare rock peak, Mt. Hight (4,675 ft.), has the best views in the range. South Carter Mountain (4,430 ft.) is wooded with no views. Middle Carter Mountain (4,610 ft.) is wooded, but there are good outlooks from various points along its ridge crest, including an excellent view of the Presidentials 70 yd. north of the summit. North Carter Mountain (4,530 ft.) has views from its summit and from ledges along the ridge north and south of the summit; the best views are east to the Baldface Range. Imp Mountain (3,730 ft.) is a trailless north spur of North Carter. Imp Profile (3,165 ft.) is an interesting cliff on a west spur of North Carter. The profile, which is named for its imagined resemblance to the grotesquely misshapen face of a part-human wood sprite, is best seen from Hayes Field in the WMNF Dolly Copp Campground. The top of the cliff affords an excellent view of the Presidentials.

From its ledgy summit block, Mt. Moriah (4,049 ft.) has fine views in all directions. A northwest spur of Moriah, Mt. Surprise (2,194 ft.), offers restricted views. The former hiking trail on Mt. Evans (1,443 ft.) is closed. Shelburne Moriah Mountain (3,735 ft.) offers magnificent views—surpassed in this range only by Mt. Hight—from acres of flat ledges at the summit and outlooks on its southwest and east ridges.

The Baldface-Royce Range extends southwest from Evans Notch, between the Wild River and the Cold River. The summits are relatively low, but so are the valleys; thus, the mountains rise impressively high above their bases. The highest peaks in the range are North Baldface (3,610 ft.) and South Baldface (3,570 ft.). Their upper slopes were swept by fire in 1903 and the resulting great expanses of open ledge make the circuit over these peaks one of the finest trips in the White Mountains. With Eagle Crag (3,030 ft.), a northeast buttress, these peaks enclose a cirque-like valley on their east. To the southwest are Sable Mountain (3,519 ft.) and Chandler Mountain (3,335 ft.), both wooded and trailless, and to the southeast is Eastman Mountain (2,939 ft.), which affords fine views from its ledgy summit.

A ridge descends northeast from Eagle Crag over Mt. Meader (2,782 ft.), which has ledgy outlooks, to the Basin Rim, where there are fine views from the brink of a cliff, then ascends to the Royces. West Royce Mountain (3,210 ft.), with good views to the east and southeast from a ledge near the summit, is located in New Hampshire, and East Royce Mountain (3,114 ft.), with good views in nearly all directions, is in Maine; the state line crosses slightly to the east of the col between them.

A number of lower mountains rise from the ridges that extend south from the main ranges. Spruce Mountain (2,270 ft.), which is trailless, and

Eagle Mountain (1,613 ft.), which has a path and views from the summit, are small peaks on a south ridge of Wildcat Mountain. Black Mountain (3,304 ft.), which lies across Perkins Notch from Carter Dome, is a long ridge with a multitude of bumps, of which seven have traditionally been considered summits—though which seven bumps should be counted as summits has never been entirely clear. The highest summit is densely wooded and trailless. Good views can be obtained from the southernmost summit, the Knoll (2,010 ft.), which is part of the Black Mountain Ski Area, and from a knob (2,757 ft.) in the middle of the ridge that is reached by the Black Mountain Ski Trail. North Doublehead (3,053 ft.), with a cabin on the summit and good views east and west from outlooks near the summit, and South Doublehead (2,939 ft.), with good views from several ledges, form a small, sharp ridge southeast of Black Mountain. Southwest of Doublehead is the low range composed of Thorn Mountain (2,282 ft.) and Tin Mountain (2,031 ft.). Tin Mountain is said to have been the site of the first discovery of tin ore in the United States, but the old mines are filled with water and cannot be easily reached. The former hiking trail on Thorn Mountain is closed. East of Doublehead lie the valleys of the East Branch of the Saco and Slippery Brook. In the valley of Slippery Brook is Mountain Pond, a crescent-shaped body of water about three-quarters of a mile long by half a mile wide, entirely surrounded by woods and overlooked by South Baldface, Mt. Shaw, and Doublehead.

Kearsarge North (3,268 ft.), sometimes called Mt. Pequawket, rises above Intervale. The open ledge summit bears an abandoned fire tower that is in good condition, and the views are magnificent in all directions, whether or not one ascends the tower; this is one of the finest viewpoints in the White Mountains. Bartlett Mountain (2,661 ft.) is a shoulder extending westward toward Intervale; it has no official trails, but a number of ledges invite exploration. A range of trailless hills extends northeast from Kearsarge North, of which the most prominent is Mt. Shaw (2,585 ft.).

Running south from Kearsarge North are the Green Hills of Conway: Hurricane Mountain (2,100 ft.), Black Cap (2,369 ft.), Peaked Mountain (1,739 ft.), Middle Mountain (1,857 ft.), Cranmore Mountain (1,690 ft.), and Rattlesnake Mountain (1,590 ft.). The summits of Black Cap, Peaked Mountain, Cranmore Mountain, and Middle Mountain afford excellent views, and there are several other good viewpoints. Except for Hurricane

Mountain, these peaks are included within the Green Hills Preserve, a tract of more than 5,000 acres of hilly terrain with several streams and cascades and a beaver pond, as well as numerous rare and endangered plants and a beautiful high-elevation stand of red pine on Peaked Mountain and Middle Mountain. This reservation, which was established in 1990 through the generosity of the Anna B. Stearns Foundation, individuals, businesses, and other foundations, is owned and managed by the Nature Conservancy, a private organization that maintains the preserve for the benefit of the public. All the major peaks except Rattlesnake Mountain are reached by well-maintained paths. Visitors are requested to park their vehicles only at designated sites. To protect this resource for the enjoyment of all, removal of rocks, minerals, plants, or artifacts from the preserve is forbidden. Information and a trail map can be obtained from the headquarters for the Green Hills Preserve; information is also posted at several kiosks along the trails (mentioned in trail descriptions), which have detailed maps on display and often have a supply of trail maps, but hikers would be well advised not to count on obtaining trail maps from this source.

HUTS

Carter Notch Hut (AMC)

The AMC constructed this stone hut in 1914. It is located at an elevation of 3,288 ft., about 60 yd. south of the smaller lake, at the southern terminus of the Nineteen-Mile Brook Trail and the northern terminus of the Wildcat River Trail. The hut, with two bunkhouses, accommodates 40 guests. Pets are not permitted in the hut. The hut will again offer a full-service season starting in 2007. The hut is open for full service from June to mid-September, and is open on a caretaker basis the rest of the year. For current information and schedule, contact the AMC's Reservations Office (603-466-2727) or visit www.outdoors.org/lodging.

CAMPING

Wild River Wilderness

The Wild River Wilderness, created in 2006, includes 23,700 acres in the great valley between the Carter and Baldface ranges. Wilderness regulations, intended to protect Wilderness resources and promote opportunities for challenge and solitude, prohibit use of motorized equipment or mechanical means of transportation of any sort. In accordance with USFS Wilderness policy, the trails in the Wild River Wilderness are in general maintained to a lower standard than trails outside Wilderness. They may be rough, overgrown, or essentially unmarked with minimal signage, and considerable care may be required to follow them. Hiking and camping group size must be no larger than 10 people. Camping and fires are also prohibited above the treeline (where trees are less than 8 ft. tall) except in winter, when camping is permitted above the treeline in places where snow cover is at least 2 ft. deep, but not on any frozen body of water. The three remaining shelters in this area may be removed in the near future; one should not count on using any of these shelters.

Forest Protection Areas

The WMNF has established a number of Forest Protection Areas (FPAs)—formerly known as Restricted Use Areas—where camping and wood or charcoal fires are prohibited throughout the year. The specific areas are under continual review, and areas are added to or subtracted from the list in order to provide the greatest amount of protection to areas subject to damage by excessive camping, while imposing the lowest level of restrictions possible. A general list of FPAs in this section follows, but because there are often major changes from year to year, one should obtain current information on FPAs from the WMNF.

(1) No camping is permitted above treeline (where trees are less than 8 ft. tall) except in winter, and then only where there is at least 2 ft. of snow cover on the ground—but not on any frozen body of water. The point where the above-treeline restricted area begins is marked on most trails with small signs, but the absence of such signs should not be construed as proof of the legality of a site.

(2) No camping is permitted within 0.25 mi. of any trailhead, picnic area, or any facility for overnight accommodation such as a hut, cabin, shelter, tentsite, or campground, except as designated at the facility itself. In the area covered by Section Nine, camping is also forbidden within 0.25 mi. of Zeta Pass.

(3) No camping is permitted within 200 ft. of certain trails. In 2006, designated trails included the first mile of the Wild River Trail south of Wild River Campground.

(4) No camping is permitted on WMNF land within 0.25 mi. of certain roads (camping on private roadside land is illegal except by permission of the landowner). In 2006, these roads included Wild River Rd. (FR 12) and NH 16 north of the Dana Place Inn, and NH 113 within .5 mi. of Hastings Campground.

Established Trailside Campsites

During peak summer and fall periods, groups of six or more planning to use AMC-managed backcountry campsites are asked to use the AMC's group notification system. For more information visit http://www.outdoors .org/lodging/campsites/campsites-notification.cfm.

Imp Campsite (AMC) is located on a spur path from the Carter-Moriah Trail between Moriah and North Carter. There is a shelter and five tent platforms. In summer, there is a caretaker and a fee is charged. Water is available in a nearby brook.

Rattle River Shelter (WMNF) is located on the Rattle River Trail 1.7 mi. from US 2.

Spruce Brook Shelter (WMNF) is located on the Wild River Trail about 3.5 mi. from Wild River Campground. Following the established policy for management of Wilderness, this shelter will be removed either in the near future or when major maintenance is required.

Perkins Notch Shelter (WMNF) is located on the southeast side of the Wild River, just south of No-Ketchum Pond, with bunk space for six. Following the established policy for management of Wilderness, this shelter will be removed either in the near future or when major maintenance is required.

Blue Brook Shelter (WMNF) is located on the Black Angel Trail (and a branch trail connecting to the Basin Trail) 0.3 mi. west of Rim Junction. Following the established policy for management of Wilderness, this shelter will be removed either in the near future or when major maintenance is required.

Baldface Shelter (WMNF) is located on the Baldface Circle Trail, just below the ledges on South Baldface. The water source near the shelter is not reliable.

Province Pond Shelter (WMNF) is located on the Province Brook Trail at Province Pond.

Mountain Pond Shelter (WMNF) is located on the Mountain Pond Loop Trail at Mountain Pond.

Doublehead Cabin (WMNF) is located at the summit of North Doublehead, with bunks for eight. The cabin is kept locked and reservations for its use must be made with the Saco Ranger District office (603-447-5448). There is no water nearby.

Black Mountain Cabin (WMNF) is located on the Black Mountain Ski Trail (which is also used for hiking) near the central summit of Black Mountain. It has bunks for eight. The cabin is kept locked and reservations for its use must be made with the Saco Ranger District office (603-447-5448). There is a spring (unreliable water source in summer, usually frozen in winter) near the cabin.

TRAIL DESCRIPTIONS

Wildcat Ridge Trail (AMC)

This trail climbs up to and across the numerous summits on the long ridge of Wildcat Mountain, then descends to the Nineteen-Mile Brook Trail 0.3 mi. north of Carter Notch Hut. The trail officially begins at the Glen Ellis Falls parking lot on NH 16 south of Pinkham Notch Visitor Center, but this end is more commonly reached by following the Lost Pond Trail from Pinkham Notch Visitor Center to avoid the often difficult and sometimes dangerous crossing of the Ellis River. From the Lost Pond Trail junction to Carter Notch, this trail is a part of the AT. The sections from the Lost Pond Trail junction to E Peak and from A Peak to Carter Notch are very steep and rough, and there are several ups and downs and other steep, rough sections along the rest of the trail that make it more difficult and time-consuming than one might infer from a casual glance at the map or the distance summary. *Caution:* The section between NH 16 and E Peak may be dangerous when wet or icy, and hikers with heavy packs should allow substantial extra time.

The trail starts on the east side of NH 16 opposite the parking area for Glen Ellis Falls (there is a pedestrian underpass for crossing the highway), and leads east across the Ellis River (may be very difficult) to a target. At 0.1 mi., the Lost Pond Trail enters on the left, and the trail shortly begins the very steep climb up the end of the ridge (use care on all ledge areas), crossing two open ledges, both with fine views of Mt. Washington across Pinkham Notch. At 0.9 mi., it passes a level, open ledge with fine views south, marked by a rock with "Sarge's Crag" engraved on it. The trail dips slightly, traverses a shoulder, then resumes the climb. At 1.2 mi., a side path (sign) leads left to a spring, and at 1.5 mi., the main trail climbs to the top of a steep ledge with a superb view of the great ravines on the east side of Mt. Washington. The trail continues to climb over several knobs and passes 3 yd. left of the summit of E Peak at 1.9 mi., then descends to the summit station of the Wildcat Ski Area in the col at 2.1 mi. From here, the easiest ski trails (those farthest to the north) descend to the Wildcat Ski Area base lodge in 2.6 mi.

The trail next climbs steeply to the summit of D Peak, where there is an observation tower; an easier trail maintained by the ski area parallels this segment to the west. The Wildcat Ridge Trail then descends into Wildcat Col, the deepest col on the main ridge, at 2.5 mi. Here it passes over a small hogback and through a second sag, then begins the climb to C Peak over several "steps"—fairly steep climbs interspersed with level sections to the summit of C Peak at 3.3 mi. The trail makes a significant descent into a col and a climb to B Peak, then a descent to a shallower col and an easy climb to A Peak at 4.2 mi. As the trail turns left near this summit, a spur path leads right 20 yd. to a spectacular view into Carter Notch. The actual summit of Wildcat Mountain is a rock in the scrub just off the spur path within a few yards of this outlook. The trail now descends rather steeply with many rock steps to meet the Nineteen-Mile Brook Trail at the height-of-land in Carter Notch; about two-thirds of the way down it crosses a large recent landslide track (potentially dangerous if icy) that provides a view north. For Carter Notch Hut, turn right (south) on the Nineteen-Mile Brook Trail.

Wildcat Ridge Trail (map 5:G9–F10)

Distances from Glen Ellis Falls parking area (1,960 ft.) to
- summit of E Peak (4,030 ft.): 1.9 mi., 2,150 ft. (rev. 100 ft.), 2 hr.
- Wildcat Col (3,770 ft.): 2.5 mi., 2,250 ft. (rev. 400 ft.), 2 hr. 25 min.
- summit of C Peak (4,298 ft.): 3.3 mi., 2,800 ft., 3 hr. 5 min.
- summit of A Peak (4,422 ft.): 4.2 mi., 3,150 ft. (rev. 200 ft.), 3 hr. 40 min.
- Nineteen-Mile Brook Trail (3,388 ft.): 4.9 mi., 3,150 ft. (rev. 1,050 ft.), 4 hr.

Lost Pond Trail (AMC)

This short link trail runs from Pinkham Notch Camp to the lower end of the Wildcat Ridge Trail, avoiding the difficult and sometimes dangerous crossing of the Ellis River at the beginning of the Wildcat Ridge Trail. It is part of the AT.

The trail leaves NH 16 opposite Pinkham Notch Camp, crosses a bridge over the Ellis River, and turns south at the end of the bridge, where the Square Ledge Trail leaves on the left. The Lost Pond Trail follows the east bank of the Ellis River, which is soon joined from the opposite side by the larger Cutler River. The trail then leaves the riverbank and climbs at a moderate grade to Lost Pond at 0.5 mi. It follows the east shore with good views, descends slightly, and ends at the Wildcat Ridge Trail.

Lost Pond Trail (map 5:F9–G9)

Distance from NH 16 opposite Pinkham Notch Visitor Center (2,030 ft.) to
• Wildcat Ridge Trail (1,980 ft.): 0.9 mi., 100 ft. (rev. 150 ft.), 30 min.

Square Ledge Trail (AMC)

This short trail (with blue blazes) leads to an excellent outlook from a ledge that rises from the floor of Pinkham Notch on the side of Wildcat Mountain. The trail diverges left where the Lost Pond Trail turns south 20 yd. beyond the east end of the footbridge across the Ellis River. It climbs moderately, and after 80 yd., a spur path leads left 50 yd. to a ledge signed Ladies' Lookout, which, though overgrown, offers a fine view of Pinkham Notch Camp. The trail bears right, then swings to the east and crosses the Square Ledge Loop Ski Trail. It then rises moderately, passes Hangover Rock, and ascends to the base of Square Ledge. It swings around to the east side of the ledge, then climbs steeply via a V-slot about 50 yd. to an outlook that offers excellent views of Pinkham Notch and Mt. Washington.

Square Ledge Trail (map 5:F9–F10)

Distance from Lost Pond Trail (2,020 ft.) to
• Square Ledge (2,500 ft.): 0.5 mi., 500 ft., 30 min.

Thompson Falls Trail (WMNF)

This trail runs from the Wildcat Ski Area to Thompson Falls, a series of cascades on a brook flowing from Wildcat Mountain. Except in wet seasons, the brook is apt to be rather low.

From the Wildcat Ski Area parking area, cross the bridge to the east side, turn left and follow the Nature Trail north; continue ahead where a branch leaves on the left at 0.1 mi. and where a loop leaves on the right and then rejoins. Leaving the Nature Trail, the trail to the falls crosses a small stream and a maintenance road, then leads up the south side of the brook to the foot of the first fall at 0.6 mi. It crosses to the north side above the fall, bears right, and continues up the brook for another 0.1 mi., with restricted views of Mt. Washington.

Thompson Falls Trail (map 5:F10)

Distance from Wildcat Ski Area (1,930 ft.) to
  • end of trail (2,100 ft.): 0.7 mi., 200 ft., 25 min.

Carter-Moriah Trail (AMC)

This trail runs 13.8 mi. from Gorham to Carter Notch, following the crest of the Carter Range. To reach the trailhead at Gorham, follow US 2 east from Gorham for 0.5 mi., take a sharp right onto Bangor St. just past the bridge and railroad track, and follow this paved road about 0.5 mi. to the turnaround at its end. Park only on the left side of the road, opposite the homes. (On foot from Gorham, follow the road that leaves the east side of NH 16 just south of the railroad tracks. Bear right in 0.1 mi. on Mill St., and in 0.1 mi. more, a path left leads across the Peabody River on a footbridge. Turn right here and follow the road to its end, where the trail enters the woods on the left.) From the Kenduskeag Trail junction near the summit of Mt. Moriah to Carter Notch, the Carter-Moriah Trail is part of the AT. Water is very scarce on many parts of this trail because it runs mostly on or near the crest of the ridge.

The following description of the path is in the southbound direction (from Gorham to Carter Notch). See later description of the path in the reverse direction.

Part I. Gorham to Mount Moriah

The trail follows a logging road up a steep bank, then climbs moderately through second-growth woods past a clear cut. It bears right, then left along the edge of another clear cut, and ascends through open hardwoods above the more recently logged area. At 2.0 mi., a ledge to the right affords good views, and the trail soon passes to the right of the insignificant summit of Mt. Surprise and its tiny box canyon. From here, the trail descends slightly, then ascends gradually at first, but soon becomes steeper as it climbs over ledges that have excellent views. The trail stays near the ridge top but winds from side to side, crossing several small ledgy humps and occasionally dipping below the crest. At 4.2 mi., there is a glimpse of Moriah's summit ahead, and at 4.5 mi., a spur path leads right 50 yd. to the ledgy summit of Mt. Moriah, which affords excellent views.

Part II. Mount Moriah to North Carter

From the junction with the Mt. Moriah summit spur path, two routes descend the ledges of the Moriah summit block. The right-hand one is probably easier, but both are rock scrambles and are dangerous when icy (in which case it may be better to bushwhack down through the woods). By either route, it is less than 100 yd. to the junction where the Kenduskeag Trail turns left, then shortly right, toward Shelburne Moriah Mountain. Here the Carter-Moriah Trail turns right (southwest). From this junction south, it is part of the AT and has white blazes. It follows the ridge crest south through woods and over an open knob, then descends moderately to excellent outlooks from the top of the south cliffs, and reaches the deep col between Moriah and the Carters at 5.9 mi. Here the Moriah Brook Trail enters left and the Carter-Moriah Trail turns right and follows a boardwalk. In 40 yd., the Stony Brook Trail enters straight ahead, and the Carter-Moriah Trail turns left. It continues with several minor ups and downs and crosses some ledges. At 6.6 mi., a spur trail descends right 0.2 mi. to Imp Campsite, which has a shelter, tent platforms, and water. The main trail crosses a small brook and passes through a wet area, ascending on the plateau south of Imp Mountain, and begins a steep and rough climb to North Carter Mountain at 7.7 mi., reaching its partly open summit at 8.2 mi.

Part III. North Carter to Zeta Pass

The path continues south, passes a fine outlook east over the Wild River valley, and winds along the crest of the ridge. At 8.5 mi., the North Carter Trail enters right, and the trail continues over several ledgy humps and boggy depressions. The best views in this area are from the ledgy knob called Mt. Lethe, a few steps to the left of the trail. A good outlook to the Presidentials is passed 70 yd. before the trail reaches the wooded summit of Middle Carter Mountain (sign) at 9.1 mi. The trail descends easily and passes an open area with a view west, then ascends a short, steep ledge and descends to the col between Middle and South Carter at 10.0 mi. It then ascends to a point 10 yd. left (east) of the wooded summit of South Carter (sign) at 10.4 mi. and descends gradually, with occasional steeper sections, to Zeta Pass, where it makes a short ascent to the junction with the Carter Dome Trail on the right at 11.2 mi. Water may occasionally be available in a small stream (usually dry in midsummer) that is accessible from the Carter Dome Trail 80 yd. below this junction.

Part IV. Zeta Pass to Carter Notch

The two trails climb easily to the south for 0.2 mi., then the Carter Dome Trail continues ahead and the Carter-Moriah Trail turns left and climbs steeply up to the summit of Mt. Hight at 11.8 mi. At this bare summit, which commands the best views in the range, the trail makes a very sharp right turn; great care must be exercised to stay on the trail if visibility is poor, particularly going north, because a beaten path that soon peters out continues north from the summit. (Compass bearings from the summit are southbound, 240 degrees magnetic; northbound, 290 degrees magnetic.) The trail passes through a shallow sag and the Carter Dome Trail reenters from the right at 12.2 mi. In another 25 yd., the Black Angel Trail enters on the left, and the Carter-Moriah Trail climbs steadily to the partly open summit of Carter Dome at 12.6 mi., where the Rainbow Trail enters on the left. The trail then descends moderately, passing a side path at 13.1 mi. that leads to the right 60 yd. to a fine spring. At 13.5 mi., a side path leads 30 yd. to the left to an excellent outlook over Carter Notch. Soon the trail begins to descend very steeply to Carter Notch, ending on the Nineteen-Mile Brook Trail at the shore of the larger Carter Lake. Carter Notch Hut is 0.1 mi. to the left.

Carter-Moriah Trail (map 5:E10–F10)

Distances from Bangor St. (800 ft.) to
- Mt. Moriah summit (4,049 ft.): 4.5 mi., 3,400 ft., 3 hr. 55 min.
- Moriah Brook and Stony Brook trails (3,127 ft.): 5.9 mi., 3,450 ft., 4 hr. 40 min.
- Imp Shelter spur trail (3,350 ft.): 6.6 mi., 3,750 ft., 5 hr. 10 min.
- North Carter Trail (4,470 ft.): 8.5 mi., 4,950 ft., 6 hr. 45 min.
- Middle Carter summit (4,610 ft.): 9.1 mi., 5,150 ft., 7 hr. 10 min.
- South Carter summit (4,430 ft.): 10.4 mi., 5,400 ft., 7 hr. 55 min.
- Zeta Pass (3,890 ft.): 11.2 mi., 5,400 ft., 8 hr. 20 min.
- Mt. Hight summit (4,675 ft.): 11.8 mi., 6,200 ft., 9 hr.
- Black Angel Trail (4,600 ft.): 12.2 mi., 6,250 ft., 9 hr. 15 min.
- Carter Dome summit (4,832 ft.): 12.6 mi., 6,500 ft., 9 hr. 35 min.
- Nineteen-Mile Brook Trail (3,300 ft.): 13.8 mi., 6,500 ft., 10 hr. 10 min.

Carter-Moriah Trail (AMC) [In Reverse]

Part I. Carter Notch to Zeta Pass

The trail begins on the Nineteen-Mile Brook Trail at the shore of the larger Carter Lake, 0.1 mi. north of Carter Notch Hut. It climbs very steeply at first, then moderates, and at 0.3 mi., a side path leads 30 yd. to the right to an excellent outlook over Carter Notch. The trail continues to climb at a moderate grade, passing a side path at 0.7 mi. that leads to the left 60 yd. to a fine spring, and at 1.2 mi., it reaches the partly open summit of Carter Dome, where the Rainbow Trail enters on the right. The Carter-Moriah Trail descends steadily, and at 1.6 mi., the Black Angel Trail enters on the right. In another 25 yd., as the Carter Dome Trail continues straight ahead, the Carter-Moriah Trail bears right, passes through a shallow sag, and ascends moderately to the summit of Mt. Hight at 2.0 mi. At this bare summit, which commands the best views in the range, the trail makes a very sharp left turn; great care must be exercised to stay on the trail if visibility is poor, particularly going north, because a beaten path that soon peters out continues north from the summit. (Compass bearings from the summit are: northbound, 290 degrees magnetic; southbound, 240 degrees magnetic.) The trail descends steeply and rejoins the Carter Dome Trail at 2.4 mi., and the two trails continue to Zeta Pass at 2.6 mi., where the Carter Dome Trail turns left and descends toward NH 16. Water may occasionally be available in a small stream (usually dry in midsummer) that is accessible from the Carter Dome Trail 80 yd. below this junction.

Part II. Zeta Pass to North Carter

From the junction with the Carter Dome Trail in Zeta Pass, the trail descends slightly to the actual low point of the pass, then ascends gradually, with occasional steeper sections, to a point 10 yd. right (east) of the wooded summit of South Carter (sign) at 3.4 mi. It descends to the col between Middle and South Carter at 3.8 mi., then ascends easily, descending a short, steep ledge and passing an open area with a view west. It reaches the wooded summit of Middle Carter Mountain (sign) at 4.7 mi. There is a good outlook to the Presidentials 70 yd. farther along the trail. The trail now descends over several ledgy humps and boggy depressions. The best views in this area are from the ledgy knob called Mt. Lethe, a few steps to the right of the trail. At 5.3 mi., the North Carter Trail enters on the left, and the Carter-Moriah Trail winds along the crest of the ridge past a fine outlook east over the Wild River valley, reaching the partly open summit of North Carter at 5.6 mi.

Part III. North Carter to Mount Moriah

The Carter-Moriah Trail makes a steep and rough descent (difficult for those with heavy packs) from North Carter, and at 6.1 mi., the grade becomes moderate to easy as the trail descends on the plateau south of Imp Mountain, passing through a wet area and crossing a small brook. At 7.2 mi., a spur trail descends to the left 0.2 mi. to Imp Campsite, which has a shelter, tent platforms, and water. The main trail crosses some ledges and continues with several minor ups and downs to the deep col between the Carters and Moriah at 7.9 mi. Here the Stony Brook Trail enters on the left, where the Carter-Moriah Trail turns sharp right on a boardwalk, and in 40 yd., the Moriah Brook Trail enters on the right. Here the Carter-Moriah Trail turns left and starts to climb up the ledgy ridge of Mt. Moriah, soon reaching excellent outlooks from the top of the south cliffs. It continues to climb moderately up ledges to a shoulder, then follows the ridge crest north through woods and over an open knob to a junction at 9.3 mi., where the Kenduskeag Trail (continuing the AT north) goes straight and shortly turns right toward Shelburne Moriah Mountain. At this junction, the Carter-Moriah Trail turns left, and two routes ascend the ledges of the Moriah summit block. The left one is probably easier, but both are rock scrambles and are dangerous when icy (in which case it may be better to bushwhack through the woods). By either route, it is less than 100 yd. to the junction with the spur path that leads left 50 yd. to the ledgy summit of Mt. Moriah, which affords excellent views.

Part IV. Mount Moriah to Gorham

The trail descends moderately, staying near the ridge top but winding from side to side, crossing several small ledgy humps and occasionally dipping below the crest. It then becomes steeper and climbs down over ledges that have excellent views. After a fairly level section below the ledges and a slight ascent, it passes to the left of the insignificant summit of Mt. Surprise and its tiny box canyon at 11.8 mi. and descends again, passing the last open ledge, which is just to the left of the trail. Soon it enters second-growth woods in a fairly recently logged area and descends on logging roads. It follows the right edge of a clear cut and then bears right, and continues on logging roads until it finally descends a steep bank to the end of Bangor St.

Carter-Moriah Trail [In Reverse] (map 5:E10–F10)

Distances from Nineteen-Mile Brook Trail (3,300 ft.) to

- Carter Dome summit (4,832 ft.): 1.2 mi., 1,550 ft., 1 hr. 25 min.
- Black Angel Trail (4,600 ft.): 1.6 mi., 1,550 ft., 1 hr. 35 min.
- Mt. Hight summit (4,675 ft.): 2.0 mi., 1,700 ft., 1 hr. 50 min.
- Zeta Pass (3,890 ft.): 2.6 mi., 1,700 ft., 2 hr. 10 min.
- South Carter summit (4,430 ft.): 3.4 mi., 2,250 ft., 2 hr. 50 min.
- Middle Carter summit (4,610 ft.): 4.7 mi., 2,700 ft., 3 hr. 40 min.
- North Carter Trail (4,470 ft.): 5.3 mi., 2,750 ft., 4 hr.
- Imp Shelter spur trail (3,350 ft.): 7.2 mi., 2,850 ft., 5 hr.
- Moriah Brook and Stony Brook trails (3,127 ft.): 7.9 mi., 2,950 ft., 5 hr. 25 min.
- Mt. Moriah summit (4,049 ft.): 9.3 mi., 3,850 ft., 6 hr. 35 min.
- Bangor St. (800 ft.): 13.8 mi., 4,000 ft., 8 hr. 55 min.

Nineteen-Mile Brook Trail (WMNF)

This trail runs from NH 16 about 1 mi. north of the Mt. Washington Auto Rd. to Carter Notch Hut and is the easiest route to the hut. (The parking area is a stop for the AMC's Hiker Shuttle.) Sections of the trail close to the brook bank sometimes become dangerously icy in the cold seasons.

Leaving NH 16, the trail follows the northeast bank of Nineteen-Mile Brook on the remains of an old road. At 1.2 mi., the main trail passes a dam in the brook, and at 1.9 mi., the Carter Dome Trail diverges left for Zeta Pass. Here the Nineteen-Mile Brook Trail crosses a tributary on a footbridge, and at 2.2 mi., it crosses another brook at a small cascade, also on a footbridge. At 3.1 mi., the trail crosses a small brook and begins to ascend more steeply to the height-of-land at 3.6 mi., where the Wildcat Ridge Trail diverges right (west). The Nineteen-Mile Brook Trail then drops steeply to the larger Carter Lake, passes the Carter-Moriah Trail left at 3.8 mi., crosses between the lakes, and reaches Carter Notch Hut and the junction with the Wildcat River Trail.

Nineteen-Mile Brook Trail (map 5:F10)

Distances from NH 16 (1,487 ft.) to

- Carter Dome Trail (2,322 ft.): 1.9 mi., 850 ft., 1 hr. 25 min.
- Wildcat Ridge Trail (3,388 ft.): 3.6 mi., 1,900 ft., 2 hr. 45 min.
- Carter Notch Hut (3,300 ft.): 3.8 mi., 1,900 ft. (rev. 100 ft.), 2 hr. 50 min.

Carter Dome Trail (WMNF)

This trail runs from the Nineteen-Mile Brook Trail 1.9 mi. from NH 16 to Zeta Pass and the summit of Carter Dome, following the route of an old road that served the long-dismantled fire tower that once stood on Carter Dome. Grades are steady and moderate all the way.

Leaving the Nineteen-Mile Brook Trail, it follows a tributary brook, crossing it at 0.5 mi., and recrossing at 0.8 mi. at a small, attractive cascade. Here it swings left, then in 50 yd. turns sharp right and ascends by a series of seven switchbacks, passing a good spring left at 1.1 mi., and reaching the junction with the Carter-Moriah Trail at Zeta Pass at 1.9 mi. The Carter Dome Trail coincides with the Carter-Moriah Trail to the right (south), then at 2.1 mi., the Carter-Moriah Trail—which offers excellent views but is steep and exposed to weather—turns left to climb to the bare summit of Mt. Hight, whereas the Carter Dome Trail continues its steady, sheltered ascent. At 2.7 mi., the Carter-Moriah Trail reenters from the left, the Black Angel Trail enters from the left in another 25 yd., and the Carter Dome and Carter-Moriah trails coincide to the junction with the Rainbow Trail at the summit of Carter Dome.

Carter Dome Trail (map 5:F10)

Distances from Nineteen-Mile Brook Trail (2,322 ft.) to
- Zeta Pass (3,890 ft.): 1.9 mi., 1,550 ft., 1 hr. 45 min.
- Carter Dome summit (4,832 ft.): 3.1 mi., 2,500 ft., 2 hr. 50 min.

Imp Trail (WMNF)

This trail makes a loop over the cliff that bears the Imp Profile, providing fine views of the Presidential Range. The ends of the loop are 0.3 mi. apart on NH 16, with the north end about 2.6 mi. north of the Mt. Washington Auto Rd. and 5.4 mi. south of Gorham.

The north branch of the trail heads east up the south side of the Imp Brook valley, through a pleasant stand of hemlocks, then crosses the brook at 0.8 mi. (difficult at high water). It angles north up to a ridge and follows its crest, nearly level for some distance. The trail then angles more steeply up the north side of the ridge and continues nearly to the bottom of a ravine northeast of the Imp Profile cliff, where it turns right and then climbs steeply, swinging to the left, to reach the Imp viewpoint at 2.2 mi.

From the cliff, the trail skirts the edge of the Imp Brook ravine and crosses a large brook in 0.3 mi. Becoming gradual but somewhat rough, it continues generally south, ascending and then descending to the junction with the North Carter Trail on the left at 3.1 mi., then passes the site of an old logging camp. The Imp Trail turns right here and descends an old logging road generally southwest, then, just before reaching Cowboy Brook, turns northwest. After another 0.8 mi., it crosses a brook and a new logging road. It meanders across a flat area, follows an old logging road north downhill to cross a small brook, then immediately crosses a larger brook. It turns sharp left, runs about level for 75 yd., and ends at NH 16.

Imp Trail (map 5:F10)

Distances from northern terminus on NH 16 (1,270 ft.) to
- viewpoint (3,100 ft.): 2.2 mi., 1,850 ft., 2 hr. to North Carter Trail (3,250 ft.): 3.1 mi., 2,100 ft. (rev. 100 ft.), 2 hr. 35 min.
- southern terminus on NH 16 (1,270 ft.): 6.3 mi., 2,100 ft. (rev. 2,000 ft.), 4 hr. 10 min.

North Carter Trail (WMNF)

This trail leaves the south branch of the Imp Trail 3.1 mi. from NH 16, just above an old logging-camp site. It follows an old logging road, and at 0.3 mi., turns to the right onto another old road. At 0.5 mi., it turns sharp left off the old road and climbs more steeply to the Carter-Moriah Trail 0.3 mi. south of the summit of North Carter.

North Carter Trail (map 5:F10)

Distance from Imp Trail (3,250 ft.) to
- Carter-Moriah Trail (4,470 ft.): 1.2 mi., 1,200 ft., 1 hr. 10 min.

Stony Brook Trail (WMNF)

This trail begins at a parking area just off NH 16 on a paved road that leaves the highway just south of the bridge over the Peabody River, about 2 mi. south of Gorham. The trail ends in the col between North Carter and Moriah and provides the best access to the beautiful south ledges of Mt. Moriah. The lower part of the trail has been relocated onto WMNF land to avoid an area of private home construction on the former route.

From NH 16 the trail crosses Stony Brook on a footbridge and follows the brook upstream for 0.8 mi., then recrosses the brook and turns left onto the old route, a logging road that becomes less and less obvious. It ascends moderately, and at 2.3 mi., the trail crosses Stony Brook at a pleasant small cascade and pool and begins to climb more steeply. At 3.1 mi., it crosses a small brook on a mossy ledge and climbs steadily to the ridge and the Carter-Moriah Trail.

Stony Brook Trail (map 5:E10–F11)

Distance from NH 16 (930 ft.) to
- Carter-Moriah Trail (3,127 ft.): 3.6 mi., 2,200 ft., 2 hr. 55 min.

Kenduskeag Trail (WMNF)

This trail runs from the Carter-Moriah Trail near the summit of Mt. Moriah to the Shelburne Trail in the col between Shelburne Moriah Mountain and Howe Peak, 4.5 mi. south of US 2. The ledges of Shelburne Moriah afford excellent views. The name of the trail is an Abenaki word meaning "a pleasant walk." From Mt. Moriah to the Rattle River Trail junction, the trail is part of the AT.

From the trail junction below the summit ledges of Mt. Moriah, the Kenduskeag Trail turns sharp right in 15 yd. and runs over a lesser summit, then descends steeply past an outlook, moderates, and continues the descent to the junction with the Rattle River Trail at 1.4 mi. The trail now climbs over a section of knobs and ledges with many plank walkways over alpine bogs and fine views, to the flat, ledgy summit of Shelburne Moriah Mountain at 2.7 mi. The upper part of this section of trail is very exposed to weather—more so than any other part of the Carter-Moriah Range. The trail runs across the summit plateau to an outlook east, then descends steadily with rough footing to a sharp, narrow col at 3.3 mi. It then climbs over two knolls with views—on the second knoll, one must scramble up a ledge on the right to obtain the fine view of the Wild River valley—and ends at the Shelburne Trail.

Kenduskeag Trail (map 5:E11–E12)

Distances from Carter-Moriah Trail (4,000 ft.) to

- Rattle River Trail (3,300 ft.): 1.4 mi., 100 ft. (rev. 800 ft.), 45 min.
- Shelburne Moriah Mountain summit (3,735 ft.): 2.7 mi., 650 ft. (rev. 100 ft.), 1 hr. 40 min.
- Shelburne Trail (2,750 ft.): 4.1 mi., 750 ft. (rev. 1,100 ft.), 2 hr. 25 min.

Rattle River Trail (WMNF)

This trail runs from US 2 to the Kenduskeag Trail in the Moriah–Shelburne Moriah col. The trailhead is on US 2 near the east end of the bridge over the Rattle River, about 300 yd. east of the North Rd. intersection and 3.5 mi. east of the eastern junction of US 2 and NH 16 in Gorham. This trail is a part of the AT.

From US 2, the trail leads generally south, following a logging road on the east side of the stream. A snowmobile trail enters on the right at 0.3 mi., the trails enter the WMNF, and the snowmobile trail leaves on the left at 0.6 mi., just before the Rattle River Trail crosses a tributary brook. At 1.7 mi., it passes the WMNF Rattle River Shelter (left) and soon crosses the Rattle River (may be difficult at high water), then crosses back over its westerly branch. At 3.2 mi., it again crosses the river and starts to climb steadily. It passes a small cascade to the left of the trail at 3.7 mi., and soon bears away from the brook and climbs steeply to the ridge top, where it meets the Kenduskeag Trail.

Rattle River Trail (map 5:E11)

Distances from US 2 (760 ft.) to

- Rattle River Shelter (1,250 ft.): 1.7 mi., 500 ft., 1 hr. 5 min.
- Kenduskeag Trail (3,300 ft.): 4.3 mi., 2,550 ft., 3 hr. 25 min.

Mount Evans Trail (AMC)

This trail has been closed by the landowner.

Shelburne Trail (WMNF)

This trail begins on FR 95 1.0 mi. from US 2 near the Maine–New Hampshire border, passes through the col between Shelburne Moriah Mountain and Howe Peak, and descends to Wild River Rd. Most of the trail south of the ridgeline is within or adjacent to the Wild River Wilderness. For the north terminus, leave US 2 about 9 mi. east of Gorham, at the west end of an abandoned wayside area just west of the Maine–New Hampshire border; go about 0.1 mi. into this area, and take FR 95 (a rough gravel road) right for 0.9 mi. to a gate. At the Wild River end, the trail leaves Wild River Rd. (FR 12) 0.6 mi. north of Wild River Campground and fords the river, which can be difficult even at moderate water levels. For this reason, the Wild River end of the trail is often approached via the Wild River Trail, the Moriah Brook Trail bridge, and the Highwater Trail.

The trail follows the continuation of FR 95 past the gate; this was an active logging road in 2006, with muddy footing, so hikers should be alert for changing conditions. The trail follows this for 2.1 mi., then it turns left off the main road (sign) onto an older logging road and begins to climb moderately above the brook. This turn was difficult to discern in 2006; it is 0.2 mi. after the first bridge. At 3.1 mi., the trail makes the first of four crossings of a branch brook and reaches the height-of-land at 4.0 mi., where it meets the eastern terminus of the Kenduskeag Trail. (For Shelburne Moriah Mountain, follow this trail to the right.) The Shelburne Trail continues over the height-of-land and descends steadily, crossing a brook and entering an old logging road. It then turns sharp left at 6.3 mi. onto another logging road, which it follows east down the valley of Bull Brook, soon crossing a branch of the brook. At 7.0 mi., the Highwater Trail enters from the right (southwest) and leaves on the left (northeast) 10 yd. farther on. This junction may be poorly signed. To avoid the Wild River crossing, follow the Highwater Trail south to the Moriah Brook Trail bridge. The Shelburne Trail continues straight across a dry channel (it may require care to follow the trail in this area) and fords the Wild River to Wild River Rd.

Shelburne Trail (map 5:E12–F12)

Distances from gate on FR 95 (900 ft.) to

- Kenduskeag Trail (2,750 ft.): 4.0 mi., 1,850 ft., 2 hr. 55 min.
- Wild River Rd. (1,079 ft.): 7.2 mi., 1,850 ft. (rev. 1,700 ft.), 4 hr. 30 min.

Wild River Trail (WMNF)

This trail begins at a parking area near the end of Wild River Rd. (FR 12) and just outside of Wild River Campground, a trailhead shared with the Basin Trail. It runs along the Wild River valley to Perkins Notch, then descends to the Wildcat River Trail between Carter Notch Rd. and Carter Notch. Wild River Rd. leaves ME 113 just south of the bridge over Evans Brook at Hastings and runs 5.7 mi. to the campground, where there is a parking area on the left just before the campground entrance. All the Wild River crossings and those of Spruce Brook and Red Brook may be difficult at moderate water levels and dangerous at high water. Between Eagle Link and Perkins Notch Shelter parts of the trail may be very muddy. From a point just beyond its junction with the Moriah Brook Trail to its junction with the Rainbow Trail, it is within the Wild River Wilderness. The two shelters on this trail may be removed in the near future.

The trail, relocated at the start to avoid passing through the campground, immediately crosses Wild River Rd., then two small streams, and follows the bank of the Wild River. At 0.2 mi., it turns right, entering and following the old logging railroad bed that extends from the end of Wild River Rd. and runs generally southwest along the southeast bank of the Wild River. At 0.4 mi., the Moriah Brook Trail leaves on the right to cross the river on a bridge, and at 1.0 mi., the trail narrows and crosses an old slide. At 2.8 mi., 70 yd. beyond the former crossing on Spider Bridge (which was washed away in 2005 and will not be replaced), the Black Angel Trail enters from the left and coincides with the Wild River Trail as both trails bear right and descend 50 yd. to a crossing of the Wild River on large rocks that may be awkward for hikers with short legs or heavy packs; this crossing may be difficult and dangerous in high water. From the west bank, the trails continue together for another 90 yd. to a four-way junction. Here the Black Angel Trail continues directly across toward Carter Dome, the Highwater Trail enters from the right, and the Wild River Trail turns left onto the old railroad grade and leads southwest on a scenic section along the bank above the river. At 3.6 mi., it passes Spruce Brook Shelter (right; may be removed) and then crosses Spruce Brook. At 4.5 mi., it crosses Red Brook, then leaves the old railroad bed and bears right. At 4.9 mi., the Eagle Link leaves on the left for Eagle Crag, and at 5.8 mi., the trail crosses to the south bank of the Wild River. At 6.4 mi., the East Branch Trail leaves on the left and the Wild River Trail crosses the Wild River to the north bank, then recrosses for the last time at 6.8 mi.

Soon the trail skirts the south side of No-Ketchum Pond (a small pool in an extensive boggy area), passes the WMNF Perkins Notch Shelter (may be removed) at 7.1 mi., heads more west, and begins a gradual climb into Perkins Notch. At 7.9 mi., after a brief descent, the Rainbow Trail leaves right for Carter Dome, and at 8.6 mi., at the Carroll-Coos county line (sign), the Bog Brook Trail leaves left for Carter Notch Rd. From this junction, the trail ascends slightly then descends gradually and ends at the Wildcat River Trail.

Wild River Trail (map 5:F12–G10)

Distances from Wild River Campground trailhead parking area (1,150 ft.) to
- Moriah Brook Trail (1,170 ft.): 0.4 mi., 0 ft., 10 min.
- Black Angel Trail /Highwater Trail junction (1,510 ft.): 2.8 mi., 350 ft., 1 hr. 35 min.
- Eagle Link (2,150 ft.): 4.9 mi., 1,000 ft., 2 hr. 55 min.
- East Branch Trail (2,400 ft.): 6.4 mi., 1,250 ft., 3 hr. 50 min.
- No-Ketchum Pond (2,560 ft.): 7.0 mi., 1,400 ft., 4 hr. 10 min.
- Rainbow Trail (2,590 ft.): 7.9 mi., 1,450 ft., 4 hr. 40 min.
- Bog Brook Trail (2,417 ft.): 8.6 mi., 1,450 ft. (rev. 150 ft.), 5 hr.
- Wildcat River Trail (2,320 ft.): 9.7 mi., 1,550 ft. (rev. 200 ft.), 5 hr. 35 min.

Hastings Trail (WMNF)

This trail has been abandoned by the WMNF.

Highwater Trail (WMNF)

This trail runs along the northwest side of the Wild River from Hastings on ME 113 to the Wild River Trail at the west side of its first river crossing, providing a means of avoiding unbridged crossings of the Wild River, which are frequently very difficult, though the crossings of Bull, Moriah, and Cypress brooks may also be difficult. Most of the way, the trail follows old logging roads with easy grades, close to the river, but it is often not blazed or signed clearly at intersections. Beyond its junction with the Moriah Brook Trail, it is within the Wild River Wilderness.

The trail starts at the west end of the suspension bridge over the Wild River across from the parking lot at Hastings. At 0.7 mi., it bears right on an old logging road that angles somewhat away from the river. The trail crosses into New Hampshire and continues up the river, then enters FR 52 and follows it for a while, passing the site of a logging bridge that formerly crossed the Wild River at 2.3 mi. to connect with the Wild River Rd. Heading generally southwest, the trail crosses Martins Brook at 4.0 mi. At 5.3 mi., it enters the Shelburne Trail, turns right and follows it for 10 yd., then turns left off it (no signs) and soon crosses Bull Brook (no bridge). At 6.7 mi., the trail reaches the footbridge where the Moriah Brook Trail crosses the Wild River, 0.4 mi. above Wild River Campground. It joins the Moriah Brook Trail and the trails descend a short, steep pitch to the left, and in another 0.1 mi., they turn sharp right. At 7.0 mi., the Highwater Trail turns left off the Moriah Brook Trail and descends to cross Moriah Brook (very difficult in high water). The trail climbs to the top of a steep bank and runs along its edge, with one descent and ascent to cross a brook and an occasional glimpse across the valley. It descends twice more to cross small brooks, then climbs again before descending to cross Cypress Brook at 9.5 mi. It soon passes the former crossing of the Wild River at Spider Bridge (which was washed away in 2005 and will not be replaced) and ends at a four-way junction with the Black Angel and Wild River trails.

Highwater Trail (map 5:E13–F11)

Distances from Wild River Rd. (830 ft.) to
- site of FR 52 bridge (950 ft.): 2.3 mi., 100 ft., 1 hr. 10 min.
- Shelburne Trail (1,090 ft.): 5.3 mi., 250 ft., 2 hr. 45 min.
- Moriah Brook Trail (1,170 ft.): 6.7 mi., 350 ft., 3 hr. 30 min.
- Wild River Trail/Black Angel Trail junction (1,510 ft.): 9.7 mi., 1,100 ft. (rev. 400 ft.), 5 hr. 25 min.

Burnt Mill Brook Trail (WMNF)

This trail ascends from a parking area off Wild River Rd. (FR 12), 2.7 mi. south of ME 113, to the Royce Trail in the col between East Royce Mountain and West Royce Mountain. From Wild River Rd., the trail ascends south on logging roads, passing a cascade to the left of the trail at 0.6 mi. At 1.4 mi., it begins to climb more steeply, crosses Burnt Mill Brook at 1.7 mi., and ascends to the col between the Royces, where it meets the Royce Trail.

Burnt Mill Brook Trail (map 5:F12)

Distance from Wild River Rd. (966 ft.) to
- Royce Trail (2,600 ft.): 2.0 mi., 1,650 ft., 1 hr. 50 min.

Moriah Brook Trail (WMNF)

This trail ascends to the col between Mt. Moriah and North Carter from the Wild River Trail 0.4 mi. south of Wild River Campground. It is an attractive trail, passing Moriah Gorge, traversing beautiful birch woods that have grown up after fires, and providing fine views up to the impressive south cliffs of Moriah. Nearly the entire trail is within the Wild River Wilderness.

The trail leaves to the right from the Wild River Trail and in 75 yd. crosses the Wild River on a suspension footbridge, where the Highwater Trail joins on the right. The trails descend a short, steep pitch to the left and follow the riverbank about 0.1 mi., then turn sharp right and generally follow the course of the former lumber railroad up the north bank of Moriah Brook. At 0.4 mi., the Highwater Trail leaves left. At 1.4 mi., the Moriah Brook Trail crosses Moriah Brook (may be difficult at high water); the gorge downstream from this crossing merits exploration. The trail follows the south bank of the brook, then recrosses at 2.8 mi., and in another 0.4 mi. passes some attractive cascades and pools, crosses a ledge, then crosses a branch of Moriah Brook just above the confluence with the main brook. The trail continues through birch woods and crosses the main brook four more times, the last crossing in a boulder area below a small cascade at 5.0 mi. The trail becomes rather wet as it winds through almost pure stands of white birch below the impressive south cliffs of Mt. Moriah, then climbs to the col and the Carter-Moriah Trail.

Moriah Brook Trail (map 5:F12–F11)

Distance from Wild River Trail (1,170 ft.) to
  • Carter-Moriah Trail (3,127 ft.): 5.5 mi., 1,950 ft., 3 hr. 45 min.

Black Angel Trail (WMNF)

This trail begins at Rim Junction—where the Basin and Basin Rim trails cross—and descends to cross the Wild River 70 yd. beyond the former crossing on Spider Bridge (which was washed away in 2005 and will not be replaced) along with the Wild River Trail, then climbs to the Carter-Moriah Trail 0.4 mi. north of Carter Dome. Nearly the entire trail is within the Wild River Wilderness. The Blue Brook Shelter may be removed in the near future.

Leaving Rim Junction, the trail descends gradually southwest 0.5 mi. to Blue Brook Shelter, where the Blue Brook Connector runs right (north) for 0.3 mi. to connect with the Basin Trail 0.3 mi. west of Rim Junction. From Blue Brook Shelter, the Black Angel Trail crosses Blue Brook, ascends moderately west and passes through a col, then descends to an old logging road and follows it generally west for 1.4 mi. down the Cedar Brook valley, remaining on the north side of the stream and making several obvious shortcuts at curves. The trail then leaves the logging road, turns more north, and joins the Wild River Trail, turning left and in 50 yd. crossing the Wild River on large rocks that may be awkward for hikers with short legs or heavy packs; this crossing may be difficult and dangerous in high water. From the west bank, the trails continue together for another 90 yd. to a four-way junction. Here the Highwater Trail enters from the right, the Wild River Trail turns left, and the Black Angel Trail continues directly ahead.

The Black Angel Trail now rises slowly through open woods. About 1.5 mi. up from the Wild River, the grade becomes steeper; at 5.2 mi., the trail crosses a north branch of Spruce Brook, and about 0.5 mi. beyond enters virgin timber. The grade lessens but the footing becomes rougher as the trail angles up the east slope of Mt. Hight, passing lookout points as it traverses a steep, ledgy section on its south-southeast slope, then swings southwest and ends at the Carter-Moriah Trail.

Black Angel Trail (map 5:F12–F10)

Distances from Rim Junction (1,950 ft.) to
- Blue Brook Shelter (1,800 ft.): 0.5 mi., 0 ft. (rev. 150 ft.), 15 min.
- Wild River Trail/Highwater Trail junction (1,510 ft.): 2.8 mi., 500 ft. (rev. 800 ft.), 1 hr. 40 min.
- Carter-Moriah Trail (4,600 ft.): 7.7 mi., 3,600 ft., 5 hr. 40 min.

Basin Trail (WMNF)

This trail runs from the parking area just outside of Wild River Campground (also the trailhead for the Wild River Trail) to Basin Pond (0.7 mi. from NH 113, near Cold River Campground), crossing the ridge connecting Mt. Meader to West Royce somewhat north of its lowest point and giving easy access to the magnificent views along the brink of the cliffs. Most of the trail west of the ridge crest is within the Wild River Wilderness.

Leaving the parking area, it follows an old lumber road. At 0.4 mi., where the road swings right, the trail continues straight ahead and soon approaches the southwest bank of Blue Brook, which it follows for about 0.8 mi. At 1.3 mi., it crosses the brook at the foot of a pretty cascade and then follows the northeast bank, passing opposite a very striking cliff to the south of the brook. The trail leaves Blue Brook, crosses another small brook, then climbs somewhat more steeply. At 2.0 mi., the Blue Brook Connector branches right 0.3 mi. to Blue Brook Shelter and the Black Angel Trail, and at 2.2 mi., the Basin Trail crosses the Basin Rim Trail and meets the Black Angel Trail at Rim Junction. The best viewpoint from the top of the cliff that overhangs the Basin is located 0.1 mi. south of this junction on the Basin Rim Trail.

The trail passes an outlook over the Basin on the right, then descends very steeply along the south side and foot of the great cliff, passing one spot where a rock slab has fallen across the trail, and crosses a wide, stony brook. At 3.0 mi., it passes the upper end of the Hermit Falls Loop, a loop path slightly longer than the main trail that descends steeply right 0.1 mi. to Hermit Falls and then returns to the main trail 0.2 mi. below its point of departure. The Basin Trail descends to an old logging road and turns right on it, then follows segments of other old roads, crosses two brooks (the first on a bridge), and at 4.0 mi., bears right on a relocation above a swampy area.

It then skirts the shore of Basin Pond with minor ups and downs, passing several side paths leading left to the shore of the pond and right to the Basin Campground, and ends at the parking area.

Basin Trail (map 5:F12)

Distances from Wild River Campground hiker parking area (1,150 ft.) to
- Rim Junction (1,950 ft.): 2.2 mi., 800 ft., 1 hr. 30 min.
- Hermit Falls loop path, lower junction (730 ft.): 3.2 mi., 800 ft. (rev. 1,200 ft.), 2 hr.
- Basin Pond parking area (670 ft.): 4.5 mi., 800 ft. (rev. 50 ft.), 2 hr. 40 min.

Eagle Link (AMC)

This trail runs from the Wild River Trail 4.8 mi. southwest of Wild River Campground to the junction with the Baldface Circle and Meader Ridge trails 0.2 mi. south of Eagle Crag. Nearly the entire trail is within the Wild River Wilderness. It leaves the Wild River Trail and soon crosses two channels of the Wild River (may be difficult at high water), then bears sharp right and ascends generally east at a moderate grade. It crosses a small brook at 1.2 mi., angles up through a birch forest on the north slope of North Baldface, and ends at the junction of the Baldface Circle and Meader Ridge trails.

Eagle Link (map 5:F11–F12)

Distance from Wild River Trail (2,150 ft.) to
- Baldface Circle Trail/Meader Ridge Trail (2,990 ft.): 2.7 mi., 1,000 ft. (rev. 150 ft.), 1 hr. 45 min.

Royce Trail (AMC)

This trail runs to the summit of West Royce Mountain from the west side of ME 113, at a point opposite the Brickett Place about 0.3 mi. north of the access road to the WMNF Cold River Campground. The first two crossings of the Cold River are difficult in high water. Leaving ME 113, it follows a narrow road about 0.3 mi., then crosses the Cold River and bears off the road to the right onto a blue-blazed footpath. The trail recrosses the river at 0.7 mi. and again at 1.4 mi. Then, after crossing the south branch of the Mad River, it rises more steeply and soon passes Mad River Falls, where a side path leads left 25 yd. to a viewpoint. The trail becomes rather rough, with large boulders, and rises steeply under the imposing ledges for which East Royce is famous. At 2.7 mi., the Laughing Lion Trail enters right, and at a height-of-land at 2.9 mi., after a very steep ascent, the Royce Connector Trail branches right, leading to the East Royce Trail for East Royce.

Royce Connector Trail (AMC). This short trail, 0.2 mi. (5 min.) long, links the Royce Trail and the East Royce Trail, permitting the ascent of either summit of Royce from either trail, and provides views from ledges along the way.

The Royce Trail bears left at this junction and descends somewhat, then climbs to the height-of-land between the Royces at 3.6 mi., where the Burnt Mill Brook Trail to Wild River Rd. bears right, whereas the Royce Trail turns abruptly left (west) and ascends the steep wall of the pass. It then continues by easy grades over ledges and through stunted spruce, passing two outlooks to the east, to the summit of West Royce, where it meets the Basin Rim Trail.

Royce Trail (map 5:F12)

Distances from ME 113 (600 ft.) to

- Mad River Falls (900 ft.): 1.6 mi., 300 ft., 55 min.
- Laughing Lion Trail (2,200 ft.): 2.7 mi., 1,600 ft., 2 hr. 10 min.
- Royce Connector Trail (2,650 ft.): 2.9 mi., 2,050 ft., 2 hr. 30 min.
- West Royce Mountain summit (3,210 ft.): 4.3 mi., 2,700 ft. (rev. 100 ft.), 3 hr. 30 min.
- East Royce Mountain summit (3,114 ft.) via Royce Connector and East Royce Trail: 3.6 mi., 2,600 ft. (rev. 100 ft.), 3 hr. 5 min.

East Royce Trail (AMC)

This trail climbs rather steeply to East Royce Mountain from the west side of ME 113 just north of the height-of-land. Leaving the parking area, it immediately crosses Evans Brook and ascends steeply, crossing several other brooks in the first 0.5 mi. At the final brook crossing at 1.0 mi., the Royce Connector Trail leaves on the left, leading in 0.2 mi. to the Royce Trail for West Royce. After a rough section with several scrambles, the East Royce Trail emerges on open ledges at 1.1 mi.; here there is a view east to Speckled Mtn. The trail soon reaches a subsidiary summit with views to the south, turns right, and climbs to a broad open ledge with wide-ranging views, where the plainly marked trail ends. Here a faintly marked beaten path turns right (north), dropping down the steep edge of the ledge, and runs generally northeast over several more ledges, passing over the true summit of East Royce in 250 yd. and continuing another 180 yd. to a large open ledge with a beautiful outlook to the north and west.

East Royce Trail (map 5:F13–F12)

Distances from ME 113 (1,420 ft.) to
- ledge at the end of the East Royce Trail (3,070 ft.): 1.3 mi., 1,650 ft., 1 hr. 30 min.
- northern viewpoint (3,090 ft.): 1.7 mi., 1,700 ft., 1 hr. 40 min.

Laughing Lion Trail (CTA)

This trail begins on the west side of ME 113, just north of a roadside picnic area and about 2.3 mi. north of the road to Cold River Campground, and ends on the Royce Trail. It descends to and crosses the Cold River then ascends west to a ridge crest, which it follows north, alternating moderate and steep sections and providing occasional fine views down the valley, then swings west and levels off just before it ends at the Royce Trail.

Laughing Lion Trail (map 5:F13–F12)

Distance from ME 113 (1,370 ft.) to
- Royce Trail (2,200 ft.): 1.1 mi., 1,000 ft. (rev. 150 ft.), 1 hr. 5 min.

Basin Rim Trail (AMC)

This trail follows the ridge that runs north from Mt. Meader, starting from the east knob at the junction with the Mt. Meader and Meader Ridge trails and ending at the summit of West Royce Mountain, where it meets the Royce Trail. It has fine views, particularly at the top of the cliff that forms the wall of the Basin.

The trail leaves the east knob of Mt. Meader, passing an outlook on the right, and descends north over the ledges. Just after crossing a small brook, it reaches a col, then ascends slightly along the east side of a prominent hump called Ragged Jacket. The trail soon descends steeply down the north slope to the lowest point of the ridge (1,870 ft.), then rises gradually over ledges. It passes the best outlook over the Basin about 0.1 mi. before reaching Rim Junction at 1.4 mi., where the Basin Trail crosses and the Black Angel Trail enters. At 1.5 mi., a short spur leads right to Basin Outlook, a restricted but interesting viewpoint at the edge of the cliffs on the east. In the next 0.3 mi., there are more good views east over the great cliff of the Basin Rim. Passing west of the prominent southeast knee of West Royce, the trail climbs, with only short intervening descents. At 2.6 mi., it climbs a very steep pitch to a restricted outlook to the Carter-Moriah Range. It then passes a small brook (unreliable), ascends easily, passes an outlook south to the Baldfaces on the right, and ends at the summit of West Royce Mountain.

Basin Rim Trail (map 5:F12)

Distances from Mt. Meader Trail/Meader Ridge Trail (2,750 ft.) to

- Rim Junction (1,950 ft.): 1.4 mi., 200 ft. (rev. 1,000 ft.), 50 min.
- West Royce Mountain summit (3,210 ft.): 3.9 mi., 1,600 ft. (rev. 150 ft.), 2 hr. 45 min.

Mount Meader Trail (AMC)

This trail runs from the west side of NH 113, about 0.5 mi. north of the entrance to the Baldface Circle Trail, to a junction with the Meader Ridge and Basin Rim trails on the ridge crest at an easterly knob of Mt. Meader. There is limited roadside parking; do not block the entrance to the trail, which starts on a private logging road.

From NH 113, it follows the logging road; in 70 yd. bear left at a fork. The trail follows the north side of Mill Brook, entering the WMNF at 0.7 mi., and crossing an overgrown skid road at 0.9 mi. At 1.0 mi., it passes a side path left (sign) that rises easily 0.1 mi. to Brickett Falls. The main trail soon turns left uphill off the logging road (sign), crosses and recrosses a small brook, and at 2.1 mi., it turns right and begins a steep climb by switchbacks up the heel of the ridge. It turns sharp left at the top of the heel at 2.5 mi., passes an outlook south, and climbs through fine spruce woods. Coming out on open ledges with fine views at 2.9 mi., it soon reaches the east knob of Mt. Meader.

Mount Meader Trail (map 5:G12–F12)

Distance from NH 113 (520 ft.) to
- Meader Ridge Trail (2,750 ft.): 3.0 mi., 2,250 ft., 2 hr. 40 min.

Meader Ridge Trail (AMC)

This trail runs along the ridge crest from the junction with the Mt. Meader and Basin Rim trails on the east knob of Mt. Meader to the junction with the Baldface Circle Trail and Eagle Link, 0.2 mi. south of Eagle Crag.

From the east knob of Mt. Meader, the trail descends slightly in a southwest direction, climbs out of a sag, and in 0.2 mi., passes just south of the true summit of Mt. Meader. Descending again, with a small intervening ascent, it passes two restricted views and then an excellent open view to the east. At 0.4 mi., just beyond the best eastern viewpoint, a side path (sign) leads west 100 yd. up to a large open ledge with a view of the Baldfaces and Carter Dome. The Meader Ridge Trail passes the deepest col of the ridge at 0.6 mi., where it crosses an unreliable small brook; sometimes there is also water upstream a short distance in a swampy place called the Bear Traps. The trail then climbs to an intermediate peak at 1.2 mi. and descends to another col at 1.4 mi. Climbing again, it emerges from timberline at 1.9 mi., passes over the summit of Eagle Crag, and then descends slightly to meet the Baldface Circle Trail and Eagle Link.

Meader Ridge Trail (map 5:F12)

Distance from Mt. Meader Trail/Basin Rim Trail (2,750 ft.) to
- Baldface Circle Trail/Eagle Link (2,990 ft.): 2.0 mi., 550 ft. (rev. 300 ft.), 1 hr. 15 min.

Baldface Circle Trail (AMC)

This trail makes a loop over North and South Baldface from NH 113 at a parking area 0.1 mi. north of the driveway to the AMC's Cold River Camp. It is one of the most attractive trips in the White Mountains, with about 4 mi. of open and semi-open ledge providing long stretches of unobstructed views and equally great exposure to storms. This is a strenuous trip that should not be underestimated.

Leaving NH 113 about 60 yd. north of the parking area, the trail runs at easy grades to Circle Junction at 0.7 mi., where a side path leads right (north) 0.1 mi. to Emerald Pool. From here, the trail is described in a clockwise direction—up South Baldface, over to North Baldface, and down from Eagle Crag—but the circuit in the reverse direction is equally fine.

From Circle Junction, the south branch follows an old road, then turns left (south), crosses a brook bed, and climbs past the junction with the Slippery Brook Trail on the left at 0.9 mi. to an old logging road that it follows for almost a mile. At 1.2 mi., a loop path 0.5 mi. long leads left to Chandler Gorge (a small flume with several pools and lesser cascades in a rocky bed) and rejoins the main trail 0.1 mi. above its departure point. The trail swings around the south side of Spruce Knoll and, at 2.5 mi., leaves the old road in a rocky area and soon reaches Last Chance Spring (unreliable) and South Baldface Shelter. In a short distance, the trail comes out on the ledges and climbs very steeply in the open on rocks that are dangerous if wet or icy; this danger can be avoided by using the Slippery Brook Trail and Baldface Knob Trail instead of this part of the Baldface Circle Trail. At 3.0 mi., the trail reaches the crest of a rounded ridge and swings left, ascending near the crest toward a knob, becoming much less steep. On that knob, at 3.2 mi., the Baldface Knob Trail enters on the left (south). The Baldface Circle Trail then ascends open ledges to the summit of South Baldface at 3.7 mi.

Bearing right at the summit of South Baldface, it follows the broad ridge, descending into the shelter of mature conifers at 4.0 mi., then coming out on a semi-open knob at 4.2 mi. From here to North Baldface, the trail runs mostly in the open, though there are several small cols where some shelter could be obtained in a storm. At 4.9 mi., it mounts the last steep pitch to the summit of North Baldface, then descends steeply to the broad, lumpy, ledgy ridge that runs toward Eagle Crag. At 5.8 mi., the Bicknell Ridge Trail leaves right, providing a scenic alternative route to NH 113.

At 6.1 mi., the trail reaches a multiple junction where the Eagle Link leaves left (west) for the Wild River valley, the Meader Ridge Trail continues straight ahead (north) for Eagle Crag and Mt. Meader, and the Baldface Circle Trail turns sharp right and descends on a steep and rough way over ledges for 0.2 mi., with two tricky scrambles. At the base of the ledges, the trail swings left and, after a short gradual section, descends moderately. At 6.9 mi., it crosses a very small brook (unreliable) with a ledgy, mossy bed and becomes less steep; at 7.3 mi., it enters an old logging road and follows it to the right. At 7.7 mi., the Eagle Cascade Link, 0.7 mi. long, leaves on the right, traverses to a short side path left that provides a view of Eagle Cascade, climbs steeply to cross the brook (use caution) above the cascade in 0.4 mi., and climbs to the Bicknell Ridge Trail. The Baldface Circle Trail continues to descend gradually, crossing a branch of Charles Brook, and at 8.4 mi., the Bicknell Ridge Trail enters right just after crossing a branch of Charles Brook on flat ledges. The Baldface Circle Trail now angles left away from the brook, then returns to it and crosses it (may be difficult in high water) at 9.0 mi., just before reaching Circle Junction.

Baldface Circle Trail (map 5:G12)

Distances from NH 113 (520 ft.) to
- Circle Junction (720 ft.): 0.7 mi., 200 ft., 25 min.
- Slippery Brook Trail junction (800 ft.): 0.9 mi., 300 ft., 35 min.
- South Baldface Shelter (2,130 ft.): 2.5 mi., 1,600 ft., 2 hr. 5 min.
- Baldface Knob Trail (3,030 ft.): 3.2 mi., 2,500 ft., 2 hr. 50 min.
- South Baldface summit (3,570 ft.): 3.7 mi., 3,050 ft., 3 hr. 25 min.
- North Baldface summit (3,610 ft.): 4.9 mi., 3,500 ft. (rev. 400 ft.), 4 hr. 10 min.
- Eagle Link/Meader Ridge Trail (2,990 ft.): 6.1 mi., 3,600 ft. (rev. 700 ft.), 4 hr. 50 min.

- Bicknell Ridge Trail, lower junction (970 ft.): 8.4 mi., 3,600 ft. (rev. 2,000 ft.), 6 hr.
- Circle Junction (720 ft.): 9.1 mi., 3,600 ft. (rev. 250 ft.), 6 hr. 20 min.
- NH 113 (520 ft.), for complete loop: 9.8 mi., 3,600 ft. (rev. 200 ft.), 6 hr. 40 min.

Bicknell Ridge Trail (CTA)

This trail begins on the north branch of the Baldface Circle Trail 1.4 mi. from NH 113 and ends on the same trail 0.9 mi. north of North Baldface. Diverging from the Baldface Circle Trail, it immediately crosses a branch of Charles Brook and ascends gradually through second-growth hardwood. After about 1.0 mi., it turns more to the west, rises more rapidly along the south side of Bicknell Ridge, and, just before the first ledges, crosses a brook bed where there is usually water among the boulders. Soon the trail emerges on the open ledges, and the Eagle Cascade Link enters right from Eagle Cascade and the Baldface Circle Trail. Above this junction, the trail climbs over broad, open ledges with excellent views, interspersed with patches of spruce woods; in places it requires care to follow. Reaching the open, flat ridge top, it swings left and rejoins the Baldface Circle Trail.

Bicknell Ridge Trail (map 5:G12)

Distances from Baldface Circle Trail, lower junction (970 ft.) to
- Eagle Cascade Link (2,020 ft.): 1.4 mi., 1,050 ft., 1 hr. 15 min.
- Baldface Circle Trail, upper junction (3,050 ft.): 2.5 mi., 2,100 ft., 2 hr. 20 min.

Baldface Knob Trail (WMNF)

This trail, in combination with the Slippery Brook Trail, provides an alternative route to South Baldface that avoids the steepest ledges on the Baldface Circle Trail. It begins at the Slippery Brook Trail in the col between Eastman Mountain and South Baldface, opposite the beginning of the Eastman Mountain Trail. It rises gradually and then climbs steeply, emerging on open ledges below the flat, open summit called Baldface Knob, an excellent viewpoint. It descends into a scrubby saddle and then climbs easily along the open ridge to the Baldface Circle Trail on the shoulder below the summit of South Baldface.

Baldface Knob Trail (map 5:G12)

Distance from Slippery Brook Trail (2,650 ft.) to
- Baldface Circle Trail (3,030 ft.): 0.7 mi., 450 ft. (rev. 50 ft.), 35 min.

Eastman Mountain Trail (CTA)

This trail ascends Eastman Mountain from the Slippery Brook Trail at the height-of-land in the col between Eastman Mountain and South Baldface, opposite the lower terminus of the Baldface Knob Trail. The trail runs through a beautiful birch forest, first descending slightly then rising at a moderate grade onto the north ridge, where outlook points provide partial views of South Baldface and Sable Mountain. It continues generally southeast to the summit, where open areas provide rewarding views in most directions.

Eastman Mountain Trail (map 5:G12)

Distance from Slippery Brook Trail (2,650 ft.) to
- Eastman Mountain summit (2,939 ft.): 0.8 mi., 400 ft. (rev. 100 ft.), 35 min.

Slippery Brook Trail (WMNF/CTA)

This trail runs from the south branch of the Baldface Circle Trail, 0.9 mi. from NH 113, through the col between South Baldface and Eastman Mountain to the north end of Slippery Brook Rd. (FR 17, called Town Hall Rd. at its south end). To reach the south trailhead, leave NH 16 1.5 mi. south of the traffic lights in Glen and go north on Town Hall Rd. Bear left at 2.6 mi. from NH 16 where the pavement ends, bear right at 6.0 mi., and continue to a gate at 7.3 mi., where the trail begins. The southern 3.0 mi. of this trail have been relocated.

Leaving the Baldface Circle Trail, it ascends a small ridge and then descends, crossing a branch of Chandler Brook and a tributary before joining the older route on an old logging road. The trail ascends generally southwest through woods, first easily then moderately, and swings left up through a beautiful birch grove to reach the col between South Baldface and Eastman Mountain at 2.6 mi. Here the Baldface Knob Trail leaves right (north) for South Baldface and the Eastman Mountain Trail leaves left (south). After a slight rise, the Slippery Brook Trail begins its moderate descent toward Slippery Brook. The relocated path crosses the lower slopes of Eastman Mountain, passing a view to South Baldface at 4.0 mi. At 4.4 mi., after a short descent, it turns left into a logging road (in the reverse direction, turn right off the road onto a woods path), then bears right at 4.6 mi. (in the reverse direction, bear left at an arrow). It continues at easy grades on this road through several small clearings to the gate at the end of Slippery Brook Rd.

Slippery Brook Trail (map 5:G12–G11)

Distances from Baldface Circle Trail (800 ft.) to
- Baldface Knob Trail/Eastman Mountain Trail (2,650 ft.): 2.6 mi., 1,850 ft., 2 hr. 15 min.
- left turn onto logging road (1,950 ft.): 4.4 mi., 1,850 ft. (rev. 700 ft.), 3 hr. 10 min.
- Slippery Brook Rd. (1,610 ft.): 6.6 mi., 1,850 ft. (rev. 350 ft.), 4 hr. 15 min.

Mountain Pond Loop Trail (WMNF)

This trail begins on Slippery Brook Rd. (FR 17, called Town Hall Rd. at its southern end), 6.3 mi. from NH 16A. (In winter the road is plowed for about 3.5 mi., after which it receives heavy use by snowmobiles.) East of Mountain Pond, the former route of the trail has been officially closed by the WMNF, and the cabin formerly located at the pond has been removed.

The trail runs 0.3 mi. from the road to a fork; bearing left, it reaches the Mountain Pond Shelter at 1.0 mi., then continues around the pond with occasional moderately rough footing. From points along the shore, there are views of Doublehead Mountain and South Baldface. Just before returning to the fork, it crosses the pond's outlet brook, where at times of high water the crossing may be difficult and the trail hard to follow (but it is fairly easy to bushwhack along the south bank of the outlet brook back to the road and parking area).

Mountain Pond Loop Trail (map 5:G11)

Distance from Slippery Brook Rd. (1,483 ft.) for
- complete loop around Mountain Pond (1,509 ft.): 2.7 mi., 50 ft., 1 hr. 25 min.

East Branch Trail (WMNF)

The upper part of this trail is in the Wild River Wilderness. This trail begins on Slippery Brook Rd. (FR 17, called Town Hall Rd. at its southern end), 4.8 mi. from NH 16A and about 0.5 mi. southwest of the junction with East Branch Rd. (FR 38). It follows the East Branch of the Saco River, crossing East Branch Rd., and making three difficult crossings of the East Branch, then rejoins East Branch Rd. (which is passable for cars up to this point). It then ascends along the East Branch and crosses a height-of-land, finally ending on the Wild River Trail at the foot of the hill east of Perkins Notch, 0.7 mi. east of Perkins Notch Shelter. It is very muddy south of the height-of-land, at times difficult to follow, and the three crossings of the East Branch are hard at normal water levels and would be hazardous at high water (but can be avoided by starting at the trailhead at the end of East Branch Rd.).

Leaving Slippery Brook Rd., the trail descends to cross Slippery Brook (may be difficult), then runs north along the east side of the East Branch, at times following an old railroad bed. It crosses East Branch Rd. at 2.3 mi. and the East Branch at 2.7 mi. The next 0.8 mi., with two more river crossings, is extremely overgrown and difficult to follow through an area of beaver meadows and swamps. At 3.5 mi. East Branch Rd. joins from the left just beyond the end of the part of this road open to vehicles. The East Branch Trail then crosses Gulf Brook, leaves the railroad bed within 0.1 mi., and follows old logging roads. At 4.9 mi., the trail crosses Black Brook and shortly bears northwest away from the river. It then climbs by easy grades, crossing a newer logging road, and continues to the height-of-land between Black Mountain and a prominent southwest spur of North Baldface at 7.2 mi. The old logging road dwindles to a trail, passes through a patch of spruce, and descends to its junction with the Wild River Trail on the south bank of the Wild River. In this section, it is followed or paralleled by a former snowmobile trail, which may be more obvious in some locations.

East Branch Trail (map 5:H11–G11)

Distances from Slippery Brook Rd. (1,205 ft.) to

- crossing of East Branch Rd. (1,650 ft.): 2.3 mi., 450 ft., 1 hr. 25 min.
- end of East Branch Rd. (1,700 ft.): 3.5 mi., 550 ft. (rev. 50 ft.), 2 hr.

Bald Land Trail (WMNF)

This trail follows an old roadway from Black Mountain Rd. to the East Branch through the divide between Black Mountain and North Doublehead. From its western trailhead to the height-of-land, it is also a cross-country ski trail and intersects several other ski trails; it is somewhat hard to follow though most of the intersections are signed or otherwise marked. The west trailhead is reached in from NH 16 in Jackson by following NH 16B for 2.2 mi., bearing right on Dundee Rd. past the Black Mountain Ski Area, then bearing left uphill on Black Mountain Rd. at 2.4 mi. and continuing to a small parking area on the right at 3.0 mi., just before driveways diverge to the left and right. The east trailhead is 0.4 mi. before the end of East Branch Rd. (FR 38), a branch of Slippery Brook Rd. (FR 17).

The trail (WMNF sign) coincides with the East Pasture (X-C ski) Trail for the first 0.4 mi. The Bald Land Trails follows a gravel road for 0.1 mi., then continues ahead past a cable gate on a rougher road where a driveway diverges left. It continues straight at a 3-way intersection, and at 0.4 mi., it turns right onto a woods road (signs), crosses Great Brook on a bridge, enters the WMNF, and runs nearly level on the old road with a stone wall on the right. It crosses a muddy area, turns right onto another old road at 0.8 mi., then bears left and ascends gradually. At 1.2 mi., it bears right at a fork (sign) and ascends to a T-intersection at 1.5 mi. Here a spur, signed "Scenic Vista," leads right to two clearings. The first, at 0.1 mi., provides a view up to North Doublehead; the second, at 0.2 mi., has a limited view west from its upper edge. At the intersection, the main trail turns left, then in 100 yd. diverges right off the wide woods road onto a footpath. It descends moderately, swings left and crosses a logging road at 2.1 mi., crosses muddy areas and a small brook, and reaches the East Branch Rd.

Bald Land Trail (map 5:G11)

Distance from Black Mountain Rd. (1,585 ft.) to
- Scenic Vista spur (2,100 ft.): 1.5 mi., 500 ft., 1 hr.
- East Branch Rd. (1,730 ft.): 2.2 mi., 500 ft. (rev. 350 ft.), 1 hr. 20 min.

Rainbow Trail (WMNF)

This trail climbs to the summit of Carter Dome from the Wild River Trail in Perkins Notch about 0.8 mi. west of the Perkins Notch Shelter near No-Ketchum Pond. After leaving the Wild River Trail, it passes through a sag then ascends steadily through birch woods on the southeast slope of Carter Dome. At 1.5 mi., it passes just east of the summit of a southerly knob and runs in the open with fine views, returns into the woods at a sag, then climbs moderately to the Carter-Moriah Trail at the summit of Carter Dome.

Rainbow Trail (map 5:G11–F10)

Distances from Wild River Trail (2,590 ft.) to

- south knob (4,274 ft.): 1.5 mi., 17,00 ft., 1 hr. 35 min.
- Carter Dome summit (4,832 ft.): 2.5 mi., 2,300 ft., 2 hr. 25 min.

Bog Brook Trail (WMNF)

This trail begins at a small, unimproved parking area on Carter Notch Rd., about 3.0 mi. from NH 16B just west of its sharp turn at the crossing of Wildcat Brook. It ends on the Wild River Trail 1.5 mi. west of Perkins Notch Shelter. Some brook crossings may be difficult at high water, but they can be avoided by following the gravel logging road extension of Carter Notch Rd. (FR 233) to the point where the Bog Brook Trail crosses it; this route is about 0.5 mi. longer. The parking area may be relocated in the near future as part of a Forest Service logging project.

The trail follows a dirt road (sign) past two camps and bears right off the road into the woods (marked here by blue diamonds) at a turnaround at the WMNF boundary. Descending slightly, it crosses Wildcat Brook, then another brook, and then the Wildcat River, a tributary of Wildcat Brook. In 60 yd., the Wildcat River Trail continues straight ahead, while the Bog Brook Trail diverges right. The trail now ascends moderately, crossing a gravel logging road (FR 233) that leads (to the left) back to Carter Notch Rd. The trail continues up at mostly easy grades with some muddy footing and makes the first of five crossings of Bog Brook at 1.9 mi. At the fifth crossing, it may be necessary to detour left across a beaver dam; a few yards farther the trail ends at the Wild River Trail.

Bog Brook Trail (map 5:G10)

Distances from Carter Notch Rd. (1,810 ft.) to

* Wildcat River Trail (1,790 ft.): 0.7 mi., 50 ft. (rev. 50 ft.), 25 min.
* Wild River Trail (2,417 ft.): 2.8 mi., 650 ft., 1 hr. 45 min.

Wildcat River Trail (AMC)

This trail runs to Carter Notch Hut from the Bog Brook Trail just east of
the Wildcat River crossing 0.7 mi. from Carter Notch Rd. Brook crossings may be difficult at high water, but those on the Bog Brook Trail can
be avoided by following the gravel logging road extension of Carter Notch
Rd. (FR 233) to the point where the Wildcat River Trail crosses it, just beyond the bridge over Wildcat River.

From the Bog Brook Trail junction, the trail follows the east bank of
Wildcat River, crossing a gravel logging road (FR 233) that leads back (to
the left) to Carter Notch Rd. The trail climbs over a rise, descends to cross
Bog Brook at 1.0 mi., and the Wild River Trail enters right at 1.9 mi. Soon
the trail crosses Wildcat River, turns sharp right in 100 yd., and continues
to ascend at a moderate grade. It climbs more steeply toward Carter Notch,
passes a side trail right that leads to the rocks of the Rampart, and in 100
yd. more reaches Carter Notch Hut and the junction with the Nineteen-
Mile Brook Trail.

Wildcat River Trail (map 5:G10–F10)

Distances from Bog Brook Trail (1,790 ft.) to

* Bog Brook crossing (2,050 ft.): 1.0 mi., 300 ft., 40 min.
* Wild River Trail (2,320 ft.): 1.9 mi., 550 ft., 1 hr. 15 min.
* Carter Notch Hut (3,288 ft.): 3.6 mi., 1,500 ft., 2 hr. 35 min.

Hutmen's Trail (HA)

This trail crosses the flat ridge between Spruce Mountain on the south and
Wildcat Mountain on the north, running from NH 16 at a point 3.9 mi.
north of the covered bridge in Jackson and 5.6 mi. south of Pinkham
Notch Camp to Carter Notch Rd. about 2.7 mi. north of its junction with
NH 16B and 0.3 mi. south of the Bog Brook Trail trailhead (which may
be relocated). Views are extremely limited. The western section follows its

traditional route as a hiking trail, though the part near the trailhead on NH 16 may be disrupted by new housing construction. The middle and eastern sections follow logging roads that become cross-country ski trails during the winter. The ski trail section is grassy and wet in places, with little evident footway; a portion of this section was scheduled for reconstruction as part of a logging operation from 2006 to 2007.

Leaving NH 16, where there is a trail sign to the left of a house, the trail follows a road for 50 yd., then bears right off the road (obscure turn), shortly swings right and left at small cairns, and enters the woods, where the footway becomes much clearer. It ascends rather steeply up the west slope of Spruce Mountain, following the left side of a small brook. After 0.4 mi., the grade decreases and the trail bears left away from the brook, turns more north, crosses a small brook, and runs nearly level through mixed softwoods. It enters the WMNF at 0.6 mi., passing through logged areas. At 0.8 mi., the Dana Place (X-C ski) Trail enters from the left and the trails coincide, passing an apple orchard on the left. At 1.1 mi., Hutmen's Trail swings left, and in 15 yd., turns left again onto a grassy logging road, the Marsh Brook (X-C ski) Trail, and follows it generally northeast along the flat ridge crest, with wet footing in places. At 1.7 mi., the UST (X-C ski) Trail diverges left, following an overgrown logging road 0.2 mi. to a limited outlook. The Hutmen's Trail descends gradually and, at 2.2 mi., follows the Marsh Brook Trail straight ahead where the Dana Place Trail branches left toward the Hall's Ledge Trail. Soon the trail enters a clearing with a view of Wildcat Mountain over the trees, where it turns to the right into the woods onto another logging road (sign for Marsh Brook), crosses the brook, and leaves the WMNF. After a flat, wet section, the trail swings left where an unmarked footpath diverges right, and descends past a dilapidated camp to Carter Notch Rd. There are two entrances to the trail 25 yd. apart; the southern entrance is marked by a sign for Marsh Brook.

Hutmen's Trail (map 5:G10)

Distances from NH 16 (1,050 ft.) to

- Marsh Brook Trail (1,750 ft.): 1.1 mi., 700 ft., 55 min.
- Carter Notch Rd. (1,800 ft.): 3.1 mi., 900 ft. (rev. 150 ft.), 2 hr.

Hall's Ledge Trail (HA)

This trail starts on the east side of NH 16, just south of the bridge over the Ellis River and 5.2 mi. north of the covered bridge in Jackson. The trail sign is on a bank behind a guard rail and is easily missed. Use the Rocky Branch Trail parking lot, 0.1 mi. north of the NH 16 bridge. The trail ends at the upper end of Carter Notch Rd., 0.1 mi. north of the Bog Brook Trail parking area (which may be relocated). There is limited parking at this trailhead where a gated logging road diverges to the right (north); do not block the gate on this road or on the road that continues ahead (west) as the Hall's Ledge Trail. Halls Ledge itself is completely overgrown, but there is a fine vista of Mt. Washington from a cleared area.

From NH 16, follow the river for 80 yd., then veer right uphill and in another 100 yd. bear right across a field. The trail runs through a brushy, swampy area, then swings left uphill and ascends to a high bank overlooking a brook with a long cascade. The yellow-blazed trail soon bears away from the brook and climbs steeply through a fine hardwood forest for about 0.3 mi. From the top of this rise, it runs generally north and northeast at an easier grade through an area scheduled for logging from 2006 to 2007. It then ascends moderately through spruce forest, levels, and, at 1.7 mi., reaches a small clearing on the left with a picnic table and a view of Mt. Washington and its eastern spurs and ravines. From here, the trail follows the wide, grassy Hall's Ledge Ski Trail, rising easily for 0.3 mi. to a junction with the Wildcat Valley Ski Trail. Here it bears right and follows the latter trail through the town of Jackson's Prospect Farm conservation area, descending moderately past several other ski trail junctions to the gate at the end of Carter Notch Rd.

Hall's Ledge Trail (map 5:G10)

Distances from NH 16 (1,150 ft.) to
- viewpoint (2,550 ft.): 1.7 mi., 1,400 ft., 1 hr. 35 min.
- Carter Notch Rd. (1,850 ft.): 3.3 mi., 1,500 ft. (rev. 800 ft.), 2 hr. 25 min.

Black Mountain Ski Trail (WMNF)

This trail leads to Black Mountain Cabin and a nearby knob (2,757 ft.) on the ridge of Black Mountain that provides views of Mt. Washington,

Carter Notch, and other peaks in its vicinity. To reach the trailhead, follow Carter Notch Rd. for 3.7 mi. from Wentworth Hall in Jackson, then turn right onto Melloon Rd. at the junction, where the WMNF trail sign is located. Follow Melloon Rd. (gravel) across the Wildcat River, then bear left uphill, passing the Wildcat Valley Ski Trail (right). Continue to a parking area on the left 0.3 mi. from Carter Notch Rd., just before a private driveway with a chain gate. The road is plowed to this point in winter. Black Mountain Cabin is kept locked and reservations for its use must be made with the Saco Ranger District office (603-447-5448). There is a spring (unreliable water source) near the cabin, and the trail crosses several small streams (also unreliable).

The trail ascends the gravel driveway and turns to the right onto an old woods road (sign) just before reaching a brown house. It crosses several small brooks, enters the WMNF, then swings right and angles up the western slope of Black Mountain, ascending moderately at first and then more steeply. At 1.3 mi., the trail reaches Black Mountain Cabin, where there is a view northwest toward Mt. Washington. The direct route to the viewpoint on the nearby knob of Black Mountain follows the main trail left (north) for 0.3 mi. to a spur path that leads 80 yd. left to the outlook. To make a scenic loop back to the cabin that is only 0.3 mi. longer than the direct route, follow a connector to the East Pasture (X-C ski) Trail, which leads left downhill from the spur path junction for 0.1 mi. Turn right here onto the Black Mountain Cutoff (X-C ski trail) and ascend, crossing the ridge crest in a beautiful softwood forest; then swing right and descend, emerging just to the south of the cabin on a path that leads to the left to a nearby spring.

Black Mountain Ski Trail (map 5:G10)

Distances from parking area on Melloon Rd. (1,300 ft.) to
- Black Mountain Cabin (2,450 ft.): 1.3 mi., 1,150 ft., 1 hr. 15 min.
- summit of knob (2,757 ft.): 1.6 mi., 1,450 ft., 1 hr. 30 min.

Eagle Mountain Path

Eagle Mountain is a small peak with a restricted but interesting view to Doublehead, Kearsarge North, and the Moat Range. It can be climbed from NH 16B, 0.8 mi. from Wentworth Hall in Jackson, by a path that starts in the upper parking lot behind the Eagle Mountain House. The path is lightly used and marked, but its green spray-paint blazes can be followed easily by careful hikers. The trail starts from the right (north) side of the parking lot, where there is a sign for the Gale (X-C ski) Trail. Eagle Mountain Path follows a woods road for 150 yd. and, just before reaching the crest of the ridge, turns right. In another 150 yd., it bears to the left of a pump house. The road becomes older, then becomes a path, and ascends to an open swampy area. Cairns mark the way along the right side of the swamp and into the woods, where the climbing becomes steeper. After passing a large boulder on the right, the trail turns left uphill and climbs a steep and rough section by switchbacks, aiming for a small gap at the top right edge of the rock face. At the top of the rock face, it turns left and climbs up the right side of a ledge, then turns left toward a false summit. It then turns right where there is a good cleared view to the south on the left, and the true summit (marked by a large cairn) is 90 yd. farther; from here an obscure path leads 60 yd. left to ledges with a similar view to the south.

Eagle Mountain Path (map 5:H10)

Distance from NH 16B (1.000 ft.) to
  • summit of Eagle Mountain (1,613 ft.): 0.9 mi., 600 ft., 45 min.

Doublehead Ski Trail (WMNF)

This trail ascends North Doublehead from Dundee Rd. From NH 16 at the Jackson covered bridge follow NH 16A, then turn right on NH 16B at the Jackson Post Office. Go up a long hill, turn right again at the Black Mountain Ski Area, then finally turn right onto Dundee Rd. and continue to the parking area on the east (left) side of the road 2.9 mi. from NH 16. The WMNF Doublehead Cabin, located on the summit, is kept locked, and reservations for its use must be made with the Saco Ranger District office (603-447-5448).

The trail follows a private road for about 100 yd., then turns right, enters the woods, swings left, and becomes steeper. At 0.6 mi., it bears slightly left where the Old Path leaves right. The ski trail ascends by a zigzag route on the west slope of North Doublehead, terminating at the Doublehead Cabin on the summit. The nearest water is alongside the trail about halfway down. Beyond the cabin, a path leads in 30 yd. to a good view east, overlooking Mountain Pond, the mountains of the Baldface Range, and the hills and lakes of western Maine.

Doublehead Ski Trail (map 5:H11)

Distance from Dundee Rd. (1,480 ft.) to
• North Doublehead summit (3,053 ft.): 1.8 mi., 1,600 ft., 1 hr. 40 min.

Old Path (JCC)

This trail ascends to North Doublehead from the Doublehead Ski Trail, 0.6 mi. from Dundee Rd. It diverges right and passes a brook left in 50 yd., rises at a moderate grade for about 0.1 mi., then becomes somewhat steeper until it reaches the height-of-land in the col between the peaks at 0.6 mi. Here the New Path enters right, and the Old Path turns left and ascends moderately, then more steeply, passing a side path that leads left somewhat downhill about 100 yd. to a splendid view west to Mt. Carrigain, Moat Mountain, and the Sandwich Range. In a short distance, it reaches the summit of North Doublehead, the cabin (which is kept locked), and the Doublehead Ski Trail.

Old Path (map 5:H11)

Distance from Doublehead Ski Trail (1,860 ft.) to
• North Doublehead summit (3,053 ft.): 0.9 mi., 1,200 ft., 1 hr. 5 min.

New Path (JCC)

This trail ascends South Doublehead and continues to the col between South and North Doublehead, where it meets the Old Path. It starts on Dundee Rd., 3.4 mi. from NH 16 at the Jackson covered bridge and 0.5 mi. beyond the parking area for the Doublehead Ski Trail. It is marked with cairns and its upper half is steep.

The trail descends slightly as it leaves the road and, in 60 yd., bears right, then left, and follows a logging road at a slight upgrade. At 0.3 mi. from Dundee Rd. bear left and in about 100 yd. descend slightly and cross a small brook. Proceed uphill for 100 yd. and bear right at a cairn. About 0.2 mi. from this point, the trail crosses a small, almost flat, ledge, and crosses a smaller ledge a short distance beyond. From here, it begins the steep climb to South Doublehead, approaching it from the southeast slope. It meets the ridge crest at a point between two knobs. To the right, a spur path leads over two knobs with open ledges; the second provides the wider view. The New Path turns left and crosses the summit of South Doublehead; just before it starts to descend it bears right, and here a spur path leads to the left about 30 yd. to a superb outlook ranging from the Sandwich Range to Carter Notch. The New Path then descends to meet the Old Path in the col to the north.

New Path (map 5:H11)

Distances from Dundee Rd. (1,590 ft.) to

• South Doublehead (2,939 ft.): 1.2 mi., 1,350 ft., 1 hr. 15 min.
• Old Path (2,700 ft.): 1.4 mi., 1,350 ft. (rev. 250 ft.), 1 hr. 25 min.

Mount Kearsarge North Trail (WMNF)

This trail ascends Kearsarge North from a small parking area on the north side of Hurricane Mountain Rd., 1.5 mi. east of NH 16 near the state highway rest area at Intervale. It is a very popular and relatively easy trail to the magnificent views of Kearsarge North, but inexperienced hikers should not underestimate the total climb of 2,600 ft., which is comparable to the ascent required for many much higher peaks.

Leaving the road, the trail runs level for a short distance, then climbs rather easily past a summer residence on an old road well up on the bank above a brook. At 1.1 mi., it passes several boulders, and the old road starts to become rougher. It climbs steadily into a ledgy area, where there are views to Mt. Chocorua and Moat Mountain, crosses the crest of the ridge connecting Kearsarge North to Bartlett Mountain at 2.4 mi., then swings right and ascends mostly along the north side of the ridge. At 2.9 mi., the trail makes a sharp right turn at a steep spot, then angles upward, circling to the left around to the west edge of the summit ledges, and climbs to the tower.

Mount Kearsarge North Trail (map 5:I11–H11)

Distances from Hurricane Mountain Rd. (680 ft.) to

• boulders (1,400 ft.): 1.1 mi., 700 ft., 55 min.
• crest of ridge (2,750 ft.): 2.4 mi., 2,050 ft., 2 hr. 15 min.
• Kearsarge North summit (3,268 ft.): 3.1 mi., 2,600 ft., 2 hr. 50 min.

Weeks Brook Trail (WMNF)

This trail ascends Kearsarge North from the east, a somewhat rough and sparsely marked route that, for experienced hikers, provides an attractive, lightly used alternative to the Mt. Kearsarge North Trail, the very popular trail that ascends this outstanding mountain from Hurricane Mountain Rd. The Weeks Brook Trail begins at a trailhead on Hardwood Hill Rd. (FR 317) 0.1 mi. from South Chatham Rd.; FR 317 leaves South Chatham Rd. at a point 4.9 mi. from ME 113 in North Fryeburg, Maine, and 0.4 mi. north of the east terminus of Hurricane Mountain Rd. Following this trail may require considerable care, particularly in the part near the road and in the upper part.

From the parking area, this trail follows FR 317 uphill and crosses Weeks Brook on a bridge at 0.4 mi. The trail soon bears left (south), then at 0.6 mi., it turns to the right off FR 317 onto a gated USFS road, then quickly bears left off the road into a hemlock forest, following old logging roads marked by yellow blazes. In an overgrown clearing at 1.5 mi., the trail reenters the USFS road and follows it to the left for about 100 yd. Here the trail joins the former route, bearing right into the woods on a logging road, then quickly left at a fork—look carefully for these obscure turns. This road quickly becomes distinctly older and rougher and begins to climb gradually, then moderately, to boggy Shingle Pond. At 3.1 mi., the trail makes its closest approach to the pond, which has been visible for some time. At 3.5 mi., the trail reaches a branch of Middle Brook, then soon crosses on a ledge and follows the north bank of the attractive brook, crossing and recrossing a branch several times. The trail enters an open boggy area in the sag between Kearsarge and Rickers Knoll at 4.2 mi., and turns sharp left (south) at a sign. It makes a winding ascent (watch for arrows), first moderately, then steeply, and enters low scrub and blueberries, passing a fine view east. Here it turns sharp right and soon reaches a ledge with views south, from which the fire tower is visible. From here to the summit, the trail may be somewhat obscure, but the direction is obvious (however, follow the trail with extreme care when descending).

Weeks Brook Trail (map 5:H12–H11)

Distances from trailhead on FR 317 (550 ft.) to
- Shingle Pond (1,700 ft.): 3.1 mi., 1,150 ft., 2 hr. 10 min.
- Kearsarge North summit (3,268 ft.): 5.1 mi., 2,700 ft., 3 hr. 55 min.

Province Brook Trail (WMNF)

This trail provides an easy hike to Province Pond, where there is a WMNF shelter. The trail begins at the north end of Peaked Hill Rd. (FR 450) 2.6 mi. from South Chatham Rd. Peaked Hill Rd. leaves South Chatham Rd. 4.4 mi. from ME 113 in North Fryeburg, Maine, and 0.9 mi. north of the east end of Hurricane Mountain Rd.

The trail leaves the north end of Peaked Hill Rd., then in 30 yd. turns right onto a wide snowmobile trail and heads northwest up Province Brook on a logging road. It traverses a muddy section and crosses a tributary on a snowmobile bridge, then crosses on another bridge shortly before reaching the boggy south end of Province Pond, where there is a view across the pond to Mt. Shaw. The trail leads north along the east shore, then turns left off the wide snowmobile trail onto a narrow yellow-blazed footpath; though marked with an arrow and cairn, this turn is easily missed. The trail passes to the right of a prominent peaked rock, then bears left well back from the north end of the pond, where it may be wet and overgrown, then swings left again and leads south to the shelter.

Province Brook Trail (map 5:H12)

Distance from north end of Peaked Hill Rd. (950 ft.) to
  • Province Pond Shelter (1,330 ft.): 1.6 mi., 400 ft., 1 hr.

Black Cap Trail (AMC/NC)

This path provides a relatively easy ascent to the bare summit of Black Cap, the highest peak in the Green Hills Preserve, which affords the best views in the Green Hills range. It begins on the south side of steep, winding Hurricane Mountain Rd. (which is closed to automobiles from November through mid-May) from a parking lot at the height-of-land, 3.8 mi. from NH 16 at the Intervale scenic vista and rest area. In winter, the trail is used by snowmobiles up to the Black Cap Connector junction.

The trail runs almost level through partly logged spruce woods, then ascends moderately through mixed hardwoods to an information kiosk at 0.5 mi. At 0.7 mi., the Cranmore Trail leaves right and runs 1.2 mi. to Cranmore Mountain, and at 0.8 mi., the Black Cap Connector diverges right to traverse the west side of Black Cap toward Peaked Mountain and

Pudding Pond. The Black Cap Trail soon reaches ledges that become more open, with excellent views westward, as the summit nears. At the summit, there are views in all directions (though not from any single spot); a spur path marked by paint blazes on the ledge leads left (east) 80 yd. to a fine view to the east toward the hills of western Maine. A link trail descends to the right to meet the Black Cap Connector in 0.2 mi., which can be followed to the right, 0.4 mi. back to the Black Cap Trail, making a short loop from the summit.

Black Cap Trail (map 5:I12)

Distance from Hurricane Mountain Rd. (1,700 ft.) to
- Black Cap summit (2,369 ft.): 1.1 mi., 650 ft., 55 min.

Cranmore Trail

This path provides access to the summit of Cranmore Mountain and the Cranmore Mountain Ski Area from Hurricane Mountain Rd. Leaving the Black Cap Trail 0.7 mi. from Hurricane Mountain Rd., the trail descends gradually, passing a junction with the Red Tail (mountain bike) Trail on the right at 0.2 mi. At 1.0 mi., it climbs over a small but steep knob and resumes its descent to the main col at 1.1 mi. Here it starts to ascend Cranmore Mountain, joining a service road coming up from the left after 30 yd. This service road climbs to the flat summit area, passing a radio tower and reaching the actual summit at the top of the chairlift. The Cranmore Ski Area base lodge can be reached in about 1.2 mi. with about 1,100 ft. of descent via ski trails.

Cranmore Trail (map 5:I12–I11)

Distance from Black Cap Trail (2,000 ft.) to
- summit of Cranmore Mountain (1,690 ft.): 1.2 mi., 100 ft. (rev. 400 ft.), 40 min.

Black Cap Connector (AMC/NC)

This trail traverses the west slope of the Green Hills and connects Peaked Mountain and Middle Mountain with Black Cap and Cranmore Mountain. It begins on the coinciding Middle Mountain and Peaked Mountain trails 0.7 mi. from their Thompson Rd. trailhead and ends on the Black Cap Trail just south of its junction with the Cranmore Trail, 0.8 mi. from Hurricane Mountain Rd. It follows old logging roads, and the northern half is multiple use, open to mountain bikes and snowmobiles.

This trail coincides with the Peaked Mountain Trail on an old road for 0.5 mi. to an information kiosk, where the Peaked Mountain Trail turns uphill to the right toward Peaked Mountain and a path (an old route of the trail) turns downhill to the left to return to Thompson Rd. at a point where parking is forbidden. The Black Cap Connector continues straight from this junction, then swings right (east) and ascends the valley of Artist Brook between Peaked Mountain and Cranmore Mountain. At 0.7 mi., it makes a right turn onto a well-defined old logging road (descending, turn left here). After crossing several small streams, it passes a junction on the right at 0.9 mi. with the Peaked Mountain Connector Trail, which climbs steeply 0.1 mi. to the Peaked Mountain Trail at the lower ledges. The main trail now climbs for about a mile to a ridge crest, where it descends briefly and then climbs again to the junction with the Mason Brook Snowmobile Trail at a snow fence at 2.1 mi. (The Mason Brook Snowmobile Trail descends 3.3 mi. to East Conway Rd. and may be used by hikers, though it is not signed and not maintained for hiking.) From here on, the trail is open to multiple uses. It continues to ascend by several switchbacks and swings gradually northward, occasionally descending into gullies. At 3.6 mi., a short link path diverges right and reaches the Black Cap Trail at the summit of Black Cap in 0.2 mi., and at 4.0 mi., after a gradual descent, the Black Cap Connector ends at its junction with the Black Cap Trail.

Black Cap Connector (map 5:I11–I12)

Distances from Middle Mountain Trail junction (700 ft.) to

- Mason Brook Snowmobile Trail (1,700 ft.): 2.1 mi., 1,050 ft. (rev. 50 ft.), 1 hr. 35 min.
- Black Cap Trail (2,100 ft.): 4.0 mi., 1,550 ft. (rev. 100 ft.), 2 hr. 45 min.

Peaked Mountain Trail (AMC/NC)

This trail offers an unusually great variety of scenic vistas and natural features, including fine open stands of red and pitch pine, for relatively little effort. The sharp, rocky knoll of Peaked Mountain, bare except for a few small pines, affords excellent views toward Mt. Washington, the Saco Valley, and nearby mountains. From NH 16 in North Conway, take Artist's Falls Rd. (just south of the town center) for 0.4 mi., then turn right and follow Thompson Rd. for 0.3 mi. to the Pudding Pond Trail parking area, just before the power-line crossing. Parking is forbidden at the former trailhead at the upper end of Thompson Rd., near the small reservoir, although the old section of path remains and can be used by walking up the road 0.6 mi. from the official parking area. There is a small flume in the brook where it is crossed by this old path about 25 yd. from Thompson Rd.

The Peaked Mountain Trail, coinciding with the Pudding Pond and Middle Mountain trails, follows a recent logging road parallel to the power lines for 0.2 mi. to an information kiosk. Here the Pudding Pond Trail diverges to the right, whereas the Peaked Mountain and Middle Mountain trails turn left, cross under the power lines, swing around a snow fence to enter the woods, and ascend gradually on an old road. At 0.7 mi., at the boundary of the Green Hills Preserve, the Middle Mountain Trail continues straight uphill, while the Peaked Mountain Trail, now coinciding with the Black Cap Connector, turns left onto another old road. It first ascends, then descends gradually to another information kiosk at 1.2 mi. Here the old route of the Peaked Mountain Trail (blue blazes) descends 0.3 mi. to Thompson Rd. at a point where parking is forbidden, while the Black Cap Connector continues straight ahead for Black Cap and Hurricane Mountain Rd.

At this junction, the Peaked Mountain Trail (blue blazes) turns right and ascends moderately, passing a junction with a closed former route of the trail on the right, to a ledge at 1.5 mi., where a short link trail descends steeply 0.1 mi. to the Black Cap Connector. Here the main trail turns sharp right and ascends scattered ledges into stands of red pine with increasing views to the west and north. The trail passes an old route that has been closed to permit the vegetation to recover (sign on right), then bears left while crossing a ledge that offers fine views of Kearsarge North and Mt. Washington (though not from one particular point). At 1.9 mi., the Middle Mountain Connector leaves on the right and descends 0.3 mi. on several switchbacks to the Middle Mountain Trail. The Peaked Mountain Trail swings left and ascends the final ledges to the summit, a pointed, grassy knoll with views east, south, and west—particularly fine of the Ossipee Range and Mt. Chocorua.

Peaked Mountain Trail (map 5:I11)

Distance from Thompson Rd. parking area (530 ft.) to
• Peaked Mountain summit (1,739 ft.): 2.1 mi., 1,200 ft., 1 hr. 40 min.

Middle Mountain Trail (AMC/NC)

This trail provides access to a fine southern outlook from Middle Mountain, and passes through a scenic hemlock ravine with several cascades in its middle section that are interesting when there is a good flow of water. The trailhead is the same as for the Peaked Mountain Trail (discussed earlier).

This trail coincides with the Peaked Mountain and Pudding Pond trails for 0.2 mi. to the information kiosk, then turns left and continues along with the Peaked Mountain Trail, crossing straight under the power lines, swinging around a snow fence into the woods, and ascending gradually on an old road to the Green Hills Preserve boundary at 0.7 mi. Here the Peaked Mountain Trail and Black Cap Connector leave on the left, whereas the Middle Mountain Trail continues to ascend straight ahead on the old road, reaching the cascades in 0.5 mi. After a short steep climb, the grade eases, and soon the Middle Mountain Connector leaves on the left and ascends by switchbacks 0.3 mi. to the Peaked Mountain Trail at a point 0.2 mi. below the summit of Peaked Mountain. The main trail continues east up the valley for another 0.2 mi., then swings right (south), crosses the brook, and ascends moderately up the north ridge of Middle Mountain. The trail bears right (sign), ascends moderately to a small ridge crest, then descends slightly and swings left around a boulder before the final ascent to the pine grove at the summit. (On the descent, be sure to swing right around the boulder where a false path continues ahead.) The best view is obtained from a ledge about 40 yd. west of the highest point—a fine outlook to the Ossipee Range, Mt. Chocorua, Mt. Passaconaway, and the Moat Range.

Middle Mountain Trail (map 5:I11)

Distance from Thompson Rd. parking area (530 ft.) to
• summit of Middle Mountain (1,857 ft.): 2.1 mi., 1,350 ft., 1 hr. 45 min.

Pudding Pond Trail (NC)

This trail provides a very easy and scenic 2.0-mi. nature walk to a beaver pond and its surrounding woodlands, particularly suited for families with small children. It passes several beaver dams and lodges, a variety of eco-systems, and numerous bird habitats, including a nesting area for the great blue heron. Views of the pond itself are very limited. The trailhead is the same as for the Peaked Mountain Trail (discussed earlier).

It leaves the trailhead and follows the old road parallel to the power lines for 0.2 mi. to the information kiosk, where the Peaked Mountain and Middle Mountain trails diverge left. The Pudding Pond Trail turns sharp right on an old road and rises slightly then descends gradually, passing several unmarked junctions with old roads and the junction on the left (may not be signed) with the section of the loop that returns from the pond. At 0.5 mi., just before a bridge over the outlet brook, a spur path continues across the bridge and leads 250 yd. to a crossing of a railroad track and the North-South Rd.; on the far side of the road a gravel path ascends the bank to a small parking area at the end of Locust Lane. The main trail does not cross this bridge, but leads to the left (south) along the east bank of the brook past several unmarked paths to viewpoints for two beaver dams with lodges. At 0.9 mi., the trail swings left where a side path runs ahead to a former outlook over the pond that is too overgrown and wet to be accessible. At 1.1 mi., the trail turns sharp left away from the pond, and at 1.4 mi., it enters a woods road and follows it downhill to the left (in the reverse direction, turn right off the woods road into woods; in the other direction, the woods road leads to the power lines south of the point where the trails to Middle Mountain and Peaked Mountain cross under the power lines near the kiosk). The trail returns to the loop junction at 1.6 mi.; turn right to return to the kiosk and Thompson Rd. trailhead.

Pudding Pond Trail (map 5:I11)

Distance from Thompson Rd. parking area (530 ft.) for
- complete loop around Pudding Pond (500 ft.): 2.0 mi., 50 ft., 1 hr.

SUGGESTED HIKES

For more information on suggested hikes, see p. ix.

Easy Hikes

Lost Pond [rt: 1.0 mi., 100 ft., 0:35]. This pleasant spot has excellent views across to the east face of Mt. Washington. It is reached by the Lost Pond Trail, which is part of the AT.

Square Ledge [rt: 1.2 mi., 500 ft., 0:50]. A fairly rugged but short trip to a fine view of Mt. Washington via Lost Pond and Square Ledge trails.

Thompson Falls [rt: 1.4 mi., 200 ft., 0:50]. The Thompson Falls Trail, which begins at the Wildcat Mountain Ski Area, visits attractive cascades flowing over flat ledges.

Mountain Pond [lp: 2.7 mi., 50 ft., 1:25]. The Mountain Pond Loop Trail provides an easy circuit, rocky in places, around this large, remote pond.

Black Cap Mountain [rt: 2.2 mi., 650 ft., 1:25]. The Black Cap Trail provides easy access from Hurricane Mountain Rd. to this excellent view-point in the Green Hills.

Moderate Hikes

Peaked Mountain [rt: 4.2 mi., 1,200 ft., 2:40]. The Peaked Mountain Trail features beautiful red pines and open ledges. Another option in the Green Hills is nearby Middle Mountain [rt: 4.2 mi., 1,350 ft., 2:45] or a loop combining both summits [lp: 5.4 mi., 1,750 ft., 3:35].

Imp Face [rt: 4.4 mi., 1,850 ft., 3:10]. The north half of the Imp Trail provides the shortest access to this spectacular cliff-top perch on the northern part of the Carter Range.

East Royce Mountain [rt: 3.0 mi., 1,700 ft., 2:20]. The East Royce Trail offers a steep and rough but relatively short ascent to excellent views in Evans Notch.

Doublehead Mountain [lp: 3.7 mi., 1,850 ft., 2:45]. The views from both the south and north peaks of this mountain in Jackson can be enjoyed with a loop using the Old Path, a short section of the New Path, and Doublehead Ski Trail.

Basin Rim [rt: 4.8 mi., 1,300 ft., 3:05]. Hermit Falls and a striking view over the cirque known as the Basin are the highlights of this hike on the east half of the Basin Trail and a short section of the Basin Rim Trail.

Wild River Loop [lp: 6.2 mi., 750 ft., 3:30]. A lowland loop through the beautiful Wild River valley (the heart of the WMNF's newest Wilderness) on the Wild River and Highwater trails. Three brook crossings may be difficult in high water, so it is best to start up the Wild River Trail and, if the crossing near the site of Spider Bridge is too difficult, return by the same route [rt: 5.6 mi., 350 ft., 3:00].

Mt. Kearsarge North [rt: 6.2 mi., 2,600 ft., 4:25]. A steady, moderate climb on the Mt. Kearsarge North Trail leads to one of the finest views in the White Mountains.

Carter Notch [rt: 7.6 mi., 2,000 ft., 4:50]. This magnificent mountain pass, with ponds and an AMC hut, is most easily accessed by the Nineteen-Mile Brook Trail.

Strenuous Hikes

Carter Dome Loop [lp: 10.2 mi., 3,600 ft., 6:55]. An excellent loop over two high summits. Follow the Nineteen-Mile Brook Trail to Carter Notch, then take the Carter-Moriah Trail over Carter Dome and Mt. Hight (the best viewpoint on the Carter Range) and descend via the relatively easy Carter Dome Trail.

Mt. Moriah [rt: 10.0 mi., 3,100 ft., 6:35]. The ascent of this peak near Gorham via the Stony Brook and Carter-Moriah trails is very scenic, affording excellent views both along the way and at the summit.

Shelburne Moriah Mountain [rt: 11.2 mi., 3,200 ft., 7:10]. An ascent of this less visited peak via the Rattle River and Kenduskeag trails offers exceptional views from the ledges on the upper part of the ridge and at the summit.

The Baldfaces [lp: 9.7 mi., 3,600 ft., 6:40]. One of the finest ridge traverses of the White Mountains, with nearly 4 mi. of open ledge walking. Follow Baldface Circle Trail on the steep climb to South Baldface and across North Baldface; descend via the ledgy Bicknell Ridge Trail and lower Baldface Circle Trail. The steep ledges on South Baldface can be avoided by using the Slippery Brook and Baldface Knob trails [lp: 10.7 mi., 3,700 ft., 7:10].

SECTION TEN
SPECKLED MOUNTAIN REGION

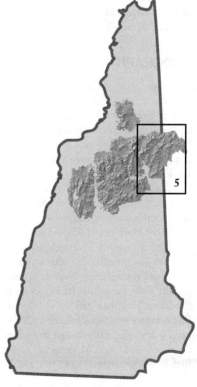

This section covers the mountains and trails in the region east of Evans Notch and the valleys of Evans Brook and the Cold River that lead up to Evans Notch from the north and south, respectively. The section is bounded on the west by ME 113/NH 113, the highway that runs through Evans Notch from Chatham, New Hampshire, to Gilead, Maine, and on the north by US 2. Except for a sliver of land near North Chatham, New Hampshire, the entire section lies in Maine. Almost all the land in this section is within the WMNF, and most of its central portion is included in the Caribou–Speckled Mountain Wilderness. The AMC's *Carter Range–Evans Notch Map* (map 5) covers the entire area. The Chatham Trails Association (CTA) publishes a detailed map of the trail system in the Cold River valley.

The Appalachian Trail (AT) does not pass through this section.

GEOGRAPHY

The major part of this region is occupied by a jumbled mass of ridges with numerous ledges; although the peaks are not high, they offer a variety of fine walks. With the exception of a few trails off ME 113, this area probably receives less hiking traffic than any comparable section of the WMNF, allowing visitors to enjoy relative solitude on trails in an area that is quite rugged and scenic, if not quite as spectacular as the Presidentials and Franconias.

Speckled Mountain (2,906 ft.) is the tallest peak of the region, one of at least three mountains in Maine that have been known by this name, and its open summit ledges have excellent views in nearly all directions. Blueberry Mountain (1,781 ft.) is a long, flat spur running southwest from Speckled Mountain. The top is mostly one big open ledge, where mature trees are slowly reclaiming what was once a burned-over summit with only sparse and stunted trees. Numerous open spaces afford excellent views, especially from the southwest ledges on the summit. In the valley between Blueberry Mountain and the west ridge of Speckled Mountain, Bickford Brook passes two sets of flumes, falls, and boulders of unusual beauty. A long, ledgy ridge extends east from Speckled Mountain to Miles Notch, running over Durgin Mountain (2,404 ft.), Butters Mountain (2,246 ft.), Red Rock Mountain (2,141 ft.), and Miles Knob (2,090 ft.). The west ridge of Speckled Mountain, which descends toward ME 113, includes Ames Mountain (2,686 ft.) and Spruce Hill (2,510 ft.).

Caribou Mountain (2,850 ft.)—called "Calabo" in the Walling map of Oxford County (1853)—is the second highest peak in the area. It also has a bare, ledgy summit that affords excellent views. South of Caribou Mountain is Haystack Notch, overlooked by the cliffs of Haystack Mountain (2,210 ft.). Peabody Mountain (2,462 ft.) is a wooded mountain that rises to the north of Caribou Mountain. Located on the eastern edge of the WMNF, Albany Mountain (1,930 ft.) has open ledges near its summit with excellent views in several directions. To the west of Albany Mountain and Albany Notch are several small but interesting rugged mountains that have no trails but invite exploration, of which the most prominent is Farwell Mountain (1,865 ft.). Round Pond is an interesting mountain pond that lies east of Albany Mountain and is easily visited from Crocker Pond Campground.

Deer Hill (1,367 ft.), often called Big Deer, is located south of Speckled Mountain and east of the Cold River. The views from the east and south ledges are excellent. Little Deer Hill (1,090 ft.), a lower hill west of Deer Hill that rises only about 600 ft. above the valley, gives fine views of the valley and the Baldfaces from its summit ledges. Pine Hill (1,250 ft.) and Lord Hill (1,257 ft.) rise southeast of Deer Hill, with scattered open ledges that afford interesting views. There are several short paths in the vicinity of the AMC's Cold River Camp not covered in this guide because they are not open to the public, though some are mentioned where they intersect other more important trails.

The Roost (1,374 ft.) is a small hill near Hastings, with open ledges that afford fine views of the Wild River valley, the Evans Brook valley, and many mountains.

CAMPING

Caribou–Speckled Mountain Wilderness

Wilderness regulations, intended to protect Wilderness resources and promote opportunities for challenge and solitude, prohibit use of motorized equipment or mechanical means of transportation of any sort. In accordance with USFS Wilderness policy, the trails in the Caribou–Speckled

Mountain Wilderness are in general maintained to a lower standard than trails outside Wilderness. They may be rough, overgrown, or essentially unmarked with minimal signage, and considerable care may be required to follow them. Hiking and camping group size must be no larger than 10 people. Camping and fires are also prohibited above the treeline (where trees are less than 8 ft. tall) except in winter, when camping is permitted above the treeline in places where snow cover is at least 2 ft. deep, but not on any frozen body of water. Caribou Shelter has been dismantled.

Forest Protection Areas

The WMNF has established a number of Forest Protection Areas (FPAs)—formerly known as Restricted Use Areas—where camping and wood or charcoal fires are prohibited throughout the year. The specific areas are under continual review, and areas are added to or subtracted from the list to provide the greatest amount of protection to areas subject to damage by excessive camping, while imposing the lowest level of restrictions possible. A general list of FPAs in this section follows, but because there are often major changes from year to year, one should obtain current information on FPAs from the WMNF.

(1) No camping is permitted above treeline (where trees are less than 8 ft. tall), except in winter, and then only in places where there is at least 2 ft. of snow cover on the ground—but not on any frozen body of water. The point where the restricted area begins is marked on most trails with small signs, but the absence of such signs should not be construed as proof of the legality of a site.

(2) No camping is permitted within 0.25 mi. of any trailhead, picnic area, or any facility for overnight accommodation such as a hut, cabin, shelter, tentsite, or campground, except as designated at the facility itself. In this section, camping is also forbidden within 0.25 mi. of ME/NH 113 for 0.50 mi. in either direction from Hastings Campground.

Established Trailside Campsites

Caribou Shelter (WMNF), formerly located on the Caribou Trail northeast of the summit of Caribou Mountain, has been removed. The spring near the shelter site is not reliable.

TRAIL DESCRIPTIONS

Roost Trail (WMNF)

This trail ascends to the Roost, a small mountain with fine views of the Wild River and Evans Brook valleys, from two trailheads 0.8 mi. apart on the east side of ME 113. The relocated north trailhead (sign, parking on shoulder) is 0.1 mi. north of a bridge over Evans Brook and 0.2 mi. north of the junction of ME 113 with Wild River Rd. at Hastings, Maine; the south trailhead is just south of another bridge over Evans Brook.

Leaving the north trailhead, the trail ascends a steep bank for 90 yd., then bears right (east) and ascends gradually along a wooded ridge, rejoining the older route at 0.1 mi. It crosses a small brook at 0.3 mi., then rises somewhat more steeply, swings right, and emerges on a ledge at the summit (no views) at 0.5 mi. Here a side trail descends 0.1 mi. and 100 ft. west through woods to spacious open ledges, where the views are excellent. The main trail descends generally southeast from the summit at a moderate grade and crosses a small brook, then turns right (west) on an old road (no sign) and follows it past a cellar hole and a brushy area back to ME 113.

Roost Trail (map 5:E13)
Distances from ME 113, north trailhead (820 ft.) to
- the Roost (1,374 ft.): 0.5 mi., 550 ft., 30 min.
- ME 113, south trailhead (850 ft.): 1.2 mi., 550 ft. (rev. 500 ft.), 55 min.

Wheeler Brook Trail (WMNF)

The trailheads for this trail are on the south side of US 2, 2.3 mi. east of the junction of US 2 and ME 113, and on Little Lary Brook Rd. (FR 8) 1.6 mi. from its junction with ME 113, which is 7.0 mi. north of the road to the WMNF Cold River Campground and 3.8 mi. south of the junction of US 2 and ME 113.

From US 2, the trail joins and follows the west side of Wheeler Brook, generally following old logging roads and crossing the brook four times. It turns left (arrow) at a logging road fork at 1.0 mi., just before the third crossing of the brook. The trail rises to its highest point, just over 2,000 ft., at the crest of the northwest ridge of Peabody Mountain (2,462 ft.) at 2.1 mi. (There is no trail to the wooded summit of Peabody Mountain.)

The trail then descends generally southwest, merges onto an old logging road that comes down from the left, and reaches Little Lary Brook Rd. Turn left on Little Lary Brook Rd. and continue about 100 yd. to a locked gate near the bridge over Little Lary Brook, 1.6 mi. from ME 113.

In the reverse direction, proceed along Little Lary Brook Rd. about 100 yd. from the locked gate, then turn right at the junction where FR 185 continues straight ahead. The trail leaves the left side of the road in another 0.3 mi.

Wheeler Brook Trail (map 5:E13)

Distance from US 2 (680 ft.) to
- gate on Little Lary Brook Rd. (1,220 ft.): 3.5 mi., 1,350 ft. (rev. 800 ft.), 2 hr. 25 min.

Caribou Trail (WMNF)

This trail provides access to the attractive ledges of Caribou Mountain. The middle section of this trail is in the Caribou–Speckled Mountain Wilderness. Its west trailhead, which it now shares with the Mud Brook Trail, is located on the east side of ME 113 6.1 mi. north of the road to WMNF Cold River Campground and 4.6 mi. south of US 2. The east trailhead is on Bog Rd. (FR 6), which leaves the south side of US 2 1.3 mi. west of the West Bethel Post Office (there is currently a sign for Pooh Corner Farm as well as a road sign at this junction) and leads 2.8 mi. to the trailhead where a gate ends public travel on the road.

From ME 113, the trail runs north. It crosses Morrison Brook at 0.4 mi. (the former bridge at this crossing was washed out in 2005) and turns east to follow the brook, crossing it five more times. The third crossing, at 2.0 mi., is at the head of Kees Falls, a 25-ft. waterfall. The trail levels off at the height-of-land as it crosses the col between Gammon Mountain and Caribou Mountain at 2.9 mi. Soon the Mud Brook Trail leaves right to return to ME 113 via the summit of Caribou Mountain, passing the site of the former Caribou Shelter and Caribou Spring (unreliable) in 0.3 mi. The Caribou Trail continues ahead at the junction, descends more rapidly, then turns northeast toward the valley of Bog Brook, which lies east of Peabody Mountain. It then follows a succession of logging roads down this valley, crossing Bog Brook at 4.3 mi. At 4.8 mi., it bears left in a clearing, crosses a tributary brook, then bears left again on the extension of Bog Rd. (FR 6) and continues to the gate.

Caribou Trail (map 5:E13–E14)

Distances from ME 113 (960 ft.) to

- Mud Brook Trail (2,420 ft.): 3.0 mi., 1,450 ft., 2 hr. 15 min.
- Bog Rd. (860 ft.): 5.5 mi., 1,450 ft. (rev. 1,550 ft.), 3 hr. 30 min.
- Caribou Mountain summit (2,850 ft.) via Mud Brook Trail: 3.6 mi., 1,900 ft., 2 hr. 45 min.

Mud Brook Trail (WMNF)

This trail begins on ME 113 at the same point as the Caribou Trail, 6.1 mi. north of the road to WMNF Cold River Campground, then passes over the summit of Caribou Mountain and ends at the Caribou Trail in the pass between Caribou Mountain and Gammon Mountain. Despite the ominous name, the footing on the trail is generally dry and good. The eastern section of this trail is in the Caribou–Speckled Mountain Wilderness.

From ME 113, the trail runs generally south, then turns east along the north side of Mud Brook, rising gradually. It crosses the headwaters of Mud Brook at 1.9 mi. and swings left (north) uphill, climbing more steeply. The trail crosses several smaller brooks and, at 3.0 mi., comes out on a small bare knob with excellent views east. It turns left into the woods and makes a short descent into a small ravine, then emerges above timberline and crosses ledges to the summit of Caribou Mountain at 3.4 mi. It then descends north, passes Caribou Spring (unreliable) left at 3.6 mi. and the site of the former Caribou Shelter right 70 yd. farther, and meets the Caribou Trail in the pass.

Mud Brook Trail (map 5:E13)

Distances from ME 113 (960 ft.) to

- Caribou Mountain summit (2,850 ft.): 3.4 mi., 1,900 ft., 2 hr. 40 min.
- Caribou Trail (2,420 ft.): 3.9 mi., 1,900 ft. (rev. 450 ft.), 2 hr. 55 min.

Haystack Notch Trail (WMNF)

This trail, with good footing and easy grades but some potentially difficult brook crossings, runs through Haystack Notch. The middle section of this trail is in the Caribou–Speckled Mountain Wilderness. Its west trailhead is on the east side of ME 113, 4.8 mi. north of the road to WMNF Cold River Campground. The east trailhead is on the Miles Notch Trail 0.2 mi. from that trail's north terminus, which is reached by following Flat Rd., which leads south from US 2 opposite the West Bethel Post Office to a crossroads at 3.1 mi., then taking the road that runs right (west). Continue straight ahead at a junction just beyond a small cemetery. The road becomes rather rough after about 1 mi. from the crossroads, and it may not be possible for some cars to drive all the way to the trailhead, which is about 2.5 mi. from the crossroads. Because of logging on private land, it may be difficult to find and follow the trail from this trailhead.

Leaving ME 113, the trail runs generally east along the east branch of Evans Brook, crossing it several times. The first crossing in particular may be difficult at high water. It enters the Wilderness and climbs to the broad height-of-land in Haystack Notch at 2.1 mi. It then descends into the valley of the West Branch of the Pleasant River, leaves the Wilderness at 3.4 mi., and at 4.4 mi., after crossing a tributary brook and leaving the WMNF, makes the first of three crossings of that stream, some of which may also be difficult at high water. The trail now crosses private land where it may be severely disrupted by logging. Eventually, it merges into an old logging road and meets the Miles Notch Trail, where it ends.

Haystack Notch Trail (map 5:F13–E14)

Distances from ME 113 (1,070 ft.) to

- Haystack Notch (1,900 ft.): 2.1 mi., 850 ft., 1 hr. 30 min.
- Miles Notch Trail (919 ft.): 5.4 mi., 850 ft. (rev. 1,000 ft.), 3 hr. 5 min.

Albany Notch Trail (WMNF)

This trail passes through the notch west of Albany Mountain. Parts of its northern section still suffer from invasion by berry bushes as a result of the loss of the mature forest in the 1980 windstorm, and beaver flooding has further complicated the situation. The southern section, which is located partly on old, rather overgrown logging roads, is poorly marked and requires much care to follow. Most use of this trail is on the north section, which in combination with the Albany Mountain Trail provides the easiest access to Albany Mountain. At present, the attractive loop hike that uses the Albany Mountain Trail in combination with the branch trail that runs from the height-of-land in Albany Notch to the base of the ledges on the Albany Mountain Trail cannot be recommended because of the recent beaver flooding on the Albany Notch Trail between its junctions with these two trails.

To reach the north trailhead, follow Flat Rd., which leads south from US 2 opposite the West Bethel Post Office and becomes FR 7 when it enters the WMNF at 4.5 mi. At 5.8 mi., turn right on FR 18, following signs for Crocker Pond Campground. The trailhead parking lot and kiosk are on the right in another 0.6 mi., just past the end of an extensive beaver swamp. The trailhead can also be reached from ME 5 just south of Songo Pond by turning west onto Patte Brook Rd., which becomes FR 8. At 2.7 mi., turn left onto FR 18 and follow it 0.6 mi. to the trailhead on the right. The south trailhead is reached by leaving ME 5 at the west end of Keewaydin Lake, 2.4 mi. west of the East Stoneham Post Office and 0.7 mi. east of the Lovell-Stoneham town line, and following Birch Ave. north. Bear right on Birch Ave. at 0.4 mi. from ME 5 and continue to the trailhead, which is on the right 1.0 mi. from ME 5. Park carefully to avoid blocking any roads; the road that the trail follows is passable in cars for another 0.2 mi. to a parking spot on the left: parking is extremely limited beyond this point.

Leaving the small clearing on FR 18, the trail follows an old logging road, with one small relocation to the left of the road, and a beaver dam crossing where it may be flooded at times. At 0.6 mi., it bears right at the junction where the Albany Mountain Trail diverges left (south). Between this junction and the junction with the branch trail to Albany Mountain at 1.7 mi., beavers have flooded the trail and it is only passable by bushwhacking around the beaver pond. (This section will probably be abandoned.) At 1.2 mi., the Albany Notch Trail enters the region damaged by the windstorm, where berry bushes are often a nuisance, though the trail becomes markedly drier underfoot. Returning to mature woods at 1.4 mi., it starts to climb at a moderate grade to the left of a small brook, and at 1.7 mi., it reaches the junction where the branch trail leads left (east) 0.4 mi. to the Albany Mountain Trail at the base of the ledges.

The trail now descends moderately, with a steeper pitch just below the pass, and crosses two small brooks; this section may be overgrown. It then runs at easy grades until it reaches a logging road used as a snowmobile trail at 2.4 mi., and turns left on this road (if ascending from the south, turn sharp right off the road onto a narrow footpath leading into the woods just before the road dips to cross a small brook; the arrow marking this turn is easily missed). This road is fairly easy to follow, but is rather wet and overgrown with tall grasses and other vegetation that permit little evidence of a footway. At 2.8 mi., the trail bears right off the logging road onto an older road (arrow), which is also wet and overgrown. At 3.1 mi., the newer road rejoins from the left and improves greatly, becoming a gravel road after passing a WMNF gate. The trail crosses Meadow Brook on a snowmobile bridge at 3.6 mi. and climbs gradually to the trailhead.

Albany Notch Trail (map 5:F15–F14)

Distances from FR 18 (800 ft.) to

- Albany Mountain Trail (990 ft.): 0.6 mi., 200 ft., 25 min.
- branch trail junction in Albany Notch (1,530 ft.): 1.7 mi., 750 ft., 1 hr. 15 min.
- trailhead on Birch Ave. (750 ft.): 4.2 mi., 800 ft. (rev. 850 ft.), 2 hr. 30 min.

Albany Mountain Trail (WMNF)

This trail ascends the north slope of Albany Mountain to an open ledge near its summit that affords a good view east and north. It begins on the Albany Notch Trail 0.6 mi. from FR 18.

Leaving the Albany Notch Trail, the Albany Mountain Trail ascends moderately. At 0.6 mi., the trail turns right at the foot of a small mossy rock face, and climbs to the junction at 0.9 mi., where the branch trail leads right (west) 0.4 mi. to the Albany Notch Trail at the height-of-land in Albany Notch; about halfway down, this path crosses a ledge with a view west. Soon the trail passes a ledge with a good view of the Baldfaces and Mt. Washington and winds upward at easy grades across ledges and through stands of red pine to the northeast outlook, where regular marking ends. The true summit, wooded and not reached by any well-defined trail, is about 100 yd. south. The summit area has other viewpoints not reached by the trail that repay efforts devoted to cautious exploration by experienced hikers. The best viewpoint on the mountain is about 0.1 mi. southwest of the true summit; a sketchy and incomplete line of cairns leads to it, with some bushwhacking required.

Albany Mountain Trail (map 5:F14)
Distance from Albany Notch Trail (990 ft.) to
  • Albany Mountain upper outlook (1,900 ft.): 1.3 mi., 900 ft., 1 hr. 5 min.

Albany Brook Trail (WMNF)

This short, easy trail follows the shore of Crocker Pond and then leads to attractive, secluded Round Pond. It begins at the turnaround at the end of the main road at Crocker Pond Campground (do not enter the actual camping area), reached by following Flat Rd., which runs south from US 2 opposite the West Bethel Post Office and becomes FR 7 when it enters the WMNF at 4.5 mi. At 5.8 mi., turn right on FR 18, following signs 1.5 mi. to the campground entrance. The trailhead can also be reached from ME 5 just south of Songo Pond by turning west onto Patte Brook Rd., which becomes FR 8. At 2.7 mi., turn left onto FR 18 and follow it 1.5 mi. to the campground entrance.

Leaving the turnaround, the trail descends to a small brook and follows the west shore of Crocker Pond for 0.2 mi., makes a short, moderate ascent, then joins and follows Albany Brook with gentle ups and downs. At 0.9 mi., it goes straight through a logging-road intersection with a clearing visible on the right, and soon reaches the north end of Round Pond.

Albany Brook Trail (map 5:F15)
Distance from Crocker Pond Campground (830 ft.) to
  • Round Pond (800 ft.): 1.0 mi., 100 ft. (rev. 150 ft.), 35 min.

Miles Notch Trail (WMNF)

This trail runs through Miles Notch, giving access to the east end of the ledgy ridge that culminates in Speckled Mountain. To reach its south terminus, near which the Great Brook Trail also begins, leave ME 5 in North Lovell, Maine, on West Stoneham Rd. and follow that road northwest for 1.8 mi., then turn right onto Hut Rd. just before the bridge over Great Brook and continue 1.5 mi. to the trailhead. To reach the north terminus, follow Flat Rd., which leads south from US 2 opposite the West Bethel Post Office to a crossroads at 3.1 mi., then take the road that runs right (west) and continue straight ahead at a junction just beyond a small cemetery. The road becomes rather rough after about 1 mi. from the crossroads, and it may not be possible for some cars to drive all the way to the trailhead, which is about 2.5 mi. from the crossroads. Because of logging on private land, it may be difficult to find and follow the trail from this trailhead.

From the south terminus, the trail follows an old logging road generally north. At 0.3 mi., it bears left off the road (arrow), then climbs over a small ridge and descends steadily into the valley of Beaver Brook. At 1.2 mi., it enters another old logging road, which it follows it to the left for 0.2 mi., then bears to the right off the old road and soon crosses a branch of Beaver Brook. At 2.3 mi., it crosses Beaver Brook, passes over a steeper section, runs in the gully of a small brook, then turns left away from the brook and reaches Miles Notch at 2.9 mi.; ascending to the notch, the cliffs of Miles Knob can be seen up to the left. The trail now descends gradually, and at 3.2 mi., the Red Rock Trail leaves on the left for the summit of Speckled Mountain. The Miles Notch Trail then descends moderately, crossing Miles Brook and its branches five times. At 4.7 mi., it leaves the WMNF, enters private land where logging may severely disrupt the trail, and crosses Miles Brook again at 5.1 mi. At 5.4 mi., the Haystack Notch Trail enters on the left, and the Miles Notch Trail soon reaches its northern end.

Miles Notch Trail (map 5:F14–E14)

Distances from south terminus (470 ft.) to

- Red Rock Trail (1,750 ft.): 3.2 mi., 1,800 ft. (rev. 500 ft.), 2 hr. 30 min.
- north terminus (800 ft.): 5.6 mi., 1,800 ft. (rev. 950 ft.), 3 hr. 40 min.

Bickford Brook Trail (CTA)

This trail ascends Speckled Mountain from the Brickett Place on ME 113, 0.2 mi. north of the road to WMNF Cold River Campground. Most of this trail is in the Caribou–Speckled Mountain Wilderness. The trail enters the woods near the garage, then at 0.3 mi. turns to the right onto an old WMNF service road built for access to the former fire tower on Speckled Mountain and follows this road for the next 2.5 mi. The trail soon enters the Wilderness, and at 0.7 mi., the Blueberry Ridge Trail leaves on the right (east) for the lower end of the Bickford Slides and Blueberry Mountain; this trail rejoins the Bickford Brook Trail 0.5 mi. below the summit of Speckled Mountain, affording the opportunity for a loop hike. At 1.1 mi., the upper end of the Bickford Slides Loop enters on the right. The Bickford Brook Trail soon swings away from the brook and winds up a southwest spur to the crest of the main west ridge of the Speckled Mountain range, where the Spruce Hill Trail enters left at 3.1 mi. The Bickford Brook Trail then passes west and north of the summit of Ames Mountain into the col between Ames Mountain and Speckled Mountain, where the Blueberry Ridge Trail rejoins right at 3.8 mi. The Bickford Brook Trail then continues upward to the summit.

Bickford Brook Trail (map 5:F12–F13)

Distances from ME 113 (600 ft.) to
- Blueberry Ridge Trail, lower junction (950 ft.): 0.7 mi., 350 ft., 30 min.
- Spruce Hill Trail (2,420 ft.): 3.1 mi., 1,800 ft., 2 hr. 25 min.
- Blueberry Ridge Trail, upper junction (2,590 ft.): 3.8 mi., 2,000 ft., 2 hr. 55 min.
- Speckled Mountain summit (2,906 ft.): 4.3 mi., 2,300 ft., 3 hr. 20 min.

Blueberry Ridge Trail (CTA)

This trail begins and ends on the Bickford Brook Trail, leaving at a sign 0.7 mi. from its trailhead at the Brickett Place on ME 113 and rejoining 0.5 mi. below the summit of Speckled Mountain. (The upper part of the Blueberry Ridge Trail may also be reached from Stone House Rd.—formerly Shell Pond Rd.—via the Stone House or White Cairn trails.) This entire trail is in the Caribou–Speckled Mountain Wilderness.

Leaving the Bickford Brook Trail, the Blueberry Ridge Trail descends toward Bickford Brook, and at 0.1 mi., the trail passes the lower end of the Bickford Slides Loop, which diverges to the left just before the main trail crosses Bickford Brook. Care should be taken to avoid (or else deliberately explore) numerous unofficial side paths from the Bickford Slides and over to the Bickford Brook Trail.

Bickford Slides Loop. This side path, 0.5 mi. long, leaves the Blueberry Ridge Trail on the left just before it crosses Bickford Brook, at a point 0.1 mi. from its lower junction with the Bickford Brook Trail. At the same point, a spur path descends 50 yd. to the right along Bickford Brook to the

Lower Slides. At a point 20 yd. from its beginning, the Bickford Slides Loop crosses Bickford Brook (may be difficult at high water) and climbs easily alongside it for 0.2 mi. It climbs steeply over a low rise and descends to a junction at 0.3 mi., where a short side path descends steeply left to a pool at the base of the Middle Slide. (The former continuation of this branching path up the steep west wall of the ravine has been abandoned.) The Bickford Slides Loop now climbs on a narrow, rough footway past the Middle and Upper Slides, then crosses the brook above the slides and ends at the Bickford Brook Trail, 0.4 mi. above that trail's lower junction with the Blueberry Ridge Trail.

From the junction with the Bickford Slides Loop and the spur path to the Lower Slides, the Blueberry Ridge Trail crosses Bickford Brook (may be difficult at high water) and ascends steeply southeast past a good western outlook to an open area just over the crest of Blueberry Ridge, where the White Cairn Trail enters right at 0.7 mi. An overlook loop 0.4 mi. long, with excellent views to the south, leaves the Blueberry Ridge Trail shortly after this junction and rejoins it shortly before the Stone House Trail enters on the right at 0.9 mi., a few steps past the high point of the trail on Blueberry Mountain. From the junction with the Stone House Trail, marked by signs and a large cairn, the Blueberry Ridge Trail bears left and descends to a spring (unreliable) a short distance from the trail on the left (north). Here it turns sharp right, and ascends over ledges with fine views, marked by cairns, and through patches of woods, passing over several humps. The best viewpoints are passed at 1.5 mi., 1.8 mi., and 2.5 mi. After crossing one more ledgy area at 2.8 mi., the trail swings right into spruce woods, climbs slightly, then turns right and descends to meet the Bickford Brook Trail in the shallow pass at the head of the Rattlesnake Brook ravine, about 0.5 mi. below the summit of Speckled Mountain.

Blueberry Ridge Trail (map 5:F13)

Distances from Bickford Brook Trail, lower junction (950 ft.) to
- Stone House Trail (1,750 ft.): 0.9 mi., 900 ft. (rev. 100 ft.), 55 min.
- Bickford Brook Trail, upper junction (2,590 ft.): 3.1 mi., 1,850 ft. (rev. 100 ft.), 2 hr. 30 min.

Spruce Hill Trail (WMNF)

This trail begins on the east side of ME 113 3.0 mi. north of the road to WMNF Cold River Campground, opposite the start of the East Royce Trail, and ascends to the Bickford Brook Trail, with which it forms the shortest route to the summit of Speckled Mountain. Most of this trail is in the Caribou–Speckled Mountain Wilderness. It ascends moderately through woods, passing the Wilderness boundary sign at 0.6 mi., to the summit of Spruce Hill at 1.5 mi. It then descends into a sag and climbs to meet the Bickford Brook Trail on the ridge crest west of Ames Mountain.

Spruce Hill Trail (map 5:F13)

Distances from ME 113 (1,450 ft.) to
- Bickford Brook Trail (2,420 ft.): 1.9 mi., 1,150 ft. (rev. 200 ft.), 1 hr. 30 min.
- Speckled Mountain summit (2,906 ft.) via Bickford Brook Trail: 3.1 mi., 1,650 ft., 2 hr. 25 min.

Cold Brook Trail (WMNF)

This trail ascends Speckled Mountain and affords fine views from numerous open ledges in its upper part, which is in the Caribou–Speckled Mountain Wilderness. Its trailhead is reached from ME 5 in North Lovell, Maine, 2 mi. south of Keewaydin Lake, by following West Stoneham Rd. (signs for Evergreen Valley) for 1.9 mi. Take the first right (Adams Rd., with an Evergreen Valley sign), just after the bridge over Great Brook, then continue to a gravel road on the right 2.2 mi. from ME 5. The WMNF sign is on the paved road, but it may be possible to drive 0.5 mi. on the rough gravel road to a parking area. It can also be approached via the Evergreen Link Trail, a shorter and more attractive alternative to the lower section of this trail.

Beyond here, the road becomes rougher, and in 0.7 mi. from the paved road, it bears left past a gate. The next 1.0 mi. is on a road, muddy in places, that circles on contour to a cabin, the Duncan McIntosh House. Continuing ahead on the road, take the left fork, then the right. The trail descends to Cold Brook and crosses it at 1.9 mi., then crosses a logging yard, bearing right on the far side. It climbs moderately, bears right at a fork, crosses a branch brook, and passes west of Sugarloaf Mountain. It climbs easily to a junction left at 2.7 mi. with the Evergreen Link Trail from Evergreen Valley, then ascends steadily up the south side of Speckled Mountain. It emerges on semi-open ledges at 3.5 mi., crosses two open ledgy areas with excellent views south, and bears right to reenter the woods at 4.4 mi. At 4.9 mi., it emerges on semi-open ledges again and soon reaches the junction with the Red Rock Trail right and the Bickford Brook Trail left, where it follows the latter trail left 30 yd. to the summit of Speckled Mountain.

Cold Brook Trail (map 5:F14–F13)

Distance from paved road (500 ft.) to
- Evergreen Link Trail (1,130 ft.): 2.7 mi., 750 ft. (rev. 100 ft.), 1 hr. 45 min.
- Speckled Mountain summit (2,906 ft.): 4.9 mi., 2,500 ft., 3 hr. 40 min.

Evergreen Link Trail (WMNF)

This trail provides the easiest access to Speckled Mountain via the scenic ledges on the upper Cold Brook Trail. It is lightly used but easily followed by experienced hikers. To reach the trailhead, leave ME 5 in North Lovell, 2 mi. south of Keewaydin Lake, and follow West Stoneham Rd. for 1.9 mi. Just beyond the bridge over Great Brook, turn right onto Adams Rd. (sign for Evergreen Valley) and follow it for 1.5 mi., passing the trailhead for Cold Brook Trail. Then turn right onto Mountain Rd. (sign for Evergreen Valley Inn), drive 0.4 mi. up this road to the inn, and park in the lot just above or in a sandy area just below.

On foot, follow the paved road uphill for about 100 yd. Where it turns left, take the dirt road (soon gated) straight ahead and continue climbing steeply. At 0.4 mi., turn left onto a grassy logging road (a sign reads, LINK), then right onto the Link Trail proper at 0.7 mi. (a sign reads, Speckled Mountain via Cold Brook Trail). The trail, blazed in yellow, leads off at a bearing of 70 degrees. It crosses a woods road at 1.0 mi. and reaches the Cold Brook Trail at 1.2 mi.; turn left for the ledges and Speckled Mountain.

Evergreen Link Trail (map 5:F13)

Distances from inn at Evergreen Valley (530 ft.) to
- Cold Brook Trail (1,130 ft.): 1.2 mi., 600 ft., 55 min.
- Speckled Mountain summit (2,906 ft.) via Cold Brook Trail: 3.4 mi., 2,400 ft., 2 hr. 55 min

Red Rock Trail (WMNF)

This trail ascends to Speckled Mountain from the Miles Notch Trail 0.3 mi. north of Miles Notch, 3.2 mi. from its southern trailhead and 2.4 mi. from its northern trailhead. It traverses the long eastern ridge of the Speckled Mountain range, affording fine views of the surrounding mountains. This entire trail is in the Caribou–Speckled Mountain Wilderness.

It leaves the Miles Notch Trail, descends to cross Miles Brook in its deep ravine, then angles up the north slope of Miles Knob and gains the ridge crest northwest of that summit. It descends to a col, then ascends to the east knob of Red Rock Mountain, where it passes an obscure side path that leads left downhill to a spectacular viewpoint (dangerous if wet or icy) at the top of the sheer south cliff of Red Rock Mountain. The main trail continues to the ledgy true summit of Red Rock Mountain at 1.2 mi., where there is a view to the north. A short distance beyond the summit, at a ledge with a view southwest, the trail swings right and descends over more ledges to a sag. It then follows the ridge, with several ups and downs, over Butters Mountain at 2.5 mi., and then on to the next sag to the west. Here, at 3.4 mi., the Great Brook Trail diverges left (east) and descends southeast to its trailhead, which is very close to the southern trailhead of the Miles Notch Trail. The Red Rock Trail swings southwest and crosses the summit of Durgin Mountain—which is ledgy with some outlooks, the best located on an obscure side path right just before the high point—at 4.4 mi. It then descends easily to a notch, climbs sharply, then runs generally southwest to the junction with the Cold Brook Trail and Bickford Brook Trail 30 yd. east of the summit of Speckled Mountain. There is a spring near the trail about 0.1 mi. east of the summit.

Red Rock Trail (map 5:F14–F13)

Distances from Miles Notch Trail (1,750 ft.) to

- Great Brook Trail (2,000 ft.): 3.4 mi., 1,000 ft. (rev. 750 ft.), 2 hr. 10 min.
- Speckled Mountain summit (2,906 ft.): 5.6 mi., 2,100 ft. (rev. 200 ft.), 3 hr. 50 min.

Great Brook Trail (WMNF)

This trail ascends to the Red Rock Trail east of Speckled Mountain. The upper part of this trail is in the Caribou–Speckled Mountain Wilderness. To reach its trailhead, leave ME 5 in North Lovell, Maine, on West Stoneham Rd. and follow that road northwest for 1.8 mi. Turn right here just before the bridge over Great Brook onto Hut Rd., and continue 1.5 mi. to the trailhead, which is about 100 yd. past the southern trailhead for the Miles Notch Trail.

The trail continues up the gravel road and bears right onto FR 4 at 0.8 mi., just after crossing Great Brook on a bridge with a gate. (It may be possible to drive vehicles to this point, where parking is available near a small cascade.) At 1.8 mi., it turns left onto a grassy older road and follows Great Brook, passing a stone wall, cellar hole, and gravesite marking the mid-1800s homestead of the Butters family on the left at 2.0 mi., just before crossing a tributary brook. At 3.0 mi., it crosses Great Brook, with some interesting cascades just below and just above the crossing. The trail then bears left (arrow), becomes steeper, and continues along Great Brook to the ridge crest, where it joins the Red Rock Trail in the col between Butters Mountain and Durgin Mountain.

Great Brook Trail (map 5:F14–F13)

Distances from trailhead (500 ft.) to
- Red Rock Trail (2,000 ft.): 3.7 mi., 1,500 ft., 2 hr. 35 min.
- Speckled Mountain summit (2,906 ft.) via Red Rock Trail: 5.8 mi., 2,600 ft. (rev. 200 ft.), 4 hr. 10 min.

Stone House Trail (CTA)

This trail ascends to the scenic ledges of Blueberry Mountain from Stone House Rd. (formerly Shell Pond Rd.) The upper part of this trail is in the Caribou–Speckled Mountain Wilderness. To reach the trailhead, leave NH 113 on the east side 1.3 mi. north of the AMC's Cold River Camp and follow Stone House Rd. 1.1 mi. to a padlocked steel gate, where there is a parking area on the right. The lower part of this trail, including Rattlesnake Flume and Rattlesnake Pool, is on private land, and hikers are requested to stay on the marked trails.

The trail leaves the road on the left (north), 0.5 mi. beyond the gate, east of an open shed. It follows a logging road and approaches Rattlesnake Brook. At 0.2 mi. from Stone House Rd., it merges with a private road (descending, bear right at arrow) and immediately reaches the junction with a spur path that leads right 30 yd. to a bridge overlooking Rattlesnake Flume, a small, attractive gorge. The main trail soon swings right (arrow), and at 0.5 mi., just after crossing a bridge over a small brook, another spur leads right 0.1 mi. to the exquisite Rattlesnake Pool, which lies at the foot of a small cascade. The main trail soon enters the WMNF, and at 1.2 mi., it swings left and begins to climb rather steeply straight up the slope, running generally northwest to the top of the ridge, where it ends at the Blueberry Ridge Trail only a few steps from the top of Blueberry Mountain. The eastern junction with the Overlook Loop is 30 yd. to the left up a ledge. For Speckled Mountain, turn right on the Blueberry Ridge Trail.

Stone House Trail (map 5:G13–F13)

Distance from Stone House Rd. (formerly Shell Pond Rd.) (600 ft.) to
• Blueberry Ridge Trail (1,750 ft.): 1.5 mi., 1,150 ft., 1 hr. 20 min.

White Cairn Trail (CTA)

This trail, steep in places, provides access to the open ledges on Blueberry Mountain and, with the Stone House Trail, makes a rewarding half-day circuit. The upper part of this trail is in the Caribou–Speckled Mountain Wilderness. It begins on Stone House Rd. (formerly Shell Pond Rd.), which leaves NH 113 on the east side 1.3 mi. north of the AMC's Cold River Camp and runs 1.1 mi. to a padlocked steel gate, where there is a parking area on the right.

The trail leaves Stone House Rd. at a small clearing 0.3 mi. beyond the gate. It follows an old logging road north across a flat area, where the trail was flooded by beaver activity in 2006, making it necessary to bushwhack to the left and cross a beaver dam. At 0.3 mi., it enters the WMNF. At 0.8 mi., it begins to climb steeply up the right (east) margin of the cliffs that are visible from the road, then turns sharp left and begins to climb on ledges. The grade soon moderates as the trail runs northwest along the crest of the cliffs to the west, with views to the south. At 1.2 mi., it passes a spring, then swings right (north) at easy grades; follow cairns carefully as the trail winds through ledgy areas. It passes another spring just before ending at the junction with the Blueberry Ridge Trail, 0.2 mi. west of the upper terminus of the Stone House Trail. An overlook loop trail that leaves the Blueberry Ridge Trail near its junction with this trail provides a scenic alternate route, 0.4 mi. long. to the Stone House Trail.

White Cairn Trail (map 5:F13)

Distance from Stone House Rd. (formerly Shell Pond Rd.) (600 ft.) to
• Blueberry Ridge Trail (1,750 ft.): 1.4 mi., 1,150 ft., 1 hr. 15 min.

Shell Pond Trail (CTA)

This trail runs between Stone House Rd. (formerly Shell Pond Rd.), at the locked gate 1.1 mi. from NH 113, and Deer Hill Rd. (FR 9), 3.5 mi. from NH 113. Stone House Rd. leaves NH 113 on the east side 1.3 mi. north of the AMC's Cold River Camp. Much of this trail is on private property, and hikers are requested to stay on the marked trails, especially in the vicinity of the Stone House. The trail itself does not come within sight of the pond, but the Shell Pond Loop provides access to a viewpoint on the shore.

From the gate on Stone House Rd., continue east on the road on foot. The Shell Pond Loop leaves right at 0.2 mi., and in another 80 yd., the White Cairn Trail leaves left. At 0.4 mi., the road emerges at the side of a large field and soon bears right at a fork onto a grassy airplane landing strip; here the Stone House Trail diverges left while the road ahead (not open to hikers) leads to a private house. The Shell Pond Trail heads east across the field with good views of the surrounding mountains, passing to the right of the Stone House at 0.6 mi.

The trail leaves the landing strip at 0.8 mi., entering a patch of woods to the left, and follows a grassy old road through an orchard. The trail is not clearly marked in this area; in the reverse direction, bear left at a fork to reach the landing strip. The trail crosses Rattlesnake Brook on a bridge at 1.1 mi., passes through a wet area, and turns left off the road at 1.2 mi., where the Shell Pond Loop bears right. From here the Shell Pond Trail ascends gradually to Deer Hill Rd.

Shell Pond Trail (map 5:G13)

Distance from gate on Stone House Rd. (600 ft.) to
• Deer Hill Rd. (850 ft.): 1.8 mi., 250 ft., 1 hr.

Shell Pond Loop (CTA)

This trail skirts the south side of Shell Pond, making possible a pleasant loop hike in combination with the Shell Pond Trail. It is located almost entirely on private property and also serves as an ATV trail; hikers are requested to stay on the marked trail. It leaves the south side of the Shell Pond Trail 0.2 mi. east of the gate on Stone House Rd. (formerly Shell Pond Rd.) and leads through woods near the edge of a field, making several turns marked by yellow blazes.

At 0.2 mi., it turns right onto a grassy road, crosses a bridge over Shell Pond Brook, and soon swings left (east) on a well-worn woods road. It traverses the slope well above the south shore of Shell Pond, with several minor ups and downs. At 1.3 mi., the trail turns left off the road and descends, then meanders through the woods behind the east shore of the pond, crossing several small brooks. At 1.7 mi., a spur path leads 25 yd. left to a clearing and a bench with a fine view across the pond to the Baldfaces and Mt. Meader. The main trail bears right here and continues at easy grades to the Shell Pond Trail, 0.6 mi. west of the latter's eastern trailhead on Deer Hill Rd. and 1.2 mi. from the gate on Stone House Rd.

Shell Pond Loop (map 5:F13–G13)

Distance from western junction with Shell Pond Trail (600 ft.) to
• eastern junction with Shell Pond Trail (630 ft.): 1.9 mi , 150 ft. (rev. 100 ft.), 1 hr.

Horseshoe Pond Trail (CTA)

This trail, blazed with bright yellow paint, starts from Deer Hill Rd. (FR 9) 4.7 mi. from NH 113 at a small parking area at a curve in the road, where the pond is visible; it ends on the Conant Trail. The former Horseshoe Pond Loop is now closed to public use, so there is no public access to the shore of this pond.

From Deer Hill Rd., it descends moderately past the Styles grave, which is on the right of the trail and enclosed by a stone wall, then enters a recent gravel logging road and turns right onto it. The trail follows this road, keeping straight at a junction in 100 yd. At 0.3 mi., just before the gravel road ends, the trail turns right onto a grassy road that leads up into a brushy area, and ascends through the clear-cut resulting from the timber salvage operations after the 1980 windstorm. It follows cairns and overgrown skid roads back into the woods to the old trail, which continues to the Conant Trail between Lord Hill and Harndon Hill.

Horseshoe Pond Trail (map 5:G13)

Distance from Deer Hill Rd. (700 ft.) to
* Conant Trail (1,100 ft.): 1.1 mi., 500 ft. (rev. 100 ft), 50 min.

Conant Trail (CTA)

This loop path to Pine Hill and Lord Hill is an interesting and fairly easy walk with a number of good outlooks. Much of the trail, especially the south loop, is on private land. It is frequently referred to (and may be signed as) the Pine-Lord-Harndon Trail, though it does not go particularly close to the summit of Harndon Hill; it should not be confused with the Conant Path, a short trail (not open to the public) near the AMC's Cold River Camp. It is reached by following Deer Hill Rd. (FR 9) and making a right turn 1.5 mi. from NH 113, then quickly turning left onto North Barbour Rd. and parking near a dike 0.1 mi. from Deer Hill Rd.; it may be easier to park at the junction with North Barbour Rd.

The trail runs straight ahead along the dike across swampy Colton Brook—Colton Dam is located several hundred yards to the right from here—and continues on a gravel road to the loop junction at 0.4 mi., where the path divides. From here, the path is described in a counterclockwise direction. The south branch turns right and follows a logging road (Hemp Hill Rd.) to a level spot at 1.0 mi. near the old Johnson cellar hole. Here it turns left on a logging road, then left again in a few steps. The trail turns left again at 1.2 mi. and ascends Pine Hill, rather steeply at times, passing a ledge with a fine view to the west at 1.4 mi. It reaches the west end of the summit ridge and continues to the most easterly knob, which has a good view north, at 2.0 mi. The trail zigzags down past logged areas. It crosses Bradley Brook at 2.3 mi., and then climbs, crossing the logging road that provides access to the mine on Lord Hill and passing an outlook over Horseshoe Pond. It reaches ledges near the summit of Lord Hill at 3.0 mi., where the Mine Loop leaves on the left.

Mine Loop. This path is 1.0 mi. long, 0.1 mi. shorter than the section of Conant Trail it bypasses. Except for the one critical turn mentioned later, it is fairly easy to follow. From the junction with the Conant Trail near the summit of Lord Hill, the path climbs briefly to the ledge at the top of the old mica mine and then descends on a woods road, and at 0.1 mi., it passes a spur path that leads right 30 yd. to the mine. At 0.5 mi., it turns sharp left on a good logging road, then at 0.7 mi., it reaches a fork and turns sharp right back on the other branch of the road, which shows much less evidence of use. This turn is easily missed because it is difficult to mark adequately and the correct side road is less obvious than the main road. (The main road, continuing straight at this fork, crosses the Conant Trail between Pine Hill and Lord Hill and continues south toward Kezar Lake.) At a clearing, the Mine Loop leaves the road on the right and descends 50 yd. to rejoin the Conant Trail 1.1 mi. from its trailhead.

From Lord Hill, the Conant Trail descends to the junction with the Horseshoe Pond Trail on the right at 3.2 mi., where it bears left, then soon turns left and runs at a fairly level grade along the south side of Harndon Hill. It passes a cellar hole, and the Mine Loop rejoins on the left at 4.1 mi. At 4.5 mi., the road passes a gate, becomes wider (in the reverse direction, avoid logging roads branching to the right), reaches the loop junction, and continues straight ahead across the dike to the trailhead.

Conant Trail (map 5:G13)

Distance from trailhead off Deer Hill Rd. (550 ft.) for
- complete loop: 5.2 mi., 1,000 ft., 3 hr. 5 min.

Deer Hills Trail (CTA)

This trail ascends Little Deer Hill and Big Deer Hill, providing a relatively easy trip that offers interesting views. Several trail sections in this area have been renamed to provide a more rational nomenclature. The trail proper runs from the AMC's Cold River Camp to Deer Hill Rd. (FR 9) 1.4 mi. from NH 113.

Members of the public who wish to use this trail starting at the north end are requested to park at the Baldface Circle Trail trailhead parking area and follow a path called the Deer Hill Connector, which runs south of Charles Brook for 0.3 mi. to a junction on the right with the Tea House Path (not open to the public) from Cold River Camp, then runs another 0.1 mi. to the dam on the Cold River near Cold River Camp. Here the trail from the AMC's camp enters on the right; its junction with the Conant Path is a few steps to the right (neither of these trails is open to the public). Distances given below include those traveled on the Deer Hill Connector.

The Deer Hills Trail crosses Cold River on the dam, soon passing the junction on the left with the Leach Link Trail and then the junction on the right with the Deer Hills Bypass. The Deer Hills Trail continues straight ahead and climbs moderately past an outlook west, then bears left onto ledges and reaches the summit of Little Deer Hill at 1.3 mi. Here the Frost Trail enters on the right, having ascended from the Deer Hills Bypass. The main trail descends into a sag, then climbs to the summit of Big Deer Hill at 2.0 mi. It then descends the south ridge with several fine outlooks, turning left at 2.5 mi., where the Deer Hills Bypass leaves on the right. Soon the Deer Hills Trail turns left again, then turns right onto an old logging road at 2.7 mi. Here a spur path (sign) follows the logging road left for 20 yd., then turns right and descends in 0.2 mi. and 100 ft. to Deer Hill Spring (also called Bubbling Spring), a shallow pool with air bubbles rising through a small area of light-colored sand. The main trail descends from the junction to Deer Hill Rd.

Deer Hills Trail (map 5:G12–G13)

Distances from ME 113 at the Baldface Circle Trail parking area (520 ft.) via Deer Hill Connector to

- Little Deer Hill summit (1,090 ft.): 1.3 mi., 550 ft., 55 min.
- Big Deer Hill summit (1,367 ft.): 2.0 mi., 1,000 ft. (rev. 200 ft.), 1 hr. 30 min.
- Deer Hill Rd. (500 ft.): 3.3 mi., 1,000 ft. (rev. 850 ft.), 2 hr. 10 min.

Deer Hills Bypass (CTA)

This trail skirts the south slopes of the Deer Hills, making possible various loop hikes over the summits. It leaves the Deer Hills Trail just east of Cold River Dam and follows a level grassy road south along the river. (This section of trail was formerly part of the Leach Link Trail.) At 0.4 mi., it turns left off the road and ascends past a ledge with a view west. At 0.6 mi., the Ledges Trail leaves left, and the Deer Hills Bypass climbs steadily alongside a stone wall. At 0.8 mi., a spur path called the Frost Trail leaves left, climbing 0.2 mi. to the summit of Little Deer Hill. The Deer Hills Bypass descends into a shallow ravine, then ascends easily to rejoin the Deer Hills Trail on the south ridge of Deer Hill, 0.5 mi. below the summit.

Deer Hills Bypass (map 5:G13)

Distance from western junction with Deer Hills Trail (500 ft.) to
- eastern junction with Deer Hills Trail (1,000 ft.): 1.4 mi (2.3 km), 550 ft (rev 50 ft.), 1 hr.

Ledges Trail (CTA)

This trail passes interesting ledges and a cave but is very steep and rough, dangerous in wet or icy conditions, and not recommended for descent. It leaves the Deer Hills Bypass, 0.6 mi. from the Cold River Dam, and climbs rather steeply with numerous outlooks. At 0.2 mi., the Ledges Trail divides; the right branch, which is slightly longer, rejoins in about 100 yd. Just above the point where these branches rejoin, the Ledges Trail meets the Frost Trail, a short spur from the Deer Hills Bypass. The summit of Little Deer Hill is 70 yd. left on the Frost Trail.

Ledges Trail (map 5:G12)

Distance from Deer Hills Bypass (700 ft.) to
- Little Deer Hill summit (1,090 ft.): 0.3 mi., 400 ft., 20 min.

Leach Link Trail (CTA)

This trail gives access to Little Deer Hill and Big Deer Hill from Stone House Rd. (formerly Shell Pond Rd.), which leaves NH 113 on the east side 1.3 mi. north of the AMC's Cold River Camp. The trail starts at a gated road on the right side of Stone House Rd. 0.3 mi. from NH 113. The northern part of the trail uses the former Shell Pond Brook Trail.

Beyond the gate, the trail follows a grassy road across a snowmobile bridge over Shell Pond Brook. At 0.2 mi., the trail turns right off the road (sign), then in another 50 yd. bears left and runs through hemlock woods along a bank high above the brook. It then descends, and at 0.5 mi., turns left at a point where the former route of the trail came across the brook from the right. The trail continues south at easy grades and ends at the Deer Hills Trail a few steps east of Cold River Dam. To ascend the Deer Hills, turn left on the Deer Hills Trail.

Leach Link Trail (map 5:G12)

Distance from Stone House Rd. (600 ft.) to
  • Deer Hills Trail (500 ft.): 1.2 mi., 0 ft. (rev. 100 ft.), 35 min.

SUGGESTED HIKES

For more information on suggested hikes, see p. ix.

Easy Hikes

The Roost [rt: 1.2 mi., 650 ft., 0:55]. A short climb up the Roost Trail to ledges with views of Evans Notch and the Wild River valley.

Round Pond [rt: 2.0 mi., 250 ft., 1:10]. An easy ramble to a pair of ponds along the Albany Brook Trail.

Deer Hills. These low hills provide good views of the Cold River valley and the Baldfaces. Options include a shorter trip out-and-back to Little Deer Hill [rt: 2.6 mi., 550 ft., 1:35] or a longer loop over Little and Big Deer Hills [lp: 4.3 mi., 1,050 ft., 2:40]. Use Deer Hill Connector, Deer Hills Trail, and connecting spurs.

Moderate Hikes

Caribou Mountain [lp: 6.9 mi., 1,900 ft., 4:25]. A loop trip over the Caribou and Mud Brook trails, with extensive views from the bare summit.

Albany Mountain [rt: 3.8 mi., 1,100 ft., 2:25]. A small mountain with good views over western Maine, accessed by the Albany Notch (north end) and Albany Mountain trails.

Blueberry Mountain [lp: 4.1 mi., 1,150 ft., 2:40]. There are many ledges with views on this loop over the Shell Pond and White Cairn trails, summit overlook loop, and Stone House Trail.

Strenuous Hikes

Speckled Mountain Loop [lp: 8.6 mi., 2,500 ft., 5:35]. A scenic circuit along the Blueberry Ridge and Bickford Brook trails, including the open summits of Blueberry and Speckled Mountains.

Red Rock Mountain Loop [lp: 10.3 mi., 2,700 ft., 6:30]. An interesting valley and ridge loop through a wild, less visited area, with views from Red Rock Mountain, using the Miles Notch, Red Rock, and Great Brook trails.

SECTION ELEVEN
THE MAHOOSUC RANGE AREA

6

This section includes the region along the Maine–New Hampshire border that lies east and north of the Androscoggin River, which runs south from Lake Umbagog near Errol to Gorham, then swings east from Gorham to Bethel, Maine. The region is bounded by NH 16 on the west, by US 2 on the south, and by ME/NH 26 on the northeast. The backbone of the region is the Mahoosuc Range, which rises from the east bank of the river above Berlin and Gorham, runs east at first, then gradually swings toward the north as it continues to its far end at Grafton Notch. This section covers the main Mahoosuc Range and all the trails on it, but does not cover some of the routes on eastern spurs of the range that lie wholly within Maine. Such mountains and routes are covered in the *AMC Maine Mountain Guide*. The most important peaks in the Mahoosuc Range are Old Speck Mountain, Mahoosuc Arm, Goose Eye Mountain, Mt. Carlo, Mt. Success, Cascade Mountain, and Mt. Hayes. The region is completely covered by the AMC's *North Country–Mahoosuc Range Map* (map 6).

In this section, the Appalachian Trail (AT) begins at the trailhead of the Rattle River Trail (Section Nine) on US 2. It follows the highway west 0.2 mi. to North Rd., then follows North Rd. for 0.5 mi., crossing the Androscoggin River, then turns left on Hogan Rd. for 0.2 mi. to the Centennial Trail. It then follows the Centennial Trail, the Mahoosuc Trail, and the Old Speck Trail to Grafton Notch, the eastern boundary of the area covered in this guide; the Baldpate Mountain Trail (see the *AMC Maine Mountain Guide*) continues the AT on the opposite side of Grafton Notch. In its course through the Mahoosucs, the AT crosses the summits of Cascade Mountain, Mt. Success, and Mt. Carlo, and passes near the summits of Mt. Hayes, Goose Eye Mountain, Mahoosuc Arm, and Old Speck Mountain.

GEOGRAPHY

The southern part of the Mahoosuc Range is a broad, ledgy, lumpy ridge, with numerous spurs extending south toward the Androscoggin valley. The main peaks, from west to east, are Mt. Hayes (2,555 ft.), Cascade Mountain (2,631 ft.), Bald Cap (3,065 ft.), and Bald Cap's two subsidiary peaks, Bald Cap Peak (2,795 ft.) and North Bald Cap (2,893 ft.); all three Bald Cap peaks are trailless. The northern part of the range is taller and narrower, with a well-defined ridge crest and two long subsidiary ridges running southeast toward the Androscoggin and Bear rivers; the Sunday River flows between these subsidiary ridges. The main peaks, from southwest to northeast, are Mt. Success (3,565 ft.), Mt. Carlo (3,565 ft.), the three peaks of Goose Eye Mountain (West Peak, the highest, 3,870 ft.; East Peak, 3,790 ft.; and North Peak, 3,675 ft.), Fulling Mill Mountain (trailless North Peak, 3,450 ft., and South Peak, 3,395 ft.), trailless Mahoosuc Mountain (3,470 ft.), Mahoosuc Arm (3,765 ft.), and Old Speck Mountain (4,170 ft.). Old Speck is the third highest mountain in Maine; its name distinguishes it from the several other Speckled mountains (so called for their scattered open ledges) in the general area. Mt. Success is named for the unincorporated township in which it is located, and Mt. Carlo is named for a dog, the faithful companion of Eugene B. Cook. Cook was a pioneer White Mountain trail builder who made several early explorations of the Mahoosuc area, often accompanied by Lucia and Marian Pychowska, whose letters concerning their experiences in the White Mountains, including their exploratory adventures with Cook, have been published under the title of *Mountain Summers*. The origin of Goose Eye Mountain's peculiar name is in doubt; the most plausible explanation maintains that Canada geese in their flight south from the Rangeley Lakes appear almost to graze its summit, and it is, therefore, "goose high."

The views from Goose Eye, a striking rock peak, are among the best in the White Mountains, and most of the other peaks have fine views, either from the summits or from the numerous open ledges scattered throughout the range. There are several fine mountain ponds, including Speck Pond (one of the highest ponds in Maine), Gentian Pond, Moss Pond, Dream Lake, and Page Pond. The most remarkable feature of the range is Mahoosuc Notch, where the trail winds around and under huge fragments of rock that have fallen from the cliffs of Mahoosuc Mountain to the northwest; Fulling Mill Mountain forms the southeast wall.

The Alpine Cascades on Cascade Brook, which flows from the northwest slope of Cascade Mountain, are an attractive sight except in dry seasons. They can be approached from the abandoned railroad grade on the east side of the Androscoggin River in Berlin. From NH 16 just south of the city, 4.5 mi. north of its eastern junction with US 2 in Gorham, follow Unity St. across the Cleveland Bridge over the Androscoggin. At traffic lights 0.7 mi. from NH 16, turn right onto Mason St., and in another 0.1 mi., turn right on Goebel St. Follow this street for 0.2 mi., then turn right onto Devens St. and in a short distance, at a junction with Shelby St., bear left and drive about 1.0 mi. south to a gate at the Berlin Pollution Control Facility, where the old railroad grade will be seen on the right. Park off the road here and walk south on the railroad grade for about 0.5 mi. to a point nearly opposite the Cascade Mill. Here a footpath diverges left, then divides into two routes; the right branch, an old road, crosses under a power line in about 100 yd. and continues to the foot of Cascade Falls.

A formerly trailless range of peaks that extends southeast from Old Speck Mountain has been made accessible by the new western section of the Grafton Loop Trail (scheduled to open in 2007). The most important of these are wooded, trailless Slide Mountain (3,250 ft.) and the spectacular open ledgy peak of Sunday River Whitecap (3,335 ft.), which is traversed by the new trail. These two peaks are separated by Miles Notch. Extending southeast from Sunday River Whitecap are Stowe Mountain (2,730 ft.) and Bald Mountain (2,085 ft.); the Grafton Loop Trail crosses both of these lower peaks.

From the major peaks of the southern part of the range, ridges run toward the Androscoggin, bearing interesting smaller peaks. Among these mountains are Middle Mountain (2,010 ft.), Mt. Crag (1,412 ft.), Mt. Ingalls (2,242 ft.), Mt. Cabot (1,512 ft.), and Crow's Nest (1,287 ft.). There are also two waterfalls on the south side of the range. Dryad Fall is reached by the Dryad Fall Trail; the name was given by pioneer explorer and path maker Eugene Cook, an incurable punster, referring to the fact that unless it has rained recently, the falls are fairly dry. Giant Falls is accessible by a spur path off the Peabody Brook Trail. Lary Flume is a wild chasm that resembles the Ice Gulch and Devils Hopyard, with many boulder caves and one fissure cave. There is no trail, but experienced bushwhackers have visited it by ascending along the brook that may be reached by following a compass course east where the Austin Brook Trail begins its last 0.5 mi. of ascent to Gentian Pond.

Success Pond Rd. is a gravel main-haul logging road that runs 19.4 mi. from Hutchins St. on the east side of the Androscoggin River in Berlin to ME 26 2.8 mi. north of the Old Speck Trail (AT) trailhead in Grafton Notch; its northern 1.8 mi. is signed as the York Pond Rd. (not to be confused with the York Pond Rd. in the Kilkenny area). Over the years this has been perhaps the most difficult road in the White Mountains for a person unfamiliar with the region to find. In recent years, the location of the first part of the road, which in the past was moved with astounding but unpredictable regularity, has become well-established, though it still requires care to find and follow. *Caution:* This road passes through an area of active logging, so drivers must always be vigilant and prepared to yield to large and fast-moving logging trucks—it is not always easy to find a place to get out of the way quickly. To find the road, leave NH 16 just south of the city of Berlin, 4.5 mi. north of its eastern junction with US 2 in Gorham, and follow Unity St. across the Androscoggin on the Cleveland Bridge. At the east end of the bridge, Unity St. swings left and passes through a set of traffic lights in 0.7 mi. from NH 16. At 0.8 mi., the road bears right across railroad tracks, and at 0.9 mi., it bears left and becomes Hutchins St. It bears left at 1.6 mi., and at 1.9 mi., where there is usually a sign on the left reading "OHRV PARKING 1 MILE," the Success Pond Rd. begins on the right (east). A short distance in from Hutchins St., there have been boulders and cables on either side of the road. The first part of the road has at times been difficult to distinguish from branch roads, though at 0.2 mi., a sign, "Success Pond Rd.," has recently been placed, and mile markers have been posted along the main road. At 0.5 mi. from Hutchins St., the road bears left under a power line, and at 1.0 mi., it passes parking for the Success ATV Trail on the right. Once past this area, it is well defined—though it is often easy to take a dead-end branch road by mistake. The road is not generally open to public vehicular use in winter, and it can be very rough and muddy, particularly in spring and early summer before yearly maintenance is carried out. At certain times of the year, the road may be gated at either end, so it would be prudent not to plan on driving all the way through. Trailheads are marked only with the AMC's small standard trail signs, often at diverging logging roads with no well-defined parking area, so one must look for them carefully. The lower parts of the trails originating on this road have been disrupted frequently in the past by construction of new logging roads; great care is necessary to follow the blazes that mark the proper roads, ascending or descending. In recent years extensive new logging operations have been underway along this road, so hikers should be prepared for changing conditions.

North Rd. provides access to the trails on the south side of the Mahoosuc Range. This road leaves US 2 about 2.8 mi. east of its easterly junction with NH 16 in Gorham and crosses the Androscoggin River on the Lead Mine Bridge; the AT follows this part of the road. North Rd. then swings east and runs along the north side of the river to rejoin US 2 just north of Bethel, Maine. Bridges connect North Rd. with US 2 at the villages of Shelburne, New Hampshire, and Gilead, Maine.

CAMPING

Except for the corridor of the AT on the ridge crest, land in this section is owned by the state of Maine (mostly the higher-elevation lands along the Mahoosuc ridge crest in Maine), and by paper companies and other private interests. Hiking is permitted through their courtesy. No part of this section is included in the WMNF, though the AT corridor along the New Hampshire section of the range is managed by the WMNF. Along the New Hampshire section camping is allowed within the AT corridor except within 0.25 mi. of shelters and designated campsites; fires are allowed only at the shelters and at designated campsites and backcountry sites. Most of the Maine portion of the Mahoosuc Range (except for Old Speck Mountain, which is in Grafton Notch State Park), including the ridge crest, the upper part of the western slopes, and much of the land to the east, is within the state-owned Mahoosuc Public Reserve Lands. On the portions of these lands above treeline, camping and fires are allowed only at shelters and designated sites. No fire permits are required at these sites or at the Goose Eye Brook campsite on the Wright Trail. Below treeline, backcountry camping is allowed, but fires are not. No camping is allowed in Grafton Notch State Park. Along the Grafton Loop Trail, much of which is located on private land, camping is allowed only at designated sites. During peak summer and fall periods, groups of six or more planning to use AMC-managed backcountry campsites are asked to use the AMC's group notification system. For more information, visit http://www.outdoors.org/lodging/campsites/campsites-notification.cfm.

Trident Col Tentsite (AMC) is located on a side path from the Mahoosuc Trail in Trident Col. There are sites for four tents. Water is available about 50 yd. below (west of) the site.

Gentian Pond Campsite (AMC) on Gentian Pond has a large shelter and four tent platforms.

Carlo Col Campsite (AMC), consisting of a shelter and five tent platforms, is located on the Carlo Col Trail 0.3 mi. below the Mahoosuc Trail at Carlo Col.

Full Goose Campsite (AMC), consisting of a shelter and four tent platforms, is located on the Mahoosuc Trail between Fulling Mill Mountain and Goose Eye Mountain. There is a spring 30 yd. east of the shelter.

Speck Pond Campsite (AMC), located at Speck Pond on the Mahoosuc Trail, includes a shelter and six tent platforms. In summer, there is a caretaker, and a fee is charged.

TRAIL DESCRIPTIONS

Mahoosuc Trail (AMC/MDP)

This trail extends along the entire length of the Mahoosuc Range from Gorham, NH, to the summit of Old Speck. Beyond its junction with the Centennial Trail, the Mahoosuc Trail is a link in the AT. Camping is available at the tentsites at Trident Col and to the four shelters: Gentian Pond, Carlo Col, Full Goose, and Speck Pond (all of which also have tentsites). These sites may have a caretaker, in which case a fee is charged. See earlier for trailside camping regulations. Water is scarce, particularly in dry weather, and its purity is always in question. Do not be deceived by the relatively low elevations; this trail is among the most rugged of its kind in the White Mountains, a very strenuous trail—particularly for those with heavy packs—with numerous minor humps and cols, and many ledges, some of them quite steep, that are likely to be slippery when wet. Many parts of the trail may require significantly more time than that provided by the formula, particularly for backpackers, and Mahoosuc Notch may require several extra hours, depending in part on how much time one spends enjoying the spectacular scenery. Mahoosuc Notch is regarded by many who have hiked the entire length of the AT as its most difficult mile. *Caution:* Mahoosuc Notch can be hazardous in wet or icy conditions and can remain impassable because of unmelted snowdrifts through the end of May and perhaps even longer. Some sections of the ridge, especially the one traversing Goose Eye Mountain, have significant weather exposure.

Part I. Gorham to Centennial Trail

The former section of the Mahoosuc Trail leading from NH 16 across the Boston & Maine railroad bridge over the Androcsoggin, and then across the powerhouse and dam over the canal to Hogan Rd. on the east side of the canal, has been closed. The Mahoosuc Trail now begins on the east side of Hogan Rd., 0.1 mi. north of the dam, which is signed as the Gorham Hydro Station. To reach this trailhead by car, follow North Rd. north from US 2 in Shelburne and in 0.5 mi., just north of the bridge over the Androscoggin River, turn left (west) onto Hogan Rd. This gravel road, rough in places but sound, passes the trailhead for the Centennial Trail at 0.2 mi. from North Rd. and follows the river southwest, then west. Bear left at 1.3 mi. and again at 2.4 mi., beyond which the road narrows and becomes rougher. At 4.5 mi., after the road has swung to the northwest, park on the right opposite the Gorham Hydro Station; do not park next to the station. Proceed north up the road on foot for 0.1 mi. to the start of the trail (sign) on the right; mileages are given from the parking area. The trail enters the woods and climbs moderately, crosses a power-line clearing at 0.2 mi., then follows a brook for 100 yd. It ascends at only a slight grade to a side path at 0.5 mi. that leads right 0.2 mi. to Mascot Pond, which lies just below Leadmine Ledge, the cliffs seen prominently from Gorham. The Mahoosuc Trail bears left and climbs moderately, crosses a gravel road at 1.0 mi., then ascends gradually along the valley of a small brook, which it crosses several times. It then swings right and ascends steadily, passing a short spur (sign) at 1.9 mi. that leads left to Popsy Spring. It now climbs steeply and emerges on the southwest side of the flat, ledgy summit of Mt. Hayes at 2.2 mi. An unmarked footway leads a few yards right to the best viewpoint south over the valley. A cairn marks the true summit of Mt. Hayes at 2.5 mi. The trail runs across open ledges with restricted views north to the junction on the right with the Centennial Trail at 2.7 mi.

Part II. Centennial Trail to Gentian Pond

From here north, the Mahoosuc Trail is part of the AT, marked with white blazes. It bears left and descends steadily, then gradually north to the col between Mt. Hayes and Cascade Mountain at 3.5 mi., where there is sometimes water. The trail then ascends Cascade Mountain by a southwest ridge, climbing steeply over large, broken rock slabs and then ledges, emerging on a ledge with excellent views south at 3.9 mi. It crosses a shoulder and a minor col, then ascends easily to the wooded summit of Cascade Mountain at 4.5 mi. At a ledge, it turns back sharply left, descending gradually with occasional slight ascents to the east end of the mountain, passing an outlook south. It then enters a fine forest and descends rapidly beside cliffs and ledges to Trident Col at 5.7 mi., where a side path leads left 0.2 mi. to Trident Col Tentsite. Water is available about 50 yd. below (west of) the site. The bare ledges of the rocky cone to the east of Trident Col repay the effort required to scramble to its top; a route ascends between two large cairns where the Mahoosuc Trail crosses open ledges a short distance east of the tentsite side path.

The trail descends rather steeply to the southeast and runs along the side of the ridge at the base of the Trident, which is made up of the previously mentioned cone, the ledgy peak just west of Page Pond, and a somewhat less prominent peak between them. The trail crosses several small brooks, at least one of which usually has water. It follows a logging road for 0.1 mi., then turns left off the road at a sign and ascends to Page Pond at 6.7 mi., where beaver activity may cause wet conditions. The trail passes the south end of the pond, crosses a beaver dam, and climbs gradually, then more steeply, to a short spur path at 7.3 mi. that leads left to a fine outlook from ledges near the summit of Wocket Ledge, a shoulder of Bald Cap. The main trail crosses the height-of-land and descends east, crosses the upper (west) branch of Peabody Brook, then climbs around the nose of a small ridge and descends gradually to the head of Dream Lake. The trail bears left here, then bears right to run around the north end of the lake, and crosses the inlet brook at 8.4 mi. Just beyond, the Peabody Brook Trail leaves on the right.

From this junction, the Mahoosuc Trail follows an old lumber road left for 100 yd. It soon recrosses the inlet brook, passes over a slight divide into the watershed of Austin Brook, ascends through some swampy places, and descends to Moss Pond at 9.9 mi. It continues past the north shore of the pond and follows an old logging road down the outlet brook, then crosses the brook, turns abruptly right downhill from the logging road, and descends to Gentian Pond. It skirts the northeast shore of the pond, then crosses the inlet stream. A few yards beyond, at 10.6 mi., is Gentian Pond Campsite (shelter and tentsites), and here the Austin Brook Trail diverges right for North Rd. in Shelburne.

Part III. Gentian Pond to Carlo Col

From Gentian Pond Shelter the trail climbs to the top of the steep-sided hump whose ledges overlook the pond from the east, then descends moderately to a sag. It then starts up the west end of Mt. Success, climbing rather steeply at first to the lumpy ridge, and passes a small stream at 12.0 mi. in the col that lies under the main mass of Mt. Success. The trail now climbs rather steeply and roughly for about 0.5 mi. to the relatively flat upper part of the mountain, then ascends over open ledges with an outlook to the southwest, passes through a belt of high scrub, crosses an alpine meadow, and finally comes out on the summit of Mt. Success at 13.4 mi.

The trail turns sharp left here and descends through scrub, then forest, to the sag between Mt. Success and a northern subpeak, where the Success Trail enters left at 14.0 mi. The main trail climbs slightly, then descends moderately to the main col between Mt. Success and Mt. Carlo at 14.7 mi. The trail then rises over a low hump and descends to a lesser col, where it turns right, then left, passes the Maine–New Hampshire border signs, and ascends moderately again. At 15.8 mi., it drops sharply past a fine outlook ledge into the little box ravine called Carlo Col. The Carlo Col Trail from Success Pond Rd. enters left here; Carlo Col Campsite is located 0.3 mi. down the Carlo Col Trail, at the head of a small brook.

Part IV. Carlo Col to Mahoosuc Notch

From Carlo Col the trail climbs steadily to the bare southwest summit of Mt. Carlo at 16.2 mi., where there is an excellent view. It then passes a lower knob to the northeast, descends through a mountain meadow—where there is a fine view of Goose Eye ahead—and reaches the col at 16.8 mi. The trail turns more north and climbs steeply to a ledgy knoll below Goose Eye, then passes through a sag and climbs steeply again to the narrow ridge of the main peak of Goose Eye Mountain at 17.6 mi. Use care on the ledges. Here, at the ridge top, the Goose Eye Trail branches sharp left, reaching the open summit and its spectacular views in 0.1 mi. and continuing to Success Pond Rd. From the ridge-top junction the Mahoosuc Trail turns sharp right (east) and follows the ridge crest through mixed ledge and scrub to a col at 17.9 mi., where it meets the south branch of the Wright Trail to Bull Branch Rd. in Ketchum, Maine. The Mahoosuc Trail then climbs steeply through woods and open areas to the bare summit of the East Peak of Goose Eye Mountain. Here, it turns north and descends steeply, then switchbacks downhill through scrub over plank walkways, meeting the north branch of the Wright Trail at 18.2 mi. Beyond the col, the trail runs in the open nearly to the foot of the North Peak, except for a box ravine, where there is often water. At the broad, open summit of the North Peak, at 19.2 mi., the trail turns sharp right (east) along the ridge crest, then swings northeast down the steep slope with fine views, winding through several patches of scrub. At the foot of the steep slope, it enters the woods and angles down the west face of the ridge to the col at 20.2 mi. The trail ascends a ladder to Full Goose Campsite, located on a ledgy shelf near the col; there is a spring 80 yd. to the right (east of the campsite). In front of the shelter the trail turns sharp left, descends a ladder, then ascends, coming into the open about 0.3 mi. below the bare summit of the South Peak of Fulling Mill Mountain, which is reached at 20.7 mi. At the broad summit ledge, the trail turns sharp left and runs through a meadow. It descends northwest through woods, first gradually, then steeply, with two ladders and many rock steps, to the head of Mahoosuc Notch at 21.7 mi. Here, the Notch Trail to Success Pond Rd. diverges sharp left (southwest).

Part V. Mahoosuc Notch to Old Speck
From the head of Mahoosuc Notch the trail turns sharp right (northeast) and descends the length of the narrow notch along a rough footway, passing through a number of boulder caverns, some with narrow openings where progress will be slow and where ice remains into summer. The trail is blazed on the rocks with white paint. *Caution:* Great care should be exercised in the notch because of the numerous slippery rocks and dangerous holes. The notch may be impassable through early June because of snow, even with snowshoes. Heavy backpacks will impede progress considerably.

At the lower end of the notch, at 22.8 mi., the trail bears left and ascends moderately but roughly under the east end of Mahoosuc Mountain along the valley that leads to Notch 2, then crosses to the north side of the brook at 23.3 mi. The trail then winds upward among rocks and ledges on the very steep wooded slope of Mahoosuc Arm with a steep, rough footway and many wet, slippery slabs. A little more than halfway up, it passes the head of a little flume, in which there is sometimes water. At 24.4 mi., a few yards past the top of the flat ledges near the summit of Mahoosuc Arm, the May Cutoff diverges left and leads 0.3 mi. over the true summit to the Speck Pond Trail. The Mahoosuc Trail swings right and wanders across the semi-open summit plateau for about 0.5 mi., then drops steeply to Speck Pond (3,430 ft.), one of the highest ponds in Maine, bordered with thick woods. The trail crosses the outlet brook and continues around the east side of the pond to Speck Pond Campsite at 25.3 mi. (in summer, there is a caretaker and a fee for overnight camping). Here the Speck Pond Trail to Success Pond Rd. leaves on the left.

The trail then climbs to the southeast end of the next hump on the ridge, passes over it, and runs across the east face of a second small hump. In the gully beyond, a few yards east of the trail, there is an unreliable spring. The trail climbs on the west shoulder of Old Speck, reaching an open area where the footway is well defined on the crest. Near the top of the shoulder, the trail bears right, reenters the woods, and follows the wooded crest with blue blazes that mark the boundary of Grafton Notch State Park. The Old Speck Trail, which continues the AT north, diverges left to Grafton Notch at 26.4 mi., and the Mahoosuc Trail runs straight ahead to the summit of Old Speck and its observation tower, where the recently cleared summit offers fine views in many directions. Here the new Grafton Loop Trail (not yet open in the fall 2006) will lead south.

Mahoosuc Trail (map 6:E10–C13)

Distances from Hogan Rd. (800 ft.) to
- Mt. Hayes summit (2,555 ft.): 2.5 mi., 1,750 ft., 2 hr. 10 min.
- Centennial Trail (2,550 ft.): 2.7 mi., 1,750 ft., 2 hr. 15 min.
- Cascade Mountain summit (2,631 ft.): 4.5 mi., 2,450 ft., 3 hr. 30 min.
- Trident Col (2,000 ft.): 5.7 mi., 2,500 ft., 4 hr. 5 min.
- Page Pond (2,220 ft.): 6.7 mi., 2,850 ft., 4 hr. 45 min.
- Wocket Ledge viewpoint (2,700 ft.): 7.3 mi., 3,350 ft., 5 hr. 20 min.
- Dream Lake, inlet brook crossing (2,620 ft.): 8.4 mi., 3,650 ft., 6 hr.
- Gentian Pond Campsite (2,166 ft.): 10.6 mi., 3,850 ft., 7 hr. 15 min.
- Mt. Success summit (3,565 ft.): 13.4 mi., 5,750 ft., 9 hr. 35 min.
- Success Trail (3,170 ft.): 14.0 mi., 5,750 ft., 9 hr. 55 min.
- Carlo Col Trail (3,170 ft.): 15.8 mi., 6,250 ft., 11 hr.
- Mt. Carlo (3,565 ft.): 16.2 mi., 6,650 ft., 11 hr. 25 min.
- Goose Eye Trail (3,800 ft.): 17.6 mi., 7,350 ft., 12 hr. 30 min.
- Wright Trail, south junction (3,620 ft.): 17.9 mi., 7,350 ft., 12 hr. 40 min.
- Goose Eye Mountain, East Peak (3,790 ft.): 18.0 mi., 7,500 ft., 12 hr. 45 min.
- Wright Trail, north junction (3,450 ft.): 18.2 mi., 7,500 ft., 12 hr. 50 min.
- Goose Eye Mountain, North Peak (3,675 ft.): 19.2 mi., 7,800 ft., 13 hr. 30 min.

▶

- Full Goose Campsite (3,030 ft.): 20.2 mi., 7,800 ft., 14 hr.
- Notch Trail (2,460 ft.): 21.7 mi., 8,150 ft., 14 hr. 55 min.
- foot of Mahoosuc Notch (2,150 ft.): 22.8 mi., 8,150 ft., 15 hr. 30 min.
- Mahoosuc Arm summit (3,770 ft.): 24.4 mi., 9,750 ft., 17 hr. 5 min.
- Speck Pond Campsite (3,400 ft.): 25.3 mi., 9,750 ft., 17 hr. 30 min.
- Old Speck Trail junction (4,000 ft.): 26.4 mi., 10,550 ft., 18 hr. 30 min.
- Old Speck Mountain summit (4,170 ft.): 26.7 mi., 10,750 ft., 18 hr. 45 min.

Distances from Old Speck Mountain summit (4,170 ft.) to

- Old Speck Trail junction (4,000 ft.): 0.3 mi., 0 ft., 10 min.
- Speck Pond Campsite (3,400 ft.): 1.4 mi., 200 ft., 50 min.
- Mahoosuc Arm summit (3,770 ft.): 2.3 mi., 550 ft., 1 hr. 25 min.
- foot of Mahoosuc Notch (2,150 ft.): 3.9 mi., 550 ft., 2 hr. 15 min.
- Notch Trail (2,460 ft.): 5.0 mi., 850 ft., 2 hr. 55 min.
- Full Goose Campsite (3,030 ft.): 6.5 mi., 1,800 ft., 4 hr. 10 min.
- Goose Eye Mountain, North Peak (3,675 ft.): 7.5 mi., 2,450 ft., 5 hr.
- Wright Trail, north junction (3,450 ft.): 8.5 mi., 2,450 ft., 5 hr. 30 min.
- Goose Eye Mountain, East Peak (3,790 ft.): 8.7 mi., 2,800 ft., 5 hr. 45 min.
- Wright Trail, south junction (3,620 ft.): 8.8 mi., 2,800 ft., 5 hr. 50 min.
- Goose Eye Trail (3,800 ft.): 9.1 mi., 3,000 ft., 6 hr. 5 min.
- Mt. Carlo (3,565 ft.): 10.5 mi., 3,450 ft., 7 hr.
- Carlo Col Trail (3,170 ft.): 10.9 mi., 3,450 ft., 7 hr. 10 min.
- Success Trail (3,170 ft.): 12.7 mi., 3,950 ft., 8 hr. 20 min.
- Mt. Success summit (3,565 ft.): 13.3 mi., 4,350 ft., 8 hr. 50 min.
- Gentian Pond Campsite (2,166 ft.): 16.1 mi., 4,850 ft., 10 hr. 30 min.
- Dream Lake, inlet brook crossing (2,620 ft.): 18.3 mi., 5,500 ft., 11 hr. 55 min.
- Wocket Ledge viewpoint (2,700 ft.): 19.4 mi., 5,900 ft., 12 hr. 40 min.
- Page Pond (2,220 ft.): 20.0 mi., 5,900 ft., 13 hr.
- Trident Col (2,000 ft.): 21.0 mi., 6,050 ft., 13 hr. 30 min.
- Cascade Mountain summit (2,631 ft.): 22.2 mi., 6,700 ft., 14 hr. 25 min.
- Centennial Trail (2,550 ft.): 24.0 mi., 7,300 ft., 15 hr. 40 min.
- Mt. Hayes summit (2,555 ft.): 24.2 mi., 7,300 ft., 15 hr. 45 min.
- Hogan Rd. (800 ft.): 26.7 mi., 7,300 ft., 17 hr.

Success Trail (AMC)

This trail ascends to the Mahoosuc Trail 0.6 mi. north of Mt. Success, starting on Success Pond Rd. 5.4 mi. from Hutchins St. in Berlin. The trail sign is easy to miss, and the lower part of the trail must be followed with care through logged areas. The trail follows a logging road, bears right at a fork (sign) at 0.2 mi., and passes straight through a clearing (in 2006, it was possible to drive up into this clearing and park), entering the woods at a sign at 0.5 mi. The trail crosses a small brook twice and runs along the bank of an eroded roadbed, then begins to climb at a moderate grade along an old woods road. At 1.4 mi., the trail reaches the upper edge of an area of small second-growth trees, swings right, and ascends steeply along an eroded streambed, where care must be taken because of slippery rocks. At 1.6 mi., a loop path 0.3 mi. long diverges right to a spectacular ledge outlook with fine views of the Presidentials and the mountains of the North Country. In a little more than 100 yd., the upper end of the loop path rejoins, and the main trail ascends to a ridge crest, from which it descends to a brook (unreliable) at an old logging camp site. The trail soon enters a wet, boggy area, climbs over a small ridge, passes through another short boggy area, and then makes a short steep ascent to the Mahoosuc Trail at the main ridge crest.

Success Trail (map 6:D12)

Distances from Success Pond Rd. (1,610 ft.) to
- Mahoosuc Trail (3,170 ft.): 2.4 mi., 1,550 ft., 2 hr.
- Mt. Success summit (3,565 ft.) via Mahoosuc Trail: 3.0 mi., 1,950 ft., 2 hr. 30 min.

Carlo Col Trail (AMC)

This trail ascends to the Mahoosuc Trail at the small box ravine called Carlo Col. It leaves Success Pond Rd., in common with the Goose Eye Trail, on a new logging road that begins 8.1 mi. from Hutchins St. In 2006, parking was available a few yards up the trail on the left. The lower part of the trail must be followed with care through logged areas.

From the road, the two trails follow a new logging road, and in 100 yd. the Goose Eye Trail diverges sharp left down an embankment, while the Carlo Col Trail continues straight ahead on the road, climbing easily through a logged area. At 0.6 mi., the trail takes the left-hand road at a fork, descends on it for 0.1 mi., then turns left (sign) onto a footpath and immediately crosses the brook that flows from Carlo Col (may be difficult at high water). It continues near the brook for about 0.3 mi., then turns left away from it and follows a branch road with a steeper grade. It swings back to the south, crossing over the north and south branches of the main brook, and bends east up the rather steep south bank of the south branch. Avoiding several false crossings of this brook, it climbs to Carlo Col Campsite at 2.4 mi. (last water, perhaps for several miles). The trail continues up the dry ravine and ends at the Mahoosuc Trail at Carlo Col. There is a fine outlook ledge a short distance to the right (southwest) on the Mahoosuc Trail.

Carlo Col Trail (map 6:C12–D12)

Distance from Success Pond Rd. (1,630 ft.) to
• Mahoosuc Trail (3,170 ft.): 2.7 mi., 1,550 ft., 2 hr. 10 min.

Goose Eye Trail (AMC)

This trail ascends Goose Eye Mountain from Success Pond Rd., starting in common with the Carlo Col Trail 8.1 mi. from Hutchins St. and reaching the Mahoosuc Trail 0.1 mi. beyond the summit. In 2006, parking was available a few yards up the trail on the left. This is a generally easy trail—with good footing and moderate grades except for a steep pitch near the top—to a very scenic summit. The lower part of the trail must be followed with care through logged areas.

From the road the two trails follow a new logging road, and in 100 yd., where the Carlo Col Trail continues straight ahead, the Goose Eye Trail diverges sharp left down an embankment, then turns sharp right onto an older logging road. The Goose Eye Trail follows this logging road through recently logged areas, crosses two brooks, and enters a more recent gravel road that comes in from the right (descending, bear right). In 0.1 mi., it diverges right (watch carefully for sign) from the gravel road, passes through a clear-cut area, and crosses a wet section. At 1.4 mi., it reaches the yellow-blazed Maine–New Hampshire state line. The trail angles up the south side of a ridge at a moderate grade through fine hardwoods, climbs more steeply uphill, then becomes gradual at the crest of the ridge; at 2.6 mi., there is a glimpse of the peak of Goose Eye ahead. The trail ascends moderately along the north side of the ridge, then climbs steeply; the main path now ascends to the left bypassing a scramble up a difficult ledge, and soon comes out on the open ledges below the summit, to which it makes a steep, scrambly ascent. From the summit, which has magnificent views in all directions, the trail descends over ledges 0.1 mi. to the Mahoosuc Trail, which turns right (southbound) and runs straight ahead at the junction (northbound).

Goose Eye Trail (map 6:C12–C13)

Distances from Success Pond Rd. (1,630 ft.) to
- Goose Eye Mountain summit (3,870 ft.): 3.1 mi., 2,250 ft., 2 hr. 40 min.
- Mahoosuc Trail (3,800 ft.): 3.2 mi., 2,250 ft. (rev. 50 ft.), 2 hr. 45 min.

Notch Trail (AMC)

This trail ascends at easy grades to the southwest end of Mahoosuc Notch, providing the easiest access to that wild and beautiful place. It begins on Shelter Brook Rd. (sign), a spur road that leaves Success Pond Rd. 10.9 mi. from Hutchins St. and runs 0.3 mi. to a junction, where there is limited parking on the left. Shelter Brook Rd. turns right here (avoid Alder Brook Rd., which continues ahead) and crosses two bridges (the second of which has been deteriorating and should be checked before one drives across). At 0.5 mi., from Success Pond Rd. there is a parking area on the right, and 50 yd. farther, the trail leaves the road on the left (sign). The trail ascends easily along a slow-running brook, crossing it three times, following logging roads much of the way with bypasses at some of the wetter spots. At the height-of-land it meets the Mahoosuc Trail; turn left to traverse the notch. Very soon after entering the Mahoosuc Trail, the valley, which has been an ordinary one, changes sharply to a chamber formation, and the high cliffs of the notch, which have not been visible at all on the Notch Trail, come into sight.

Notch Trail (map 6:C12–C13)

Distance from parking area on Shelter Brook Rd. (1,650 ft.) to
- Mahoosuc Trail (2,460 ft.): 2.0 mi., 800 ft., 1 hr. 25 min.

Speck Pond Trail (AMC)

This trail ascends to Speck Pond from Success Pond Rd.; take the right fork of the road 11.4 mi. from Hutchins St. (marked by "SPECK MT. TRAIL, RT. 26" painted on a boulder) and continue 0.8 mi. to the trailhead (sign). There is parking on the left just beyond the trailhead, opposite the entrance to Speck Pond Rd.

The trail leaves Success Pond Rd., enters the woods, and in 100 yd. makes a crossing of Sucker Brook that may be difficult; in another 75 yd., it recrosses the brook. (In high water conditions, it may be best to walk 100 yd. up Speck Pond Rd. and then bushwhack south to the trail, which runs a short distance away on the near side of the brook, parallel to the road and the brook.) The trail follows its north side for 1.4 mi., then swings left away from the brook and traverses northward across logged areas where markings should be followed with care. It then bears right (east) and climbs rather steeply at times. After passing a relatively level section, it climbs rather steeply and roughly to the junction at 3.1 mi. with the May Cutoff, which diverges right.

May Cutoff (AMC). This short trail runs 0.3 mi. (10 min.) from the Speck Pond Trail to the Mahoosuc Trail with only minor ups and downs, crossing a hump that is probably the true summit of Mahoosuc Arm along the way.

The Speck Pond Trail continues over ledges, passes an excellent outlook over the pond and up to Old Speck, then descends steeply to the pond and reaches the campsite and the Mahoosuc Trail.

Speck Pond Trail (map 6:C12–C13)

Distance from Success Pond Rd. (1,700 ft.) to

• Speck Pond Campsite (3,400 ft.): 3.6 mi., 2,050 ft. (rev. 350 ft.), 2 hr. 50 min.

Old Speck Trail (AMC)

This trail, part of the AT, ascends Old Speck Mountain from a well-signed parking area (small fee) on ME 26 at the height-of-land in Grafton Notch. From the north side of the parking lot follow the trail leading to the left; the right-hand trail goes to Baldpate Mountain. In 0.1 mi., the Eyebrow Trail leaves right to circle over the top of an 800-ft. cliff shaped like an eyebrow and rejoin the Old Speck Trail. The main trail crosses a brook and soon begins to climb, following a series of switchbacks to approach the falls on Cascade Brook. Above the falls, the trail, now heading more north, crosses the brook for the last time (last water), turns left at a ledge with a view up to Old Speck, and at 1.1 mi. it passes the upper terminus of the Eyebrow Trail on the right. The main trail bears left and ascends gradually to the north ridge, where it swings more to the left and follows the ridge, with numerous short descents interspersed through the ascent. High up, the trail turns southeast toward the summit, and at 3.0 mi., there is an outlook east from the top of a ledgy hump. The trail descends again briefly, then ascends steadily to the south, passing the abandoned and closed Link Trail on the left. The Old Speck Trail passes an excellent north outlook just before its junction with the Mahoosuc Trail, where it ends. The flat, wooded summit of Old Speck, where an observation tower and the recently cleared summit plateau afford fine views, is 0.3 mi. left (east); Speck Pond Shelter is 1.1 mi. to the right.

Old Speck Trail (map 6:B13–C13)

Distances from ME 26 (1,500 ft.) to

- Eyebrow Trail, upper junction (2,550 ft.): 1.1 mi., 1,050 ft., 1 hr. 5 min.
- Mahoosuc Trail (4,030 ft.): 3.5 mi., 2,650 ft. (rev. 100 ft.), 3 hr. 5 min.
- Old Speck Mountain summit (4,170 ft.) via Mahoosuc Trail: 3.8 mi., 2,800 ft., 3 hr. 20 min.

Grafton Loop Trail (AMC)

This major new trail was constructed over a six-year period by the AMC and other members of the Grafton Loop Trail Coalition, including the Maine Bureau of Parks and Lands, the Maine Appalachian Trail Club, the Appalachian Trail Conservancy, the Maine Conservation Corps, Hurricane Island Outward Bound School, several timber management companies, Sunday River Ski Resort, and other private landowners. The group's goal was to develop multi-day hiking opportunities that offer alternatives to heavily used sections of the AT. This unique public-private partnership was the AMC's first major new trail construction project in the White Mountains since the Centennial Trail was opened in 1976. About 30 mi. of new trail have been constructed on either side of Grafton Notch, which, along with an 8-mi. section of the AT between Old Speck Mountain and Baldpate Mountain, has created a 38-mi. loop that connects a series of scenic peaks and other natural features. The eastern half of the Grafton Loop Trail opened to public use in 2003 and is described in the ninth edition of the *AMC Maine Mountain Guide.*

The western half of the trail, about 13 mi. in length, opened in 2007. Camping will be allowed only at designated campsites. From its trailhead on ME 26, south of North Newry, the trail ascends westward to Bald

Mountain (2,085 ft.), then climbs very steeply northwest to Stowe Mountain (2,730 ft.). It then swings north, passes Sargent Brook Campsite, and climbs to the open, ledgy summit of Sunday River Whitecap (3,335 ft.), with excellent views in all directions. It descends northward over open ledges, where the AMC's trail crews have used innovative construction techniques to protect the fragile alpine vegetation, then enters the woods and swings west, descending to Miles Notch. It loops to the south around the base of Slide Mountain (3,250 ft.), then turns northwest along the west side of the mountain, passing a spur to Slide Tentsite. It gains the crest of a southeastern spur of Old Speck Mountain, then climbs by switchbacks to the summit and its observation tower, where it meets the Mahoosuc Trail. For a full description of the western part of the Grafton Loop Trail, visit www.outdoors.org/conservation/trails/work/grafton.

Link Trail

This trail on Old Speck Mountain is no longer maintained and has been closed by the Maine Bureau of Parks and Lands.

East Spur Trail

This trail on Old Speck Mountain is no longer maintained and has been closed by the Maine Bureau of Parks and Lands.

Eyebrow Trail (MDP/AMC)

This trail provides a steep and rough alternative route to the lower part of the Old Speck Trail, passing along the edge of the cliff called the Eyebrow that overlooks Grafton Notch. It is better suited for ascent than descent. The trail leaves the Old Speck Trail on the right 0.1 mi. from the parking area off ME 26. It climbs moderately northwest and north for 0.4 mi., then swings left and ascends more steeply with the aid of cable handrails. It turns right at the base of a rock face, crosses a rock slab where iron rungs and a small ladder have been placed to assist hikers (but is still potentially dangerous if icy), then turns sharp left and ascends steeply, bearing right where a side path leaves straight ahead for an outlook. Soon the trail runs at a moderate grade along the top of the cliff, with good views, then descends to an outlook and runs mostly level until it ends at the Old Speck Trail.

Wright Trail (MBPL)

This trail, steep and rough in places, provides access to Goose Eye Mountain and the Mahoosuc Range via a scenic route from the east that begins in a place known as Ketchum, located on a branch of the Sunday River. The upper part of the trail has two separate branches that make possible a loop hike; the north branch passes through old-growth forest and a small glacial cirque, while the south branch follows a scenic ridge. To reach the trailhead, leave US 2 2.8 mi. north of Bethel, Maine, and follow Sunday River Rd. At a fork at 2.2 mi., bear right (signs for Jordan Bowl and covered bridge), and at 3.3 mi., bear right again (sign for covered bridge) and continue past Artist Covered Bridge (left) at 3.8 mi., from US 2. At 6.5 mi., the road becomes gravel. At 7.8 mi., turn left across the two steel bridges, then immediately take the first right, which is Bull Branch Rd. (no sign). At 9.3 mi., Goose Eye Brook is crossed on a bridge, and the trailhead is on the left (sign) at 9.5 mi. from US 2; parking is available a short distance farther up the road.

The blue-blazed trail leaves the south side of the parking area and descends toward Goose Eye Brook, then follows its north side upstream past several large pools and a 30-ft. gorge. At 0.5 mi., it makes a left turn onto a woods road and follows it for 0.2 mi., then makes a right turn onto an older road. At 0.9 mi., it bears left off the road and descends gradually 100 yd. to Goose Eye Brook at its confluence with a tributary, where it bears right and follows the tributary for 0.1 mi., then turns sharp left and crosses it. From this point the trail roughly follows the north side of Goose Eye Brook until it reaches the junction of the two parts of the loop at 2.5 mi. There is a designated MBPL tentsite on the right just before the junction.

North Branch. The north branch crosses a small brook and continues a gradual ascent on an old logging road along Goose Eye Brook for

0.2 mi., crossing it twice, then bears right and climbs moderately up away from the floor of the small glacial cirque in which Goose Eye Brook originates. It passes beneath several large rock slabs, then at 3.0 mi., comes out on the base of an open ledge from which the whole cirque is visible. The trail descends from this ledge, crosses Goose Eye Brook, and climbs a steep and rough slope on the headwall with a number of wooden steps, crossing the small streambed six more times; some of these crossings are slippery and require caution. Finally, it reaches the ridge crest and descends gradually for 100 yd. to the junction with the Mahoosuc Trail at 4.0 mi. For the south branch of the Wright Trail, follow the Mahoosuc Trail south for 0.3 mi., switchbacking up the ledgy East Peak of Mt. Goose Eye and descending the other side of the peak to the junction in the col. From this point, the West Peak (main summit) of Mt. Goose Eye can be reached in 0.4 mi. by following the Mahoosuc Trail (southbound) and the Goose Eye Trail.

South Branch. The south branch immediately crosses Goose Eye Brook and starts its climb, gradually at first and then moderately by switchbacks with rough sections and wooden steps, to the ridge crest at 3.1 mi. At 3.4 mi., after a rough ascent, it reaches an open spot, then descends slightly back into the woods. It then resumes a steep, rough ascent on ledges to an open knob with beautiful views at 3.6 mi. The trail continues along the ridge with several open areas and occasional minor descents to cross small sags, then finally climbs moderately to the Mahoosuc Trail in the small gap between the East Peak and the West Peak (main summit) of Mt. Goose Eye at 4.4 mi. The main summit can be reached in 0.4 mi. by following the Mahoosuc Trail to the left (southbound) and then the Goose Eye Trail. The upper end of the north branch of the Wright Trail is on the far side of the steep, ledgy East Peak, 0.3 mi. to the right (northbound) via the Mahoosuc Trail.

Wright Trail (map 6:C13)

Distances from parking area on Bull Branch Rd. (1,240 ft.)
- to loop junction (2,300 ft.): 2.5 mi., 1,050 ft., 1 hr. 45 min.
- to Mahoosuc Trail (3,450 ft.) via north branch: 4.0 mi., 2,200 ft., 3 hr. 5 min.
- to Mahoosuc Trail (3,620 ft.) via south branch: 4.4 mi., 2,400 ft., 3 hr. 25 min.
- for complete loop with side trip to West Peak of Mt. Goose Eye via Mahoosuc Trail and Goose Eye Trail: 9.5 mi., 2,800 ft., 6 hr. 10 min.

Centennial Trail (AMC)

This trail, a part of the AT, was constructed by the AMC in 1976, its centennial year. The trail begins on Hogan Rd., a dirt road that turns west from North Rd. north of its crossing of the Androscoggin River, just before it swings abruptly to the east. There is a small parking area 0.2 mi. from North Rd., and parking is also permitted at the junction of North Rd. and Hogan Rd.; in any case, do not block the road.

From the parking area on Hogan Rd., the trail runs generally northwest. After 50 yd. on an old road, it bears left up a steep bank into the woods, levels off, and reaches the first of many stone steps in 0.1 mi. The trail ascends rather steeply, then more gradually, with a limited view of the Androscoggin River. It turns left onto a woods road and crosses a brook at 0.7 mi. (last water). The trail then crosses a logging road and climbs steadily past several restricted viewpoints, swings right and passes an open outlook on the right, then descends to a sag in a birch grove at 1.6 mi. After a long gradual climb angling up the side of the ridge, it turns sharp left and continues upward past ledges that provide restricted views. At 2.8 mi., the trail reaches an easterly summit of Mt. Hayes, where there is a restricted view south. The trail descends slightly, then ascends across a series of open ledges to end at the Mahoosuc Trail at 3.1 mi. Here the AT turns right (north) on the Mahoosuc Trail. The summit of Mt. Hayes, with limited views, is 0.2 mi. to the left; the fine open ledges at the southwest end of the summit, with the best views on the mountain, are 0.3 mi. farther.

Centennial Trail (map 6:E11)

Distance from Hogan Rd. (750 ft.) to
• Mahoosuc Trail (2,550 ft.): 3.1 mi., 1,900 ft. (rev. 100 ft.), 2 hr. 30 min.

Peabody Brook Trail (AMC)

This trail ascends to the Mahoosuc Trail at Dream Lake from North Rd., 1.3 mi. east of its junction with US 2. Park on the shoulder on the south side of the road, taking care not to block driveways; overnight parking is not permitted at the base of this trail, most of which is on private land.

The trail follows a logging road between two houses, passing a gate, bears right at a four-way intersection, and crosses Peabody Brook on a logging bridge at 0.2 mi. It follows a logging road up along the brook through recently logged areas, skirts the left side of a large logging yard at 0.4 mi., and continues up the road. At 0.8 mi., it bears left at a fork, soon becomes a footpath, and ascends moderately up the side of the ravine. At 1.2 mi., a side path (unsigned, but there is a sign for the Peabody Brook Trail on the right) leaves left for Giant Falls, 0.3 mi., 150 ft. (rev. 100 ft.) from the main trail. The main trail rises more steeply and crosses a recent slide at 1.5 mi. where caution is required; here there is a fine view of the Presidentials beyond the Androscoggin valley. The trail climbs a short ladder just beyond the slide. At 2.1 mi., the trail crosses the east branch of the brook, then recrosses it at 2.4 mi. From here, it climbs easily through a wet area to Dream Lake and the junction on the right with the Dryad Fall Trail at 3.0 mi., and continues along the southeast shore of the lake, with views across the water to the Presidential Range, to the Mahoosuc Trail.

Peabody Brook Trail (map 6:E11–D11)

Distance from North Rd. (750 ft.) to
- side path to Giant Falls (1,450 ft.): 1.2 mi., 700 ft., 55 min.
- Mahoosuc Trail (2,620 ft.): 3.1 mi., 1,900 ft., 2 hr. 30 min.

Austin Brook Trail (AMC)

This trail ascends to the Mahoosuc Trail at Gentian Pond from North Rd., 0.6 mi. west of Meadow Rd. (which crosses the Androscoggin at Shelburne village). There is limited parking on the south side of the road. The trail passes through a turnstile on private land and follows the west side of Austin Brook, crossing the Yellow Trail at 0.4 mi. The Austin Brook Trail follows logging roads along the brook, then crosses it and reaches the gravel Mill Brook Rd. at 1.1 mi. (Austin Brook and Mill Brook are different names for the same stream.) This private gravel road leaves North Rd. 0.5 mi. east of the Austin Brook Trail trailhead and just west of the junction with Meadow Rd. In the past, this road has been gated at times and open to public vehicular use at other times. In 2006, it was possible to drive in on this road for 2.1 mi. to a turnout on the left with room for parking; parking may also be available 1.4 mi. up the road, at a point 80 yd. south of where the trail enters the road. However, logging operations could change this road access at any time, and drivers should heed any signs posted by the landowner.

From the point where the trail enters the road, it turns left onto the road and in 0.1 mi. bears left at a fork (sign). In another 0.1 mi., shortly after crossing a bridge, it bears right at a second fork (sign). At 2.1 mi., after crossing a bridge that was deteriorating in 2006, the trail turns left onto an older road and ascends moderately. At 2.5 mi., the Dryad Fall Trail diverges left. Here the Austin Brook Trail bears right, and at 2.7 mi., it turns right off the old road and enters the woods. At 2.9 mi., it makes a hairpin turn left and ascends along the edge of a logged area to a plateau. At 3.1 mi., it crosses the brook that drains Gentian Pond and runs on bog bridges through an area of beaver activity where the trail may be flooded. It swings right to the base of a steep slope, then bears left and climbs rather steeply to the Mahoosuc Trail at Gentian Pond Shelter.

Austin Brook Trail (map 6:E12–D12)

Distance from North Rd. (700 ft.) to
- Mill Brook Rd. (930 ft.): 1.1 mi., 250 ft., 40 min.
- Dryad Fall Trail (1,500 ft.): 2.5 mi., 800 ft., 1 hr. 40 min.
- Gentian Pond Campsite (2,166 ft.): 3.5 mi., 1,450 ft., 2 hr. 30 min.

Dryad Fall Trail (AMC)

This yellow-blazed trail runs from the Austin Brook Trail to the Peabody Brook Trail near Dream Lake, passing Dryad Fall, one of the highest cascades in the mountains—particularly interesting for a few days after a rainstorm, because its several cascades fall at least 300 ft. over steep ledges.

The trail leaves the Austin Brook Trail on the left 2.5 mi. from North Rd., where that trail turns right. The trail immediately crosses a brook and follows an old woods road, climbing moderately across the slope. At 0.4 mi., a spur trail (sign) descends 60 yd. left to ledges near the top of the falls, where there is a fine view southeast. *Caution:* Rocks in the vicinity of the falls are very slippery and hazardous. The main trail climbs above the falls, and at 0.6 mi., it turns left on an old road (descending, make sure to turn right here), crosses Dryad Brook, and in another 0.3 mi. turns sharp right. It then climbs at mostly moderate grades to a height-of-land, then descends slightly to the Peabody Brook Trail near Dream Lake 0.1 mi. southeast of the Mahoosuc Trail.

Dryad Fall Trail (map 6:D12–D11)

Distances from Austin Brook Trail (1,500 ft.) to
- spur trail to Dryad Fall and view (1,800 ft.): 0.4 mi., 300 ft., 20 min.
- Peabody Brook Trail (2,620 ft.): 1.5 mi., 1,100 ft., 1 hr. 20 min.

Scudder Trail

This trail has been severely disrupted by logging and has been abandoned.

Middle Mountain Path

This trail has been abandoned.

Mount Crag

This small mountain (1,412 ft.) is easily climbed and offers an excellent view up and down the Androscoggin valley. It has two trails.

(1) Take Gates Brook Rd., a woods road that leaves North Rd. on the north just east of Gates Brook, 2.4 mi. from the west junction of North Rd. and US 2. There is a trail sign a short distance up this road. The nameless trail, marked only by a cairn, leaves this road 0.4 mi. from North Rd., on the right, and climbs steeply 0.3 mi. to the Yellow Trail a few steps below the summit.

(2) *Yellow Trail.* This attractive trail gives convenient access to the Austin Brook Trail and Mt. Crag from the Philbrook Farm Inn on North Rd. (For the shortest route to Mt. Crag via the Yellow Trail, follow the Austin Brook Trail 0.4 mi. in from North Rd., then go left on the Yellow Trail to Mt. Crag.) The Yellow Trail leads northwest from the north end of the access road (0.1 mi. long) behind the cottages connected with the inn. It coincides with the Red Trail to Mt. Cabot for 90 yd., then branches left onto a footpath, crosses a gravel road and a small brook, and at 0.1 mi., turns right onto a grassy logging road. (In the reverse direction, turn left on a footpath descending into the woods.) The Yellow Trail now runs northwest at a practically level grade. At 0.4 mi., it passes an unmarked

path on the right that leads 0.2 mi. to the Red Trail. At 0.6 mi., it crosses a major logging road (formerly the route of the Scudder Trail), then continues across Mill Brook Rd., Austin Brook, and the Austin Brook Trail. After the Austin Brook Trail junction, at 1.0 mi., it climbs easily at first, then at a steady grade. Swinging right, then left, it reaches the summit of Mt. Crag at 1.8 mi.

Mount Crag (map 6:E12–D12)

Mount Cabot and Crow's Nest

This range runs south and southeast from Mt. Ingalls. Several trails, distinguished by color, start from the access road at the Philbrook Farm Inn on North Rd. in Shelburne. Hikers are permitted to park at the inn but are requested to speak with the inn management before leaving their vehicles. The path farthest to the east is the White Trail, which leads to Crow's Nest (1,287 ft.), which has limited views; several of the turns on this trail were poorly marked in 2006 and this route is recommended for experienced hikers only. The Blue and Red trails both lead to the summit of Mt. Cabot (1,512 ft.), making a loop trip possible. The Yellow Trail, described above, runs northwest to Mt. Crag.

White Trail. This trail is best approached from the dirt road that starts immediately west of the fire pond east of the Philbrook Farm Inn. Follow the dirt road to a point behind the first cottage, where the White Trail turns right by a large rock. In 75 yd. it bears left onto a grassy logging road, and at 0.1 mi. from the dirt road the Wiggin Rock Trail (Orange Trail) leaves left, whereas the White Trail bears right and ascends along a succession of old and newer logging roads through logged areas. At 1.2 mi., it turns right off the last logging road and makes a short, steep ascent to the wooded summit of Crow's Nest at 1.3 mi. The trail ends a few yards farther at a very limited viewpoint to the northeast.

Wiggin Rock Trail (Orange Trail). This trail begins at a junction with the White Trail. It climbs for 0.2 mi., then turns left onto an old logging road and in 5 yd. diverges right and continues another 60 yd. up, then slightly down to Wiggin Rock, a small ledge with a view southeast across the Androscoggin valley; from the junction, the logging road, an alternate route, descends 0.2 mi. to the north end of the fire road where the Red, Yellow, and Blue trails begin. Beyond the viewpoint, the Orange Trail swings right and drops steeply for 0.2 mi. to the Blue Trail, 80 yd. north of its beginning.

Blue Trail. This trail starts from the north end of the access road immediately to the west of the Philbrook Farm Inn. Here, the Blue Trail continues straight ahead on a good woods road, while the coinciding Red and Yellow trails lead to the left and an alternate access trail to Wiggin Rock leads to the right. In 80 yd. the Blue Trail passes the Wiggin Rock (Orange) Trail on the right, and at 0.1 mi., it crosses a road with a clearing on the right. It continues ahead on an older road for 60 yd., then diverges right onto another old road and climbs moderately. It narrows to a footpath and meanders across a plateau, turns left onto a woods road, passes a boundary marker at 1.0 mi., and climbs more steeply to the summit of Mt. Cabot and the Red Trail at 1.3 mi. The summit is wooded, but a ledge on the right shortly before the summit gives a view east, and an outlook path (sign) descends 60 yd. left, then right from the summit to a ledge with a restricted view southwest.

Red Trail. This trail diverges left from the north end of the access road west of the Philbrook Farm Inn, coinciding for 90 yd. with the Yellow Trail, which then diverges left. Following a woods road, the Red Trail crosses a gravel road and a small brook, and at 0.2 mi., it turns right onto another old road; the road continuing ahead leads 0.2 mi. to the Yellow Trail. The Red Trail ascends moderately, and at 0.6 mi., a path (marked by a cairn) leads right up a bank and continues 75 yd. to a limited viewpoint known as Mary's Aerie. In another 30 yd., the main trail turns left off the road and follows a footpath into the woods, soon crossing a small brook. It follows footpaths and old logging roads, circling around the slope, and finally climbs steeply to approach Mt. Cabot from the north, passing the junction with the abandoned Judson Pond Trail on the left 100 yd. before reaching the summit at 1.2 mi. (See Blue Trail for description of views.)

Mount Cabot and Crow's Nest (map 6:E12–D12)

SUGGESTED HIKES

For more information on suggested hikes, see p. ix.

Easy Hikes

Mascot Pond [rt: 1.4 mi., 250 ft., 0:50]. An unusual hike on the Mahoosuc Trail and a spur path to a pond at the base of Leadmine Ledge.

Mt. Crag [rt: 2.4 mi., 700 ft., 1:35]. This small peak has excellent views over the Androscoggin valley; use the Austin Brook Trail and Yellow Trail.

Giant Falls [rt: 3.0 mi., 950 ft., 2:00]. This high waterfall is accessible via the Peabody Book Trail and a spur path.

Moderate Hikes

Eyebrow Loop [lp: 2.4 mi., 1,150 ft., 1:45]. This loop over the Eyebrow and the Old Speck trails features some steep climbing and fine views of Grafton Notch.

Mt. Success [rt: 6.2 mi., 1,950 ft., 4:00]. This trip from Success Pond Rd. via the Success and Mahoosuc trails must include the side loop to the beautiful, unusual outlook on the way up to the open summit.

Mt. Hayes [rt: 7.2 mi., 2,100 ft., 4:40]. This low, ledgy mountain provides wide views of the Gorham region and the Presidentials; use the Centennial Trail and a short section of the Mahoosuc Trail, to reach the open ledges at the southwest end of the flat summit.

Strenuous Hikes

Goose Eye and Carlo Mountains [lp: 7.6 mi., 2,700 ft., 5:10]. A rewarding loop over two open peaks via the Goose Eye, Mahoosuc, and Carlo Col trails, with some steep spots.

Old Speck Mountain [rt: 7.6 mi., 2,900 ft., 5:15]. The Old Speck Trail offers a moderate route to fire tower views from Maine's third highest peak.

Mahoosuc Ponds [lp: 9.8 mi., 2,100 ft., 6:00]. This loop uses the Austin Brook, Dryad Fall, Peabody Brook, and Mahoosuc trails to visit a waterfall and three high-mountain ponds; it may be possible to shorten this loop by as much as 3.6 mi. [lp: 6.2 mi., 1,650 ft., 3:55] by driving up the Mill Brook Rd.

SECTION TWELVE
NORTHERN NEW HAMPSHIRE

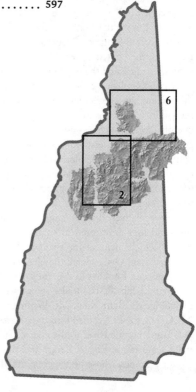

This section covers the entire part of New Hampshire that lies west of NH 16 and north of US 2. At the heart of this section is the triangle formed by US 2, US 3, and NH 110; the corners of this triangle are located roughly at the towns of Lancaster, Groveton, and Gorham. Within the triangle are the Pliny, Pilot, and Crescent ranges. The Cherry-Dartmouth Range, which rises south of US 2 between Jefferson and Twin Mountain, is also included here. These are relatively compact mountain ranges, with officially maintained trail networks, on or adjacent to lands of the WMNF. North of NH 110 lies the North Country proper, a sparsely populated region with extensive woodlands owned mostly by large corporations and managed for lumber and pulpwood production. This region, so similar to the small adjacent corner of Vermont and the much vaster woodlands of northern Maine to the east, is on the southern edge of the great band of boreal forest that covers much of Ontario, Quebec, and the northern part of the Great Lakes Region in the United States. There are only a few trails to widely scattered natural features, and the region is far better known for hunting, fishing, and snowmobiling than for hiking. Even the southern part of the area covered in this section has a higher level of logging activity than in the main ranges of the White Mountains to the south and east, along with hiking trails that frequently receive much less use and less intensive maintenance. This area can perhaps best be understood as a transitional zone between the main ranges, with their heavily used, intensively maintained trail systems that visit almost every significant feature, and the vast commercial woodlands of the north, where logging roads are the principal routes of travel both by wheel and on foot, and logging activity is visible almost everywhere.

Four relatively distinct ranges and trail networks are covered in this section, and they are treated in separate subsections: the Cherry-Dartmouth Range, which includes the main peak of Cherry Mountain and its fine northern crag, Owl's Head; the Crescent Range, including Mt. Randolph, Mt. Crescent, Lookout Ledge, the Ice Gulch, and the rest of the Randolph Mountain Club (RMC) trail system north of US 2; the Pilot-Pliny Range, including Mt. Starr King, Mt. Waumbek, Mt. Weeks, Terrace Mountain, Mt. Cabot, the Bulge, the Horn, and the region of the headwaters of the Upper Ammonoosuc River to the east of Unknown Pond, whose most prominent features are Rogers Ledge and the Devils Hopyard; and the North Country proper, whose principal points of interest are the Percy Peaks and

Sugarloaf, Dixville Notch and Table Rock, the Diamond Peaks, and Magalloway Mountain. The Cherry-Dartmouth Range is completely covered by the AMC's *Franconia–Pemigewasset Map* (map 2); the Crescent Range and the Pilot-Pliny Range (except for the trails on Mt. Prospect) are completely covered by the AMC's *North Country–Mahoosuc Range Map* (map 6); and the North Country requires USGS maps as indicated for each objective.

CAMPING

Substantial portions of the territory covered in the Cherry-Dartmouth Range, the Crescent Range, and the Pilot-Pliny Range subsections are included in the WMNF, and in such areas normal WMNF camping regulations apply. Most of the remaining forested areas in these subsections and all of the territory covered by the North Country subsection are private commercial woodlands or New Hampshire state parks or state forests. On state lands camping is usually restricted to official campgrounds, while on private lands camping requires the permission of the landowner, which normally cannot be obtained because of owners' justifiable unwillingness to risk forest fire.

Forest Protection Areas

The WMNF has established a number of Forest Protection Areas (FPAs)—formerly known as Restricted Use Areas—where camping and wood or charcoal fires are prohibited throughout the year. The specific areas are under continual review, and areas are added to or subtracted from the list to provide the greatest amount of protection to areas subject to damage by excessive camping, while imposing the lowest level of restrictions possible. A general list of FPAs in this section follows, but because there are often major changes from year to year, one should obtain current information on FPAs from the WMNF.

(1) No camping is permitted above treeline (where trees are less than 8 ft. tall), except in winter, and then only in places where there is at least 2 ft. of snow cover on the ground—but not on any frozen body of water. The point where the restricted area begins is marked on most trails with small signs, but the absence of such signs should not be construed as proof of the legality of a site.

(2) No camping is permitted within 0.25 mi. of any trailhead, picnic area, or any facility for overnight accommodation such as a hut, cabin, shelter, tentsite, or campground, except as designated at the facility itself, or Unknown Pond except at the designated sites. In this section, camping is also forbidden at the South Pond Recreation Area.

(3) No camping is permitted on WMNF land within 0.25 mi. of certain roads (camping on private roadside land is illegal except by permission of the landowner). In 2006, these roads included the Old Cherry Mountain Rd. (FR 14).

Established Trailside Campsites

Cabot Firewarden's Cabin (WMNF) is located on the Kilkenny Ridge Trail just south of the cleared south summit of Mt. Cabot where the fire tower used to stand. It has bunks for about eight people. The nearest reliable water source is Bunnell Brook, at the crossing 1.3 mi. below the cabin.

Unknown Pond Campsite (WMNF) is a designated campsite with several tent pads and an outhouse located on a spur path off the Unknown Pond Trail near the southeast corner of Unknown Pond. Camping is prohibited within 0.25 mi. of Unknown Pond except at the designated sites.

Rogers Ledge Campsite (WMNF) is a designated campsite with an outhouse located on a spur path off the Kilkenny Ridge Trail 0.5 mi. south of Rogers Ledge.

Percy Loop Campsite (TCTA) is a designated campsite with a tent platform and outhouse located on a spur path off the Percy Loop Trail in Nash Stream State Forest. Fires are not permitted.

TRAIL DESCRIPTIONS

The Cherry-Dartmouth Range

Though technically speaking this range is the western extension of the Presidential Range, in its terrain, the type and amount of use, as well as the nature of its trail system—in sum, its general flavor for hiking visitors—it is far more similar to its neighbors to the north than to the great mountains connected to it on the east. Cherry Mountain is a prominent mountain located in the town of Carroll, west of the Presidential Range. The highest peak is Mt. Martha (3,573 ft.), which has good outlooks from the summit area, although the former fire tower has been dismantled. A northern spur, Owl's Head (3,258 ft.), has a spectacular view from a fine ledge just south of the wooded summit. The Dartmouth Range is a ridge with numerous humps running southwest to northeast between Cherry Mountain and the Presidentials. The range is completely trailless; Mt. Dartmouth (3,727 ft.) and Mt. Deception (3,671 ft.) are the most important summits. Cherry Mountain Rd. (FR 14), 6.9 mi. long, runs from US 302 about 0.8 mi. west of the Above the Notch Motel to the junction of NH 115 and NH 115A, passing through the high notch that separates the two mountain masses. This area is covered by the AMC's *Franconia–Pemigewasset Map* (map 2).

The Pondicherry National Wildlife Refuge (a division of the Silvio O. Conte National Fish & Wildlife Refuge) is a fine 5,500-acre wild tract of forest with a pond and a bog located in Jefferson and Whitefield; it has been greatly expanded in recent years. It consists of Big Cherry Pond (about 100 acres) and Little Cherry Pond (about 20 acres). As "Great Ponds," these are in the custody of the state. Surrounding each are bands of open bog and bog-swamp forest belonging to the Audubon Society of New Hampshire. Pondicherry is the old name for Cherry Pond and nearby Cherry Mountain. The refuge is managed jointly by the U.S. Fish and Wildlife Service, the New Hampshire Fish and Game Department, and the Audubon Society. Fishing is allowed, but not hunting or trapping. At least 230 species of birds, including uncommon land and water species, have been seen here. Pondicherry is also interesting for its vegetation and its spectacular views of the Presidential Range. The main access route to the Pondicherry refuge follows the Pondicherry Rail Trail along an abandoned Maine Central Railroad right of way to Cherry Pond. (See map 2:E6.) From NH 115, 4.4 mi north of its junction with US 3 in Carroll, turn left (west) on Airport Rd. At 1.5 mi from NH 115, turn right into a parking area. The Pondicherry Rail Trail begins beyond a kiosk and gate and follows the railroad grade generally northeast through woods and brush, crossing under a power line at 0.8 mi. At 1.3 mi., a spur trail diverges right and follows a connecting section of railroad grade for 0.1 mi., then crosses an abandoned railroad track (which is the Presidential Range Rail Trail and the route of the Cohos Trail approaching Cherry Pond from the southeast) and follows an elevated walkway for 40 yd. to a new viewing platform on the southwest shore of Cherry Pond, where there are magnificent views. At 1.4 mi., the Pondicherry Rail Trail meets the Presidential Range Rail Trail at a location known as Waumbek Junction. (This is the western terminus of the Presidential Range Rail Trail, which leads 19 mi. east to Gorham; in its first mile, it skirts Moorhen Marsh, an excellent area for birding and wildlife viewing.) The main route to the Cherry Ponds continues straight ahead (northeast) beyond the junction, crossing the Johns River on a railroad bridge where a still-active railroad track joins from the left. Walk along the right edge of the tracks past a swamp. At 1.5 mi., the Shore Path (no sign) diverges right into the woods, reaching the shore of Cherry Pond and a view of the Presidential Range in 100 yd. The Shore Path then turns left, passing more vistas and a National Natural Landmark plaque, and loops back to rejoin the railroad track at 0.1 mi. By continuing north along the tracks, two more trails are accessible. About 150 yd. beyond the north end of the Shore Path, the Rampart Trail (no sign) leads right 80 yd. to a superb viewpoint on the shore of Cherry Pond, with a sweeping view of the Pliny, Crescent, Presidential, and Dartmouth ranges and Cherry Mountain. The Rampart Trail then runs north for about 0.2 mi. on a natural upthrust known as an ice push rampart. The continuation of the trail beyond this point, very wet in places, is the northbound Cohos Trail (a section known as the Colonel Whipple Trail), leading in about 1.7 mi. to Whipple Rd. in Jefferson.

The well-worn Little Cherry Pond Loop Trail, which was designated in 2006 as a National Recreation Trail, leaves the left (west) side of the tracks about 100 yd. north of the outlook spur described earlier. It runs nearly level through conifers and reaches the first loop junction in 0.2 mi. Here the east loop continues straight ahead but the west loop turns sharp left. The east loop passes over a boardwalk through an attractive black spruce forest and descends slightly to rejoin the west loop in 0.3 mi. near the edge of the bog surrounding Little Cherry Pond. From the first loop junction the west loop runs west, then swings gradually north to meet the east loop in 0.4 mi. From the second loop junction, the trail descends gently to the bog, traverses wooden walkways for 100 yd., and ends 0.1 mi. from the junction at an observation platform on the shore of Little Cherry Pond. Distance from the railroad tracks to Little Cherry Pond is 0.6 mi. via the east loop and 0.7 mi. via the west loop.

Cherry Mountain Trail (WMNF)

This trail runs across the ridge of Cherry Mountain just south of the summit (which is reached by a spur path). The west trailhead is at a parking area opposite Lennon Rd. on NH 115, 1.9 mi. from its junction with US 3; the east trailhead, which is far less frequently used, is on Cherry Mountain Rd. (FR 14) (which is narrow—use care) just north of its height-of-land, 3.2 mi. from US 302 and 3.7 mi. from NH 115. The eastern part of the trail, from the height-of-land to Cherry Mountain Rd., is heavily used by snowmobiles in winter.

Leaving NH 115 on a logging road, the trail passes straight through an old log yard at 0.3 mi., and continues straight ahead at 0.5 mi., where another road diverges right. In 0.7 mi., it becomes a footpath and ascends steadily on an old roadbed, climbing higher above the brook that it parallels, and passes a spring left at 1.3 mi. At 1.7 mi., the trail reaches the ridge crest, and a spur path turns left and climbs 0.2 mi. to the summit of Mt. Martha, where it meets Martha's Mile.

From the junction with the summit spur, the Cherry Mountain Trail turns right (south) and descends moderately with an occasional minor ascent on an old road with excellent footing in the upper part. At 3.1 mi., it turns left (east), and at 3.3 mi., it passes the junction on the right with the abandoned Black Brook Trail. The Cherry Mountain Trail continues down the slope on the old road, becoming muddy at times, and ends at Cherry Mountain Rd.

Cherry Mountain Trail (map 2:F6–F7)

Distances from NH 115 (1,650 ft.) to

- Mt. Martha summit spur trail (3,370 ft.): 1.7 mi., 1,700 ft., 1 hr. 40 min.
- Mt. Martha summit (3,573 ft.) via spur trail: 1.9 mi., 1,900 ft., 1 hr. 55 min.
- Cherry Mountain Rd. (2,190 ft.): 5.3 mi., 1,900 ft. (rev. 1,400 ft.), 3 hr. 35 min.

Owl's Head Trail (RMC)

This trail ascends to the fine outlook on Owl's Head. It begins on NH 115 at a parking lot with the Stanley Slide historical marker, 5.9 mi. from the junction with US 3 and 0.7 mi. from the junction with NH 115A. Logging operations have taken place over much of the lower slopes of this mountain in recent years. Much of the trail has been recently relocated, and the footway may still be obscured through cutover areas in the first mile—the yellow blazes should be followed carefully along skid roads and through second growth.

From the parking area the trail crosses a small stream, turns right on an old road, then quickly left across a large clearing (signs). It leads east through brushy logged areas, descending slightly. Remaining nearly level, it swings back to the west, then at 0.7 mi. bears left (south) toward the mountain. It rises at easy grades, dips to cross a brook at 1.1 mi., then climbs the far bank and turns sharp left. After crossing an old logging road it climbs steadily through hardwoods. At 2.0 mi., it turns right off the old route of the trail and slabs west across a rocky slope. It climbs steeply past a WMNF boundary marker and turns sharp left at 2.2 mi., gaining the crest of a northwest ridge. The grade is easy at first, then steep as the trail zig-zags up the cone to meet the Martha's Mile trail at the wooded summit. The outlook ledges are a short distance right (south) on Martha's Mile.

Owl's Head Trail (map 2:E7)

Distance from NH 115 (1,250 ft.) to
• Owl's Head summit (3,258 ft.): 2.5 mi., 2,000 ft., 2 hr. 15 min.

Martha's Mile (WMNF)

Martha's Mile is a link trail between the summits of Mt. Martha and Owl's Head. It leaves the ledge at the summit of Owl's Head, swings north, then sharp left. It descends a very short steep pitch, then descends easily to a col and climbs moderately, with excellent footing, to the summit of Mt. Martha.

Martha's Mile (map 2:E7–E6)

Distance from Owl's Head (3,258 ft.) to
• Mt. Martha summit (3,573 ft.): 0.8 mi., 450 ft. (rev. 100 ft.), 40 min.

The Crescent Range

The Crescent Range lies north of US 2 and west of NH 16 in the towns of Jefferson, Randolph, and Berlin. This area is covered by the AMC's *North Country–Mahoosuc Range Map* (map 6). The chief summits, from southwest to northeast, are Mt. Randolph, Mt. Crescent, Black Crescent Mountain, Mt. Jericho, and Mt. Forist. Deriving its name from the shape of the ridge on which it is the highest summit, Mt. Crescent (3,251 ft.) offers good views south and north. It is ascended by the Mt. Crescent and Crescent Ridge trails. The heavily wooded peak at the southern end of the Crescent Ridge, Mt. Randolph (3,081 ft.) is reached by the Crescent Ridge Trail. Black Crescent Mountain (3,264 ft.) lies to the north across the deep notch called Hunter's Pass. It is the highest peak in the range but has no trails; hikers with sufficient map and compass skills can ascend it fairly easily from the Bog Dam Rd. on the west, or by a much more difficult but more interesting route from the head of the Ice Gulch, climbing up a slide that affords excellent views. Lookout Ledge (2,260 ft.) is a granite cliff on a knob of the southeast ridge of Mt. Randolph that affords one of the best views of the floor of King Ravine and its rock glacier, with moderate effort. It is reached by the Pasture Path, Ledge Trail, Sargent Path, Vyron D. Lowe Trail, and Crescent Ridge Trail. The ledge is on private property and no fires are permitted. Boy (Bois) Mountain (2,234 ft.) is a small peak at the west edge of the Crescent Range that offers an interesting view.

At the northeast end of the Crescent Range, just west of Berlin, New Hampshire, lies Mt. Jericho (2,487 ft.). Like many northern mountains, its summit was burned over to bare rock by the forest fires of the early 1900s. Now partially overgrown, it still offers a fine view east to the Mahoosucs and an obstructed view of the Carter Range, the northern Presidentials, and the Tinker Brook valley. An impressive east cliff that rises from the edge of the city of Berlin, Mt. Forist (2,068 ft.) is known locally as Elephant Mountain because of its shape. The mountain was named for Merrill C. Forist, an early settler. (Note that the name of this mountain is misspelled on the USGS Berlin quad.) The summit is on the elephant's "head," and there is an outlook on its "rear end." There is no maintained hiking trail to the summit of either Mt. Jericho or Mt. Forist, but experienced hikers with map and compass skills may be able to make some use of old paths and more recent snowmobile trails while bushwhacking up these mountains; a snowmobile trail network generally to the north of the ridge line may help provide access to these two mountains.

The Ice Gulch, one of the wildest and most beautiful places in the White Mountains, is a deep cut on the southeast slope of the Crescent

Range, between Mt. Crescent and Black Crescent Mountain. The bed of the gulch is strewn with great boulders that lie in picturesque confusion, similar in many respects to those scattered over the floor of King Ravine. Among the boulders are many caves, some with perpetual ice. Springs and the melting ice form the headwaters of Moose Brook. Two paths lead to the gulch: the Cook Path to the head, and the Ice Gulch Path to the foot and from there up through the gulch. A short trail, the Peboamauk Loop, follows Moose Brook below the Ice Gulch, past Peboamauk Fall and several fine springs back to the Ice Gulch Path. The walk along the gulch itself is very strenuous with constant scrambling over wet, possibly icy, slippery rocks, requiring great care. This trip is not appropriate for dogs—canine rescues are common.

The Pond of Safety is a small but attractive pond that lies just north of the Crescent Range and east of the Pliny Range in the town of Randolph. It derived its name from an incident that occurred during the American Revolution. Four local men who had joined the Continental army were captured by the British and paroled on condition that they not participate further in the conflict. The Continental authorities felt that their parole papers were spurious and insisted that they return to their units. Because they feared severe punishment if they were recaptured by the British, they retired to this isolated region to hunt and fish, and remained out of reach until there was no further danger that they might be apprehended as deserters. Many years after the end of the war, having become respected citizens in the region, they were exonerated of the desertion charges and placed on the pension rolls. The pond has continued to be a place of refuge from the woes of civilization for those who love fishing, hunting, hiking, cross-country skiing, and snowmobiling. It may be reached from Jefferson by Pond of Safety Rd., which is passable by four-wheel-drive vehicle (though it is sometimes gated) and from Randolph by two RMC footpaths, the Four Soldiers Path and the Underhill Path. The WMNF Pond of Safety Trail from Bog Dam Rd. to the north is a snowmobile trail that is no longer maintained for hiking.

Most of the paths in this region are part of the Randolph Mountain Club (RMC) trail system. The town of Randolph consists of two sections: the lower section lies along Durand Rd. (the former US 2), in the Moose River valley, and the upper section is situated on Randolph Hill—a plateau extending southeast from the foot of Mt. Crescent, from which there are excellent views of the Northern Presidentials—reached by Randolph Hill Rd. (also known as Mt. Crescent Rd.). Lowe's Store and the Ravine House site are located in the lower section, and the Mt. Crescent House site is in the upper section. On the south slope of the hill, connecting the two sections of the town and providing access from various points to major mountain trails, is a well-developed network of paths maintained by the RMC. Some of these short and less important trails—those that are mainly connecting links to places in the town for local residents—are omitted from this guide, but they are described in detail, along with the other RMC trails that are covered in this guide, in the RMC guidebook *Randolph Paths* (8th ed., 2005). They also are shown on the RMC map of the Randolph Valley and the Northern Peaks, which covers this area with somewhat more detail than the AMC map.

In 2001, more than 13,000 acres of private timberland in the Crescent Range and Pond of Safety area came into public ownership. About 3,000 acres, including the land around the Pond of Safety, were added to the WMNF. The remaining 10,000 acres are now owned by the town of Randolph as the Randolph Community Forest and will remain open for traditional uses, including public recreation and sustainable timber harvesting. Many of the trails on the Crescent Range are partly or wholly within the Randolph Community Forest. For regulations on use, contact the town of Randolph offices (603-466-5771). On the northeast side of the Crescent Range is the town of Gorham's Paul Doherty Memorial Forest, named for a longtime Fish and Game Conservation Officer in the region. The spectacular Ice Gulch is included within this tract.

Active lumbering and residential developments on the south slopes outside the Randolph Community Forest may intrude on some of the following trails, many of which are partly or wholly on private land. Watch carefully for markers and signs; it may be useful to inquire locally for further information.

Boy Mountain Path

This path ascends Boy (Bois) Mountain (2,234 ft.), a small mountain, located east of Jefferson Highlands, with an open ledge near the summit that provides a fine and easily accessible view of the northern Presidential

Range. It is on private land maintained by the Carter-Bridgman family. There is no trail sign where it leaves US 2, 1.1 mi. east of the junction of US 2 and NH 115. Park on the shoulder of the highway, just west of Carter Cut Rd., and not in the driveway to the Carter estate. Cross the highway, go up the first driveway (unpaved) to the west, at the edge of a field, and pass between the house and barn to the trail sign. Beyond the sign walk a few yards up a grassy slope to the point where the trail (small sign) enters the woods to the right and ascends. At 0.2 mi., turn left (arrow) across a traversing woods road and onto an old logging road that climbs up the slope. At 0.4 mi., turn right onto a path (descending, bear left here). The path climbs moderately past a cement marker and bears right to the ledge near the summit.

Boy Mountain Path (map 6:E8)

Distance from US 2 (1,575 ft.) to
* Boy Mountain summit (2,234 ft.): 0.7 mi., 650 ft., 40 min.

Bee Line (RMC)

This path is an important connecting link between the Appalachia parking area, the Ravine House site, and the trails on Randolph Hill.

Beginning on US 2 directly opposite the Appalachia parking area, the trail descends through an opening in the chain-link fence. It swings left, then right, and runs around the west shore of Durand Lake. It crosses the Moose River on Baldwin Bridge, then at 0.3 mi. crosses Durand Rd. just east of the Ravine House site. The trail briefly ascends on a driveway, bears right into the woods (sign), passes an excellent spring, then crosses a woods road and reaches a junction on the right with the Diagonal at 0.8 mi. From here, Mossy Glen can be reached in a short distance by following the Diagonal and then the Glenside downhill. The Bee Line bears left and crosses Carlton Brook on the Peeko Folsom Memorial Bridge, passes a junction on the right with the Burnbrae Path, and turns to the right onto a logging road, which it follows for 0.4 mi. Shortly after leaving this logging road, it turns to the left onto a dirt road and in 0.1 mi. meets the Pasture Path on Glover Spring Rd. at 1.5 mi. For the Mt. Crescent House site, follow Highacres Rd. straight ahead for 0.2 mi. to Randolph

Hill Rd.; the Mt. Crescent House site is a short distance to the right (east) via Randolph Hill Rd., and the Ice Gulch Path begins about 0.4 mi. east of that site. The various paths to Lookout Ledge and the Crescent Range, as well as the Cook Path to the Ice Gulch, can be reached by turning left on Randolph Hill Rd.

Bee Line (map 6:E9)

Distance from US 2 (1,300 ft.) to
- Randolph Hill Rd. (1,820 ft.): 1.6 mi., 500 ft., 1 hr. 5 min.

Short Paths in Randolph Village Area

The Diagonal (RMC). This path begins on the Bee Line 0.5 mi. from the Ravine House site on Durand Rd. and runs northeast uphill, linking many of the paths on the lower part of Randolph Hill. From the Bee Line, it descends gradually to a junction with the Glenside, which continues straight ahead. The Diagonal turns sharp left here, crosses Carlton Brook, and begins a gentle to moderate ascent. It crosses the Burnbrae Path, soon bears left, and ascends moderately. At 0.5 mi., the trail crosses the EZ Way and its grade becomes level. It crosses the Wood Path at 0.9 mi. and continues to its end at 1.3 mi. at the Pasture Path, which it reaches a short distance west of Pasture Path Rd. Ascent from Bee Line is 250 ft. Randolph Hill Rd. is 0.1 mi. north via the Short Circuit Path, which begins a short distance to the right (east) near the end of Pasture Path Rd.

Burnbrae Path (RMC). This path begins on Durand Rd. just east of Carlton Brook and the Randolph Public Library. It crosses a field, ascends through woods, crosses a driveway, passes a junction on the left with the Glenside, and then crosses the Diagonal at 0.3 mi. It ends at 0.5 mi. on the Bee Line just above the Bee Line's crossing of Carlton Brook. Ascent from Durand Rd. is 250 ft.

The Glenside (RMC). This extremely scenic short path leaves the Burnbrae Path 0.2 mi. north of Durand Rd. and follows Carlton Brook up through beautiful Mossy Glen. There are several short side paths and loops within Mossy Glen. The Glenside crosses to the west side of the brook, bears right as the Bluffway enters left, and ends at 0.2 mi. on the Diagonal a short distance east of the junction of the Diagonal and Bee Line.

Wood Path (RMC). This path connects the east end of Durand Rd. with the Pasture Path. It climbs through a field and then through woods, joins a woods road, and crosses the Diagonal at 0.6 mi. It then climbs easily to end at 0.9 mi. at the Pasture Path, 0.3 mi. west of Pasture Path Rd. Ascent from Durand Rd. is 500 ft.

EZ Way (RMC). This path leads from Durand Rd. near its east end to Randolph Hill Rd. just east of the Mt. Crescent House site. It leaves Durand Rd. just east of a cemetery, runs along the edge of a field, and enters the woods. It climbs easily, then more steadily, crossing the Diagonal at 0.5 mi. It ascends at an easier grade through wet areas, crosses the Pasture Path at 0.9 mi., and ends at Randolph Hill Rd. at 1.0 mi. Ascent from Durand Rd. is 550 ft.

Groveway (RMC). This path, just 0.2 mi. long, climbs from Durand Rd. just west of the town library to the Glenside at Mossy Glen. It starts up a driveway, then ascends through woods, passing a staircase that leads down to the right to a natural amphitheater in Mossy Glen. It passes a junction left with the Bluffway, crosses the Nepalese Bridge over Carlton Brook, and ends at the Glenside. Ascent from Durand Rd. is 150 ft.

Bluffway (RMC). This short trail, less than 0.1 mi. long, runs along the west side of Mossy Glen between the Groveway and the Glenside.

Church Path (RMC). This path, 0.5 mi. long, runs from behind the Randolph Church on US 2 to Randolph Hill Rd. across from Boothman Lane. It starts behind the church, crosses a new cemetery with a view south, enters the woods and runs at easy grades to a dirt road, where it turns left and leads 100 yd. to Randolph Hill Rd.

Short paths in Randolph Village area (map 6:E9)

Vyron D. Lowe Trail (RMC)

This orange-blazed path ascends from Durand Rd. to the Crescent Ridge Trail near Lookout Ledge. It starts at the parking area for Randolph Spring on the north side of the road, 0.3 mi. east of Lowe's Store. Nearly the entire trail was relocated by the RMC in 2004–2005. Until the footway becomes worn in, the blazes should be followed with care. It enters the woods behind the spring (sign) and climbs moderately northeast, crossing two small brooks and entering the Randolph Community Forest (blue blazes) at 0.4 mi. It crosses an overgrown logging road, climbs by switchbacks, and crosses another old road at 0.8 mi., with a limited view southwest. It swings right through a cluster of boulders at 1.3 mi., then climbs easily through an open area of ice-damaged forest and berry bushes. At 1.5 mi., it bears right onto an old road, joining the former route of the trail, and continues 0.1 mi. to the Crescent Ridge Trail. For Lookout Ledge, follow the Crescent Ridge Trail ahead (east) for 0.1 mi.

Vyron D. Lowe Trail (map 6:E9)

Distances from Durand Rd. (1,400 ft.) to
- Crescent Ridge Trail (2,300 ft.): 1.6 mi., 900 ft., 1 hr. 15 min.
- Lookout Ledge (2,260 ft.): 1.7 mi., 900 ft. (rev. 50 ft.), 1 hr. 20 min.

Sargent Path (RMC)

This is the most direct route to Lookout Ledge, as well as the steepest. The trail is little used but well blazed, and with care, it can be readily followed. Leave Durand Rd. opposite a dark red cottage 0.8 mi. west of the Ravine House site and 1.0 mi. east of Randolph Spring. The path immediately bears left and rises steadily to the ledge, where it meets the Ledge and Crescent Ridge trails.

Sargent Path (map 6:E9)

Distance from Durand Rd. (1,310 ft.) to
- Lookout Ledge (2,260 ft.): 0.8 mi., 950 ft., 55 min.

Ledge Trail (RMC)

Leading from Durand Rd. at the Ravine House site to Lookout Ledge, this trail forms a steep but direct route to the outlook. Park at a small trailhead just west of the former hotel's site. The trail starts up a paved driveway, quickly turns right onto an abandoned driveway and then diverges right into the woods. It climbs northwest through a recently logged area to the notch at 0.6 mi., where the Notchway diverges right for Randolph Hill. The Ledge Trail turns sharp left here, becomes steeper, and follows an overgrown lumber road through second growth. It then bears off the road to the right and shortly intersects the Pasture Path on the right at 1.2 mi. The trail climbs steeply over some rocks, then descends slightly, passing the Eyrie (a small outlook), and continues a few yards more to its end at the Crescent Ridge Trail. Just below is Lookout Ledge.

Ledge Trail (map 6:E9)

Distance from Ravine House site (1,289 ft.) to
- Lookout Ledge (2,260 ft.): 1.3 mi., 1,000 ft., 1 hr. 10 min.

Pasture Path (RMC)

This trail leads from Pasture Path Rd. (formerly Stearns Rd.) to the Ledge Trail near Lookout Ledge. The Pasture Path begins at the end of Pasture Path Rd., 0.4 mi. west of Randolph Hill Rd., and runs west through old pastures and woods, passing junctions with several local paths: Diagonal, Wood Path, and EZ Way. Shortly after passing EZ Way at 0.6 mi., the trail briefly coincides with Glover Spring Rd. and High Acres Rd.; follow signs carefully. Where these two roads intersect at 0.7 mi., the Bee Line enters from the left; to the right High Acres Rd. leads 0.2 mi. to Randolph Hill Rd. near the Mt. Crescent House site. At 0.8 mi., the Pasture Path turns right off High Acres Rd. Grassy Lane diverges right at 1.0 mi., providing a shortcut 0.1 mi. long to Randolph Hill Rd. (Grassy Lane affords the most direct route from Randolph Hill Rd. to Lookout Ledge via the upper part of the Pasture Path; parking is available across from the intersection of Grassy Lane and Randolph Hill Rd.) The Pasture Path traverses a level swampy area through young second growth and turns sharp left onto a logging road at 1.5 mi., passing a junction with the Four Soldiers Path on the right. Soon it turns sharp right off the road where the Notchway continues straight ahead. The Pasture Path runs across several branches of Carlton Brook, then ascends to meet the Ledge Trail 0.2 mi. below Lookout Ledge; turn right to reach the ledge.

Pasture Path (map 6:E9)

Distances from end of Pasture Path Rd. (1,680 ft.) to
- Ledge Trail (2,070 ft.): 2.3 mi., 400 ft., 1 hr. 20 min.
- Lookout Ledge (2,260 ft.) via Ledge Trail: 2.5 mi., 600 ft., 1 hr. 35 min.

Notchway (RMC)

This is a connecting path from the Ledge Trail 0.6 mi. from Durand Rd. to the Pasture Path 1.6 mi. from Pasture Path Rd. The Notchway leaves the Ledge Trail at the notch and ascends slightly, then passes through a lumbered area, an old forest, and a swamp. It descends to cross two branches of Carlton Brook and climbs. Follow arrows to the left to a logging road and from there to the Pasture Path 0.9 mi. below Lookout Ledge.

Notchway (map 6:E9)

Distance from Ledge Trail (1,800 ft.) to
  • Pasture Path (1,800 ft.): 0.5 mi., 100 ft. (rev. 100 ft.), 20 min.

Mount Crescent Trail (RMC)

This trail begins at Randolph Hill Rd. about 0.3 mi. west of the Mt. Crescent House site, opposite the head of Grassy Lane. A small parking area is located just east of the trailhead on the north side of the road; alternative parking is at the Mt. Crescent House site.

Coinciding with the Cook Path, the trail briefly follows a relocation around a house, then turns right onto the original route. At 0.1 mi., the Cook Path diverges right. The Mt. Crescent Trail continues on the logging road for another 0.1 mi. to the junction with the Carlton Notch Trail, which continues straight ahead, while the Mt. Crescent Trail turns right and begins to ascend the mountain. Markings through recently logged areas should be followed with care. At 0.3 mi., from Randolph Hill Rd., the Jimtown logging road is crossed, the Boothman Spring Cutoff enters right from the Mt. Crescent House site, and the main trail becomes steeper. At 0.7 mi., it passes Castleview Loop, which leads left 80 yd. to Castleview Rock.

Castleview Loop (RMC). The Castleview Loop, 0.4 mi. long, diverges left from the Mt. Crescent Trail 0.7 mi. from Randolph Hill Rd. In a few feet, a side trail leads left to Castleview Rock, an interesting boulder. The main trail descends gently through light woods, passing Castleview Ledge, which is named for its unique view of the Castellated Ridge of Mt. Jefferson. Entering thick forest, the loop then descends steeply, losing about 200 ft. of elevation, crosses a logging road, and leads through logged areas (follow markings carefully) to its end at the Carlton Notch Trail near the Mt. Crescent Water Co. reservoir, 0.7 mi. from Randolph Hill Rd.

At 1.1 mi., the Crescent Ridge Trail, an alternate route that rejoins at the north summit of Mt. Crescent, branches right. The Mt. Crescent Trail climbs northwest, occasionally becoming steep and rough over ledges, to the south viewpoint, where there is an excellent view of the Northern Presidentials. It then ascends to the wooded south summit of Mt. Crescent and continues for 0.2 mi. to the north summit, also wooded, with an outlook from which the Pliny and Pilot ranges can be seen across the broad valley of the Upper Ammonoosuc. The trail ends here, at the second junction with the Crescent Ridge Trail.

Mount Crescent Trail (map 6:E9)

Distances from Randolph Hill Rd. (1,850 ft.) to
- Crescent Ridge Trail, lower junction (2,800 ft.): 1.1 mi., 950 ft., 1 hr. 5 min.
- Crescent Ridge Trail, upper junction (3,210 ft.): 1.7 mi., 1,350 ft., 1 hr. 30 min.

Crescent Ridge Trail (RMC)

This trail branches right from the Mt. Crescent Trail 1.1 mi. from Randolph Hill Rd. and crosses the east flank of the mountain. From there it turns west and climbs steeply to the north outlook, where it again meets the Mt. Crescent Trail at 0.6 mi. Continuing southwest, it descends gradually, passing through brushy logged areas where markings should be followed carefully. At 1.3 mi., it crosses Carlton Brook and continues down to Carlton Notch, where it passes a junction on the left with the Carlton Notch Trail at 1.6 mi. and on the right with the Underhill Path at 1.8 mi. The Crescent Ridge Trail then ascends the ridge that rises west from Carlton Notch and passes Lafayette View, an outlook with a view of the northern Presidentials. The trail then descends into the col between Mt. Randolph and the slightly higher unnamed peak north of it, crosses the headwaters of a branch of Carlton Brook, and climbs to the wooded summit of Mt. Randolph. At the south end of the flat summit, the trail swings left to descend, soon passing a ledge on the right with a view of the Northern Presidentials. From here the trail descends steeply, crosses the Four Soldiers Path and a snowmobile trail, then briefly follows an old logging road passing a junction on the right with the Vyron D. Lowe Trail, and continues to the Ledge Trail just above Lookout Ledge.

Crescent Ridge Trail (map 6:E9)

Distances from Mt. Crescent Trail, lower junction (2,800 ft.) to
- Mt. Crescent, north outlook (3,210 ft.): 0.6 mi., 400 ft., 30 min.
- Carlton Notch Trail (2,820 ft.): 1.6 mi., 400 ft. (rev. 400 ft.), 1 hr.
- Lafayette View (3,050 ft.): 2.3 mi., 650 ft., 1 hr. 30 min.
- Mt. Randolph summit (3,081 ft.): 2.9 mi., 900 ft. (rev. 200 ft.), 1 hr. 55 min.
- Lookout Ledge (2,260 ft.): 3.8 mi., 900 ft. (rev. 800 ft.), 2 hr. 20 min.

Carlton Notch Trail (RMC)

The Carlton Notch Trail leads from the Mt. Crescent Trail to the Crescent Ridge Trail in Carlton Notch, the pass between Mt. Randolph and Mt. Crescent. The trail diverges from the Mt. Crescent Trail 0.1 mi. above its junction with the Cook Path and 0.2 mi. from Randolph Hill Rd. The Mt. Crescent Trail turns right at this point, and the Carlton Notch Trail continues straight ahead. The trail rises gently on an old logging road through logged areas (follow markings carefully), crossing two logging roads and passing the Mt. Crescent Water Co. reservoir and the Castleview Loop (right) at 0.7 mi. from Randolph Hill Rd. It then crosses Carlton Brook and ascends moderately over a relocated section with several switchbacks to Carlton Notch, where it ends at the Crescent Ridge Trail.

Carlton Notch Trail (map 6:E9)

Distance from Mt. Crescent Trail (1,880 ft.) to
- Carlton Notch (2,820 ft.): 1.7 mi., 950 ft., 1 hr. 20 min.

Four Soldiers Path (RMC)

This recently built trail, located on land recently acquired by the Town of Randolph and the WMNF, leads from the Pasture Path, 1.5 mi. west of its trailhead on Pasture Path Rd., over the Crescent Range to the Pond of Safety Trail, 0.3 mi. from the pond. (The most direct access to the trail from Randolph Hill is from trailhead parking for the Mt. Crescent Trail on Randolph Hill Rd.; follow Grassy Lane for 0.1 mi. and Pasture Path for

0.5 mi.) In combination with the new Underhill Path and other trails on the Crescent Range, the Four Soldiers Path makes possible various loop hikes from Randolph to the Pond of Safety. The trail is named for the quartet of American soldiers who, during the Revolutionary War, were unjustly accused of desertion and sought refuge at the pond. The RMC plans to develop interpretive stops along this trail in the near future.

The Four Soldiers Path leaves the Pasture Path on the right (west) 10 yd. beyond a sharp left turn. It soon crosses Carlton Brook and ascends west through hardwoods at easy grades, crossing an old logging road, an abandoned snowmobile trail, and several small brooks. It then ascends moderately along the southeast slope of Mt. Randolph. At 1.3 mi., it levels where a boulder on the left provides a cleared view south. In 130 yd., it crosses the Crescent Ridge Trail, and in another 20 yd., it turns right and climbs gradually northwest through an extensive logged area where openings will provide views of the Northern Presidentials for a few years. The trail reenters the woods and at 1.9 mi. swings right where a spur path leads 50 yd. left to a fine cleared view across the valley to the high peaks. The main trail climbs easily for 0.1 mi. to the height-of-land and "The Eye of the Needle," a spot where there is a unique perspective on Mt. Washington through Edmands Col. The trail now descends gradually, swinging more to the north, and enters another open logged area with partial views of the Pliny Range and a glimpse of the Pond of Safety. It reenters the woods and descends easily, crossing a gravel road at 3.3 mi.; the Underhill Path begins 25 yd. right (east) along this road. The Four Soldiers Path meanders down to the northwest, then crosses a series of bog bridges in a dense, wet conifer grove. It crosses two branches of the outlet brook from the Pond of Safety and ends at the Pond of Safety (snowmobile) Trail, here a gravel road. To reach the pond, follow the road left for 0.1 mi., then a spur road right for 0.2 mi., and descend a path to the shore.

Four Soldiers Path (map 6:E8–E9)

Distances from Pasture Path (1,830 ft.) to
- Crescent Ridge Trail (2,500 ft.): 1.3 mi., 700 ft., 1 hr.
- Eye of the Needle (2,800 ft.): 2.0 mi., 1,000 ft., 1 hr. 30 min.
- Underhill Path (2,275 ft.): 3.3 mi., 1,000 ft. (rev. 500 ft.), 2 hr. 10 min.
- Pond of Safety (2,190 ft.): 4.1 mi., 1,000 ft. (rev. 100 ft.), 2 hr. 35 min.

Underhill Path (RMC)

This recently built trail leads from the Four Soldiers Path, 0.8 mi. south of Pond of Safety, to the Crescent Ridge Trail, 0.2 mi. west of Carlton Notch. It is named for Miriam Underhill, a pioneer in women's mountaineering and, with her husband Robert, a longtime resident of Randolph.

It begins on a gravel logging road 25 yd. east of the point where the Four Soldiers Path crosses the road and climbs gradually east and southeast through hardwoods. At 0.7 mi., it turns right and climbs through a series of switchbacks in a beautiful forest of fir and birch. It crosses a height-of-land at 1.2 mi. and descends, soon turning to the left (east). It then swings briefly to the south and ends at the Crescent Ridge Trail.

> **Underhill Path (map 6:E9)**
> Distance from Four Soldiers Path (2,275 ft.) to
> • Crescent Ridge Trail (2,850 ft.): 1.4 mi., 700 ft. (rev. 150 ft.), 1 hr. 5 min.

Boothman Spring Cutoff (RMC)

This short path provides access to the Cook Path and Mt. Crescent Trail from the Mt. Crescent House site on Randolph Hill Rd., which is a good starting point with parking spaces. The trail is level or gradual throughout. It starts up a driveway at the west end of the Mt. Crescent House site, passing a house, continues across a field as the driveway bears left, then enters the woods. At 0.3 mi., it passes the excellent Boothman Spring, then at 0.5 mi., it crosses the Cook Path (to the Ice Gulch), then the Jimtown lumber road, and ends at the Mt. Crescent Trail.

> **Boothman Spring Cutoff (map 6:E9)**
> Distance from Randolph Hill Rd. at the Mt. Crescent House site (1,800 ft.) to
> • Mt. Crescent Trail (1,900 ft.): 0.6 mi., 100 ft., 20 min.

Cook Path (RMC)

This trail begins on Randolph Hill Rd. opposite Grassy Lane, about 0.3 mi. west of the Mt. Crescent House site. There is a small parking area on the north side of the road just east of the trailhead; alternative parking is at the Mt. Crescent House site. The Boothman Spring Cutoff may be used to avoid the road walk at the start of the Cook Path for those who park at the Mt. Crescent House site.

Coinciding with the Mt. Crescent Trail, the Cook Path first follows a short relocation around a house, then turns right onto the original route. At 0.1 mi., it diverges right from the Mt. Crescent Trail, and at 0.3 mi., it crosses the Boothman Spring Cutoff, which comes directly from the Mt. Crescent House site, and then the Jimtown logging road. The Cook Path ascends over a low ridge, passing through a recently logged area (watch carefully for blazes), and then descends easily to the head of Ice Gulch, where it ends. The Ice Gulch Path begins here and descends through the Ice Gulch.

Cook Path (map 6:E9–D9)

Distance from Randolph Hill Rd. (1,850 ft.) to
- Ice Gulch Path (2,460 ft.): 2.5 mi., 900 ft. (rev. 300 ft.), 1 hr. 40 min.

Ice Gulch Path (RMC)

This path gives access to the wild, beautiful Ice Gulch from Randolph Hill Rd., starting at an old farm with a prominent sign, Sky Meadows, located about 0.4 mi. east of the Mt. Crescent House site (please park cars off the south side of the road). It runs to the bottom of the Ice Gulch and then up through it. The following description assumes that the trip will be made in the traditional direction; that is, by following the Cook Path to the head of the gulch, then descending through it and returning to Randolph Hill Rd. via the Ice Gulch Path. However, many hikers will feel more comfortable ascending, rather than descending, the slippery rocks in the gulch, so the ascent via the Ice Gulch Path and return via the Cook Path should be seriously considered. *Caution:* The trip through the gulch itself is one of the most difficult and strenuous trail segments in the White Mountains, involving nearly constant scrambling over wet, slippery rocks, and it may take much more time than the standard formula allows. There is no way to exit from the ravine in the mile between the Vestibule and Fairy Spring; hikers must either retrace their steps to the end they started from or continue to the other end, and should take this fact into account when considering the suitability of this trip for their party or estimating the amount of time they should allow for it. The trail is not suitable for dogs.

From the Cook Path at the head of the Ice Gulch, the descent is very steep for 0.1 mi. to the Vestibule, where there is an excellent spring. Toward the bottom, the trail passes along the base of a large open talus slope on the left. The steep descent continues generally southeast, with views toward Gorham and down the gulch. At the foot of the gulch, the trail passes Fairy Spring. Just below this spring, at 0.9 mi., the Peboamauk Loop leaves on the left to follow the brook down to Peboamauk Fall. The Ice Gulch Path turns right here and climbs steeply for a short distance up the west bank of the ravine, then descends to the south across several wet areas to the "Marked Birch," where it bears right as the Peboamauk Loop rejoins on the left. The Ice Gulch Path runs southwest with several minor ups and downs. It crosses another brook, rises gradually, emerges in a field by a red barn, and follows a driveway to Randolph Hill Rd.

Ice Gulch Path (map 6:E9–D9)

Distances from head of Ice Gulch (2,460 ft.) to
- site of "Marked Birch" (1,770 ft.): 1.4 mi., 0 ft. (rev. 700 ft.), 45 min.
- Randolph Hill Rd. (1,780 ft.): 3.4 mi., 200 ft. (rev. 200 ft.), 1 hr. 50 min.

Distance from Randolph Hill Rd. (1,800 ft.) for
- complete loop via Boothman Spring Cutoff, Cook Path, and Ice Gulch Path: 6.6 mi., 1,150 ft., 3 hr. 55 min.

Peboamauk Loop (RMC)

This path is an alternate route to the main Ice Gulch Path at the lower end of the gulch, longer and more strenuous but much more rewarding than the main route. It travels beside a pleasant stream and passes Peboamauk Fall, a fine cascade fed by the slowly melting ice in the gulch (Peboamauk means "winter's home"). On the descent, the path leaves the Ice Gulch Path on the left at the foot of the Ice Gulch just below Fairy Spring and descends moderately along Moose Brook for 0.4 mi., crossing it four times, then drops steeply to the foot of Peboamauk Fall. It rises steeply to rejoin the Ice Gulch Path at the "Marked Birch."

Peboamauk Loop (map 6:E9)

Distance from Ice Gulch Path, upper junction (1,860 ft.) to
- Ice Gulch Path, lower junction (1,770 ft.): 0.5 mi., 100 ft. (rev. 200 ft.), 20 min.

The Pliny and Pilot Ranges

These two ranges are essentially one mountain mass, extending north and south between the Israel and Upper Ammonoosuc rivers, east of Lancaster. The Pliny Range forms the semicircular southern end of this mass; its chief summits are Mt. Starr King, Mt. Waumbek, and the three peaks of Mt. Weeks. Across Willard Notch from Mt. Weeks, the Pilot Range begins, including Terrace Mountain, Mt. Cabot, Mt. Mary, and Hutchins Mountain, which is often known as Mt. Pilot. A spur that extends northeast from Mt. Cabot carries the Bulge and the Horn. The tallest peak in the entire North Country is Mt. Cabot. Two fire towers accessible by auto provide excellent views that may be helpful to hikers planning trips in this region. Mt. Prospect (2,077 ft.) is located in Weeks State Park, the former estate of John W. Weeks, reached by a paved road (small fee charged for vehicles) that leaves US 3 at its high point between Whitefield and Lancaster. There is now also a small trail network on this mountain. Milan Hill (1,737 ft.) is located in Milan Hill State Park (campground) on NH 110B west of Milan village; its fire tower offers a panoramic view that includes the Mahoosucs and the mountains north of NH 110 as well as the region covered in this subsection. This entire subsection is covered by the AMC's *North Country–Mahoosuc Range Map* (map 6); the USGS Pliny Range and Stark quads may also be useful.

Thomas Starr King, a minister in Boston and San Francisco who was the author of *The White Hills*—one of the most important and influential books ever written about the White Mountains—gave his name to Mt. Starr King (3,907 ft.); King Ravine on Mt. Adams and a peak in the Sierra Nevada of California are also named for him. New Hampshire's Mt. Starr King is located northeast of Jefferson village, from which it is reached by the Starr King Trail. The summit is wooded, but there is a fine cleared vista toward the Presidentials. Immediately east of Mt. Starr King is Mt. Waumbek (4,006 ft.), which is also reached by the Starr King Trail, as well as being the southern terminus of the Kilkenny Ridge Trail. Formerly called Pliny Major, Mt. Waumbek is the highest point of the Pliny Range but has only a very restricted view to the east. Located northeast of Mt. Waumbek, Mt. Weeks has three distinct peaks—the North Peak (3,901 ft.), the Middle Peak (3,684 ft.), and the South Peak (3,885 ft.)—all of which are wooded with no significant views and are traversed by the Kilkenny Ridge Trail. Formerly known as Round Mountain, it was renamed to honor John W. Weeks, who was the sponsor and chief proponent of the Weeks Act (1911), the piece of federal legislation that authorized the purchase of lands for national forests and thereby made possible the establishment of the WMNF.

The Pilot Range begins on the north side of Willard Notch with Terrace Mountain (3,655 ft.), a narrow ridge with several summits, named for its appearance when seen from the west. It is traversed by the Kilkenny Ridge Trail, and its principal summit affords an interesting if somewhat restricted view. The tallest peak of the North Country, Mt. Cabot (4,170 ft.), is located north of Terrace Mountain across Bunnell Notch. Its true summit is wooded with no views, but good outlooks east and west have been cleared at the site of the former fire tower, 0.3 mi. southeast of the true summit, and there is an excellent vista from the ledges above Bunnell Notch. The Bulge (3,950 ft.) and the Horn (3,905 ft.) lie just northeast of Mt. Cabot. They are reached via the Kilkenny Ridge Trail, which follows the ridge that joins them to Mt. Cabot over the Bulge and then circles around the northwest side of the Horn, which is ascended by a spur path. The Bulge is a wooded hump with no views. The Horn is a fine sharp peak composed of a jumble of bare rocks that afford views in all directions; it is unquestionably one of the finest summits in the region.

Hutchins Mountain (3,730 ft.), sometimes also called Mt. Pilot, was named for Alpheus Hutchins, an early settler. It lies at the northwest end of the Pilot Range, separated from Mt. Cabot by Mt. Mary and several unnamed peaks. It has no regular trail but can be ascended by experienced bushwhackers by following a private logging road that leaves the road from Grange to Groveton via Lost Nation at a sharp turn near an old schoolhouse at the foot of the mountain (use care not to block any roads). The most frequently used route follows the logging road that runs up the southeast side of Cummings Brook into the basin below the summit, then ascends to the southwest ridge of Hutchins Mountain and follows it to the summit. See the USGS Stark quad.

The wide valley east of the Pilot Range and north of the Crescent Range, drained by the headwaters of the Upper Ammonoosuc River, has been traditionally known to local residents as "the Kilkenny," from the uninhabited township in which many of the peaks of the Pilot and Pliny ranges, including Mt. Waumbek and Mt. Cabot, are located. Ironically, most of the region usually called by the name of Kilkenny lies in the towns of Berlin, Randolph, Milan, and Stark, with very little in Kilkenny itself; though if the Pilot and Pliny ranges are included in the region (as is sometimes the case) the name of Kilkenny is then amply justified. It is a rather flat, densely forested region known well by loggers and those who love to hunt and fish, but not to nearly the same extent by hikers. Historically this region has been a major timber-harvest area, and many of the features of interest reflect past and present logging activity both on private inholdings and on the national forest lands, which are managed for multiple use. The trails in this region generally follow an extensive network of old, older, and ancient logging roads or railroad grades. Primary trails are usually blazed with yellow paint. The visual environment on the maintained trails has generally been screened from logging activity, but the longer view often includes vegetational diversity resulting from timber harvest and reforestation, and access roads may be in evidence. As a result of the variety of vegetation types, chances are excellent that one will see many kinds of native wildlife. The Kilkenny Ridge Trail links some of the main attractions of this area, including the Devil's Hopyard and Rogers Ledge. There are primitive campsites at Rogers Ledge and Unknown Pond. This is a backcountry area in which trails are normally maintained only once annually. It may be useful to check with the Androscoggin Ranger District office in Gorham for the current status of particular trails.

The center of this area is accessible by York Pond Rd. (FR 13) to the Berlin Fish Hatchery at York Pond, and by Bog Dam Rd. (FR 15), which makes a 15.5-mi. loop south of York Pond. Bog Dam Rd. follows in part the earlier Upper Ammonoosuc Trail and logging-road network, passing the sites of several former logging camps. York Pond Rd. leaves NH 110 7.4 mi. northwest of its beginning at NH 16 in Berlin. There is a gate at the Berlin Fish Hatchery that is locked from 4 P.M. to 8 A.M. Hikers who plan to leave cars at the trailheads west of this gate should make prior arrangements in person at the gatehouse, or by phone with the hatchery (603-449-3412). Foot travel past the gate is not restricted. This road has been open and plowed in recent winters, with a plowed parking area at the Unknown Pond Trail trailhead or the York Pond Trail trailhead.

The South Pond Recreation Area is a picnic and swimming area operated by the WMNF at South Pond, south of NH 110 in Stark; camping is not permitted here. This is the northern terminus of the Kilkenny Ridge

Trail and the Devil's Hopyard Trail. The access road to South Pond Recreation Area has a gate 1.1 mi. from the trailhead in the picnic area; this
gate is kept locked from 8 P.M. to 9 A.M. during the season when the beach
and picnic area are open. At other times, it is usually locked, but it is normally left open from Labor Day to the end of hunting season. Foot travel
is always permitted. Check with the Androscoggin Ranger District office
of the WMNF for details.

The Devils Hopyard is a picturesque gorge on a brook that empties
into South Pond. It resembles the Ice Gulch in Randolph but is shorter
and narrower. Rogers Ledge (2,965 ft.), one of the most interesting little-
known mountains in the White Mountains, lies about 3.5 mi. northwest of
York Pond. It was named in honor of Major Robert Rogers, leader of Rogers's Rangers in the French and Indian Wars. The entire southwest face of
the mountain is a cliff, and the view from the top includes the Kilkenny
area, the Pilot Range, the Mahoosucs, and the Presidential Range. It may
be reached from South Pond by the Kilkenny Ridge Trail, or from the York
Pond Fish Hatchery by the Mill Brook Trail and the Kilkenny Ridge Trail.
Unknown Pond, which is reached by the Kilkenny Ridge Trail or the Unknown Pond Trail, is one of the jewels of the White Mountains—a beautiful mountain tarn in a birch forest carpeted with dense ferns, offering a
spectacular view up to the rugged and picturesque Horn from its shore.

Mount Prospect Auto Road (NHDP)

This road runs from US 3 between Lancaster and Whitefield to the summit of Mt. Prospect in Weeks State Park, where the picturesque fieldstone
tower provides excellent views. It is usually open to vehicles (fee charged)
daily from mid-June to Labor Day, and on weekends from Memorial Day
to mid-June and from Labor Day to Columbus Day. At other times, it is
gated and open to pedestrian use (and to skiers in winter) only. When the
gate is closed, parking is available on the west side of US 3. Refer to the
USGS Lancaster quad.

Leaving US 3 at the top of the hill between Whitefield and Lancaster,
it ascends in a counterclockwise direction, crossing the Around the Mountain Trail (of which this section is a part of the New Hampshire Heritage
Trail, a path that is planned to extend the entire length of the state) in

0.1 mi. At 0.6 mi., the Davidge Path diverges right and descends in 0.2 mi. to the Around the Mountain Trail. At 0.7 mi., the road passes a viewpoint to Blood Pond and Mountain Meadow Pond, and at 1.1 mi., it passes an excellent outlook to the Presidentials with a mountain identification sign. At 1.3 mi., at a hairpin turn to the left, the Old Carriage Rd. diverges on the right and descends along the north slope of the mountain, crossing the Around the Mountain Trail in 0.4 mi. and reaching Reed Rd. in 0.7 mi. The Auto Rd. continues to the summit and its buildings.

Mount Prospect Auto Road (USGS Lancaster quad)

Distance from US 3 (1,430 ft.) to
- Mt. Prospect summit (2,077 ft.): 1.6 mi., 650 ft., 1 hr. 10 min.

Around the Mountain Trail (NHDP)

This trail runs completely around the lower slopes of Mt. Prospect, providing a pleasant 3-mi. loop on interconnecting woods roads that is particularly useful as a cross-country ski route. It begins at the entrance gate to the Mt. Prospect Ski Area on US 3 0.2 mi. north of the lower end of the Mt. Prospect Auto Rd.; it is described here in the counterclockwise direction.

Leaving the ski area, the trail follows an old grassy road southward, marked by yellow blazes as part of the New Hampshire Heritage Trail. At 0.3 mi., it crosses the Mt. Prospect Auto Rd., and at 0.4 mi., the New Hampshire Heritage Trail diverges right, whereas the Around the Mountain Trail swings left and runs eastward through a logged area. At 1.2 mi. it crosses an opening above a log yard, then the Davidge Path (much disrupted by logging) diverges left, ascending 0.2 mi. and 150 ft. to the Auto Rd. The Around the Mountain Trail then turns left (north) onto an old woods road bordered with stone walls. It bears left off the road and ascends to a semi-open outlook to the east near a stone wall. The trail continues to climb across a small stream and reaches its high point at 1.8 mi., then descends left (west). It crosses over several small streams and under maple-sugaring sap lines, then swings left past old building foundations (right) and crosses the Old Carriage Rd. at 2.6 mi. (The summit of Mt. Prospect is 0.7 mi. to the left via the Old Carriage Rd. and the Auto Rd. The New

Hampshire Heritage Trail, which has followed the Old Carriage Rd. 0.3 mi. up from Reed Rd., now coincides with the Around the Mountain Trail for the rest of its distance.) Soon the Around the Mountain Trail swings left (south) and continues to the starting point at the ski area.

Around the Mountain Trail (USGS Lancaster quad)

Distance from Mt. Prospect Ski Area (1,410 ft.) for
  • complete loop: 3.0 mi., 300 ft., 1 hr. 40 min.

Kilkenny Ridge Trail (WMNF)

The Kilkenny Ridge Trail is a ridge-crest trail that runs from South Pond Recreation Area off NH 110 to the summit of Mt. Waumbek. From South Pond, it climbs over Rogers Ledge, traverses a nameless ridge and descends to Unknown Pond, then circles to the northwest side of the Horn to gain the crest of the Pilot-Pliny ridge at the col between the Bulge and the Horn (the Horn is reached by a spur path). It then follows the backbone of the main ridge over the Bulge, Mt. Cabot, Terrace Mountain, and the three peaks of Weeks to its southern end on Mt. Waumbek. This trail was designed primarily to provide an extended route for backpackers interested in avoiding crowds of day-hikers, because, except for the section that coincides with the Mt. Cabot Trail, use of those sections and features that are accessible to day-hikers is very light. The trail has generally easy to moderate grades and reaches several fine viewpoints—notably the Horn and Rogers Ledge—but has long stretches of woods walking that are pleasant but lacking in significant views.

From the parking lot at South Pond, go right (south) toward the west shore to the sign for the Devils Hopyard. The trail follows the shore for 0.4 mi., then bears to the right away from the pond. At 0.7 mi., shortly after the trail crosses Devil's Hopyard Stream, the Devil's Hopyard Trail diverges right (west) and the Kilkenny Ridge Trail continues straight ahead. It crosses two brooks on bridges and runs southeast and south following old logging roads. At 2.5 mi., the trail bears sharp right (west), crossing from one logging road to another, then resumes its generally southerly course, crossing the town boundary between Stark and Kilkenny at 3.2 mi. At 3.4 mi., the grade becomes steeper along the crest of a narrowing ridge, and the trail ascends to a sharp left turn at 4.1 mi., with the summit of Rogers Ledge a few steps ahead. The best view is at the edge of the cliff, reached by a short spur on the right just before this turn. From the south-facing ledge, the view includes the Presidential Range, the Androscoggin River valley, the Mahoosuc Range, the entire Kilkenny basin, and the northern shoulder of Mt. Cabot.

Descending steeply from Rogers Ledge, the trail curves east around the foot of the ledge and passes a side path left to a designated campsite at 4.6 mi., then continues to its junction with Mill Brook Trail at 4.7 mi. from South Pond. The trail continues west, traversing a muddy section and passing a beaver pond called Kilback Pond at 5.3 mi., and at 6.0 mi., begins the steady ascent to the ridge east of Unknown Pond. It reaches the crest of the ridge at 6.4 mi. and descends to the pond at 6.8 mi., where it meets the Unknown Pond Trail. At the southeast corner of the pond, a side trail leads to several designated tentsites.

The Kilkenny Ridge Trail follows the Unknown Pond Trail to the right for 100 yd., then turns sharp left off it and runs around the north shore of the pond. It descends to a wet sag, then swings west around the end of the ridge and begins the climb up the north slope of the Horn to the sag between the Bulge and the Horn at 8.5 mi. Here a side trail climbs to the left (east) 0.3 mi. and 250 ft. to the open rocks of the Horn, from which there are magnificent views; the upper part of the side trail has several ledge scrambles, including a fairly difficult one to reach the summit ledge. The Kilkenny Ridge Trail turns right (west) and ascends to the wooded summit of the Bulge, drops to the saddle, and climbs steadily to the true summit of Mt. Cabot at 9.6 mi., where it joins the Mt. Cabot Trail.

The two trails descend together, passing a side trail left (sign) that drops steeply for 250 yd. to an unreliable spring. At 10.0 mi., they cross the viewpoint at the lower but more open summit of Cabot and pass the cabin just below it, which also has views. They continue to descend moderately past the fine outlook from Bunnell Rock on the left as the trail makes a great curving 180 degree turn to the right. At 11.0 mi., where the Mt. Cabot Trail turns sharp right and continues its descent to East Lancaster (the lower section of this trail has been closed by the landowner since 2000), the Kilkenny Ridge Trail bears slightly left and runs southeast with gentle ups and downs. At 11.3 mi., it meets the Bunnell Notch Trail, follows it to the left for 0.1 mi., and then leaves it on the right to begin the ascent of Terrace Mountain, climbing moderately to the overgrown clearing once opened for emergency helicopter landings in the event of a forest fire (called a "helspot") at the summit of the northern knob. It then continues along the ridge with a significant climb and descent over a lesser peak. At 13.3 mi., where a spur path continues straight 0.1 mi. to the interesting but restricted southeast outlook at the summit of Terrace Mountain, the main trail turns sharp left and drops off the ridge, then begins a long circling descent to the York Pond Trail.

Crossing a small brook at its low point in Willard Notch, where there is a trailside campsite, the trail ascends slightly to the York Pond Trail at 14.4 mi., follows it left (east) for 100 yd., then leaves it on the right and begins a rather long and winding ascent of North Weeks, reaching the summit at 15.7 mi. The trail descends at easy to moderate grades past a small spring (unreliable) at 16.0 mi. to a potential campsite in the main col at 16.5 mi. Ascending again, it passes over Middle Weeks at 17.1 mi. and crosses through a much shallower col to South Weeks at 18.1 mi. Here a short spur continues straight to the blowdown-infested summit, while the main trail turns left and descends to the col between Weeks and Waumbek at 18.7 mi. From here it swings to the west and ascends along the crest of the ridge, slowly gaining elevation despite occasional losses, then crosses the interesting, rather steep-sided east knob of Waumbek and continues another 0.2 mi. to the true summit, where it meets the Starr King Trail.

Kilkenny Ridge Trail (map 6:B8–D7)

Distances from South Pond Recreation Area (1,120 ft.) to
- Rogers Ledge (2,965 ft.): 4.1 mi., 1,850 ft., 3 hr.
- Mill Brook Trail (2,400 ft.): 4.7 mi., 1,850 ft. (rev. 550 ft.), 3 hr. 15 min.
- Unknown Pond (3,177 ft.): 6.8 mi., 2,800 ft. (rev. 150 ft.), 4 hr. 50 min.
- the side trail to the Horn (3,650 ft.): 8.5 mi., 3,350 ft. (rev. 100 ft.), 5 hr. 55 min.
- Mt. Cabot summit (4,170 ft.): 9.6 mi., 4,100 ft. (rev. 250 ft.), 6 hr. 50 min.
- departure from Mt. Cabot Trail (2,975 ft.): 11.0 mi., 4,150 ft. (rev. 1,250 ft.), 7 hr. 35 min.
- Terrace Mountain summit spur (3,550 ft.): 13.3 mi., 5,050 ft. (rev. 350 ft.), 9 hr. 10 min.
- York Pond Trail, west junction (2,720 ft.): 14.4 mi., 5,050 ft. (rev. 850 ft.), 9 hr. 45 min.
- North Weeks summit (3,901 ft.): 15.7 mi., 6,250 ft., 11 hr. ▶

- South Weeks summit (3,885 ft.): 18.1 mi., 7,050 ft. (rev. 800 ft.), 12 hr. 35 min.
- Mt. Waumbek summit (4,006 ft.): 20.6 mi., 7,650 ft. (rev. 500 ft.), 14 hr. 5 min.

Devil's Hopyard Trail (WMNF)

This trail begins at the South Pond Recreation Area off NH 110 and provides access to the wild and beautiful Devils Hopyard, a small gorge with cliffy walls and a boulder-strewn floor. At the start, it coincides with the Kilkenny Ridge Trail, which leads south from the picnic area, skirting the west side of the pond, and crosses Devil's Hopyard Stream in 0.6 mi. After another 60 yd., the Devil's Hopyard Trail diverges right (west) from the Kilkenny Ridge Trail (sign). At 0.8 mi., it recrosses the brook to the north side and soon enters the Hopyard. The small stream that drains the gorge is for the most part completely out of sight beneath moss-covered boulders, while ledges overhang the path. (Use caution where rocks are wet or covered with moss.) At 1.2 mi., the path rises steeply on the rocks at the west end of the Hopyard and ends at a cascade.

Devil's Hopyard Trail (map 6:B8)

Distance from South Pond (1,120 ft.) to
- end of trail (1,350): 1.3 mi., 250 ft., 50 min.

Starr King Trail (RMC)

This trail begins on Starr King Rd., a gravel road to several houses that leaves the north side of US 2 (trail sign) 0.2 mi. east of its junction with NH 115A. Go up the road, always bearing left to avoid driveways on the right. At 0.2 mi. pass on the left the former route of the trail, an overgrown road that may be used by pedestrians, and continue to a small parking lot. If the parking lot cannot be reached by car (as when the access road is unplowed in winter), park in the lot for the Jefferson village swimming pool, just east of the junction of US 2 and NH 115A, and walk up the road; do not obstruct the roads by parking cars on them. The trail is generally fairly easy all the way up, with moderate grades and good footing.

From the parking area, ascend gradually on a grassy logging road for 100 yd., then turn left (arrow) and ascend another 100 yd. to meet the old route of the trail, a logging road on which the trail turns uphill to the right and soon passes the stone foundations of a springhouse (right). At 0.4 mi., the trail bears right and ascends the broad southwest ridge of the mountain. At 1.4 mi., it angles left and runs north on a long traverse of the west flank of the mountain, passing a spring on the left (downhill side) of the trail at 2.1 mi. Swinging right and leaving the traverse at 2.5 mi., the trail climbs to the summit at 2.6 mi., then continues another 60 yd. to a cleared vista south and west (slowly being encroached upon by tree growth) at the site of a former shelter. From the remains of the old cabin's fireplace, the trail enters the woods again, angling left, then swings right (east) and follows close to the crest of the ridge or slightly below it on one side or the other, dipping just below the col on the south and then rising to the summit of Mt. Waumbek, where it meets the south end of the Kilkenny Ridge Trail.

Starr King Trail (map 6:D7)

Distances from trailhead parking area (1,600 ft.) to

- beginning of traverse (2,900 ft.): 1.4 mi., 1,300 ft., 1 hr. 20 min.
- Mt. Starr King summit (3,907 ft.): 2.6 mi., 2,300 ft., 2 hr. 25 min.
- Mt. Waumbek summit (4,006 ft.): 3.6 mi., 2,550 ft. (rev. 150 ft.), 3 hr. 5 min.

Mount Cabot Trail (WMNF)

Note: The lower section of this trail has been closed by the landowner for the past few years and so must not be used at the present time. There is therefore no legal access to this trail from the west side. It is retained in this book in the hope that it will again be open in the near future. Hikers wishing to climb Mt. Cabot should consider routes from the York Pond Rd. or Mill Brook Rd.

In addition to ascending Mt. Cabot, this trail provides access to the York Pond, Kilkenny Ridge, and Bunnell Notch trails. From the junction of US 2 and NH 116 just west of the village of Jefferson, go west 0.2 mi., then turn right (north) on North Rd. for 2.3 mi., then turn right again on Gore Rd. (which becomes Garland Rd. at a sharp left turn). At 4.0 mi. from US 2, turn right again on Pleasant Valley Rd., and at 4.8 mi. turn right on Arthur White Rd. and continue 0.4 mi. to the parking area (sign) about 50 yd. before the end of the road at Heath's Gate; do not block the road or the driveway. Any or all of the road signs at intersections may be missing, so the directions given should be followed with care. The trail follows logging roads and the old tractor road to the former fire tower almost all the way, with steady moderate grades; footing is fair to good on the upper part, but the lower part has a severely eroded stretch of logging road.

From Heath's Gate, the Mt. Cabot Trail follows a logging road through a cut-over area 0.4 mi. to the old Kilkenny logging railroad bed. Here the York Pond Trail to York Pond and the Berlin Fish Hatchery by way of Willard Notch goes right (southeast) along the railroad bed. The Mt. Cabot Trail continues ahead on a recent road for another 0.4 mi., then the newer road ends and the trail becomes a footway on much older roads to the Bunnell Brook crossing at 2.2 mi. Just past the brook, the Bunnell Notch Trail (sign) leaves on the right. After zigzagging up from the brook, the trail passes a junction at 2.5 mi. where it turns left as the Kilkenny Ridge Trail joins from the right. Soon the trail swings right (southeast) and ascends past a limited southwest outlook. In another 100 yd., after swinging to the left, the trail passes a spur path right (sign) at 2.9 mi. that leads a few steps to Bunnell Rock, a ledge at the cliff-top that offers an excellent vista to the south—probably the best view on the trail. From here, the trail turns left (northeast) and climbs through evergreens, with two switchbacks, to the old firewarden's cabin. From the cabin, the trail climbs a few steps to the open rocky area where the fire tower was formerly located (views), then passes through a shallow sag and climbs gradually past a side path right (sign) that descends steeply 250 yd. to an unreliable spring to the true summit (sign). The Kilkenny Ridge Trail continues northward from here, leading over the Bulge and past a side trail to the Horn, then on to Unknown Pond, Rogers Ledge, and South Pond.

Mount Cabot Trail (map 6:D7–C8)

Distances from Heath's Gate (1,510 ft.) to

- York Pond Trail (1,640 ft.): 0.4 mi., 150 ft., 15 min.
- Bunnell Brook crossing (2,650 ft.): 2.2 mi., 1,150 ft., 1 hr. 40 min.
- outlook at Bunnell Rock (3,350 ft.): 2.9 mi., 1,850 ft., 2 hr. 25 min.
- cabin (4,070 ft.): 3.5 mi., 2,550 ft., 3 hr.
- Mt. Cabot summit (4,170 ft.): 3.9 mi., 2,700 ft. (rev. 50 ft.), 3 hr. 20 min.

York Pond Trail (WMNF)

Note: The lower west section of this trail has been closed by the landowner for the past few years and so must not be used at the present time. There is therefore no legal access to this trail from the west side. It is retained in this book in the hope that it will again be open in the near future.

This trail leaves York Pond Rd. (FR 13) near its west end and follows old logging roads through Willard Notch and down to the old Kilkenny logging railroad bed, on which it continues to East Lancaster at Heath's Gate (see Mt. Cabot Trail). It is blazed with yellow paint. The eastern and western ends are in generally excellent condition with good footing, but much of the central part of the trail from the Kilkenny Ridge Trail to the logging railroad bed is very wet and muddy.

From the fish hatchery gate at York Pond (see the earlier warning concerning, the times this gate is locked), continue west 2.1 mi. on York Pond Rd. to a fenced raceway. The trailhead (sign) is on the road to the left. The entrance to the trail is gated, but foot travel is not restricted. The York Pond Trail follows a good gravel road for 0.2 mi., then bears left (arrow) where the Bunnell Notch Trail diverges right. In 100 yd., it crosses a small concrete dam, then continues up the south side of the brook, crossing two branches. At 0.9 mi., it begins to swing up a hardwood ridge, following a well-defined old logging road in excellent condition. At 2.4 mi., it reaches its highest point, just east of Willard Notch on a minor ridge from North Weeks. Descending slightly, it passes two junctions with the Kilkenny Ridge Trail 100 yd. apart; at the first, the Kilkenny Ridge Trail leads left (south) to Mt. Weeks and Mt. Waumbek, and at the second it leads right (north) to Terrace Mountain, Mt. Cabot, and South Pond. The York Pond Trail contours along the south side of the notch, rising and falling gently and remaining somewhat above the floor of the notch. It then descends gradually through several swampy areas and crosses a number of small streams, becoming very muddy at times, then crosses a fairly substantial branch of Garland Brook at 4.6 mi. and joins the old logging railroad grade, where the footing improves greatly. At 5.6 mi., it crosses the WMNF boundary and at 6.6 mi., just after crossing a stream on a culvert bridge, it bears right at a fork (the more obvious left branch is the Tekwood Rd., which continues down Garland Brook to Pleasant Valley Rd.). The trail continues on the old railroad grade in a northwesterly direction and joins the Mt. Cabot Trail at 7.0 mi. Turn right (east) for Mt. Cabot or left (west) to reach the parking area at Heath's Gate (the former White's farm) in East Lancaster at 7.4 mi.

York Pond Trail (map 6:D8–D7)

Distances from York Pond Rd. trailhead (1,670 ft.) to
- high point of trail (2,750 ft.): 2.4 mi., 1,100 ft., 1 hr. 45 min.
- WMNF boundary (1,920 ft.): 5.6 mi., 1,100 ft. (rev. 850 ft.), 3 hr. 20 min.
- Mt. Cabot Trail (1,640 ft.): 7.0 mi., 1,100 ft. (rev. 300 ft.), 4 hr. 5 min.
- Heath's Gate (1,510 ft.): 7.4 mi., 1,100 ft. (rev. 150 ft.), 4 hr. 15 min.

Bunnell Notch Trail (WMNF)

This trail connects the York Pond Rd. with the Kilkenny Ridge Trail in Bunnell Notch; the former extension of the trail to the Mt. Cabot Trail has been abandoned. In recent years, this trail has seen a considerable increase in usage as an alternative route to Mt. Cabot, because the standard western route to that peak has been closed to the public since 2000 (though the northern approach via Unknown Pond Trail from Stark is much more attractive); it also makes possible a rather long but very attractive loop trip to Unknown Pond, the Horn, and Mt. Cabot. In 2004, the Forest Service made considerable improvements on the trail, including a short relocation. While still wet in places, the trail is better maintained and easier to follow than it has been in the past.

Leaving the York Pond Trail on the right in a clearing 0.2 mi. from York Pond Rd., it follows a logging road, bearing right at a fork at 0.3 mi. It descends gradually, crossing several small streams and the larger stream that flows down from Bunnell Notch. At 0.9 mi., it turns left (sign) off the logging road onto a relocated section; the turn is 70 yd. beyond where the trail formerly turned off the road. At 1.1 mi., it rejoins the original route, swings right to climb to a high bank, then descends slightly to the edge of the brook flowing down from the notch. It follows the north side of the brook up the valley, alternately close beside the stream and higher up on the slope. At 2.4 mi., it bears right at an arrow and climbs into Bunnell Notch, reaching the height-of-land at 2.8 mi. After a slight dip, the Kilkenny Ridge Trail leaves on the left (south) for Terrace Mountain, Mt. Weeks, and Mt. Waumbek. In another 0.1 mi. of gentle descent the maintained section of the Bunnell Notch Trail ends where the Kilkenny Ridge Trail leaves on the right (north) for Mt. Cabot and South Pond.

Bunnell Notch Trail (map 6:D8–D7)

Distance from York Pond Trail (1,690 ft.) to
- Kilkenny Ridge Trail, west junction (3,000 ft.): 2.9 mi., 1,400 ft. (rev. 100 ft.), 2 hr. 10 min.

Distance from York Pond Rd. (1,670 ft.) to
- Mt. Cabot summit (4,170 ft.) via York Pond Trail, Bunnell Notch Trail and Kilkenny Ridge Trail: 4.8 mi., 2,700 ft. (rev. 200 ft.), 3 hr. 45 min.

Unknown Pond Trail (WMNF)

This trail connects York Pond Rd. with Mill Brook Rd. near the village of Stark, passing beautiful Unknown Pond and crossing the Kilkenny Ridge Trail. The south terminus is on York Pond Rd. 2.0 mi. west of the fish hatchery gate (sign) at a parking area on the right just beyond a small pond (see the earlier warning for the York Pond Trail concerning the locked gate at the fish hatchery, locked 4 P.M. to 8 A.M.). The north terminus is on Mill Brook Rd. (FR 11) 4.5 mi. south of NH 110. There is a sign (hiker symbol) on NH 110 at the beginning of Mill Brook Rd. and a trail sign at the trailhead, which is just east of a bridge across Mill Brook. Parking is available beyond the bridge on the right.

Leaving the parking area on York Pond Rd., the trail reaches an old railroad grade at 0.2 mi. and turns left on it. It then leaves the grade, crosses a small brook twice, and climbs generally northwest up the valley of the brook that drains Unknown Pond. At 1.9 mi., it crosses the main brook, then a tributary, then recrosses the main brook at 2.1 mi. At about 2.5 mi., the trail begins a steeper ascent to Unknown Pond, which it reaches at 3.3 mi. At the southeast corner of the pond, a side trail leads to several designated tent sites.

The Kilkenny Ridge Trail enters right (east) at the northeast corner of the pond and coincides with the Unknown Pond Trail for 100 yd. The two paths swing west around the pond through birch woods carpeted with ferns, passing a beautiful view up to the picturesque Horn rising over the pond. At the northwest corner of the pond, the Kilkenny Ridge Trail leaves left (west) toward Mt. Cabot and the Unknown Pond Trail goes north toward Mill Brook Rd. in Stark, crossing a moist area and descending moderately in beautiful birch woods for a mile. It then becomes more gradual, soon crossing the Kilkenny-Stark town line. It traverses the slope east of Mill Brook and ends at the gravel Mill Brook Rd. (FR 11) at 5.5 mi.

Unknown Pond Trail (map 6:D8–C8)

Distances from York Pond Rd. trailhead (1,640 ft.) to

* Unknown Pond (3,177 ft.): 3.3 mi., 1,550 ft., 2 hr. 25 min.
* Mill Brook Rd. (1,755 ft.): 5.5 mi., 1,550 ft. (rev. 1,400 ft.), 3 hr. 30 min.

Mill Brook Trail (WMNF)

Formerly a through route from Stark village to York Pond, the north section of this trail, from the junction with the Kilkenny Ridge Trail at the height-of-land to Stark, has been abandoned by the WMNF, and beaver activity and logging have obliterated the old footway. The remaining part of the trail is important mostly because it provides the most convenient route from the south to the spectacular views from Rogers Ledge. It now begins near the main building of the Berlin Fish Hatchery on York Pond Rd. (FR 9). (The lower part of the trail may be difficult to locate; if so, ask at the hatchery for directions.)

From the trail sign on York Pond Rd., ascend gradually on a paved road for 0.2 mi., then follow a dirt road (sign) to the left of a fish hatchery building. After 100 yd., bear right off the dirt road (no sign) and go behind an old brown pump house on a concrete dam by a small pond, then turn left onto an old grassy woods road. The trail joins Cold Brook and ascends along it for about 1.3 mi., then diverges right (east) up a side stream, passing through several wet areas with luxuriant undergrowth. It crosses the Berlin-Milan town boundary at 1.7 mi. and the Milan-Kilkenny boundary at 2.7 mi. It descends west from the height-of-land and ends at the Kilkenny Ridge Trail. To the right (east) it is 0.6 mi. to Rogers Ledge; to the left (west) it is 2.1 mi. to Unknown Pond.

Mill Brook Trail (map 6:C8)

Distance from York Pond Rd. (1,550 ft.) to

* Kilkenny Ridge Trail (2,400 ft.): 3.8 mi., 950 ft. (rev. 100 ft.), 2 hr. 20 min.

Pond of Safety Trail (WMNF)

This is now a snowmobile trail that is no longer maintained for hiking by the WMNF.

Upper Ammonoosuc Trail (WMNF)

This trail has been abandoned by the WMNF.

Landing Camp Trail (WMNF)

This trail is the remnant of an old trail that once connected Bog Dam (built to provide a "head" of water for spring logging drives on the Upper Ammonoosuc River, and later used as a town water supply) with Randolph through Hunter's Pass. It is lightly used, very wet in places, and was obstructed by numerous blowdowns in late 2006; it is unsuitable for most hikers and must be followed with great care even by experienced ones. It leaves the west side of the east leg of Bog Dam Rd. 6.3 mi. south of its eastern junction with York Pond Rd. It descends gradually to the site of the former Camp 18 at 0.4 mi. and bears right through the brushy clearing. It crosses a wet area and a small stream, turns left where an obscure path comes in from the right, and crosses two more brooks, the second of which may require bushwhacking right to a better crossing. It then leads through a very swampy area, crosses another brook, rises over a knoll and descends briefly, then runs nearly level to its end at the former junction with the abandoned Upper Ammonoosuc Trail.

Landing Camp Trail (map 6:D9)

Distance from Bog Dam Rd. (1,820 ft.) to
- former junction with abandoned Upper Ammonoosuc Trail (1,610 ft.): 1.9 mi., 0 ft. (rev. 200 ft.), 55 min.

West Milan Trail (WMNF)

This is now a snowmobile trail that is no longer maintained for hiking by the WMNF.

The North Country

As C. F. Belcher commented (*Appalachia* XXXIII:37) when referring to the Kilkenny region, "this area has built up a legend of isolation and mystery...even though for years it has been the intimate hunting and fishing preserve of those living nearby and a knowing few"—and, one might add, a source of income for the wood-products industries and their employees and suppliers. These remarks apply, with emphasis, to the true North Country, the region north of NH 110 and NH 110A between Groveton and Milan. The appearance of wilderness masks the active presence of logging operations, and the lack of marked and signed trails disguises the extensive network of roads and paths known very well to many local residents and others who enjoy the sense of being far from the crowds. To the south of this region, the mountain backcountry is mostly within the WMNF and has a well-developed trail system. In the great tracts of the North Country, there are only a few hiking trails, even on mountains over 3,000 ft., and most of these are not regularly maintained by any organization. Many experienced hikers will find pleasure in the area's remoteness, but those who expect to find their trails groomed and manicured are doomed to disappointment, and possibly to the inconvenience of getting lost. The scarcity of settlements and the confusing river drainages make inappropriate the usual advice about following a stream when lost; one must have a map and compass, know how to use them, and be prepared to traverse considerable distances on a compass course to the nearest road, possibly obstructed by swamps or logged areas with slash piles and dense second growth of blackberry, raspberry, and cherry. In general, camping and fires are prohibited throughout the region; because of the large amounts of drying slash in the extensive logged-over areas, the risk of a large forest fire is far greater than in the selectively logged areas to the south, and most landowners are intensely concerned about the possibility of a careless hiker or camper starting a major fire.

From the Presidential Range, this vast wooded region extends more than 60 mi. north to the Canadian border. The North Country proper is about 30 mi. long from north to south and varies in width from 20 mi. at the southern end to less than 15 mi. at Pittsburg. Its natural boundaries are the Upper Ammonoosuc, Androscoggin, and Magalloway rivers on the south and east and the Connecticut River on the west. To the south of this region, below the line made by NH 110 and NH 110A between the towns of Groveton and Milan, the mountains are still relatively high—two just over 4,000 ft.—and grouped compactly into ranges, like those farther south. Above this line lies the true North Country, a region very similar to the adjacent section of Maine. The mountains are lower—only about 10 exceed 3,500 ft.—and most have wooded summits. The noteworthy mountains, for example the Percy Peaks, Mt. Magalloway, and Rump Mountain, are scattered, separated by long stretches of less interesting terrain. Although the main backbone of the White Mountains—the divide between the Connecticut River and the streams and lakes to the east—continues north through this country all the way to the Canadian border, it crosses for the most part a broad upland jumbled with medium-sized rounded mountains, with no outstanding summits directly on the divide. Except for Dixville Notch, there is little rugged mountain scenery, although there are several large lakes.

South of NH 110, good public roads are always within a reasonable distance, but there are only three main highways in this northern section. Following the Connecticut Valley to its uppermost headwaters on the Canadian border beyond the Connecticut Lakes is US 3; NH 145 is an alternate road between the towns of Colebrook and Pittsburg. On the east side of the state, NH 16, which continues as ME 16, accompanies the Androscoggin and Magalloway rivers north to the outlet of Lake Aziscohos, then swings east to the Rangeley Lakes. The only east-west paved road north of NH 110, NH 26 crosses from Errol to Colebrook through Dixville Notch. Even public secondary roads are few and short, although the paper companies have constructed an intricate system of good main-haul gravel roads. Many of these have gates or are restricted, and heavy log trucks have the right of way on all of them. These roads are not signed, and the lack of striking landmarks makes travel on them confusing for the inexperienced. Because this northern section is managed for the continuous production of timber, roads and trails may change radically from one year to the next. Visitors may well find it helpful to obtain specific information about current conditions in advance. Among official sources that may be of help are the New Hampshire Fish and Game District Chief and Conservation Officers; information on who these people are and how to contact them can be obtained from New Hampshire Fish and Game in Concord.

Hikers in this region may well have occasion to contact representatives of the chief landowners, but while the vast majority of land in this region is still owned by large timber companies, ownership has changed so rapidly in recent years that any attempt to list these contacts would likely be out of date in a year or two.

In 2001, a consortium of government and nonprofit agencies acquired 171,500 acres in the town of Pittsburg, now called the Connecticut Lakes Headwaters tract; most of this was sold to another timber company with conservation easements to ensure continued public access and sustainable timber harvesting, while the state of New Hampshire retained 25,000 acres at the northern tip of the state to be managed as a wilderness reserve. A recreation management plan for the Connecticut Lakes Headwaters tract is under development. Many of the main haul roads will be open to public vehicular use, though subject to closure during timber harvests. Under the plan, hiking trails will be maintained to Magalloway Mountain and Garfield Falls, and short trails to other natural features may also be developed. Also significant was the purchase by the Nature Conservancy of 10,600 acres southwest of Dixville Notch as the Vicki Bunnell Preserve. Many natural features in this area, particularly ponds, are reached by woods roads passable to four-wheel-drive vehicles or by snowmobile trails, with limited appeal to pedestrian users; but many others, including most mountain summits, are simply pathless. Many trails, including several to fire towers that used to be operated in the North Country, have fallen into disuse or been abandoned, and can no longer be followed except by hikers with fairly sophisticated navigational skills. Still, given the landownership changes noted, this situation seems about to undergo major change.

Traversing this region is the Cohos Trail, a challenging 160-mi. route intended to run the length of Coos County from Crawford Notch to the Canadian border. As of 2006, the Cohos Trail Association (TCTA) had opened nearly all of the trail from Crawford Notch to Coleman State Park in Stewartstown, using a combination of existing hiking trails, snowmobile and cross-country ski trails, logging and skid roads, old railroad grades, paved and gravel roads, and newly cut sections of trail. By walking on a variety of older and newer roads, the route can be extended to First Connecticut Lake in Pittsburg. Some sections of the Cohos Trail have changed rapidly in the first few years of its development, and north of Stewartstown the route is intermittent—indeed, conceptual in places—so no detailed description can be given here. The final routing of the northern part of the trail will not be finalized until the Connecticut Lakes Headwaters management plan is completed. TCTA has published a guidebook, *The Cohos Trail* (2nd ed., 2004), and a set of nine maps (updated annually); these may be ordered from the TCTA. Hikers should be aware that some sections of the Cohos Trail are poorly defined, overgrown, wet, and muddy, though TCTA has been working to improve blazing, signage, drainage, and footing in problem areas. Parts of the trail (such as in the remote country at the north end of the Nash Stream Forest) have little or no evident footway as yet, and numerous intersecting logging roads and snowmobile trails can cause considerable confusion. Hikers who venture into these areas should have adequate supplies and be proficient with map and compass. Of particular interest to hikers, especially backpackers, is the section of the Cohos Trail through the Nash Stream Forest and the Dixville Notch area, where there are a number of viewpoints and interesting natural features. A designated campsite has been opened beside the Percy Loop Trail on the northeast side of North Percy, and two shelters have been built: the Baldhead lean-to on the south peak of Baldhead Mountain, about 5 mi. south of Dixville Peak, and the Panorama lean-to near the north peak of Sanguinary Mountain, about 3.5 mi. north of the high point of the Sanguinary Ridge Trail. Fires are not permitted at any of these sites. At present, these are the only permitted backcountry camping sites on the Cohos Trail north of the WMNF, much of which crosses private timberlands.

In the valley of Nash Stream north of NH 110 between Groveton and Stark, a tract of nearly 40,000 acres is managed by the state of New Hampshire as the Nash Stream Forest. It is approached via the gravel Nash Stream Rd., which leaves Emerson Rd. 2.2 mi. from NH 110; Emerson Rd. leaves NH 110 2.6 mi. east of Groveton. Although major benefits to hikers have yet to develop, there are certainly many enticing possibilities within this tract. Included in this tract are the Percy Peaks and their trails, and most of the trail to Sugarloaf, but not its summit. The Percy Peaks, located northeast of Groveton, are the most conspicuous mountains in the northern view from Mt. Washington. The summit of the North Peak (3,430 ft.) is bare, except for low scrub; that of the South Peak (3,234 ft.) is wooded, but there are several good viewpoints. The trails described in this guide are on North Percy, as well as a rough trail to South Percy. Sugarloaf Mountain (3,710 ft.) rises east of North Stratford at the head of Nash Stream, and its bare rocky peak commands an extensive view, particularly of the Percy Peaks. Long Mountain (3,661 ft.) is a broad trailless ridge just to the northeast of the Percy Peaks; in the saddle between its two principal summits is Long Mountain Pond, one of the highest water bodies in the state. Victor Head (2,265 ft.) is a low peak south of Long Mountain with interesting views near its summit; it is now easily accessible from the Cohos Trail. Bunnell Mountain (3,730 ft.), formerly called Blue Mountain, is a trailless peak in the same mountain mass and is the highest peak in New Hampshire outside the WMNF; it is located in the Bunnell Preserve. The mountain and preserve are named for Vicki Bunnell, a local lawyer and judge who was murdered in 1997. Other trailless peaks in this range include West Peak (3,590 ft.), Castle Mountain (3,569 ft.), Notch Mountain (3,402 ft.), Gore Mountain (3,610 ft.) and Fitch Mountain (3,414 ft.). Eastward across the valley of Nash Stream are the several summits of trailless Whitcomb Mountain (3,615 ft.). Pond Brook Falls, an attractive series of cascades where an eastern tributary of Nash Stream slides over broad ledges, can be accessed by a trail 0.1 mi. long that leaves the east side of Nash Stream Rd. 5.7 mi. from Emerson Rd. Use caution because the ledges can be slippery when wet. Other interesting natural features of the Nash Stream Forest include the Devil's Jacuzzi, an interesting rock formation in Nash Stream, and Nash Stream Bog, a 200-acre wetland created when the dam holding back Nash Bog Pond gave way in 1969. Both of these features can easily be visited by following the Cohos Trail about 1.5 mi. north from the trailhead for Sugarloaf Mountain. The Nash Stream Forest also contains several attractive high mountain ponds; of particular interest to hikers is Whitcomb Pond, accessible on foot via a 0.7 mi. walk up old roads from the end of Little Bog Pond Rd., which leaves the east side of Nash Stream Rd. 5.1 mi. from Emerson Rd. and is rough but usually drivable for 3.0 mi. to the outlet of Little Bog Pond. Devil's Slide (1,590 ft.) is a small mountain with a sheer cliff that rises 600 ft. on the north edge of Stark village. An unmaintained beaten path makes a very steep and rough ascent up the west slope, and there are plans to construct and maintain an official trail.

North of Berlin and east of the main divide lies a region of rivers and lakes of special interest to those who love fishing and canoeing. Among these waterways, which include Lake Umbagog (much of the land around this lake is now part of a National Wildlife Refuge) and the Androscoggin, Magalloway, and Diamond rivers, there are a few hills from which the view is worth the visit. Much of this land is in private hands, with gates on the access roads. The chief landowners are Dartmouth College and woods products corporations. Both are hospitable to hikers but do not usually permit vehicular traffic over their roads, which limits access to the region because of the considerable distances that are frequently involved. The Thirteen Mile Woods, along the Androscoggin River between Milan and Errol, is managed by a consortium of landowners and state agencies. This provides a scenic drive along the river, access to fishing and canoeing, and a public campground at Mollidgewock. The former fire warden's trail to Signal Mountain, a small mountain west of Errol with an abandoned and unsafe fire tower that overlooks this region, has been devastated by logging and can no longer be recommended to the general hiker.

Far to the north of Hanover, above the headwaters of the Androscoggin River, lies the Second College Grant, given to Dartmouth College by the state in 1807 "for the assistance of indigent students." On this grant, between Errol, New Hampshire, and Wilsons Mills, Maine, the Swift Diamond and the Dead Diamond come together to form the Diamond River, which then enters the Magalloway River from the west. This in turn joins the Androscoggin River at Umbagog Lake. Branches of the Dead Diamond extend well up into the Connecticut Lakes region. (Refer to the USGS Wilsons Mills quad.) Immediately below the confluence of its two branches, the Diamond has carved a wild and beautiful gorge between the Diamond Peaks on the north and Mt. Dustan on the south. This valley is served by Dartmouth's private logging road, open to pedestrians but not to vehicles without a permit. In the village of Wentworth Location, New Hampshire, 8.7 mi. north of Errol or 0.5 mi. west of the Maine–New Hampshire state line, this gravel road leaves NH 16 on the west near a small cemetery. Hikers may leave their cars at the gate 0.2 mi. in from NH 16; public travel beyond this gate is on foot only. The College Grant gatehouse, the former location of the main gate, is reached in 0.7 mi., where the road soon crosses the Diamond River on a bridge and proceeds up through the gorge. Good viewpoints are not abundant; but the best—a clear outlook down into the gorge with the stream rushing about 50 ft. below—is reached at about 1.6 mi., the Dartmouth Peaks Camp at 1.8 mi., and the Management Center at 2.2 mi. Hellgate, another scenic gorge, named because of the trouble river drivers had getting their logs through its narrow channel without jamming, is 12.5 mi. from the gatehouse. For hikers, the principal feature of interest is the path that runs from the Management Center to the fine ledges on the Diamond Peaks (2,050 ft.). Other short paths to points of interest have also been opened. For further information, contact the Dartmouth Outdoor Programs Office.

Dixville Notch, the most spectacular spot in the North Country, lies between Sanguinary Mountain (north) and Mt. Gloriette (south). With the Mohawk River flowing west and Clear Stream east, the notch itself is less than 2 mi. in length with a steep grade on each side, and is only wide enough to admit the highway. The cliff formations, composed of vertical strata, are impressively jagged. Just west of the notch is the Balsams, a hotel and resort complex that includes most of the land west of the notch on both sides of NH 26. The management maintains a number of summer and winter trails—and is actively increasing the network of available paths at the present time—including both cross-country ski and snowmobile trails and some paths that are suitable for horse travel and mountain biking, in addition to hiking opportunities. Part of their operation is the Wilderness Ski Area on the west slopes of Dixville Peak. The Balsams has a guide to paths in the notch, available in summer from the information booth on NH 26 just across from the hotel entrance road or from the outdoor recreation center to the rear of the hotel (in season). The Cohos Trail and New Hampshire Heritage Trail now pass through this region, traversing the summit of Dixville Peak and descending over Table Rock to the notch.

The mountains in the vicinity of Dixville Notch are relatively low and have no open summits. The south side of the notch is Mt. Gloriette (2,630 ft.), which bears the rock formations Table Rock, Old King, Third Cliff, and Profile Cliff. There were once paths to all of them, but only that to Table Rock is now maintained and signed, and hiking to the others is not encouraged because the terrain is very rough and it is easy to stray into dangerous areas. Table Rock (2,510 ft.) is a cliff that juts out from the north side of Mt. Gloriette, south of the highway. Formed of vertical slabs, it is less than 10 ft. wide at its narrowest point and extends more than 100 ft. from the shoulder of the mountain. The view is spectacular and extensive. It can be climbed by a trail that begins and ends at points 0.5 mi. apart on NH 26 in the heart of the notch. The rock formation known as the Profile can be seen high up on the cliffs by looking south from the high point in the notch. On the north side of the road just west of the high point is Lake Gloriette (1,846 ft.), an artificial lake on the grounds of the Balsams, formed from the headwaters of the Mohawk River.

Dixville Peak (3,490 ft.) is the highest mountain in the vicinity of Dixville Notch, but it is wooded except for the cleared summit. It is accessible by snowmobile trails that are now part of the Cohos Trail. The shortest route is about 3.5 mi. (one way) from NH 26 following the Table Rock Trail and trails designated 9, 65, and 63 on the Balsams map; inquire at the Balsams information booth or outdoor recreation center. Sanguinary Mountain (2,710 ft.) forms the north wall of Dixville Notch and is named for the color of its cliffs at sunset. The Sanguinary Ridge Trail, which does not go to the summit, traverses the cliffs north of the notch, running between one trailhead at the hotel entrance road and another at a picnic area north of the highway 1 mi. east of the Balsams. A very short trail (sign) from the same picnic area leads to a small but attractive flume. A little farther east on the south side of the highway is a second picnic area from which a trail leads 0.4 mi. to Huntington Cascades. From the cascades, the Three Brothers Trail runs 1.0 mi. to Table Rock, passing an excellent outlook and the Ice Cave along the way. There are no maintained trails to Cave Mountain (3,191 ft.). After a lapse of many years, there is once again a trail to Mt. Abeniki (2,723 ft.). Some 10 mi. above Colebrook, the Connecticut River Valley bends northeast and, just beyond the village of Beecher Falls, Vermont, comes wholly within New Hampshire. Between its source near the Canadian line and the village of Pittsburg, the river passes through a chain of lakes of increasing size, numbered first to fourth in upstream order from the south. A high dam at Pittsburg created Lake Francis—the lowest lake in the series, below First Lake—and dams are responsible for the present size of both First and Second Lakes. First Lake (5.5 mi. long and 2.5 mi. wide at its broadest) and Lake Francis are the largest bodies of water in New Hampshire north of the Presidential

Range. US 3, the only major highway in the region, passes close to all of the lakes except Fourth Lake, crossing the river from west to east between Second Lake and Third Lake, and eventually entering Canada. Refer to USGS Second Lake, Indian Stream, and Moose Bog quads. Much of the land in the Connecticut Lakes region is privately owned. Although the owners do not discourage the use of their lands for hiking, they do request that these activities be limited to the daylight hours. Overnight camping and open fires are prohibited. Use of registered vehicles is limited to those roads that are not gated and not posted for road closure. Use of ATVs is prohibited at all times.

The town of Pittsburg is a notable historical curiosity because it was once—in the minds of its residents, at least—an independent republic. Lying in a region that was claimed by both the United States and Canada until the Webster-Ashburton Treaty of 1842 awarded it to the United States, the township was proclaimed by its residents as the Republic of Indian Stream in 1832; this tiny republic, which had its own written constitution, managed its own affairs for three years until trouble with the large, quarrelsome neighbor to the north led to its occupation by the large, quarrelsome neighbor to the south. This fascinating piece of New England frontier history is chronicled in *Indian Stream Republic* by Daniel Doan (who was best known as a writer of hiking trail guides) and published by the University Press of New England. Magalloway Mountain (3,383 ft.), located east of First Connecticut Lake, overlooks the Middle Branch of the Dead Diamond River; it has the only existing mountain trails of any consequence in the Connecticut Lakes region. A fire tower (no longer operated most of the time) affords excellent views; there are also good views from a ledge near the summit, at the top of the mountain's east cliff, with an impressive talus slope below. Garfield Falls is a remote and picturesque waterfall on the East Branch of the Dead Diamond that is accessible by two short paths. Fourth Connecticut Lake (2,670 ft.), a little mountain tarn northwest of Third Lake and just south of the Canadian border, is the ultimate source of the Connecticut River. Once considered as remote a spot as the mountains had to offer, it is located in a 78-acre reservation given by Champion International to the Nature Conservancy in 1990, and is now accessible from US 3 by a maintained trail.

Rump Mountain (3,654 ft.) is located in Maine just east of the New Hampshire border, 7 mi. south of the Canadian line. Rump Mountain was formerly known as Mt. Carmel, or Camel's Rump, from its appearance from the southwest; it can best be viewed from the far side of the dam on Second Connecticut Lake a few yards from US 3. This attractive but remote mountain has views of three states and Quebec province, and an unusual view of Bigelow Mountain near Stratton, Maine; the dubious claim is sometimes made that in clear weather Katahdin may be visible. Rump Mountain is on private land. Although the owners do not object to hikers crossing their lands, there may be restrictions on vehicle travel, and camping is not permitted. The most convenient approach to Rump Mountain is probably from the East Inlet Rd., ascending to the narrow east–west ridge near the state line and following this ridge to the summit ledge on the far eastern knob, but only hikers thoroughly experienced in wilderness navigation should consider this trip because route finding is not easy and it is possible to wind up a very long way from the starting point. Refer to the USGS Rump Mountain quad.

Percy Peaks Trail

This trail ascends North Percy Peak from Nash Stream Rd. Leaving NH 110 2.6 mi. east of Groveton, go north on Emerson Rd. 2.2 mi. until the paved road makes a prominent curve to the right (east); here the gravel Nash Stream Rd. turns left (north). Formerly owned and maintained by Diamond International, this road has usually been closed during the winter and almost always from spring thaw through Memorial Day weekend in the past. Follow the road for 2.7 mi. to a small parking area (sign) on the east side; the trail (sign) begins 50 yd. farther up, also on the east side of the road. Refer to the AMC's *North Country–Mahoosuc Range Map* (map 6) and the USGS Percy Peaks quad.

The current trail is a combination of the lower part of the former West Side Trail and the Notch Trail. The upper part of the former West Side Trail has been officially closed. This section of trail, one of the most spectacular and challenging in New England, was laid out by Robert and Miriam Underhill, both noted rock climbers who delighted in finding short but challenging routes to good viewpoints. Though it crossed rock slabs that are steep and exposed where use of hands is required, it was not a rock climb in the technical sense, nor was it more difficult than some other officially maintained trails, such as the North Slide of Tripyramid or the Huntington Ravine Trail or the Holt Trail on Cardigan, although like those trails it was hazardous in wet or icy weather. (The only recorded hiking fatality on this mountain occurred on the slippery slabs below the former trail junction, along which the trail still passes.) The route can probably still be followed by those interested in undertaking a rewarding challenge at their own risk; particular caution should be exercised on wet spots, and the much steeper slabs to the south (right side) of the route should be avoided.

Leaving Nash Stream Rd., the trail ascends moderately for 0.3 mi., then bears right, crosses a small stream, and follows logging roads at easy to moderate grades, generally parallel to and north of Slide Brook. At 1.0 mi., the trail turns left at a large boulder, becomes steeper and rougher, and soon reaches the base of the lower slabs. The slabs in this area are mossy and extremely slippery when wet; stay to the right (south) of the slabs, ignoring any remaining blazes painted on the rocks to the left (such blazes were placed in an unusually dry year). At 1.2 mi., the trail reaches the former trail junction, where the old trail continued straight up the ledges; the current trail now turns right and follows the former Notch Trail.

The trail now traverses several ledges, staying north of the low point in the notch. At 1.7 mi., the Old Summer Club Trail (the Cohos Trail, southbound) enters on the right; the rough trail to South Percy leaves this trail 0.1 mi. from this junction. The orange-blazed Percy Peaks Trail soon swings left (north) and in 100 yd. bears left again as the yellow-blazed Percy Loop Trail (the Cohos Trail, northbound) diverges right. At 1.9 mi., the Percy Peaks Trail emerges at the base of open slabs, turns left, and ascends steeply up the ledges with wide views south. The ledges are potentially dangerous if wet or icy. The trail continues climbing generally northwest over ledges and through scrub, making several turns—look carefully for cairns and blazes. The grade eases on the approach to the flat summit, where there are good views in all directions around the rim. Descending, the trail heads south at first, then veers left (southeast) in the direction of Christine Lake.

Percy Peaks Trail (map 6:B7)

Distances from Nash Stream Rd. (1,242 ft.) to
- former Notch Trail junction (2,500 ft.): 1.2 mi., 1,250 ft., 1 hr. 15 min.
- Old Summer Club Trail (2,930 ft.): 1.7 mi., 1,700 ft., 1 hr. 40 min.
- North Percy summit (3,430 ft.): 2.2 mi., 2,200 ft., 2 hr. 10 min.

Percy Loop Trail (TCTA)

This recently built trail, a link in the Cohos Trail, provides a pleasant northern approach to the Percy Peaks from Nash Stream Rd. 1.1 mi. north of the Percy Peaks Trail trailhead. It can be combined with the Percy Peaks Trail to create a 6-mi. loop over North Percy. The trail, marked by a small CT sign and yellow blaze, leaves the right (east) side of Nash Stream Rd. 3.8 mi. from Emerson Rd., just before the crossing of Long Mountain Brook. Best parking is on the west side of the road just north of the brook, at a grassy spot beside the driveway to a private camp; do not block access to the driveway.

The trail climbs moderately on an old logging road on the south side of Long Mountain Brook, with good footing. At 0.3 mi., it bears left onto another old road and climbs up the side of Boman Valley through hardwood forest, well above the brook. At 0.8 mi., it descends slightly and swings right; the grade is mostly easy until the trail turns sharp right (south) off the road at 1.5 mi. It soon passes a 100-yd. spur trail left that leads across a small brook to the Percy Loop Campsite (tent platform and privy, no fires allowed), then climbs steadily on a winding course up the northeast slope of North Percy—blazes should be followed carefully, as the footway is not well worn in some places. Higher up there are some rough sections with rocks and holes; watch footing carefully, especially at one short, fairly difficult scramble. At 2.2 mi., the grade eases and the footing improves, and the trail swings right (southwest) and contours around the side of North Percy to the Percy Peaks Trail, 0.4 mi. below the summit of North Percy.

Percy Loop Trail (map 6:A7–B7)

Distances from Nash Stream Rd. (1,360 ft.) to
- right turn off logging road (2,250 ft.): 1.5 mi., 900 ft., 1 hr. 10 min.
- Percy Peaks Trail (2,975 ft.): 2.3 mi., 1,600 ft., 2 hr.
- North Percy summit (3,430 ft.) via Percy Peaks Trail: 2.7 mi., 2,050 ft., 2 hr. 20 min.

Old Summer Club Trail (TCTA)

This trail, a section of the Cohos Trail, follows in part a restored section of an old trail to the Percy Peaks from the Percy Summer Club on Christine

Lake. In combination with a route on woods roads from a public parking lot on Christine Lake, it provides hikers with a new route to the Percy Peaks and offers access via a side trail to the cliffs of Victor Head, where there are interesting views. To reach the trailhead, turn north off NH 110 in the village of Stark, 6.8 mi. east of US 3 in Groveton. Drive through the covered bridge, turn right (east) on Percy Rd. and follow it for 2.2 mi., then turn left (north) on Christine Lake Rd., and in 0.4 mi., bear left at a fork into the parking area at the east end of the lake, where there is a beach with a fine view across the water to Victor Head and South Percy.

Walk 100 yd. back to the fork just east of the parking area and turn left on Summer Club Rd. (No Trespassing signs do not apply to hikers who stay on the trails.) In 0.1 mi., where the road curves left, bear right onto an older woods road, soon passing a metal gate. At 0.4 mi. from the parking area, stay straight where a snowmobile trail diverges right. At 0.5 mi., turn sharp left (west) onto another woods road and follow it at easy grades, crossing Rowell Brook on a bridge at 1.0 mi. The grass-grown road now climbs more steadily, passing the blue-blazed boundary of the Nash Stream State Forest at 1.3 mi., and meets the Cohos Trail at a T-junction with a wide, grassy logging road (the Jimmy Cole Brook Rd.) at 1.7 mi. To the right, this road coincides with the southbound Cohos Trail, which leads through a notch behind Bald Mountain and reaches NH 110 in 4.1 mi. The Old Summer Club Trail (also the northbound Cohos Trail) enters the woods across the road and slightly to the left (yellow blaze). The yellow-blazed trail ascends moderately on an ancient logging road. At 2.0 mi., the blue-blazed side trail to Victor Head leaves right (sign).

Victor Head Side Trail. This well-worn trail climbs steadily, and at times steeply, swinging left into a deep spruce forest on the north side of the peak. It bears right and climbs a short steep, rough section through wooded ledges, then levels and reaches the wooded summit, where one spur path leads 20 yd. right to a cleared outlook toward the Percy Peaks, and another path descends 50 yd. left to a ledge with views east to the Mahoosucs and south over Christine Lake to the Pilot Range. Distance from Old Summer Club Trail (1,775 ft.) to Victor Head (2,265 ft.): 0.4 mi., 500 ft., 25 min.

The Old Summer Club Trail continues up the old road, then turns sharp right off it at 2.3 mi., entering a recently cut section of trail. At

2.5 mi., it turns left onto another old road, follows it for 140 yd., then turns sharp right into the woods. At 2.7 mi., the trail turns left onto another road, then turns right off it in 40 yd. (All the turns are well blazed.) At 2.8 mi., it crosses a branch of Jimmy Cole Brook and in 100 yd. crosses another branch. The recently cut trail now climbs moderately up the east slope of South Percy, crossing an overgrown road at 3.2 mi., following several twists and turns, then traversing a rough section with rocks and holes. After passing a small cave on the right the trail becomes steep and rough in a rocky area. It follows the edge of a ledge shelf, then drops to the col between the Percy Peaks at 3.7 mi., where it turns sharp right. At this turn, a rough, narrow orange-blazed path (no sign) diverges left, climbing steeply in 0.3 mi. (350 ft.) to the summit of South Percy, with occasional views as it ascends through scrub near the top. Ledges around the summit provide good views, especially toward the bare cone of North Percy. From the junction the Old Summer Club Trail rises easily to meet the Percy Peaks Trail; to reach the summit of North Percy, 0.5 mi. away, turn right.

Old Summer Club Trail (map 6:B8-B7)

Distances from Christine Lake parking area (1,210 ft.) to
- Victor Head side trail (1,775 ft.): 2.0 mi., 600 ft. (rev. 50 ft.), 1 hr. 20 min.
- Percy Peaks Trail (2,930 ft.): 3.8 mi., 1,850 ft. (rev. 100 ft.), 2 hr. 50 min.
- North Percy Peak (3,430 ft.) via Percy Peaks Trail: 4.3 mi., 2,350 ft., 3 hr. 20 min.

Sugarloaf Trail

This trail provides access to the bare rock summit of Sugarloaf Mountain, which commands sweeping views of the Nash Stream valley and surrounding areas. The trail ascends the east side of the mountain by a direct route, following a logging road that was the fire warden's trail to the former fire tower. From NH 110 2.6 mi. east of Groveton, take Emerson Rd. north until it swings right (east) at 2.2 mi., then follow the gravel Nash Stream Rd. left (north) for 8.3 mi. to a point 60 yd. beyond its crossing of Nash Stream. The trail begins on the left as the driveway to a private camp (a sign reads, Finally Inn). Park in a grassy area near the driveway entrance, taking care not to block the driveway, or on the right (east) side of the road just south of the bridge. Refer to the USGS Percy Peaks quad.

The trail (sign) passes to the left of a camp, crosses a small brook, goes around a gate and through a clearing, and enters the woods. At 0.2 mi., it bears right at a fork where the yellow-blazed Cohos Trail (southbound) goes left. The Sugarloaf Trail ascends generally northwest at a steady grade on the wide, old road to the remains of the fire warden's cabins at 1.6 mi. A short distance farther, near a spring, the trail bears right at a fork (the left branch is an overgrown alternate route to the summit). It climbs to the ridge north of the summit, turns left (south), and reaches the summit ledges.

Sugarloaf Trail (USGS Percy Peaks quad)

Distances from Nash Stream Rd. (1,530 ft.) to
- the warden's cabins (3,220 ft.): 1.6 mi., 1,700 ft., 1 hr. 40 min.
- Sugarloaf Mountain summit (3,710 ft.): 2.1 mi., 2,200 ft., 2 hr. 10 min.

Diamond Peaks Trail (DOC)

The Diamond Peaks are three small peaks (West Peak, 2,010 ft., East Peak, 2,050 ft., and South Peak, 1,994 ft.) capping a nearly semicircular ridge that rises between the Dead Diamond and Magalloway rivers. Their most attractive feature is a high cliff on the concave side of the ridge, facing south, with a number of good viewpoints. The trail to the summit is short but has a number of fairly steep, rough sections. Refer to the USGS Wilsons Mills quad.

The trail begins on the north side of the clearing across the road from the Dartmouth Management Center, 2.2 mi. from the gate near NH 16. It crosses a wet, mossy area on plank bridges, then ascends fairly steeply to a ridge crest at 0.3 mi. Here a side trail (not well cleared but fairly easy to follow) leads left 70 yd. to the summit of a small crag then down slightly another 20 yd. to Alice Ledge, with a view across and down the Diamond River valley. The main trail turns sharp right and climbs, reaching at 0.5 mi. the first of several fine cliffy outlooks on the side of Linda Ledge (use caution here in wet or icy conditions). The trail continues to climb, rather steeply at times, to a fork at 0.9 mi. Here a trail used as a winter bypass of the lower ledges enters on the left; the lower part is not marked or cleared for non-winter use. The main trail, which is less obvious at this point (mostly because of the lack of mature trees to receive blazes) bears somewhat to the right, crosses a ledgy area near the ridge crest, and reaches a fine outlook ledge in 50 yd. The trail continues, first descending slightly then climbing, and passes a short distance to the right of the highest point of the mountain. It then continues 120 yd. to another viewpoint, which offers a particularly fine vista of the Magalloway River meandering peacefully through the broad, mostly undeveloped valley at the foot of the mountain.

Diamond Peaks Trail (USGS Wilsons Mills quad)

Distance from the Management Center (1,350 ft.) to
  • Diamond Peaks, East Peak (2,050 ft.): 1.1 mi., 700 ft., 55 min.

Table Rock Trail (NHDP)

This short, rough loop path begins and ends on NH 26 and gives access to Table Rock, which is perhaps the most spectacular viewpoint in the White Mountains, consisting of a narrow ledge rising several hundred feet over a cliff face. There may be better scenery in the White Mountains, but few trails reach airier spots from which to view it. The trail is shown on the USGS Dixville Notch quad. The east trailhead, which gives access to the much steeper section of the loop (called by the Balsams map the Table Rock Climbing Trail, trail 57, and now a part of the New Hampshire Heritage Trail), is in a parking lot 0.1 mi. east of the main entrance to the Balsams. The west trailhead (where the trail is called the Table Rock Hiking Trail, trail 50, and is also designated as part of the Dixville Heritage Trail loop) is 0.6 mi. west of the main entrance to the Balsams near a Pedestrian Crossing sign. Because of the recent and ongoing expansion of the Balsams trail network, hikers may encounter more trail junctions and different trail designations than those described later, but the Table Rock Trail is now well signed and marked and can be easily followed.

From the east trailhead, the trail climbs extremely steeply (not recommended for descent) with rough and often slippery footing, rising 600 ft. in 0.3 mi. It emerges just behind Table Rock (no sign); turn right and scramble up a few yards to the open ledge.

From the west trailhead, the trail (recommended for the average hiker) follows a cross-country ski trail (signed as E, or #5) for 25 yd., then diverges left on the trail signed as 50 and climbs steadily, with some loose derfoot, easing as it approaches the height-of-land. At 0.7 mi., it bears left where a trail signed 9 (the southbound Cohos Trail) diverges right for the top of the Wilderness Ski Area and Dixville Peak. The Table Rock Trail descends 50 yd. to a junction where the Three Brothers Trail (the northbound Cohos Trail) diverges right. Here a spur path (signed To View) turns left and descends steeply for 25 yd., meets the east trail—which virtually plunges down to NH 26—and ascends briefly to Table Rock.

Table Rock Trail (USGS Dixville Notch quad)

Distances from parking area for east trailhead (1,930 ft.) to
- Table Rock (2,510 ft.): 0.3 mi., 600 ft., 25 min.
- west trailhead (1,870 ft.): 1.0 mi., 600 ft. (rev. 650 ft.), 50 min.

Three Brothers Trail (NHDP)

This trail leads from the end of the Huntington Cascade Trail to Table Rock, passing two other viewpoints along the way. It begins on the north bank of Cascade Brook, 0.4 mi. from the Cascade Brook picnic area. It is trail K on the Balsams trail map, and is a link in the Cohos Trail.

Huntington Cascade Trail. This short trail begins on the south side of NH 26 at the Cascade Brook picnic area by the eastern entrance to Dixville Notch State Park. Drive into the wayside area, and in 0.1 mi., bear left into the picnic area. The trail (sign) begins at the far side of a loop at the end of this road. Leaving the picnic area, the trail meanders through hardwoods then turns right (a sign reads 61), crosses Cascade Brook, and climbs steeply up the south bank, passing an overlook of a mossy cascade. It continues climbing high above the brook through spruces, where other beaten paths parallel the trail, and at 0.4 mi., it turns right and descends, crosses Cascade Brook, and meets the Three Brothers Trail on the north bank.

From the junction with the Huntington Cascade Trail, the Three Brothers Trail climbs up the east ridge of Mt. Gloriette at a moderate grade through hardwoods. At 0.5 mi., it crosses a blue-blazed state park boundary line and stays near it for some distance. The grade becomes easy on a shoulder, and after a slight dip the trail climbs to a spur trail right at 0.8 mi. leading to Middle Brother Outlook. This spur, 0.1 mi. long, descends 75 ft. then swings right to a cliff-top outlook with a spectacular view of Table

Rock and the Balsams resort. The main trail climbs to a high point, passes another view of Table Rock on the right, then turns right and descends to the Ice Cave, an interesting chasm in a ledge on the left. Here the trail turns left and meets the Table Rock Trail just behind Table Rock.

Three Brothers Trail (USGS Dixville Notch quad)

Distance from Cascade Brook picnic area (1,510 ft.) to
- Table Rock (2,510 ft.) via Huntington Cascade Trail: 1.4 mi., 1,100 ft. (rev. 100 ft.), 1 hr. 15 min.

Sanguinary Ridge Trail (NHDP)

This trail provides access to the spectacular views from the open rocks of Sanguinary Ridge on the north side of Dixville Notch. Beginning and ending on NH 26, it is marked with directional signs and white blazes, and is designated as trail 58 on the Balsams trail map; the eastern section is also part of the Cohos Trail. It is shown on the USGS Dixville Notch quad. The western trailhead is at the main entrance to the Balsams resort. The eastern trailhead is 1.0 mi. to the east at the Flume Brook picnic area of the Dixville Notch State Wayside, a rest area on the north side of NH 26 east of the notch. The lower end of the eastern part may be signed as the Flume Brook Trail (60 on the Balsams trail map).

Leaving the east end of the wayside area (CT sign and white blazes), the trail climbs alongside Clear Brook, passing a small flume on the right in 50 yd. It soon turns sharp left away from the brook, crosses an old road at 0.1 mi., and in another 100 yd. passes a spur trail left leading to the west end of the wayside. It begins climbing up a scenic ridge at easy to moderate grades, passing the first outlook on the left at 0.4 mi. Three more outlooks are passed in the next 0.3 mi., with good views of Table Rock and Old King cliffs, and also east down the valley toward the Mahoosuc Range. At 0.8 mi., the trail turns right and ascends more steeply through hardwoods, reaching its high point on the ridge at 1.2 mi. Here the Sanguinary Summit Trail (64 on the Balsams trail map, also the northbound Cohos Trail) diverges right, leading about 3.5 mi. along the ridge to the Panorama lean-to, built in 2002 by TCTA; 40 yd. up this trail, there is an outlook west on the left. The Sanguinary Ridge Trail bears left at the junction and switchbacks down to two spectacular rocky viewpoints overlooking Lake Gloriette and the Balsams resort at 1.4 mi. Here it turns left and soon emerges on an open slope of gravel and loose rock, where the footing is poor. It descends to the right past needlelike Index Rock, with good views up to the cliffs across the notch, reenters the woods, and switchbacks down a steep slope to the Balsams entrance.

Sanguinary Ridge Trail (USGS Dixville Notch quad)

Distances from Flume Brook picnic area (1,580 ft.) to
- junction at height-of-land (2,530 ft.): 1.2 mi., 950 ft., 1 hr. 5 min.
- Balsams entrance road (1,860 ft.): 1.7 mi., 950 ft. (rev. 700 ft.), 1 hr. 20 min.

Coot Trail

This trail follows the old firewarden's jeep road to the fire tower on the summit of Magalloway Mountain. Refer to the USGS Magalloway Mountain quad. From US 3, 4.7 mi. north of the dam on First Connecticut Lake, take gravel Magalloway Rd. (sign for lookout tower) to the southeast. This is a wide, well-graded main-haul private logging road; drivers must always be vigilant and prepared to yield to large and fast-moving logging trucks— it is not always easy to find a place to get out of the way quickly. At 1.2 mi., cross the Connecticut River on a bridge and continue straight. Bear left at 2.3 mi. and again at 2.9 mi. At 5.3 mi., turn sharp right onto a branch road that is narrower and rougher, and bear right again at 6.3 mi. The road ends in a turnaround at 8.4 mi., where hikers should park.

The Coot Trail (sign) starts on the right across from a privy and follows the rough, eroded jeep road, passing a cabin and spring at 0.1 mi. It ascends steadily with a few relatively steep grades and two short bypasses that quickly rejoin the main trail. Higher up it passes two short connecting paths on the right that climb to the Bobcat Trail, and at 0.6 mi., it passes the junction with the upper end of the Bobcat Trail on the right; here there is a view back over First Connecticut Lake. The Coot Trail soon swings left at an easy grade and reaches the grassy summit clearing and the fire tower at 0.8 mi. The extensive views include portions of New Hampshire, Vermont, Maine, and Quebec. From the clearing an unmarked side path descends right for 0.1 mi. to a spring, and an overlook path diverges left, passes to the right of the warden's cabins, and descends easily for 0.2 mi. to an excellent viewpoint at the top of the mountain's east cliff.

Bobcat Trail

This trail, in combination with the Coot Trail, makes possible a loop hike on Magalloway Mountain. Its footing is generally better than that on the old jeep road. It leaves the gravel road (no sign) 60 yd. to the right (west) of the Coot Trail. It crosses a log bridge, climbs a brushy bank and enters the woods. The grade is fairly easy for 0.2 mi., then the trail swings left and climbs steadily, with an occasional short breather. At 0.6 mi., there is a good viewpoint overlooking Second Connecticut Lake 10 yd. to the left. The trail passes two short connecting paths that descend left to the Coot Trail and ends at the Coot Trail at the top of a steep pitch, 0.2 mi. below the summit.

Garfield Falls Path

Garfield Falls is a beautiful, remote waterfall on the East Branch of the Dead Diamond River. It can be reached from either of two trailheads 0.4 mi. apart. From US 3, 4.7 mi. north of the dam on First Connecticut Lake, follow Magalloway Rd. as described earlier for the Coot Trail. At 5.3 mi., where the route to Magalloway Mountain turns right, continue ahead on the main-haul road. At 6.4 mi., there is a fine view of Magalloway Mountain to the right. Bear left with the main road at 8.4 mi., and at 10.7 mi., stay straight at a major intersection on the road signed "112-S" (sign for Garfield Falls). The northern trailhead for the falls is at a kiosk and parking area on the left at 12.0 mi. For the southern trailhead, bear left at a fork just beyond the kiosk and follow a grassy road downhill to its end at 12.4 mi.

From the southern trailhead (no sign), the trail enters the woods and in 35 yd. bears left at a fork onto a newly constructed route. It rises gently along the East Branch with one brief descent and reaches a pool below the falls at 0.4 mi. Here it turns left and climbs log steps to a bluff with an excellent view of the falls, which drops 40 ft. amidst pools and steep ledges. The trail climbs well above the falls, swings right, and ascends easily, then bears left to the kiosk at the northern trailhead.

Garfield Falls Path (Bosebuck Mountain quad)

Distances from southern trailhead (1,670 ft.) or northern trailhead (1,862 ft.) for
  • entire loop to Garfield Falls (1,710 ft.) via Garfield Falls Path and grassy road: 1.0 mi., 200 ft., 35 min.

Fourth Connecticut Lake Trail (NC)

This path begins at the U.S. Customs station at the Canadian border on US 3. Parking is available in a designated area on the east side of the road. Refer to the USGS Second Connecticut Lake and Prospect Hill quads. Hikers should check in with customs personnel before hiking the trail, which begins at a signboard on a grassy bank just north of the customs building; a brochure with map may be available at the signboard. Follow a worn footway along the international boundary uphill to the left (west). The boundary is a wide swath cut through the forest and marked at irregular intervals by brass discs set in concrete. The trail climbs steeply with rough footing, swings left (southwest) at 0.1 mi. and eases, then resumes the climb, with occasional views of the border mountains to the northeast. The trail levels again and at 0.5 mi., it continues ahead into the woods at a sign as the boundary swath swings to the right. It descends gradually through dense woods to a loop junction at 0.7 mi. From here, the trail makes a 0.6 mi. loop around the small, boggy lake, with minor ups and downs; for the best view of the lake, follow the loop 10 yd. to the right and then a short side path left to the shore. On the southeast side of the pond, the loop crosses two small outlet streams that form the initial flow of the Connecticut River.

Fourth Connecticut Lake Trail (USGS Second Connecticut Lake and Prospect Hill quads)

Distance from U.S. Customs station (2,360 ft.) for
  • loop around Fourth Connecticut Lake (2,670 ft.) and return: 2.0 mi., 400 ft., 1 hr. 10 min.

SUGGESTED HIKES

For more information on suggested hikes, see p. ix.

Easy Hikes

Table Rock [rt: 1.4 mi., 650 ft., 1:05]. The west section of the Table Rock Trail provides the easiest approach to this spectacular perch on the rim of Dixville Notch.

Magalloway Mountain [rt: 2.2 mi., 900 ft., 1:35]. The drive is longer than the hike up this remote peak that overlooks an extensive uninhabited region, with sweeping views from a fire tower and the superb viewpoint at the top of the east cliff. The Coot and Bobcat trails make a convenient loop along with the side trip to the east cliff viewpoint.

Lookout Ledge [rt: 2.6 mi., 1,000 ft., 1:50]. A fairly steep climb along the Ledge Trail to an excellent view of the Northern Presidentials.

Devils Hopyard [rt: 2.6 mi., 250 ft., 1:25]. From South Pond off NH 110, the Kilkenny Ridge and Devil's Hopyard trails provide easy access to this miniature version of the more spectacular but much more difficult gorges at the Ice Gulch and Mahoosuc Notch.

Moderate Hikes

Diamond Peaks [rt: 6.6 mi., 800 ft., 3:40]. An interesting small ridge with good views in the Dartmouth College Grant.

North Percy Peak [rt: 4.4 mi., 2,200 ft., 3:20]. The Percy Peaks Trail provides a fairly rugged climb up this ledgy mountain with excellent views over the Nash Stream Forest. A fine loop can be made by using the Percy Loop Trail for the descent and returning along the Nash Stream Rd. [lp: 6.0 mi., 2,200 ft., 4:05].

Sugarloaf Mountain [rt: 4.2 mi., 2,200 ft., 3:10]. A steady ascent up the Sugarloaf Trail to an open peak in the upper Nash Stream valley.

Owl's Head [rt: 5.0 mi., 2,000 ft., 3:30]. A relocation of the Owl's Head Trail has eased the climb to this ledgy knob and its fine view of the

Presidentials. For a longer hike, Martha's Mile leads to the summit of Cherry Mountain and more views [rt: 6.6 mi., 2,550 ft., 4:35].

Strenuous Hikes

Rogers Ledge [rt: 8.8 mi., 1,600 ft., 5:10]. This spectacular, remote, and seldom-visited viewpoint can be reached from the York Pond Rd. via the Mill Brook and Kilkenny Ridge trails. If the gate is open, it can also be approached from South Pond via the Kilkenny Ridge Trail [rt: 8.2 mi., 1,850 ft., 5:00].

Mt. Cabot [rt: 9.6 mi., 2,900 ft., 6:15]. With the lower Mt. Cabot Trail closed, the shortest route to the northernmost 4,000-footer is from the east via the York Pond, Bunnell Notch, and Kilkenny Ridge trails, with two good viewpoints en route. A loop can also be made including the magnificent views from The Horn and beautiful Unknown Pond, descending via the Unknown Pond Trail [lp: 11.6 mi., 3,300 ft., 7:25]. Unknown Pond and The Horn can also be accessed from FR 11 off NH 110 via the Unknown Pond and Kilkenny Ridge trails [rt: 8.4 mi., 2,350 ft., 5:25]. Mt. Cabot can be added to this trip [rt: 10.6 mi., 3,350 ft., 7:00].

Appendix

Four Thousand Footers

The Four Thousand Footer Club was formed in 1957 to bring together hikers who had traveled to some of the less frequently visited sections of the White Mountains. The Four Thousand Footer Committee recognizes three lists of peaks: the White Mountain Four Thousand Footers, the New England Four Thousand Footers, and the New England Hundred Highest. Applicants for the White Mountain Four Thousand Footer Club must climb all 48 peaks in New Hampshire. To qualify for membership, a hiker must climb on foot to and from each summit on the list. The official lists of the Four Thousand Footers in New Hampshire, Maine, and Vermont are included at the end of this appendix. Criteria for mountains on the official list are: (1) each peak must be 4,000 ft. high, and (2) each peak must rise 200 ft. above the low point of its connecting ridge with a higher neighbor. The latter qualification eliminates peaks such as Clay, Franklin, North Carter, Guyot, Little Haystack, South Tripyramid, Lethe, Blue, and Jim. All 67 Four Thousand Footers are reached by well-defined trails, although the paths to Owl's Head and Redington as well as some short spur trails to other summits are not officially maintained. Applicants for the New England Four Thousand Footer Club must also climb the 14 peaks in Maine and the 5 in Vermont. Separate awards are given to those who climb all peaks on a list in winter; to qualify as a winter ascent, the hike must not begin before the hour and minute of the beginning of winter or end after the hour and minute of the end of winter.

If you are interested in becoming a member of one or more of the clubs sponsored by the Four Thousand Footer Committee, please send a self-addressed stamped envelope to the Four Thousand Footer Committee, Appalachian Mountain Club, 5 Joy Street, Boston, MA 02108, and an information packet including application forms will be sent to you. If you are interested in the New England Four Thousand Footer Club and/or the New England Hundred Highest Club, please specify this in your letter, because these lists are not routinely included in the basic information packet. After climbing each peak, please record the date of the ascent, companions, if any, and other remarks.

On the following lists, elevations have been obtained from the latest USGS maps, some of which are now metric, requiring conversion from meters to feet. Where no exact elevation is given on the map, the elevation has been estimated by adding half the contour interval to the highest contour shown on the map; elevations so obtained are marked on the list with an asterisk. The elevations given here for several peaks in the Presidential region differ from those given elsewhere in this book, because the Four Thousand Footer Committee uses the USGS maps as the authority for all elevations, while in the rest of the book the Bradford Washburn map of the Presidential Range supersedes the USGS maps in the area it covers.

Four Thousand Footers in New Hampshire

Mountain	Elevation (feet)	(meters)	Date Climbed
1. Washington	6,288	1,916.6	
2. Adams	5,774	1,760	
3. Jefferson	5,712	1,741	
4. Monroe	5,384*	1,641*	
5. Madison	5,367	1,636	
6. Lafayette	5,260*	1,603*	
7. Lincoln	5,089	1,551	
8. South Twin	4,902	1,494	
9. Carter Dome	4,832	1,473	
10. Moosilauke	4,802	1,464	
11. Eisenhower	4,780*	1,457*	
12. North Twin	4,761	1,451	
13. Carrigain	4,700*	1,433*	
14. Bond	4,698	1,432	
15. Middle Carter	4,610*	1,405*	
16. West Bond	4,540*	1,384*	
17. Garfield	4,500*	1,372*	
18. Liberty	4,459	1,359	
19. South Carter	4,430*	1,350*	
20. Wildcat	4,422	1,348	
21. Hancock	4,420*	1,347*	
22. South Kinsman	4,358	1,328	
23. Field	4,340*	1,323*	
24. Osceola	4,340*	1,323*	
25. Flume	4,328	1,319	
26. South Hancock	4,319	1,316	
27. Pierce (Clinton)	4,310	1,314	
28. North Kinsman	4,293	1,309	
29. Willey	4,285	1,306	
30. Bondcliff	4,265	1,300	
31. Zealand	4,260*	1,298*	
32. North Tripyramid	4,180*	1,274*	
33. Cabot	4,170*	1,271*	
34. East Osceola	4,156	1,267	
35. Middle Tripyramid	4,140*	1,262*	
36. Cannon	4,100*	1,250*	
37. Hale	4,054	1,236	

Mountain	Elevation (feet)	(meters)	Date Climbed
38. Jackson	4,052	1,235	
39. Tom	4,051	1,235	
40. Wildcat D	4,050*	1,234*	
41. Moriah	4,049	1,234	
42. Passaconaway	4,043	1,232	
43. Owl's Head	4,025	1,227	
44. Galehead	4,024	1,227	
45. Whiteface	4,020*	1,225*	
46. Waumbek	4,006	1,221	
47. Isolation	4,004	1,220	
48. Tecumseh	4,003	1,220	

Four Thousand Footers in Maine

Mountain	Elevation (feet)	(meters)	Date Climbed
1. Katahdin, Baxter Peak	5,268	1,606	
2. Katahdin, Hamlin Peak	4,756	1,450	
3. Sugarloaf	4,250*	1,295*	
4. Old Speck	4,170*	1,271*	
5. Crocker	4,228	1,289	
6. Bigelow, West Peak	4,145	1,263	
7. North Brother	4,151	1,265	
8. Saddleback	4,120	1,256	
9. Bigelow, Avery Peak	4,090*	1,247*	
10. Abraham	4,050*	1,234*	
11. Saddleback, the Horn	4,041	1,232	
12. South Crocker	4,050*	1,234*	
13. Redington	4,010*	1,222*	
14. Spaulding	4,010*	1,222*	

Four Thousand Footers in Vermont

Mountain	Elevation (feet)	(meters)	Date Climbed
1. Mansfield	4,393	1,339	
2. Killington	4,235	1,291	
3. Camel's Hump	4,083	1,244	
4. Ellen	4,083	1,244	
5. Abraham	4,006	1,221	

INDEX

Where multiple page references appear, bold numbering indicates the main entry for the trail or feature. Bracketed information indicates which of the six maps displays the feature and where, by section letter and number.